Classics of
Organizational Behavior

Fourth Edition

Classics of Organizational Behavior

Fourth Edition

Walter E. Natemeyer
North American Training and Development, Inc.

Paul Hersey
Center for Leadership Studies

WAVELAND

PRESS, INC.

Long Grove, Illinois

For information about this book, contact:
Waveland Press, Inc.
4180 IL Route 83, Suite 101
Long Grove, IL 60047-9580
(847) 634-0081
info@waveland.com
www.waveland.com

Contents

SECTION I
Origins of Organizational Behavior   1

SECTION II
Motivation and Performance

73

SECTION III
Interpersonal and Group Behavior

163

SECTION IV
Leadership

SECTION V
Power and Influence

SECTION VII
Increasing Leadership and Organizational Effectiveness 543

Foreword

Marshall Goldsmith

Walt Natemeyer and Paul Hersey have been my friends and colleagues for more than 30 years. I am honored to write the foreword to the Fourth Edition of their outstanding book, *Classics of Organizational Behavior.* Years ago, Paul Hersey taught me the meaning of the phrase *operational definition.* In his classes, he would discuss terms such as "leadership" and "management." He knew that such open-ended terms were often perceived differently depending on who was listening. So he always started with an operational definition. He didn't claim that his definitions were the only definitions of these terms; he merely noted that for the purpose of the class, his definition was the basis for the discussion. This saved hours of debate and clarified Dr. Hersey's key points!

Classics of Organizational Behavior is based on the same principle. Dr. Natemeyer and Dr. Hersey have compiled 54 distinguished readings in the field of organizational behavior. The contributing authors spent significant time and energy creating operational definitions in their areas of expertise, and their ideas became among the most important in advancing our understanding of management and organizational behavior. That is what makes each of the wonderful readings in this book a "classic."

With the selections included in this book, one can gain a sound understanding of well-known concepts and ideas on numerous aspects of organizational behavior, from motivating employees and goal setting to servant leadership and emotional intelligence to power and influence, as well as how to increase leadership and organizational effectiveness. Everyone working in an organization or studying organizational behavior should have this resource in his or her collection!

Marshall Goldsmith
Author of these best-selling titles:
What Got You Here Won't Get You There
Succession: Are You Ready?
MOJO: How to Get It, How to Keep It, and How to Get It Back If You Lose It

Preface

"Management" is typically defined as the process of utilizing numerous resources (people, materials, physical plant, equipment, information, time, and money) to accomplish organizational goals. Maximum organizational effectiveness clearly requires the competent management of all resources. None, however, is more important in determining the long-term effectiveness of an organization than the human resource, for people control how well all of the other resources are managed. If an organization utilizes its human talent effectively, the successful management of the organization's other resources becomes much more likely.

The importance of the human element in the practice of management has been increasingly recognized since Frederick W. Taylor conducted his pioneering scientific management experiments more than 100 years ago. During that time, the behavioral sciences have become an integral part of the field of management, and the professional literature of organizational behavior has proliferated. Within this immense body of knowledge, certain works stand out as more important than others, as "classics." The purpose of this book is to familiarize the reader with some of the outstanding contributions to the knowledge and literature of organizational behavior.

Selecting this set of "classics" has not been an easy task. Not only is there no consensus on what constitutes the "classics" of organizational behavior, but limitations of space and balance necessitated that many excellent articles be omitted. While the editors fully expect to be challenged for these exclusions, it should be considerably more difficult to question the inclusions, for what remains is a collection of readable, time-tested, and oft-referenced readings from many of the most important writers in the field.

Ten years have passed since the Third Edition of *Classics of Organizational Behavior* was published. Of the 54 readings in the Fourth Edition, 36 were retained from the Third Edition. The additional articles include important topics such as self-directed work teams, servant leadership, and emotional intelligence. This entire collection explains, usually in the originator's own words, concepts that have profoundly changed management thinking and practice. "Classic" implies a work of recognized and enduring worth. The editors believe that each of the selections contained herein has achieved such status.

xiii

The book is organized into seven sections, each beginning with a brief introduction. Within each section, the selections are presented in chronological order to enhance the reader's understanding of the evolution of thought in the field of organizational behavior. Section I provides an overview of the origins of organizational behavior. Section II examines motivation and performance. In section III, the readings focus on interpersonal and group behavior, while section IV contains selections on leadership. Section V focuses on power and influence. Section VI addresses the interaction between organizations, work processes, and people, and section VII concludes with thoughts on how to increase leadership and organizational effectiveness.

Classics of Organizational Behavior could not have been published without the help of numerous others. We wish to thank the authors and publishers of these "classics" for permission to reproduce their work. The suggestions and comments of Lloyd Greene (Texas State University), Steve LaCivita (The University of Chicago), and other colleagues were much appreciated. The advice from Neil Rowe and Diane Evans at Waveland Press was very helpful. Barbara Dressler, Debbie Sprague, and Barbara Gorman provided invaluable assistance in preparing the manuscript. We are grateful to Marshall Goldsmith for kindly writing the foreword to our book. Finally, we would like to thank our families for their support and encouragement throughout this project.

Walter E. Natemeyer
Paul Hersey
January 2011

Chronological Contents

Our Contributors

Clayton P. Alderfer
Chris Argyris
Warren G. Bennis
Eric Berne*
Robert Blake
Kenneth H. Blanchard
James MacGregor Burns
Tom Burns
John P. Campbell
Dorwin Cartwright
James Champy
Lester Coch
Jim Collins
Marvin D. Dunnette
Peter F. Drucker
Amitai Etzioni
Mary Parker Follett
Wendell French
John R. P. French Jr
Marshall Goldsmith
Daniel Goleman
Alvin W. Gouldner
Robert K. Greenleaf
Jay Hall
Gary Hamel
Michael Hammer
Jerry B. Harvey
Paul Hersey
Frederick Herzberg
Harry Ingham*
Arthur G. Jago
Muriel James
Irving L. Janis
Mary Ann C. Jensen
Spencer Johnson*
Dorothy Jongeward
Robert L. Katz
Steven Kerr

John P. Kotter
James M. Kouzes
Gary P. Latham
Edward E. Lawler III
Paul R. Lawrence
Rensis Likert
Edwin A. Locke
Jay W. Lorsch
Joseph Luft*
Niccolo Machiavelli
Norman R. F. Maier
Abraham H. Maslow
David C. McClelland
Douglas M. McGregor
Jane Mouton
Walter E. Natemeyer
George S. Odiorne
Thomas J. Peters
Jeffrey Pfeffer
Barry Z. Posner
C. K. Prahalad
Bertram Raven
Fritz J. Roethlisberger
Gerald R. Salancik
Edgar H. Schein
Warren H. Schmidt
Peter M. Senge
G. M. Stalker
Ralph Stayer
Robert Tannenbaum
Frederick Winslow Taylor
Robert J. Thomas
Bruce W. Tuckman
Victor H. Vroom
Robert H. Waterman
Max Weber
Karl E. Weick Jr.
Alvin Zander

*Originators of concepts discussed by others

xix

About the Editors

Dr. Walter E. Natemeyer is the CEO of North American Training and Development, Inc. He received his BBA and MBA from Ohio University and his PhD in organizational behavior from the University of Houston. Dr. Natemeyer was a professor of management and organizational behavior at Ohio University and the University of Houston, and he currently teaches in the EMBA Program at the University of Chicago. Also, he served for five years as Director of the NASA Johnson Space Center Management Development Program. He has designed and conducted management development programs for more than 100 major organizations in the United States and abroad, including Alcoa, American Red Cross, Aramco, BP, Chase Bank, Coca-Cola, ExxonMobil, FedEx, Ford, IBM, NASA, Schlumberger, Shell, and United Technologies. Dr. Natemeyer lives with his wife Mona on Galveston Bay near Houston, Texas. He has three children and four grandchildren.

Dr. Paul Hersey is Chairman of the Board of the Center for Leadership Studies, the home of Situational Leadership®. He is also Distinguished Professor of Leadership Studies at Nova Southeastern University, University Professor at Alliant University, and the first Scholar in Residence at the Booth School of Business at the University of Chicago. He received his bachelor's degree from Seton Hall University, master's degrees from the University of Chicago and the University of Arkansas, and a doctorate from the University of Massachusetts. Dr. Hersey has been a business executive, a professor of management and organizational behavior, a department chairman, a dean, and a university president. Over the past 50 years, he has conducted leadership development programs in over 100 countries. Dr. Hersey lives with his wife Suzanne in Escondido, California. He is the father of six, grandfather of seventeen, and great-grandfather of three.

Dr. Walt Natemeyer
North American Training and
    Development, Inc.
17041 El Camino Real, Suite 103
Houston, Texas 77058 USA
1-281-488-7000
www.natraining.com

Dr. Paul Hersey
Center for Leadership Studies
230 West Third Avenue
Escondido, California 92025 USA
1-760-741-6595
www.situational.com

Origins of Organizational Behavior

O rganizational behavior emerged as an academic discipline in the early 1900s. Its research has focused on understanding human behavior and performance within organizations. This section reviews the contributions of several pioneers whose research and writings established the importance and legitimacy of this field of study.

Frederick Winslow Taylor is considered to be the "father of scientific management." He examined how to increase employee productivity by "scientifically" designing how work should be done. Taylor pioneered the use of time-and-motion studies to determine the most efficient work methods and experimented with incentive pay systems. While his approach tended to de-personalize the workplace, Taylor and other "scientific management" researchers helped many industries increase employee productivity.

Mary Parker Follett was among the first to address the psychological aspects of employee motivation and behavior. In "The Giving of Orders," she suggested that employees would have more positive attitudes and be more productive if those "giving the orders" were to create a work environment based on trust and mutual respect.

The Hawthorne experiments are generally considered the first application of the behavioral sciences to organizations. The famous experiments—conducted at the Western Electric Company's plant in Cicero, Illinois—began in the late 1920s as an attempt to determine the impact of working conditions on employee productivity. What evolved during nearly a decade of research was the scientifically based realization that psychological and social factors had more significant effects on the work behavior of employees than physiological factors. A definitive account of these experiments is contained in *Management and the*

Worker (1939) by Fritz J. Roethlisberger and William J. Dickson. Reprinted here is the more concise description of the studies as given by Roethlisberger in a chapter from his book *Management and Morale* (1941).

Lester Coch and John R. P. French Jr. deal with a common problem associated with organizational change. Their article, "Overcoming Resistance to Change," addresses why people resist change and how this resistance is manifested in their behavior. As an example, they describe their experiment with participative management at the Harwood Manufacturing Company, which had groups of workers involved in designing changes to be made in their jobs. The results show that the "rate of recovery" to changes in a job is directly proportional to the amount of worker participation, and rates of turnover and aggression are inversely proportional to the amount of participation. Coch and French conclude by suggesting that it is possible for management to overcome resistance to change if the need for change is communicated effectively and if group participation is encouraged during planning for the change. This 1948 study is often considered to be the genesis of the participative management movement.

Thirty years after the Hawthorne studies began, Douglas M. McGregor published his article "The Human Side of Enterprise." McGregor contrasted the more traditional view of the worker as lazy and resistant (Theory X) with a more positive and humanistic view (Theory Y). He contended that significant increases in human effort will result in organizational settings that create opportunities, remove obstacles, encourage growth, and provide guidance. No author has done more to popularize the notion of industrial humanism. McGregor's 1957 article presents the main themes of his more famous 1960 book of the same title.

1

The Principles of Scientific Management

Frederick Winslow Taylor

By far the most important fact which faces the industries of our country, the industries, in fact, of the civilized world, is that not only the average worker, but nineteen out of twenty workmen throughout the civilized world firmly believe that it is for their best interests to go slow instead of to go fast. They firmly believe that it is for their interest to give as little work in return for the money that they get as is practical. The reasons for this belief are twofold, and I do not believe that the working-men are to blame for holding these fallacious views.

If you will take any set of workmen in your own town and suggest to those men that it would be a good thing for them in their trade if they were to double their output in the coming year, each man turn out twice as much work and become twice as efficient, they would say, "I do not know anything about other people's trades; what you are saying about increasing efficiency being a good thing may be good for other trades, but I know that the only result if you come to our trade would be that half of us would be out of a job before the year was out." That to the average workingman is an axiom; it is not a matter subject to debate at all. And even among the average business men of this country that opinion is almost universal. They firmly believe that that would be the result of a great increase in efficiency, and yet directly the opposite is true.

The Effect of Labor-Saving Devices

Whenever any labor-saving device of any kind has been introduced into any trade—go back into the history of any trade and see it—even though that labor-saving device may turn out ten, twenty, thirty times that output that was originally turned out by men in that trade, the result has universally been to make work for more men in that trade, not work for less men.

Let me give you one illustration. Let us take one of the staple businesses, the cotton industry. About 1840 the power loom succeeded the old hand loom in the

Reprinted from *Bulletin of the Taylor Society*, December 1916.

cotton industry. It was invented many years before, somewhere about 1780 or 1790, but it came in very slowly. About 1840 the weavers of Manchester, England, saw that the power loom was coming, and they knew it would turn out three times the yardage of cloth in a day that the hand loom turned out. And what did they do, these five thousand weavers of Manchester, England, who saw starvation staring them in the face? They broke into the establishments into which those machines were being introduced, they smashed them, they did everything possible to stop the introduction of the power loom. And the same result followed that follows every attempt to interfere with the introduction of any labor-saving device, if it is really a labor-saving device. Instead of stopping the introduction of the power loom, their opposition apparently accelerated it, just as opposition to scientific management all over the country, bitter labor opposition today, is accelerating the introduction of it instead of retarding it. History repeats itself in that respect. The power loom came right straight along.

And let us see the result in Manchester. Just what follows in every industry when any labor-saving device is introduced. Less than a century has gone by since 1840. The population of England in that time has not more than doubled. Each man in the cotton industry in Manchester, England, now turns out, at a restricted estimate ten yards of cloth for every yard of cloth that was turned out in 1840. In 1840 there were 5,000 weavers in Manchester. Now there are 265,000. Has that thrown men out of work? Has the introduction of labor-saving machinery, which has multiplied the output per man by tenfold, thrown men out of work?

What is the real meaning of this? All that you have to do is to bring wealth into this world and the world uses it. That is the real meaning. The meaning is that where in 1840 cotton goods were a luxury to be worn only by rich people when they were hardly ever seen on the street, now every man, woman and child all over the world wears cotton goods as a daily necessity.

Nineteen-twentieths of the real wealth of this world is used by the poor people, and not the rich, so that the workingman who sets out as a steady principle to restrict output is merely robbing his own kind. That group of manufacturers which adopts as a permanent principle restriction of output, in order to hold up prices, is robbing the world. The one great thing that marks the improvement of this world is measured by the enormous increase in output of the individuals in this world. There is fully twenty times the output per man now that there was three hundred years ago. That marks the increase in the real wealth of the world; that marks the increase of the happiness of the world; that gives us the opportunity for shorter hours, for better education, for amusement, for art, for music, for everything that is worthwhile in this world—goes right straight back to this increase in the output of the individual. The workingmen of today live better than the king did three hundred years ago. From what does the progress the world has made come? Simply from the increase in the output of the individual all over the world.

The Development of Soldiering

The second reason why the workmen of this country and of Europe deliberately restrict output is a very simple one. They, for this reason, are even less to blame than they are for the other. If, for example, you are manufacturing a pen, let us assume for simplicity that a pen can be made by a single man. Let us say that the workman is turning out ten pens per day, and that he is receiving $2.50 a day for his wages. He has a progressive foreman who is up to date, and that foreman goes to the workman and suggests, "Here, John, you are getting $2.50 a day, and you are turning out ten pens. I would suggest that I pay you 25 cents for making that pen." The man takes the job, and through the help of his foreman, through his own ingenuity, through his increased work, through his interest in his business, through the help of his friends, at the end of the year he finds himself turning out twenty pens instead of ten. He is happy, he is making $5, instead of $2.50 a day. His foreman is happy because, with the same room, with the same men he had before, he has doubled the output of his department, and the manufacturer himself is sometimes happy, but not often. Then someone on the board of directors asks to see the payroll, and he finds that we are paying $5 a day where other similar mechanics are only getting $2.50, and in no uncertain terms he announces that we must stop ruining the labor market. We cannot pay $5 a day when the standard rate of wages is $2.50; how can we hope to compete with surrounding towns? What is the result? Mr. Foreman is sent for, and he is told that he has got to stop ruining the labor market of Cleveland. And the foreman goes back to his workman in sadness, in depression, and tells his workman, "I am sorry, John, but I have got to cut the price down for that pen; I cannot let you earn $5 a day; the board of directors has got on to it, and it is ruining the labor market; you ought to be willing to have the price reduced. You cannot earn more than $3 or $2.75 a day, and I will have to cut your wages so that you will only get $3 a day." John, of necessity, accepts the cut, but he sees to it that he never makes enough pens to get another cut.

Characteristics of the Union Workman

There seem to be two divergent opinions about the workmen of this country. One is that a lot of the trade unions' workmen, particularly in this country, have become brutal, have become dominating, careless of any interests but their own, and are a pretty poor lot. And the other opinion which those same trade unionists hold of themselves is that they are pretty close to little gods. Whichever view you may hold of the workingmen of this country, and my personal view of them is that they are a pretty fine lot of fellows, they are just about the same as you and I. But whether you hold the bad opinion or the good opinion, it makes no difference. Whatever the workingmen of this country are or whatever they are not, they are not fools. And all that is necessary is for a workingman to have but one object lesson, like that I have told you, and he soldiers for the rest of his life.

There are a few exceptional employers who treat their workmen differently, but I am talking about the rule of the country. Soldiering is the absolute rule with all workmen who know their business. I am not saying it is for their interest to soldier. You cannot blame them for it. You cannot expect them to be large enough minded men to look at the proper view of the matter. Nor is the man who cuts the wages necessarily to blame. It is simply a misfortune in industry.

The Development of Scientific Management

There has been, until comparatively recently, no scheme promulgated by which the evils of rate cutting could be properly avoided, so soldiering has been the rule.

Now the first step that was taken toward the development of those methods, of those principles, which rightly or wrongly have come to be known under the name of scientific management—the first step that was taken in an earnest endeavor to remedy the evils of soldiering; an earnest endeavor to make it unnecessary for workmen to be hypocritical in this way, to deceive themselves, to deceive their employers, to live day in and day out a life of deceit, forced upon them by conditions—the very first step that was taken toward the development was to overcome that evil. I want to emphasize that, because I wish to emphasize the one great fact relating to scientific management, the greatest factor, namely, that scientific management is no new set of theories that has been tried on by any one at every step. Scientific management at every step has been an evolution, not a theory. In all cases the practice has preceded the theory, not succeeded it. In every case one measure after another has been tried out, until the proper remedy has been found. That series of proper eliminations, that evolution, is what is called scientific management. Every element of it has had to fight its way against the elements that preceded it, and prove itself better or it would not be there tomorrow.

All the men that I know of who are in any way connected with scientific management are ready to abandon any scheme, any theory in favor of anything else that could be found that is better. There is nothing in scientific management that is fixed. There is no one man, or group of men, who have invented scientific management.

What I want to emphasize is that all of the elements of scientific management are an evolution, not an invention. Scientific management is in use in an immense range and variety of industries. Almost every type of industry in this country has scientific management working successfully. I think I can safely say that on the average in those establishments in which scientific management has been introduced, the average workman is turning out double the output he was before. I think that is a conservative statement.

The Chief Beneficiaries

Three or four years ago I could have said there were about fifty thousand men working under scientific management, but now I know there are many more. Company after company is coming under it, many of which I know nothing about. Almost universally they are working successfully. This increasing of the output per individual in the trade, results, of course, in cheapening the product; it results, therefore, in larger profit usually to the owners of the business; it results also, in many cases, in a lowering of the selling price, although that has not come to the extent it will later. In the end the public gets the good. Without any question, the large good which so far has come from scientific management has come to the worker. To the workman has come, practically right off as soon as scientific management is introduced, an increase in wages amounting from 33 to 100 per cent, and yet that is not the greatest good that comes to the workmen from scientific management. The great good comes from the fact that, under scientific management, they look upon their employers as the best friends they have in the world; the suspicious watchfulness which characterizes the old type of management, the semi-antagonism, or the complete antagonism between workmen and employers is entirely superseded, and in its place comes genuine friendship between both sides. That is the greatest good that has come under scientific management. As a proof of this in the many businesses in which scientific management has been introduced, I know of not one single strike of workmen working under it after it had been introduced, and only two or three while it was in process of introduction. In this connection I must speak of the fakers, those who have said they can introduce scientific management into a business in six months or a year. That is pure nonsense. There have been many strikes stirred up by that type of man. Not one strike has ever come, and I do not believe ever will come, under scientific management.

What Scientific Management Is

What is scientific management? It is no efficiency device, nor is it any group of efficiency devices. Scientific management is no new scheme for paying men, it is no bonus system, no piecework system, no premium system of payment; it is no new method of figuring costs. It is no one of the various elements by which it is commonly known, by which people refer to it. It is not time study nor man study. It is not the printing of a ton or two of blanks and unloading them on a company and saying, "There is your system, go ahead and use it." Scientific management does not exist and cannot exist until there has been a complete mental revolution on the part of the workmen working under it, as to their duties toward themselves and toward their employers, and a complete mental revolution in the outlook for the employers, toward their duties, toward themselves, and toward their workmen. And until this great mental change takes place, scientific management does not exist. Do you think you can make a great mental revolution in a large group of workmen in a year, or do you think you can make it in a large group of foremen and superintendents in a year? If you do, you are very much mistaken. All of us hold mighty close to our ideas and principles in life, and we change very slowly toward the new, and very properly too.

Let me give you an idea of what I mean by this change in mental outlook. If you are manufacturing a hammer or a mallet, into the cost of that mallet goes a certain amount of raw materials, a certain amount of wood and metal. If you will take the cost of the raw materials and then add to it that cost which is frequently called by various names—overhead expenses, general expense, indirect expense; that is, the proper share of taxes, insurance, light, heat, salaries of officers and advertising—and you have a sum of money. Subtract that sum from the selling price, and what is left over is called the surplus. It is over this surplus that all of the labor disputes in the past have occurred. The workman naturally wants all he can get. His wages come out of that surplus. The manufacturer wants all he can get in the shape of profits, and it is from the division of this surplus that all the labor disputes have come in the past—the equitable division.

The new outlook that comes under scientific management is this: The work-men, after many object lessons, come to see and the management come to see that this surplus can be made so great, providing both sides will stop their pulling apart, will stop their fighting and will push as hard as they can to get as cheap an output as possible, that there is no occasion to quarrel. Each side can get more than ever before. The acknowledgment of this fact represents a complete mental revolution.

Intelligent Old-Style Management

There is one more illustration of the new and great change which comes under scientific management. I can make it clearer, perhaps, by contrasting it with what I look upon as the best of the older types of management. If you have a com-pany employing five hundred or a thousand men, you will have in that company perhaps fifteen different trades. The workmen in those trades have learned abso-lutely all that they know, not from books, not by being taught, but they have learned it traditionally. It has been handed down to them, not even by word of mouth in many cases, but by seeing what other men do. One man stands alongside of another man and imitates him. That is the way the trades are handed down, and my impres-sion is that trades are now picked up just as they were in the Middle Ages.

The manufacturer, the manager, or the foreman who knows his business real-izes that his chief function as a manager—I am talking now of the old-fashioned manager—ought to be to get the true initiative of his workman. He wants the initia-tive of the workman, their hard work, their good will, their ingenuity, their determi-nation to do all they can for the benefit of his firm. If he knows anything about human nature, if he has thought over the problems, he must realize that in order to get the initiative of his workman, in order to modify their soldiering, he must do something more for his men than other employers are doing for their men under similar circumstances. The wise manager, under the old type of management, delib-erately sets out to do something better for his workmen than his competitors are doing, better than he himself has ever done before. . . . When he sets out to do better for his men than other people do for theirs, the workmen respond liberally when that time comes. I refer to this case as being the highest type of management, the case in which the managers deliberately set out to do something better for their workmen than other people are doing, and to give them a special incentive of some kind, to which the workmen respond by giving a share at least of their initiative.

What Scientific Management Will Do

I am going to try to prove to you that the old style of management has not a ghost of a chance in competition with the principles of scientific management. Why? In the first place, under scientific management, the initiative of the work-men, their hard work, their goodwill, their best endeavors are obtained with abso-lute regularity. There are cases all the time where men will soldier, but they become the exception, as a rule, and they give their true initiative under scientific management. That is the least of the two sources of gain. The greatest source of gain under scientific management comes from the new and almost unheard-of duties and burdens which are voluntarily assumed, not by the workmen, but by the men on the management side. These are the things which make scientific management a success. These new duties, these new burdens undertaken by the management have rightly or wrongly been divided into four groups, and have been called the principles of scientific management.

The first of the great principles of scientific management, the first of the new burdens which are voluntarily undertaken by those on the management side is the deliberate gathering together of the great mass of traditional knowledge which, in the past, has been in the heads of the workmen, recording it, tabulating it, reducing it in most cases to rules, laws, and in many cases to mathematical formulae, which, with these new laws, are applied to the cooperation of the management to the work of the workmen. This results in an immense increase in the output, we may say, of the two. The gathering in of this great mass of traditional knowledge, which is done by the means of motion study, time study, can be truly called the science.

Let me make a prediction. I have before me the first book, so far as I know, that has been published on motion study and on time study. That is, the motion study and time study of the cement and concrete trades. It contains everything relating to concrete work. It is of about seven hundred pages and embodies the motions of men, the time and the best way of doing that sort of work. It is the first case in which a trade has been reduced to the same condition that engineering data of all kinds have been reduced, and it is this sort of data that is bound to sweep the world.

I have before me something which has been gathering for about fourteen years, the time or motion study of the machine shop. It will take probably four or five years more before the first book will be ready to publish on that subject. There is a collection of sixty or seventy thousand elements affecting machine-shop work. After a few years, say three, four or five years more, some one will be ready to publish the first book giving the laws of the movements of men in the machine shop— all the laws, not only a few of them. Let me predict, just as sure as the sun shines, that is going to come in every trade. Why? Because it pays, for no other reason. That results in doubling the output in any shop. Any device which results in an increased output is bound to come in spite of all opposition, whether we want it or not. It comes automatically.

The Selection of the Workman

The next of the four principles of scientific management is the scientific selection of the workman, and then his progressive development. It becomes the duty under scientific management of not one, but of a group of men on the management side, to deliberately study the workmen who are under them; study them in the most careful, thorough and painstaking way; and not just leave it to the poor, overworked foreman to go out and say, "Come on, what do you want? If you are cheap enough I will give you a trial."

That is the old way. The new way is to take a great deal of trouble in selecting the workmen. The selection proceeds year after year. And it becomes the duty of those engaged in scientific management to know something about the workmen under them. It becomes their duty to set out deliberately to train the workmen in their employ to be able to do a better and still better class of work than ever before, and to then pay them higher wages than ever before. This deliberate selection of the workmen is the second of the great duties that devolve on the management under scientific management.

Bringing Together the Science and the Man

The third principle is the bringing together of this science of which I have spoken and the trained workmen. I say bringing because they don't come together unless some one brings them. Select and train your workmen all you may, but unless there is some one who will make the men and the science come together, they will stay apart. The "make" involves a great many elements. They are not all disagreeable elements. The most important and largest way of "making" is to do something nice for the man whom you wish to make come together with the science. Offer him a plum, something that is worthwhile. There are many plums offered to those who come under scientific management—better treatment, more kindly treatment, more consideration for their wishes, and an opportunity for them to express their wants freely. That is one side of the "make." An equally important side is, whenever a man will not do what he ought, to either make him do it or stop it. If he will not do it, let him get out. I am not talking of any mollycoddle. Let me disabuse your minds of any opinion that scientific management is a mollycoddle scheme.

I have a great many union friends. I find they look with especial bitterness on this word "make." They have been used to doing the "making" in the past. That is the attitude of the trade unions, and it softens matters greatly when you can tell them the facts, namely, that in our making the science and the men come together, nine-tenths of our trouble comes with the men on the management side in making them do their new duties. I am speaking of those who have been trying to change from the old system to the new. Nine-tenths of our troubles come in trying to make the men on the management side do what they ought to do, to make them do the new duties, and take on these new burdens, and give up their old duties. That softens this word "make."

The Principle of the Division of Work

The fourth principle is the plainest of all. It involves a complete re-division of the work of the establishment. Under the old scheme of management, almost all of the work was done by the workmen. Under the new, the work of the establishment is divided into two large parts. All of that work which formerly was done by the workmen alone is divided into two large sections, and one of those sections is handed over to the management. They do a whole division of the work formerly done by the workmen. It is this real cooperation, this genuine division of the work between the two sides, more than any other element which accounts for the fact that there never will be strikes under scientific management. When the workman realizes that there is hardly a thing he does that does not have to be preceded by some act of preparation on the part of management, and when that workman realizes when the management falls down and does not do its part, that he is not only entitled to a kick, but that he can register that kick in the most forcible possible way, he cannot quarrel with the men over him. It is team work. There are more complaints made every day on the part of the workmen that the men on the management side fail to do their duties than are made by the management that the men fail. Every one of the complaints of the men has to be heeded, just as much as the complaints from the management that the workmen do not do their share. That is characteristic of scientific management. It represents a democracy, cooperation, a genuine division of work which never existed before in this world.

The Proof of the Theory

I am through now with the theory. I will try to convince you of the value of these four principles by giving you some practical illustrations. I hope that you will look for these four elements in the illustrations. I shall begin by trying to show the power of these four elements when applied to the greatest kind of work I know of that is done by man. The reason I have heretofore chosen pig-iron for an illustration is that it is the lowest form of work that is known.

A pig of iron weighs about ninety-two pounds on an average. A man stoops down and, with no other implement than his hands, picks up a pig of iron, walks a few yards with it, and drops it on a pile. A large part of the community has the impression that scientific management is chiefly handling pig-iron. The reason I first chose pig-iron for an illustration is that, if you can prove to any one the strength, the effect, of those four principles when applied to such rudimentary work as handling pig-iron, the presumption is that it can be applied to something better. The only way to prove it is to start at the bottom and show those four principles all along the line. I am sorry I cannot, because of lack of time, give you the illustration of handling pig-iron. Many of you doubt whether there is much of any science in it. I am going to try to prove later with a high-class mechanic that the workman who is fit to work at any type of work is almost universally incapable of understanding the principles without the help of some one else. I will use shoveling because it is a shorter illustration, and I will try to show what I mean by the science of shoveling, and the power which comes to the man who knows the science of shoveling. It is a high art compared with pig-iron handling.

The Science of Shoveling

When I went to the Bethlehem Steel Works, the first thing I saw was a gang of men unloading rice coal. They were a splendid set of fellows, and they shoveled fast. There was no loafing at all. They shoveled as hard as you could ask any man to work. I looked with the greatest of interest for a long time, and finally they moved off rapidly down into the yard to another part of the yard and went right at handling iron ore. One of the main facts connected with that shoveling was that the work those men were doing was that, in handling the rice coal, they had on their shovels a load of 3¾ pounds, and when the same men went to handling ore with the same shovel, they had over 38 pounds on their shovels. Is it asking too much of anyone to inquire whether 3¾ pounds is the right load for a shovel, or whether 38 pounds is the right load for a shovel? Surely if one is right the other must be wrong. I think that is a self-evident fact, and yet I am willing to bet that that is what workmen are doing right now in Cleveland.

That is the old way. Suppose we notice that fact. Most of us do not notice it because it is left to the foreman. At the Midvale works, we had to find out these facts. What is the old way of finding them out? The old way was to sit down and write one's friends and ask them the question. They got answers from contractors about what they thought it ought to be, and then they averaged them up, or took the most reliable man, and said, "That is all right; now we have a shovel load of so much." The more common way is to say, "I want a good shovel foreman." They will send for the foreman of the shovelers and put the job up to him to find what is the proper load to put on a shovel. He will tell you right off the bat. I want to show you the difference under scientific management.

Under scientific management you ask no one. Every little trifle—there is nothing too small—becomes the subject of experiment. The experiments develop into a law; they save money; they increase the output of the individual and make the thing worthwhile. How is this done? What we did in shoveling experiments was to deliberately select two first class shovelers, the best we knew how to get. We brought them into the office and said, "Jim and Mike, you two fellows are both good shovelers. I have a proposition to make to you. I am going to pay you double wages if you fellows will go out and do what I want you to do. There will be a young chap go along with you with a pencil and a piece of paper, and he will tell you to do a lot of fool things, and you will do them, and he will write down a lot of fool things, and you will think it is a joke, but it is nothing of the kind. Let me tell you one thing: if you fellows think that you can fool that chap you are very much mistaken, you cannot fool him at all. Don't get it through your heads you can fool him. If you take this double wages, you will be straight and do what you are told." They both promised and did exactly what they were told. What we told them was this: "We want you to start in and do whatever shoveling you are told to do, and work at just the pace, all day long, that when it comes night you are going to be good and tired, but not tired out. I do not want you exhausted or anything like that, but properly tired. You know what a good day's work is. In other words, I do not want any loafing business or any overwork business. If you find yourself overworked and getting too tired, slow down." Those men did that and did it in the most splendid kind of way day in and day out. We proved their cooperation because they were in different parts of the yard, and they both got near enough the same results. Our results were duplicated.

I have found that there are a lot of schemes among my working friends, but no more among them than among us. They are good, straight fellows if you only treat them right, and put the matter up squarely to them. We started in at a pile of material, with a very large shovel. We kept innumerable accurate records of all kinds, some of them useless. Thirty or forty different items were carefully observed about the work of those two men. We counted the number of shovelfuls thrown in a day. We found with a weight of between thirty-eight and thirty-nine pounds on the shovel, the man made a pile of material of a certain height. We then cut off the shovel, and he shoveled again and with a thirty-four pound load his pile went up and he shoveled more in a day. We again cut off the shovel to thirty pounds, and the pile went up again. With twenty-six pounds on the shovel, the pile again went up, and at twenty-one and one-half pounds the men could do their best. At twenty pounds the pile went down, at eighteen it went down, and at fourteen it went down, so that they were at the peak of twenty-one and one-half pounds. There is a scientific fact. A first class shoveler ought to take twenty-one and one-half pounds on his shovel in order to work to the best possible advantage. You are not giving that man a chance unless you give him a shovel which will hold twenty-one pounds.

The men in the yard were run by the old fashioned foreman. He simply walked about with them. We at once took their shovels away from them. We built a large labor tool room which held ten to fifteen different kinds of shoveling implements so that for each kind of material that was handled in that yard, all the way from rice coal, ashes, coke, all the way up to ore, we would have a shovel that would just hold twenty-one pounds, or average twenty-one. One time it would hold eighteen, the next twenty-four, but it will average twenty-one.

When you have six hundred men laboring in the yard, as we had there, it becomes a matter of quite considerable difficulty to get, each day, for each one of those six hundred men, engaged in a line one and one-half to two miles long and a half mile wide, just the right shovel for shoveling material. That requires organization to lay out and plan for those men in advance. We had to lay out the work each day. We had to have large maps on which the movements of the men were plotted out a day in advance. When each workman came in the morning, he took out two pieces of paper. One of the blanks gave them a statement of the implements which they had to use, and the part of the yard in which they had to work. That required organization planning in advance.

One of the first principles we adopted was that no man in that labor gang could work on the new way unless he earned sixty per cent higher wages than under the old plan. It is only just to the workman that he shall know right off whether he is doing his work right or not. He must not be told a week or month after, that he fell down. He must know it the next morning. So the next slip that came out of the pigeon hole was either a white or yellow slip. We used the two colors because some of the men could not read. The yellow slip meant that he had not earned his sixty per cent higher wages. He knew that he could not stay in that gang and keep on getting yellow slips.

Teaching the Men

I want to show you again the totally different outlook there is under scientific management by illustrating what happened when that man got his yellow slips. Under the old scheme, the foreman could say to him, "You are no good, get out of this; no time for you, you cannot earn sixty per cent higher wages; get out of this! Go!" It was not done politely, but the foreman had no time to palaver. Under the new scheme what happened? A teacher of shoveling went down to see that man. A teacher of shoveling is a man who is handy with a shovel, who has made his mark in life with a shovel, and yet who is a kindly fellow and knows how to show the other fellow what he ought to do. When that teacher went there he said, "See here, Jim, you have a lot of those yellow slips, what is the matter with you? What is up? Have you been drunk? Are you tired? Are you sick? Anything wrong with you? Because if you are tired or sick we will give you a show somewhere else." "Well, no, I am all right." "Then if you are not sick, or there is nothing wrong with you, you have forgotten how to shovel. I showed you how to shovel. You have forgotten something, now go ahead and shovel and I will show you what is the matter with you." Shoveling is a pretty big science, it is not a little thing.

If you are going to use the shovel right you should always shovel off an iron bottom; if not an iron bottom, a wooden bottom; and if not a wooden bottom a hard dirt bottom. Time and again the conditions are such that you have to go right into the pile. When that is the case, with nine out of ten materials it takes more trouble and more time and more effort to get the shovel into the pile than to do all the rest of the shoveling. That is where the effort comes. Those of you again who have taught the art of shoveling will have taught your workmen to do this. There is only one way to do it right. Put your forearm down onto the upper part of your leg, and when you push into the pile, throw your weight against it. That relieves your arm of work. You then have an automatic push, we will say, about eighty pounds, the weight of your body thrown on to it. Time and again we would find men whom we had taught to shovel right were going at it in the old way, and of course they could not do a day's work. The teacher would simply stand over that fellow and say, "There is what is the matter with you, Jim, you have forgotten to shovel into the pile."

You are not interested in shoveling, you are not interested in whether one way or the other is right, but I do hope to interest you in the difference of the mental attitude of the men who are teaching under the new system. Under the new system, if a man falls down, the presumption is that it is our fault at first, that we probably have not taught the man right, have not given him a fair show, have not spent time enough in showing him how to do his work.

Let me tell you another thing that is characteristic of scientific management. In my day, we were smart enough to know when the boss was coming, and when he came up we were apparently really working. Under scientific management, there is none of that pretense. I cannot say that in the old days we were delighted to see the boss coming around. We always expected some kind of roast if he came too close. Under the new, the teacher is welcomed; he is not an enemy, but a friend. He comes there to try to help the man get bigger wages, to show him how to do something. It is the great mental change, the change in the outlook that comes, rather than the details of it.

Does Scientific Management Pay?

It took the time of a number of men for about three years to study the art of shoveling in that yard at the Bethlehem Steel Works alone. They were carefully trained college men, and they were busy all the time. That costs money, the tool room costs money, the clerks we had to keep there all night figuring up how much the men did the day before cost money, the office in which the men laid out and planned the work cost money. The very fair and proper question, the only question to ask is "Does it pay?" because if scientific management does not pay, there is nothing in it; if it does not pay in dollars and cents, it is the rankest kind of nonsense. There is nothing philanthropic about it. It has got to pay, because business which cannot be done on a profitable basis ought not to be done on a philanthropic basis, for it will not last. At the end of three and one-half years we had a very good chance to know whether or not it paid.

Fortunately in the Bethlehem Steel Works they had records of how much it cost to handle the materials under the old system, where the single foreman led a group of men around the works. It costs them between seven and eight cents a ton to handle materials, on an average throughout the year. After paying for all this extra work I have told you about, it cost between three and four cents a ton to handle materials, and there was a profit of between seventy-five and eighty thousand dollars a year in that yard by handling those materials in the new way. What the men got out of it was this: Under the old system there were between four and six hundred men handling the material in that yard, and when we got through there were about one hundred and forty. Each one was earning a great deal more money. We made careful investigation and found they were almost all saving money, living better, happier; they are the most contented set of laborers to be seen anywhere. It is only by this kind of justification, justification of a profit for both sides, an advantage to both sides, that scientific management can exist.

I would like to give you one more illustration. I want to try to prove to you that even the highest-class mechanic cannot possibly understand the philosophy of his work, cannot possibly understand the laws under which he has to operate. There is a man who has had a high school education, an ingenious fellow who courts variety in life, to whom it is pleasant to change from one kind of work to another. He is not a cheap man, he is rather a high-grade man among the machinists of this country. The case of which I am going to tell you is one in which my friend Barth went to introduce scientific management in the works of an owner, who, at between 65 and 70 years of age, had built up his business from nothing to almost five thousand men. They had a squabble, and after they got through, Mr. Barth made the proposition, "I will take any machine that you use in your shop, and I will show you that I can double the output of that machine." A very fair machine was selected. It was a lathe on which the workman had been working about twelve years. The product of that shop is a patented machine with a good many parts, 350 men working making those parts year in and year out. Each man had ten or a dozen parts a year.

The first thing that was done was in the presence of the foreman, the superintendent and the owner of the establishment. Mr. Barth laid down the way in which all of the parts were to be machined on that machine by the workman. Then Mr. Barth, with one of his small slide rules, proceeded to analyze the machine. With the aid of this analysis, which embodies the laws of cutting metals, Mr. Barth was able to take his turn at the machine; his gain was from two and one-half times to three times the amount of work turned out by the other man. This is what can be done by science as against the old rule of thumb knowledge. That is not exaggeration; the gain is as great as that in many cases.

Let me tell you something. The machines of this country, almost universally in the machine shops of our country, are speeded two or three hundred percent wrong. I made that assertion before the tool builders in Atlantic City. I said, "Gentlemen, in your own shops, many of your machines are two and three hundred percent wrong in speeds. Why? Because you have guessed at it." I am trying to show you what are the losses under the old opinions, the difference between knowledge on the one hand and guesswork on the other.

In 1882, at the end of a long fight with the machinists of the Midvale Steel Works, I went there as a laborer, and finally became a machinist after serving my apprenticeship outside. I finally got into the shop, and worked up to the place of a clerk who had something wrong with him. I then did a little bit more work than the others were doing, not too much. They came to me and said, "See here, Fred, you are not going to be a piecework hog." I said, "You fellows mean that you think I am not going to try to get any more work off these machines? I certainly am. Now I am on the other side, and I am going to be straight with you, and I will tell you so in advance." They said, "All right then, we will give you fair notice you will be outside the fence inside of six weeks." Let me tell you gentlemen, if any of you have been through a fight like that, trying to get workmen to do what they do not want to do, you will know the meanness of it, and you will never want to go into another one. I never would have gone into it if I had known what was ahead of me. After the meanest kind of a bitter fight, at the end of three years, we fairly won out and got a big increase in output. I had no illusion at the end of that time as to my great ability or anything else. I knew that those workmen knew about ten times as much as I did about doing the work. I set out deliberately to get on our side some of that knowledge that those workmen had.

Mr. William Sellers was the president, and he was a man away beyond his generation in progress. I went to him and said, "I want to spend quite a good deal of money trying to educate ourselves on the management side of our works. I do not know much of anything, and I am just about in the same condition as all the rest of the foremen around here." Very reluctantly, I may say, he allowed us to start to spend money. That started the study of the art of cutting metals. At the end of six months, from the standpoint of how to cut the metal off faster, the study did not amount to anything, but we unearthed a gold mine of information. Mr. Sellers laughed at me, but when I was able to show him the possibilities that lay ahead of us, the number of things we could find out, he said, "Go ahead." So until 1889, that experiment went straight ahead day in and day out. That was done because it paid in dollars and cents.

After I left the Midvale Steel Works, we had no means of figuring those experiments except the information which we had already gotten. Ten different machines were built to develop the art of cutting metals, so that almost continuously from 1882 for twenty-six years, all sorts of experiments went on to determine the twelve great elements that go to make up the art of cutting metals. I am trying to show you just what is going to take place in every industry throughout this world. You must know those facts if you are going to manufacture cheaply, and the only way to know them is to pay for them.

The Discovery of High Speed Steel

Twelve elements do not sound very many, but they are difficult elements. One of the twelve elements was the discovery of high speed steel, that is, it resulted from a careful series of experiments to determine the proper chemical composition, plus the proper heat treatment of tool steel in order to get the highest cutting speed out of it. It was a series of most carefully tried scientific experiments lasting through three years, which led gradually up to the discovery of high speed steel. Most people think it was an accident. Not at all. It was at the expense of about $50,000 in work, in wages, and in the manufacture of steels. That is one of the twelve elements. There are eleven others. Among the others is this one, simplest of all. We found very early that if we threw a heavy stream of cold water on the tip of the tool, the cooling effect was such that we could run forty percent faster. Mr. Sellers was skeptical, and it was pretty hard to make him believe the truth. He tore down the old shop and built an entirely new shop in order to get that forty percent increase. He had his overhead supply of water brought down to each machine so that it could be adjusted quickly, and by means of that it gave us that forty percent increase. Gentlemen, think of it, only one machine shop in twenty years followed that. It was explained to the manufacturers, and the average man said, "Oh, hell, what's the use?" There is the answer.

I also want to try to show you why the high class mechanic cannot possibly compete with this science. The working out of those twelve elements resulted in the development of twelve large mathematical formulas, and in order to figure out the two great things that every mechanic has to know when he sets a tool in a lathe and goes to cutting metals—what speed and what feed shall be used—requires the solution of a mathematical problem containing twelve unknown quantities. If any one tries to solve those twelve unknown quantities with a pencil and paper, it takes about six hours. For eighteen years we had mathematicians all the time employed trying to solve that problem, and it paid because we got nearer and nearer to the solution. At the end of eighteen years, instead of taking six hours to solve the problem, it can be solved in twenty seconds by all of the workmen. That brings this problem right down to the level of everyday practical common sense.

The Effect on the Workman

Almost everyone says, "Why, yes, that may be a good thing for the manufacturer, but how about the workmen? You are taking all the initiative away from that workman, you are making a machine out of him; what are you doing for him? He becomes merely a part of the machine." That is the almost universal impression. Again let me try to sweep aside the fallacy of that view by an illustration. The modern surgeon without a doubt is the finest mechanic in the world. He combines the greatest manual dexterity with the greatest knowledge of implements and the greatest knowledge of the materials on which he is working. He is a true scientist, and he is a very highly skilled mechanic.

How does the surgeon teach his trade to the young men who come to the medical school? Does he say to them, "Now, young men, we belong to an older generation than you do, but the new generation is going to far outstrip anything that has been done in our generation; therefore, what we want of you is your initiative. We must have your brains, your thought, with your initiative. Of course, you know we old fellows have certain prejudices. For example, if we were going to amputate a leg, when we come down to the bone we are accustomed to take a saw, and we use it in that way and saw the bone off. But, gentlemen, do not let that fact one minute interfere with your originality, with your initiative, if you prefer an axe or a hatchet." Does the surgeon say this? He does not. He says, "You young men are going to outstrip us, but we will show you how. You shall not use a single implement in a single way until you know just which one to use, and we will tell you which one to use, and until you know how to use it, we will tell you how to use that implement, and after you have learned to use that implement our way, if you then see any defects in the implements, any defects in the method, then invent; but, invent so that you can invent upwards. Do not go inventing things which we discarded years ago."

That is just what we say to our young men in the shops. Scientific Management makes no pretense that there is any finality in it. We merely say that the collective work of thirty or forty men in this trade through eight or ten years has gathered together a large amount of data. Every man in the establishment must start that way, must start our way, then if he can show us any better way, I do not care what it is, we will make an experiment to see if it is better. It will be named after him, and he will get a prize for having improved on one of our standards. There is the way we make progress under scientific management. There is your justification for all this. It does not dwarf initiative, it makes true initiative. Most of our progress comes through our workmen, but it comes in a legitimate way.

2

The Giving of Orders

Mary Parker Follett

To some men the matter of giving orders seems a very simple affair; they expect to issue their own orders and have them obeyed without question. Yet, on the other hand, the shrewd common sense of many a business executive has shown him that the issuing of orders is surrounded by many difficulties; that to demand an unquestioning obedience to orders not approved, not perhaps even understood, is bad business policy. Moreover, psychology, as well as our own observation, shows us not only that you cannot get people to do things most satisfactorily by ordering them or exhorting them; but also that even reasoning with them, even convincing them intellectually, may not be enough. Even the "consent of the governed" will not do all the work it is supposed to do, an important consideration for those who are advocating employee representation. For all our past life, our early training, our later experience, all our emotions, beliefs, prejudices, every desire that we have, have formed certain habits of mind what the psychologists call habit-patterns, action-patterns, motor-sets.

Therefore it will do little good merely to get intellectual agreement; unless you change the habit-patterns of people, you have not really changed your people. Business administration, industrial organization, should build up certain habit-patterns, that is, certain mental attitudes. For instance, the farmer has a general disposition to "go it alone," and this is being changed by the activities of the cooperatives, that is, note, *by the farmer's own activities*. So the workman has often a general disposition of antagonism to his employers which cannot be changed by argument or exhortation, but only through certain activities which will create a different disposition. One of my trade union friends told me that he remembered when he was a quite small boy hearing his father, who worked in a shoe-shop, railing daily against his boss. So he grew up believing that it was inherent in the nature of things that the workman should be against his employer. I know many working men who have a prejudice against getting college men into factories. You could all give me examples of attitudes among your employees which you would like to change. We want, for instance, to create an attitude of respect for expert opinion.

If we analyze this matter a little further we shall see that we have to do three things, I am now going to use psychological language: (1) build up certain attitudes; (2) provide for the release of these attitudes; (3) augment the released response as it is being carried out. What does this mean in the language of business? A psychologist has given us the example of the salesman. The salesman first creates in you the attitude that you want his article; then, at just the "psychological" moment, he produces his contract blank which you may sign and thus release that attitude; then if, as you are preparing to sign, some one comes in and tells you how pleased he has been with his purchase of this article, that augments the response which is being released.

If we apply this to the subject of orders and obedience, we see that people can obey an order only if previous habit-patterns are appealed to or new ones created. When the employer is considering an order, he should also be thinking of the way to form the habits which will ensure its being carried out. We should first lead the salesmen selling shoes or the bank clerk cashing cheques to see the desirability of a different method. Then the rules of the store or bank should be so changed as to make it possible for salesman or cashier to adopt the new method. In the third place they could be made more ready to follow the new method by convincing in advance some one individual who will set an example to the others. You can usually convince one or two or three ahead of the rank and file. This last step you all know from your experience to be good tactics; it is what the psychologists call intensifying the attitude to be released. But we find that the released attitude is not by one release fixed as a habit; it takes a good many responses to do that.

This is an important consideration for us, for from one point of view business success depends largely on this—namely, whether our business is so organized and administered that it tends to form certain habits, certain mental attitudes. It has been hard for many old-fashioned employers to understand that *orders will not take the place of training.* I want to italicize that. Many a time an employer has been angry because, as he expressed it, a workman "wouldn't" do so and so, when the truth of the matter was that the workman couldn't, actually couldn't, do as ordered because he could not go contrary to life-long habits. This whole subject might be taken up under the heading of education, for there we could give many instances of the attempt to make arbitrary authority take the place of training. In history, the aftermath of all revolutions shows us the results of the lack of training.

In this matter of prepared-in-advance behaviour patterns—that is, in preparing the way for the reception of orders, psychology makes a contribution when it points out that the same words often rouse in us a quite different response when heard in certain places and on certain occasions. A boy may respond differently to the same suggestion when made by his teacher and when made by his schoolmate. Moreover, he may respond differently to the same suggestion made by the teacher in the schoolroom and made by the teacher when they are taking a walk together. Applying this to the giving of orders, we see that the place in which orders are given, the circumstances under which they are given, may make all the difference in the world as to the response which we get. Hand them down a long way from President or Works Manager and the effect is weakened. One might say that the strength of favourable response to an order is in inverse ratio to the distance the order travels. Production efficiency is always in danger of being affected whenever the long-distance order is substituted for the face-to-face suggestion. There is, however, another reason for that which I shall consider in a moment.

All that we said in the foregoing paper of integration and circular behaviour applies directly to the anticipation of response in giving orders. We spoke then of what the psychologists call linear and circular behaviour. Linear behaviour would be, to quote from Dr. Cabot's review of my book, *Creative Experience,* when an order is accepted as passively as the woodshed accepts the wood. In circular behaviour you get a "come-back." But we all know that we get the come-back every day of our life, and we must certainly allow for it, or for what is more elegantly called circular behaviour, in the giving of orders. Following out the thought of the previous paper, I should say that the giving of orders and the receiving of orders ought to be a matter of integration through circular behaviour, and that we should seek methods to bring this about.

Psychology has another important contribution to make on this subject of issuing orders or giving directions: before the integration can be made between order-giver and order-receiver, there is often an integration to be made within one or both of the individuals concerned. There are often two dissociated paths in the individual; if you are clever enough to recognize these, you can sometimes forestall a Freudian conflict, make the integration appear before there is an acute stage.

To explain what I mean, let me run over briefly a social worker's case. The girl's parents had been divorced and the girl placed with a jolly, easy-going, slack and untidy family, consisting of the father and mother and eleven children, sons and daughters. Gracie was very happy here, but when the social worker in charge of the case found that the living conditions involved a good deal of promiscuity, she thought the girl should be placed elsewhere. She therefore took her to call on an aunt who had a home with some refinement of living, where they had "high tastes," as one of the family said. This aunt wished to have Gracie live with her, and Gracie decided that she would like to do so. The social worker, however, in order to test her, said, "But I thought you were so happy where you are." "Can't I be happy and high, too?" the girl replied. There were two wishes here, you see. The social worker by removing the girl to the aunt may have forestalled a Freudian conflict, the dissociated paths may have been united. I do not know the outcome of this story, but it indicates a method of dealing with our co-directors—make them "happy and high, too."

Business administration has often to consider how to deal with the dissociated paths in individuals or groups, but the methods of doing this successfully have been developed much further in some departments than in others. We have as yet hardly recognized this as part of the technique of dealing with employees, yet the clever salesman knows that it is the chief part of his job. The prospective buyer wants the article and does not want it. The able salesman does not suppress the arguments in the mind of the purchaser against buying, for then the purchaser might be sorry afterwards for his purchase, and that would not be good salesmanship. Unless he can unite, integrate, in the purchaser's mind, the reasons for buying and the reasons for not buying, his future sales will be imperilled, he will not be the highest grade salesman.

Please note that this goes beyond what the psychologist whom I quoted at the beginning of this section told us. He said, "The salesman must create in you the attitude that you want his article." Yes, but only if he creates this attitude by integration not by suppression.

Apply all this to orders. An order often leaves the individual to whom it is given with two dissociated paths; an order should seek to unite, to integrate, dissociated paths. Court decisions often settle arbitrarily which of two ways is to be followed without showing a possible integration of the two, that is, the individual is often left with an internal conflict on his hands. This is what both courts and business administration should try to prevent, the internal conflicts of individuals or groups.

In discussing the preparation for giving orders, I have not spoken at all of the appeal to certain instincts made so important by many writers. Some writers, for instance, emphasize the instinct of self-assertion; this would be violated by too rigid orders or too clumsily-exercised authority. Other writers, of equal standing, tell us that there is an instinct of submission to authority. I cannot discuss this for we should first have to define instincts, too long an undertaking for us now. Moreover, the exaggerated interest in instincts of recent years, an interest which in many cases has received rather crude expression, is now subsiding. Or, rather, it is being replaced by the more fruitful interest in habits.

There is much more that we could learn from psychology about the forming of habits and the preparation for giving orders than I can even hint at now. But there is one point, already spoken of by implication, that I wish to consider more explicitly—namely, the manner of giving orders. Probably more industrial trouble has been caused by the manner in which orders are given than in any other way. In the *Report on Strikes and Lockouts*, a British Government publication, the cause of a number of strikes is given as "alleged harassing conduct of the foreman," "alleged tyrannical conduct of an under-foreman," "alleged overbearing conduct of officials." The explicit statement, however, of the tyranny of superior officers as the direct cause of strikes is I should say, unusual, yet resentment smoulders and breaks out in other issues. And the demand for better treatment is often explicit enough. We find it made by the metal and woodworking trades in an aircraft factory, who declared that any treatment of men without regard to their feelings of self-respect would be answered by a stoppage of work. We find it put in certain agreements with employers that "the men must be treated with proper respect, and threats and abusive language must not be used."

What happens to man, *in* a man, when an order is given in a disagreeable manner by foreman, head of department, his immediate superior in store, bank or factory? The man addressed feels that his self-respect is attacked, that one of his most inner sanctuaries is invaded. He loses his temper or becomes sullen or is on the defensive; he begins thinking of his "rights"—a fatal attitude for any of us. In the language we have been using, the wrong behaviour pattern is aroused, the wrong motor-set; that is, he is now "set" to act in a way which is not going to benefit the enterprise in which he is engaged.

There is a more subtle psychological point here, too; the more you are "bossed" the more your activity of thought will take place within the bossing-pattern, and your part in that pattern seems usually to be opposition to the bossing.

This complaint of the abusive language and the tyrannical treatment of the one just above the worker is an old story to us all, but there is an opposite extreme which is far too little considered. The immediate superior officer is often so close to the worker that he does not exercise the proper duties of his position. Far from taking on himself an aggressive authority, he has often evaded one of the chief problems of his job: how to do what is implied in the fact that he has been put in a position over others. The head of the woman's cloak department in a store will call out, "Say, Sadie, you're 36, aren't you? There's a woman down in the Back Bay kicking about something she says you promised yesterday." "Well, I like that," says Sadie. "Some of those Back Bay women would kick in Heaven." And that perhaps is about all that happens. Of course, the Back Bay lady has to be appeased, but there is often no study of what has taken place for the benefit of the store. I do not mean that a lack of connection between such incidents and the improvement of store technique is universal, but it certainly exists far too often and is one of the problems of those officials who are just above the heads of departments. Naturally, a woman does not want to get on bad terms with her fellow employees with whom she talks and works all day long. Consider the chief operator of the telephone exchanges, remembering that the chief operator is a member of the union, and that the manager is not.

Now what is our problem here? How can we avoid the two extremes: too great bossism in giving orders, and practically no orders given? I am going to ask how you are avoiding these extremes. My solution is to depersonalize the giving of orders, to unite all concerned in a study of the situation, to discover the law of the situation and obey that. Until we do this I do not think we shall have the most successful business administration. This is what does take place, what has to take place, when there is a question between two men in positions of equal authority. The head of the sales departments does not give orders to the head of the production department, or vice versa. Each studies the market and the final decision is made as the market demands. This is, ideally, what should take place between foremen and rank and file, between any head and his subordinates. One *person* should not give orders to another *person*, but both should agree to take their orders from the situation. If orders are simply part of the situation, the question of someone giving and someone receiving does not come up. Both accept the orders given by the situation. Employers accept the orders given by the situation; employees accept the orders given by the situation. This gives, does it not, a slightly different aspect to the whole of business administration through the entire plant?

We have here, I think, one of the largest contributions of scientific management: it tends to depersonalize orders. From one point of view, one might call the essence of scientific management the attempt to find the law of the situation.

With scientific management the managers are as much under orders as the workers, for both obey the law of the situation. Our job is not how to get people to obey orders, but how to devise methods by which we can best *discover* the order integral to a particular situation. When that is found, the employee can issue it to the employer, as well as employer to employee. This often happens easily and naturally. My cook or my stenographer points out the law of the situation, and I, if I recognize it as such, accept it, even although it may reverse some "order" I have given.

If those in supervisory positions should depersonalize orders, then there would be no overbearing authority on the one hand, nor on the other that dangerous *laissez-aller* which comes from the fear of exercising authority. Of course we should exercise authority, but always the authority of the situation. I do not say that we have found the way to a frictionless existence, far from it, but we now understand the place which we mean to give to friction. We intend to set it to work for us as the engineer does when he puts the belt over the pulley. There will be just as much, probably more, room for disagreement in the method I am advocating. The situation will often be seen differently, often be interpreted differently. But we shall know what to do with it, we shall have found a method of dealing with it.

I call it depersonalizing because there is not time to go any further into the matter. I think it really is a matter of *repersonalizing*. We, persons, have relations with each other, but we should find them in and through the whole situation. We cannot have any sound relations with each other as long as we take them out of that setting which gives them their meaning and value. This divorcing of persons and the situation does a great deal of harm. I have just said that scientific management depersonalizes; the deeper philosophy of scientific management shows us personal relations within the whole setting of that thing of which they are a part.

There is much psychology, modern psychology particularly, which tends to divorce person and situation. What I am referring to is the present zest for "personality studies." When some difficulty arises we often hear the psychologist whose specialty is personality studies say, "Study the psychology of that man." And this is very good advice, but only if at the same time we study the entire situation. To leave out the whole situation, however, is so common a blunder in the studies of these psychologists that it constitutes a serious weakness in their work. And as those of you who are personnel directors have more to do, I suppose, with those psychologists who have taken personality for their specialty than with any others, I wish you would watch and see how often you find that this limitation detracts from the value of their conclusions.

I said above that we should substitute for the long-distance order the face-to-face suggestion. I think we can now see a more cogent reason for this than the one then given. It is not the face-to-face suggestion that we want so much as the joint study of the problem, and such joint study can be made best by the employee and his immediate superior or employee and special expert on that question.

I began this talk by emphasizing the advisability of preparing in advance the attitude necessary for the carrying out of orders, as in the previous paper we considered preparing the attitude for integration; but we have now, in our consideration of the joint study of situations, in our emphasis on obeying the law of the situation, perhaps got a little beyond that, or rather we have now to consider in what sense we wish to take the psychologist's doctrine of prepared-in-advance attitudes. By itself this would not take us far, for everyone is studying psychology nowadays, and our employees are going to be just as active in preparing us as we in preparing them. Indeed, a girl working in a factory said to me, "We had a course in psychology last winter, and I see now that you have to be pretty careful how you put things to the managers if you want them to consider favourably what you're asking for." If this prepared-in-advance idea were all that the psychologists think it, it would have to be printed privately as secret doctrine. But the truth is that the best preparation for integration in the matter of orders or in anything else, is a joint study of the situation. We should not try to create the attitude we *want*, although that is the usual phrase, but the attitude required for cooperative study and decision. This holds good even for the salesman. We said above that when the salesman is told that he should create in the prospective buyer the attitude that he wants the article, he ought also to be told that he should do this by integration rather than by suppression. We have now a hint of *how* he is to attain this integration.

I have spoken of the importance of changing some of the language of business personnel relations. We considered whether the words "grievances," "complaints," or Ford's "trouble specialists" did not arouse the wrong behaviour-patterns. I think "order" certainly does. If that word is not to mean any longer external authority, arbitrary authority, but the law of the situation, then we need a new word for it. It is often the order that people resent as much as the thing ordered. People do not like to be ordered even to take a holiday. I have often seen instances of this. The wish to govern one's own life is, of course, one of the most fundamental feelings in every human being. To call this "the instinct of self-assertion," "the instinct of initiative," does not express it wholly. I think it is told in the life of some famous American that when he was a boy and his mother said, "Go get a pail of water," he always replied, "I won't," before taking up the pail and fetching the water. This is significant; he resented the command, the command of a person; but he went and got the water, not, I believe, because he had to, but because he recognized the demand of the situation. *That*, he knew he had to obey; *that*, he was willing to obey. And this kind of obedience is not opposed to the wish to govern one's self, but each is involved in the other; both are part of the same fundamental urge at the root of one's being. We have here something far more profound than "the egoistic impulse" or "the instinct of self-assertion." We have the very essence of the human being.

This subject of orders has led us into the heart of the whole question of authority and consent. When we conceive of authority and consent as parts of an inclusive situation, does that not throw a flood of light on this question? The point of view here presented gets rid of several dilemmas which have seemed to puzzle people in dealing with consent. The feeling of being "under" someone, of "subordination," of "servility," of being "at the will of another," comes out again and again in the shop stewards movement and in the testimony before the Coal Commission. One man said before the Coal Commission, "It is all right to work *with* anyone; what is disagreeable is to feel too distinctly that you are working *under* anyone." *With* is a pretty good preposition, not because it connotes democracy, but because it connotes functional unity, a much more profound conception than that of democracy as usually held. The study of the situation involves the *with* preposition. Then Sadie is not left alone by the head of the cloak department, nor does she have to obey her. The head of the department says, "Let's see how such cases had better be handled, then we'll abide by that." Sadie is not under the head of the department, but both are *under* the situation.

Twice I have had a servant applying for a place ask me if she would be treated as a menial. When the first woman asked me that, I had no idea what she meant, I thought perhaps she did not want to do the roughest work, but later I came to the conclusion that to be treated as a menial meant to be obliged to be under someone, to follow orders without using one's own judgment. If we believe that what heightens self-respect increases efficiency, we shall be on our guard here.

Very closely connected with this is the matter of pride in one's work. If an order goes against what the craftsman or the clerk thinks is the way of doing his work which will bring the best results, he is justified in not wishing to obey that order. Could not that difficulty be met by a joint study of the situation? It is said that it is characteristic of the British workman to feel, "I know my job and won't be told how." The peculiarities of the British workman might be met by a joint study of the situation, it being understood that he probably has more to contribute to that study than anyone else. . . .

There is another dilemma which has to be met by everyone who is in what is called a position of authority: how can you expect people merely to obey orders and at the same time to take that degree of responsibility which they should take? Indeed, in my experience, the people who enjoy following orders blindly, without any thought on their own part, are those who like thus to get rid of responsibility. But the taking of responsibility, each according to his capacity, each according to his function in the whole . . . , this taking of responsibility is usually the most vital matter in the life of every human being, just as the allotting of responsibility is the most important part of business administration.

A young trade unionist said to me, "How much dignity can I have as a mere employee?" He can have all the dignity in the world if he is allowed to make his fullest contribution to the plant *and to assume definitely the responsibility therefor.*

I think one of the gravest problems before us is how to make the reconciliation between receiving orders and taking responsibility. And I think the reconciliation can be made through our conception of the law of the situation. . . .

We have considered the subject of symbols. It is often very apparent that an order is a symbol. The referee in the game stands watch in hand, and says, "Go." It is an order, but order only as symbol. I may say to an employee, "Do so and so," but I should say it only because we have both agreed, openly or tacitly, that that which I am ordering done is the best thing to be done. The order is then a symbol. And if it is a philosophical and psychological truth that we owe obedience only to a functional unity to which we are contributing, we should remember that a more accurate way of stating that would be to say that our obligation is to a *unifying*, to a process.

This brings us now to one of our most serious problems in this matter of orders. It is important, but we can touch on it only briefly; it is what we spoke of . . .

as the evolving situation. I am trying to show here that the order must be integral to the situation and must be recognized as such. But we saw that the situation was always developing. If the situation is never stationary, then the order should never be stationary, so to speak; how to prevent it from being so is our problem. The situation is changing while orders are being carried out, because, by and through orders being carried out. How is the order to keep up with the situation? External orders never can, only those drawn fresh from the situation.

Moreover, if taking a *responsible* attitude toward experience involves recognizing the evolving situation, a *conscious* attitude toward experience means that we note the change which the developing situation makes in ourselves; the situation does not change without changing us.

To summarize, . . . integration being the basic law of life, orders should be the composite conclusion of those who give and those who receive them; more than this, that they should be the integration of the people concerned and the situation; more even than this, that they should be the integrations involved in the evolving situation. If you accept my three fundamental statements on this subject: (1) that the order should be the law of the situation; (2) that the situation is always evolving; (3) that orders should involve circular not linear behaviour—then we see that our old conception of orders has somewhat changed, and that there should therefore follow definite changes in business practice.

There is a problem so closely connected with the giving of orders that I want to put it before you for future discussion. After we have decided on our orders, we have to consider how much and what kind of supervision is necessary or advisable in order that they shall be carried out. We all know that many workers object to being watched. What does that mean, how far is it justifiable? How can the objectionable element be avoided and at the same time necessary supervision given? I do not think that this matter has been studied sufficiently. When I asked a very intelligent girl what she thought would be the result of profit-sharing and employee representation in the factory where she worked, she replied joyfully, "We shan't need foremen any more." While her entire ignoring of the fact that the foreman has other duties than keeping workers on their jobs was amusing, one wants to go beyond one's amusement and find out what this objection to being watched really means.

In a case in Scotland arising under the Minimum Wage Act, the overman was called in to testify whether or not a certain workman did his work properly. The examination was as follows:

Magistrate: "But isn't it your duty under the Mines Act to visit each working place twice a day?"

Overman: "Yes."

Magistrate: "Don't you do it?"

Overman: "Yes."

Magistrate: "Then why didn't you ever see him work?"

Overman: "They always stop work when they see an overman coming and sit down and wait till he's gone—even take out their pipes, if it's a mine free from gas. They won't let anyone watch them."

An equally extreme standard was enforced for a part of the war period at a Clyde engineering works. The chairman of shop stewards was told one morning that there was a grievance at the smithy. He found one of the blacksmiths in a rage because the managing director in his ordinary morning's walk through the works had stopped for five minutes or so and watched this man's fire. After a shop meeting the chairman took up a deputation to the director and secured the promise that this should not happen again. At the next works meeting the chairman reported the incident to the body of workers, with the result that a similar demand was made throughout the works and practically acceded to, so that the director hardly dared to stop at all in his morning's walk.

I have seen similar instances cited. Many workmen feel that being watched is unbearable. What can we do about it? How can we get proper supervision without this watching which a worker resents? Supervision is necessary; supervision is resented—how are we going to make the integration there? Some say, "Let the workers elect the supervisors." I do not believe in that.

There are three other points closely connected with the subject of this paper which I should like merely to point out. First, when and how do you point out mistakes, misconduct? One principle can surely guide us here: don't blame for the sake of blaming, make what you have to say accomplish something; say it in that form, at that time, under those circumstances, which will make it a real education to your subordinate. Secondly, since it is recognized that the one who gives the orders is not as a rule a very popular person, the management sometimes tries to offset this by allowing the person who has this onus upon him to give any pleasant news to the workers, to have the credit of any innovation which the workers very much desire. One manager told me that he always tried to do this. I suppose that this is good behaviouristic psychology, and yet I am not sure that it is a method I wholly like. It is quite different, however, in the case of a mistaken order having been given; then I think the one who made the mistake should certainly be the one to rectify it, not as a matter of strategy, but because it is better for him too. It is better for all of us not only to acknowledge our mistakes, but to do something about them. If a foreman discharges someone and it is decided to reinstate the man, it is obviously not only good tactics but a square deal to the foreman to allow him to do the reinstating.

There is, of course, a great deal more to this matter of giving orders than we have been able to touch on; far from exhausting the subject, I feel that I have only given hints. I have been told that the artillery men suffered more mentally in the war than others, and the reason assigned for this was that their work was directed from a distance. The combination of numbers by which they focused their fire was telephoned to them. The result was also at a distance. Their activity was not closely enough connected with the actual situation at either end.

3

The Hawthorne Experiments

Fritz J. Roethlisberger

At a recent meeting the researches in personnel at the Hawthorne plant of the Western Electric Company were mentioned by both a management man and a union man. There seemed to be no difference of opinion between the two regarding the importance or relevance of these research findings for effective management-employee relations. This seemed to me interesting because it suggested that the labor situation can be discussed at a level where both sides can roughly agree. The question of what this level is can be answered only after closer examination of these studies.

In the February, 1941, issue of the *Reader's Digest* there appeared a summary statement of these researches by Stuart Chase, under the title, "What Makes the Worker Like to Work?" At the conclusion of his article, Stuart Chase said, "There is an idea here so big that it leaves one gasping." Just what Mr. Chase meant by this statement is not explained, but to find out one can go back to the actual studies and see what was learned from them. In my opinion, the results were very simple and obvious—as Sherlock Holmes used to say to Dr. Watson, "Elementary, my dear Watson." Now this is what may have left Stuart Chase "gasping"—the systematic exploitation of the simple and the obvious which these studies represent.

There seems to be an assumption today that we need a complex set of ideas to handle the complex problems of this complex world in which we live. We assume that a big problem needs a big idea; a complex problem needs a complex idea for its solution. As a result, our thinking tends to become more and more tortuous and muddled. Nowhere is this more true than in matters of human behavior. It seems to me that the road back to sanity—and here is where my title comes in—lies

(1) In having a few simple and clear ideas about the world in which we live.

Originally titled "The Road Back to Sanity." Reprinted by permission of the publisher from *Management and Morale* by F. J. Roethlisberger, pp. 7–26, Cambridge, MA: Harvard University Press. Copyright © 1941 by the President and Fellows of Harvard College, Copyright © renewed 1969 by F. J. Roethlisberger.

(2) In complicating our ideas, not in a vacuum, but only in reference to things we can observe, see, feel, hear, and touch. Let us not generalize from verbal definitions; let us know in fact what we are talking about.

(3) In having a very simple method by means of which we can explore our complex world. We need a tool which will allow us to get the data from which our generalizations are to be drawn. We need a simple skill to keep us in touch with what is sometimes referred to as "reality."

(4) In being "tough-minded," i.e., in not letting ourselves be too disappointed because the complex world never quite fulfills our most cherished expectations of it. Let us remember that the concrete phenomena will always elude any set of abstractions that we can make of them.

(5) In knowing very clearly the class of phenomena to which our ideas and methods relate. Now, this is merely a way of saying, "Do not use a saw as a hammer." A saw is a useful tool precisely because it is limited and designed for a certain purpose. Do not criticize the usefulness of a saw because it does not make a good hammer.

Although this last statement is obvious with regard to such things as "saws" and "hammers," it is less well understood in the area of human relations. Too often we try to solve human problems with nonhuman tools and, what is still more extraordinary, in terms of nonhuman data. We take data from which all human meaning has been deleted and then are surprised to find that we reach conclusions which have no human significance.

It is my simple thesis that a human problem requires a human solution. First, we have to learn to recognize a human problem when we see one; and, second, upon recognizing it, we have to learn to deal with it as such and not as if it were something else. Too often at the verbal level we talk glibly about the importance of the human factor; and too seldom at the concrete level of behavior do we recognize a human problem for what it is and deal with it as such. *A human problem to be brought to a human solution requires human data and human tools.* It is my purpose to use the Western Electric researches as an illustration of what I mean by this statement, because, if they deserve the publicity and acclaim which they have received, it is because, in my opinion, they have so conclusively demonstrated this point. In this sense they are the road back to sanity in management-employee relations.

Experiments in Illumination

The Western Electric researches started about sixteen years ago, in the Hawthorne plant, with a series of experiments on illumination. The purpose was to find out the relation of the quality and quantity of illumination to the efficiency of industrial workers. These studies lasted several years, and I shall not describe them in detail. It will suffice to point out that the results were quite different from what had been expected.

In one experiment the workers were divided into two groups. One group, called the "test group," was to work under different illumination intensities. The other group, called the "control group," was to work under an intensity of illumination as nearly constant as possible. During the first experiment, the test group was submitted to three different intensities of illumination of increasing magnitude, 24, 46, and 70 foot candles. What were the results of this early experiment? Production increased in both rooms—in both the test group and the control group—and the rise in output was roughly of the same magnitude in both cases.

In another experiment, the light under which the test group worked was decreased from 10 to 3 foot candles, while the control group worked, as before, under a constant level of illumination intensity. In this case the output rate in the test group went up instead of down. It also went up in the control group.

In still another experiment, the workers were allowed to believe that the illumination was being increased, although, in fact, no change in intensity was made. The workers commented favorably on the improved lighting condition, but there was no appreciable change in output. At another time, the workers were allowed to believe that the intensity of illumination was being decreased, although again, in fact, no actual change was made. The workers complained somewhat about the poorer lighting, but again there was no appreciable effect on output.

And finally, in another experiment, the intensity of illumination was decreased to .06 of a foot candle, which is the intensity of illumination approximately equivalent to that of ordinary moonlight. Not until this point was reached was there any appreciable decline in the output rate.

What did the experimenters learn? Obviously, as Stuart Chase said, there was something "screwy," but the experimenters were not quite sure who or what was screwy—they themselves, the subjects, or the results. One thing was clear: the results were negative. Nothing of a positive nature had been learned about the relation of illumination to industrial efficiency. If the results were to be taken at their face value, it would appear that there was no relation between illumination and industrial efficiency. However, the investigators were not yet quite willing to draw this conclusion. They realized the difficulty of testing for the effect of a single variable in a situation where there were many uncontrolled variables. It was thought therefore that another experiment should be devised in which other variables affecting the output of workers could be better controlled.

A few of the tough-minded experimenters already were beginning to suspect their basic ideas and assumptions with regard to human motivation. It occurred to them that the trouble was not so much with the results or with the subjects as it was with their notion regarding the way their subjects were supposed to behave—the notion of a simple cause-and-effect, direct relationship between certain physical changes in the workers' environment and the responses of the workers to these changes. Such a notion completely ignored the human meaning of these changes to the people who were subjected to them.

In the illumination experiments, therefore, we have a classic example of trying to deal with a human situation in nonhuman terms. The experimenters had obtained no human data; they had been handling electric-light bulbs and plotting average output curves. Hence their results had no human significance. That is why they seemed screwy. Let me suggest here, however, that the results were not screwy, but the experimenters were—a "screwy" person being by definition one who is not acting in accordance with the customary human values of the situation in which he finds himself.

The Relay Assembly Test Room

Another experiment was framed, in which it was planned to submit a segregated group of workers to different kinds of working conditions. The idea was very simple: A group of five girls were placed in a separate room where their conditions of work could be carefully controlled, where their output could be measured, and where they could be closely observed. It was decided to introduce at specified intervals different changes in working conditions and to see what effect these innovations had on output. Also, records were kept, such as the temperature and humidity of the room, the number of hours each girl slept at night, the kind and amount of food she ate for breakfast, lunch, and dinner. Output was carefully measured, the time it took each girl to assemble a telephone relay of approximately forty parts (roughly a minute) being automatically recorded each time; quality records were kept; each girl had a physical examination at regular intervals. Under these conditions of close observation the girls were studied for a period of five years. Literally tons of material were collected. Probably nowhere in the world has so much material been collected about a small group of workers for such a long period of time.

But what about the results? They can be stated very briefly. When all is said and done, they amount roughly to this: A skillful statistician spent several years trying to relate variations in output with variations in the physical circumstances of these five operators. For example, he correlated the hours that each girl spent in bed the night before with variations in output the following day. Inasmuch as some people said that the effect of being out late one night was not felt the following day but the day after that, he correlated variations in output with the amount of rest the operators had had two nights before. I mention this just to point out the fact that he missed no obvious tricks and that he did a careful job and a thorough one, and it took him many years to do it. The attempt to relate changes in physical circumstances to variations in output resulted in not a single correlation of enough statistical significance to be recognized by any competent statistician as having any meaning.

Now, of course, it would be misleading to say that this negative result was the only conclusion reached. There were positive conclusions, and it did not take the experimenters more than two years to find out that they had missed the boat. After two years of work, certain things happened which made them sit up and take notice. Different experimental conditions of work, in the nature of changes in the number and duration of rest pauses and differences in the length of the working day and week, had been introduced in this Relay Assembly Test Room. For example, the investigators first introduced two five-minute rests, one in the morning and one in the afternoon. Then they increased the length of these rests, and after that they introduced the rests at different times of the day. During one experimental period they served the operators a specially prepared lunch during the rest. In the later periods, they decreased the length of the working day by one-half hour and then by one hour. They gave the operators Saturday morning off for a while. Altogether, thirteen such periods of different working conditions were introduced in the first two years.

During the first year and a half of the experiment, everybody was happy, both the investigators and the operators. The investigators were happy because as conditions of work improved the output rate rose steadily. Here, it appeared, was strong evidence in favor of their preconceived hypothesis that fatigue was the major factor limiting output. The operators were happy because their conditions of work were being improved, they were earning more money, and they were objects of considerable attention from top management. But then one investigator—one of those tough-minded fellows—suggested that they restore the original conditions of work, that is, go back to a full forty-eight-hour week without rests, lunches and what not. This was Period XII. Then the happy state of affairs, when everything was going along as it theoretically should, went sour. Output, instead of taking the expected nosedive, maintained its high level.

Again the investigators were forcibly reminded that human situations are likely to be complex. In any human situation, whenever a simple change is introduced—a rest pause, for example—other changes, unwanted and unanticipated, may also be brought about. What I am saying here is very simple. If one experiments on a stone, the stone does not know it is being experimented upon—all of which makes it simple for people experimenting on stones. But if a human being is being experimented upon, he is likely to know it. Therefore, his attitudes toward the experiment and toward the experimenters become very important factors in determining his responses to the situation.

Now that is what happened in the Relay Assembly Test Room. To the investigators, it was essential that the workers give their full and wholehearted coöperation to the experiment. They did not want the operators to work harder or easier depending upon their attitude toward the conditions that were imposed. They wanted them to work as they felt, so that they could be sure that the different physical conditions of work were solely responsible for the variations in output. For each of the experimental changes, they wanted subjects whose responses would be uninfluenced by so-called "psychological factors."

In order to bring this about, the investigators did everything in their power to secure the complete coöperation of their subjects, with the result that almost all the practices common to the shop were altered. The operators were consulted about the changes to be made, and, indeed, several plans were abandoned because they met with the disapproval of the girls. They were questioned sympathetically about their reactions to the conditions imposed, and many of these conferences took place in the office of the superintendent. The girls were allowed to talk at work; their "bogey" was eliminated. Their physical health and well-being became matters of great concern. Their opinions, hopes, and fears were eagerly sought. What happened was that in the very process of setting the conditions for the test—a so-called "controlled" experiment—the experimenters had completely altered the social situation of the room. Inadvertently a change had been introduced which was far more important than the planned experimental innovations: the customary supervision in the room had been revolutionized. This accounted for the better attitudes of the girls and their improved rate of work.

The Development of a New and More Fruitful Point of View

After Period XII in the Relay Assembly Test Room, the investigators decided to change their ideas radically. What all their experiments had dramatically and conclusively demonstrated was the importance of employee attitudes and sentiments. It was clear that the responses of workers to what was happening about them were dependent upon the significance these events had for them. In most work situations the meaning of a change is likely to be as important, if not more so, than the change itself. This was the great *éclaircissement*, the new illumination that came from the research. It was an illumination quite different from what they had expected from the illumination studies. Curiously enough, this discovery is nothing very new or startling. It is something which anyone who has had some concrete experience in handling other people intuitively recognizes and practices. Whether or not a person is going to give his services whole-heartedly to a group depends, in good part, on the way he feels about his job, his fellow workers, and supervisors—the meaning for him of what is happening about him.

However, when the experimenters began to tackle the problem of employee attitudes and the factors determining such attitudes—when they began to tackle the problem of "meaning"—they entered a sort of twilight zone where things are never quite what they seem. Moreover, overnight, as it were, they were robbed of all the tools they had so carefully forged; for all their previous tools were nonhuman tools concerned with the measurement of output, temperature, humidity, etc., and these were no longer useful for the human data that they now wanted to obtain. What the experimenters now wanted to know was how a person felt, what his intimate thinking, reflections, and preoccupations were, and what he liked and disliked about his work environment. In short, what did the whole blooming business—his job, his supervision, his working conditions—mean to him? Now this was human stuff, and there were no tools, or at least the experimenters knew of none, for obtaining and evaluating this kind of material.

Fortunately, there were a few courageous souls among the experimenters. These men were not metaphysicians, psychologists, academicians, professors, intellectuals, or what have you. They were men of common sense and of practical affairs. They were not driven by any great heroic desire to change the world. They were true experimenters, that is, men compelled to follow the implications of their own monkey business. All the evidence of their studies was pointing in one direction. Would they take the jump? They did.

Experiments in Interviewing Workers

A few tough-minded experimenters decided to go into the shops and—completely disarmed and denuded of their elaborate logical equipment and in all humility—to see if they could learn how to get the workers to talk about things that were important to them and could learn to understand what the workers were trying to tell them. This was a revolutionary idea in the year 1928, when this interviewing program started—the idea of getting a worker to talk to you and to listen sympathetically, but intelligently, to what he had to say. In that year a new era of personnel relations began. It was the first real attempt to get human data and to forge human tools to get them. In that year a novel idea was born; dimly the experimenters perceived a new method of human control. In that year the Rubicon was crossed from which there could be no return to the "good old days." Not that the experimenters ever wanted to return, because they now entered a world so exciting, so intriguing, and so full of promise that it made the "good old days" seem like the prattle and play of children.

When these experimenters decided to enter the world of "meaning," with very few tools, but with a strong sense of curiosity and a willingness to learn, they had many interesting adventures. It would be too long a story to tell all of them, or even a small part of them. They made plenty of mistakes, but they were not afraid to learn.

At first, they found it difficult to learn to give full and complete attention to what a person had to say without interrupting him before he was through. They found it difficult to learn not to give advice, not to make or imply moral judgments about the speaker, not to argue, not to be too clever, not to dominate the conversation, not to ask leading questions. They found it difficult to get the person to talk about matters which were important to him and not to the interviewer. But, most important of all, they found it difficult to learn that perhaps the thing most significant to a person was not something in his immediate work situation.

Gradually, however, they learned these things. They discovered that sooner or later a person tends to talk about what is uppermost in his mind to a sympathetic and skillful listener, and they became more proficient in interpreting what a person is saying or trying to say. Of course they protected the confidences given to them and made absolutely sure that nothing an employee said could ever be used against him. Slowly they began to forge a simple human tool—imperfect, to be sure—to get the kind of data they wanted. They called this method "interviewing." I would hesitate to say the number of manhours of labor which went into the forging of this tool. There followed from studies made through its use a gradually changing conception of the worker and his behavior.

A New Way of Viewing Employee Satisfaction and Dissatisfaction

When the experimenters started to study employee likes and dislikes, they assumed, at first, that they would find a simple and logical relation between a person's likes or dislikes and certain items and events in his immediate work situation. They expected to find a simple connection, for example, between a person's complaint and the object about which he was complaining. Hence, the solution would be easy: correct the object of the complaint, if possible, and presto! the complaint would disappear. Unfortunately, however, the world of human behavior is not so simple as this conception of it; and it took the investigators several arduous and painful years to find this out. I will mention only a few interesting experiences they had.

Several times they changed the objects of the complaint only to find that the attitudes of the complainants remained unchanged. In these cases, correcting the object of the complaint did not remedy the complaint or the attitude of the person expressing it. A certain complaint might disappear, to be sure, only to have another one arise. Here the investigators were running into so-called "chronic kickers," people whose dissatisfactions were more deeply rooted in factors relating to their personal histories. For such people the simple remedy of changing the object of the complaint was not enough.

Several times they did absolutely nothing about the object of the complaint, but after the interview, curiously enough, the complaint disappeared. A typical example of this was that of a woman who complained at great length and with considerable feeling about the poor food being served in the company restaurant. When, a few days later, she chanced to meet the interviewer, she commented with great enthusiasm upon the improved food and thanked the interviewer for communicating her grievance to management and for securing such prompt action. Here no change had been made in the thing criticized; yet the employee felt that something had been done.

Many times they found that people did not really want anything done about the things of which they were complaining. What they did want was an opportunity to talk about their troubles to a sympathetic listener. It was astonishing to find the number of instances in which workers complained about things which had happened many, many years ago, but which they described as vividly as if they had happened just a day before.

Here again, something was "screwy," but this time the experimenters realized that it was their assumptions which were screwy. They were assuming that the meanings which people assign to their experience are essentially logical. They were carrying in their heads the notion of the "economic man," a man primarily motivated by economic interest, whose logical capacities were being used in the service of this self-interest.

Gradually and painfully in the light of the evidence, which was overwhelming, the experimenters had been forced to abandon this conception of the worker and his behavior. Only with a new working hypothesis could they make sense of the data they had collected. The conception of the worker which they developed is actually nothing very new or startling; it is one which any effective administrator intuitively recognizes and practices in handling human beings.

First, they found that the behavior of workers could not be understood apart from their feelings or sentiments. I shall use the word "sentiment" hereafter to refer not only to such things as feelings and emotions, but also to a much wider range of phenomena which may not be expressed in violent feelings or emotions—phenomena that are referred to by such words as "loyalty," "integrity," "solidarity."

Secondly, they found that sentiments are easily disguised, and hence are difficult to recognize and to study. Manifestations of sentiment take a number of different forms. Feelings of personal integrity, for example, can be expressed by a handshake; they can also be expressed, when violated, by a sitdown strike. Moreover, people like to rationalize their sentiments and to objectify them. We are not so likely to say "I feel bad," as to say "The world is bad." In other words, we like to endow the world with those attributes and qualities which will justify and account for the feelings and sentiments we have toward it; we tend to project our sentiments on the outside world.

Thirdly, they found that manifestations of sentiment could not be understood as things in and by themselves, but only in terms of the total situation of the person. To comprehend why a person felt the way he did, a wider range of phenomena had to be explored. The following three diagrams illustrate roughly the development of this point of view.

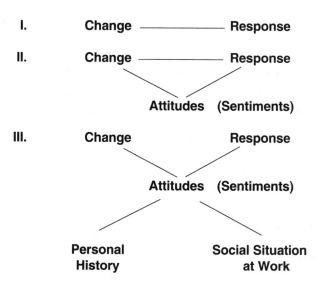

It will be remembered that at first the investigators assumed a simple and direct relation between certain physical changes in the worker's environment and his responses to them. This simple state of mind is illustrated in diagram I. But all the evidence of the early experiments showed that the responses of employees to changes in their immediate working environment can be understood only in terms of their attitudes—the "meaning" these changes have for them. This point of view is represented in diagram II. However, the "meaning" which these changes have for the worker is not strictly and primarily logical, for they are fraught with human feelings and values. The "meaning," therefore, which any individual worker assigns to a particular change depends upon (1) his social "conditioning," or what sentiments (values, hopes, fears, expectations, etc.) he is bringing to the work situation because of his previous family and group associations, and hence the relation of the change to these sentiments; and (2) the kind of human satisfactions he is deriving from his social participation with other workers and supervisors in the immediate work group of which he is a member, and hence the effect of the change on his customary interpersonal relations. This way of regarding the responses of workers (both verbal and overt) is represented in diagram III. It says briefly: Sentiments do not appear in a vacuum; they do not come out of the blue; they appear in a social context. They have to be considered in terms of that context, and apart from it they are likely to be misunderstood.

One further point should be made about that aspect of the worker's environment designated "Social Situation at Work" in diagram III. What is meant is that the worker is not an isolated, atomic individual; he is a member of a group, or of groups. Within each of these groups the individuals have feelings and sentiments toward each other, which bind them together in collaborative effort. Moreover, these collective sentiments can, and do, become attached to every item and object in the industrial environment—even to output. Material goods, output, wages, hours of work, and so on, cannot be treated as things in themselves. Instead, they must be interpreted as carriers of social value.

Output as a Form of Social Behavior

That output is a form of social behavior was well illustrated in a study made by the Hawthorne experimenters, called the Bank Wiring Observation Room. This room contained fourteen workmen representing three occupational groups—wiremen, soldermen, and inspectors. These men were on group piecework, where the more they turned out the more they earned. In such a situation one might have expected that they would have been interested in maintaining total output and that the faster workers would have put pressure on the slower workers to improve their efficiency. But this was not the case. Operating within this group were four basic sentiments, which can be expressed briefly as follows: (1) You should not turn out too much work; if you do, you are a "rate buster." (2) You should not turn out too little work; if you do, you are a "chiseler." (3) You should not say anything to a supervisor which would react to the detriment of one of your associates; if you do, you are a "squealer." (4) You should not be too officious; that is, if you are an inspector you should not act like one.

To be an accepted member of the group a man had to act in accordance with these social standards. One man in this group exceeded the group standard of what constituted a fair day's work. Social pressure was put on him to conform, but without avail, since he enjoyed doing things the others disliked. The best-liked person in the group was the one who kept his output exactly where the group agreed it should be.

Inasmuch as the operators were agreed as to what constituted a day's work, one might have expected rate of output to be about the same for each member of the group. This was by no means the case; there were marked differences. At first the experimenters thought that the differences in individual performance were related to differences in ability, so they compared each worker's relative rank in output with his relative rank in intelligence and dexterity as measured by certain tests. The results were interesting: the lowest producer in the room ranked first in intelligence and third in dexterity; the highest producer in the room was seventh in dexterity and lowest in intelligence. Here surely was a situation in which the native capacities of the men were not finding expression. From the viewpoint of logical, economic behavior, this room did not make sense. Only in terms of powerful sentiments could these individual differences in output level be explained. Each worker's level of output reflected his position in the informal organization of the group.

What Makes the Worker Not Want to Cooperate?

As a result of the Bank Wiring Observation Room, the Hawthorne researchers became more and more interested in the informal employee groups which tend to form within the formal organization of the company, and which are not likely to be represented in the organization chart. They became interested in the beliefs and creeds which have the effect of making each individual feel an integral part of the group and which make the group appear as a single unit, in the social codes and norms of behavior by means of which employees automatically work together in a group without any conscious choice as to whether they will or will not coöperate. They studied the important social functions these groups perform for their members, the histories of these informal work groups, how they spontaneously appear, how they tend to perpetuate themselves, multiply, and disappear, how they are in constant jeopardy from technical change, and hence how they tend to resist innovation. In particular, they became interested in those groups whose norms and codes of behavior are at variance with the technical and economic objectives of the company as a whole. They examined the social conditions under which it is more likely for the employee group to separate itself out in opposition to the remainder of the groups which make up the total organization. In such phenomena they felt that they had at last arrived at the heart of the problem of effective collaboration. They obtained a new enlightenment of the present industrial scene; from this point of view, many perplexing problems became more intelligible.

Some people claim, for example, that the size of the pay envelope is the major demand which the employee is making of his job. All the worker wants is to be told what to do and to get paid for doing it. If we look at him and his job in terms of sentiments, this is far from being as generally true as we would like to believe. Most of us want the satisfaction that comes from being accepted and recognized as people of worth by our friends and work associates. Money is only a small part of this social recognition. The way we are greeted by our boss, being asked to help a newcomer, being asked to keep an eye on a difficult operation, being given a job requiring special skill—all of these are acts of social recognition. They tell us how we stand in our work group. We all want tangible evidence of our social importance. We want to have a skill that is socially recognized as useful. We want the feeling of security that comes not so much from the amount of money we have in the bank as from being an accepted member of a group. A man whose job is without social function is like a man without a country; the activity to which he has to give the major portion of his life is robbed of all human meaning and significance.

If this is true—and all the evidence of the Western Electric researches points in this direction—have we not a clue as to the possible basis for labor unrest and disputes? Granted that these disputes are often stated in terms of wages, hours of work, and physical conditions of work, is it not possible that these demands are disguising, or in part are the symptomatic expression of, much more deeply rooted human situations which we have not as yet learned to recognize, to understand, or to control? It has been said there is an irresistible urge on the part of workers to tell the boss off, to tell the boss to go to hell. For some workers this generalization may hold, and I have no reason to believe it does not. But, in those situations where it does, it is telling us something very important about these particular workers and their work situations. Workers who want to tell their boss to go to hell sound to me like people whose feelings of personal integrity have been seriously injured. What in their work situations has shattered their feelings of personal integrity? Until we understand better the answer to this question, we cannot handle effectively people who manifest such sentiments. Without such understanding we are dealing only with words and not with human situations—as I fear our over-logicized machinery for handling employee grievances sometimes does.

The matters of importance to workers which the Hawthorne researches disclosed are not settled primarily by negotiating contracts. If industry today is filled with people living in a social void and without social function, a labor contract can do little to make coöperation possible. If, on the other hand, the workers are an integral part of the social situations in which they work, a legal contract is not of the first importance. Too many of us are more interested in getting our words legally straight than in getting our situations humanly straight.

In summary, therefore, the Western Electric researches seem to me like a beginning on the road back to sanity in employee relations because (1) they offer a fruitful working hypothesis, a few simple and relatively clear ideas for the study and understanding of human situations in business; (2) they offer a simple method by means of which we can explore and deal with the complex human problems in a business organization—this method is a human method: it deals with things which are important to people; and (3) they throw a new light on the precondition for effective collaboration. Too often we think of collaboration as something which can be logically or legally contrived. The Western Electric studies indicate that it is far more a matter of sentiment than a matter of logic. Workers are not isolated, unrelated individuals; they are social animals and should be treated as such.

This statement—the worker is a social animal and should be treated as such—is simple, but the systematic and consistent practice of this point of view is not. If it were systematically practiced, it would revolutionize present-day personnel work. Our technological development in the past hundred years has been tremendous. Our methods of handling people are still archaic. If this civilization is to survive, we must obtain a new understanding of human motivation and behavior in business organizations—an understanding which can be simply but effectively practiced. The Western Electric researches contribute a first step in this direction.

4

Overcoming Resistance to Change

Lester Coch and John R. P. French Jr.

Introduction

It has always been characteristic of American industry to change products and methods of doing jobs as often as competitive conditions or engineering progress dictates. This makes frequent changes in an individual's work necessary. In addition, the markedly greater turnover and absenteeism of recent years result in unbalanced production lines which again makes for frequent shifting of individuals from one job to another. One of the most serious production problems faced at the Harwood Manufacturing Corporation has been the resistance of production workers to the necessary changes in methods and jobs. This resistance expressed itself in several ways, such as grievances about the piece rates that went with the new methods, high turnover, very low efficiency, restriction of output, and marked aggression against management. Despite these undesirable effects, it was necessary that changes in methods and jobs continue.

Efforts were made to solve this serious problem by the use of a special monetary allowance for transfers, by trying to enlist the cooperation and aid of the union, by making necessary lay-offs on the basis of efficiency, etc. In all cases, these actions did little or nothing to overcome the resistance to change. On the basis of these data, it was felt that the pressing problem of resistance to change demanded further research for its solution. From the point of view of factory management, there were two purposes to the research: (1) Why do people resist change so strongly? and (2) What can be done to overcome this resistance?

Starting with a series of observations about the behavior of changed groups, the first step in the overall program was to devise a preliminary theory to account for the resistance to change. Then on the basis of the theory, a real-life action experiment was devised and conducted within the context of the factory situation. Finally, the results of the experiment were interpreted in the light of the preliminary theory and the new data.

Background

The main plant of the Harwood Manufacturing Corporation, where the present research was done, is located in the small town of Marion, Virginia. The plant produces pajamas and, like most sewing plants, employs mostly women. The plant's population is about 500 women and 100 men. The workers are recruited from the rural, mountainous areas surrounding the town, and are usually employed without previous industrial experience. The average age of the workers is 23; the average education is eight years of grammar school.

The policies of the company in regard to labor relations are liberal and progressive. A high value has been placed on fair and open dealing with the employees and they are encouraged to take up any problems or grievances with the management at any time. Every effort is made to help foremen find effective solutions to their problems in human relations, using conferences and role-playing methods. Carefully planned orientation, designed to help overcome the discouragement and frustrations attending entrance upon the new and unfamiliar situation, is used. Plantwide votes are conducted where possible to resolve problems affecting the whole working population. The company has invested both time and money in employee services such as industrial music, health services, lunchroom, and recreation programs. In the same spirit, the management has been conscious of the importance of public relations in the local community; they have supported both financially and otherwise any activity which would build up good will for the company. As a result of these policies, the company has enjoyed good labor relations since the day it commenced operations.

Harwood employees work on an individual incentive system. Piece rates are set by time study and are expressed in terms of units. One unit is equal to one minute of standard work: 60 units per hour equal the standard efficiency rating. Thus, if on a particular operation the piece rate for one dozen is 10 units, the operator would have to produce 6 dozen per hour to achieve the standard efficiency rating of 60 units per hour. The skill required to reach 60 units per hour is great. On some jobs, an average trainee may take 34 weeks to reach the skill level necessary to perform at 60 units per hour. Her few weeks of work may be on an efficiency level of 5 to 20 units per hour.

The amount of pay received is directly proportional to the weekly average efficiency rating achieved. Thus, an operator with an average efficiency rating of 75 units per hour (25 percent more than standard) would receive 25 percent more than base pay. However, there are two minimum wages below which no operator may fall. The first is the plantwide minimum, the hiring-in wage; the second is a minimum wage based on six months' employment and is 22 percent higher than the plantwide minimum wage. Both minima are smaller than the base pay for 60 units per hour efficiency rating.

The rating of every piece worker is computed every day and the results are published in a daily record of production which is shown to every operator. This daily record of production for each production line carries the names of all the operators on that line arranged in rank order of efficiency rating, with the highest rating girl at the top of the list. The supervisors speak to each operator each day about her unit ratings. Because of the above procedures, many operators do not claim credit for all work done in a given day. Instead, they save a few of the piece rate tickets as a "cushion" against a rainy day when they may not feel well or may have a great amount of machine trouble.

When it is necessary to change an operator from one type of work to another, a transfer bonus is given. The bonus is so designed that the changed operator who relearns at an average rate will suffer no loss in earnings after the change. Despite this allowance, the general attitudes toward job changes in the factory are markedly negative. Such expressions as, "When you make your units (standard production), they change your job," are all too frequent. Many operators refuse to change, preferring to quit.

The Transfer Learning Curve

An analysis of the after-change relearning curves of several hundred experienced operators rating standard or better prior to change showed that 38 percent of the changed operators recovered to the standard unit rating of 60 units per hour. The other 62 percent either became chronically substandard operators or quit during the relearning period.

The average relearning curve for those who recover to standard production on the simplest type job in the plant (see figure 1) is eight weeks long, and, when smoothed, provides the basis for the transfer bonus. The bonus is the percent difference between this expected efficiency rating and the standard of 60 units per hour. Progress is slow for the first two or three weeks, as the relearning curve shows, and then accelerates markedly to about 50 units per hour with an increase of 15 units in two weeks. Another slow progress area is encountered at 50 units per hour, the operator improving only 3 units in two weeks. The curve ends in a spurt of 10 units progress in one week, a marked goal gradient behavior. The individual curves, of course, vary widely in length according to the simplicity or difficulty of the job to be relearned; but in general, the successful curves are consistent with the average curve in form.

It is interesting to note in figure 1 that the relearning period for an experienced operator is longer than the learning period for a new operator. This is true despite the fact that the majority of transfers—the failures, who never recover to standard—are omitted from the curve. However, changed operators rarely complain of "wanting to do it the old way," etc., after the first week or two of change; and time and motion studies show few false moves after the first week of change. From this evidence it is deduced that proactive inhibition or the interference of previous habits in learning the new skill is either nonexistent or very slight after the first two weeks of change.

Figure 1
Learning Curve Comparisons for New, Inexperienced Employees
with Relearning Curve for Only Those Transfers (38 percent)
Who Eventually Recover to Standard Production

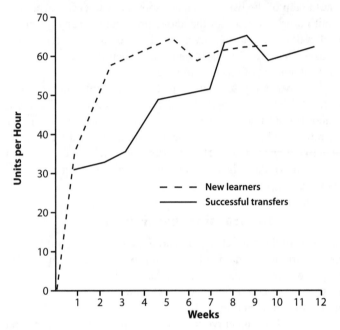

Figure 2
Drop in Production and Recovery Rate after Transfer
(Skillful and Substandard Operators)

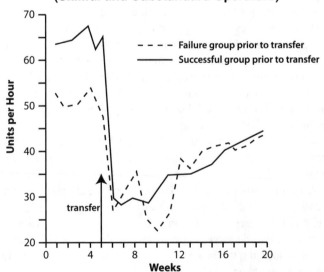

Figure 2, which presents the relearning curves for 41 experienced operators who were changed to very difficult jobs, gives a comparison between the recovery rates for operators making standard or better prior to change, and those below standard prior to change. Both classes of operators dropped to a little below 30 units per hour and recovered at a very slow but similar rate. These curves show a general (though by no means universal) phenomenon: that the efficiency rating prior to change does not indicate a faster or slower recovery rate after change.

A Preliminary Theory of Resistance to Change

The fact that relearning after transfer to a new job is so often slower than initial learning on first entering the factory would indicate, on the face of it, that the resistance to change and the slow relearning is primarily a motivational problem. The similar recovery rates of the skilled and unskilled operators shown in figure 2 tend to confirm the hypothesis that skill is a minor factor and motivation is the major determinant of the rate of recovery. Earlier experiments at Harwood by Alex Bavelas demonstrated this point conclusively. He found that the use of group decision techniques on operators who had just been transferred resulted in very marked increases in the rate of relearning, even though no skill training was given and there were no other changes in working conditions.[1]

Interviews with operators who have been transferred to a new job reveal a common pattern of feelings and attitudes which are distinctly different from those of successful nontransfers. In addition to resentment against the management for transferring them, the employees typically show feelings of frustration, loss of hope of ever regaining their former level of production and status in the factory, feelings of failure, and a very low level of aspiration. In this respect these transferred operators are similar to the chronically slow workers studied previously.

Earlier unpublished research at Harwood has shown that the nontransferred employees generally have an explicit goal of reaching and maintaining an efficiency rating of 60 units per hour. A questionnaire administered to several groups of operators indicated that a large majority of them accept as their goal the management's quota of 60 units per hour. This standard of production is the level of aspiration according to which the operators measure their own success or failure; and those who fall below standard lose status in the eyes of their fellow employees. Relatively few operators set a goal appreciably above 60 units per hour.

The actual production records confirm the effectiveness of this goal of standard production. The distribution of the total population of operators in accordance with their production levels is by no means a normal curve. Instead there is a very large number of operators who rate 60 to 63 units per hour and relatively few operators who rate just above or just below this range. Thus we may conclude that:

(1) There is a force acting on the operator in the direction of achieving a production level of 60 units per hour or more. It is assumed that the strength of this driving force (acting on an operator below standard) increases as she gets nearer the goal—a typical goal gradient (see figure 1).

On the other hand restraining forces operate to hinder or prevent her from reaching this goal. These restraining forces consist among other things of the difficulty of the job in relation to the operator's level of skill. Other things being equal, the faster an operator is sewing the more difficult it is to increase her speed by a given amount. Thus we may conclude that:

(2) The strength of the restraining force hindering higher production increases with increasing level of production.

In line with previous studies, it is assumed that the conflict of these two opposing forces—the driving force corresponding to the goal of reaching 60 and the restraining force of the difficulty of the job—produces frustration. In such a conflict situation, the strength of frustration will depend on the strength of these forces. If the restraining force against increasing production is weak, then the frustration will be weak. But if the driving force toward higher production (*i.e.,* the motivation) is weak, then the frustration will also be weak. Probably both of the conflicting forces must be above a certain minimum strength before any frustration is produced; for all goal-directed activity involves some degree of conflict of this type, yet a person is not usually frustrated so long as he is making satisfactory progress toward his goal. Consequently we assume that:

(3) The strength of frustration is a function of the weaker of these two opposing forces, provided that the weaker force is stronger than a certain minimum necessary to produce frustration.[2]

An analysis of the effects of such frustration in the factory showed that it resulted, among other things, in high turnover and absenteeism. The rate of turnover for successful operators with efficiency ratings above standard was much lower than for unsuccessful operators. Likewise, operators on the more difficult jobs quit more frequently than those on the easier jobs. Presumably the effect of being transferred is a severe frustration which should result in similar attempts to escape from the field.

In line with this theory of frustration and the finding that job turnover is one resultant of frustration, an analysis was made of the turnover rate of transferred operators as compared with the rate among operators who had not been transferred recently. For the year September 1946, to September 1947 there were 198 operators who had not been transferred recently, that is, within the 34-week period allowed for relearning after transfer. There was a second group of 85 operators who had been transferred recently, that is, within the time allowed for relearning the new job. Each of the two groups was divided into several classifications according to their unit rating at the time of quitting. For each classification the percent turnover per month, based on the total number of employees in that classification, was computed.

The results are given in figure 3. Both the levels of turnover and the form of the curves are strikingly different for the two groups. Among operators who have not been transferred recently the average turnover per month is about 4.5 percent; among recent transfers the monthly turnover is nearly 12 percent. Consistent with the previous studies, both groups show a very marked drop in the

Figure 3
Rate of Turnover at Various Levels of Production
(Transfers Compared with Nontransfers)

turnover curve after an operator becomes a success reaching 60 units per hour or standard production. However, the form of curves at lower unit ratings is markedly different for the two groups. The nontransferred operators show a gradually increasing rate of turnover up to a rating of 55 to 59 units per hour. The transferred operators, on the other hand, show a high peak at the lowest unit rating of 30 to 34 units per hour, decreasing sharply to a low point at 45 to 49 units per hour. Since most changed operators drop to a unit rating of around 30 units per hour when changed and then drop no further, it is obvious that the rate of turnover was highest for these operators just after they were changed and again much later just before they reached standard. Why?

It is assumed that the strength of frustration for an operator who has *not* been transferred gradually increases because both the driving force towards the goal of reaching 60 and the restraining force of the difficulty of the job increase with increasing unit rating. This is in line with hypotheses (1), (2) and (3) above. For the transferred operator on the other hand the frustration is greatest immediately after transfer, when the contrast of her present status with her former status is most evident. At this point the strength of the restraining forces is at a maximum because the difficulty is unusually great due to proactive inhibition. Then as she overcomes the interference effects between the two jobs and learns the new job, the difficulty and the frustration gradually decrease and the rate of turnover declines until the operator reaches 45–49 units per hour. Then at higher levels of production the difficulty starts to increase again and the transferred operator shows the same peak in frustration and turnover at 55–59 units per hour.

Though our theory of frustration explains the forms of the two turnover curves in figure 3, it hardly seems adequate to account for the markedly higher level of turnover for transfers as compared to nontransfers. On the basis of the difficulty of the job, it is especially difficult to explain the higher rate of turnover at 55–59 units per hour for transfers. Evidently additional forces are operating.

Another factor which seems to affect recovery rates of changed operators is the amount of we-feeling. Observations seem to indicate that a strong psychological subgroup with negative attitudes toward management will display the strongest resistance to change. On the other hand, changed groups with high we-feeling and positive cooperative attitudes are the best relearners. Collections of individuals with little or no we-feeling display some resistance to change but not so strongly as the groups with high we-feeling and negative attitudes toward management. However, turnover for the individual transfers is much higher than in the latter groups. This phenomenon of the relationship between we-feeling and resistance to change is so overt that for years the general policy of the management of the plant was never to change a group as a group but rather to scatter the individuals in different areas throughout the factory.

An analysis of turnover records for changed operators with high we-feeling showed a 4 percent turnover rate per month at 30 to 34 units per hour, not significantly higher than in unchanged operators but significantly lower than in changed operators with little or no we-feeling. However, the acts of aggression are far more numerous among operators with high we-feeling than among operators with little we-feeling. Since both types of operators experience the same frustration as individuals but react to it so differently, it is assumed that the effect on the in-group feeling is to set up a restraining force against leaving the group and perhaps even to set up driving forces toward staying in the group. In these circumstances, one would expect some alternative reaction to frustration rather than escape from the field. This alternative is aggression. Strong we-feeling provides strength so that members dare to express aggression which would otherwise be suppressed.

One common result in a subgroup with strong we-feeling is the setting of a group standard concerning production. Where the attitudes toward management are antagonistic, this group standard may take the form of a definite restriction of production to a given level. This phenomenon of restriction is particularly likely to happen in a group that has been transferred to a job where a new piece rate has been set; for they have some hope that if production never approaches the standard, the management may change the piece rate in their favor.

A group standard can exert extremely strong forces on an individual member of a small subgroup. That these forces can have a powerful effect on production is indicated in the production record of one presser during a period of 40 days.

Table 1

Days	Production Per Day
In the Group	
1–3	46
4–6	52
7–9	53
10–12	56
Scapegoating Begins	
13–16	55
17–20	48
Becomes a Single Worker	
21–24	83
25–28	92
29–32	92
33–36	91
37–40	92

For the first 20 days she was working in a group of other pressers who were producing at the rate of about 50 units per hour. Starting on the thirteenth day, when she reached standard production and exceeded the production of the other members, she became a scapegoat of the group. During this time her production decreased toward the level of the remaining members of the group. After 20 days the group had to be broken up and all the other members were transferred to other jobs, leaving only the scapegoat operator. With the removal of the group, the group standard was no longer operative, and the production of the one remaining operator shot up from the level of about 45 to 96 units per hour in a period of 4 days. Her production stabilized at a level of about 92 and stayed there for the remainder of the 20 days. Thus it is clear that the motivational forces induced in the individual by a strong subgroup may be more powerful than those induced by management.

The Experiment

On the basis of the preliminary theory that resistance to change is a combination of an individual reaction to frustration with strong group-induced forces it seemed that the most appropriate methods for overcoming the resistance to change would be group methods. Consequently an experiment was designed employing two variations of democratic procedure in handling groups to be transferred. The first variation involved participation through representation of the workers in designing the changes to be made in the jobs. The second variation consisted of total participation by all members of the group in designing the changes. A third control group was also used. Two experimental groups received the total participation treatment. The three experimental groups and the control group were roughly matched with respect to: (1) the efficiency ratings of the groups before transfer; (2) the degree of change involved in the transfer; (3) the amount of we-feeling observed in the groups.

In no case was more than a minor change in the work routines and time allowances made. The control group, the 18 hand pressers, had formerly stacked their work in one-half dozen lots on a flat piece of cardboard the size of the finished product. The new job called for stacking their work in one-half dozen lots in a box the size of the finished product. The box was located in the same place the cardboard had been. An additional two minutes per dozen was allowed (by the time study) for this new part of the job. This represented a total job change of 8.8 percent.

Experimental group 1, the 13 pajama folders, had formerly folded coats with prefolded pants. The new job called for the folding of coats with unfolded pants. An additional 1.8 minutes per dozen was allowed (by time study) for this new part of the job. This represented a total job change of 9.4 percent.

Experimental groups 2 and 3, consisting of 8 and 7 pajama examiners respectively, had formerly clipped threads from the entire garment and examined every seam. The new job called for pulling only certain threads off and examining every seam. An average of 1.2 minutes per dozen was subtracted (by time study) from the total time on these two jobs. This represented a total job change of 8 percent.

The control group of hand pressers went through the usual factory routine when they were changed. The production department modified the job, and a new piece rate was set. A group meeting was then held in which the control group was told that the change was necessary because of competitive conditions and that a new piece rate had been set. The new piece rate was thoroughly explained by the time study man, questions were answered, and the meeting dismissed.

Experimental group 1 was changed in a different manner. Before any changes took place, a group meeting was held with all the operators to be changed. The need for the change was presented as dramatically as possible, showing two identical garments produced in the factory; one was produced in 1946 and had sold for 100 percent more than its fellow in 1947. This demonstration effectively shared with the group the entire problem of the necessity of cost reduction. A general agreement was reached that a savings could be effected by removing the "frills" and "fancy" work from the garment without affecting the folders' opportunity to achieve a high efficiency rating. Management then presented a plan to set the new job and piece rate:

1. Make a check study of the job as it was being done.
2. Eliminate all unnecessary work.
3. Train several operators in the correct methods.
4. Set the piece rate by time studies on these specially trained operators.
5. Explain the new job and rate to all the operators.

6. Train all operators in the new method so they can reach a high rate of production within a short time.

The group approved this plan (though no formal group decision was reached) and chose the operators to be specially trained. A submeeting with the "special" operators was held immediately following the meeting with the entire group. They displayed a cooperative and interested attitude and immediately presented many good suggestions. This attitude carried over into the working out of the details of the new job; and when the new job and piece rates were set, the "special" operators referred to the resultants as "our job," "our rate," etc. The new job and piece rates were presented at a second group meeting to all the operators involved. The "special" operators served to train the other operators on the new job.

Experimental groups 2 and 3 went through much the same kind of change meetings. The groups were smaller than experimental group 1, and a more intimate atmosphere was established. The need for a change was once again made dramatically clear; the same plan was presented by management. However, since the groups were small, all operators were chosen as "special" operators; that is, all operators were to participate directly in the designing of the new jobs and all operators would be studied by the time study man. It is interesting to note that in the meetings with these two groups, suggestions were immediately made in such quantity that the stenographer had great difficulty in recording them. The group approved of the plans, but again no formal group decision was reached.

Results

The results of the experiment are summarized in graphic form in figure 4. The gaps in the production curves occur because these groups were paid on a time-work basis for a day or two. The control group improved little beyond their early efficiency ratings. Resistance developed almost immediately after the change occurred. Marked expressions of aggression against management occurred, such as conflict with the methods engineer, expression of hostility against the supervisor, deliberate restriction of production, and lack of cooperation with the supervisor. There were 17 percent quits in the first 40 days. Grievances were filed about the piece rate but when the rate was checked, it was found to be a little "loose."

Experimental group 1 showed an unusually good relearning curve. At the end of 14 days, the group averaged 61 units per hour. During the 14 days, the attitude was cooperative and permissive. They worked well with the methods engineer, the training staff, and the supervisor. (The supervisor was the same person in the cases of the control group and experimental group 1.) There were no quits in this group in the first 40 days. This group might have presented a better learning record if work had not been scarce during the first 7 days. There was one act of aggression against the supervisor recorded in the first 40 days. It is interesting to note that the three special representative operators in experimental group 1 recovered at about the same rate as the rest of their group.

Figure 4
Effects of Participation through Representation (Group 1) and Total Participation (Groups 2 and 3) on Recovery after an Easy Transfer

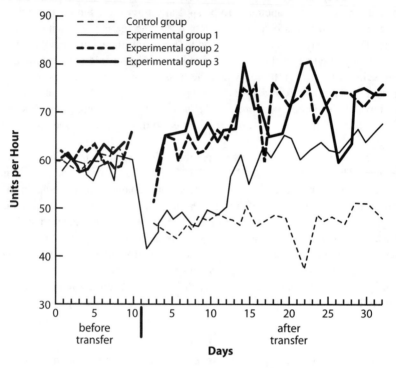

Experimental groups 2 and 3 recovered faster than experimental group 1. After a slight drop on the first day of change, the efficiency ratings returned to a prechange level and showed sustained progress thereafter to a level about 14 per-cent higher than the prechange level. No additional training was provided them after the second day. They worked well with their supervisors and no indications of aggression were observed from these groups. There were no quits in either of these groups in the first 40 days.

A fourth experimental group, composed of only two sewing operators, was transferred by the total participation technique. Their new job was one of the most difficult jobs in the factory, in contrast to the easy jobs for the control group and the other three experimental groups. As expected, the total participation tech-nique again resulted in an unusually fast recovery rate and a final level of produc-tion well above the level before transfer. Because of the difficulty of the new job, however, the rate of recovery was slower than for experimental groups 2 and 3, but faster than for experimental group 1.

In the first experiment, the control group made no progress after transfer for a period of 32 days. At the end of this period the group was broken up and the individuals were reassigned to new jobs scattered throughout the factory. Two and a half months after their dispersal, the 13 remaining members of the original control group were again brought together as a group for a second experiment.

This second experiment consisted of transferring the control group to a new job, using the total participation technique in meetings which were similar to those held with experimental groups 2 and 3. The new job was a pressing job of comparable difficulty to the new job in the first experiment. On the average it involved about the same degree of change. In the meetings no reference was made to the previous behavior of the group on being transferred.

The results of the second experiment were in sharp contrast to the first (see figure 5). With the total participation technique, the same control group now recovered rapidly to their previous efficiency rating, and, like the other groups under this treatment, continued on beyond it to a new high level of production. There was no aggression or turnover in the group for 19 days after change, a marked modification of their previous behavior after transfer. Some anxiety concerning their seniority status was expressed, but this was resolved in a meeting of their elected delegate, the union business agent, and a management representative. It should be noted in figure 5 that the prechange level on the second experiment is just above 60 units per hour; thus the individual transfers had progressed to just above standard during the two and a half months between the two experiments.

Figure 5
Comparison of the Effect of the Control Procedure with the Total Participation Procedure on the Same Group

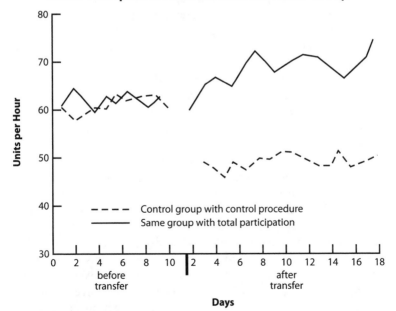

Interpretation

The purpose of this section is to explain the drop in production resulting from transfer, the differential recovery rates of the control and the experimental groups, the increases beyond their former levels of production by the experimental groups, and the differential rates of turnover and aggression.

The first experiment showed that the rate of recovery is directly proportional to the amount of participation, and that the rates of turnover and aggression are inversely proportional to the amount of participation. The second experiment demonstrated more conclusively that the results obtained depended on the experimental treatment rather than on personality factors like skill or aggressiveness, for identical individuals yielded markedly different results in the control treatment as contrasted with the total participation treatment.

Apparently total participation has the same type of effect as participation through representation, but the former has a stronger influence. In regard to recovery rates, this difference is not unequivocal because the experiment was unfortunately confounded. Right after transfer, experimental group number 1 had insufficient material to work on for a period of seven days. Hence their slower recovery during this period is at least in part due to insufficient work. In succeeding days, however, there was an adequate supply of work and the differential recovery rate still persisted. Therefore we are inclined to believe that participation through representation results in slower recovery than does total participation.

Before discussing the details of why participation produces high morale, we will consider the nature of production levels. In examining the production records of hundreds of individuals and groups in this factory, one is struck by the constancy of the level of production. Though differences among individuals in efficiency rating are very large, nearly every experienced operator maintains a fairly steady level of production given constant physical conditions. Frequently the given level will be maintained despite rather large changes in technical working conditions.

As Lewin has pointed out, this type of production can be viewed as a quasi-stationary process—in the ongoing work the operator is forever sewing new garments, yet the level of the process remains relatively stationary. Thus there are constant characteristics of the production process permitting the establishment of general laws.

In studying production as a quasi-stationary equilibrium, we are concerned with two types of forces: (1) forces on production in a downward direction, (2) forces on production in an upward direction. In this situation we are dealing with a variety of both upward forces tending to increase the level of production and downward forces tending to decrease the level of production. However, in the present experiment we have no method of measuring independently all of the component forces either downward or upward. These various component forces upward are combined into one resultant force upward. Likewise the several downward component forces combine into one resultant force downward. We can infer a good deal about the relative strengths of these resultant forces.

Where we are dealing with a quasi-stationary equilibrium, the resultant forces upward and the forces downward are opposite in direction and equal in strength at the equilibrium level. Of course either resultant forces may fluctuate over a short period of time, so that the forces may not be equally balanced at a given moment. However over a longer period of time and on the average the forces balance out. Fluctuations from the average occur but there is a tendency to return to the average level.

Just before being transferred, all of the groups in both experiments had reached a stable equilibrium level at just above the standard production of 60 units per hour. This level was equal to the average efficiency rating for the entire factory during the period of the experiments. Since this production level remained constant, neither increasing nor decreasing, we may be sure that the strength of the resultant force upward was equal to the strength of the resultant force downward. This equilibrium of forces was maintained over the period of time when production was stationary at this level. But the forces changed markedly after transfer and these new constellations of forces were distinctly different for the control and the experimental groups.

For the control group the period after transfer is a quasi-stationary equilibrium at a lower level, and the forces do not change during the period of thirty days. The resultant force upward remains equal to the resultant force downward and the level of production remains constant. The force field for this group is represented schematically in figure 6. Only the resultant forces are shown. The

Figure 6
Schematic Diagram of the Quasi-Stationary Equilibrium
(Control Group after Transfer)

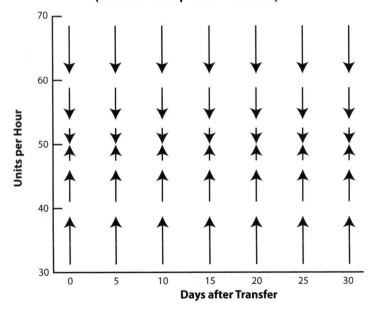

length of the vector represents the strength of the force; and the point of the arrow represents the point of application of the force, that is, the production level and the time at which the force applies. Thus the forces are equal and opposite only at the level of 50 units per hour. At higher levels of production the forces downward are greater than the forces upward; and at lower levels of production the forces upward are stronger than the forces downward. Thus there is a tendency for the equilibrium to be maintained at an efficiency rating of 50.

The situation for the experimental groups after transfer can be viewed as a quasi-stationary equilibrium of a different type. Figure 7 gives a schematic diagram of the resultant forces for the experimental groups. At any given level of production, such as 50 units per hour or 60 units per hour, both the resultant forces upward and the resultant forces downward change over the period of 30 days. During this time the point of equilibrium, which starts at 50 units per hour, gradually rises until it reaches a level of over 70 units per hour after 30 days. Yet here again the equilibrium level has the character of a "central force field" where at any point in the total field the resultant of the upward and the downward forces is in the direction of the equilibrium level.

To understand how the difference between the experimental and the control treatments produced the differences in force fields represented in figures 6 and 7,

Figure 7
Schematic Diagram of the Quasi-Stationary Equilibrium
(Experimental Groups after Transfer)

it is not sufficient to consider only the resultant forces. We must also look at the component forces for each resultant force.

There are three main component forces influencing production in a downward direction: (1) the difficulty of the job . . .; (2) a force corresponding to avoidance of strain; (3) a force corresponding to a group standard to restrict production to a given level. The resultant force upward in the direction of greater production is composed of three additional component forces: (1) the force corresponding to the goal of standard production . . .; (2) a force corresponding to pressures induced by the management through supervision; (3) a force corresponding to a group standard of competition. Let us examine each of these six component forces.

1. Job Difficulty

For all operators the difficulty of the job is one of the forces downward on production. The difficulty of the job, of course, is relative to the skill of the operator. The given job may be very difficult for an unskilled operator but relatively easy for a highly skilled one. In the case of a transfer a new element of difficulty enters. For some time the new job is much more difficult, for the operator is unskilled at that particular job. In addition to the difficulty experienced by any learner, the transfer often encounters the added difficulty of proactive inhibition. Where the new job is similar to the old job there will be a period of interference between the two similar but different skills required. For this reason a very efficient operator whose skills have become almost unconscious may suffer just as great a drop as a much less efficient operator (see figure 2). Except for group 4, the difficulty of these easy jobs does not explain the differential recovery rate because both the initial difficulty and the amount of change were equated for these groups. The two operators in group 4 probably dropped further and recovered more slowly than any of the other three groups under total participation because of the greater difficulty of the job.

2. Strain Avoidance

The force toward lower production corresponding to the difficulty of the job (or the lack of skill of the person) has the character of a restraining force—that is, it acts to prevent locomotion rather than as a driving force causing locomotion. However, in all production there is a closely related driving force toward lower production, namely, "strain avoidance." We assume that working too hard and working too fast is an unpleasant strain; and corresponding to this negative valence there is a driving force in the opposite direction, namely, towards taking it easy or working slower. The higher the level of production the greater will be the strain and other things being equal, the stronger will be the downward force of strain avoidance. Likewise, the greater the difficulty of the job the stronger will be the force corresponding to strain avoidance. But the greater the operator's skill the smaller will be the strain and the strength of the force of strain avoidance. Therefore:

(4) The strength of the force of strain avoidance =

$$\frac{\text{job difficulty} \times \text{production level}}{\text{skill of operator}}$$

The differential recovery rates of the control group in both experiments and the three experimental groups in Experiment I cannot be explained by strain avoidance because job difficulty, production level, and operator skill were matched at the time immediately following transfer. Later, however, when the experimental treatments had produced a much higher level of production, these groups were subjected to an increased downward force of strain avoidance which was stronger than in the control group in Experiment I. Evidently other forces were strong enough to overcome this force of strain avoidance.

3. The Goal of Standard Production

In considering the negative attitudes toward transfer and the resistance to being transferred, there are several important aspects on the complex goal of reaching and maintaining a level of 60 units per hour. For an operator producing below standard, this goal is attractive because it means success, high status in the eyes of her fellow employees, better pay, and job security. . . . On the other hand, there is a strong force against remaining below standard because this lower level means failure, low status, low pay, and the danger of being fired. Thus it is clear that the upward force corresponding to the goal of standard production will indeed be strong for the transfer who has dropped below standard.

It is equally clear why any operator who accepts the stereotype about transfer shows such strong resistance to being changed. She sees herself as becoming a failure and losing status, pay, and perhaps the job itself. The result is a lowered level of aspiration and a weakened force toward the goal of standard production.

Just such a weakening of the force toward 60 units per hour seems to have occurred in the control group in Experiment I. The participation treatments, on the other hand, seem to have involved the operators in designing the new job and setting the new piece rates in such a way that they did not lose hope of regaining the goal of standard production. Thus the participation resulted in a stronger force toward higher production. However, this force alone can hardly account for the large differences in recovery rate between the control group and the experimental groups; certainly it does not explain why the latter increased to a level so high above standard.

4. Management Pressure

On all operators below standard the management exerts a pressure for higher production. This pressure is no harsh and autocratic treatment involving threats. Rather it takes the form of persuasion and encouragement by the supervisors. They attempt to induce the low rating operator to improve her performance and to attain standard production.

Such an attempt to induce a psychological force on another person may have several results. In the first place the person may ignore the attempt of the inducing agent, in which case there is no induced force acting on the person. On the other hand, the attempt may succeed so that an induced force on the person exists. Other things being equal, whenever there is an induced force acting on a person, the person will locomote in the direction of the force. An induced force, which depends on the power field of an inducing agent—some other individual or group—will cease to exist when the inducing power field is withdrawn. In this report it is different from an "own" force which stems from a person's own needs and goals.

The reaction of a person to an effective induced force will vary depending, among other things, on the person's relation to the inducing agent. A force induced by a friend may be accepted in such a way that it acts more like an own force. An effective force induced by an enemy may be resisted and rejected so that the person complies unwillingly and shows signs of conflict and tension. Thus in addition to what might be called a "neutral" induced force, we also distinguish an *accepted* induced force and a *rejected* induced force. Naturally the acceptance and the rejection of an induced force can vary in degree from zero (*i.e.,* a neutral induced force) to very strong acceptance or rejection. To account for the difference in character between the acceptance and the rejection of an induced force, we make the following assumptions:

(5) The acceptance of an induced force sets up additional own forces in the same direction.

(6) The rejection of an induced force sets up additional own forces in the opposite direction.

The grievances, aggression, and tension in the control group in Experiment I indicate that they rejected the force toward higher production induced by the management. The group accepted the stereotype that transfer is a calamity, but the control procedure did not convince them that the change was necessary and they viewed the new job and the new piece rates set by management as arbitrary and unreasonable.

The experimental groups, on the contrary, participated in designing the changes and setting the piece rates so that they spoke of the new job as "our job" and the new piece rates as "our rates." Thus they accepted the new situation and accepted the management induced force toward higher production.

From the acceptance by the experimental groups and the rejection by the control group of the management induced forces, we may derive [by (5) and (6) above] that the former had additional own forces toward higher production whereas the latter had additional own forces toward lower production. This difference helps to explain the better recovery rate of experimental groups.

5. Group Standards

Probably the most important force affecting the recovery under the control procedure was a group standard, set by the group restricting the level of production to 50 units per hour. Evidently this explicit agreement to restrict production is related to the group's rejection of the change and of the new job as arbitrary and unreasonable. Perhaps they had faint hopes of demonstrating that standard production could not be attained and thereby obtain a more favorable piece rate. In any case there was a definite group phenomenon which affected all the members of the group. We have already noted the striking example of the presser whose production was restricted in the group situation to about half the level she attained as an individual. . . . In the control group, too, we would expect the group to induce strong forces on the members. The more the member deviates above the standard the stronger would be the group induced force to conform to the standard, for such deviations both negate any possibility of management increasing the piece rate and at the same time expose the other members to increased pressure from management. Thus individual differences in levels of production should be sharply curtailed in the control group after transfer.

An analysis was made for all groups of the individual differences within the group in levels of production. In Experiment I the 40 days before change were compared with the 30 days after change; in Experiment II the 10 days before change were compared to the 17 days after change. As a measure of variability, the standard deviation was calculated each day for each group. The average daily standard deviation *before* and *after* change were as follows:

There is indeed a marked decrease in individual differences within the control group after their first transfer. In fact the restriction of production resulted in a lower variability than in any other group. Thus we may conclude that the group standard at 60 units per hour set up strong group-induced forces which were important components in the central force field shown in figure 6. It is now evident that for the control group the quasi-stationary equilibrium after transfer has a steep gradient around the equilibrium level of 50 units per hour—the strength of the forces increases rapidly above and below this level. It is also clear that the group standard to restrict production is a major reason for the lack of recovery in the control group.

The table of variability also shows that the experimental treatments markedly reduced variability in the other four groups after transfer. In experimental group 1 (participation by representation) this smallest reduction of variability was produced by a group standard of individual competition. Competition among members of the group was reported by the supervisor soon after transfer. This competition was a force toward higher production which resulted in good recovery to standard and continued progress beyond standard.

Experimental groups 2 and 3 showed a greater reduction in variability following transfer. These two groups under total participation were transferred on the same day. Group competition developed between the two groups. This group competition, which evidently resulted in stronger forces on the members than did the individual competition, was an effective group standard. The standard gradually moved to higher and higher levels of production with the result that the groups not only reached but far exceeded their previous levels of production.

Table 2

Group	Variability	
Experiment I	Before Change	After Change
Control group	9.8	1.9
Experimental 1	9.7	3.8
Experimental 2	10.3	2.7
Experimental 3	9.9	2.4
Experiment II		
Control group	12.7	2.9

Turnover and Aggression

Returning now to our preliminary theory of frustration, we can see several revisions. The difficulty of the job and its relation to skill and strain avoidance has been clarified in proposition (4). It is now clear that the driving force toward 60 is a complex affair; it is partly a negative driving force corresponding to the negative valence of low pay, low status, failure, and job insecurity. Turnover results not only from the frustration produced by the conflict of these two forces, but also as a direct attempt to escape from the region of these negative valences. For the members of the control group, the group standard to restrict production prevented escape by increasing production, so that quitting their jobs was the only remaining escape. In the participation groups, on the contrary, both the group standards and the additional own forces resulting from the acceptance of management-induced forces combined to make increasing production the distinguished path of escape from this region of negative valence.

In considering turnover as a form of escape from the field, it is not enough to look only at the psychological present; one must also consider the psychological future. The employee's decision to quit the job is rarely made exclusively on the basis of a momentary frustration or an undesirable present situation; she usually quits when she also sees the future as equally hopeless. The operator transferred by the usual factory procedure (including the control group) has in fact a realistic view of the probability of continued failure because, as we have already noted, 62 percent of transfers do in fact fail to recover to standard production. Thus the higher rate of quitting for transfers as compared to nontransfers results from a more pessimistic view of the future.

The control procedure had the effect for the members of setting up management as a hostile power field. They rejected the forces induced by this hostile power field, and group standards to restrict production developed within the group in opposition to management. In this conflict between the power field of management and the power field of the group, the control group attempted to reduce the strength of the hostile power field relative to the strength of their own power field. This change was accomplished in three ways: (1) the group increased its own power by developing a more cohesive and well-disciplined group, (2) they secured "allies" by getting the backing of the union in filing a formal grievance about the new piece rate, (3) they attacked the hostile power field directly in the form of aggression against the supervisor, the time study engineer, and the higher management. Thus the aggression was derived not only from individual frustration but also from the conflict between two groups. Furthermore, this situation of group conflict both helped to define management as the frustration agent and gave the members strength to express any aggressive impulses produced by frustration.

Conclusions

It is possible for management to modify greatly or to remove completely group resistance to changes in methods of work and the ensuing piece rates. This change can be accomplished by the use of group meetings in which management effectively communicates the need for change and stimulates group participation in planning the changes.

For Harwood's management, and presumably for managements of other industries using an incentive system, this experiment has important implications in the field of labor relations. A majority of all grievances presented at Harwood have always stemmed from a change situation. By preventing or greatly modifying group resistance to change, this concomitant to change may well be greatly reduced. The reduction of such costly phenomena as turnover and slow relearning rates presents another distinct advantage.

Harwood's management has long felt that action research such as the present experiment is the only key to better labor-management relations. It is only by discovering the basic principles and applying them to the true causes of conflict that an intelligent, effective effort can be made to correct the undesirable effects of the conflict.

Notes

[1] John R. P. French, Jr., "The Behavior of Organized and Unorganized Groups under Conditions of Frustration and Fear, Studies in Topological and Vector Psychology, III," *University of Iowa Studies in Child Welfare*, Vol. 20 (1944), pp. 229–308.

[2] Kurt Lewin, "Frontiers in Group Dynamics," *Human Relations*, Vol. 1, No. 1 (1947), pp. 5–41.

5

The Human Side of Enterprise

Douglas M. McGregor

It has become trite to say that industry has the fundamental know-how to utilize physical science and technology for the material benefit of mankind and that we must now learn how to utilize the social sciences to make our human organizations truly effective.

To a degree, the social sciences today are in a position like that of the physical sciences with respect to atomic energy in the thirties. We know that past conceptions of the nature of man are inadequate and, in many ways, incorrect. We are becoming quite certain that, under proper conditions, unimagined resources of creative human energy could become available within the organizational setting.

We cannot tell industrial management how to apply this new knowledge in simple, economic ways. We know it will require years of exploration, much costly development research, and a substantial amount of creative imagination on the part of management to discover how to apply this growing knowledge to the organization of human effort in industry.

Management's Task: The Conventional View

The conventional conception of management's task in harnessing human energy to organizational requirements can be stated broadly in terms of three propositions. In order to avoid the complications introduced by a label, let us call this set of propositions "Theory X":

1. Management is responsible for organizing the elements of productive enterprise—money, materials, equipment, people—in the interest of economic ends.

2. With respect to people, this is a process of directing their efforts, motivating them, controlling their actions, modifying their behavior to fit the needs of the organization.

3. Without this active intervention by management, people would be passive—even resistant—to organizational needs. They must therefore be persuaded, rewarded, punished, controlled—their activities must be directed. This is management's task. We often sum it up by saying that management consists of getting things done through other people.

Behind this conventional theory there are several additional beliefs—less explicit, but widespread:

4. The average man is by nature indolent—he works as little as possible.

5. He lacks ambition, dislikes responsibility, prefers to be led.

6. He is inherently self-centered, indifferent to organizational needs.

7. He is by nature resistant to change.

8. He is gullible, not very bright, the ready dupe of the charlatan and the demagogue.

The human side of economic enterprise today is fashioned from propositions and beliefs such as these. Conventional organization structures and managerial policies, practices, and programs reflect these assumptions.

In accomplishing its task—with these assumptions as guides—management has conceived of a range of possibilities.

At one extreme, management can be "hard" or "strong." The methods for directing behavior involve coercion and threat (usually disguised), close supervision, tight controls over behavior. At the other extreme, management can be "soft" or "weak." The methods for directing behavior involve being permissive, satisfying people's demands, achieving harmony. Then they will be tractable, accept direction.

This range has been fairly completely explored during the past half century, and management has learned some things from the exploration. There are difficulties in the "hard" approach. Force breeds counter-forces: Restriction of output, antagonism, militant unionism, subtle but effective sabotage of management objectives. This "hard" approach is especially difficult during times of full employment.

There are also difficulties in the "soft" approach. It leads frequently to the abdication of management—to harmony, perhaps, but to indifferent performance. People take advantage of the soft approach. They continually expect more, but they give less and less.

Currently, the popular theme is "firm but fair." This is an attempt to gain the advantages of both the hard and the soft approaches. It is reminiscent of Teddy Roosevelt's "speak softly and carry a big stick."

Is the Conventional View Correct?

The findings which are beginning to emerge from the social sciences challenge this whole set of beliefs about man and human nature and about the task of management. The evidence is far from conclusive, certainly, but it is suggestive. It comes from the laboratory, the clinic, the schoolroom, the home, and even to a limited extent from industry itself.

The social scientist does not deny that human behavior in industrial organization today is approximately what management perceives it to be. He has, in fact, observed it and studied it fairly extensively. But he is pretty sure that this behavior is *not* a consequence of man's inherent nature. It is a consequence rather of the nature of industrial organizations, of management philosophy, policy, and practice. The conventional approach of Theory X is based on mistaken notions of what is cause and what is effect.

Perhaps the best way to indicate why the conventional approach of management is inadequate is to consider the subject of motivation.

Physiological Needs

Man is a wanting animal—as soon as one of his needs is satisfied, another appears in its place. This process is unending. It continues from birth to death.

Man's needs are organized in a series of levels—a hierarchy of importance. At the lowest level, but pre-eminent in importance when they are thwarted, are his *physiological needs*. Man lives for bread alone, when there is no bread. Unless the circumstances are unusual, his needs for love, for status, for recognition are inoperative when his stomach has been empty for a while. But when he eats regularly and adequately, hunger ceases to be an important motivation. The same is true of the other physiological needs of man—for rest, exercise, shelter, protection from the elements.

A satisfied need is not a motivator of behavior! This is a fact of profound significance that is regularly ignored in the conventional approach to the management of people. Consider your own need for air. Except as you are deprived of it, it has no appreciable motivating effect upon your behavior.

Safety Needs

When the physiological needs are reasonably satisfied, needs at the next higher level begin to dominate man's behavior—to motivate him. These are called *safety needs*. They are needs for protection against danger, threat, deprivation. Some people mistakenly refer to these as needs for security. However, unless man is in a dependent relationship where he fears arbitrary deprivation, he does not demand security. The need is for the "fairest possible break." When he is confident of this, he is more than willing to take risks. But when he feels threatened or dependent, his greatest need is for guarantees, for protection, for security.

The fact needs little emphasis that, since every industrial employee is in a dependent relationship, safety needs may assume considerable importance. Arbitrary management actions, behavior which arouses uncertainty with respect to continued employment or which reflects favoritism or discrimination, unpredictable administration of policy—these can be powerful motivators of the safety needs in the employment relationship *at every level,* from worker to vice president.

Social Needs

When man's physiological needs are satisfied and he is no longer fearful about his physical welfare, his *social needs* become important motivators of his behavior—needs for belonging, for association, for acceptance by his fellows, for giving and receiving friendship and love.

Management knows today of the existence of these needs, but it often assumes quite wrongly that they represent a threat to the organization. Many studies have demonstrated that the tightly knit, cohesive work group may, under proper conditions, be far more effective than an equal number of separate individuals in achieving organizational goals.

Yet management, fearing group hostility to its own objectives, often goes to considerable lengths to control and direct human efforts in ways that are inimical to the natural "groupiness" of human beings. When man's social needs—and perhaps his safety needs, too—are thus thwarted, he behaves in ways which tend to defeat organizational objectives. He becomes resistant, antagonistic, uncooperative. But this behavior is a consequence, not a cause.

Ego Needs

Above the social needs—in the sense that they do not become motivators until lower needs are reasonably satisfied—are the needs of greatest significance to management and to man himself. They are the *egoistic needs*, and they are of two kinds:

1. Those needs that relate to one's self-esteem—needs for self-confidence, for independence, for achievement, for competence, for knowledge.

2. Those needs that relate to one's reputation—needs for status, for recognition, for appreciation, for the deserved respect of one's fellows.

Unlike the lower needs, these are rarely satisfied; man seeks indefinitely for more satisfaction of these needs once they have become important to him. But they do not appear in any significant way until physiological, safety, and social needs are all reasonably satisfied.

The typical industrial organization offers few opportunities for the satisfaction of these egoistic needs to people at lower levels in the hierarchy. The conventional methods of organizing work, particularly in mass-production industries, give little heed to these aspects of human motivation. If the practices of scientific management were deliberately calculated to thwart these needs, they could hardly accomplish this purpose better than they do.

Self-Fulfillment Needs

Finally—a capstone, as it were, on the hierarchy of man's needs—there are what we may call the *needs for self-fulfillment*. These are the needs for realizing one's own potentialities, for continued self-development, for being creative in the broadest sense of that term.

It is clear that the conditions of modern life give only limited opportunity for these relatively weak needs to obtain expression. The deprivation most people experience with respect to other lower-level needs diverts their energies into the struggle to satisfy *those* needs, and the needs for self-fulfillment remain dormant.

Management and Motivation

We recognize readily enough that a man suffering from a severe dietary deficiency is sick. The deprivation of physiological needs has behavioral consequences. The same is true—although less well recognized—of deprivation of higher-level needs. The man whose needs for safety, association, independence, or status are thwarted is sick just as surely as the man who has rickets. And his sickness will have behavioral consequences. We will be mistaken if we attribute his resultant passivity, his hostility, his refusal to accept responsibility to his inherent "human nature." These forms of behavior are *symptoms* of illness—of deprivation of his social and egoistic needs.

The man whose lower-level needs are satisfied is not motivated to satisfy those needs any longer. For practical purposes they exist no longer. Management often asks, "Why aren't people more productive? We pay good wages, provide good working conditions, have excellent fringe benefits and steady employment. Yet people do not seem to be willing to put forth more than minimum effort."

The fact that management has provided for these physiological and safety needs has shifted the motivational emphasis to the social and perhaps to the egoistic needs. Unless there are opportunities *at work* to satisfy these higher-level needs, people will be deprived; and their behavior will reflect this deprivation. Under such conditions, if management continues to focus its attention on physiological needs, its efforts are bound to be ineffective.

People *will* make insistent demands for more money under these conditions. It becomes more important than ever to buy the material goods and services which can provide limited satisfaction of the thwarted needs. Although money has only limited value in satisfying many higher-level needs, it can become the focus of interest if it is the *only* means available.

The Carrot-and-Stick Approach

The carrot-and-stick theory of motivation (like Newtonian physical theory) works reasonably well under certain circumstances. The *means* for satisfying man's physiological and (within limits) his safety needs can be provided or withheld by management. Employment itself is such a means, and so are wages, working conditions, and benefits. By these means the individual can be controlled so long as he is struggling for subsistence.

But the carrot-and-stick theory does not work at all once man has reached an adequate subsistence level and is motivated primarily by higher needs. Management cannot provide a man with self-respect, or with the respect of his fellows, or with the satisfaction of needs for self-fulfillment. It can create such conditions that he is encouraged and enabled to seek such satisfactions for *himself*, or it can thwart him by failing to create those conditions.

But this creation of conditions is not "control." It is not a good device for directing behavior. And so management finds itself in an odd position. The high standard of living created by our modern technological know-how provides quite adequately for the satisfaction of physiological and safety needs. The only significant exception is where management practices have not created confidence in a "fair break"—and thus where safety needs are thwarted. But by making possible the satisfaction of low-level needs, management has deprived itself of the ability to use as motivators the devices on which conventional theory has taught it to rely—rewards, promises, incentives, or threats and other coercive devices.

The philosophy of management by direction and control—*regardless of whether it is hard or soft*—is inadequate to motivate because the human needs on which this approach relies are today unimportant motivators of behavior. Direction and control are essentially useless in motivating people whose important needs are social and egoistic. Both the hard and the soft approach fail today because they are simply irrelevant to the situation.

People, deprived of opportunities to satisfy at work the needs which are now important to them, behave exactly as we might predict—with indolence, passivity, resistance to change, lack of responsibility, willingness to follow the demagogue, unreasonable demands for economic benefits. It would seem that we are caught in a web of our own weaving.

A New Theory of Management

For these and many other reasons, we require a different theory of the task of managing people based on more adequate assumptions about human nature and human motivation. I am going to be so bold as to suggest the broad dimensions of such a theory. Call it "Theory Y," if you will.

1. Management is responsible for organizing the elements of productive enterprise—money, materials, equipment, people—in the interest of economic ends.

2. People are *not* by nature passive or resistant to organizational needs. They have become so as a result of experience in organizations.

3. The motivation, the potential for development, the capacity for assuming responsibility, the readiness to direct behavior toward organizational goals are all present in people. Management does not put them there. It is a responsibility of management to make it possible for people to recognize and develop these human characteristics for themselves.

4. The essential task of management is to arrange organizational conditions and methods of operation so that people can achieve their own goals *best* by directing *their own* efforts toward organizational objectives.

This is a process primarily of creating opportunities, releasing potential, removing obstacles, encouraging growth, providing guidance. It is what Peter Drucker has called "management by objectives" in contrast to "management by control." It does *not* involve the abdication of management, the absence of leadership, the lowering of standards, or the other characteristics usually associated with the "soft" approach under Theory X.

Some Difficulties

It is no more possible to create an organization today which will be a full, effective application of this theory than it was to build an atomic power plant in 1945. There are many formidable obstacles to overcome.

The conditions imposed by conventional organization theory and by the approach of scientific management for the past half century have tied men to limited jobs which do not utilize their capabilities, have discouraged the acceptance of responsibility, have encouraged passivity, have eliminated meaning from work. Man's habits, attitudes, expectations—his whole conception of membership in an industrial organization—have been conditioned by his experience under these circumstances.

People today are accustomed to being directed, manipulated, controlled in industrial organizations and to finding satisfaction for their social, egoistic, and self-fulfillment needs away from the job. This is true of much of management as well as of workers. Genuine "industrial citizenship"—to borrow again a term from Drucker—is a remote and unrealistic idea, the meaning of which has not even been considered by most members of industrial organizations.

Another way of saying this is that Theory X places exclusive reliance upon external control of human behavior, while Theory Y relies heavily on self-control and self-direction. It is worth noting that this difference is the difference between treating people as children and treating them as mature adults. After generations of the former, we cannot expect to shift to the latter overnight.

Steps in the Right Direction

Before we are overwhelmed by the obstacles, let us remember that the application of theory is always slow. Progress is usually achieved in small steps. Some innovative ideas which are entirely consistent with Theory Y are today being applied with some success.

Decentralization and Delegation

These are ways of freeing people from the too-close control of conventional organization, giving them a degree of freedom to direct their own activities, to assume responsibility, and, importantly, to satisfy their egoistic needs. In this connection, the flat organization of Sears, Roebuck and Company provides an interesting example. It forces "management by objectives," since it enlarges the number of people reporting to a manager until he cannot direct and control them in the conventional manner.

Job Enlargement

This concept, pioneered by I.B.M. and Detroit Edison, is quite consistent with Theory Y. It encourages the acceptance of responsibility at the bottom of the organization; it provides opportunities for satisfying social and egoistic needs. In fact, the reorganization of work at the factory level offers one of the more challenging opportunities for innovation consistent with Theory Y.

Participation and Consultative Management

Under proper conditions, participation and consultative management provide encouragement to people to direct their creative energies toward organizational objectives, give them some voice in decisions that affect them, provide significant opportunities for the satisfaction of social and egoistic needs. The Scanlon Plan is the outstanding embodiment of these ideas in practice.

Performance Appraisal

Even a cursory examination of conventional programs of performance appraisal within the ranks of management will reveal how completely consistent they are with Theory X. In fact, most such programs tend to treat the individual as though he were a product under inspection on the assembly line.

A few companies—among them General Mills, Ansul Chemical, and General Electric—have been experimenting with approaches which involve the individual in setting "targets" or objectives *for himself* and in a *self*-evaluation of performance semiannually or annually. Of course, the superior plays an important leadership role in this process—one, in fact, which demands substantially more competence than the conventional approach. The role is, however, considerably more congenial to many managers than the role of "judge" or "inspector" which is usually forced upon them. Above all, the individual is encouraged to take a greater responsibility for planning and appraising his own contribution to organizational objectives; and the accompanying effects on egoistic and self-fulfillment needs are substantial.

Applying the Ideas

The not infrequent failure of such ideas as these to work as well as expected is often attributable to the fact that a management has "bought the idea" but applied it within the framework of Theory X and its assumptions.

Delegation is not an effective way of exercising management by control. Participation becomes a farce when it is applied as a sales gimmick or a device for kidding people into thinking they are important. Only the management that has confidence in human capacities and is itself directed toward organizational objectives rather than toward the preservation of personal power can grasp the implications of this emerging theory. Such management will find and apply successfully other innovative ideas as we move slowly toward the full implementation of a theory like Y.

The Human Side of Enterprise

It is quite possible for us to realize substantial improvements in the effectiveness of industrial organizations during the next decade or two. The social sciences can contribute much to such developments; we are only beginning to grasp the implications of the growing body of knowledge in these fields. But if this conviction is to become a reality instead of a pious hope, we will need to view the process much as we view the process of releasing the energy of the atom for constructive human ends—as a slow, costly, sometimes discouraging approach toward a goal which would seem to many to be quite unrealistic.

The ingenuity and the perseverance of industrial management in the pursuit of economic ends have changed many scientific and technological dreams into commonplace realities. It is now becoming clear that the application of these same talents to the human side of enterprise will not only enhance substantially these materialistic achievements, but will bring us one step closer to "the good society."

Section

II

Motivation and Performance

As evidenced by the selections in section I, an understanding of human behavior is imperative if managers are to maximize the performance of their organization's human resources. This section contains some of the major theories of individual behavior and motivation. The first of these is probably the best known—Abraham H. Maslow's "A Theory of Human Motivation." It was in this article that Maslow originally set forth his famous "hierarchy of needs," which classifies all human needs into five categories—physiological, safety, love, esteem, and self-actualization. Needs at the lowest level (physiological) must be at least minimally satisfied before the next higher level of needs (safety) will become the primary determinant of behavior. In turn, safety needs must be satisfied before love or social needs can become highest in importance, and so on. Maslow's theory also holds that a satisfied need is no longer a motivator—an insight that has enlightened many managers to the fact that continued emphasis on the satisfaction of lower-level needs may result in diminishing returns.

David C. McClelland, in "Achievement Motivation," suggests that people can be divided into two groups: a minority that is challenged by opportunity and is willing to work hard to achieve, and a majority that really does not care all that much about achievement. Focusing on those people who possess a high degree of "achievement motivation" (or high n Ach), McClelland cites several characteristics of such individuals: (1) they set challenging but attainable goals for themselves; (2) they prefer to work at a problem, thus influencing the outcome rather than leaving it to chance or to others; (3) they are more concerned with personal achievement than with the rewards of success; and (4) they welcome concrete feedback on how well they are doing. McClelland concludes by suggesting individuals with low achievement motivation can develop the need to achieve if the environment in which they live and work is supportive of such change.

Frederick Herzberg's "One More Time: How Do You Motivate Employees?" originally appeared in the *Harvard Business Review* in 1968 and earned the distinction of being that journal's all-time best-selling reprint. In it, Herzberg recounts his famous "hygiene-motivation theory," which suggests that while "hygiene" factors (such as company policies and administration, supervision, working conditions, interpersonal relations, salary, status, and security) are important (poor hygiene factors cause job dissatisfaction), it is growth or "motivation" factors (such as achievement, recognition, interesting work, increased responsibility, and promotion) that lead to improved job satisfaction and performance. Thus, the only way to motivate an employee to excel is with challenging work in which responsibility can be assumed. This is typically done by means of job enrichment. Herzberg cautions the reader not to confuse job enrichment with job enlargement—merely increasing the number of meaningless tasks performed by a worker. Job enrichment, in marked contrast, is the deliberate upgrading of the scope, challenge, and responsibility of a job. Herzberg cites an example of a successful job-enrichment experiment and concludes by providing a step-by-step guide to job enrichment.

The next selection in this section is "Existence, Relatedness, and Growth Model" by Clayton P. Alderfer. The author contends that human needs can be divided into three categories: existence, relatedness, and growth. "Existence" needs include all the various forms of material and physiological desires. "Relatedness" needs involve relationships with significant others, including family, friends, and coworkers. "Growth" needs relate to the inner desire to utilize one's capacities more fully and to grow and develop as a human being. Alderfer sets forth ten propositions relating to how the satisfaction of one need affects the intensity of the others.

"Expectancy Theory," written by John P. Campbell, Marvin D. Dunnette, Edward E. Lawler III, and Karl E. Weick Jr., holds that individuals have cognitive "expectancies" regarding outcomes that are likely to occur as a result of their actions, and that they have preferences among these various outcomes. Consequently, motivation occurs on the basis of what an individual expects to occur as a result of what he or she chooses to do. The authors review the evolution of the expectancy theory of motivation and then focus on their "hybrid expectancy model," which views the motivation to work as the end result of a complex perceptual process that includes: (1) expectancy I (the perceived probability that an individual can do the job); (2) the nature of the task goals (categorized as external or internal); (3) expectancy II (the perceived probability of receiving a reward given achievement of the task goal); (4) the nature of the rewards that can be obtained for achieving the task goal; (5) the instrumentality or importance of the rewards to the satisfaction of the individual's needs; and (6) the needs of the individual. While this theory is clearly more complex than other motivation theories, it provides managers with a comprehensive checklist of factors that affect an individual's motivation to work. An improvement in any of the elements of the expectancy theory model is likely to lead to a corresponding improvement in motivation and performance.

Steven Kerr is the author of the next article, "On the Folly of Rewarding A, While Hoping for B." The key point is "what you reward is what you get." Kerr provides numerous examples of how what companies hope for is sacrificed because they reward something else. For example, organizations hope for long-term growth but reward quarterly earnings. Or they espouse teamwork but celebrate individual accomplishments far more. Innovation and risk-taking are preached, but mistakes are punished. Kerr concludes by suggesting that a formal reward system should positively reinforce desired behavior, and not constitute an obstacle to be overcome.

The final reading in this section is "Goal Setting—A Motivational Technique That Works" by Gary Latham and Edwin Locke. The authors contend that effective goal-setting significantly enhances productivity. Goals should be specific rather than vague and they should be challenging yet attainable. Combined with effective management and adequate compensation, clear and reachable goals are likely to motivate employees to higher levels of performance.

1

A Theory of Human Motivation

Abraham H. Maslow

I. Introduction

In a previous paper[1] various propositions were presented which would have to be included in any theory of human motivation that could lay claim to being definitive. These conclusions may be briefly summarized as follows:

1. The integrated wholeness of the organism must be one of the foundation stones of motivation theory.

2. The hunger drive (or any other physiological drive) was rejected as a centering point or model for a definitive theory of motivation. Any drive that is somatically based and localizable was shown to be atypical rather than typical in human motivation.

3. Such a theory should stress and center itself upon ultimate or basic goals rather than partial or superficial ones, upon ends rather than means to these ends. Such a stress would imply a more central place for unconscious than for conscious motivations.

4. There are usually available various cultural paths to the same goal. Therefore conscious, specific, local-cultural desires are not as fundamental in motivation theory as the more basic, unconscious goals.

5. Any motivated behavior, either preparatory or consummatory, must be understood to be a channel through which many basic needs may be simultaneously expressed or satisfied. Typically an act has *more* than one motivation.

6. Practically all organismic states are to be understood as motivated and as motivating.

7. Human needs arrange themselves in hierarchies of prepotency. That is to say, the appearance of one need usually rests on the prior satisfaction of

Reprinted from *Psychological Review*, vol. 50 (July 1943), pp. 370–396.

another, more pre-potent need. Man is a perpetually wanting animal. Also no need or drive can be treated as if it were isolated or discrete; every drive is related to the state of satisfaction or dissatisfaction of other drives.

8. *Lists* of drives will get us nowhere for various theoretical and practical reasons. Furthermore any classification of motivations must deal with the problem of levels of specificity or generalization of the motives to be classified.

9. Classifications of motivations must be based upon goals rather than upon instigating drives or motivated behavior.

10. Motivation theory should be human-centered rather than animal-centered.

11. The situation or the field in which the organism reacts must be taken into account but the field alone can rarely serve as an exclusive explanation for behavior. Furthermore the field itself must be interpreted in terms of the organism. Field theory cannot be a substitute for motivation theory.

12. Not only the integration of the organism must be taken into account, but also the possibility of isolated, specific, partial or segmental reactions.

It has since become necessary to add to these another affirmation.

13. Motivations theory is not synonymous with behavior theory. The motivations are only one class of determinants of behavior. While behavior is almost always motivated, it is also almost always biologically, culturally and situationally determined as well.

The present paper is an attempt to formulate a positive theory of motivation which will satisfy these theoretical demands and at the same time conform to the known facts, clinical and observational as well as experimental. It derives most directly, however, from clinical experience. This theory is, I think, in the functionalist tradition of James and Dewey, and is fused with the holism of Wertheimer,[2] Goldstein,[3] and Gestalt Psychology, and with the dynamicism of Freud[4] and Adler.[5] This fusion or synthesis may arbitrarily be called a "general-dynamic" theory.

It is far easier to perceive and to criticize the aspects in motivation theory than to remedy them. Mostly this is because of the very serious lack of sound data in this area. I conceive this lack of sound facts to be due primarily to the absence of a valid theory of motivation. The present theory then must be considered to be a suggested program or framework for future research and must stand or fall, not so much on facts available or evidence presented, as upon researches yet to be done, researches suggested perhaps, by the questions raised in this paper.

II. The Basic Needs

The "Physiological" Needs. The needs that are usually taken as the starting point for motivation theory are the so-called physiological drives. Two recent lines of research make it necessary to revise our customary notions about these needs, first, the development of the concept of homeostasis, and second, the finding that appetites (preferential choices among foods) are a fairly efficient indication of actual needs or lacks in the body.

Homeostasis refers to the body's automatic efforts to maintain a constant, normal state of the blood stream. Cannon[6] has described this process for (1) the water content of the blood, (2) salt content, (3) sugar content, (4) protein content, (5) fat content, (6) calcium content, (7) oxygen content, (8) constant hydrogen-ion level (acid-base balance) and (9) constant temperature of the blood. Obviously this list can be extended to include other minerals, the hormones, vitamins, etc.

Young in a recent article[7] has summarized the work on appetite in its relation to body needs. If the body lacks some chemical, the individual will tend to develop a specific appetite or partial hunger for that food element.

Thus it seems impossible as well as useless to make any list of fundamental physiological needs for they can come to almost any number one might wish, depending on the degree of specificity of description. We can not identify all physiological needs as homeostatic. That sexual desire, sleepiness, sheer activity and maternal behavior in animals, are homeostatic, has not yet been demonstrated. Furthermore, this list would not include the various sensory pleasures (tastes, smells, tickling, stroking) which are probably physiological and which may become the goals of motivated behavior.

In a previous paper[8] it has been pointed out that these physiological drives or needs are to be considered unusual rather than typical because they are isolable, and because they are localizable somatically. That is to say, they are relatively independent of each other, of other motivations and of the organism as a whole, and secondly, in many cases, it is possible to demonstrate a localized, underlying somatic base for the drive. This is true less generally than has been thought (exceptions are fatigue, sleepiness, maternal responses) but it is still true in the classic instances of hunger, sex, and thirst.

It should be pointed out again that any of the physiological needs and the consummatory behavior involved with them serve as channels for all sorts of other needs as well. That is to say, the person who thinks he is hungry may actually be seeking more for comfort, or dependence, than for vitamins or proteins. Conversely, it is possible to satisfy the hunger need in part by other activities such as drinking water or smoking cigarettes. In other words, relatively isolable as these physiological needs are, they are not completely so.

Undoubtedly these physiological needs are the most prepotent of all needs. What this means specifically is, that in the human being who is missing everything in life in an extreme fashion, it is most likely that the major motivation would be the physiological needs rather than any others. A person who is lacking food, safety, love, and esteem would most probably hunger for food more strongly than for anything else.

If all the needs are unsatisfied, and the organism is then dominated by the physiological needs, all other needs may become simply non-existent or be pushed into the background. It is then fair to characterize the whole organism by saying simply that it is hungry, for consciousness is almost completely preempted by hunger. All capacities are put into the service of hunger-satisfaction, and the organization of these capacities is almost entirely determined by the one purpose of satisfying hunger. The receptors and effectors, the intelligence, memory, habits, all may now be defined simply as hunger-gratifying tools. Capacities that are not useful for this purpose lie dormant, or are pushed into the background. The urge to write poetry, the desire to acquire an automobile, the interest in American history, the desire for a new pair of shoes are, in the extreme case, forgotten or become of secondary importance. For the man who is extremely and dangerously hungry, no other interests exist but food. He dreams food, he remembers food, he thinks about food, he emotes only about food, he perceives only food and he wants only food. The more subtle determinants that ordinarily fuse with the physiological drives in organizing even feeding, drinking or sexual behavior, may now be so completely overwhelmed as to allow us to speak at this time (but *only* at this time) of pure hunger drive and behavior, with the one unqualified aim of relief.

Another peculiar characteristic of the human organism when it is dominated by a certain need is that the whole philosophy of the future tends also to change. For our chronically and extremely hungry man, Utopia can be defined very simply as a place where there is plenty of food. He tends to think that, if only he is guaranteed food for the rest of his life, he will be perfectly happy and will never want anything more. Life itself tends to be defined in terms of eating. Anything else will be defined as unimportant. Freedom, love, community feeling, respect, philosophy, may all be waved aside as fripperies which are useless since they fail to fill the stomach. Such a man may fairly be said to live by bread alone.

It cannot possibly be denied that such things are true but their *generality* can be denied. Emergency conditions are, almost by definition, rare in the normally functioning peaceful society. That this truism can be forgotten is due mainly to two reasons. First, rats have few motivations other than physiological ones, and since so much of the research upon motivation has been made with these animals, it is easy to carry the rat-picture over to the human being. Secondly, it is too often not realized that culture itself is an adaptive tool, one of whose main functions is to make the physiological emergencies come less and less often. In most of the known societies, chronic extreme hunger of the emergency type is rare, rather than common. In any case, this is still true in the United States. The average American citizen is experiencing appetite rather than hunger when he says "I am hungry." He is apt to experience sheer life-and-death hunger only by accident and then only a few times through his entire life.

Obviously a good way to obscure the "higher" motivations, and to get a lopsided view of human capacities and human nature, is to make the organism extremely and chronically hungry or thirsty. Anyone who attempts to make an emergency picture into a typical one, and who will measure all of man's goals and desires by his behavior during extreme physiological deprivation is certainly being blind to many things. It is quite true that man lives by bread alone—when there is no bread. But what happens to man's desires when there *is* plenty of bread and when his belly is chronically filled?

At once other (and "higher") needs emerge and these, rather than physiological hungers, dominate the organism. And when these in turn are satisfied, again new (and still "higher") needs emerge and so on. This is what we mean by saying that the basic human needs are organized into a hierarchy of relative prepotency.

One main implication of this phrasing is that gratification becomes as important a concept as deprivation in motivation theory, for it releases the organism from the domination of a relatively more physiological need, permitting thereby the emergence of other more social goals. The physiological needs, along with their partial goals, when chronically gratified cease to exist as active determinants or organizers of behavior. They now exist only in a potential fashion in the sense that they may emerge again to dominate the organism if they are thwarted. But a want that is satisfied is no longer a want. The organism is dominated and its behavior organized only by unsatisfied needs. If hunger is satisfied, it becomes unimportant in the current dynamics of the individual.

This statement is somewhat qualified by a hypothesis to be discussed more fully later, namely that it is precisely those individuals in whom a certain need has always been satisfied who are best equipped to tolerate deprivation of that need in the future, and that furthermore, those who have been deprived in the past will react differently to current satisfactions than the one who has never been deprived.

The Safety Needs. If the physiological needs are relatively well gratified, there then emerges a new set of needs, which we may categorize roughly as the safety needs. All that has been said of the physiological needs is equally true, although in lesser degree, of these desires. The organism may equally well be wholly dominated by them. They may serve as the almost exclusive organizers of behavior, recruiting all the capacities of the organism in their service, and we may then fairly describe the whole organism as a safety-seeking mechanism. Again we may say of the receptors, the effectors, of the intellect and the other capacities that they are primarily safety-seeking tools. Again, as in the hungry man, we find that the dominating goal is a strong determinant not only of his current world-outlook and philosophy but also of his philosophy of the future. Practically everything looks less important than safety, (even sometimes the physiological needs which being satisfied, are now underestimated). A man, in this state, if it is extreme enough and chronic enough, may be characterized as living almost for safety alone.

Although in this paper we are interested primarily in the needs of the adult, we can approach an understanding of his safety needs perhaps more efficiently by observation of infants and children, in whom these needs are much more simple and obvious. One reason for the clearer appearance of the threat or danger reaction in infants is that they do not inhibit this reaction at all, whereas adults in our society have been taught to inhibit it at all costs. Thus even when adults do feel their safety to be threatened we may not be able to see this on the surface. Infants will react in a total fashion and as if they were endangered, if they are disturbed or dropped suddenly, startled by loud noises, flashing light, or other unusual sensory stimulation, by rough handling, by general loss of support in the mother's arms, or by inadequate support.[9]

In infants we can also see a much more direct reaction to bodily illnesses of various kinds. Sometimes these illnesses seem to be immediately and *per se* threatening and seem to make the child feel unsafe. For instance, vomiting, colic or other sharp pains seem to make the child look at the whole world in a different way. At such a moment of pain, it may be postulated that, for the child, the appearance of the whole world suddenly changes from sunniness to darkness, so to speak, and becomes a place in which anything at all might happen, in which previously stable things have suddenly become unstable. Thus a child who because of some bad food is taken ill may, for a day or two, develop fear, nightmares, and a need for protection and reassurance never seen in him before his illness.

Another indication of the child's need for safety is his preference for some kind of undisrupted routine or rhythm. He seems to want a predictable, orderly world. For instance, injustice, unfairness, or inconsistency in the parents seems to make a child feel anxious and unsafe. This attitude may be not so much because of the injustice *per se* or any particular pains involved, but rather because this treatment threatens to make the world look unreliable, or unsafe, or unpredictable. Young children seem to thrive better under a system which has at least a skeletal outline of rigidity, in which there is a schedule of a kind, some sort of routine, something that can be counted upon, not only for the present but also far into the future. Perhaps one could express this more accurately by saying that the child needs an organized world rather than an unorganized or unstructured one.

The central role of the parents and the normal family setup are indisputable. Quarreling, physical assault, separation, divorce or death within the family may be particularly terrifying. Also parental outbursts of rage or threats of punishment directed to the child, calling him names, speaking to him harshly, shaking him, handling him roughly, or actual physical punishment sometimes elicit such total panic and terror in the child that we must assume more is involved than the physical pain alone. While it is true that in some children this terror may represent also a fear of loss of parental love, it can also occur in completely rejected children, who seem to cling to the hating parents more for sheer safety and protection than because of hope of love.

Confronting the average child with new, unfamiliar, strange, unmanageable stimuli or situations will too frequently elicit the danger or terror reaction, as for example, getting lost or even being separated from the parents for a short time, being confronted with new faces, new situations or new tasks, the sight of strange, unfamiliar or uncontrollable objects, illness or death. Particularly at such times, the child's frantic clinging to his parents is eloquent testimony to their role as protectors (quite apart from their roles as food-givers and love-givers).

From these and similar observations, we may generalize and say that the average child in our society generally prefers a safe, orderly, predictable, organized world, which he can count on, and in which unexpected, unmanageable or other dangerous things do not happen, and in which, in any case, he has all-powerful parents who protect and shield him from harm.

That these reactions may so easily be observed in children is in a way a proof of the fact that children in our society, feel too unsafe (or, in a word, are badly brought up). Children who are reared in an unthreatening, loving family do *not* ordinarily react as we have described above.[10] In such children the danger reactions are apt to come mostly to objects or situations that adults too would consider dangerous.[11]

The healthy, normal, fortunate adult in our culture is largely satisfied in his safety needs. The peaceful, smoothly running, "good" society ordinarily makes its members feel safe enough from wild animals, extremes of temperature, criminals, assault and murder, tyranny, etc. Therefore, in a very real sense, he no longer has any safety needs as active motivators. Just as a sated man no longer feels hungry, a safe man no longer feels endangered. If we wish to see these needs directly and clearly we must turn to neurotic or near-neurotic individuals, and to the economic and social underdogs. In between these extremes, we can perceive the expressions of safety needs only in such phenomena as, for instance, the common preference for a job with tenure and protection, the desire for a savings account, and for insurance of various kinds (medical, dental, unemployment, disability, old age).

Other broader aspects of the attempt to seek safety and stability in the world are seen in the very common preference for familiar rather than unfamiliar things, or for the known rather than the unknown. The tendency to have some religion or world-philosophy that organizes the universe and the men in it into some sort of satisfactorily coherent, meaningful whole is also in part motivated by safety-seeking. Here too we may list science and philosophy in general as partially motivated by the safety needs (we shall see later that there are also other motivations to scientific, philosophical or religious endeavor).

Otherwise the need for safety is seen as an active and dominant mobilizer of the organism's resources only in emergencies, *e.g.*, war, disease, natural catastrophes, crime waves, societal disorganization, neurosis, brain injury, chronically bad situation.

Some neurotic adults in our society are, in many ways, like the unsafe child in their desire for safety, although in the former it takes on a somewhat special appearance. Their reaction is often to unknown, psychological dangers in a world that is perceived to be hostile, overwhelming and threatening. Such a person behaves as if a great catastrophe were almost always impending, *i.e.*, he is usually responding as if to an emergency. His safety needs often find specific expression in a search for a protector, or a stronger person on whom he may depend, or perhaps, a Fuehrer.

The neurotic individual may be described in a slightly different way with some usefulness as a grown-up person who retains his childish attitudes toward the world. That is to say, a neurotic adult may be said to behave "as if" he were actually afraid of a spanking, or of his mother's disapproval, or of being abandoned by his parents, or having his food taken away from him. It is as if his childish attitudes of fear and threat reaction to a dangerous world had gone underground, and untouched by the growing up and learning processes, were now ready to be called out by any stimulus that would make a child feel endangered and threatened.[12]

The neurosis in which the search for safety takes its clearest form is in the compulsive-obsessive neurosis. Compulsive-obsessives try frantically to order and stabilize the world so that no unmanageable, unexpected or unfamiliar dangers will ever appear.[13] They hedge themselves about with all sorts of ceremonials, rules and formulas so that every possible contingency may be provided for and so that no new contingencies may appear. They are much like the brain injured cases, described by Goldstein,[14] who manage to maintain their equilibrium by avoiding everything unfamiliar and strange and by ordering their restricted world in such a neat, disciplined, orderly fashion that everything in the world can be counted upon. They try to arrange the world so that anything unexpected (dangers) cannot possibly occur. If, through no fault of their own, something unexpected does occur, they go into a panic reaction as if this unexpected occurrence constituted a grave danger. What we can see only as a none-too-strong preference in the healthy person, *e.g.*, preference for the familiar, becomes a life-and-death necessity in abnormal cases.

The Love Needs. If both the physiological and the safety needs are fairly well gratified, then there will emerge the love and affection and belongingness needs, and the whole cycle already described will repeat itself with this new center. Now the person will feel keenly, as never before, the absence of friends, or a sweetheart, or a wife, or children. He will hunger for affectionate relations with people in general, namely, for a place in his group, and he will strive with great intensity to achieve this goal. He will want to attain such a place more than anything else in the world and may even forget that once, when he was hungry, he sneered at love.

In our society the thwarting of these needs is the most commonly found core in cases of maladjustment and more severe psychopathology. Love and affection, as well as their possible expression in sexuality, are generally looked upon with ambivalence and are customarily hedged about with many restrictions and inhibitions. Practically all theorists of psychopathology have stressed thwarting of the love needs as basic in the picture of maladjustment. Many clinical studies have therefore been made of this need and we know more about it perhaps than any of the other needs except the physiological ones.[15]

One thing that must be stressed at this point is that love is not synonymous with sex. Sex may be studied as a purely physiological need. Ordinarily sexual behavior is multi-determined, that is to say, determined not only by sexual but also by other needs, chief among which are the love and affection needs. Also not to be overlooked is the fact that the love needs involve both giving *and* receiving love.[16]

The Esteem Needs. All people in our society (with a few pathological exceptions) have a need or desire for a stable, firmly based, (usually) high evaluation of themselves, for self-respect, or self-esteem, and for the esteem of others. By firmly based self-esteem, we mean that which is soundly based upon real capacity, achievement and respect from others. These needs may be classified into two subsidiary sets. These are, first, the desire for strength, for achievement, for adequacy, for confidence in the face of the world, and for independence and freedom.[17] Secondly, we have what we may call the desire for reputation or prestige (defining it as respect or esteem from other people), recognition, attention, importance or appreciation.[18] These needs have been relatively stressed by Alfred Adler and his followers, and have been relatively neglected by Freud and the psychoanalysts. More and more today however there is appearing widespread appreciation of their central importance.

Satisfaction of the self-esteem need leads to feelings of self-confidence, worth, strength, capability and adequacy of being useful and necessary in the world. But thwarting of these needs produces feelings of inferiority, of weakness and of helplessness. These feelings in turn give rise to either basic discouragement or else compensatory or neurotic trends. An appreciation of the necessity of basic self-confidence and an understanding of how helpless people are without it, can be easily gained from a study of severe traumatic neurosis.[19]

The Need for Self-Actualization. Even if all these needs are satisfied, we may still often (if not always) expect that a new discontent and restlessness will soon develop, unless the individual is doing what he is fitted for. A musician must make music, an artist must paint, a poet must write, if he is to be ultimately happy. What a man *can* be, he *must* be. This need we may call self-actualization.

This term, first coined by Kurt Goldstein, is being used in this paper in a much more specific and limited fashion. It refers to the desire for self-fulfillment, namely, to the tendency for him to become actualized in what he is potentially. This tendency might be phrased as the desire to become more and more what one is, to become everything that one is capable of becoming.

The specific form that these needs will take will of course vary greatly from person to person. In one individual it may take the form of the desire to be an ideal mother, in another it may be expressed athletically, and in still another it may be expressed in painting pictures or in inventions. It is not necessarily a creative urge although in people who have any capacities for creation it will take this form.

The clear emergence of these needs rests upon prior satisfaction of the physiological, safety, love and esteem needs. We shall call people who are satisfied in these needs, basically satisfied people, and it is from these that we may expect the fullest (and healthiest) creativeness.[20] Since, in our society, basically satisfied people are the exception, we do not know much about self-actualization, either experimentally or clinically. It remains a challenging problem for research.

The Preconditions for the Basic Need Satisfactions. There are certain conditions which are immediate prerequisites for the basic need satisfactions. Danger to these is reacted to almost as if it were a direct danger to the basic needs themselves. Such conditions as freedom to speak, freedom to do what one wishes so long as no harm is done to others, freedom to express one's self, freedom to investigate and seek for information, freedom to defend one's self, justice, fairness, honesty, orderliness in the group are examples of such preconditions for basic need satisfactions. Thwarting in these freedoms will be reacted to with a threat or emergency response. These conditions are not ends in themselves but they are *almost* so since they are so closely related to the basic needs, which are apparently the only ends in themselves. These conditions are defended because without them the basic satisfactions are quite impossible, or at least, very severely endangered.

If we remember that the cognitive capacities (perceptual, intellectual, learning) are a set of adjustive tools, which have, among other functions, that of satisfaction of our basic needs, then it is clear that any danger to them, any deprivation or blocking of their free use, must also be indirectly threatening to the basic needs themselves. Such a statement is a partial solution of the general problems of curiosity, the search for knowledge, truth and wisdom, and the ever-persistent urge to solve the cosmic mysteries.

We must therefore introduce another hypothesis and speak of degrees of closeness to the basic needs, for we have already pointed out that *any* conscious desires (partial goals) are more or less important as they are more or less close to the basic needs. The same statement may be made for various behavior acts. An act is psychologically important if it contributes directly to satisfaction of basic needs. The less directly it so contributes, or the weaker this contribution is, the less important this act must be conceived to be from the point of view of dynamic psychology. A similar statement may be made for the various defense or coping mechanisms. Some are very directly related to the protection or attainment of the basic needs; others are only weakly and distantly related. Indeed if we wished, we could speak of more basic and less basic defense mechanisms, and then affirm that danger to the more basic defenses is more threatening than danger to less basic defenses (always remembering that this is so only because of their relationship to the basic needs).

The Desires to Know and to Understand.   So far, we have mentioned the cognitive needs only in passing. Acquiring knowledge and systematizing the universe have been considered as, in part, techniques for the achievement of basic safety in the world, or, for the intelligent man, expressions of self-actualization. Also freedom of inquiry and expression have been discussed as preconditions of satisfactions of the basic needs. True though these formulations may be, they do not constitute definitive answers to the question as to the motivation role of curiosity, learning, philosophizing, experimenting, etc. They are, at best, no more than partial answers.

This question is especially difficult because we know so little about the facts. Curiosity, exploration, desire for the facts, desire to know may certainly be observed easily enough. The fact that they often are pursued even at great cost to the individual's safety is an earnest of the partial character of our previous discussion. In addition, the writer must admit that, though he has sufficient clinical evidence to postulate the desire to know as a very strong drive in intelligent people, no data are available for unintelligent people. It may then be largely a function of relatively high intelligence. Rather tentatively, then, and largely in the hope of stimulating discussion and research, we shall postulate a basic desire to know, to be aware of reality, to get the facts, to satisfy curiosity, or as Wertheimer phrases it, to see rather than to be blind.

This postulation, however, is not enough. Even after we know, we are impelled to know more and more minutely and microscopically on the one hand, and on the other, more and more extensively in the direction of world philosophy, religion, etc. The facts that we acquire, if they are isolated or atomistic, inevitably get theorized about, and either analyzed or organized or both. This process has been phrased by some as the search for "meaning." We shall then postulate a desire to understand, to systematize, to organize, to analyze, to look for relations and meanings.

Once these desires are accepted for discussion, we see that they too form themselves into a small hierarchy in which the desire to know is prepotent over the desire to understand. All the characteristics of a hierarchy of prepotency that we have described above, seem to hold for this one as well.

We must guard ourselves against the too easy tendency to separate these desires from the basic needs we have discussed above, *i.e.*, to make a sharp dichotomy between "cognitive" and "conative" needs. The desire to know and to understand are themselves conative, *i.e.*, have a striving character, and are as much personality needs as the "basic needs" we have already discussed.[21]

III. Further Characteristics of the Basic Needs

The Degree of Fixity of the Hierarchy of Basic Needs.   We have spoken so far as if this hierarchy were a fixed order, but actually it is not nearly as rigid as we may have implied. It is true that most of the people with whom we have worked have seemed to have these basic needs in about the order that has been indicated. However, there have been a number of exceptions.

(1) There are some people in whom, for instance, self-esteem seems to be more important than love. This most common reversal in the hierarchy is usually due to the development of the notion that the person who is most likely to be loved is a strong or powerful person, one who inspires respect or fear, and who is self confident or aggressive. Therefore such people who lack love and seek it, may try hard to put on a front of aggressive, confident behavior. But essentially they seek high self-esteem and its behavior expressions more as a means-to-an-end than for its own sake; they seek self-assertion for the sake of love rather than for self-esteem itself.

(2) There are other, apparently innately creative people in whom the drive to creativeness seems to be more important than any other counterdeterminant. Their creativeness might appear not as self-actualization released by basic satisfaction, but in spite of lack of basic satisfaction.

(3) In certain people the level of aspiration may be permanently deadened or lowered. That is to say, the less prepotent goals may simply be lost, and may disappear forever, so that the person who has experienced life at a very low level, *i.e.*, chronic unemployment, may continue to be satisfied for the rest of his life if only he can get enough food.

(4) The so-called "psychopathic personality" is another example of permanent loss of the love needs. These are people who, according to the best data available,[22] have been starved for love in the earliest months of their lives and have simply lost forever the desire and the ability to give and to receive affection (as animals lose sucking or pecking reflexes that are not exercised soon enough after birth).

(5) Another cause of reversal of the hierarchy is that when a need has been satisfied for a long time, this need may be underevaluated. People who have never experienced chronic hunger are apt to underestimate its effects and to look upon food as a rather unimportant thing. If they are dominated by a higher need, this

higher need will seem to be the most important of all. It then becomes possible, and indeed does actually happen, that they may, for the sake of this higher need, put themselves into the position of being deprived in a more basic need. We may expect that after a long-time deprivation of the more basic need there will be a tendency to reevaluate both needs so that the more prepotent need will actually become consciously prepotent for the individual who may have given it up very lightly. Thus, a man who has given up his job rather than lose his self-respect, and who then starves for six months or so, may be willing to take his job back even at the price of losing his self-respect.

(6) Another partial explanation of *apparent* reversals is seen in the fact that we have been talking about the hierarchy of prepotency in terms of consciously felt wants or desires rather than of behavior. Looking at behavior itself may give us the wrong impression. What we have claimed is that the person will *want* the more basic of two needs when deprived in both. There is no necessary implication here that he will act upon his desires. Let us say again that there are many determinants of behavior other than the needs and desires.

(7) Perhaps more important than all these exceptions are the ones that involve ideals, high social standards, high values and the like. With such values people become martyrs; they will give up everything for the sake of a particular ideal, or value. These people may be understood, at least in part, by reference to one basic concept (or hypothesis) which may be called "increased frustration-tolerance through early gratification." People who have been satisfied in their basic needs throughout their lives, particularly in their earlier years, seem to develop exceptional power to withstand present or future thwarting of these needs simply because they have strong, healthy character structure as a result of basic satisfaction. They are the "strong" people who can easily weather disagreement or opposition, who can swim against the stream of public opinion and who can stand up for the truth at great personal cost. It is just the ones who have loved and been well loved, and who have had many deep friendships who can hold out against hatred, rejection or persecution.

I say all this in spite of the fact that there is a certain amount of sheer habituation which is also involved in any full discussion of frustration tolerance. For instance, it is likely that those persons who have been accustomed to relative starvation for a long time, are partially enabled thereby to withstand food deprivation. What sort of balance must be made between these two tendencies, of habituation on the one hand, and of past satisfaction breeding present frustration tolerance on the other hand, remains to be worked out by further research. Meanwhile we may assume that they are both operative, side by side, since they do not contradict each other. In respect to this phenomenon of increased frustration tolerance, it seems probable that the most important gratifications come in the first two years of life. That is to say, people who have been made secure and strong in the earliest years tend to remain secure and strong thereafter in the face of whatever threatens.

Degrees of Relative Satisfaction.   So far, our theoretical discussion may have given the impression that these five sets of needs are somehow in a step-wise, all-or-none relationship to each other. We have spoken in such terms as the following: "If one need is satisfied, then another emerges." This statement might give the false impression that a need must be satisfied 100 percent before the next need emerges. In actual fact, most members of our society who are normal, are partially satisfied in all their basic needs and partially unsatisfied in all their basic needs at the same time. A more realistic description of the hierarchy would be in terms of decreasing percentages of satisfaction as we go up the hierarchy of prepotency. For instance, if I may assign arbitrary figures for the sake of illustration, it is as if the average citizen is satisfied perhaps 85 percent in his physiological needs, 70 percent in his safety needs, 50 percent in his love needs, 40 percent in his self-esteem needs, and 10 percent in his self-actualization needs.

As for the concept of emergence of a new need after satisfaction of the prepotent need, this emergence is not a sudden, saltatory phenomenon but rather a gradual emergence by slow degrees from nothingness. For instance, if prepotent need A is satisfied only 10 percent then need B may not be visible at all. However, as this need A becomes satisfied 25 percent, need B may emerge 5 percent, as need A becomes satisfied 75 percent need B may emerge 90 percent, and so on.

Unconscious Character of Needs. These needs are neither necessarily conscious nor unconscious. On the whole, however, in the average person, they are more often unconscious rather than conscious. It is not necessary at this point to overhaul the tremendous mass of evidence which indicates the crucial importance of unconscious motivation. It would by now be expected, on a priori grounds alone, that unconscious motivations would on the whole be rather more important than the conscious motivations. What we have called the basic needs are very often largely unconscious although they may, with suitable techniques, and with sophisticated people become conscious.

Cultural Specificity and Generality of Needs. This classification of basic needs makes some attempt to take account of the relative unity behind the superficial differences in specific desires from one culture to another. Certainly in any particular culture an individual's conscious motivational content will usually be extremely different from the conscious motivational content of an individual in another society. However, it is the common experience of anthropologists that people, even in different societies, are much more alike than we would think from our first contact with them, and that as we know them better we seem to find more and more of this commonness. We then recognize the most startling differences to be superficial rather than basic, e.g., differences in style of hairdress, clothes, tastes in food, etc. Our classification of basic needs is in part an attempt to account for this unity behind the apparent diversity from culture to culture. No claim is made that it is ultimate or universal for all cultures. The claim is made only that it is relatively *more* ultimate, more universal, more basic, than the superficial conscious desires from culture to culture, and makes a somewhat closer approach to common-human characteristics. Basic needs are *more* common-human than superficial desires or behaviors.

Multiple Motivations of Behavior.   These needs must be understood *not* to be *exclusive* or single determiners of certain kinds of behavior. An example may be found in any behavior that seems to be physiologically motivated, such as eating, or sexual play or the like. The clinical psychologists have long since found that any behavior may be a channel through which flow various determinants. Or to say it in another way, most behavior is multi-motivated. Within the sphere of motivational determinants any behavior tends to be determined by several or *all* of the basic needs simultaneously rather than by only one of them. The latter would be more an exception than the former. Eating may be partially for the sake of filling the stomach, and partially for the sake of comfort and amelioration of other needs. One may make love not only for pure sexual release, but also to convince one's self of one's masculinity, or to make a conquest, to feel powerful, or to win more basic affection. As an illustration, I may point out that it would be possible (theoretically if not practically) to analyze a single act of an individual and see in it the expression of his physiological needs, his safety needs, his love needs, his esteem needs and self-actualization. This contrasts sharply with the more naive brand of trait psychology in which one trait or one motive accounts for a certain kind of act, *i.e.*, an aggressive act is traced solely to a trait of aggressiveness.

Multiple Determinants of Behavior.   Not all behavior is determined by the basic needs. We might even say that not all behavior is motivated. There are many determinants of behavior other than motives.[23] For instance, one other important class of determinants is the so-called "field" determinants. Theoretically, at least, behavior may be determined completely by the field, or even by specific isolated external stimuli, as in association of ideas, or certain conditioned reflexes. If in response to the stimulus word "table," I immediately perceive a memory image of a table, this response certainly has nothing to do with my basic needs.

Secondly, we may call attention again to the concept of "degree of closeness to the basic needs" or "degree of motivation." Some behavior is highly motivated, other behavior is only weakly motivated. Some is not motivated at all (but all behavior is determined).

Another important point[24] is that there is a basic difference between expressive behavior and coping behavior (functional striving, purposive goal seeking). An expressive behavior does not try to do anything; it is simply a reflection of the personality. A stupid man behaves stupidly, not because he wants to, or tries to, or is motivated to, but simply because he *is* what he is. The same is true when I speak in a bass voice rather than tenor or soprano. The random movements of a healthy child, the smile on the face of a happy man even when he is alone, the springiness of the healthy man's walk, and the erectness of his carriage are other examples of expressive, non-functional behavior. Also the *style* in which a man carries out almost all his behavior, motivated as well as unmotivated, is often expressive.

We may then ask, is *all* behavior expressive or reflective of the character structure? The answer is "No." Rote, habitual, automatized, or conventional behavior may or may not be expressive. The same is true for most "stimulus-bound" behaviors.

It is finally necessary to stress that expressiveness of behavior, and goal-directedness of behavior are not mutually exclusive categories. Average behavior is usually both.

Goals as Centering Principle in Motivation Theory. It will be observed that the basic principle in our classification has been neither the instigation nor the motivated behavior but rather the function, effects, purposes, or goals of the behavior. It has been proven sufficiently by various people that this is the most suitable point for centering in any motivation theory.[25]

Animal- and Human-Centering. This theory starts with the human being rather than any lower and presumably "simpler" animal. Too many of the findings that have been made in animals have been proven to be true for animals but not for the human being. There is no reason whatsoever why we should start with animals in order to study human motivation. The logic or rather illogic behind this general fallacy of "pseudosimplicity" has been exposed often enough by philosophers and logicians as well as by scientists in each of the various fields. It is no more necessary to study animals before one can study man than it is to study mathematics before one can study geology or psychology or biology.

We may also reject the old, naive, behaviorism which assumed that it was somehow necessary, or at least more "scientific" to judge human beings by animal standards. One consequence of this belief was that the whole notion of purpose and goal was excluded from motivational psychology simply because one could not ask a white rat about his purposes. Tolman[26] has long since proven in animal studies themselves that this exclusion was not necessary.

Motivation and the Theory of Psychopathogenesis. The conscious motivational content of everyday life has, according to the foregoing, been conceived to be relatively important or unimportant accordingly as it is more or less closely related to the basic goals. A desire for an ice cream cone might actually be an indirect expression of a desire for love. If it is, then this desire for the ice cream cone becomes extremely important motivation. If however the ice cream is simply something to cool the mouth with, or a casual appetitive reaction, then the desire is relatively unimportant. Everyday conscious desires are to be regarded as symptoms, as *surface indicators of more basic needs*. If we were to take these superficial desires at their face value we would find ourselves in a state of complete confusion which could never be resolved, since we would be dealing seriously with symptoms rather than with what lay behind the symptoms.

Thwarting of unimportant desires produces no psychopathological results; thwarting of a basically important need does produce such results. Any theory of psychopathogenesis must then be based on a sound theory of motivation. A conflict or a frustration is not necessarily pathogenic. It becomes so only when it threatens or thwarts the basic needs, or partial needs that are closely related to the basic needs.[27]

The Role of Gratified Needs. It has been pointed out above several times that our needs usually emerge only when more prepotent needs have been gratified.

Thus gratification has an important role in motivation theory. Apart from this, however, needs cease to play an active determining or organizing role as soon as they are gratified.

What this means is that, *e.g.*, a basically satisfied person no longer has the needs for esteem, love, safety, etc. The only sense in which he might be said to have them is in the almost metaphysical sense that a sated man has hunger, or a filled bottle has emptiness. If we are interested in what *actually* motivates us, and not in what has, will, or might motivate us, then a satisfied need is not a motivator. It must be considered for all practical purposes simply not to exist, to have disappeared. This point should be emphasized because it has been either overlooked or contradicted in every theory of motivation I know.[28] The perfectly healthy, normal, fortunate man has no sex needs or hunger needs, or needs for safety, or for love, or for prestige, or self-esteem, except in stray moments of quickly passing threat. If we were to say otherwise, we should also have to aver that every man had all the pathological reflexes, *e.g.*, Babinski, etc., because if his nervous system were damaged, these would appear.

It is such considerations as these that suggest the bold postulation that a man who is thwarted in any of his basic needs may fairly be envisaged simply as a sick man. This is a fair parallel to our designation as "sick" of the man who lacks vitamins or minerals. Who is to say that a lack of love is less important than a lack of vitamins? Since we know the pathogenic effects of love starvation, who is to say that we are invoking value-questions in an unscientific or illegitimate way, any more than the physician does who diagnoses and treats pellagra or scurvy? If I were permitted this usage, I should then say simply that a healthy man is primarily motivated by his needs to develop and actualize his fullest potentialities and capacities. If a man has any other basic needs in any active, chronic sense, then he is simply an unhealthy man. He is as surely sick as if he had suddenly developed a strong salt-hunger or calcium hunger.[29]

If this statement seems unusual or paradoxical the reader may be assured that this is only one among many such paradoxes that will appear as we revise our ways of looking at man's deeper motivations. When we ask what man wants of life, we deal with his very essence.

IV. Summary

(1) *There are at least five sets of goals, which we may call basic needs.* These are briefly physiological, safety, love, esteem, and self-actualization. In addition, we are motivated by the desire to achieve or maintain the various conditions upon which these basic satisfactions rest and by certain more intellectual desires.

(2) *These basic goals are related to each other, being arranged in a hierarchy of prepotency.* This means that the most prepotent goal will monopolize consciousness and will tend of itself to organize the recruitment of the various capacities of the organism. The less prepotent needs are minimized, even forgotten or denied. But when a need is fairly well satisfied, the next prepotent ("higher") need emerges, in turn to dominate the conscious life and to serve as the center of

organization of behavior, since gratified needs are not active motivators. Thus man is a perpetually wanting animal. Ordinarily the satisfaction of these wants is not altogether mutually exclusive, but only tends to be. The average member of our society is most often partially satisfied and partially unsatisfied in all of his wants. The hierarchy principle is usually empirically observed in terms of increasing percentages of non-satisfaction as we go up the hierarchy. Reversals of the average order of the hierarchy are sometimes observed. Also it has been observed that an individual may permanently lose the higher wants in the hierarchy under special conditions. There are not only ordinarily multiple motivations for usual behavior, but in addition many determinants other than motives.

(3) *Any thwarting or possibility of thwarting of these basic human goals, or danger to the defenses which protect them, or to the conditions upon which they rest, is considered to be a psychological threat.* With a few exceptions, all psychopathology may be partially traced to such threats. A basically thwarted man may actually be defined as a "sick" man, if we wish.

(4) *It is such basic threats which bring about the general emergency reactions.*

(5) *Certain other basic problems have not been dealt with because of limitations of space.* Among these are *(a)* the problem of values in any definitive motivation theory, *(b)* the relation between appetites, desires, needs and what is "good" for the organism, *(c)* the etiology of the basic needs and their possible derivation in early childhood, *(d)* redefinition of motivational concepts, *i.e.,* drive, desire, wish, need, goal, *(e)* implication of our theory for hedonistic theory, *(f)* the nature of the uncompleted act, or success and failure, and of aspiration-level, *(g)* the role of association, habit and conditioning, *(h)* relation to the theory of inter-personal relations, *(i)* implications for psychotherapy, *(j)* implication for theory of society, *(k)* the theory of selfishness, *(l)* the relation between needs and cultural patterns, *(m)* the relation between this theory and Allport's theory of functional autonomy. These as well as certain other less important questions must be considered as motivation theory attempts to become definitive.

Notes

[1] Maslow, A. H. A preface to motivation theory. *Psychosomatic Med.*, 1943, 5, 85–92.

[2] Wertheimer, M. Unpublished lectures at the New School for Social Research.

[3] Goldstein, K. *The organism.* New York: American Book Co., 1939.

[4] Freud, S. *New introductory lectures on psychoanalysis.* New York: Norton, 1933.

[5] Adler, A. *Social interest.* London: Faber & Faber, 1938.

[6] Cannon, W. B. *Wisdom of the body.* New York: Norton, 1932.

[7] Young, P. T. The experimental analysis of appetite. *Psychol. Bull.*, 1941, 38, 129–164.

[8] Maslow, A preface to motivation theory, *op cit.*

[9] As the child grows up, sheer knowledge and familiarity as well as better motor development make these "dangers" less and less dangerous and more and more manageable. Throughout life it may be said that one of the main cognitive functions of education is this neutralizing of apparent dangers through knowledge, *e.g.,* I am not afraid of thunder because I know something about it.

[10] Shirley, M. Children's adjustments to a strange situation. *J. Abnorm. (soc.) Psychol.*, 1942, 37, 201–217.

[11] A "test battery" for safety might be confronting the child with a small exploding firecracker, or with a bewhiskered face, having the mother leave the room, putting him upon a high ladder, a hypodermic

injection, having a mouse crawl up to him, etc. Of course I cannot seriously recommend the deliberate use of such "tests" for they might very well harm the child being tested. But these and similar situations come up by the score in the child's ordinary day-to-day living and may be observed. There is no reason why these stimuli should not be used with, for example, young chimpanzees.

[12] Not all neurotic individuals feel unsafe. Neurosis may have at its core a thwarting of the affection and esteem needs in a person who is generally safe.

[13] Maslow, A. H., & Mittelmann, B. *Principles of abnormal psychology.* New York: Harper & Bros., 1941.

[14] Goldstein, *op cit.*

[15] Maslow & Mittelmann, *op cit.*

[16] For further details see Maslow, A. H. The dynamics of psychological security-insecurity. *Character & Pers.*, 1942, 10, 331–344 and Plant, J. *Personality and the cultural pattern.* New York: Commonwealth Fund, 1937, Chapter 5.

[17] Whether or not this particular desire is universal we do not know. The crucial question, especially important today, is "Will men who are enslaved and dominated, inevitably feel dissatisfied and rebellious?" We may assume on the basis of commonly known clinical data that a man who has known true freedom (not paid for by giving up safety and security but rather built on the basis of adequate safety and security) will not willingly or easily allow his freedom to be taken away from him. But we do not know that this is true for the person born into slavery. The events of the next decade should give us our answer. See discussion of this problem in Fromm, E. *Escape from freedom.* New York: Farrar and Rinehart, 1941.

[18] Perhaps the desire for prestige and respect from others is subsidiary to the desire for self-esteem or confidence in oneself. Observation of children seems to indicate that this is so, but clinical data give no clear support for such a conclusion.

[19] Kardiner, A. *The traumatic neuroses of our time.* New York: Hoeber, 1941. For more extensive discussion of normal self-esteem, as well as for reports of various researchers, see Maslow, A. H., Dominance, personality and social behavior in women, *J. Soc. Psychol.*, 1939, 10, 3–39.

[20] Clearly creative behavior, like painting, is like any other behavior in having multiple determinants. It may be seen in "innately creative" people whether they are satisfied or not, happy or unhappy, hungry or sated. Also it is clear that creative activity may be compensatory, ameliorative or purely economic. It is my impression (as yet unconfirmed) that it is possible to distinguish the artistic and intellectual products of basically satisfied people from those of basically unsatisfied people by inspection alone. In any case, here too we must distinguish, in a dynamic fashion, the overt behavior itself from its various motivations or purposes.

[21] Wertheimer, *op cit.*

[22] Levy, D. M. Primary affect hunger. *Amer. J. Psychiat.*, 1937, 94, 643–652.

[23] I am aware that many psychologists and psychoanalysts use the term "motivated" and "determined" synonymously, *e.g.*, Freud. But I consider this an obfuscating usage. Sharp distinctions are necessary for clarity of thought, and precision in experimentation.

[24] To be discussed fully in a subsequent publication.

[25] The interested reader is referred to the very excellent discussion of this point in Murray, H. A., *et al.*, *Explorations in personality.* New York: Oxford University Press, 1938.

[26] Tolman, E. C. *Purposive behavior in animals and men.* New York: Century, 1932.

[27] Maslow, A. H. Conflict, frustration, and the theory of threat. *J. Abnorm. (soc.) Psychol.*, 1943, 38, 81–86.

[28] Note that acceptance of this theory necessitates basic revision of the Freudian theory.

[29] If we were to use the word "sick" in this way, we should then also have to face squarely the relations of man to his society. One clear implication of our definition would be that (1) since a man is to be called sick who is basically thwarted, and (2) since such basic thwarting is made possible ultimately only by forces outside the individual, then (3) sickness in the individual must come ultimately from a sickness in the society. The "good" or healthy society would then be defined as one that permitted man's highest purposes to emerge by satisfying all his prepotent basic needs.

2

Achievement Motivation

David C. McClelland

Most people in this world, psychologically, can be divided into two broad groups. There is that minority which is challenged by opportunity and willing to work hard to achieve something, and the majority which really does not care all that much.

For nearly twenty years now, psychologists have tried to penetrate the mystery of this curious dichotomy. Is the need to achieve (or the absence of it) an accident, is it hereditary, or is it the result of environment? Is it a single, isolatable human motive, or a combination of motives—the desire to accumulate wealth, power, fame? Most important of all, is there some technique that could give this will to achieve to people, even whole societies, who do not now have it?

While we do not yet have complete answers for any of these questions, years of work have given us partial answers to most of them and insights into all of them. There is a distinct human motive, distinguishable from others. It can be found, in fact tested for, in any group.

Let me give you one example. Several years ago, a careful study was made of 450 workers who had been thrown out of work by a plant shutdown in Erie, Pennsylvania. Most of the unemployed workers stayed home for a while and then checked back with the United States Employment Service to see if their old jobs or similar ones were available. But a small minority among them behaved differently: the day they were laid off, they started job-hunting.

They checked both the United States and the Pennsylvania Employment Office; they studied the "Help Wanted" sections of the papers; they checked through their union, their church, and various fraternal organizations; they looked into training courses to learn a new skill; they even left town to look for work, while the majority when questioned said they would not under any circumstances move away from Erie to obtain a job. Obviously the members of that active minority were differently motivated. All the men were more or less in the same

Reprinted from *Think Magazine*, 1966, pp. 82–89. Originally titled "That Urge to Achieve." Courtesy of International Business Machines Corporation, Copyright 1966, 2009.

situation objectively: they needed work, money, food, shelter, job security. Yet only a minority showed initiative and enterprise in finding what they needed. Why? Psychologists, after years of research, now believe they can answer that question. They have demonstrated that these men possessed in greater degree a specific type of human motivation. For the moment let us refer to this personality characteristic as "Motive A" and review some of the other characteristics of the men who have more of the motive than other men.

Suppose they are confronted by a work situation in which they can set their own goals as to how difficult a task they will undertake. In the psychological laboratory, such a situation is very simply created by asking them to throw rings over a peg from any distance they may choose. Most men throw more or less randomly, standing now close, now far away, but those with Motive A seem to calculate carefully where they are most likely to get a sense of mastery.

They stand nearly always at moderate distances, not so close as to make the task ridiculously easy, nor so far away as to make it impossible. They set moderately difficult, but potentially achievable goals for themselves, where they objectively have only about a one-in-three chance of succeeding. In other words, they are always setting challenges for themselves, tasks to make them stretch themselves a little. But they behave like this only if *they* can influence the outcome by performing the work themselves. They prefer not to gamble at all. Say they are given a choice between rolling dice with one in three chances of winning and working on a problem with a one-in-three chance of solving in the time allotted, they choose to work on the problem even though rolling the dice is obviously less work and the odds of winning are the same. They prefer to work at a problem rather than leave the outcome to chance or to others.

Obviously they are concerned with personal achievement rather than with the rewards of success *per se*, since they stand just as much chance of getting those rewards by throwing the dice. This leads to another characteristic the Motive A men show—namely, a strong preference for work situations in which they get concrete feedback on how well they are doing, as one does, say in playing golf, or in being a salesman, but as one does not in teaching, or in personnel counseling. A golfer always knows his score and can compare how well he is doing with par or with his own performance yesterday or last week. A teacher has no such concrete feedback on how well he is doing in "getting across" to his students.

The *n* Ach Men

But why do certain men behave like this? At one level the reply is simple: because they habitually spend their time thinking about doing things better. In fact, psychologists typically measure the strength of Motive A by taking samples of a man's spontaneous thoughts (such as making up a story about a picture they have been shown) and counting the frequency with which he mentions doing things better. The count is objective and can even be made these days with the help of a computer program for content analysis. It yields what is referred to technically as an individual's *n* Ach score (for "need for Achievement"). It is not difficult to understand why people who think constantly about "doing better" are more apt to do better at job-hunting, to set moderate, achievable goals for themselves, to dislike gambling (because they get no achievement satisfaction from success), and to prefer work situations where they can tell easily whether they are improving or not. But why some people and not others come to think this way is another question. The evidence suggests it is not because of special training they get in the home from parents who set moderately high achievement goals but who are warm, encouraging, and nonauthoritarian in helping their children reach these goals.

Such detailed knowledge about one motive helps correct a lot of common sense ideas about human motivation. For example, much public policy (and much business policy) is based on the simple-minded notion that people will work harder "if they have to." As a first approximation, the idea isn't totally wrong, but it is only a half-truth. The majority of unemployed workers in Erie "had to" find work as much as those with higher *n* Ach but they certainly didn't work as hard at it. Or again, it is frequently assumed that *any* strong motive will lead to doing things better. Wouldn't it be fair to say that most of the Erie workers were just "unmotivated"? But our detailed knowledge of various human motives shows that each one leads a person to behave in *different* ways. The contrast is not between being "motivated" or "unmotivated" but between being motivated toward A or toward B or C, etc.

A simple experiment makes the point nicely: subjects were told that they could choose as a working partner either a close friend or a stranger who was known to be an expert on the problem to be solved. Those with higher *n* Ach (more "need to achieve") chose the experts over their friends, whereas those with more *n* Aff (the "need to affiliate with others") chose friends over experts. The latter were not "unmotivated"; their desire to be with someone they liked was simply a stronger motive than their desire to excel at the task. Other such needs have been studied by psychologists. For instance, the need for Power is often confused with the need for Achievement because both may lead to "outstanding" activities. There is a distinct difference. People with a strong need for Power want to command attention, get recognition, and control others. They are more active in political life and tend to busy themselves primarily with controlling the channels of communication both up to the top and down to the people so that they are more "in charge." Those with high *n* Power are not as concerned with improving their work performance daily as those with high *n* Ach.

It follows, from what we have been able to learn, that not all "great achievers" score high in *n* Ach. Many generals, outstanding politicians, great research scientists do not, for instance, because their work requires other personality characteristics, other motives. A general or a politician must be more concerned with power relationships, a research scientist must be able to go for long periods without the immediate feedback the person with high *n* Ach requires, etc. On the other hand, business executives, particularly if they are in positions of real responsibility or if they are salesmen, tend to score high in *n* Ach. This is true even in a Communist country like Poland: apparently there, as well as in a private economy, a manager succeeds if he is concerned about improving all the time, setting moderate goals, keeping track of his or the company's performance, etc.

Motivation and Half-Truths

Since careful study has shown that common sense notions about motivation are at best half-truths, it also follows that you cannot trust what people tell you about their motives. After all, they often get their ideas about their own motives from common sense. Thus a general may say he is interested in achievement (because he has obviously achieved), or a businessman that he is interested only in making money (because he has made money), or one of the majority of unemployed in Erie that he desperately wants a job (because he knows he needs one); but a careful check of what each one thinks about and how he spends his time may show that each is concerned about quite different things. It requires special measurement techniques to identify the presence of *n* Ach and other such motives. Thus what people say and believe is not very closely related to these "hidden" motives which seem to affect a person's "style of life" more than his political, religious or social attitudes. Thus *n* Ach produces enterprising men among labor leaders or managers, Republicans or Democrats, Catholics or Protestants, capitalists or Communists.

Wherever people begin to think often in *n* Ach terms, things begin to move. Men with high *n* Ach get more raises and are promoted more rapidly, because they keep actively seeking ways to do a better job. Companies with many such men grow faster. In one comparison of two firms in Mexico, it was discovered that all but one of the top executives of a fast growing firm had higher *n* Ach scores than the highest scoring executive in an equally large but slow-growing firm. Countries with many such rapidly growing firms tend to show above average rates of national economic growth. This appears to be the reason why correlations have regularly been found between the *n* Ach content in popular literature (such as popular songs or stories in children's textbooks) and subsequent rates of national economic growth. A nation which is thinking about doing better all the time (as shown in its popular literature) actually does do better economically speaking. Careful quantitative studies have shown this to be true in Ancient Greece, in Spain in the Middle Ages, in England from 1400–1800, as well as among contemporary nations, whether capitalist or Communist, developed or underdeveloped.

Contrast these two stories for example. Which one contains more *n* Ach? Which one reflects a state of mind which ought to lead to harder striving to improve the way things are?

Excerpt from Story A (4th grade reader)

"Don't Ever Owe a Man—The world is an illusion. Wife, children, horses, and cows are all just ties of fate. They are ephemeral. Each after fulfilling his part in life disappears. So we should not clamour after riches which are not permanent. As long as we live it is wise not to have any attachments and just think of God. We have to spend our lives without trouble, for is it not time that there is an end to grievances? So it is better to live knowing the real state of affairs. Don't get entangled in the meshes of family life."

Excerpt from Story B (4th grade reader)

"How I Do Like to Learn—I was sent to an accelerated technical high school. I was so happy I cried. Learning is not very easy. In the beginning I couldn't understand what the teacher taught us. I always got a red cross mark on my papers. The boy sitting next to me was very enthusiastic and also an outstanding student. When he found I couldn't do the problems he offered to show me how he had done them. I could not copy his work. I must learn through my own reasoning. I gave his paper back and explained I had to do it myself. Sometimes I worked on a problem until midnight. If I couldn't finish, I started early in the morning. The red cross marks on my work were getting less common. I conquered my difficulties. My marks rose. I graduated and went on to college."

Most readers would agree, without any special knowledge of the *n* Ach coding system, that the second story shows more concern with improvement than the first, which comes from a contemporary reader used in Indian public schools. In fact the latter has a certain Horatio Alger quality that is reminiscent of our own McGuffey readers of several generations ago. It appears today in the textbooks of Communist China. It should not, therefore, come as a surprise if a nation like Communist China, obsessed as it is with improvement, tended in the long run to outproduce a nation like India, which appears to be more fatalistic.

The *n* Ach level is obviously important for statesmen to watch and in many instances to try to do something about, particularly if a nation's economy is lagging. Take Britain, for example. A generation ago (around 1925) it ranked fifth among 25 countries where children's readers were scored for *n* Ach—and its economy was doing well. By 1950 the *n* Ach level had dropped to 27th out of 39 countries—well below the world average—and today, its leaders are feeling the severe economic effects of this loss in the spirit of enterprise.

Economics and *n* Ach

If psychologists can detect *n* Ach levels in individuals or nations, particularly before their effects are widespread, can't the knowledge somehow be put to use to foster economic development? Obviously detection or diagnosis is not enough. What good is it to tell Britain (or India for that matter) that it needs more *n* Ach, a greater spirit of enterprise? In most such cases, informed observers of the local scene know very well that such a need exists, though they may be slower to discover it than the psychologist hovering over *n* Ach scores. What is needed is some method of developing *n* Ach in individuals or nations.

Since about 1960, psychologists in my research group at Harvard have been experimenting with techniques designed to accomplish this goal, chiefly among business executives whose work requires the action characteristics of people with high *n* Ach. Initially, we had real doubts as to whether we could succeed, partly because like most American psychologists we had been strongly influenced by the psychoanalytic view that basic motives are laid down in childhood and cannot really be changed later, and partly because many studies of intensive psychotherapy and counseling have shown minor if any long-term personality effects. On the other hand we were encouraged by the nonprofessionals: those enthusiasts like Dale Carnegie, the Communist idealogue or the Church mission- ary, who felt they could change adults and in fact seemed to be doing so. At any rate we ran some brief (7 to 10 days) "total push" trailing courses for busi- nessmen designed to increase their *n* Ach.

Four Main Goals

In broad outline the courses had four main goals: (1) They were designed to teach the participants how to think, talk, and act like a person with high *n* Ach, based on our knowledge of such people gained through 17 years of research. For instance, men learned how to make up stories that would code high in *n* Ach (i.e., how to think in *n* Ach terms), how to set moderate goals for themselves in the ring toss game (and in life). (2) The courses stimulated the participants to set higher but carefully planned and realistic work goals for themselves over the next two years. Then we checked back with them every six months to see how well they were doing in terms of their own objectives. (3) The courses also utilized techniques for giving the participants knowledge about themselves. For instance, in playing the ring toss game, they could observe that they behaved differently from others—perhaps in refusing to adjust a goal downward after failure. This would then become a matter for group discussion and the man would have to explain what he had in mind in setting such unrealistic goals. Discussion could then lead on to what a man's ultimate goals in life were, how much he cared about actually improving performance versus making a good impression or hav- ing many friends. In this way the participants would be freer to realize their achievement goals without being blocked by old habits and attitudes. (4) The courses also usually created a group *esprit de corps* from learning about each other's hopes and fears, successes and failures, and from going through an emo- tional experience together, away from everyday life, in a retreat setting. This membership in a new group helps a man achieve his goals, partly because he knows he has their sympathy and support and partly because he knows they will be watching to see how well he does. The same effect has been noted in other therapy groups like Alcoholics Anonymous. We are not sure which of these course "inputs" is really absolutely essential—that remains a research question— but we were taking no chances at the outset in view of the general pessimism about such efforts, and we wanted to include any and all techniques that were thought to change people.

The courses have been given: to executives in a large American firm, and in several Mexican firms, to underachieving high school boys; and to business- men in India from Bombay and from a small city—Kakinada in the state of Andhra Pradesh. In every instance save one (the Mexican case), it was possible to demonstrate statistically, some two years later, that the men who took the course had done better (made more money, got promoted faster, expanded their busi- nesses faster) than comparable men who did not take the course or who took some other management course.

Consider the Kakinada results, for example. In the two years preceding the course 9 men, 18 percent of the 52 participants, had shown "unusual" enterprise in their businesses. In the 18 months following the course 25 of the men, in other words nearly 50 percent, were unusually active. And this was not due to a general upturn of business in India. Data from a control city, some forty-five miles away, show the same base rate of "unusually active" men as in Kakinada before the course—namely, about 20 percent. Something clearly happened in Kakinada: the owner of a small radio shop started a chemical plant; a banker was so successful in making commercial loans in an enterprising way that he was promoted to a much larger branch of his bank in Calcutta; the local political leader accomplished his goal (it was set in the course) to get the federal government to deepen the harbor and make it into an all-weather port; plans are far along for establishing a steel rolling mill, etc. All this took place without any substantial capital from the outside. In fact, the only costs were for our 10-day courses plus some brief follow-up visits every six months. The men are raising their own capital and using their own resources for getting business and industry moving in a city that had been considered stagnant and unenterprising.

The promise of such a method of developing achievement motivation seems very great. It has obvious applications in helping underdeveloped countries, or "pockets of poverty" in the United States, to move faster economically. It has great potential for businesses that need to "turn around" and take a more enterprising approach toward their growth and development. It may even be helpful in developing more *n* Ach among low-income groups. For instance, data show that lower-class Negro Americans have a very low level of *n* Ach. This is not surprising. Society has systematically discouraged and blocked their achievement striving. But as the barriers to upward mobility are broken down, it will be necessary to help stimulate the motivation that will lead them to take advantage of new opportunities opening up.

Extreme Reactions

But a word of caution: Whenever I speak of this research and its great potential, audience reaction tends to go to opposite extremes. Either people remain skeptical and argue that motives can't really be changed, that all we are doing is dressing Dale Carnegie up in fancy "psychologese," or they become converts and want instant course descriptions by a return mail to solve their local motivation problems. Either response is unjustified. What I have described here in a few pages has taken 20 years of patient research effort, and hundreds of thousands of dollars in basic research costs. What remains to be done will involve even larger sums and more time for development to turn a promising idea into something of wide practical utility.

Encouragement Needed

To take only one example, we have not yet learned how to develop *n* Ach really well among low-income groups. In our first effort—a summer course for bright underachieving 14-year-olds—we found that boys from the middle class improved steadily in grades in school over a two-year period, but boys from the lower class showed an improvement after the first year followed by a drop back to their beginning low grade average (see figure 1). Why? We speculated that it was because they moved back into an environment in which neither parents nor friends encouraged achievement or upward mobility. In other words, it isn't enough to change a man's motivation if the environment in which he lives doesn't support at least to some degree his new efforts. Negroes striving to rise out of the ghetto frequently confront this problem: they are often faced by skepticism at home and suspicion on the job, so that even if their *n* Ach is raised, it can be lowered again by the heavy odds against their success. We must learn not only to raise *n* Ach but also to find methods of instructing people in how to manage it, to create a favorable environment in which it can flourish.

Many of these training techniques are now only in the pilot testing stage. It will take time and money to perfect them, but society should be willing to invest heavily in view of their tremendous potential for contributing to human betterment.

Figure 1

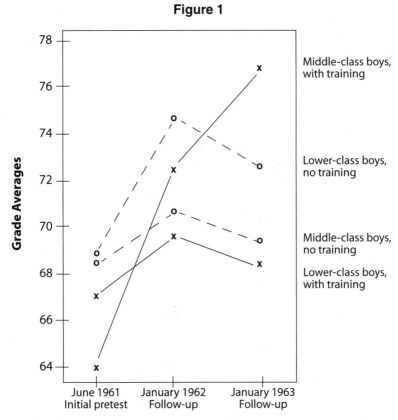

In a Harvard study, a group of underachieving 14-year-olds was given a six-week course designed to help them do better in school. Some of the boys were also given training in achievement motivation, or *n* Ach (solid lines). As graph reveals, the only boys who continued to improve after a two-year period were the middle-class boys with the special *n* Ach training. Psychologists suspect the lower-class boys dropped back, even with *n* Ach training, because they returned to an environment in which neither parents nor friends encouraged achievement.

3

One More Time
How Do You Motivate Employees?

Frederick Herzberg

How many articles, books, speeches, and workshops have pleaded plaintively, "How do I get an employee to do what I want him to do?"

The psychology of motivation is tremendously complex, and what has been unraveled with any degree of assurance is small indeed. But the dismal ratio of knowledge to speculation has not dampened the enthusiasm for new forms of snake oil that are constantly coming on the market, many of them with academic testimonials. Doubtless this article will have no depressing impact on the market for snake oil, but since the ideas expressed in it have been tested in many corporations and other organizations, it will help—I hope—to redress the imbalance in the aforementioned ratio.

"Motivating" with KITA

In lectures to industry on the problem, I have found that the audiences are anxious for quick and practical answers, so I will begin with a straightforward, practical formula for moving people.

What is the simplest, surest, and most direct way of getting someone to do something? Ask him? But if he responds that he does not want to do it, then that calls for a psychological consultation to determine the reason for his obstinacy. Tell him? His response shows that he does not understand you, and now an expert in communication methods has to be brought in to show you how to get through to him. Give him a monetary incentive? I do not need to remind the reader of the complexity and difficulty involved in setting up and administering an incentive system. Show him? This means a costly training program. We need a simple way.

Every audience contains the "direct action" manager who shouts, "Kick him!" And this type of manager is right. The surest and least circumlocuted way of getting someone to do something is to kick him in the pants—give him what might be called the KITA.

There are various forms of KITA, and here are some of them.

Negative Physical KITA

This is a literal application of the term and was frequently used in the past. It has, however, three major drawbacks: (1) it is inelegant; (2) it contradicts the precious image of benevolence that most organizations cherish; and (3) since it is a physical attack, it directly stimulates the autonomic nervous system, and this often results in negative feedback—the employee may just kick you in return. These factors give rise to certain taboos against negative physical KITA.

The psychologist has come to the rescue of those who are no longer permitted to use negative physical KITA. He has uncovered infinite sources of psychological vulnerabilities and the appropriate methods to play tunes on them. "He took my rug away"; "I wonder what he meant by that"; "The boss is always going around me"—these symptomatic expressions of ego sores that have been rubbed raw are the result of application of:

Negative Psychological KITA

This has several advantages over negative physical KITA. First, the cruelty is not visible; the bleeding is internal and comes much later. Second, since it affects the higher cortical centers of the brain with its inhibitory powers, it reduces the possibility of physical backlash. Third, since the number of psychological pains that a person can feel is almost infinite, the direction and site possibilities of the KITA are increased many times. Fourth, the person administering the kick can manage to be above it all and let the system accomplish the dirty work. Fifth, those who practice it receive some ego satisfaction (one-upmanship), whereas they would find drawing blood abhorrent. Finally, if the employee does complain, he can always be accused of being paranoid, since there is no tangible evidence of an actual attack.

Now, what does negative KITA accomplish? If I kick you in the rear (physically or psychologically), who is motivated? *I* am motivated; *you* move! Negative KITA does not lead to motivation, but to movement. So:

Positive KITA

Let us consider motivation. If I say to you, "Do this for me or the company, and in return I will give you a reward, an incentive, more status, a promotion, all the quid pro quos that exist in the industrial organization," am I motivating you? The overwhelming opinion I receive from management people is, "Yes, this is motivation."

I have a year-old Schnauzer. When it was a small puppy and I wanted it to move, I kicked it in the rear and it moved. Now that I have finished its obedience training, I hold up a dog biscuit when I want the Schnauzer to move. In this instance, who is motivated—I or the dog? The dog wants the biscuit, but it is I who want it to move. Again, I am the one who is motivated, and the dog is the one who moves. In this instance all I did was apply KITA frontally; I exerted a pull instead of a push. When industry wishes to use such positive KITAs, it has available an incredible number and variety of dog biscuits (jelly beans for humans) to wave in front of the employee to get him to jump.

Why is it that managerial audiences are quick to see that negative KITA is *not* motivation, while they are almost unanimous in their judgment that positive KITA *is* motivation? It is because negative KITA is rape, and positive KITA is seduction. But it is infinitely worse to be seduced than to be raped; the latter is an unfortunate occurrence, while the former signifies that you were a party to your own downfall. This is why positive KITA is so popular; it is a tradition; it is in the American way. The organization does not have to kick you; you kick yourself.

Myths about Motivation

Why is KITA not motivation? If I kick my dog (from the front or the back), he will move. And when I want him to move again, what must I do? I must kick him again. Similarly, I can charge a man's battery, and then recharge it, and recharge it again. But it is only when he has his own generator that we can talk about motivation. He then needs no outside stimulation. He *wants* to do it.

With this in mind, we can review some positive KITA personnel practices that were developed as attempts to instill "motivation."

1. Reducing Time Spent at Work

This represents a marvelous way of motivating people to work—getting them off the job! We have reduced (formally and informally) the time spent on the job over the last 50 or 60 years until we are finally on the way to the "6½-day weekend." An interesting variant of this approach is the development of off-hour recreation programs. The philosophy here seems to be that those who play together, work together. The fact is that motivated people seek more hours of work, not fewer.

2. Spiraling Wages

Have these motivated people? Yes, to seek the next wage increase. Some medievalists still can be heard to say that a good depression will get employees moving. They feel that if rising wages don't or won't do the job, perhaps reducing them will.

3. Fringe Benefits

Industry has outdone the most welfare-minded of welfare states in dispensing cradle-to-the-grave succor. One company I know of had an informal "fringe benefit of the month club" going for a while. The cost of fringe benefits in this country has reached approximately 25 percent of the wage dollar, and we still cry for motivation.

People spend less time working for more money and more security than ever before, and the trend cannot be reversed. These benefits are no longer rewards; they are rights. A 6-day week is inhuman, a 10-hour day is exploitation, extended medical coverage is a basic decency; and stock options are the salvation of American initiative. Unless the ante is continuously raised, the psychological reaction of employees is that the company is turning back the clock.

When industry began to realize that both the economic nerve and the lazy nerve of their employees had insatiable appetites, it started to listen to the behavioral scientists who, more out of a humanist tradition than from scientific study, criticized management for not knowing how to deal with people. The next KITA easily followed.

4. Human Relations Training

Over 30 years of teaching and, in many instances, of practicing psychological approaches to handling people have resulted in costly human relations programs and, in the end, the same question: How do you motivate workers? Here, too, escalations have taken place. Thirty years ago it was necessary to request "Please don't spit on the floor." Today the same admonition requires three "pleases" before the employee feels that his superior has demonstrated the psychologically proper attitudes toward him.

The failure of human relations training to produce motivation led to the conclusion that the supervisor or manager himself was not psychologically true to himself in his practice of interpersonal decency. So an advanced form of human relations KITA, sensitivity training, was unfolded.

5. Sensitivity Training

Do you really, really understand yourself? Do you really, really, really trust the other man? Do you really, really, really, really cooperate? The failure of sensitivity training is now being explained, by those who have become opportunistic exploiters of the technique, as a failure to really (five times) conduct proper sensitivity training courses.

With the realization that there are only temporary gains from comfort and economic and interpersonal KITA, personnel managers concluded that the fault lay not in what they were doing, but in the employee's failure to appreciate what they were doing. This opened up the field of communications, a whole new area of "scientifically" sanctioned KITA.

6. Communications

The professor of communications was invited to join the faculty of management training programs and help in making employees understand what management was doing for them. House organs, briefing sessions, supervisory instruction on the importance of communication, and all sorts of propaganda have proliferated until today there is even an International Council of Industrial Editors. But no motivation resulted, and the obvious thought occurred that perhaps management was not hearing what the employees were saying. That led to the next KITA.

7. Two-Way Communication

Management ordered morale surveys, suggestion plans, and group participation programs. Then both employees and management were communicating and listening to each other more than ever, but without much improvement in motivation.

The behavioral scientists began to take another look at their conceptions and their data, and they took human relations one step further. A glimmer of truth was beginning to show through in the writings of the so-called higher-order-need psychologists. People, so they said, want to actualize themselves. Unfortunately, the "actualizing" psychologists got mixed up with the human relations psychologists, and a new KITA emerged.

8. Job Participation

Though it may not have been the theoretical intention, job participation often became a "give them the big picture" approach. For example, if a man is tightening 10,000 nuts a day on an assembly line with a torque wrench, tell him he is building a Chevrolet. Another approach had the goal of giving the employee a *feeling* that he is determining, in some measure, what he does on his job. The goal was to provide a *sense* of achievement rather than a substantive achievement in his task. Real achievement, of course, requires a task that makes it possible.

But still there was no motivation. This led to the inevitable conclusion that the employees must be sick, and therefore to the next KITA.

9. Employee Counseling

The initial use of this form of KITA in a systematic fashion can be credited to the Hawthorne experiment of the Western Electric Company during the early 1930s. At that time, it was found that the employees harbored irrational feelings that were interfering with the rational operation of the factory. Counseling in this instance was a means of letting the employees unburden themselves by talking to someone about their problems. Although the counseling techniques were primitive, the program was large indeed.

The counseling approach suffered as a result of experiences during World War II, when the programs themselves were found to be interfering with the operation of the organizations; the counselors had forgotten their role of benevolent listeners and were attempting to do something about the problems that they heard about. Psychological counseling, however, has managed to survive the negative impact of World War II experiences and today is beginning to flourish with renewed sophistication. But, alas, many of these programs, like all the others, do not seem to have lessened the pressure of demands to find out how to motivate workers.

Since KITA results only in short-term movement, it is safe to predict that the cost of these programs will increase steadily and new varieties will be developed as old positive KITAs reach their satiation points.

Hygiene vs. Motivators

Let me rephrase the perennial question this way: How do you install a generator in an employee? A brief review of my motivation-hygiene theory of job attitudes is required before theoretical and practical suggestions can be offered. The theory was first drawn from an examination of events in the lives of engineers and accountants. At least 16 other investigations, using a wide variety of populations (including some in the Communist countries), have since been completed, making the original research one of the most replicated studies in the field of job attitudes.

The findings of these studies, along with corroboration from many other investigations using different procedures, suggest that the factors involved in producing job satisfaction (and motivation) are separate and distinct from the factors that lead to job dissatisfaction. Since separate factors need to be considered, depending on whether job satisfaction or job dissatisfaction is being examined, it follows that these two feelings are not opposites of each other. The opposite of job satisfaction is not job dissatisfaction but, rather, *no* job satisfaction; and, similarly, the opposite of job dissatisfaction is not job satisfaction, but *no* job dissatisfaction.

Stating the concept presents a problem in semantics, for we normally think of satisfaction and dissatisfaction as opposites—*i.e.*, what is not satisfying must be dissatisfying, and vice versa. But when it comes to understanding the behavior of people in their jobs, more than a play on words is involved.

Two different needs of man are involved here. One set of needs can be thought of as stemming from his animal nature—the built-in drive to avoid pain from the environment, plus all the learned drives which become conditioned to the basic biological needs. For example, hunger, a basic biological drive, makes it necessary to earn money, and then money becomes a specific drive. The other set of needs relates to that unique human characteristic, the ability to achieve and, through achievement, to experience psychological growth. The stimuli for the growth needs are tasks that induce growth; in the industrial setting, they are the *job content.* Contrariwise, the stimuli inducing pain avoidance behavior are found in the *job environment.*

The growth or *motivator* factors that are intrinsic to the job are: achievement, recognition for achievement, the work itself, responsibility, and growth or advancement. The dissatisfaction-avoidance or *hygiene* (KITA) factors that are extrinsic to the job include: company policy and administration, supervision, interpersonal relationships, working conditions, salary, status, and security.

A composite of the factors that are involved in causing job satisfaction and job dissatisfaction, drawn from samples of 1,685 employees, is shown in figure 1. The results indicate that motivators were the primary cause of satisfaction, and hygiene factors the primary cause of unhappiness on the job. The employees, studied in 12 different investigations, included lower-level supervisors, professional women, agricultural administrators, men about to retire from management positions, hospital maintenance personnel, manufacturing supervisors, nurses, food handlers, military officers, engineers, scientists, house-

Figure 1
Factors Affecting Job Attitudes, as Reported in 12 Investigations

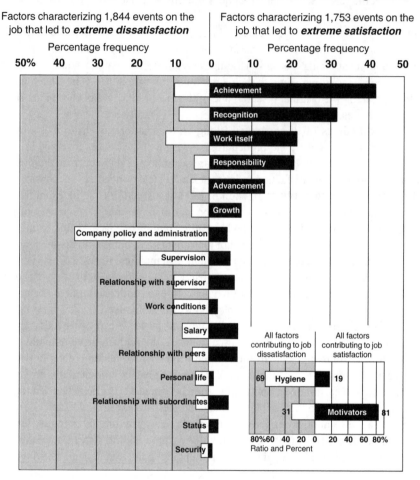

| Factors characterizing 1,844 events on the job that led to *extreme dissatisfaction* | Factors characterizing 1,753 events on the job that led to *extreme satisfaction* |

keepers, teachers, technicians, female assemblers, accountants, Finnish foremen, and Hungarian engineers.

They were asked what job events had occurred in their work that had led to extreme satisfaction or extreme dissatisfaction on their part. Their responses are broken down in the exhibit into percentages of total "positive" job events and total "negative" job events. (The figures total more than 100 percent on both the "hygiene" and "motivators" sides because often at least two factors can be attributed to a single event; advancement, for instance, often accompanies assumption of responsibility.)

To illustrate, a typical response involving achievement that had a negative effect for the employee was, "I was unhappy because I didn't do the job successfully." A typical response in the small number of positive job events in the Company Policy and Administration grouping was, "I was happy because the company reorganized the section so that I didn't report any longer to the guy I didn't get along with."

As the lower right-hand part of the exhibit shows, of all the factors contributing to job satisfaction, 81 percent were motivators. And of all the factors contributing to the employees' dissatisfaction over their work, 69 percent involved hygiene elements.

Eternal Triangle

There are three general philosophies of personnel management. The first is based on organizational theory, the second on industrial engineering, and the third on behavioral science.

The organizational theorist believes that human needs are either so irrational or so varied and adjustable to specific situations that the major function of personnel management is to be as pragmatic as the occasion demands. If jobs are organized in a proper manner, he reasons the result will be the most efficient job structure, and the most favorable job attitudes will follow as a matter of course.

The industrial engineer holds that man is mechanistically oriented and economically motivated and his needs are best met by attuning the individual to the most efficient work process. The goal of personnel management therefore should be to concoct the most appropriate incentive system and to design the specific working conditions in a way that facilitates the most efficient use of the human machine. By structuring jobs in a manner that leads to the most efficient operation, the engineer believes that he can obtain the optimal organization of work and the proper work attitudes.

The behavioral scientist focuses on group sentiments, attitudes of individual employees, and the organization's social and psychological climate. According to his persuasion, he emphasizes one or more of the various hygiene and motivator needs. His approach to personnel management generally emphasizes some form of human relations education, in the hope of instilling healthy employee attitudes and an organizational climate which he considers to be felicitous to human values. He believes that proper attitudes will lead to efficient job and organizational structure.

There is always a lively debate as to the overall effectiveness of the approaches of the organizational theorist and the industrial engineer. Manifestly they have achieved much. But the nagging question for the behavioral scientist has been: What is the cost in human problems that eventually cause more expense to the organization—for instance, turnover, absenteeism, errors, violation of safety rules, strikes, restriction of output, higher wages, and greater fringe benefits? On the other hand, the behavioral scientist is hard put to document much manifest improvement in personnel management, using his approach.

The three philosophies can be depicted as a triangle, as is done in figure 2, with each persuasion claiming the apex angle. The motivation-hygiene theory claims the same angle as industrial engineering, but for opposite goals. Rather than rationalizing the work to increase efficiency, the theory suggests that work be

Figure 2
"Triangle" of Philosophies of Personnel Management

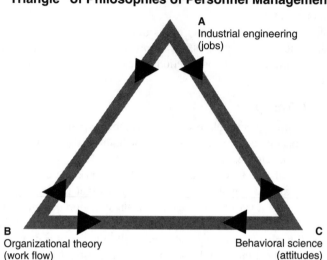

A
Industrial engineering
(jobs)

B
Organizational theory
(work flow)

C
Behavioral science
(attitudes)

enriched to bring about effective utilization of personnel. Such a systematic attempt to motivate employees by manipulating the motivator factors is just beginning.

The term *job enrichment* describes this embryonic movement. An older term, job enlargement, should be avoided because it is associated with past failures stemming from a misunderstanding of the problem. Job enrichment provides the opportunity for the employee's psychological growth, while job enlargement merely makes a job structurally bigger. Since scientific job enrichment is very new, this article only suggests the principles and practical steps that have recently emerged from several successful experiments in industry.

Job Loading

In attempting to enrich an employee's job, management often succeeds in reducing the man's personal contribution, rather than giving him an opportunity for growth in his accustomed job. Such an endeavor, which I shall call horizontal job loading (as opposed to vertical loading, or providing motivator factors), has been the problem of earlier job enlargement programs. This activity merely enlarges the meaninglessness of the job. Some examples of this approach, and their effect are:

- Challenging the employee by increasing the amount of production expected of him. If he tightens 10,000 bolts a day, see if he can tighten 20,000 bolts a day. The arithmetic involved shows that multiplying zero by zero still equals zero.

- Adding another meaningless task to the existing one, usually some routine clerical activity. The arithmetic here is adding zero to zero.

- Rotating the assignments of a number of jobs that need to be enriched. This means washing dishes for a while, then washing silverware. The arithmetic is substituting one zero for another zero.

- Removing the most difficult parts of the assignment in order to free the worker to accomplish more of the less challenging assignments. This traditional industrial engineering approach amounts to subtraction in the hope of accomplishing addition.

These are common forms of horizontal loading that frequently come up in preliminary brainstorming sessions on job enrichment. The principles of vertical loading have not all been worked out as yet, and they remain rather general, but I have furnished seven useful starting points for consideration in table 1.

A Successful Application

An example from a highly successful job enrichment experiment can illustrate the distinction between horizontal and vertical loading of a job. The subjects of this study were the stockholder correspondents employed by a very large corporation. Seemingly, the task required of these carefully selected and highly trained correspondents was quite complex and challenging. But almost all indexes of performance and job attitudes were low, and exit interviewing confirmed that the challenge of the job existed merely as words.

A job enrichment project was initiated in the form of an experiment with one group, designated as an achieving unit, having its job enriched by the principles described in table 1. A control group continued to do its job in the traditional

Table 1
Principles of Vertical Job Loading

Principle	Motivators involved
A. Removing some controls while retaining accountability	Responsibility and personal achievement
B. Increasing the accountability of individuals for own work	Responsibility and recognition
C. Giving a person a complete natural unit of work (module, division, area, and so on)	Responsibility, achievement, and recognition
D. Granting additional authority to an employee in his activity; job freedom	Responsibility, achievement, and recognition
E. Making periodic reports directly available to the worker himself rather than to the supervisor	Internal recognition
F. Introducing new and more difficult tasks not previously handled	Growth and learning
G. Assigning individuals specific or specialized tasks, enabling them to become experts	Responsibility, growth, and advancement

way. (There were also two "uncommitted" groups of correspondents formed to measure the so-called Hawthorne Effect—that is, to gauge whether productivity and attitudes toward the job changed artificially merely because employees sensed that the company was paying more attention to them in doing something different or novel. The results for these groups were substantially the same as for the control group, and for the sake of simplicity I do not deal with them in this summary.) No changes in hygiene were introduced for either group other than those that would have been made anyway, such as normal pay increases.

The changes for the achieving unit were introduced in the first two months, averaging one per week of the seven motivators listed in table 1. At the end of six months the members of the achieving unit were found to be outperforming their counterparts in the control group, and in addition indicated a marked increase in their liking for their jobs. Other results showed that the achieving group had lower absenteeism and, subsequently, a much higher rate of promotion.

Figure 3 illustrates the changes in performance, measured in February and March, before the study period began, and at the end of each month of the study period. The shareholder service index represents quality of letters, including accuracy of information, and speed of response to stockholders' letters of inquiry. The index of a current month was averaged into the average of the two prior months, which means that improvement was harder to obtain if the indexes of the previous months were low. The "achievers" were performing less well before the six-month period started, and their performance service index continued to decline after the introduction of the motivators, evidently because of

Figure 3
Shareholder Service Index in Company Experiment
(Three-month cumulative average)

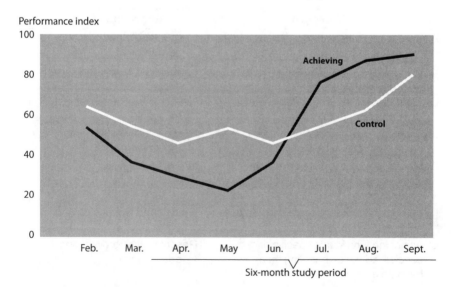

uncertainty over their newly granted responsibilities. In the third month, however, performance improved, and soon the members of this group had reached a high level of accomplishment.

Figure 4 shows the two groups' attitudes toward their job, measured at the end of March, just before the first motivator was introduced, and again at the end of September. The correspondents were asked 16 questions, all involving motivation. A typical one was, "As you see it, how many opportunities do you feel that you have in your job for making worthwhile contributions?" The answers were scaled from 1 to 5, with 80 as the maximum possible score. The achievers became much more positive about their job, while the attitude of the control unit remained about the same (the drop is not statistically significant).

Figure 4
Changes in Attitudes Toward Tasks in Company Experiment
(Changes in mean scores over six-month period)

How was the job of these correspondents restructured? Table 2 lists the suggestions made that were deemed to be horizontal loading, and the actual vertical loading changes that were incorporated in the job of the achieving unit. The capital letters under "Principle" after "Vertical loading" refer to the corresponding letters in table 1. The reader will note that the rejected forms of horizontal loading correspond closely to the list of common manifestations of the phenomenon [under the subheading "Job Loading"].

Table 2
Enlargement vs. Enrichment of Correspondents' Tasks in Company Experiment

Horizontal loading suggestions (rejected)	Vertical loading suggestions (adopted)	Principle
Firm quotas could be set for letters to be answered each day, using a rate which would be hard to reach.	Subject matter experts were appointed within each unit for other members of the unit to consult with before seeking supervisory help. (The supervisor had been answering all specialized and difficult questions.)	G
The women could type the letters themselves, as well as compose them, or take on any other clerical functions.	Correspondents signed their own names on letters. (The supervisor had been signing all letters.)	B
All difficult or complex inquiries could be channeled to a few women so that the remainder could achieve high rates of output. These jobs could be exchanged from time to time.	The work of the more experienced correspondents was proofread less frequently by supervisors and was done at the correspondents' desks, dropping verification from 100% to 10%. (Previously, all correspondents' letters had been checked by the supervisor.)	A
The women could be rotated through units handling different customers, and then sent back to their own units.	Production was discussed, but only in terms such as "a full day's work is expected." As time went on, this was no longer mentioned. (Before, the group had been constantly reminded of the number of letters that needed to be answered.)	D
	Outgoing mail went directly to the mailroom without going over supervisors' desks. (The letters had always been routed through the supervisors.)	A
	Correspondents were encouraged to answer letters in a more personalized way. (Reliance on the form-letter approach had been standard practice.)	C
	Each correspondent was held personally responsible for the quality and accuracy of letters. (This responsibility had been the province of the supervisor and the verifier.)	B, E

Steps to Job Enrichment

Now that motivator idea has been described in practice, here are the steps that managers should take in instituting the principle with their employees *[italic first sentences not in original]*:

1. *Select those jobs in which (a) the investment in industrial engineering does not make changes too costly, (b) attitudes are poor, (c) hygiene is becoming very costly, and (d) motivation will make a difference in performance.*

2. *Approach these jobs with the conviction that they can be changed.* Years of tradition have led managers to believe that the content of the jobs is

sacrosanct and the only scope of action that they have is in ways of stimulating people.

3. *Brainstorm a list of changes that may enrich the jobs, without concern
   for their practicality.*

4. *Screen the list to eliminate suggestions that involve hygiene, rather than
   actual motivation.*

5. *Screen the list for generalities such as "give them more responsibility," that
   are rarely followed in practice.* This might seem obvious, but the motivator
   words have never left industry; the substance has just been rationalized and
   organized out. Words like "responsibility," "growth," "achievement," and
   "challenge," for example, have been elevated to the lyrics of the patriotic
   anthem for all organizations. It is the old problem typified by the pledge of
   allegiance to the flag being more important than contributions to the country—of following the form, rather than the substance.

6. *Screen the list to eliminate any* horizontal [emphasis in original] *loading
   suggestions.*

7. *Avoid direct participation by the employees whose jobs are to be
   enriched.* Ideas they have expressed previously certainly constitute a
   valuable source for recommended changes, but their direct involvement
   contaminates the process with human relations *hygiene* and, more specifically, gives them only a *sense* of making a contribution. The job is to
   be changed, and it is the content that will produce the motivation, not
   attitudes about being involved or the challenge inherent in setting up a
   job. The process will be over shortly, and it is what the employees will
   be doing from then on that will determine their motivation. A sense of
   participation will result only in short-term movement.

8. *In the initial attempts at job enrichment, set up a controlled experiment.*
   At least two equivalent groups should be chosen, one an experimental
   unit in which the motivators are systematically introduced over a period
   of time, and the other one a control group in which no changes are
   made. For both groups, hygiene should be allowed to follow its natural
   course for the duration of the experiment. Pre- and post-installation tests
   of performance and job attitudes are necessary to evaluate the effectiveness of the job enrichment program. The attitude test must be limited to
   motivator items in order to divorce the employee's view of the job he is
   given from all the surrounding hygiene feelings that he might have.

9. *Be prepared for a drop in performance in the experimental group the
   first few weeks.* The changeover to a new job may lead to a temporary
   reduction in efficiency.

10. *Expect your first-line supervisors to experience some anxiety and hostil-
    ity over the changes you are making.* The anxiety comes from their fear
    that the changes will result in poorer performance for their unit. Hostil-
    ity will arise when the employees start assuming what the supervisors

regard as their own responsibility for performance. The supervisor without checking duties to perform may then be left with little to do.

After a successful experiment, however, the supervisor usually discovers the supervisory and managerial functions he has neglected, or which were never his because all his time was given over to checking the work of his subordinates. For example, in the R&D division of one large chemical company I know of, the supervisors of the laboratory assistants were theoretically responsible for their training and evaluation. These functions, however, had come to be performed in a routine, unsubstantial fashion. After the job enrichment program, during which the supervisors were not merely passive observers of the assistants' performance, the supervisors actually were devoting their time to reviewing performance and administering thorough training.

What has been called an employee-centered style of supervision will come about not through education of supervisors, but by changing the jobs that they do.

Concluding Note

Job enrichment will not be a one-time proposition, but a continuous management function. The initial changes, however, should last for a very long period of time. There are a number of reasons for this:

- The changes should bring the job up to the level of challenge commensurate with the skill that was hired.

- Those who have still more ability eventually will be able to demonstrate it better and win promotion to higher-level jobs.

- The very nature of motivators, as opposed to hygiene factors, is that they have a much longer-term effect on employees' attitudes. Perhaps the job will have to be enriched again, but this will not occur as frequently as the need for hygiene.

Not all jobs can be enriched, nor do all jobs need to be enriched. If only a small percentage of the time and money that is now devoted to hygiene, however, were given to job enrichment efforts, the return in human satisfaction and economic gain would be one of the largest dividends that industry and society have ever reaped through their efforts at better personnel management.

The argument for job enrichment can be summed up quite simply: If you have someone on a job, use him. If you can't use him on the job, get rid of him, either via automation or by selecting someone with lesser ability. If you can't use him and you can't get rid of him, you will have a motivation problem.

4

Existence, Relatedness, and Growth Model

Clayton P. Alderfer

The purpose of this chapter is to present E.R.G. theory and show how it is similar to and different from related viewpoints.

The theory deals primarily with two classes of variables—satisfactions and desires. It postulates three basic need categories which provide the basis for enumerating specific satisfactions and desires. It contains propositions which predict how satisfaction relates to desire, and it deals with the question of how chronic desires relate to satisfaction.

E.R.G. Theory

Basic Concepts

The definition of terms such as "need," "drive," "instinct," and "motive" has been a point of controversy for some time among students of motivation. Some have actively advocated the abandonment of some or all of such terms. Others have avoided a firm position in the discussion. And still others have continued to struggle with the numerous conceptual problems associated with the terms. For the purposes of presenting E.R.G. theory, a number of distinctions should be made so that the scope and purpose of the theory can be clarified.

A common distinction used by those who are willing to utilize need-like concepts is that between primary and secondary motives. Primary needs refer to innate tendencies which an organism possesses by the nature of being the type of creature it is. Sometimes this distinction also includes the notion that primary needs are biologically or physiologically rooted. E.R.G. theory holds the view that existence, relatedness, and growth needs are primary needs in the sense of their being innate, but holds open the question of whether all three are biologi-

Reprinted from "An Empirical Test of a New Theory of Human Needs," *Organizational Behavior and Human Performance*, Vol. 4, No. 2, pp. 142–156, 1969, by Clayton P. Alderfer. Copyright © 1969 by Elsevier Science and Technology Journals. Reproduced with permission of Elsevier Science and Technology Journals in the format other book via Copyright Clearance Center.

cally based. Secondary needs refer to acquired or learned tendencies to respond. E.R.G. needs can be increased in strength by learning processes but they do not come into being as a result of learning.

E.R.G. is *not* intended to be a theory to explain how people learn, make choices, or perform. It is a theory about the subjective states of satisfaction and desire. Campbell, Dunnette, Lawler, and Weick have made a useful distinction between two types of motivation theory. One type they term "mechanical" or "process" theories, while the other type is called "substantive" or "content" theories. The first type attempts to define major classes of variables that are important for explaining motivated behavior. The second type is more concerned with what it is within an individual or his environment that energizes and sustains behavior. E.R.G. theory is a content theory.

Although both satisfaction and desire are subjective states of a person, they differ in the degree of subjectivity. Satisfaction concerns the outcome of an event between a person and his environment. It refers to the internal state of a person who has obtained what he was seeking and is synonymous with getting and fulfilling. Because satisfaction involves interaction with a person's environment, its assessment (for both the person and a researcher) hinges in part on the objective nature of a person's external world. Satisfaction depends both upon the way the world "actually" is and how this reality is perceived by the person.

Frustration is the opposite condition from satisfaction. For some operational purposes, one might wish to distinguish between satisfaction and frustration. If one produced an experimental manipulation which attempted to *increase* the gratification of subjects he would call this satisfaction, but if he attempted to *decrease* the gratification of subjects he would call this frustration. A similar point has been made by Rosenzweig, who made a distinction between primary and secondary frustration. In his view, "primary frustration involves the sheer existence of an active need. . . . Secondary frustration more strictly embraces the definition given above, emphasis being placed upon supervenient obstacles or obstructions in the path of the active need."

Compared to satisfaction, desire is even more subjective, for it does not have a necessary external referent. The term refers exclusively to an internal state of a person which may be synonymous with concepts, such as want, preference, need strength, need intensity, and motive. There is no necessary parallel external state for a desire as there is for a satisfaction. Consequently measurement of desires is more difficult. A person may have defenses which prohibit his own awareness of his desires. Even if he is aware of his desires, he may not choose to report them because he doubts if he would benefit from doing so. Fundamentally, a person is alone with his desires. He cannot rely on a shared consensus of social reality to find out what he wants.

A further distinction may be made between *episodic* and *chronic desires*. *Episodic* desires tend to be situation specific, and they change in response to relevant changes in the situation. Statements about episodic changes in desires are intended to apply across people, without regard for individual differences. *Chronic* desires, on the other hand, reflect more or less enduring states of a person. They are seen as being a consequence both of episodic desires and of learning. To partial out the effects of chronic and episodic desires would require a study which, to some degree, was longitudinal.

According to this definitional system, the term "need" is a concept subsuming both desires and satisfactions (frustrations). For example, when a statement contains the words "existence needs," it includes both existence desires and existence satisfactions (frustrations). Depending on one's theory, there may be no reason to distinguish between the terms "desire," "satisfaction," and "need." If there were always a correspondence between lack of satisfaction (or frustration) and desire, one might abandon these terms and simply refer to "need" as the presence of a deficiency or excess which, if not altered, would impair the health of the organism.

In recent years, there has been an increasing tendency to make use of open-systems concepts for understanding the human personality. This approach offers the possibility of bridging the gap between those views of man which tend to view him primarily in reactive, tension-producing ways and those orientations which tend to focus on his proactive, stimulus-seeking qualities. Acting as a metatheory or broader framework, open-systems theory stands behind E.R.G. theory. All the major concepts and propositions of E.R.G. should be consistent with the logic of open-systems theory. In a loose sense, E.R.G. theory is derived from an open-systems view of man.

The primary categories of human needs follow from the criteria of personality as an open system outlined by Allport. Existence needs reflect a person's requirement for material and energy exchange and for the need to reach and maintain a homeostatic equilibrium with regard to the provision of certain material substances. Relatedness needs acknowledge that a person is not a self-contained unit but must engage in transactions with his human environment. Growth needs emerge from the tendency of open systems to increase in internal order and differentiation over time as a consequence of going beyond steady states and interacting with the environment.

Existence needs include all the various forms of material and physiological desires. Hunger and thirst represent deficiencies in existence needs. Pay, fringe benefits, and physical working conditions are other types of existence needs. One of the basic characteristics of existence needs is that they can be divided among people in such a way that one person's gain is another's loss when resources are limited. If two people are hungry, for example, the food eaten by one is not available to the other. When a salary decision is made that provides one person or group of people with more pay, it eliminates the possibility of some other person or group getting extra money. This property of existence needs frequently means that a person's (or group's) satisfaction, beyond a bare minimum, depends upon the comparison of what he gets with what others get in the same situation.

However, this comparison is not "interpersonal" in the sense of necessitating comparison with known significant others. The interpersonal aspect of equity is not an issue for existence needs. The comparison process for material goods is simply among piles of goods, without necessarily attaching the added dimension of knowing who the others are who would obtain smaller or larger shares. It turns out in our society that people have learned to state such comparisons in interpersonal terms. Consequently, in developing operational definitions, some existence-need comparisons were stated as interpersonal comparisons. However, this reflects a realistic limitation of the measures, stemming from certain aspects of our culture for which the theory, not being a learning theory, does not account.

Relatedness needs involve relationships with significant other people. Family members are usually significant others, as are superiors, coworkers, subordinates, friends, and enemies. One of the basic characteristics of relatedness needs is that their satisfaction depends on a process of sharing or mutuality. People are assumed to satisfy relatedness needs by mutually sharing their thoughts and feelings. Acceptance, confirmation, understanding, and influence are elements of the relatedness process. Significant others include groups as well as individuals. Any human unit can become a significant other for a person if he has sustained interaction with this person either by virtue of his own choice or because of the setting in which he is located. Families, work groups, friendship groups, and professional groups are examples of significant groups with which a person might have a relationship and therefore relatedness needs.

The theoretical roots of the relatedness concept are twofold. One set of theorists have focused primarily on what occurs between persons when they relate to each other. Out of this work has come Rogers' theory of interpersonal relationships and Argyris' concepts of authentic relationships and interpersonal competence. Complementary to the emphasis on what happens between the parties is the attention to what happens within each person. Freudian and neo-Freudian theorists such as Sullivan, Horney, and Klein have given particular attention to how significant others may be represented intrapsychically and what emotions these representations may carry.

This conception of relatedness needs does not necessitate equal formal power between (or among) people for satisfaction to occur, although for some emotions, such as anger, power equalization tends to aid authentic expression. The essential conditions involve the willingness of both (or all) persons to share their thoughts and feelings as fully as possible while trying to enable the other(s) to do the same thing. Certainly not all interpersonal relationships are characterized by the mutual sharing and concern implied by this definition. However, I wish to suggest that this is the direction toward which relationships move when people wish to be meaningfully related to each other and when the relationship is not marred by defensiveness or lack of commitment by one or more of the parties.

Furthermore, the outcome of satisfying relatedness needs need not always be a positive affectual state for both or either person. The exchange or expression of anger and hostility is a very important part of meaningful interpersonal relationships, just as is the expression of warmth and closeness. Thus, the opposite of relatedness satisfaction is not necessarily anger, but it is a sense of distance or lack of connection.

A major difference between relatedness and existence needs arises under conditions of scarcity with respect to either satisfaction. For existence needs, a limited supply of material goods can result in one party being highly satisfied if, for example, he obtains all or nearly all of the scarce supply. However, for relatedness satisfaction a scarce supply is hypothesized to affect both parties in similar ways. That is to say, if a relationship is not working, both (or all) parties suffer. This is not to say that the parties suffer equally. The relationship may be more central for one of the parties than for the other. However, the degree of suffering or satisfaction among the parties always tends to be positively correlated for relatedness needs. For existence needs, however, the degree of suffering among parties tends to be inversely related when there is scarcity and uncorrelated when there is no scarcity.

Growth needs impel a person to make creative or productive effects on himself and the environment. Satisfaction of growth needs comes from a person engaging problems which call upon him to utilize his capacities fully and may include requiring him to develop additional capacities. A person experiences a greater sense of wholeness and fullness as a human being by satisfying growth needs. Thus, satisfaction of growth needs depends on a person finding the opportunities to be what he is most fully and to become what he can. This concept owes much to the existential psychologists, such as Maslow, Allport, and Rogers; the ego-oriented psycho-analysts such as Fromm and White; and the laboratory psychologists concerned with a varied experience, curiosity, and activation.

Specific growth needs are defined in terms of environmental settings with which a person contends. Barker's work on the ecological environment offers a relatively precise definition of what is meant here by environmental settings.

> The ecological environment of a person's molar behavior, the molar environment, consists of bounded, physical-temporal locales and variegated but stable patterns in the behavior of people en masse.

Most people's lives contain several environmental settings in the form of organizational roles and leisure-time activities. Some of the settings studied in this research include jobs, college fraternity life, academic work, and extracurricular activities.

E.R.G. theory assumes that these broad categories of needs are active in all living persons. How strong each need is is one question the theory addresses. All people are alike in that they possess some degree of each need, but they differ in the strength of their needs. There is no postulate of strict prepotency as Maslow has offered, but there are propositions relating lower-level need satisfaction to higher-level desires.

Summary.—Each of the three basic needs in E.R.G. theory were defined in terms of a target toward which efforts at gratification were aimed and in terms of a process through which, and only through which, satisfaction could be obtained. For existence needs, the targets were material substances, and the process was simply getting enough. When the substances are scarce, the process quickly becomes "win-lose," and one person's gain is correlated with another's loss. For relatedness needs, the targets were significant others (persons or groups) and the process was mutual sharing of thoughts and feelings. For growth needs, the targets were environmental settings, and there were joint processes of a person becoming more differentiated and integrated as a human being.

Propositions Relating Satisfaction to Desire

Seven major propositions in the E.R.G. theory provide a basis from which empirically testable hypotheses relating satisfaction to desire can be logically derived. The form of this derivation is as follows. If *A* is an operational indicator of an E., an R., or a G. satisfaction and *B* is an operational indicator of an E., an R., or a G. desire, then *A* should show an empirically verifiable relationship to *B* in such a way as predicted by one of the E.R.G. propositions. If empirical results provide support for the *A* to *B* relationship, one would have more confidence in the theory. If the empirical results do not provide support for the *A* to *B* relationship, then one can have less confidence in the theory. The structure of this theory is such that the results can provide support for some propositions while not for others.

The major propositions in E.R.G. theory are as follows:

P1. The less existence needs are satisfied, the more they will be desired.

P2. The less relatedness needs are satisfied, the more existence needs will be desired.

P3. The more existence needs are satisfied, the more relatedness needs will be desired.

P4. The less relatedness needs are satisfied, the more they will be desired.

P5. The less growth needs are satisfied, the more relatedness needs will be desired.

P6. The more relatedness needs are satisfied, the more growth needs will be desired.

P7. The more growth needs are satisfied, the more they will be desired.

These propositions indicate that any desire can have several types of satisfaction (including some outside its particular category) affecting its strength. Any satisfaction also affects more than one type of desire (including some outside its particular category). This multiple determination property is shown in figure 1, which gives a summary of the propositions in diagrammatic form.

An additional aspect of the theory, however, concerns providing explanatory concepts or mechanisms which lie behind the various propositions. These explanatory concepts are intended to help answer the "why" questions for the various propositions. As such, they add richness to the theoretical framework. They may be seen as analogous to axioms which provide a basis from which the main propositions can be derived.

Within need categories.   Proposition 1, which deals with the impact of the existence need satisfaction on existence desires, has an assumption of the *interchangeability* of various satisfiers of existence needs. Pay and fringe benefits are obvious examples where an organization actually makes choices about how to compensate its employees. The investigations of Nealey and others have been based on this assumption. Where the interchangeability assumption may not be as obvious is with such things as physical working conditions or physical demands of the job. However, most job-evaluation systems contain provisions

Figure 1
Satisfaction to Desire Propositions from E.R.G. Theory*

Need frustration	Strength of desires	Need satisfaction
(lack of satisfaction)		

*Numbers on the diagram refer to the proposition numbers in the text.

where an employee is paid more because he has dirty, hazardous, or physically taxing duties in his job. Moreover, Jacques has formulated a view of payment based upon the time span of discretion. According to his view, there is a correspondence between equitable payment and discretion. He reported that there is evidence to support the view that the length of discretionary time span corresponds with the financial loss which would be caused by sub-standard discretion.

Dunnette and Lawler and Porter have argued that pay can stimulate and satisfy needs other than for material goods. Lawler and Porter showed correlations between managers' pay and their esteem and autonomy satisfaction. Reasoning from expectancy theory, Dunnette suggested that pay can be used as a reward for those who seek power, status, and achievement. His view was that pay could be instrumental for satisfying these other needs.

Some of the implications of these views conflict with E.R.G. theory while others do not. According to the E.R.G. definitional system, pay is an existence need; it is a material substance which can be scarce and thereby promote a win-lose orientation among people who do not have enough. Pay *per se* cannot satisfy relatedness or growth needs but could be part of a process which results in these needs being satisfied. Giving a person a raise, for example, might be a way of communicating a feeling of esteem for him. It might also be a tactic for "keeping him quiet." Additional pay might be a way for a person to obtain greater autonomy but only if he is able to use the money to create an environmental setting conducive to his being independent and self-directive. The discussion of *P2* will deal further with this issue.

The structure of *P*4 is similar to that of *P*1 when it states that lack of satisfaction of relatedness needs leads to higher relatedness desires. The explanatory mechanism in this proposition is *transferability* of significant others. Persons who lack a basic scheme of connectedness and sharing in their emotional lives with significant others will seek to obtain that need satisfaction. If they are unable to obtain the satisfaction with the original person where the satisfaction is missing, they will tend to transfer the desire to others. Some of the earliest clues about the operation of this process are found in Freud's work on transference.

> Expectant libidinal impulses will inevitably be roused, in anyone whose need for love is not being satisfactorily gratified in reality, by each new person coming upon the scene, and it is more than probable that both parts of the libido, the conscious and the unconscious, will participate in this attitude.

Proposition 7 is like *P*1 and *P*4 in that it implies that satisfaction of growth needs in one environmental setting affects a person's desires in other settings. But it is also different because the sign of the relationship between satisfaction and desire is positive rather than negative. The explanatory mechanism in this proposition is the notion of *expanding environments*. Persons who experience growth in one setting tend not only to seek more opportunities in that setting but also seek more settings in which to rise and develop their talents.

Downward and upward movement in the hierarchy.   The concepts of existence, relatedness, and growth needs were presented as separate and distinct categories. One of the ways in which the needs can be ordered, however, is on a continuum in terms of their concreteness. Existence needs are the most concrete. Their presence or absence is the easiest for the person to verify due to the fact that they can be reduced to material substances. Relatedness needs are less concrete than existence needs. Their presence or absence depends on the state of a relationship between two or more people. To verify the state of relatedness needs depends on the consensual validation of the people involved in the relationship. Finally, growth needs are the least concrete. Ultimately, their specific objectives depend on the uniqueness of each person. At the most precise level, the state of a person's growth can be fully known only to him and only when he is not deluding himself. The continuum from more to less concreteness is also a continuum from more to less verifiability and from less to more potential uncertainty for the person.

Propositions 2 and 5 follow from the concept of *frustration-regression* which played such an important part in Lewinian field theory. Regression meant a more primitive, less mature way of behaving, not necessarily behavior that had been produced earlier in life. Frustration-regression is employed in E.R.G. theory to identify one motivational basis for explaining primitivity of some desires.

The sense in which *frustration-regression* is employed in E.R.G. theory concerns the tendency of persons to desire more concrete ends as a consequence of being unable to obtain more differentiated, less concrete ends. Thus, a person wants material substances when his relatedness needs are not satisfied because he is using them as a more concrete way of establishing his connectedness with other people. He wants relationships with significant others when his growth needs are not being met because he is using them for alternative sources of stimulation. In neither case will substitute gratification satisfy the original desire, but rationality is only part of the picture in understanding motivation.

It is in this sense that a person may use the size of his pay check as an indicator of the esteem in which he is held by his boss, colleagues, or organization. At the cultural level, Fromm has called this kind of phenomenon the "market orientation." From her work with psychiatric patients, Horney proposed that the neurotic quest for material possessions not only followed from anxiety about interpersonal relationships but also served as an indirect way of expressing hostility.

Propositions 3 and 6 follow from the concept of *satisfaction-progression* which played an important part in Maslow's original concept of the need hierarchy. In the case of E.R.G. theory, however, the movement up the hierarchy from relatedness satisfaction to growth desires does not presume satisfaction of existence needs. The assumption implied in the satisfaction-progression mechanism is that a person has more energy available for the more personal and less certain aspects of living if he has obtained gratification in the more concrete areas. Movement from existence satisfaction to relatedness desires is possible because a person fears others as competitors for scarce material goods less as he satisfies his existence needs. Satisfaction of relatedness needs provides a source of social support for persons seeking to develop and use their skills and talents. As his relatedness needs become satisfied, a person is freed to want to grow by a sense of greater authenticity in his relations with others.

Propositions Relating Desires to Satisfaction

Any theory that takes a position by stating that certain human characteristics (such as needs) apply to all people must also deal with the fact that people are different. Assuming that all persons have existence, relatedness, and growth needs is not the same as assuming that all people have these needs in the same degree. E.R.G. theory does not assume that all people have the same chronic strength of the various needs. However, the theory does assume that to *some* degree all people do have all three broad categories of needs.

The relationship between chronic desires and satisfaction in E.R.G. theory depends both on the particular need in question and on the nature of the material, interpersonal, and ecological conditions facing the person. The various needs and relevant conditions will be taken up according to need category. Each of the following propositions is based on the conceptual definitions of the needs, both the targets and the processes for obtaining need satisfaction.

Existence needs. Satisfaction of existence needs depends on a person's getting enough of the various material substances that he wants. When there is scarcity (as is most often the case), a person with high needs will be able to obtain a lower proportion of his desires than a person with low needs. When there is no scarcity, then everyone can get what he wants, and there would be no difference in degree of satisfaction between those with different chronic existence needs. An example can be taken from the case of oxygen, an existence need that is normally but not always in very abundant supply. When there is no shortage of oxygen, then everyone can get all he needs. People rarely express much dissatisfaction under these conditions. However, when oxygen exists in limited supply, as is true in a submarine, then those people with higher needs, such as a person with a heart condition, would suffer more as the amount available diminished than those with lower needs. To summarize:

P8a. When existence materials are scarce, then the higher chronic existence desires are, the less existence satisfaction.

P8b. When existence materials are not scarce, then there will be no differential existence satisfaction as a function of chronic existence desires.

Relatedness needs. Satisfaction of relatedness needs depends on people establishing relationships in which they can mutually share their relevant thoughts and feelings. Most people are to some degree responsive to the thoughts and feelings of others with whom they interact. Consequently, persons with varying needs almost always have the possibility of increasing the amount of mutual exchange that occurs by being more empathic and sharing more of themselves. At the same time, people differ in the degree of exchange that they want or can tolerate comfortably. These preferences set limits on the satisfaction they can obtain and also on the satisfaction others who interact with them can obtain.

In the optimally satisfying relationship, a person is able to share and be heard on all relevant matters to him. In a highly dissatisfying relationship, a person is able to share and be heard on a very small proportion of relevant issues. Persons who are very high on chronic relatedness needs may find it more difficult to achieve satisfaction under normal conditions because they may be perceived as overwhelming others with their thoughts and feelings, while persons very low on chronic relatedness needs may find it difficult to achieve satisfaction under normal conditions because they do not invest enough of themselves in the relationship for it to become very satisfying. In a very satisfying relationship, the degree of chronic relatedness needs may have no impact on satisfaction because a person is able to establish conditions which permit him to share and be heard as much as he wants, however much that is. In a very dissatisfying relationship, a person with very high relatedness needs may be able to get more satisfaction because he is more willing to invest himself, and even the most deteriorating relationship can benefit by the efforts of one party.

In order to state these ideas in propositional form, a distinction among the three kinds of interpersonal states is employed as a moderating variable between chronic relatedness desires and relatedness satisfaction. The terms "highly satisfying," "normal," and "highly dissatisfying" are loosely defined at this point, but they do provide a point from which to begin research.

P9a. In highly satisfying relationships, there is no differential relatedness satisfaction as a function of chronic relatedness desires.

P9*b*. In normal relationships, persons very high and very low on chronic relatedness desires tend to obtain lower satisfaction than persons with moderate desires.

P9*c*. In highly dissatisfying relationships, then, the higher chronic relatedness desires, the more relatedness satisfaction.

Growth needs. Satisfaction of growth needs depends on a person's being able to find ways to utilize his capabilities and to develop new talents. Ecological environments vary in the degree to which they permit or encourage the use of a person's full capabilities. Some settings contain very little opportunity for discretion and offer little stimulation or challenge. A prototypic example of this kind of setting would be an assembly-line job. Other settings offer a high degree of stimulation and choice to persons. The job of a high level executive might be a case of this type of setting. Growth satisfaction depends on a person's taking a proactive stance toward his environment, but if the setting is unresponsive, it matters little if the person wants to produce effects because he cannot. Thus, the major mediating effect of the environment concerns whether the setting offers challenge and choice.

P10*a*. In challenging discretionary settings, then, the higher chronic growth desires, the more growth satisfaction.

P10*b*. In nonchallenging, nondiscretionary settings, there will be no differential growth satisfaction as a function of chronic growth desires.

Summary and implications. By combining propositions 1 to 7 with 8 to 10, one obtains a set of answers to the questions of how need satisfaction relates to desire and how chronic desires relate to need satisfaction. According to this view, the relationship between satisfaction and desire is essentially instantaneous. As soon as a person is aware of whether his needs are being satisfied, his desires change according to the propositions outlined above. But the relationships between chronic desires and satisfaction are not instantaneous. Because of the mediating effects of external conditions, there is a time delay (of unknown degree at this time) between how quickly a person of given chronic desires obtains the possible satisfactions available to him.

The impact of combining propositions 1 and 8*a* is to define an existence-need deficiency cycle: Under scarcity, the less a person is satisfied the more he desires, and the more he desires the less he is satisfied. As a result a person could become fixated on material needs.

The impact of combining propositions 7 and 10*a* is to define a growth-need enrichment cycle: In challenging discretionary settings, the more a person is satisfied the more he desires, and the more he desires the more he is satisfied. As a result, a person who is already growth oriented is likely to become increasingly so.

Although relatedness satisfactions do not play a direct role in either of these cycles, they can play a supporting or suppressing part in both. If relatedness satisfaction decreases, then the existence desires tend to increase while growth desires tend to decrease, thereby supporting the growth enrichment cycle while suppressing the existence deficiency cycle.

5

Expectancy Theory

John P. Campbell, Marvin D. Dunnette, Edward E. Lawler III, and Karl E. Weick Jr.

Early Cognitive Theories

Concomitant with the development of drive x habit theory, Lewin[1] and Tolman[2] developed and investigated cognitive, or expectancy, theories of motivation. Even though Lewin was concerned with human subjects and Tolman worked largely with animals, much of their respective theorizing contained common elements. Basic to the cognitive view of motivation is the notion that individuals have cognitive *expectancies* concerning the outcomes that are likely to occur as the result of what they do and that individuals have preferences among outcomes. That is, an individual has an "idea" about possible consequences of his acts, and he makes conscious choices among consequences according to their probability of occurrence and their value to him.

Thus for the cognitive theorist it is the anticipation of reward that energizes behavior and the perceived value of various outcomes that gives behavior its direction. Tolman spoke of a belief-value matrix that specifies for each individual the value he places on particular outcomes and his belief that they can be attained.

Atkinson[3] has compared drive theory and expectancy theory. Although he points out some differences, he emphasizes that both theories are actually quite similar and contain many of the same concepts. Both include the notion of a reward or favorable outcome that is desired, and both postulate a learned connection contained within the organism. For expectancy theory this learned connection is a behavior-outcome expectancy, and for drive theory it is an *S-R* habit strength.

However, the theories differ in two ways which are important for research on motivation in an organizational setting. For example, they differ in what they state is activated by the anticipation of reward. Expectancy theory sees the anticipation of a reward as functioning selectively on actions expected to lead to it. Drive theory views the magnitude of the anticipated goals as a source of general excitement—a nonselective influence on performance.

Expectancy theory is also much looser in specifying how expectancy-outcome connections are built up. Drive theory postulates that *S-R* habit strengths are built up through repeated associations of stimulus and response; that is, the reward or outcome must actually have followed the response to a particular stimulus in order for the *S-R* connection to operate in future choice behavior. Such a process is sufficient but not necessary for forming expectancy-outcome relationships. An individual may form expectancies vicariously (someone may tell him that complimenting the boss's wife leads to a promotion, for example) or by other symbolic means. This last point is crucial since the symbolic (cognitive) manipulation of various *S-R* situations seems quite descriptive of a great deal of human behavior.

These two differences make the cognitive or expectancy point of view much more useful for studying human motivation in an organizational setting. In fact, it is the one which has been given the most attention by theorists concerned with behavior in organizations.

Instrumentality–Valence Theory

Building on expectancy theory and its later amplifications by Atkinson,[4] W. Edwards,[5] Peak,[6] and Rotter,[7] Vroom[8] has presented a process theory of work motivation that he calls *instrumentality theory*. His basic classes of variables are expectancies, valences, choices, outcomes, and instrumentalities.

Expectancy is defined as a belief concerning the likelihood that a particular act will be followed by a particular outcome. Presumably, the degree of belief can vary between 0 (complete lack of belief that it will follow) and 1 (complete certainty that it will). Note that it is the perception of the individual that is important, not the objective reality. This same concept has been referred to as *subjective probability* by others (*e.g.*, W. Edwards).

Valence refers to the strength of an individual's preference for a particular outcome. An individual may have either a positive or a negative preference for an outcome; presumably, outcomes gain their valence as a function of the degree to which they are seen to be related to the needs of the individual. However, this last point is not dealt with concretely in Vroom's formulation. As an example of these two concepts, one might consider an increase in pay to be a possible outcome of a particular act. The theory would then deal with the valence of a wage increase for an individual and his expectancy that particular behaviors will be followed by a wage increase outcome. Again, valence refers to the perceived or expected value of an outcome, not its real or eventual value.

According to Vroom, outcomes take on a valence value because of their *instrumentality* for achieving other outcomes. Thus he is really postulating two classes of outcomes. In the organizational setting, the first class of outcomes might include such things as money, promotion, recognition, etc. Supposedly, these outcomes are directly linked to behavior. However, as Vroom implicitly suggests, wage increases or promotion may have no value by themselves. They are valuable in terms of their instrumental role in securing second level outcomes such as food, clothing, shelter, entertainment, and status, which are not obtained as the direct result of a particular action.

According to Vroom, instrumentality, like correlation, varies between +1.0 and –1.0. Thus a first level outcome may be seen as always leading to some desired second level outcome (+1.0) or as never leading to the second level outcome (–1.0). In Vroom's theory the formal definition of valence for a first level outcome is the sum of the products between its instrumentalities for all possible second level outcomes and their respective valences.

To sum up, Vroom's formulation postulates that the motivational force, or effort, an individual exerts is a function of (1) his expectancy that certain outcomes will result from his behavior (*e.g.*, a raise in pay for increased effort) and (2) the valence, for him, of those outcomes. The valence of an outcome is in turn a function of its instrumentality for obtaining other outcomes and the valence of these other outcomes.

A Hybrid Expectancy Model

Since his formulation first appeared, a number of investigators have attempted to extend Vroom's model to make it more explicit and more inclusive in terms of relevant variables (Graen,[9] L. W. Porter and Lawler[10]). Although we shall not discuss the contributions of these writers in detail, we would like to incorporate a number of their ideas in our own composite picture of an expanded expectancy model. However, any imperfections in what follows should be ascribed to us and not to them.

One major addition to Vroom's model is the necessity for a more concrete specification of the task or performance goals toward which work behavior is directed. Graen[11] refers to this class of variables as *work roles*, but we prefer to retain the notion of *task goals*. Task goals may be specified externally by the organization or the work group, or internally by the individual's own value system. Examples of task goals include such things as production quotas, time limits for projects, quality standards, showing a certain amount of loyalty to the organization, exhibiting the right set of attitudes, etc.

We would also like to make more explicit a distinction between first and second level outcomes. First level outcomes are outcomes contingent on achieving the task goal or set of task goals. A potential first level outcome is synonymous with the term "incentive," and an outcome which is actually realized is synonymous with the term "reward." The distinction is temporal. Like task goals, first level outcomes may be external or internal. Some examples of external first level outcomes granted by the organization are job security, pay, promotions, recognition, and increased autonomy. An individual may also set up his own internal incentives or reward himself with internally mediated outcomes such as ego satisfaction.

As pointed out in the discussion of Vroom's model first level outcomes may or may not be associated with a plethora of second level outcomes; that is, the externally or internally mediated rewards are instrumental in varying degrees for obtaining second level outcomes, such as food, housing, material goods, community status, and freedom from anxiety.

The concepts of valence for first and second level outcomes and the instrumentality of first or second level outcomes are defined as before, but the notion of expectancy decomposes into two different variables. First, individuals may have expectancies concerning whether or not they will actually accomplish the task goal if they expend effort (expectancy I); that is, an individual makes a subjective probability estimate concerning his chances for reaching a particular goal, given a particular situation. For example, a manufacturing manager may think the odds of his getting a new product into production by the first of the year are about 3 to 1 (*i.e.,* expectancy I = 0.75). Perhaps the primary determiner of expectancy I is how the individual perceives his own job skills in the context of what is specified as his task goals and the various difficulties and external constraints standing in the way of accomplishing them. Certainly, then, an employee's perceptions of his own talents determine to a large degree the direction and intensity of his job behavior. This first kind of expectancy should be more salient for more complex and higher level tasks such as those involved in managing.

Second, individuals possess expectancies concerning whether or not achievement of specified task goals will actually be followed by the first level outcome (expectancy II). In other words, they form subjective probability estimates of the degree to which rewards are *contingent* on achieving task goals. The individual must ask himself what the probability is that his achievement of the goal will be rewarded by the organization. For example, the manufacturing manager may be virtually certain (expectancy II = 1.0) that if he does get the new product into production by the first of the year, he will receive a promotion and a substantial salary increase. Or, and this may be the more usual case, he may see no relationship at all between meeting the objective and getting a promotion and salary increase.

None of the authors cited so far have explicitly labeled these two kinds of expectancies. Indeed, in a laboratory or other experimental setting the distinction may not be necessary since the task may be so easy that accomplishing the goal is always a certainty (*i.e.,* expectancy I is 1.0 for everybody) or the contingency of reward on behavior may be certain and easily verified by the subject (*i.e.,* expectancy II is 1.0 for everybody). Vroom[12] defines expectancy as an action-outcome relationship which is represented by an individual's subjective probability estimate that a particular set of behaviors will be followed by a particular outcome. Since Vroom presents no concrete definitions for the terms "action" and "outcome," his notion of expectancy could include both expectancy I and expectancy II as defined above. Thus effort expenditure could be regarded as an action, and goal performance as an outcome; or performance could be considered behavior, and money an outcome. Vroom uses both kinds of examples to illustrate the expectancy variable and makes no conceptual distinction between them. However, in the organizational setting, the distinction seems quite necessary. Rewards may or may not be contingent on goal accomplishment, and the individual may or may not believe he has the wherewithal to reach the goal. A schematic representation of this hybrid is shown in figure 1.

We have purposely been rather vague concerning the exact form of the relationships between these different classes of variables. This schematic model is no way meant to be formal theory. To propose explicit multiplicative combinations or other configural or higher order functions is going a bit too far beyond our present measurement capability. Rather, we shall sum up the relationships contained in our expanded model as follows:

Figure 1
Schematic Representation of Hybrid Expectancy Model of Work Motivation Outlining Determinants of Direction, Amplitude, and Persistence of Individual Effort

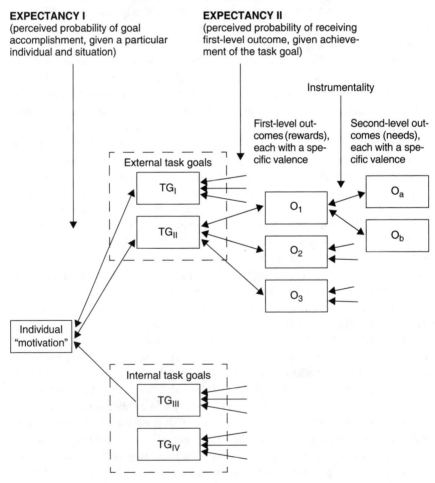

EXPECTANCY I
(perceived probability of goal accomplishment, given a particular individual and situation)

EXPECTANCY II
(perceived probability of receiving first-level outcome, given achievement of the task goal)

Instrumentality

First-level outcomes (rewards), each with a specific valence

Second-level outcomes (needs), each with a specific valence

External task goals

TG_I

TG_{II}

O_1

O_2

O_3

O_a

O_b

Individual "motivation"

Internal task goals

TG_{III}

TG_{IV}

1. The valence of a first level outcome (incentive or reward) is a function of the instrumentality of that outcome for obtaining second level outcomes (need satisfactions) and the valences of the relevant second level outcomes.

2. The decision by an individual to work on a particular task and expend a certain amount of effort in that direction is a function of *(a)* his personal probability estimate that he can accomplish the task (expectancy I), *(b)* his personal probability estimate that his accomplishment of the task goal will be followed by certain first level outcomes or rewards (expectancy II), and *(c)* the valence of the first level outcomes.

3. The distinction between external and internal goals and rewards leads to a number of potential conflict situations for the individual. For example, an individual might estimate his chances for accomplishing a particular task is virtually certain (*i.e.*, expectancy = 1.0). However, the internal rewards which are virtually certain to follow (*i.e.*, expectancy = 1.0) may have a very low or even negative valence (*e.g.*, feelings of extreme boredom or distants). If external rewards, such as a lot of money, have a very high valence, a serious stress situation could result from outcomes which have conflicting valences. It would be to an organization's advantage to ensure positive valences for both internal and external rewards. Other conflict situations could be produced by high positive valences for outcomes and low estimates of type I expectancies (*i.e.*, the individual does not think he can actually do the job).

Even though this kind of hybrid expectancy model seems to be a useful way of looking at organizational behavior and even though we have devoted more space to it, the reader should keep in mind that it is not the only process theory that one could use. Equity theory is its major competitor. . . .

Notes

[1] K. Lewin, *The Conceptual Representation and the Measurement of Psychological Forces* (Durham, NC: Duke University Press, 1938).

[2] E. C. Tolman, *Purposive Behavior in Animals and Men* (New York: Century. By permission of the University of California Press, 1932).

[3] J. W. Atkinson, *An Introduction to Motivation* (Princeton, NJ: Van Nostrand, 1964).

[4] J. W. Atkinson (ed.), *Motives in Fantasy, Action and Society* (Princeton, NJ: Van Nostrand, 1958).

[5] W. Edwards, "The Theory of Decision Making," *Psychological Bulletin*, Vol. 51 (1954), pp. 380–417.

[6] H. Peak, "Attitude and Motivation," in M. R. Jones (ed.) *Nebraska Symposium on Motivation* (Lincoln, NE: University of Nebraska Press, 1955), pp. 149–188.

[7] J. B. Rotter, "The Role of the Psychological Situation In Determining the Direction of Human Behavior," in M. R. Jones (ed.) *Nebraska Symposium on Motivation* (Lincoln, NE: University of Nebraska Press, 1955).

[8] V. H. Vroom, *Work and Motivation* (New York: Wiley, 1964).

[9] G. B. Graen, Work Motivation: The Behavioral Effects of Job Content and Job Context Factors in an Employment Situation. Unpublished doctoral dissertation (University of Minnesota, 1967).

[10] L. W. Porter and E. E. Lawler, *Managerial Attitudes and Performance* (Homewood, IL: Dorsey-Irwin, 1968).

[11] Graen, *op cit.*

[12] Vroom, *op cit.*

6

On the Folly of Rewarding A, While Hoping for B

Steven Kerr

Whether dealing with monkeys, rats, or human beings, it is hardly controversial to state that most organisms seek information concerning what activities are rewarded, and then seek to do (or at least pretend to do) those things, often to the virtual exclusion of activities not rewarded. The extent to which this occurs of course will depend on the perceived attractiveness of the rewards offered, but neither operant nor expectancy theorists would quarrel with the essence of this notion.

Nevertheless, numerous examples exist of reward systems that are fouled up, in that behaviors which are rewarded are those which the rewarder is trying to *discourage*, while the behavior he desires is not being rewarded at all.

In an effort to understand and explain this phenomenon, this paper presents examples from society, from organizations in general, and from profit-making firms in particular. Data from a manufacturing company and information from an insurance firm are examined to demonstrate the consequences of such reward systems for the organizations involved, and possible reasons why such reward systems continue to exist are considered.

Societal Examples

Politics

Official goals are "purposely vague and general and do not indicate . . . the host of decisions that must be made among alternative ways of achieving official goals and the priority of multiple goals . . ." (Perrow, 1969, p. 66). They usually may be relied on to offend absolutely no one, and in this sense can be considered high-acceptance, low-quality goals. An example might be "build better schools." Operative goals are higher in quality but lower in acceptance, since they specify where the money will come from, what alternative goals will be ignored, etc.

The American citizenry supposedly wants its candidates for public office to set forth operative goals, making their proposed programs "perfectly clear," specifying sources and uses of funds, etc. However, since operative goals are lower in acceptance, and since aspirants to public office need acceptance (from at least 50.1 percent of the people), most politicians prefer to speak only of official goals, at least until after the election. They, of course, would agree to speak at the operative level if "punished" for not doing so. The electorate could do this by refusing to support candidates who do not speak at the operative level.

Instead, however, the American voter typically punishes (withholds support from) candidates who frankly discuss where the money will come from, rewards politicians who speak only of official goals, but hopes that candidates (despite the reward system) will discuss the issues operatively. It is academic whether it was moral for Nixon, for example, to refuse to discuss his 1968 "secret plan" to end the Vietnam war, his 1972 operative goals concerning the lifting of price controls, the reshuffling of his cabinet, etc. The point is that the reward system made such refusal rational.

It seems worth mentioning that no manuscript can adequately define what is "moral" and what is not. However, examination of costs and benefits, combined with knowledge of what motivates a particular individual, often will suffice to determine what for him is "rational." [1] If the reward system is so designed that it is irrational to be moral, this does not necessarily mean that immorality will result. But is this not asking for trouble?

War

If some oversimplification may be permitted, let it be assumed that the primary goal of the organization (Pentagon, Luftwaffe, or whatever) is to win. Let it be assumed further that the primary goal of most individuals on the front lines is to get home alive. Then there appears to be an important conflict in goals—personally rational behavior by those at the bottom will endanger goal attainment by those at the top.

But not necessarily! It depends on how the reward system is set up. The Vietnam war was indeed a study of disobedience and rebellion, with terms such as "fragging" (killing one's own commanding officer) and "search and evade" becoming part of the military vocabulary. The difference in subordinates' acceptance of authority between World War II and Vietnam is reported to be considerable, and veterans of the Second World War often have been quoted as being outraged at the mutinous actions of many American soldiers in Vietnam.

Consider, however, some critical differences in the reward system in use during the two conflicts. What did the GI in World War II want? To go home. And when did he get to go home? When the war was won! If he disobeyed the orders to clean out the trenches and take the hills, the war would not be won and he would not go home. Furthermore, what were his chances of attaining his goal (getting home alive) if he obeyed the orders compared to his chances if he did not? What is being suggested is that the rational soldier in World War II, *whether patriotic or not*, probably found it expedient to obey.

Consider the reward system in use in Vietnam. What did the man at the bottom want? To go home. And when did he get to go home? When his tour of duty was over! This was the case *whether or not* the war was won. Furthermore, concerning the relative chance of getting home alive by obeying orders compared to the chance if they were disobeyed, it is worth noting that a mutineer in Vietnam was far more likely to be assigned rest and rehabilitation (on the assumption that fatigue was the cause) than he was to suffer any negative consequence.

In his description of the "zone of difference," Barnard stated that "a person can and will accept a communication as authoritative only when . . . at the time of his decision, he believes it to be compatible with his personal interests as a whole" (Barnard, 1968, p. 165). In light of the reward system used in Vietnam, would it not have been personally irrational for some orders to have been obeyed? Was not the military implementing a system which *rewarded* disobedience, while *hoping* that soldiers (despite the reward system) would obey orders?

Medicine

Theoretically, a physician can make either of two types of error, and intuitively one seems as bad as the other. A doctor can pronounce a patient sick when he is actually well, thus causing him needless anxiety and expense, curtailment of enjoyable foods and activities, and even physical danger by subjecting him to needless medication and surgery. Alternately, a doctor can label a sick person well, and thus avoid treating what may be a serious, even fatal ailment. It might be natural to conclude that physicians seek to minimize both types of error.

Such a conclusion would be wrong.[2] It is estimated that numerous Americans are presently afflicted with iatrogenic (physician-*caused*) illnesses (Scheff, 1965). This occurs when the doctor is approached by someone complaining of a few stray symptoms. The doctor classifies and organizes these symptoms, gives them a name, and obligingly tells the patient what further symptoms may be expected. This information often acts as a self-fulfilling prophecy, with the result that from that day on the patient for all practical purposes is sick.

Why does this happen? Why are physicians so reluctant to sustain a type 2 error (pronouncing a sick person well) that they will tolerate many type 1 errors? Again, a look at the reward system is needed. The punishments for a type 2 error are real: guilt, embarrassment, and the threat of lawsuit and scandal. On the other hand, a type 1 error (labeling a well person sick) "is sometimes seen as sound clinical practice, indicating a healthy conservative approach to medicine" (Scheff, 1965, p. 69). Type 1 errors also are likely to generate increased income and a stream of steady customers who, being well in a limited physiological sense, will not embarrass the doctor by dying abruptly.

Fellow physicians and the general public therefore are really *rewarding* type 1 errors and at the same time *hoping* fervently that doctors will try not to make them.

General Organizational Examples

Rehabilitation Centers and Orphanages

In terms of the prime beneficiary classification (Blau and Scott, 1962, p. 42) organizations such as these are supposed to exist for the "public-in-contact," that is, clients. The orphanage, therefore, theoretically is interested in placing as many children as possible in good homes. However, often orphanages surround themselves with so many rules concerning adoption that it is nearly impossible to pry a child out of the place. Orphanages may deny adoption unless the applicants are a married couple, both of the same religion as the child, without history of emotional or vocational instability, with a specified minimum income and a private room for the child, etc.

If the primary goal is to place children in good homes, then the rules ought to constitute means toward that goal. Goal displacement results when these "means become ends-in-themselves that displace the original goals" (Blau and Scott, 1962, p. 229).

To some extent these rules are required by law. But the influence of the reward system on the orphanage's management should not be ignored. Consider, for example, that the:

1. Number of children enrolled often is the most important determinant of the size of the allocated budget.

2. Number of children under the director's care will also affect the size of his staff.

3. Total organizational size will determine largely the director's prestige at the annual conventions, in the community, etc.

Therefore, to the extent that staff size, total budget, and personal prestige are valued by the orphanage's executive personnel, it becomes rational for them to make it difficult for children to be adopted. After all, who wants to be the director of the smallest orphanage in the state?

If the reward system errs in the opposite direction, paying off only for placements, extensive goal displacement again is likely to result. A common example of vocational rehabilitation in many states, for example, consists of placing someone in a job for which he has little interest and few qualifications, for two months or so, and then "rehabilitating" him again in another position. Such behavior is quite consistent with the prevailing reward system, which pays off for the number of individuals placed in any position for 60 days or more. Rehabilitation counselors also confess to competing with one another to place relatively skilled clients, sometimes ignoring persons with few skills who would be harder to place. Extensively disabled clients find that counselors often prefer to work with those whose disabilities are less severe.[3]

Universities

Society *hopes* that teachers will not neglect their teaching responsibilities but *rewards* them almost entirely for research and publications. This is most true at the large and prestigious universities. Clichés, such as "good research and good teaching go together" notwithstanding, professors often find that they must choose between teaching and research-oriented activities when allocating their time. Rewards for good teaching usually are limited to outstanding teacher awards, which are given to only a small percentage of good teachers and which usually bestow little money and fleeting prestige. Punishments for poor teaching also are rare.

Rewards for research and publications, on the other hand, and punishments for failure to accomplish these, are commonly administered by universities at which teachers are employed. Furthermore, publication-oriented résumés usually will be well received at other universities, whereas teaching credentials, harder to document and quantify, are much less transferable. Consequently, it is rational for university teachers to concentrate on research, even if to the detriment of teaching and at the expense of their students.

By the same token, it is rational for students to act based upon the goal displacement which has occurred within universities concerning what they are rewarded for. If it is assumed that a primary goal of a university is to transfer knowledge from teacher to student, then grades become identifiable as a means toward that goal, serving as motivational, control, and feedback devices to expedite the knowledge transfer. Instead, however, the grades themselves have become much more important for entrance to graduate school, successful employment, tuition refunds, parental respect, etc., than the knowledge or lack of knowledge they are supposed to signify.

It, therefore, should come as no surprise that information has surfaced in recent years concerning fraternity files for examinations, term-paper writing services, organized cheating at the service academies, and the like. Such activities constitute a personally rational response to a reward system which pays off for grades, rather than knowledge.

Business-Related Examples

Ecology

Assume that the president of XYZ Corporation is confronted with the following alternatives:

1. Spend $11 million for antipollution equipment to keep from poisoning fish in the river adjacent to the plant; or
2. Do nothing, in violation of the law, and assume a 1-in-10 chance of being caught; with a resultant $1 million fine plus the necessity of buying the equipment.

Under this not unrealistic set of choices it requires no linear program to determine that XYZ Corporation can maximize its probabilities by flouting the law. Add the fact that XYZ's president is probably being rewarded (by creditors, stockholders, and other salient parts of his task environment) according to criteria totally unrelated to the number of fish poisoned, and his probable course of action becomes clear.

Evaluation of Training

It is axiomatic that those who care about a firm's well-being should insist that the organization get fair value for its expenditures. Yet it is commonly known that firms seldom bother to evaluate a new GRID, MBO, job enrichment program, or whatever, to see if the company is getting its money's worth. Why? Certainly it is not because people have not pointed out that this situation exists; numerous practitioner-oriented articles are written each year to just this point.

The individuals (whether in personnel, manpower planning, or wherever) who normally would be responsible for conducting such evaluations are the same ones often charged with introducing the change effort in the first place. Having convinced top management to spend the money, they usually are quite animated afterwards in collecting rigorous vignettes and anecdotes about how successful the program was. The last thing many desire is a formal, systematic, and revealing evaluation. Although members of top management may actually *hope* for such systematic evaluation, their reward systems continue to *reward* ignorance in this area. And if the personnel department abdicates its responsibility, who is to step into the breach? The change agent himself? Hardly! He is likely to be too busy collecting anecdotal "evidence" of his own, for use with his next client.

Miscellaneous

Many additional examples could be cited of systems which in fact are rewarding other behaviors than those supposedly desired by the rewarder. A few of these are described briefly [below].

Most coaches disdain to discuss individual accomplishments, preferring to speak of teamwork, proper attitude, and a one-for-all spirit. Usually, however, rewards are distributed according to individual performance. The college basketball player who feeds his teammates instead of shooting will not compile impressive scoring statistics and is less likely to be drafted by the pros. The ballplayer who hits to right field to advance the runners will win neither the batting nor home run titles, and will be offered smaller raises. It, therefore, is rational for players to think of themselves first and the team second.

In business organizations where rewards are dispensed for unit performance or for individual goals achieved, without regard for overall effectiveness, similar attitudes often are observed. Under most Management by Objectives (MBO) systems, goals in areas where quantification is difficult often go unspecified. The organization, therefore, often is in a position where it *hopes* for employee effort in the areas of team building, interpersonal relations, creativity, etc., but it formally *rewards* none of these. In cases where promotions and raises are formally tied to MBO, the system itself contains a paradox in that it "asks employees to set challenging, risky goals, only to face smaller paychecks and possibly damaged careers if these goals are not accomplished" (Kerr, 1973a, p. 40).

It is *hoped* that administrators will pay attention to long-run costs and opportunities and will institute programs which will bear fruit later on. However, many organizational reward systems pay off for short-run sales and earnings only. Under such circumstances it is personally rational for officials to sacrifice long-term growth and profit (by selling off equipment and property, or by stifling research and development) for short-term advantages. This probably is most pertinent in the public sector, with the result that many public officials are unwilling to implement programs which will not show benefits by election time.

As a final, clear-cut example of a fouled-up reward system, consider the cost-plus contract or its next of kin, the allocation of next year's budget as a direct function of this year's expenditures. It probably is conceivable that those who award such budgets and contracts really hope for economy and prudence in spending. It is obvious, however, that adopting the proverb "to him who spends shall more be given," rewards not economy but spending itself.

Two Companies' Experiences

A Manufacturing Organization

A Midwest manufacturer of industrial goods had been troubled for some time by aspects of its organizational climate it believed dysfunctional. For research purposes, interviews were conducted with many employees and a questionnaire was administered on a company-wide basis, including plants and offices in several American and Canadian locations. The company strongly encouraged employee participation in the survey and made available time and space during the workday for completion of the instrument. All employees in attendance during the day of the survey completed the questionnaire. All instruments were collected directly by the researcher, who personally administered each session. Since no one employed by the firm handled the questionnaires, and since respondent names were not asked for, it seems likely that the pledge of anonymity given was believed.

A modified version of the Expect Approval scale (Litwin and Stringer, 1968) was included as part of the questionnaire. The instrument asked respondents to indicate the degree of approval or disapproval they could expect if they performed each of the described actions. A seven-point Likert scale was used, with 1 indicating that the action would probably bring strong disapproval and 7 signifying likely strong approval.

Although normative data for this scale from studies of other organizations are unavailable, it is possible to examine fruitfully the data obtained from this survey in several ways. First, it may be worth noting that the questionnaire data corresponded closely to information gathered through interviews. Furthermore, as can be seen from the results summarized in Table 1, sizable differences between various work units, and between employees at different job levels within the same work unit, were obtained. This suggests that response bias effects (social desirability in particular loomed as a potential concern) are not likely to be severe.

Most importantly, comparisons between scores obtained on the Expect Approval scale and a statement of problems which were the reason for the survey revealed that the same behaviors which managers in each division thought dysfunctional were those which lower level employees claimed were rewarded. As compared to job levels 1 to 8 in Division B (see Table 1), those in Division A claimed a much higher acceptance by management of "conforming" activities. Between 31 and 37 percent of Division A employees at levels 1–8 stated that going along with the majority, agreeing with the boss, and staying on everyone's good side brought approval; only once (level 5–8 responses to one of the three items) did a majority suggest that such actions would generate disapproval.

Furthermore, responses from Division A workers at levels 1–4 indicate that behaviors geared toward risk avoidance were as likely to be rewarded as to be punished. Only at job levels 9 and above was it apparent that the reward system was positively reinforcing behaviors desired by top management. Overall, the same "tendencies toward conservatism and apple-polishing at the lower levels" which divisional management had complained about during the interviews were those claimed by subordinates to be the most rational course of action in light of the existing reward system. Management apparently was not getting the behaviors it was *hoping* for, but it certainly was getting the behaviors it was perceived by subordinates to be *rewarding*.

An Insurance Firm

The Group Health Claims Division of a large eastern insurance company provides another rich illustration of a reward system which reinforces behaviors not desired by top management.

Attempting to measure and reward accuracy in paying surgical claims, the firm systematically keeps track of the number of returned checks and letters of complaint received from policyholders. However, underpayments are likely to provoke cries of outrage from the insured, while overpayments often are accepted in courteous silence. Since it often is impossible to tell from the physician's statement which of two surgical procedures, with different allowable benefits, was performed, and since writing for clarifications will interfere with other standards used by the firm concerning "percentage of claims paid within two days of receipt," the new hire in more than one claims section is soon acquainted with the informal norm: "When in doubt, pay it out!"

The situation would be even worse were it not for the fact that other features of the firm's reward system tend to neutralize those described. For example, annual "merit" increases are given to all employees, in one of the following three amounts:

1. If the worker is "outstanding" (a select category, into which no more than two employees per section may be placed): 5 percent

2. If the worker is "above average" (normally all workers not "outstanding" are so rated): 4 percent

Table 1

Summary of Two Divisions' Data Relevant to Conforming and Risk-Avoidance Behaviors
(extent to which subjects expect approval)

Dimension	Item	Division and Sample	Total Responses	Percentage of Workers Responding		
				1, 2, or 3 (Disapproval)	4	5, 6, or 7 (Approval)
Risk avoidance	Making a risky decision based on the best information available at the time, but which turns out wrong.	A, levels 1–4 (lowest)	127	61%	25%	14%
		A, levels 5–8	172	46	31	23
		A, levels 9 and above	17	41	30	30
		B, levels 1–4 (lowest)	31	58	26	16
		B, levels 5–8	19	42	42	16
		B, levels 9 and above	10	50	20	30
Risk	Setting extremely high and challenging standards and goals, and then narrowly failing to make them.	A, levels 1–4	122	47	28	25
		A, levels 5–8	168	33	26	41
		A, levels 9+	17	24	6	70
		B, levels 1–4	31	48	23	29
		B, levels 5–8	18	17	33	50
		B, levels 9+	10	30	0	70

Table 1 (continued)

Dimension	Item	Division and Sample	Total Responses	Percentage of Workers Responding		
				1, 2, or 3 (Disapproval)	4	5, 6, or 7 (Approval)
	Setting goals which are extremely easy to make and then making them.	A, levels 1–4	124	35%	30%	35%
		A, levels 5–8	171	47	27	26
		A, levels 9+	17	70	24	6
		B, levels 1–4	32	58	26	16
		B, levels 5–8	19	63	16	21
		B, levels 9+	10	80	0	20
	Being a "yes man" and always agreeing with the boss.	A, levels 1–4	126	46	17	37
		A, levels 5–8	180	54	14	31
		A, levels 9+	17	88	12	0
		B, levels 1–4	32	53	28	19
		B, levels 5–8	19	68	21	11
		B, levels 9+	10	80	10	10

Table 1 (continued)

Dimension	Item	Division and Sample	Total Responses	Percentage of Workers Responding		
				1, 2, or 3 (Disapproval)	4	5, 6, or 7 (Approval)
				40%	25%	35%
	Always going along with the majority.	A, levels 1–4	125	47	21	32
		A, levels 5–8	173	70	12	18
		A, levels 9+	17	61	23	16
		B, levels 1–4	31	68	11	21
		B, levels 5–8	19	80	10	10
		B, levels 9+	10			
	Being careful to stay on the good side of everyone, so that everyone agrees that you are a great guy.	A, levels 1–4	124	45	18	37
		A, levels 5–8	173	45	22	33
		A, levels 9+	17	64	6	30
		B, levels 1–4	31	54	23	23
		B, levels 5–8	19	73	11	16
		B, levels 9+	10	80	10	10

3. If the worker commits gross acts of negligence and irresponsibility for which he might be discharged in many other companies: 3 percent.

Now, since (*a*) the difference between the 5 percent theoretically attainable through hard work and the 4 percent attainable merely by living until the review date is small, and (*b*) since insurance firms seldom dispense much of a salary increase in cash (rather, the worker's insurance benefits increase, causing him to be further overinsured), many employees are rather indifferent to the possibility of obtaining the extra one percent reward and, therefore, tend to ignore the norm concerning indiscriminant payments.

However, most employees are not indifferent to the rule which states that, should absences or latenesses total three or more in any six-month period, the entire 4 or 5 percent due at the next "merit" review must be forfeited. In this sense the firm may be described as *hoping* for performance, while *rewarding* attendance. What it gets, of course, is attendance. (If the absence-lateness rule appears to the reader to be stringent, it really is not. The company counts "times," rather than "days" absent, and a 10-day absence, therefore, counts the same as one lasting 2 days. A worker in danger of accumulating a third absence within six months merely has to remain ill (away from work) during his second absence until his first absence is more than six months old. The limiting factor is that at some point his salary ceases, and his sickness benefits take over. This usually is sufficient to get the younger workers to return, but for those with 20 or more years' service, the company provides sickness benefits of 90 percent of normal salary, tax free! Therefore . . .)

Causes

Extremely diverse instances of systems which reward behavior A although the rewarder apparently hopes for behavior B have been given. These are useful to illustrate the breadth and magnitude of the phenomenon, but the diversity increases the difficulty of determining commonalities and establishing causes. However, four general factors may be pertinent to an explanation of why fouled-up reward systems seem to be so prevalent.

Fascination with an "Objective" Criterion

It has been mentioned elsewhere that:

Most "objective" measures of productivity are objective only in that their subjective elements are (*a*) determined in advance, rather than coming into play at the time of the formal evaluation, and (*b*) well concealed on the rating instrument itself. Thus industrial firms seeking to devise objective rating systems first decide, in an arbitrary manner, what dimensions are to be rated, . . . usually including some items having little to do with organizational effectiveness while excluding others that do. Only then does Personnel Division churn out official-looking documents on which all dimensions chosen to be rated are assigned point values, categories, or whatever. (Kerr, 1973b, p. 92)

Nonetheless, many individuals seek to establish simple, quantifiable standards against which to measure and reward performance. Such efforts may be successful in highly predictable areas within an organization, but are likely to cause goal displacement when applied anywhere else. Overconcern with attendance and lateness in the insurance firm and with number of people placed in the vocational rehabilitation division may have been largely responsible for the problems described in those organizations.

Overemphasis on Highly Visible Behaviors

Difficulties often stem from the fact that some parts of the task are highly visible while other parts are not. For example, publications are easier to demonstrate than teaching, and scoring baskets and hitting home runs are more readily observable than feeding teammates and advancing base runners. Similarly, the adverse consequences of pronouncing a sick person well are more visible than those sustained by labeling a well person sick. Team building and creativity are other examples of behaviors which may not be rewarded simply because they are hard to observe.

Hypocrisy

In some of the instances described, the rewarder may have been getting the desired behavior, notwithstanding claims that the behavior was not desired. This may be true, for example, of management's attitude toward apple-polishing in the manufacturing firm (a behavior which subordinates felt was rewarded, despite management's avowed dislike of the practice). This also may explain politicians' unwillingness to revise the penalties for disobedience of ecology laws, and the failure of top management to devise reward systems which would cause systematic evaluation of training and development programs.

Emphasis on Morality or Equity, Rather Than Efficiency

Some consideration of other factors prevents the establishment of a system which rewards behaviors desired by the rewarder. The felt obligation of many Americans to vote for one candidate or another, for example, may impair their ability to withhold support from politicians who refuse to discuss the issues. Similarly, the concern for spreading the risks and costs of wartime military service may outweigh the advantage to be obtained by committing personnel to combat until the war is over.

It should be noted that only with respect to the first two causes are reward systems really paying off for other than desired behaviors. In the case of the third and fourth causes, the system *is* rewarding behaviors desired by the rewarder, and the systems are fouled up only from the standpoints of those who believe the rewarder's public statements (cause 3), or those who seek to maximize efficiency, rather than other outcomes (cause 4).

Conclusions

Modern organization theory requires a recognition that the members of organizations and society possess divergent goals and motives. It, therefore, is unlikely that managers and their subordinates will seek the same outcomes. Three possible remedies for this potential problem are suggested.

Selection

It is theoretically possible for organizations to employ only those individuals whose goals and motives are wholly consonant with those of management. In such cases the same behaviors judged by subordinates to be rational would be perceived by management as desirable. State-of-the-art reviews of selection techniques, however, provide scant grounds for hope that such an approach would be successful (e.g., see Webster, 1964).

Training

Another theoretical alternative is for the organization to admit those employees whose goals are not consonant with those of management and then, through training, socialization, or whatever, alter employee goals to make them consonant. However, research on the effectiveness of such training programs, though limited, provides further grounds for pessimism (e.g., see Fiedler, 1972).

Altering the Reward System

What would have been the result if:

1. Nixon had been assured by his advisors that he could not win reelection except by discussing the issues in detail?
2. Physicians' conduct was subjected to regular examination by review boards for type 1 errors (calling healthy people ill) and to penalties (fines, censure, etc.) for errors of either type?
3. The president of XYZ Corporation had to choose between (*a*) spending $11 million for antipollution equipment and (*b*) incurring a 50–50 chance of going to jail for five years?

Managers who complain that their workers are not motivated might do well to consider the possibility that they have installed reward systems which are paying off for other behaviors than those they are seeking. This, in part, is what happened in Vietnam, and this is what regularly frustrates societal efforts to bring about honest politicians, civic-minded managers, etc. This certainly is what happened in both the manufacturing and the insurance companies.

A first step for such managers might be to find out what behaviors currently are being rewarded. Perhaps an instrument similar to that used in the manufacturing firm could be useful for this purpose. Chances are excellent that these managers will be surprised by what they find—that their firms are not rewarding what they assume they are. In fact, such undesirable behavior by organizational members as they have observed may be explained largely by the reward systems in use.

This is not to say that all organizational behavior is determined by formal rewards and punishments. Certainly it is true that in the absence of formal reinforcement some soldiers will be patriotic, some presidents will be ecology-minded, and some orphanage directors will care about children. The point, however, is that in such cases the rewarder is not *causing* the behaviors desired but is only a fortunate bystander. For an organization to *act* upon its members, the formal reward system should positively reinforce desired behaviors, not constitute an obstacle to be overcome.

It might be wise to underscore the obvious fact that there is nothing really new in what has been said. In both theory and practice these matters have been mentioned before. Thus, in many states good samaritan laws have been installed to protect doctors who stop to assist a stricken motorist. In states without such laws it is commonplace for doctors to refuse to stop, for fear of involvement in a subsequent lawsuit. In college basketball additional penalties have been instituted against players who foul their opponents deliberately. It has long been argued by Milton Friedman and others that penalties should be altered so as to make it irrational to disobey the ecology laws, and so on.

By altering the reward system the organization escapes the necessity of selecting only desirable people or of trying to alter undesirable ones, in Skinnerian terms (as described in Swanson, 1972, p. 704), "As for responsibility and goodness—as commonly defined—no one . . . would want or need them. They refer to a man's behaving well despite the absence of positive reinforcement that is obviously sufficient to explain it. Where such reinforcement exists, 'no one needs goodness.'"

Notes

[1] In Simon's (1957, pp. 76–77) terms, a decision is "subjectively rational" if it maximizes an individual's valued outcomes so far as his knowledge permits. A decision is "personally rational" if it is oriented toward the individual's goals.

[2] In one study (Garland, 1959) of 14,867 films for signs of tuberculosis, 1,216 positive readings turned out to be clinically negative; only 24 negative readings proved clinically active, a ratio of 50 to 1.

[3] Personal interviews conducted during 1972–73.

References

Barnard, Chester I. *The Functions of the Executive.* Cambridge, MA: Harvard University Press, 1968. (First published in 1936.)

Blau, Peter M., and W. Richard Scott. *Formal Organizations.* San Francisco: Chandler, 1962.

Fiedler, Fred E. "Predicting the Effects of Leadership Training and Experience from the Contingency Model." *Journal of Applied Psychology* 56 (1972), pp. 114–19.

Garland, L. H. "Studies of the Accuracy of Diagnostic Procedures." *American Journal Roentgenological, Radium Therapy Nuclear Medicine* 82 (1959), pp. 25–28.

Kerr, Steven. "Some Modifications in MBO as an OD Strategy." *Academy of Management Proceedings*, 1973a, pp. 39–42.

Kerr, Steven. "What Price Objectivity?" *American Sociologist* 8 (1973b), pp. 92–93.

Litwin, G. H., and R. A. Stringer, Jr. *Motivation and Organizational Climate.* Cambridge, MA: Harvard University Press, 1968.

Perrow, Charles. "The Analysis of Goals in Complex Organizations." In *Readings on Modern Organizations*, ed. A. Etzioni. Englewood, Cliffs, NJ: Prentice-Hall, 1969.

Scheff, Thomas J. "Decision Rules, Types of Error, and Their Consequences in Medical Diagnosis." In *Mathematical Explorations in Behavioral Science*, ed. F. Massarik and P. Ratoosh. Homewood, IL: Richard D. Irwin, 1965.

Simon, Herbert A. *Administrative Behavior.* New York: Free Press, 1957.

Swanson, G. E. "Review Symposium: Beyond Freedom and Dignity." *American Journal of Sociology* 78 (1972), pp. 702–5.

Webster, E. *Decision Making in the Employment Interview.* Montreal: Industrial Relations Center, McGill University, 1964.

7

Goal Setting— A Motivational Technique That Works

Gary P. Latham and Edwin A. Locke

The problem of how to motivate employees has puzzled and frustrated managers for generations. One reason the problem has seemed difficult, if not mysterious, is that motivation ultimately comes from within the individual and therefore cannot be observed directly. Moreover, most managers are not in a position to change an employee's basic personality structure. The best they can do is try to use incentives to direct the energies of their employees toward organizational objectives.

Money is obviously the primary incentive, since without it few if any employees would come to work. But money alone is not always enough to motivate high performance. Other incentives, such as participation in decision making, job enrichment, behavior modification, and organizational development, have been tried with varying degrees of success. A large number of research studies have shown, however, that one very straightforward technique—goal setting—is probably not only more effective than alternative methods, but may be the major mechanism by which these other incentives affect motivation. For example, a recent experiment on job enrichment demonstrated that unless employees in enriched jobs set higher, more specific goals than do those with unenriched jobs, job enrichment has absolutely no effect on productivity. Even money has been found most effective as a motivator when the bonuses offered are made contingent on attaining specific objectives.

The Goal-Setting Concept

The idea of assigning employees a specific amount of work to be accomplished—a specific task, a quota, a performance standard, an objective, or a deadline—is not new. The task concept, along with time and motion study and incentive pay, was the cornerstone of scientific management, founded by Frederick W. Taylor more than 70 years ago. He used his system to increase the productivity of blue collar workers. About 20 years ago the idea of goal setting reappeared under a new name, management by objectives, but this technique was designed for managers.

In a 14-year program of research, we have found that goal setting does not necessarily have to be part of a wider management system to motivate performance effectively. It can be used as a technique in its own right.

Laboratory and Field Research

Our research program began in the laboratory. In a series of experiments, individuals were assigned different types of goals on a variety of simple tasks—addition, brainstorming, assembling toys. Repeatedly it was found that those assigned hard goals performed better than did people assigned moderately difficult or easy goals. Furthermore, individuals who had specific, challenging goals outperformed those who were given such vague goals as to "do your best." Finally, we observed that pay and performance feedback led to improved performance only when these incentives led the individual to set higher goals.

While results were quite consistent in the laboratory, there was no proof that they could be applied to actual work settings. Fortunately, just as Locke published a summary of the laboratory studies in 1968, Latham began a separate series of experiments in the wood products industry that demonstrated the practical significance of these findings. The field studies did not start out as a validity test of a laboratory theory, but rather as a response to a practical problem.

In 1968, six sponsors of the American Pulpwood Association became concerned about increasing the productivity of independent loggers in the South. These loggers were entrepreneurs on whom the multimillion-dollar companies are largely dependent for their raw material. The problem was twofold. First, these entrepreneurs did not work for a single company; they worked for themselves. Thus they were free to (and often did) work two days one week, four days a second week, five half-days a third week, or whatever schedule they preferred. In short, these workers could be classified as marginal from the standpoint of their productivity and attendance, which were considered highly unsatisfactory by conventional company standards. Second, the major approach taken to alleviate this problem had been to develop equipment that would make the industry less dependent on this type of worker. A limitation of this approach was that many of the logging supervisors were unable to obtain the financing necessary to purchase a small tractor, let alone a rubber-tired skidder.

Consequently, we designed a survey that would help managers determine "what makes these people tick." The survey was conducted orally in the field with 292 logging supervisors. Complex statistical analyses of the data identified three basic types of supervisor. One type stayed on the job with their men, gave them instructions and explanations, provided them with training, read the trade magazines, and had little difficulty financing the equipment they needed. Still, the productivity of their units was at best mediocre.

The operation of the second group of supervisors was slightly less mechanized. These supervisors provided little training for their workforce. They simply drove their employees to the woods, gave them a specific production goal to attain for the day or week, left them alone in the woods unsupervised, and returned at night to take them home. Labor turnover was high and productivity was again average.

The operation of the third group of supervisors was relatively unmechanized. These leaders stayed on the job with their men, provided training, gave instructions and explanations, and in addition, set a specific production goal for the day or week. Not only was the crew's productivity high, but their injury rate was well below average.

Two conclusions were discussed with the managers of the companies sponsoring this study. First, mechanization alone will not increase the productivity of logging crews. Just as the average tax payer would probably commit more mathematical errors if he were to try to use a computer to complete his income tax return, the average logger misuses, and frequently abuses, the equipment he purchases (for example, drives a skidder with two flat tires, doesn't change the oil filter). This increases not only the logger's downtime, but also his costs which, in turn, can force him out of business. The second conclusion of the survey was that setting a specific production goal combined with supervisory presence to ensure goal commitment will bring about a significant increase in productivity.

These conclusions were greeted with the standard, but valid, cliché, "Statistics don't prove causation." And our comments regarding the value of machinery were especially irritating to these managers, many of whom had received degrees in engineering. So one of the companies decided to replicate the survey in order to check our findings.

The company's study placed each of 892 independent logging supervisors who sold wood to the company into one of three categories of supervisory styles our survey had identified—namely, (1) stays on the job but does not set specific production goals; (2) sets specific production goals but does not stay on the job; and (3) stays on the job and sets specific production goals. Once again, goal setting, in combination with the on-site presence of a supervisor, was shown to be the key to improved productivity.

Testing for the Hawthorne Effect

Management may have been unfamiliar with different theories of motivation, but it was fully aware of one label—the Hawthorne effect. Managers in these wood products companies remained unconvinced that anything so simple as staying on the job with the men and setting a specific production goal could have an appreciable effect on productivity. They pointed out that the results simply reflected the positive effects any supervisor would have on the work unit after giving his crew attention. And they were unimpressed by the laboratory experiments we cited—experiments showing that individuals who have a specific goal solve more arithmetic problems or assemble more tinker toys than do people who are told to "do your best." Skepticism prevailed.

But the country's economic picture made it critical to continue the study of inexpensive techniques to improve employee motivation and productivity. We were granted permission to run one more project to test the effectiveness of goal setting.

Twenty independent logging crews who were all but identical in size, mechanization level, terrain on which they worked, productivity, and attendance were located. The logging supervisors of these crews were in the habit of staying on the job with their men, but they did not set production goals. Half the crews were randomly selected to receive training in goal setting; the remaining crews served as a control group.

The logging supervisors who were to set goals were told that we had found a way to increase productivity at no financial expense to anyone. We gave the ten supervisors in the training group production tables developed through time-and-motion studies by the company's engineers. These tables made it possible to determine how much wood should be harvested in a given number of manhours. They were asked to use these tables as a guide in determining a specific production goal to assign their employees. In addition, each sawhand was given a tallymeter (counter) that he could wear on his belt. The sawhand was asked to punch the counter each time he felled a tree. Finally, permission was requested to measure the crew's performance on a weekly basis.

The ten supervisors in the control group—those who were not asked to set production goals—were told that the researchers were interested in learning the extent to which productivity is affected by absenteeism and injuries. They were urged to "do your best" to maximize the crew's productivity and attendance and to minimize injuries. It was explained that the data might be useful in finding ways to increase productivity at little or no cost to the wood harvester.

To control for the Hawthorne effect, we made an equal number of visits to the control group and the training group. Performance was measured for 12 weeks. During this time, the productivity of the goal-setting group was significantly higher than that of the control group. Moreover, absenteeism was significantly lower in the groups that set goals than in the groups who were simply urged to do their best. Injury and turnover rates were low in both groups.

Why should anything so simple and inexpensive as goal setting influence the work of these employees so significantly? Anecdotal evidence from conversations with both the loggers and the company foresters who visited them suggested several reasons.

Harvesting timber can be a monotonous, tiring job with little or no meaning for most workers. Introducing a goal that is difficult, but attainable, increases the challenge of the job. In addition, a specific goal makes it clear to the worker what it is he is expected to do. Goal feedback via the tallymeter and weekly recordkeeping provide the worker with a sense of achievement, recognition, and accomplishment. He can see how well he is doing now as against his past performance and, in some cases, how well he is doing in comparison with others. Thus the worker not only may expend greater effort, but may also devise better or more creative tactics for attaining the goal than those he previously used.

New Applications

Management was finally convinced that goal setting was an effective motivational technique for increasing the productivity of the independent woods worker in the South. The issue now raised by the management of another wood products company was whether the procedure could be used in the West with company logging operations in which the employees were unionized and paid by the hour. The previous study had involved employees on a piece-rate system, which was the practice in the South.

The immediate problem confronting this company involved the loading of logging trucks. If the trucks were underloaded, the company lost money. If the trucks were overloaded, however, the driver could be fined by the Highway Department and could ultimately lose his job. The drivers opted for underloading the trucks.

For three months management tried to solve this problem by urging the drivers to try harder to fill the truck to its legal net weight, and by developing weighing scales that could be attached to the truck. But this approach did not prove cost effective, because the scales continually broke down when subjected to the rough terrain on which the trucks traveled. Consequently, the drivers reverted to their former practice of underloading. For the three months in which the problem was under study the trucks were seldom loaded in excess of 58 to 63 percent of capacity.

At the end of the three-month period, the results of the previous goal-setting experiments were explained to the union. They were told three things—that the company would like to set a specific net weight goal for the drivers, that no monetary reward or fringe benefits other than verbal praise could be expected for improved performance, and that no one would be criticized for failing to attain the goal. Once again, the idea that simply setting a specific goal would solve a production problem seemed too incredible to be taken seriously by the union. However, they reached an agreement that a difficult, but attainable, goal of 94 percent of the truck's legal net weight would be assigned to the drivers, provided that no one could be reprimanded for failing to attain the goal. This latter point was emphasized to the company foremen in particular.

Within the first month, performance increased to 80 percent of the truck's net weight. After the second month, however, performance decreased to 70 percent. Interviews with the drivers indicated that they were testing management's statement that no punitive steps would be taken against them if their performance suddenly dropped. Fortunately for all concerned, no such steps were taken by the foremen, and performance exceeded 90 percent of the truck's capacity after the third month. Their performance has remained at this level to this day, seven years later.

The results over the nine-month period during which this study was conducted saved the company $250,000. This figure, determined by the company's accountants, is based on the cost of additional trucks that would have been required to deliver the same quantity of logs to the mill if goal setting had not been implemented. The dollars-saved figure is even higher when you factor in the cost of the additional diesel fuel that would have been consumed and the expenses incurred in recruiting and hiring the additional truck drivers.

Why could this procedure work without the union's demanding an increase in hourly wages? First, the drivers did not feel that they were really doing anything differently. This, of course, was not true. As a result of goal setting, the men began to record their truck weight in a pocket notebook, and they found themselves bragging about their accomplishments to their peers. Second, they viewed goal setting as a challenging game: "It was great to beat the other guy."

Competition was a crucial factor in bringing about goal acceptance and commitment in this study. However, we can reject the hypothesis that improved performance resulted solely from competition, because no special prizes or formal recognition programs were provided for those who came close to, or exceeded, the goal. No effort was made by the company to single out one "winner." More important, the opportunity for competition among drivers had existed before goal setting was instituted; after all, each driver knew his own truck's weight, and the truck weight of each of the 36 other drivers every time he hauled wood into the yard. In short, competition affected productivity only in the sense that it led to the acceptance of, and commitment to, the goal. It was the setting of the goal itself and the working toward it that brought about increased performance and decreased costs.

Participative Goal Setting

The inevitable question always raised by management was raised here: "We know goal setting works. How can we make it work better?" Was there one best method for setting goals? Evidence for a "one best way" approach was cited by several managers, but it was finally concluded that different approaches would work best under different circumstances.

It was hypothesized that the woods workers in the South, who had little or no education, would work better with assigned goals, while the educated workers in the West would achieve higher productivity if they were allowed to help set the goals themselves. Why the focus on education? Many of the uneducated workers in the South could be classified as culturally disadvantaged. Such persons often lack self-confidence, have a poor sense of time, and are not very competitive. The cycle of skill mastery, which in turn guarantees skill levels high enough to prevent discouragement, doesn't apply to these employees. If, for example, these people were allowed to participate in goal setting, the goals might be too difficult or they might be too easy. On the other hand, participation for the educated worker was considered critical in effecting maximum goal acceptance. Since these conclusions appeared logical, management initially decided that no research was necessary. This decision led to hours of further discussion.

The same questions were raised again and again by the researchers. What if the logic were wrong? Can we afford to implement these decisions without evaluating them systematically? Would we implement decisions regarding a new approach to tree planting without first testing it? Do we care more about trees than we do about people? Finally, permission was granted to conduct an experiment.

Logging crews were randomly appointed to either participative goal setting, assigned (nonparticipative) goal setting, or a do-your-best condition. The results were startling. The uneducated crews, consisting primarily of black employees who participated in goal setting, set significantly higher goals and attained them more often than did those whose goals were assigned by the supervisor. Not surprisingly, their performance was higher. Crews with assigned goals performed no better than did those who were urged to do their best to improve their productivity. The performance of white, educationally advantaged workers was higher with assigned rather than participatively set goals, although the difference was not statistically significant. These results were precisely the opposite of what had been predicted.

Another study comparing participative and assigned goals was conducted with typists. The results supported findings obtained by researchers at General Electric years before. It did not matter so much *how* the goal was set. What mattered was *that* a goal was set. The study demonstrated that both assigned and participatively set goals led to substantial improvements in typing speed. The process by which these gains occurred, however, differed in the two groups.

In the participative group, employees insisted on setting very high goals regardless of whether they had attained their goal the previous week. Nevertheless, their productivity improved—an outcome consistent with the theory that high goals lead to high performance.

In the assigned-goal group, supervisors were highly supportive of employees. No criticism was given for failure to attain the goals. Instead, the supervisor lowered the goal after failure so that the employee would be certain to attain it. The goal was then raised gradually each week until the supervisor felt the employee was achieving his or her potential. The result? Feelings of accomplishment and achievement on the part of the worker and improved productivity for the company.

These basic findings were replicated in a subsequent study of engineers and scientists. Participative goal setting was superior to assigned goal setting only to the degree that it led to the setting of higher goals. Both participative and assigned-goal groups outperformed groups that were simply told to "do your best."

An additional experiment was conducted to validate the conclusion that participation in goal setting may be important only to the extent that it leads to the setting of difficult goals. It was performed in a laboratory setting in which the task was to brainstorm uses for wood. One group was asked to "do your best" to think of as many ideas as possible. A second group took part in deciding, with the experimenter, the specific number of ideas each person would generate. These goals were, in turn, assigned to individuals in a third group. In this way, goal difficulty was held constant between the assigned-goal and participative groups. Again, it was found that specific, difficult goals—whether assigned or set through participation—led to higher performance than did an abstract or generalized goal such as "do your best." And, when goal difficulty was held constant, there was no significant difference in the performance of those with assigned as compared with participatively set goals.

These results demonstrate that goal setting in industry works just as it does in the laboratory. Specific, challenging goals lead to better performance than do easy or vague goals, and feedback motivates higher performance only when it leads to the setting of higher goals.

It is important to note that participation is not only a motivational tool. When a manager has competent subordinates, participation is also a useful device for increasing the manager's knowledge and thereby improving decision quality. It can lead to better decisions through input from subordinates.

A representative sample of the results of field studies of goal setting conducted by Latham and others is shown in figure 1. Each of these ten studies compared the performance of employees given specific challenging goals with those given "do best" or no goals. Note that goal setting has been successful across a wide variety of jobs and industries. The effects of goal setting have been recorded for as long as seven years after the onset of the program, although the results of most studies have been followed for only a few weeks or months. The median improvement in performance in the ten studies shown in figure 1 was 17 percent.

Figure 1
Representative Field Studies of Goal Setting

Researcher(s)	Task	Duration of Study or of Significant Effects	Percent of Change in performance[a]
Blumenfeld & Leidy	Servicing soft drink coolers	Unspecified	+27
Dockstader	Keypunching	3 mos.	+27
Ivancevich	Skilled technical jobs	9 mos.	+15
Ivancevich	Sales	9 mos.	+24
Kim and Hamner	5 telephone service jobs	3 mos.	+13
Latham and Baldes	Loading trucks	9 mos.[b]	+26
Latham and Yukl	Logging	2 mos.	+18
Latham and Yukl	Typing	5 weeks	+11
Migliore	Mass production	2 years	+16
Umstot, Beg, and Mitchell	Coding land parcels	1–2 days[c]	+16

[a] Percentage changes were obtained by subtracting pre-goal-setting performance from post-goal-setting performance and dividing by pre-goal-setting performance. Different experimental groups were combined where appropriate. If a control group was available, the percentage figure represents the difference of the percentage changes between the experimental and control groups. If multiple performance measures were used, the median improvement on all measures was used. The authors would like to thank Dena Feren and Vicki McCaleb for performing these calculations.
[b] Performance remained high for seven years.
[c] Simulated organization.

A Critical Incidents Survey

To explore further the importance of goal setting in the work setting, Dr. Frank White conducted another study in two plants of a high-technology, multinational corporation on the East Coast. Seventy-one engineers, 50 managers, and 31 clerks were asked to describe a specific instance when they were especially productive and a specific instance when they were especially unproductive on their present jobs. Responses were classified according to a reliable coding scheme. Of primary interest here are the external events perceived by employees as being responsible for the high-productivity and low-productivity incidents. The results are shown in figure 2.

Figure 2
Events Perceived as Causing High and Low Productivity*

Event	Percent of Times Event Caused	
	High Productivity	Low Productivity
Goal pursuit/Goal blockage	17.1	23.0
Large amount of work/Small amount of work	12.5	19.0
Deadline or schedule/No deadline	15.1	3.3
Smooth work routine/Interrupted routine	5.9	14.5
Intrinsic/Extrinsic factors	50.6	59.8
Interesting task/Uninteresting task	17.1	11.2
Increased responsibility/Decreased responsibility	13.8	4.6
Anticipated promotion/Promotion denied	1.3	0.7
Verbal recognition/Criticism	4.6	2.6
People/Company conditions	36.8	19.1
Pleasant personal relationships/ Unpleasant personal relationships	10.5	9.9
Anticipated pay increase/Pay increase denied	1.3	1.3
Pleasant working conditions/ Unpleasant working conditions	0.7	0.7
Other (miscellaneous)	—	9.3

* $N = 152$ in this study by Frank White.

The first set of events—pursuing a specific goal, having a large amount of work, working under a deadline, or having an uninterrupted routine—accounted for more than half the high-productivity events. Similarly, the converse of these—goal blockage, having a small amount of work, lacking a deadline, and suffering work interruptions—accounted for nearly 60 percent of the low-productivity events. Note that the first set of four categories are all relevant to goal setting and the second set to a lack of goals or goal blockage. The goal category itself—that of pursuing an attainable goal or goal blockage—was the one most frequently used to describe high- and low-productivity incidents.

The next four categories, which are more pertinent to Frederick Herzberg's motivator-hygiene theory—task interest, responsibility, promotion, and recognition—are less important, accounting for 36.8 percent of the high-productivity incidents (the opposite of these four categories accounted for 19.1 percent of the lows). The remaining categories were even less important.

Employees were also asked to identify the responsible agent behind the events that had led to high and low productivity. In both cases, the employees themselves, their immediate supervisors, and the organization were the agents most frequently mentioned.

The concept of goal setting is a very simple one. Interestingly, however, we have gotten two contradictory types of reaction when the idea was introduced to managers. Some claimed it was so simple and self-evident that everyone, including themselves, already used it. This, we have found, is not true. Time after time we have gotten the following response from subordinates after goal setting was introduced: "This is the first time I knew what my supervisor expected of me on this job." Conversely, other managers have argued that the idea would not work, precisely because it is so simple (implying that something more radical and complex was needed). Again, results proved them wrong.

But these successes should not mislead managers into thinking that goal setting can be used without careful planning and forethought. Research and experience suggest that the best results are obtained when the following steps are followed:

Setting the goal.   The goal set should have two main characteristics. First, it should be specific rather than vague: "Increase sales by 10 percent" rather than "Try to improve sales." Whenever possible, there should be a time limit for goal accomplishment: "Cut costs by 3 percent in the next six months."

Second, the goal should be challenging yet reachable. If accepted, difficult goals lead to better performance than do easy goals. In contrast, if the goals are perceived as unreachable, employees will not accept them. Nor will employees get a sense of achievement from pursuing goals that are never attained. Employees with low self-confidence or ability should be given more easily attainable goals than those with high self-confidence and ability.

There are at least five possible sources of input, aside from the individual's self-confidence and ability, that can be used to determine the particular goal to set for a given individual.

The scientific management approach pioneered by Frederick W. Taylor uses time and motion study to determine a fair day's work. This is probably the most objective technique available, but it can be used only where the task is reasonably repetitive and standardized. Another drawback is that this method often leads to employee resistance, especially in cases where the new standard is substantially higher than previous performance and where rate changes are made frequently.

More readily accepted, although less scientific than time and motion study, are standards based on the average past performance of employees. This method was used successfully in some of our field studies. Most employees consider this approach fair but, naturally, in cases where past performance is far below capacity, beating that standard will be extremely easy.

Since goal setting is sometimes simply a matter of judgment, another technique we have used is to allow the goal to be set jointly by supervisor and subordinate. The participative approach may be less scientific than time and motion study, but it does lead to ready acceptance by both employee and immediate superior in addition to promoting role clarity.

External constraints often affect goal setting, especially among managers. For example, the goal to produce an item at a certain price may be dictated by the actions of competitors, and deadlines may be imposed externally in line with contract agreements. Legal regulations, such as attaining a certain reduction in pollution levels by a certain date, may affect goal setting as well. In these cases, setting the goal is not so much the problem as is figuring out a method of reaching it.

Finally, organizational goals set by the board of directors or upper management will influence the goals set by employees at lower levels. This is the essence of the MBO process.

Another issue that needs to be considered when setting goals is whether they should be designed for individuals or for groups. Rensis Likert and a number of other human relations experts argue for group goal setting on grounds that it promotes cooperation and team spirit. But one could argue that individual goals better promote individual responsibility and make it easier to appraise individual performance. The degree of task interdependence involved would also be a factor to consider.

Obtaining goal commitment. If goal setting is to work, then the manager must ensure that subordinates will accept and remain committed to the goals. Simple instruction backed by positive support and an absence of threats or intimidation were enough to ensure goal acceptance in most of our studies. Subordinates must perceive the goals as fair and reasonable and they must trust management, for if they perceive the goals as no more than a means of exploitation, they will be likely to reject the goals.

It may seem surprising that goal acceptance was achieved so readily in the field studies. Remember, however, that in all cases the employees were receiving wages or a salary (although these were not necessarily directly contingent on goal attainment). Pay in combination with the supervisor's benevolent authority and supportiveness were sufficient to bring about goal acceptance. Recent research indicates that whether goals are assigned or set participatively, supportiveness on the part of the immediate superior is critical. A supportive manager or supervisor does not use goals to threaten subordinates, but rather to clarify what is expected of them. His or her role is that of a helper and goal facilitator.

As noted earlier, the employee gets a feeling of pride and satisfaction from the experience of reaching a challenging but fair performance goal. Success in reaching a goal also tends to reinforce acceptance of future goals. Once goal setting is introduced, informal competition frequently arises among the employees. This further reinforces commitment and may lead employees to raise the goals spontaneously. A word of caution here, however: We do not recommend setting up formal competition, as this may lead employees to place individual goals ahead of company goals. The emphasis should be on accomplishing the task, getting the job done, not "beating" the other person.

When employees resist assigned goals, they generally do so for one of two reasons. First, they may think they are incapable of reaching the goal because they lack confidence, ability, knowledge, and the like. Second, they may not see any personal benefit—either in terms of personal pride or in terms of external rewards like money, promotion, recognition—in reaching assigned goals.

There are various methods of overcoming employee resistance to goals. One possibility is more training designed to raise the employee's level of skill and self-confidence. Allowing the subordinate to participate in setting the goal—deciding on the goal level—is another method. This was found most effective among uneducated and minority group employees, perhaps because it gave them a feeling of control over their fate. Offering monetary bonuses or other rewards (recognition, time off) for reaching goals may also help.

The last two methods may be especially useful where there is a history of labor-management conflict and where employees have become accustomed to a lower level of effort than currently considered acceptable. Group incentives may also encourage goal acceptance, especially where there is a group goal, or when considerable cooperation is required.

Providing support elements. A third step to take when introducing goal setting is to ensure the availability of necessary support elements. That is, the employee must be given adequate resources—money, equipment, time, help—as well as the freedom to utilize them in attaining goals, and company policies must not work to block goal attainment.

Before turning an employee loose with these resources, however, it's wise to do a quick check on whether conditions are optimum for reaching the goal set. First, the supervisor must make sure that the employee has sufficient ability and knowledge to be able to reach the goal. Motivation without knowledge is useless. This, of course, puts a premium on proper selection and training and requires that the supervisor know the capabilities of subordinates when goals are assigned. Asking an employee to formulate an action plan for reaching the goal, as in MBO, is very useful, as it will indicate any knowledge deficiencies.

Second, the supervisor must ensure that the employee is provided with precise feedback so that he will know to what degree he's reaching or falling short of his goal and can thereupon adjust his level of effort or strategy accordingly. Recent research indicates that, while feedback is not a sufficient condition for improved performance, it is a necessary condition. A useful way to present periodic feedback is through the use of charts or graphs that plot performance over time.

Elements involved in taking the three steps described are shown in figure 3, which illustrates in outline form our model of goal setting.

Figure 3
Goal-Setting Model

Interpersonal and Group Behavior

The Hawthorne experiments formally "discovered" the impact of social and psychological factors on workers' behavior. Since that time, managers have become increasingly aware that interpersonal and group behavior can have negative as well as positive effects on the organizations in which they exist.

In his article, "Cosmopolitans and Locals," Alvin Gouldner discusses two social roles among employees in organizations. Professional employees tend to adopt a "cosmopolitan" role, which is characterized by identification with reference groups outside of the organization, a high commitment to their specialty, and less loyalty to their employer. "Locals," conversely, tend to be nonprofessionals who identify with groups within their organization, are less committed to specialized skills, and are more loyal to their employer.

Although the utilization of groups as decision-making entities in organizations has become more common in recent decades—due primarily to the realization that groups often make better decisions—there are potential hazards in group decision making. Norman R. F. Maier, in "Assets and Liabilities in Group Decision Making," assesses both the assets (greater sum total of knowledge and information, greater number of approaches to a problem, increased acceptance through participation, better comprehension of the decision) and the liabilities (social pressure, influence of a vocal minority, individual domination, conflicting secondary goals) of group problem solving. Maier finds that several factors can serve as assets *or* liabilities and concludes by examining the role of the group leader in capitalizing on group assets and avoiding group liabilities.

It is generally accepted that Kurt Lewin "invented" the field of group dynamics—that is, he was responsible, either directly or indirectly, for most of the pioneering research on group dynamics. Two of Lewin's close associates, Dorwin Cartwright and Alvin Zander, went on to produce what was for many years the standard text on the subject, *Group Dynamics.* They defined "group dynamics" as the field of inquiry dedicated to advancing knowledge about the nature of groups, how they develop, and their relationships to individuals, other groups, and larger institutions. Included here, the first chapter of their text, "Origins of Group Dynamics," traces the evolution of the field of group dynamics and reviews several of the more significant pioneering research studies on group behavior.

"Group and Intergroup Relationships," a selection from Edgar H. Schein's 1970 book, *Organizational Psychology,* focuses on the nature of groups in organizations. After defining a group as any number of people who interact with one another, are aware of one another, and perceive themselves to be a group, Schein examines the nature of formal and informal groups in organizations, as well as the functions fulfilled by organizational groups. Factors that determine the kinds of groups that exist in an organization are discussed, and the questions of whether these groups fulfill organizational functions, personal functions, or both are analyzed.

While "groupthink"—the psychological drive for consensus that suppresses dissent and appraisal of alternatives in cohesive decision-making groups—has always been with us, the conceptualization of the phenomenon is credited to Irving L. Janis. In the preface to his 1972 book, *Victims of Groupthink,* Janis says the basic idea occurred to him while he was reading an account of the ill-fated Bay of Pigs invasion of Cuba in a biography of President John F. Kennedy. Janis asked himself, "How could bright, shrewd men like John F. Kennedy and his advisors be taken in by the CIA's stupid, patchwork plan?" In his article "Groupthink," published one year before his book, Janis discusses the main symptoms of groupthink, using the Bay of Pigs invasion, Vietnam, and Pearl Harbor as examples of the dire consequences that can occur when groupthink stalks the corridors of power. He concludes by citing a list of remedies drawn from two highly successful examples of group decision making—the formulation of the Marshall Plan during the Truman administration and the handling of the Cuban Missile Crisis by President Kennedy and his advisors. Given the current popularity of "cooperative," or "consensus," approaches to group decision making, the chance that a group will deteriorate into groupthink is significant. Unlike the true "consensus" approach, groupthink suppresses conflict and independent critical thinking.

The next selection in section III is from the best-selling book, *Born to Win.* In "Transactional Analysis," Muriel James and Dorothy Jongeward review Eric Berne's theory that all people have three ego states that are separate and distinct sources of behavior: the Parent ego state, the Adult ego state, and the Child ego state.

The Parent ego state contains the attitudes and behaviors incorporated from external sources, primarily parents. When you are acting, thinking, and feeling as your parents did, you are in your Parent ego state. The Adult ego state is oriented to current reality and an objective assessment of information. When you are focusing on current reality, gathering facts, and computing objectively, you are in your Adult ego state. The Child ego state contains all of the impulses that come naturally to a child. When you are feeling and acting as you did as a child, you are in your Child ego state. James and Jongeward describe how interactions between people can be analyzed using a transactional analysis model. These "transactions" can be classified as complementary, crossed, or ulterior.

Jay Hall's article discusses "the Johari Window" developed by Joe Luft and Harry Ingham. Their model is based on two dimensions of interpersonal behavior: the degree to which you openly expose information to others and the degree to which you actively solicit feedback from others. The Johari Window consists of four categories of interpersonal awareness. Region 1 focuses on that which is "known to self" and "known to others" and is labeled as "Open." Region 2, referred to as "Blind," relates to "not known to self" but "known to others." Region 3, the "Hidden" category, deals with situations "known to self" but "not known to others." Region 4, called "Unknown," refers to aspects of interpersonal relations that are "not known to self" and "not known to others." Hall points out how a change in one's awareness level impacts numerous aspects of intra- and intergroup behavior, and discusses the relationship between management style and the Johari Window.

In "The Abilene Paradox," Jerry Harvey tells the story of how his family ended up taking an unpleasant trip to Abilene when no one really wanted to go. The article points out the danger of allowing casual suggestions and assumptions to go unchallenged, how those ideas can gain momentum and how they can lead to unintended consequences. Harvey clearly explains the causes of self-censorship, a method for diagnosing the paradox, and suggestions for overcoming the problem.

The next reading, "Stages of Group Development" by Bruce Tuckman and Mary Ann Jensen, suggests that teams evolve through five distinct stages:

1. The *"forming" stage.* This initial stage is marked by uncertainty and even confusion. Group members usually are highly motivated, but they are unsure about the group's purpose, structure, and goals.
2. The *"storming" stage.* This stage is characterized by conflict and confrontation as the group strives to clarify its structure, goals, and roles.
3. The *"norming" stage.* In this stage, group members begin to settle into cooperation and collaboration. They start evolving into a "team" characterized by high cohesion and group identity.
4. The *"performing" stage.* At this stage, the team has developed into a fully functioning group that is highly committed to accomplishing its goals.
5. *Termination.* At this stage, the group disbands because it has achieved its goals, its responsibilities have been transferred, or the group is no longer needed.

In "Self-Directed Work Teams," Ralph Stayer describes how he learned to let his workers lead at his family business, Johnsonville Foods. Stayer observed that in spite of his company's financial success, employees were bored with their roles, made stupid mistakes, and took no responsibility for their work. They showed up in the morning, halfheartedly did what they were told to do, and then went home.

Stayer discusses how he transformed Johnsonville Foods from a profitable, traditionally managed enterprise into an innovative, rapidly growing, and enormously successful organization by relinquishing control and empowering employees and teams to be all they wanted to be. Stayer's guidelines for improving performance include the following observations:

- People want to be great.
- Performance hinges on individuals' expectations.
- Expectations are driven by many things, including vision, goals, compensation systems, production practices, and decision making.
- The actions of managers shape expectations.
- Learning is an ongoing process.
- To change performance, managers and employees must change themselves first.

1

Cosmopolitans and Locals

Alvin W. Gouldner

Sociologists have long since documented the empirical utility of role theory. It may be, however, that concepts stagnate when small theoretical investments yield large empirical dividends. The very currency of role concepts may invite complacency concerning their theoretical clarity.

Although the larger theory of social roles could doubtless profit from serious recasting and systematic reappraisal,[1] this is not the place for so ambitious an undertaking. All that will be essayed here are some limited questions relating to role analysis. In particular, an attempt will be made to develop certain distinctions between what will be termed "manifest" and "latent" identities and roles.

Since role theory already encompasses a welter of concepts,[2] the introduction of new concepts requires firm justification. Concepts commend themselves to social scientists only as tools with which to resolve problematic situations. Unless this criterion is insisted upon, there inevitably eventuates a sterile formalism and a needless proliferation of neologisms. We must therefore justify the proposed distinction between manifest and latent roles by indicating the theoretic context from which it emerged and by showing its use in various studies.

Theoretical Considerations

A social role is commonly defined as a set of expectations oriented toward people who occupy a certain "position" in a social system or group. It is a rare discussion of social role that does not at some point make reference to the "position" occupied by a group member. Despite its frequent use, however, the notion of a social "position" is obscure and not likely to provide clean-cut directives for social research. Often, it is used as little more than a geometrical metaphor with little value for guiding the empirical studies of behavioral scientists.

It seems that what is meant by a "position" is the social identity which has been assigned to a person by members of his group. That is, group members may be regarded as acting in the following manner: (1) They observe or impute to a person certain characteristics; they observe certain aspects of his behavior or appearance which they employ as clues to enable themselves to answer the question "Who is he?" (2) These observed or imputed characteristics are then related to and interpreted in terms of a set of culturally prescribed *categories* which have been learned during the course of socialization. Conversely, the culturally learned categories focus attention upon certain aspects of the individual's behavior and appearance. (3) In this manner the individual is "pigeonholed"; that is, he is held to be a certain "type" of person, a teacher, boy, man, or woman. The assignment of a "social identity" is the process of applying culturally prescribed categories. The types or categories to which he has been assigned are his social identities. (4) When this assignment of identity is consensually or otherwise validated in the group, people then "ask themselves" what they know about such a type; they mobilize their beliefs concerning it. Corresponding to different social identities are differing sets of expectations, differing configurations of rights and obligations. In these terms, then, a social role is a shared set of expectations directed toward people who are assigned a given social identity.

Obviously the people in any one group have a variety of social identities. In a classroom, for example, there are those identified as "students," but these same people are also identified as men, women, young, mature, and so on. In the classroom situation, it is primarily their identity as students that others in the group regard as central and properly salient. It is also the expectations congruent with this salient identity that are most appropriately activated and have the fullest claim to application. But while the expectations congruent with the student identity are most institutionally relevant and legitimately mobilizable, it is clear that in various ways certain of the other identities do "intrude" and affect the group's behavior in sociologically interesting ways. For example, there is usually something happening between the students that is influenced by their sexual identities.

It is necessary to distinguish, then, between those social identities of group members which are consensually regarded as relevant to them in a given setting and those which group members define as being irrelevant, inappropriate to consider, or illegitimate to take into account. The former can be called the *manifest* social identities, the latter, the *latent* social identities. Let us be clear that "social identities," manifest or latent, are not synonymous with the concept of social status. Social identities have to do with the way in which an individual is in fact *perceived* and classified by others in terms of a system of culturally standardized categories. Social statuses, however, refer to the complex of culturally standardized categories to which individuals in a group may be assigned; they are sometimes also defined as the hierarchical "position" of the individual in relation to others, as well as the culturally prescribed expectations directed toward those in this position.[3]

Expectations which are associated with the manifest social identities can be termed the manifest social *roles*, while expectations oriented toward the latent identities can be called the latent social roles. Just as others can be oriented toward an individual's latent identities, so, too, can the individual himself be oriented to his own latent identities. This is, of course, to be expected in the light of Mead's role theory, which stresses that an individual's self-conception is a function of the judgments and orientations which significant others have toward him.

At the present time, little systematic attention is given to the functioning of either latent identities or roles. It is too easy to focus on the more evident manifest identities and roles in a group. As a result, even in a world on which Freudian theory has made its impact, many sociologists give little indication of the fact that the people they study in offices, factories, schools, or hospitals are also males and females. The sociologist's assumption often seems to be that the latent identities and roles are as irrelevant as the people whom they are studying conventionally pretend. The fact seems to be however, that these do affect group behavior.

This is, of course, obvious from the most commonplace of questions. For example: Are the career chances of industrial workers affected by their ethnic identity? Are "old-timers" in a group more or less friendly toward each other than with those of less tenure? Do college professors take note of and behave somewhat differently toward members of the college football team who are taking their courses? Do Unitarian ministers sometimes refer to their "Jewish" parishioners?

While it is obvious that individuals in a group have a variety of social identities, and not merely one, we need conceptual tools that firmly distinguish between different types of social identities and facilitate analysis of the varying ways in which they influence group behavior. While it is obvious that a group member may have many social identities, it needs to be stressed that not all of them are regarded as equally relevant or legitimately activated in that group. This is precisely the point to which the concepts of latent identities and roles direct attention.

This implies that when group members orient themselves to the latent identities of others in their group, they are involved in a relationship with them which is not culturally *prescribed* by the group norms governing their manifest roles. It implies, also, that they are utilizing reference persons or groups which are not culturally prescribed for those in their roles. Thus the concepts of latent identities and roles focus research on those patterns of social interaction, and lines of orientation, which are not prescribed by the group under study. It would also seem clear that latent identities and roles are important because they exert pressure upon the manifest roles, often impairing conformity with their requirements and endemically threatening the equilibrium of the manifest role system. In contrast, the concept of manifest roles focuses on the manner in which group norms yield *prescribed* similarities in the behavior and beliefs of those performing the same role.

The role of "elders" in a gerontocratic society, with the deference and respect due them by their juniors, is in these terms a manifest role. For, in this case, the rights and obligations of elders are culturally prescribed. Here to be an "elder" is a societally relevant identity. Note, however, that even in the American factory elders may also receive some special consideration and similar if not equal deference from their juniors. Here, however, the role of the elder is a latent one, being based upon an assignment of identity which is not regarded as fully legitimate or as clearly relevant in the factory, even if fully acknowledged in the larger society.

This distinction between manifest and latent roles directs us to search out and specify the latent identities, and the expectations corresponding to them, which crosscut and underlie those which are culturally prescribed in the group under study. The concept of latent roles suggests that people playing *different* manifest roles may be performing *similar* latent roles and, conversely, that those performing the same manifest role may be playing *different* latent roles. The concept of latent role may then aid in accounting for some of the differences (in behavior or belief) among those in the same manifest role or for some of the similarities among those having different manifest roles. Neither the similarities nor the differences mentioned above need be due to the intrusion of "personality" factors or other individual attributes. They may derive from the nature of the latent roles, that is, from the responses to the latent identities of group members, which yield culturally unprescribed yet structured interactions and orientations with others.

The problem that will be explored in the following analysis is whether there are latent identities and roles of general significance for the study of the modern complex organization. That is, can we discern latent identities and roles which are common to a number of different complex organizations? In this connection, we will explore the possibility that, as distinguished from and in addition to their manifest identities, members of formal organizations may have two latent social identities, here called "cosmopolitan" and "local."[4] Development of these concepts may enable organizational analysis to proceed without focusing solely on the relatively visible, culturally differentiated, manifest organizational identities and roles, but without confining analysis to an undifferentiated blob of "bureaucrats." There are of course other latent identities that are of organizational significance.

Concerning Cosmopolitans and Locals

A number of prior researches have identified certain role-playing patterns which appear convergent with each other and which, further, seem to be commonly based upon those latent identities which will be called "cosmopolitans."

In a study of a factory,[5] "The General Gypsum Company," I noted a type of company executive which I called the "expert." Experts tend to be staff men who never seem to win the complete confidence of the company's highest authorities and are kept removed from the highest reaches of power. Much like staff men in other companies, these experts can advise but cannot command. They are expected to "sell" management on their plans, but cannot order them put into effect. It is widely recognized that these experts are not given the "real promotions." The expert is under pressure to forego the active pursuit of his specialty if he wishes to ascend in the company hierarchy. Among the reasons for the experts' subordination may be the fact that they are less frequently identified as "company men" than others in the executive group. The "company man," a pervasive category for the informal classification of industrial personnel, is one who is regarded as having totally committed his career aspirations to his employing company and as having indicated that he wishes to remain with it indefinitely. In effect, then, company personnel were using a criterion of "loyalty to the company" in assigning social identities to members of their organization. A company man is one who is identified as "loyal."

Experts are less likely to be identified in this manner in part because their relatively complex, seemingly mysterious skills, derived from long formal training, lead them to make a more basic commitment to their job than to the organization in which they work. Furthermore, because of their intensive technical training, experts have greater opportunities for horizontal job mobility and can fill jobs in many different organizations. As E. C. Hughes would say, they are more likely to be "itinerants." Consequently, experts are less likely to be committed to their employing organization than to their specialty.

The expert's skills are continually being refined and developed by professional peers outside of his employing organization. Moreover, his continued standing as a competent professional often cannot be validated by members of his own organization, since they are not knowledgeable enough about it. For these reasons, the expert is more likely than others to esteem the good opinion of professional peers elsewhere; he is disposed to seek recognition and acceptance from "outsiders." We can say that he is more likely to be oriented to a reference group composed of others not a part of his employing organization, that is, an "outer reference group."

Leonard Reissman's study of the role conceptions of government bureaucrats provides another case in point.[6] Among these is the "functional bureaucrat" who is found to be oriented toward groups outside of his employing bureaucracy and is especially concerned with securing recognition from his professional peers elsewhere. If he is an economist, for example, he wants other economists to think well of him, whether or not they are his organizational associates. The functional bureaucrats are also more likely to associate with their professional peers than with their bureaucratic colleagues. They are less likely than other types of bureaucrats to have sentiments of loyalty to their employing bureaucracy. Finally, more than other bureaucrats their satisfaction with their job depends upon the degree to which their work conforms with professional standards, and they seem to be more deeply committed to their professional skills. In short, Reissman's "functional bureaucrat" is much the same as our "expert," insofar as both tend to manifest lesser organizational loyalty, deeper job commitment, and an outer reference group orientation, as compared with their colleagues.

A third study, by Vernon J. Bentz,[7] of a city college faculty, again indicates the interrelationship of these variables and suggests their relevance in another organizational setting. Bentz divided the college faculty into two groups, those who publish much and those publishing little or nothing. Publication as such is not of course theoretically interesting but it becomes so if taken as an index of something else. The difficulty is that it is an ambiguous index. Within limits, it seems reasonable to treat it as an index of the degree of commitment to professional skills. However, "high" publication might also indicate a desire to communicate with other, like professionals in different organizations. The high publisher must also take cognizance of the publications which others elsewhere are producing. Thus high publication may also be an index of an outer reference group orientation. High publishers also tend to deemphasize the importance which their own college department had to them and to express the feeling that it had comparatively little control over them. This might be taken to imply a lower degree of commitment or loyalty to that particular group.

Although Bentz's research findings are less direct than the others examined, they do seem to point in the same direction, indicating similarities between the high publisher, the functional bureaucrat, and the expert. They were also particularly useful to my own later study of a college by suggesting indices for some of the significant variables.

These three cases suggested the importance of three variables for analyzing latent identities in organizations: (1) loyalty to the employing organization, (2) commitment to specialized or professional skills, and (3) reference group orientations. Considerations of space do not permit this to be developed here, but each of these studies also found role-playing patterns polar to those discussed. This led us to hypothesize that *two* latent organizational identities could be found. These were:

1. *Cosmopolitans*: those low on loyalty to the employing organization, high on commitment to specialized role skills, and likely to use an outer reference group orientation.

2. *Locals*: those high on loyalty to the employing organization, low on commitment to specialized role skills, and likely to use an inner reference group orientation.

Cosmopolitans and locals are regarded as *latent* identities because they involve criteria which are not fully institutionalized as bases for classifying people in the modern organization, though they are in fact often used as such. For example, "loyalty" usually tends to be taken for granted and is, under normal circumstances, a latent social identity in a rational bureaucracy. For example, it may be preferred, but it is not usually prescribed, that one should be a "company man." While loyalty criteria do become activated at irregular intervals, as, for example, at occasional "testimonial dinners" or during outbursts of organizational conflict and crisis, other criteria for identifying personnel are routinely regarded as more fully legitimate and relevant. For example, skill and competence or training and experience are usually the publicly utilized standards in terms of which performances are judged and performers identified.

While organizations are in fact concerned with the loyalty of their personnel, as indicated by the ritual awarding of gold watches for lengthy years of "faithful service," the dominant organizational orientation toward rationality imposes a ban of pathos on the use of loyalty criteria. Organizational concern with the skill and competence of its personnel exerts pressure against evaluating them in terms of loyalty. Indeed, one of the major dilemmas of the modern organization is the tension between promotions based on skill versus promotions based on seniority, the latter often being an informal index of loyalty. Despite the devotion to rational criteria in the modern organization, however, considerations of loyalty can never be entirely excluded and loyalty criteria frequently serve as a basis for assigning latent identities. In some measure, loyalty to the organization often implies the other two criteria, (1) a willingness to limit or relinquish the commitment to a specialized professional task and (2) a dominant career orientation to the employing organization as a reference group. This linking of organizational criteria is only barely understood by the group members. Thus cosmopolitans and locals are also latent identities because the *conjunction* of criteria involved is not normatively prescribed by the organization.

Each of the other two criteria involved may, however, become an independent basis for assigning organizational identities. For example, in the modern organization people tend to be distinguished in terms of their commitment to their work as well as to their employing organization. A distinction is commonly made between the "cynics" and "clock watchers" or those who are just "doing time," on the one hand, and those who "believe in" or are "fired up" by their task.[8] This distinction is based on the common, if not entirely documented, assumption that the latter are likely to be superior role performers.

It is, however, relatively difficult to know how a person feels about his job; it is easier, and is therefore frequently regarded as more important, to know how he *does* it. Performance rather than belief more commonly becomes the formal criterion for assigning organizational identity. Nonetheless, belief is never totally neglected or discarded but tends, instead, to become a basis on which more latent identities are assigned.

While the significance of reference group orientation varies from one type of organization to another, it remains a commonplace if somewhat subtle criterion for assigning latent identities. In colleges, groups distinguish between "insiders" and "outsiders," sometimes using such informal indices as whether or not individuals orient themselves to certain "schools of thought" or people, share familiarity with a prestigious literature, or utilize certain styles of research. In trade unions, different identities may be assigned to those who orient themselves to political movements or to professional peers in other types of organizations and to those who are primarily oriented to the more limited goals of the union—the "union men." Such identities are not fully institutionalized or legitimated, although they may obliquely impinge on promotions, election to office, and evaluation of performance.

Notes

[1] Such an overhauling seems well begun in the recent volume by S. F. Nadel, *Theory of Social Structure* (Glencoe, IL, 1957). Efforts moving in a similar direction may also be found in Marion J. Levy, Jr., *The Structure of Society* (Princeton, 1952), pp. 157–166, and in Robert K. Merton, *Social Theory and Social Structure* (Glencoe, 1957), pp. 368–380, 415–420.

[2] The variety of these role concepts is well displayed in Erving Goffman, *The Presentation of Self in Everyday Life* (Edinburgh, 1956), and is discussed with great cogency in Joseph R. Gusfield, General Education as a Career, *Journal of General Education*, 10 Jan. (1957), 37–48.

[3] The terminological disparities with respect to the definition of "status" barely fall short of being appalling. Among the varying definitions which may be found are the following: (1) "a position in the social aggregate identified with a pattern of prestige symbols. . . ." D. Martindale and E. D. Monachesi, *Elements of Sociology* (New York, 1951), p. 540; (2) the "successful realization of claims to prestige . . . the distribution of prestige in a society . . ." H. Gerth and C. W. Mills, *Character and Social Structure* (New York, 1953), p. 307; (3) "a measure of the worth or the importance of the role," R. Freedman, A. H. Hawley, W. S. Landecker, and H. M. Miner, eds., *Principles of Sociology* (New York, 1952), p. 148; (4) "the rank position with respect chiefly to income, prestige, and power—one or all of these," G. Knupfer in R. O'Brien, C. C. Shrag, and W. T. Martin,

Readings in General Sociology (New York, 1951), p. 274; (5) "a collection of rights and obligations . . ." R. Linton, *The Study of Man* (New York, 1945), p. 113; (6) a "complex of mutual rights, obligations, and functions as defined by the pertinent ideal patterns," T. Parsons, *Essays in Sociological Theory Pure and Applied* (Glencoe, IL, 1949), p. 42; (7) "a position in the general institutional system, recognized and supported by the entire society . . ." K. Davis, *Human Society* (New York, 1949), p. 87. One could go on. That these varying definitions are not necessarily contradictory is small consolation and certainly no guarantee that they all refer to the same things. Nowhere do these definitions become more opaque than when—as they frequently do—they refer to a status as a "position" in something. The ready familiarity of the word position seems to induce paralysis of the analytic nerve. Needless to say such terminological confusion begets efforts at neologistic clarification which may then only further becloud the field. We can only hope that this has not happened here.

[4] These terms are taken from Robert K. Merton, "Patterns of Influence, Local and Cosmopolitan Influentials," in Merton, *op cit.* Merton's terms are used with respect to types of roles within communities rather than in connection with formal organizations, as they are here. Moreover, Merton's focus is on the conjunction between influence and cosmopolitans-locals, whereas our analysis applies cosmopolitan and local orientations to role players apart from considerations of their influence. Note, also, the similarity between my own discussion of "latent" identities and roles and that of R. Linton, in T. N. Newcomb and E. L. Hartley, eds., *Readings in Sociology* (New York, 1947), p. 368.

[5] Alvin W. Gouldner, *Patterns of Industrial Bureaucracy* (Glencoe, IL, 1954). It may be worth mentioning that the research published here represents an effort at deliberate continuity and development of some of the conceptions that emerged in the *Patterns* volume.

[6] Leonard Reissman, A Study of Role Conceptions in Bureaucracy, *Social Forces*, 27(1949), 305–310.

[7] Vernon J. Bentz, "A Study of Leadership in a Liberal Arts College" (Columbus: Ohio State University, 1950; mimeo).

[8] For a broader discussion of this problem, see Howard S. Becker and Blanche Geer, "The Fate of Idealism in Medical School" (unpublished paper, available from authors at Community Studies, Inc., Kansas City, MO).

2

Assets and Liabilities in Group Decision Making

Norman R. F. Maier

A number of investigations have raised the question of whether group problem solving is superior, inferior, or equal to individual problem solving. Evidence can be cited in support of each position so that the answer to this question remains ambiguous. Rather than pursue this generalized approach to the question, it seems more fruitful to explore the forces that influence problem solving under the two conditions.[1] It is hoped that a better recognition of these forces will permit clarification of the varied dimensions of the problem-solving process, especially in groups.

The forces operating in such groups include some that are assets, some that are liabilities, and some that can be either assets or liabilities, depending upon the skills of the members, especially those of the discussion leader. Let us examine these three sets of forces.[2]

Group Assets

Greater Sum Total of Knowledge and Information

There is more information in a group than in any of its members. Thus problems that require the utilization of knowledge should give groups an advantage over individuals. Even if one member of the group (*e.g.,* the leader) knows much more than anyone else, the limited unique knowledge of lesser-informed individuals could serve to fill in some gaps in knowledge. For example, a skilled machinist might contribute to an engineer's problem solving and an ordinary workman might supply information on how a new machine might be received by workers.

Greater Number of Approaches to a Problem

It has been shown that individuals get into ruts in their thinking.[3] Many obstacles stand in the way of achieving a goal, and a solution must circumvent these. The individual is handicapped in that he tends to persist in his approach and

From *Psychological Review*, Vol. 74, No. 4 (July 1967), pp. 239–249. Copyright © 1967 by the American Psychological Association.

thus fails to find another approach that might solve the problem in a simpler manner. Individuals in a group have the same failing, but the approaches in which they are persisting may be different. For example, one researcher may try to prevent the spread of a disease by making man immune to the germ, another by finding and destroying the carrier of the germ, and still another by altering the environment so as to kill the germ before it reaches man. There is no way of determining which approach will best achieve the desired goal, but undue persistence in any one will stifle new discoveries. Since group members do not have identical approaches, each can contribute by knocking others out of ruts in thinking.

Participation in Problem Solving Increases Acceptance

Many problems require solutions that depend upon the support of others to be effective. Insofar as group problem solving permits participation and influence, it follows that more individuals accept solutions when a group solves the problem than when one person solves it. When one individual solves a problem he still has the task of persuading others. It follows, therefore, that when groups solve such problems, a greater number of persons accept and feel responsible for making the solution work. A low-quality solution that has good acceptance can be more effective than a higher-quality solution that lacks acceptance.

Better Comprehension of the Decision

Decisions made by an individual, which are to be carried out by others, must be communicated from the decision-maker to the decision-executors. Thus individual problem solving often requires an additional stage—that of relaying the decision reached. Failures in this communication process detract from the merits of the decision and can even cause its failure or create a problem of greater magnitude than the initial problem that was solved. Many organizational problems can be traced to inadequate communication of decisions made by superiors and transmitted to subordinates, who have the task of implementing the decision.

The chances for communication failures are greatly reduced when the individuals who must work together in executing the decision have participated in making it. They not only understand the solution because they saw it develop, but they are also aware of the several other alternatives that were considered and the reasons why they were discarded. The common assumption that decisions supplied by superiors are arbitrarily reached therefore disappears. A full knowledge of goals, obstacles, alternatives, and factual information is essential to communication, and this communication is maximized when the total problem-solving process is shared.

Group Liabilities

Social Pressure

Social pressure is a major force making for conformity. The desire to be a good group member and to be accepted tends to silence disagreement and favors consensus. Majority opinions tend to be accepted regardless of whether or not their objective quality is logically and scientifically sound. Problems requiring solutions based upon facts, regardless of feelings and wishes, can suffer in group problem-solving situations.

It has been shown that minority opinions in leaderless groups have little influence on the solution reached, even when these opinions are the correct ones.[4] Reaching agreement in a group often is confused with finding the right answer, and it is for this reason that the dimensions of a decision's acceptance and its objective quality must be distinguished.[5]

Valence of Solutions

When leaderless groups (made up of three or four persons) engage in problem solving, they propose a variety of solutions. Each solution may receive both critical and supportive comments, as well as descriptive and explorative comments from other participants. If the number of negative and positive comments for each solution are algebraically summed, each may be given a *valence index*.[6] The first solution that receives a positive valence value of 15 tends to be adopted to the satisfaction of all participants about 85 percent of the time, regardless of its quality. Higher quality solutions introduced after the critical value for one of the solutions has been reached have little chance of achieving real consideration. Once some degree of consensus is reached, the jelling process seems to proceed rather rapidly.

The critical valence value of 15 appears not to be greatly altered by the nature of the problem or the exact size of the group. Rather, it seems to designate a turning point between the idea-getting process and the decision-making process (idea evaluation). A solution's valence index is not a measure of the number of persons supporting the solution, since a vocal minority can build up a solution's valence by actively pushing it. In this sense, valence becomes an influence in addition to social pressure in determining an outcome.

Since a solution's valence is independent to its objective quality, this group factor becomes an important liability in group problem solving, even when the value of a decision depends upon objective criteria (facts and logic). It becomes a means whereby skilled manipulators can have more influence over the group process than their proportion of membership deserves.

Individual Domination

In most leaderless groups a dominant individual emerges and captures more than his share of influence on the outcome. He can achieve this end through a greater degree of participation (valence), persuasive ability, or stubborn persistence (fatiguing the opposition). None of these factors is related to problem-solving ability, so that the best problem solver in the group may not have the influence to upgrade the quality of the group's solution (which he would have had if left to solve the problem by himself).

Hoffman and Maier found that the mere fact of appointing a leader causes this person to dominate a discussion.[7] Thus, regardless of his problem-solving ability a leader tends to exert a major influence on the outcome of a decision.

Conflicting Secondary Goal: Winning the Argument

When groups are confronted with a problem, the initial goal is to obtain a solution. However, the appearance of several alternatives causes individuals to have preferences and once these emerge the desire to support a position is created. Converting those with neutral viewpoints and refuting those with opposed viewpoints now enters into the problem-solving process. More and more the goal becomes that of winning the decision rather than finding the best solution. This new goal is unrelated to the quality of the problem's solution and therefore can result in lowering the quality of the decision [*footnote omitted*].

Factors That Serve as Assets or Liabilities, Depending Largely upon the Skill of the Discussion Leader

Disagreement

The fact that discussion may lead to disagreement can serve either to create hard feelings among members or lead to a resolution of conflict and hence to an innovative solution.[9] The first of these outcomes of disagreement is a liability, especially with regard to the acceptance of solutions; while the second is an asset, particularly where innovation is desired. A leader can treat disagreement as undesirable and thereby reduce the probability of both hard feelings and innovation, or he can maximize disagreement and risk hard feelings in his attempts to achieve innovation. The skill of a leader requires his ability to create a climate for disagreement which will permit innovation without risking hard feelings. The leader's perception of disagreement is one of the critical factors in this skill area.[10] Others involve permissiveness,[11] delaying the reaching of a solution,[12] techniques for processing information and opinions,[13] and techniques for separating idea-getting from idea-evaluation.[14]

Conflicting Interests versus Mutual Interests

Disagreement in discussion may take many forms. Often participants disagree with one another with regard to solutions, but when issues are explored one finds that these conflicting solutions are designed to solve different problems. Before one can rightly expect agreement on a solution, there should be agreement on the nature of the problem. Even before this, there should be agreement on the goal, as well as on the various obstacles that prevent the goal from being reached. Once distinctions are made between goals, obstacles, and solutions (which represent ways of overcoming obstacles), one finds increased opportunities for cooperative problem solving and less conflict.[15]

Often there is also disagreement regarding whether the objective of a solution is to achieve quality or acceptance,[16] and frequently a stated problem reveals a complex of separate problems, each having separate solutions so that a search for a single solution is impossible.[17] Communications often are inadequate because the discussion is not synchronized and each person is engaged in discussing a different aspect. Organizing discussion to synchronize the exploration of different aspects of the problem and to follow a systematic procedure increases solution quality.[18] The leadership function of influence discussion procedure is quite distinct from the function of evaluating or contributing ideas.[19]

When the discussion leader aids in the separation of the several aspects of the problem-solving process and delays the solution-mindedness of the group,[20] both solution quality and acceptance improve; when he hinders or fails to facilitate the isolation of these varied processes, he risks a deterioration in the group process.[21] His skill thus determines whether a discussion drifts toward conflicting interests or whether mutual interests are located. Cooperative problem solving can only occur after the mutual interests have been established and it is surprising how often they can be found when the discussion leader makes this his task.[22]

Risk Taking

Groups are more willing than individuals to reach decisions involving risks.[23] Taking risks is a factor in acceptance of change, but change may either represent a gain or a loss. The best guard against the latter outcome seems to be primarily a matter of a decision's quality. In a group situation this depends upon the leader's skill in utilizing the factors that represent group assets and avoiding those that make for liabilities.

Time Requirements

In general, more time is required for a group to reach a decision than for a single individual to reach one. Insofar as some problems require quick decisions, individual decisions are favored. In other situations acceptance and quality are requirements, but excessive time without sufficient returns also represents a loss. On the other hand, discussion can resolve conflicts, whereas reaching consensus has limited value.[24] The practice of hastening a meeting can prevent full discussion, but failure to move a discussion forward can lead to boredom and fatigue-type solutions, in which members agree merely to get out of the meeting. The effective utilization of discussion time (a delicate balance between permissiveness and control on the part of the leader), therefore, is needed to make the time factor an asset rather than a liability. Unskilled leaders tend to be too concerned with reaching a solution and therefore terminate a discussion before the group potential is achieved.[25]

Who Changes

In reaching consensus or agreement, some members of a group must change. Persuasive forces do not operate in individual problem solving in the same way they operate in a group situation; hence, the changing of someone's mind is not an issue. In group situations, however, who changes can be an asset or a liability. If persons with the most constructive views are induced to change the end-product suffers; whereas if persons with the least constructive points of view change the end-product is upgraded. The leader can upgrade the quality of a decision because his position permits him to protect the person with a minority view and increase his opportunity to influence the majority position. This protection is a constructive factor because a minority viewpoint influences only when facts favor it.[26]

The leader also plays a constructive role insofar as he can facilitate communications and thereby reduce misunderstandings.[27] The leader has an adverse effect on the end-product when he suppresses minority views by holding a contrary position and when he uses his office to promote his own views.[28] In many problem-solving discussions, the untrained leader plays a dominant role in influencing the outcome, and when he is more resistant to changing his views than are the other participants, the quality of the outcome tends to be lowered. This negative leader-influence was demonstrated by experiments in which untrained leaders were asked to obtain a second solution to a problem after they had obtained their first one.[29] It was found that the second solution tended to be superior to the first. Since the dominant individual had influenced the first solution, he had won his point and therefore ceased to dominate the subsequent discussion which led to the second solution. Acceptance of a solution also increases as the leader sees disagreement as idea-producing rather than as a source of difficulty or trouble.[30] Leaders who see some of their participants as trouble-makers obtain fewer innovative solutions and gain less acceptance of decisions made than leaders who see disagreeing members as persons with ideas.

The Leader's Role for Integrated Groups

Two Differing Types of Group Process

In observing group problem solving under various conditions it is rather easy to distinguish between cooperative problem-solving activity and persuasion or selling approaches. Problem-solving activity includes searching, trying out ideas on one another, listening to understand rather than to refute, making relatively short speeches, and reacting to differences in opinion as stimulating. The general pattern is one of rather complete participation, involvement, and interest. Persuasion activity includes the selling of opinions already formed, defending a position held, either not listening at all or listening in order to be able to refute, talking dominated by a few members, unfavorable reactions to disagreement, and a lack of involvement of some members. During problem solving the behavior observed seems to be that of members interacting as segments of a group. The interaction pattern is not between certain individual members, but with the group as a whole. Sometimes it is difficult to determine who should be credited with an idea. "It just developed," is a response often used to describe the solution reached. In contrast, discussions involving selling or persuasive behavior seem to consist of a series of interpersonal interactions with each individual retaining his identity. Such groups do not function as integrated units but as separate individuals, each with an agenda. In one situation the solution is unknown and is sought; in the other, several solutions exist and conflict occurs because commitments have been made.

The Starfish Analogy

The analysis of these two group processes suggests an analogy with the behavior of the rays of a starfish under two conditions; one with the nerve ring intact, the other with the nerve ring sectioned.[31] In the intact condition, locomotion and righting behavior reveal that the behavior of each ray is not merely a function of local stimulation. Locomotion and righting behavior reveal a degree of coordination and interdependence that is centrally controlled. However, when the nerve ring is sectioned, the behavior of one ray still can influence others, but internal coordination is lacking. For example, if one ray is stimulated, it may step forward, thereby exerting pressure on the sides of the other four rays. In response to these external pressures (tactile stimulation), these rays show stepping responses on the stimulated side so that locomotion successfully occurs without the aid of neural coordination. Thus integrated behavior can occur on the basis of external control. If, however, stimulation is applied to opposite rays, the specimen may be "locked" for a time, and in some species the conflicting locomotions may divide the animal, thus destroying it.[32]

Each of the rays of the starfish can show stepping responses even when sectioned and removed from the animal. Thus each may be regarded as an individual. In a starfish with a sectioned nerve ring the five rays become members of a group. They can successfully work together for locomotion purposes by being controlled by the dominant ray. Thus if uniformity of action is desired, the group of five rays can sometimes be more effective than the individual ray in moving the group toward a source of stimulation. However, if "locking" or the division of the organism occurs, the group action becomes less effective than individual action. External control, through the influence of a dominant ray, therefore can lead to adaptive behavior for the starfish as a whole, but it can also result in a conflict that destroys the organism. Something more than external influence is needed.

In the animal with an intact nerve ring, the function of the rays is coordinated by the nerve ring. With this type of internal organization the group is always superior to that of the individual actions. When the rays function as a part of an organized unit, rather than as a group that is physically together, they become a higher type of organization—a single intact organism. This is accomplished by the nerve ring, which in itself does not do the behaving. Rather, it receives and processes the data which the rays relay to it. Through this central organization, the responses of the rays become part of a larger pattern so that together they constitute a single coordinated total response rather than a group of individual responses.

The Leader as the Group's Central Nervous System

If we now examine what goes on in a discussion group we find that members can problem-solve as individuals, they can influence others by external pushes and pulls, or they can function as a group with varying degrees of unity. In order for the latter function to be maximized, however, something must be introduced to serve the function of the nerve ring. In our conceptualization of group problem solving and group decision,[33] we see this as the function of the leader. Thus the leader does not serve as a dominant ray and produce the solution. Rather, his function is to receive information, facilitate communications between the individuals, relay messages, and integrate the incoming responses so that a single unified response occurs.

Solutions that are the product of good group discussions often come as surprises to discussion leaders. One of these is unexpected generosity. If there is a weak member, this member is given less to do, in much the same way as an organism adapts to an injured limb and alters the function of other limbs to keep locomotion on course. Experimental evidence supports the point that group decisions award special consideration to needy members of groups.[34] Group decisions in industrial groups often give smaller assignments to the less gifted.[35] A leader could not effectually impose such differential treatment on group members without being charged with discriminatory practices.

Another unique aspect of group discussion is the way fairness is resolved. In a simulated problem situation involving the problem of how to introduce a new truck into a group of drivers, the typical group solution involves a trading of trucks so that several or all members stand to profit. If the leader makes the decision the number of persons who profit is often confined to one.[36] In industrial practice, supervisors assign a new truck to an individual member of a crew after careful evaluation of needs. This practice results in dissatisfaction, with the charge of *unfair* being leveled at him. Despite these repeated attempts to do justice, supervisors in the telephone industry never hit upon the notion of a general reallocation of trucks, a solution that crews invariably reach when the decision is theirs to make.

In experiments involving the introduction of change, the use of group discussion tends to lead to decisions that resolve differences.[37] Such decisions tend to be different from decisions reached by individuals because of the very fact that disagreement is common in group problem solving and rare in individual problem solving. The process of resolving difference in a constructive setting causes the exploration of additional areas and leads to solutions that are integrative rather than compromises.

Finally, group solutions tend to be tailored to fit the interests and personalities of the participants; thus group solutions to problems involving fairness, fears, face saving, etc., tend to vary from one group to another. An outsider cannot process these variables because they are not subject to logical treatment.

If we think of the leader as serving a function in the group different from that of its membership, we might be able to create a group that can function as an intact organism. For a leader, such functions as rejecting or promoting ideas according to his personal needs are out of bounds. He must be receptive to information contributed, accept contributions without evaluating them (posting contributions on a chalkboard to keep them alive), summarize information to facilitate integration, stimulate exploratory behavior, create awareness of problems of one member by others, and detect when the group is ready to resolve differences and agree to a unified solution.

Since higher organisms have more than a nerve ring and can store information, a leader might appropriately supply information, but according to our model of a leader's role, he must clearly distinguish between supplying information and promoting a solution. If his knowledge indicates the desirability of a particular solution, sharing this knowledge might lead the group to find this solution, but the solution should be the group's discovery. A leader's contributions do not receive the same treatment as those of a member of the group. Whether he likes it or not, his position is different. According to our conception of the leader's contribution to discussion, his role not only differs in influence, but gives him an entirely different function. He is to serve much as the nerve ring in the starfish and to further refine this function so as to make it a higher type of nerve ring.

This model of a leader's role in group process has served as a guide for many of our studies in group problem solving. It is not our claim that this will lead to the best possible group function under all conditions. In sharing it we hope to indicate the nature of our guidelines in exploring group leadership as a function quite different and apart from group membership. Thus the model serves as a stimulant for research problems and as a guide for our analyses of leadership skills and principles.

Conclusions

On the basis of our analysis, it follows that the comparison of the merits of group versus individual problem solving depends on the nature of the problem, the goal to be achieved (high quality solution, highly accepted solution, effective communication and understanding of the solution, innovation, a quickly reached solution, or satisfaction), and the skill of the discussion leader. If liabilities inherent in groups are avoided, assets capitalized upon, and conditions that can serve either favorable or unfavorable outcomes are effectively used, it follows that groups have a potential which in many instances can exceed that of a superior individual functioning alone, even with respect to creativity.

This goal was nicely stated by Thibaut and Kelley when they

> wonder whether it may not be possible for a rather small, intimate group to establish a problem solving process that capitalizes upon the total pool of information and provides for great interstimulation of ideas without any loss of innovative creativity due to social restraints.[38]

In order to accomplish this high level of achievement, however, a leader is needed who plays a role quite different from that of the members. His role is analogous to that of the nerve ring in the starfish which permits the rays to execute a unified response. If the leader can contribute the integrative requirement, group problem solving may emerge as a unique type of group function. This type of approach to group processes places the leader in a particular role in which he must cease to contribute, avoid evaluation, and refrain from thinking about solutions or group *products*. Instead he must concentrate on the group *process*, listen in order to understand rather than to appraise or refute, assume responsibility for accurate communication between members, be sensitive to unexpressed feelings, protect minority points of view, keep the discussion moving, and develop skills in summarizing.

Notes

[1] L. R. Hoffman, "Group Problem Solving," In *Advances in Experimental Social Psychology*, vol. 2, ed. L. Berkowitz (New York: Academic Press, 1965), pp. 99–132. H. H. Kelley and J. W. Thibaut, "Experimental Studies of Group Problem Solving and Process," in *Handbook of Social Psychology*, ed. G. Lindzey (Cambridge, MA: Addison-Wesley, 1954), pp. 735–85.

[2] The research reported here was supported by Grant No. MH-02704 from the United States Public Health Service. Grateful acknowledgment is made for the constructive criticism of Melba Colgrove, Junie Janzen, Mara Julius, and James Thurber.

[3] K. Duncker, "On Problem Solving," *Psychological Monographs*, 1945, 58 (5, Whole No. 270). N. R. F. Maier, "Reasoning in Humans. I. On Direction," *Journal of Comparative Psychology* 10 (1930): 115–43. M. Wertheimer, *Productive Thinking* (New York: Harper, 1959).

[4] N. R. F. Maier and A. R. Solem, "The Contribution of a Discussion Leader to the Quality of Group Thinking: The Effective Use of Minority Opinions," *Human Relations* 5 (1952): 277–88.

[5] N. R. F. Maier, *Problem Solving Discussions and Conferences: Leadership Methods and Skills* (New York: McGraw-Hill, 1963).

[6] L. R. Hoffman and N. R. F. Maier, "Valence in the Adoption of Solutions by Problem-Solving Groups: Concept, Method, and Results," *Journal of Abnormal and Social Psychology* 69 (1964): 264–71.

[7] L. R. Hoffman and N. R. F. Maier, "Valence in the Adoption of Solutions by Problem-Solving Groups: II. Quality and Acceptance as Goals of Leaders and Members," mimeographed (1967).

[8] Footnote omitted; unclear reference in original.

[9] L. R. Hoffman, "Conditions for Creative Problem Solving," *Journal of Psychology* 52 (1961): 429–44. L. R. Hoffman, E. Harburg, and N. R. F. Maier, "Differences and Disagreement as Factors in Creative Group Problem Solving," *Journal of Abnormal and Social Psychology* 64 (1962): 206–14. L. R. Hoffman and N. R. F. Maier, "Quality and Acceptance of Problem Solutions by Members of Homogeneous and Heterogeneous Groups," *Journal of Abnormal and Social Psychology* 62 (1961): 401–07. N. R. F. Maier, *The Appraisal Review* (New York: Wiley, 1958). Maier, *Problem . . .* (1963). N. R. F. Maier and L. R. Hoffman, "Acceptance and Quality of Solutions as Related to Leaders' Attitudes toward Disagreement in Group Problem Solving," *Journal of Applied Behavioral Science* 1 (1965): 373–86.

[10] *Ibid.*

[11] N. R. F. Maier, "An Experimental Test of the Effect of Training on Discussion Leadership," *Human Relations* 6 (1953): 161–73.

[12] N. R. F. Maier and L. R. Hoffman, "Quality of First and Second Solutions in Group Problem Solving," *Journal of Applied Psychology* 44 (1960): 278–83. N. R. F. Maier and A. R. Solem, "Improving Solutions by Turning Choice Situations into Problems," *Personnel Psychology* 15 (1962): 151–57.

[13] Maier, *Problem . . .* (1963). N. R. F. Maier and L. R. Hoffman, "Using Trained 'Developmental' Discussion Leaders to Improve Further the Quality of Group Decisions," *Journal of Applied Psychology* 44 (1960): 247–51. N. R. F. Maier and R. A. Maier, "An Experimental Test of the Effects of 'Developmental' vs. 'Free' Discussions on the Quality of Group Decisions," *Journal of Applied Psychology* 41 (1957): 320–23.

[14] N. R. F. Maier, "Screening Solutions to Upgrade Quality: A New Approach to Problem Solving Under Conditions of Uncertainty," *Journal of Psychology* 49 (1960): 217–31. Maier, *Problem . . .* (1963). A. F. Osborn, *Applied Imagination* (New York: Scribner's, 1953).

[15] L. R. Hoffman and N. R. F. Maier, "The Use of Group Decision to Resolve a Problem of Fairness," *Personnel Psychology* 12 (1959): 545–59. Maier, "Screening . . ." (1960). Maier, *Problem . . .* (1963). Maier and Solem, "Improving . . ." (1962). A. R. Solem, "1965: Almost Anything I Can Do, We Can Do Better," *Personnel Administration* 28 (1965): 6–16.

[16] N. R. F. Maier and L. R. Hoffman, "Types of Problems Confronting Managers," *Personnel Psychology* 17 (1964): 261–69.

[17] Maier, *Problem . . .* (1963).

[18] Maier and Hoffman, "Using . . ." (1960). Maier and Maier, "An Experimental . . ." (1957).

[19] N. R. F. Maier, "The Quality of Group Decisions as Influenced by the Discussion Leader," *Human Relations* 3 (1950): 155–74. Maier, "An Experimental . . ." (1953).

[20] Maier, "The Appraisal . . ." (1958). Maier, *Problem . . .* (1963). Maier and Solem, "Improving . . ." (1962).

[21] Solem, "Almost . . ." (1965).

[22] N. R. F. Maier, *Principles of Human Relations* (New York: Wiley, 1952). Maier, *Problem . . .* (1963). N. R. F. Maier and J. J. Hayes, *Creative Management* (New York: Wiley, 1962).

[23] M. A. Wallach and N. Kogan, "The Roles of Information, Discussion and Consensus in Group Risk Taking," *Journal of Experimental and Social Psychology* 1 (1965): 1–19. M. A. Wallach, N.

Kogan, and D. J. Bem, "Group Influence on Individual Risk Taking," *Journal of Abnormal and Social Psychology* 65 (1962): 75–86.

24 Wallach and Kogan, "The Roles . . ." (1965).

25 Maier and Hoffman, "Quality . . ." (1960).

26 Maier, "The Quality . . ." (1950). Maier, *Principles* . . . (1952). Maier and Solem, "The Contribution . . ." (1952).

27 Maier, *Principles* . . . (1952). Solem, *1965* . . .

28 Maier and Hoffman, "Quality . . ." (1960). N. R. F. Maier and L. R. Hoffman, "Group Decision in England and the United States," *Personnel Psychology* 15 (1962): 75–87. Maier and Solem, "The Contribution . . ." (1952).

29 Maier and Hoffman, "Using . . ." (1960).

30 Maier and Hoffman, "Acceptance . . ." (1965).

31 W. F. Hamilton, "Coordination in the Starfish. III. The Righting Reaction as a Phase of Locomotion (Righting and Locomotion)," *Journal of Comparative Psychology* 2 (1922): 81–94. A. R. Moore, "The Nervous Mechanism of Coordination in the Crinoid *Antedon rosaceus*," *Journal of Genetic Psychology* 6 (1924): 281–88. A. R. Moore and M. Doudoroff, "Injury, Recovery and Function in an Aganglionic Central Nervous System," *Journal of Comparative Psychology* 28 (1939), 313–28. T. C. Schneirla and N. R. F. Maier, "Concerning the Status of the Starfish," *Journal of Comparative Psychology* 30 (1940): 103–10.

32 W. J. Crozier, "Notes on Some Problems of Adaptation," *Biological Bulletin* 39 (1920): 116–29. Moore and Doudoroff, "Injury . . ." (1939).

33 Maier, *Problem* . . . (1963).

34 Hoffman and Maier, "The Use . . ." (1959).

35 Maier, *Principles* . . . (1952).

36 Maier and Hoffman, "Group . . ." (1962). N. R. F. Maier and L. F. Zerfoss, "MRP: A Technique for Training Large Groups of Supervisors and Its Potential Use in Social Research," *Human Relations* 5 (1952): 177–86.

37 Maier, *Principles* . . . (1952). Maier, "An Experimental . . ." (1953). N. R. F. Maier and L. R. Hoffman, "Organization and Creative Problem Solving," *Journal of Applied Psychology* 45 (1961): 277–80. N. R. F. Maier and L. R. Hoffman, "Financial Incentives and Group Decision in Motivating Change," *Journal of Social Psychology* 64 (1964): 369–78. N. R. F. Maier and L. R. Hoffman, "Types of Problems Confronting Managers," *Personnel Psychology* 17 (1964): 261–69.

38 J. W. Thibaut and H. H. Kelley, *The Social Psychology of Groups* (New York: Wiley, 1961), p. 268.

3

Origins of Group Dynamics

Dorwin Cartwright and Alvin Zander

If it were possible for the overworked hypothetical man from Mars to take a fresh view of the people of Earth, he would probably be impressed by the amount of time they spend doing things together in groups. He would note that most people cluster into relatively small groups, with the members residing together in the same dwelling, satisfying their basic biological needs within the group, depending upon the same source for economic support, rearing children, and mutually caring for the health of one another. He would observe that the education and socialization of children tend to occur in other, usually larger, groups in churches, schools, or other social institutions. He would see that much of the work of the world is carried out by people who perform their activities in close interdependence within relatively enduring associations. He would perhaps be saddened to find groups of men engaged in warfare, gaining courage and morale from pride in their unit and a knowledge that they can depend upon their buddies. He might be gladdened to see groups of people enjoying themselves in recreations and sports of various kinds. Finally he might be puzzled why so many people spend so much time in little groups talking, planning, and being "in conference." Surely he would conclude that if he wanted to understand much about what is happening on Earth he would have to examine rather carefully the ways in which groups form, function, and dissolve.

Now if we turn to a more customary perspective and view our society through the eyes of Earth's inhabitants, we discover that the functioning or malfunctioning of groups is recognized increasingly as one of society's major problems. In business, government, and the military, there is great interest in improving the productivity of groups. Many thoughtful people are alarmed by the apparent weakening and disintegration of the family. Educators are coming to believe that they cannot carry out their responsibilities fully unless they understand better how the classroom functions as a social group. Those concerned with social welfare are diligently seeking ways to reduce intergroup conflicts between labor and management. The operation of juvenile gangs is a most troublesome obstacle in attempts to prevent crime. It is becoming clear that much mental illness derives in some way from the individual's relations with groups and that groups may be used effectively in mental therapy.

Whether one wishes to understand or to improve human behavior, it is necessary to know a great deal about the nature of groups. Neither a coherent view of man nor an advanced social technology is possible without dependable answers to a host of questions concerning the operation of groups, how individuals relate to groups, and how groups relate to larger society. When, and under what conditions, do groups form? What conditions are necessary for their growth and effective functioning? What factors foster the decline and disintegration of groups? How do groups affect the behavior, thinking, motivation, and adjustment of individuals? What makes some groups have powerful influence over members while other groups exert little or none? What characteristics of individuals are important determinants of the properties of groups? What determines the nature of relations between groups? When groups are part of a larger social system, what circumstances make them strengthen or weaken the more inclusive organization? How does the social environment of a group affect its properties? Questions like these must be answered before we will have a real understanding of human nature and human behavior. They must be answered, too, before we can hope to design an optimal society and bring it into being.

The student of group dynamics is interested in acquiring knowledge about the nature of groups and especially about the psychological and social forces associated with groups. Such an interest has, of course, motivated intellectual activities of thoughtful people for centuries. The earliest recorded philosophical literature contains a great deal of wisdom about the nature of groups and the relations between individuals and groups. It also contains a variety of specifications concerning the "best" ways of managing group life. During the period from the sixteenth through the nineteenth centuries there was created in Europe an impressive literature dealing with the nature of man and his place in society. In this literature one can find most of the major orientations, or "basic assumptions," which guide current research and thinking about groups. It is evident that the modern student of group dynamics is not essentially different in his interests from scholars writing at various times over the centuries. And yet, it is equally clear that the approach to the study of groups known as "group dynamics" is strictly a twentieth-century development; it is significantly different from that of preceding centuries.

What, then, is group dynamics? The phrase has gained popular familiarity since World War II but, unfortunately, with its increasing circulation its meaning has become imprecise. According to one rather frequent usage, group dynamics refers to a sort of political ideology concerning the ways in which groups should be organized and managed. This ideology emphasizes the importance of democratic leadership, the participation of members in decisions, and the gains both to society and to individuals to be obtained through cooperative activities in groups. The critics of this view have sometimes caricatured it as making "togetherness" the supreme virtue, advocating that everything be done jointly in groups that have and need no leader because everyone participates fully and equally. A second popular usage of the term group dynamics has it refer to a set of techniques, such as role playing, buzz-sessions, observation and feedback of group process, and group decision, which have been employed widely during the past decade or two in training programs designed to improve skill in human relations and in the management of conferences and committees. These techniques have been identified most closely with the National Training Laboratories whose annual training programs at Bethel, Maine, have become widely known. According to the third usage of the term group dynamics, it refers to a field of inquiry dedicated to achieving knowledge about the nature of groups, the laws of their development, and their interrelations with individuals, other groups, and larger institutions.

It is not possible, of course, to legislate how terms are to be used in a language. Nevertheless, it is important for clarity of thinking and communication to distinguish among these three quite distinct things which have been given the same label in popular discussions. Everyone has an ideology, even though he may not be able to state it very explicitly, concerning the ways in which group life should be organized. Those responsible for the management of groups and the training of people for participation in groups can fulfill their responsibilities only by the use of techniques of one sort or another. But there is no rigidly fixed correspondence between a particular ideology about the "ideal" nature of groups and the use of particular techniques of management and training. And it should be obvious that the search for a better understanding of the nature of group life need not be linked to a particular ideology or adherence to certain techniques of management. In this book we shall limit our usage of the term group dynamics to refer to the field of inquiry dedicated to advancing knowledge about the nature of group life.

Group dynamics, in this sense, is a branch of knowledge or an intellectual specialization. Being concerned with human behavior and social relationships, it can be located within the social sciences. And yet it cannot be identified readily as a subpart of any of the traditional academic disciplines. In order to gain a better understanding of how group dynamics differs from other familiar fields, let us consider briefly some of its distinguishing characteristics. [*Initial sentences in following list not italic in original.*]

1. *Emphasis on theoretically significant empirical research.* We noted above that an interest in groups can be found throughout history and that such an interest cannot, therefore, distinguish group dynamics from its predecessors. The difference lies, rather, in the way this interest is exploited. Until the beginning of the present century those who were curious about the nature of groups relied primarily upon personal experience and historical records to provide answers to their questions. Not being burdened by the necessity of accounting for an accumulation of carefully gathered empirical data, writers in this speculative era devoted their energies to the creation of comprehensive theoretical treatments of groups. These theoretical systems, especially the ones produced during

the nineteenth century, were elaborate and widely inclusive, having been created by men of outstanding intellectual ability. The list of names from this era contains such impressive thinkers as Cooley, Durkheim, Freud, Giddings, LeBon, McDougall, Ross, Tarde, Tönnies, and Wundt. Their ideas can still be seen in contemporary discussions of group life.

By the second decade of this century an empiricist rebellion had begun in social science, principally in the United States and especially in psychology and sociology. Instead of being content with speculation about the nature of groups, a few people began to seek out facts and to attempt to distinguish between objective data and subjective impression. Although rather simple empirical questions initially guided this research, a fundamentally new criterion for evaluating knowledge about groups was established. Instead of asking merely whether some proposition about the nature of groups is plausible and logically consistent, those interested in groups began to demand that the proposition be supported by reliable data that can be reproduced by an independent investigator. Major effort went into the devising and improving of techniques of empirical research that would provide reliability of measurement, standardization of observation, effective experimental design, and the statistical analysis of data. When, in the late 1930s, group dynamics began to emerge as an identifiable field the empiricist rebellion was well along in social psychology and sociology, and from the outset group dynamics could employ the research methods characteristic of an empirical science. In fact, group dynamics is to be distinguished from its intellectual predecessors primarily by its basic reliance on careful observation, quantification, measurement, and experimentation.

But one should not identify group dynamics too closely with extreme empiricism. Even in its earliest days, work in group dynamics displayed an interest in the construction of theory and the derivation of testable hypotheses from theory, and it has come progressively to maintain a close interplay between data collection and the advancement of theory.

2. *Interest in dynamics and interdependence of phenomena.* Although the phrase group dynamics specifies groups as the object of study, it also focuses attention more sharply on questions about the dynamics of group life. The student of group dynamics is not satisfied with just a description of the properties of groups or of events associated with groups. Nor is he content with a classification of types of groups or of forms of group behavior. He wants to know how the phenomena he observes depend on one another and what new phenomena might result from the creation of conditions never before observed. In short, he seeks to discover general principles concerning what conditions produce what effects.

This search requires the asking of many detailed questions about the interdependence among specific phenomena. If a change of membership occurs in a group, which other features of the group will change and which will remain stable? Under what conditions does a group tend to undergo a change of leadership? What are the pressures in a group which bring about uniformity of thinking among its members? What conditions inhibit creativity among group members? What changes in a group will heighten productivity, lower it, or not affect it at all? If the cohesiveness of a group is raised, which other of its features will change? Answers to questions like these reveal how certain properties and processes depend on others.

Theories of group dynamics attempt to formulate lawful relations among phenomena such as these. As these theories have been elaborated, they have guided work in group dynamics toward the intensive investigation of such things as change, resistance to change, social pressures, influence, coercion, power, cohesion, attraction, rejection, interdependence, equilibrium, and instability. Terms like these, by suggesting the operation of psychological and social forces, refer to the dynamic aspects of groups and play an important role in theories of group dynamics.

3. *Interdisciplinary relevance.* It is important to recognize that research on the dynamics of groups has not been associated exclusively with any one of the social science disciplines. Sociologists have, of course, devoted great energy to the study of groups, as illustrated by investigations of the family, gangs, work groups, military units, and voluntary associations. Psychologists have directed their attention to many of the same kinds of groups, concentrating for the most part on the ways groups influence the behavior, attitudes, and personalities of individuals and the effects of characteristics of individuals on group functioning. Cultural anthropologists, while investigating many of the same topics as sociologists and psychologists, have contributed data on groups living under conditions quite different from those of modern industrial society. Political scientists have extended their traditional interest in large institutions to include studies of the functioning of legislative groups, pressure groups, and the effects of group membership on voting. And economists have come increasingly to collect data on the way decisions to spend or save money are made in the family, how family needs and relationships affect the size of the labor force, how goals of unions affect policies in business, and how decisions having economic consequences are reached in businesses of various kinds. Since an interest in groups is shared by the various social science disciplines, it is clear that any general knowledge about the dynamics of groups has significance widely throughout the social sciences.

4. *Potential applicability of findings to social practice.* Everyone who feels a responsibility for improving the functioning of groups and the quality of their consequences for individuals and society must base his actions upon some more or less explicit view of the effects that will be produced by

different conditions and procedures. Anyone who is concerned with improving the quality of work in a research team, the effectiveness of a Sunday school class, the morale of a military unit, with decreasing the destructive consequences of intergroup conflict, or with attaining any socially desirable objective through groups, can make his efforts more effective by basing them on a firm knowledge of the laws governing group life.

The various professions that specialize in dealing with particular needs of individuals and of society have much to gain from advances in the scientific study of groups. One outstanding development in the more advanced societies during the past century has been the increasing differentiation undergone by the traditional professions of medicine, law, education, and theology. Today there are people who receive extensive training and devote their lives to such professional specialties as labor-management mediation, public health education, marriage counseling, human relations training, intergroup relations, social group work, pastoral counseling, hospital administration, adult education, public administration, psychiatry, and clinical psychology—just to mention a few. The professionalization of practice in these many areas has brought about a self-conscious desire to improve standards and the establishment of requirements for proper training. The major universities now have professional schools in many of these fields to provide such training. As this training has been extended and rationalized, members of these professions have become increasingly aware of the need for knowledge of the basic findings and principles produced in the social sciences. All of these professions must work with people, not simply as individuals but in groups and through social institutions. It should not be surprising, therefore, to find that courses in group dynamics are becoming more and more common in the professional schools, that people trained in group dynamics are being employed by agencies concerned with professional practice, and that group dynamics research is often carried out in connection with the work of such agencies.

In summary, then, we have proposed that group dynamics should be defined as a field of inquiry dedicated to advancing knowledge about the nature of groups, the laws of their development, and their interrelations with individuals, other groups, and larger institutions. It may be identified by four distinguishing characteristics (*a*) an emphasis on theoretically significant empirical research, (*b*) an interest in dynamics and the interdependence among phenomena, (*c*) a broad relevance to all the social sciences, and (*d*) the potential applicability of its findings in efforts to improve the functioning of groups and their consequences on individuals and society. Thus conceived, group dynamics need not be associated with any particular ideology concerning the ways in which groups should be organized and managed nor with the use of any particular techniques of group management. In fact, it is a basic objective of group dynamics to provide a better scientific basis for ideology and practice.

Conditions Fostering the Rise of Group Dynamics

Group dynamics began, as an identifiable field of inquiry, in the United States toward the end of the 1930s. Its origination as a distinct specialty is associated primarily with Kurt Lewin (1890–1947) who popularized the term group dynamics, made significant contributions to both research and theory in group dynamics, and in 1945 established the first organization devoted explicitly to research on group dynamics. Lewin's contribution was of great importance, but, as we shall see in detail, group dynamics was not the creation of just one person. It was, in fact, the result of many developments that occurred over a period of several years and in several different disciplines and professions. Viewed in historical perspective, group dynamics can be seen as the convergence of certain trends within the social sciences and, more broadly, as the product of the particular society in which it arose.

The time and place of the rise of group dynamics were, of course, not accidental. American society in the 1930s provided the kind of conditions required for the emergence of such an intellectual movement. And, over the years since that time, only certain countries have afforded a favorable environment for its growth. To date, group dynamics has taken root primarily in the United States and the countries of northwestern Europe, although there have also been important developments in Israel, Japan, and India. Three major conditions seem to have been required for its rise and subsequent growth.

A Supportive Society

If any field of inquiry is to prosper, it must exist in a surrounding society which is sufficiently supportive to provide the institutional resources required. By the end of the 1930s cultural and economic conditions in the United States were favorable for the emergence and growth of group dynamics. Great value was placed on science, technology, rational problem-solving, and progress. There was a fundamental conviction that in a democracy human nature and society can be deliberately improved by education, religion, legislation, and hard work. American industry had grown so rapidly, it was believed, not only because of abundant natural resources but especially because it had acquired technological and administrative "know how." The heroes of American progress were inventors, like Bell, Edison, Franklin, Fulton, and Whitney, and industrialists who fashioned new social organizations for efficient mass production. Although there had grown up a myth about the inventor as a lone wolf working in his own tool shed, research was already becoming a large-scale operation—just how big may be seen in the fact that private and public expenditures for research in the United States in 1930 amounted to more than $160,000,000 and increased, even during the depression years, to nearly $350,000,000 by 1940.

Most of this research was, of course, in the natural and biological sciences and in engineering and medicine. The idea that research could be directed profitably to the solution of social problems gained acceptance much more slowly. But even in the 1930s significant resources were being allotted to the social sciences.

The dramatic use of intelligence testing during World War I had stimulated research on human abilities and the application of testing procedures in school systems, industry, and government. "Scientific management," though slow to recognize the importance of social factors, was laying the groundwork for a scientific approach to the management of organizations. The belief that the solution of "social problems" could be facilitated by systematic fact-finding was gaining acceptance. Thomas and Znaniecki had, by 1920, demonstrated that the difficulties accompanying the absorption of immigrants into American society could be investigated systematically;[1] several research centers had been created to advance knowledge and to improve practice with respect to the welfare of children; by the early 1930s practices in social work and juvenile courts were being modified on the basis of findings from an impressive series of studies on juvenile gangs in Chicago that had been conducted by Thrasher[2] and Shaw;[3] and, enough research had been completed on intergroup relations by 1939 so that Myrdal could write a comprehensive treatment of the "Negro problem" in America.[4] Symptomatic of the belief in the feasibility of empirical research on social problems was the establishment in 1936 of the Society for the Psychological Study of Social Issues with 333 charter members. Thus, when the rapid expansion of group dynamics began after World War II, there were important segments of American society prepared to provide financial support for such research. Support came not only from academic institutions and foundations but also from business, the federal government, and various organizations concerned with improving human relations.

Developed Professions

The attempt to formulate a coherent view of the nature of group life may be motivated by intellectual curiosity or by the desire to improve social practice. A study of the conditions bringing the field of group dynamics into existence reveals that both of these motivations played an important role. Interest in groups and a recognition of their importance in society were apparent early among social scientists, who according to a common stereotype are motivated by idle curiosity. But it should be also noted that some of the most influential early systematic writing about the nature of groups came from the pens of people working in the professions, people whose motivation has often been said to be purely practical. Before considering the social scientific background of group dynamics, we will describe briefly some of the developments within the professions that facilitated its rise.

By the 1930s a large number of distinct professions had come into existence in the United States, probably more than in any other country. Many of these worked directly with groups of people, and as they became concerned with improving the quality of their practice they undertook to codify procedures and to discover general principles for dealing with groups. It gradually became evident, more quickly in some professions than in others, that generalizations from experience can go only so far and that systematic research is required to produce a deeper understanding of group life. Thus, when group dynamics began to emerge as a distinct field, the leaders of some of the professions were well prepared to foster the idea that systematic research on group life could make a significant contribution to their professions. As a result, several professions helped to create a favorable atmosphere for the financing of group dynamics research, provided from their accumulated experience a broad systematic conception of group functioning from which hypotheses for research could be drawn, afforded facilities in which research could be conducted, and furnished the beginnings of a technology for creating and manipulating variables in experimentation on groups. Four professions played an especially important part in the origin and growth of group dynamics.

Social Group Work. This profession should be mentioned first because it was one of the earliest to recognize explicitly that groups can be managed so as to bring about desired changes in members. Being responsible for the operation of clubs, recreational groups, camps and athletic teams, group workers came to realize that their techniques of dealing with groups had important effects on group processes and on the behaviors, attitudes, and personalities of those participating in these groups. Although the objective of group work included such diverse purposes as "character building," "providing constructive recreation," "keeping the kids off the street and out of trouble," and, later, "psychotherapy," it gradually became evident that, whatever the objective, some techniques of group management were more successful than others. One of the earliest experimental studies of groups concerned the effects of several leadership practices on the adjustment of boys in their summer camp cabins.[5] The wealth of experience acquired by group workers has been systemized by Busch,[6] Coyle,[7] and Wilson and Ryland.[8] Group dynamics drew heavily on this experience at the outset, and group dynamicists have continued to collaborate with group workers on various research projects.

Group Psychotherapy. Although group psychotherapy is commonly considered a branch of psychiatry, the use of groups for psychotherapeutic purposes has grown up in other than strictly medical settings, the Alcoholics Anonymous movement being one outstanding example. In the development of a professional approach to psychotherapeutic work with groups, psychoanalytic theory has exerted the major, though not exclusive, influence. Freud's writing (especially his *Group Psychology and the Analysis of the Ego*) has set the tone, but many of the techniques for dealing with groups and much of the emphasis upon group processes have been contributed by people drawing from the field of group work—see, for example, the writings of Redl,[9] Scheidlinger,[10] and Slavson.[11] A rather different tradition, although strongly psychoanalytic in its orientation, has grown up in England under the influence of Bion[12] and a group of people associated with the Tavistock Institute of Human Relations.[13] An important feature of this approach is the application of psychoanalytic group work to "natural" groups in the military establishment, industry, and the community. Still another approach in group psychotherapy was established by the unusually creative and pioneering work of Moreno.[14] His techniques of role-playing (more precisely, psychodrama and sociodrama) and sociometry were among the earliest contributions to the field and have been of great value both in group psychotherapy and in research on group dynamics. Although many of the developments in group psychotherapy and in group dynamics have been simultaneous, the early work in group psychotherapy had a clear and distinct influence on the initial work in group dynamics. And the two lines of endeavor have continued to influence each other, as can be seen, for example, in the systematic treatment of group psychotherapy by Bach.[15]

Education.   The revolution in American public education that occurred in the first quarter of this century, influenced strongly by the writings of Dewey, broadened the conception of both the purposes and the procedures of education. The goal of education in the public schools became the preparation of children for life in society rather than merely the transmission of knowledge. "Learning by doing" became a popular slogan and was implemented by such things as group projects, extracurricular activities, and student government. Teachers became interested in installing skills of leadership, cooperation, responsible membership, and human relations. It gradually became apparent that teachers, like group workers, were having to take actions affecting the course of events in children's groups and needed principles to guide these events toward constructive ends. A similar trend was developing simultaneously in adult education, where the problems were made even more apparent by the voluntary nature of participation in adult-education programs. There began to emerge the conception of the teacher as a group leader who affects his students' learning not merely by his subject-matter competence but also by his ability to heighten motivation, stimulate participation, and generate morale. Although controversy over this general approach to education has persisted up to the present time, the education profession had, by the late 1930s, accumulated a considerable fund of knowledge about group life. Group dynamics drew upon this experience in formulating hypotheses for research, and group dynamics established close working relations with educators and schools of education. Both educational practice and research in group dynamics have benefited from this association.

Administration.   Under this label is a whole cluster of specialties, all concerned with the management of large organizations. Included are such specific professions as business administration, public administration, hospital administration, and educational administration. Although each of these must develop expertise in its particular sphere of operation, all share the necessity of designing effective procedures for coordinating the behavior of people. For this reason, they share a common interest in the findings of social science. It might be expected, therefore, that systematic treatments of management would early come to a recognition of the importance of groups in large enterprises and that management practices for dealing with groups would become highly developed. Actually, the historical facts are rather different. Until the 1930s efforts to develop principles of management were remarkably blind to the existence of groups. One noteworthy exception is found in the writings of Mary P. Follett,[16] who after World War I attempted to construct a systematic approach to administration, and more generally to government, in which groups were recognized as important elements. Her ideas, however, gained little acceptance.

In fact, the individualistic orientation held sway until about 1933 when the first of several books by Mayo and his associates[17] made its appearance. These publications reported an extensive program of research begun in 1927 at the Hawthorne plant of the Western Electric Company. The initial objective of this research was to study the relation between conditions of work and the incidence of fatigue among workers. A variety of experimental variations was introduced—frequency of rest pauses, length of working hours, nature of wage incentives—with the intention of discovering their influence on fatigue and productivity. It is to the great credit of these investigators that they were alert to the existence of effects not anticipated, for the important changes actually produced by their experiments turned out to be in interpersonal relations among workers and between workers and management. The results of this program of research led Mayo and his associates to place major emphasis on the social organization of the work group, on the social relations between the supervisor and his subordinates, on informal standards governing the behavior of members of the work group, and on the attitudes and motives of workers existing in a group context.

The impact of this research upon all branches of administration can hardly be exaggerated. Haire has described it in the following way:

> After the publication of these researches, thinking about industrial problems was radically and irrevocably changed. It was no longer possible to see a decrement in productivity simply as a function of changes in illumination, physical fatigue, and the like. It was no longer possible to look for explanation of turnover simply in terms of an economic man maximizing dollar income. The role of the leader began to shift from one who directed work to one who enlisted co-operation. The incentive to work was no longer seen as simple and unitary but rather infinitely varied, complex, and changing. The new view opened the way for, and demanded, more research and new conceptualizations to handle the problems.[18]

Another important contribution to this new view of management was the systematic theory of management published in 1938 by Barnard,[19] which was the product of his many years of experience as a business executive. Although this book did not put primary stress on groups as such, it placed human needs and social processes in the forefront of consideration. Barnard made it clear that management practice can be satisfactorily understood and effectively fashioned only if large organizations are conceived as social institutions composed of people in social interrelations. The emergence of group dynamics in the late 1930s came, then, at the very time when administrators and organization theorists were beginning to emphasize the importance of groups and of "human relations" in administration. In subsequent years the findings from research in group dynamics have been incorporated increasingly into systematic treatments of administration and a growing number of administrators have supported group dynamics research in various ways.

Before leaving the discussion of the role of the professions in the origin and growth of group dynamics, we should note that the developments reported here had counterparts to varying degrees in other areas of social practice, many of which were not highly professionalized. Special mention should be made of the support that has come from those concerned with providing a scientific basis for work in intergroup relations, public health, the military, religious education, community organization, and speech.[20]

Developed Social Science

In considering the conditions that stimulated the present approach to group dynamics within the social sciences, it is essential to recognize that this approach could originate only because certain advances had been accomplished in the social sciences at large. Thus, the rise of group dynamics required not only a supportive society and developed professions but also developed social sciences.

A basic premise of group dynamics is that the methods of science can be employed in the study of groups. This assumption could be entertained seriously only after the more general belief had gained acceptance that man, his behavior, and his social relations can be properly subjected to scientific investigation. And, any question about the utilization of scientific methods for learning about human behavior and social relations could not rise, of course, before the methods of science were well developed. It was only in the nineteenth century that serious discussions of this possibility occurred. Comte's extensive treatment of positivism in 1830 provided a major advance in the self-conscious examination of basic assumptions about the possibility of subjecting human and social phenomena to scientific investigation; and the controversies over evolutionary theories of man in the last half of the century resulted in a drastically new view of the possibility of extending the scientific enterprise to human behavior. Not until the last decades of the nineteenth century were there many people actually observing, measuring, or conducting experiments on human behavior. The first psychological laboratory was established only in 1879.

One can hardly imagine how group dynamics could have come into existence before the belief had taken root that empirical research can be conducted on groups of people, that important social phenomena can be measured, that group variables can be manipulated for experimental purposes, and that laws governing group life can be discovered. These beliefs gained acceptance only in recent years, though they had been advocated now and then by writers since the seventeenth century, and they are not universally held even today. There remain those who assert that human behavior does not operate according to laws, that important social phenomena cannot be quantified, and that experimentation on groups is impossible or immoral, or even both. William H. Whyte, Jr., in his attack on "the organization man," has spoken most eloquently for those who remain skeptical about the applicability of the methods of science to the study of man.[21] He defines scientism as "the promise that with the same techniques that have worked in the physical sciences we can eventually create an exact science of man." He identifies scientism as a major component of the Social Ethic which, in his opinion, is weakening American society. And, the tragedy of scientism, he maintains, is that it is based on an illusion, for "'a science of man' cannot work in the way its believers think it can." Were such views to prevail, group dynamics could not thrive.

The Reality of Groups.   An important part of the early progress in social science consisted in clarifying certain basic assumptions about the reality of social phenomena. The first extensions of the scientific method of human behavior occurred in close proximity to biology. Techniques of experimentation and measurement were first applied to investigations of the responses of organisms to stimulation of the sense organs and to modification of responses due to repeated stimulation. There was never much doubt about the "existence" of individual organisms, but when attention turned to groups of people and to social institutions, a great confusion arose. Discussion of these matters invoked terms like "group mind," "collective representations," "collective unconscious," and "culture." And people argued heatedly as to whether such terms refer to any real phenomena or whether they are mere "abstractions" or "analogies." On the whole, the disciplines concerned with institutions (anthropology, economics, political science, and sociology) have freely attributed concrete reality to supra-individual entities, whereas psychology, with its interest in the physiological bases of behavior, has been reluctant to admit existence to anything other than the behavior of organisms. But in all these disciplines there have been conflicts between "institutionalists" and "behavioral scientists."

The sharpest cleavage occurred in the early days of social psychology, naturally enough since it is a discipline concerned directly with the relations between the individual and society. Here the great debate over the "group mind" reached its climax in the 1920s. Although many people took part, the names of William McDougall and Floyd Allport are most closely associated with this controversy. At one extreme was the position that groups, institutions, and culture have reality quite apart from the particular individuals who participate in them. It was maintained that a group may continue to exist even after there has been a complete turnover of membership, that it has properties, such as a division of labor, a system of values, and a role structure, that cannot be conceived as properties of individuals, and that laws governing these group-level properties must be stated at the group level. A slogan reflecting this approach is the statement, attributed to Durkheim, that "every time a social phenomenon is directly explained by a psychological phenomenon, we may be sure that the explanation is false." In strong reaction to all this was the view, advanced most effectively by Allport, that only individuals are real and that groups or institutions are "sets of ideals, thoughts, and habits repeated in each individual mind and existing only in those minds."[22] Groups, then, are abstractions from collections of individual organisms. "Group mind" refers to nothing but similarities among individual minds, and individuals cannot be parts of groups, for groups exist only in the minds of men.

It may appear strange that social scientists should get involved in philosophical considerations about the nature of reality. As a matter of fact, however, the social scientist's view of reality makes a great deal of difference to his scientific behavior. In the first place, it determines what things he is prepared to subject to empirical investigation. Lewin pointed out this fact succinctly in the following statement:

> Labeling something as "nonexistent" is equivalent to declaring it "out of bounds" for the scientist. Attributing "existence" to an item automatically makes it a duty of the scientist to consider this item as an object of research; it includes the necessity of considering its properties as "facts" which cannot be neglected in the total system of theories: finally, it implies that the terms with which one refers to the item are acceptable as scientific "concepts" (rather than as "mere words").[23]

Secondly, the history of science shows a close interaction between the techniques of research which at any time are available and the prevailing assumptions about reality. Insistence on the existence of phenomena that cannot at that time be objectively observed, measured, or experimentally manipulated accomplishes little scientific value if it does not lead to the invention of appropriate techniques of empirical research. As a practical matter, the scientist is justified in excluding from consideration allegedly real entities whose empirical investigation appears impossible. And yet, as soon as a new technique makes it possible to treat empirically some new entity, this entity immediately acquires "reality" for the scientist. As Lewin noted, "The taboo against believing in the existence of a social entity is probably most effectively broken by handling this entity experimentally." [24]

The history of the "group mind" controversy well illustrates these points. The early insistence on the reality of the "group mind," before techniques for investigating such phenomena were developed, contributed little to their scientific study. Allport's denial of the reality of the group actually had a strongly liberating influence on social psychologists, for he was saying, in effect, "Let us not be immobilized by insisting on the reality of things which we cannot now deal with by means of existing techniques of research." He, and like-minded psychologists, were then able to embark upon a remarkably fruitful program of research on the attitudes of individuals toward institutions and on the behavior of individuals in social settings. Although this view of reality was too limited to encourage the empirical study of properties of groups, it did stimulate the development of research techniques that subsequently made a broader view of reality scientifically feasible. Until these techniques were in existence those who persisted in attributing reality to groups and institutions were forced to rely on purely descriptive studies or armchair speculation from personal experience, and such work was legitimately criticized as being "subjective" since the objective techniques of science were rarely applied to such phenomena.

Development of Techniques of Research.   Of extreme importance for the origin of group dynamics, then, was the shaping of research techniques that could be extended to research on groups. This process, of course, took time. It began in the last half of the nineteenth century with the rise of experimental psychology. Over the subsequent years more and more aspects of human experience and behavior were subjected to techniques of measurement and experimentation. Thus, for example, during the first third of this century impressive gains were made in the measurement of attitudes. Noteworthy among these were the scale of "social distance" developed by Bogardus,[25] the comprehensive treatment of problems of scaling by Thurstone[26] and Thurstone and Chave,[27] and the much simpler scaling technique of Likert.[28] Parallel to these developments, and interacting with them, were major advances in statistics. By the late 1930s powerful statistical methods had been fashioned, which made possible efficient experimental designs and the evaluation of the significance of quantitative findings. These advances were important, of course, not only for the rise of group dynamics but for progress in all the behavioral sciences.

Within this general development we may note three methodological gains contributing specifically to the rise of group dynamics. [*Initial sentences in following list not italic in original.*]

1. *Experiments on individual behavior in groups.* As noted above, research in group dynamics is deeply indebted to experimental psychology for the invention of techniques for conducting experiments on the conditions affecting human behavior. But experimental psychology did not concern itself at first with social variables; it was only toward the beginning of the present century that a few investigators embarked upon experimental research designed to investigate the effects of social variables upon the behavior of individuals. The nature of this early experimental social psychology has been described by G. W. Allport this way:

   The first experimental problem—indeed the only problem for the first three decades of experimental research—was formulated as follows: What *change in an individual's normal solitary performance occurs when other people are present?*[29]

   And according to Allport, the first laboratory answer to this question came from Triplett, who compared the performance of children in winding fishing reels when working alone and when working together with other children.[30] Triplett concluded from this experience that the group situation tended to generate an increase in output of energy and achievement.

   Of greater significance for the development of experimental social psychology was the work of Moede, begun at Leipzig in 1913, in which he undertook a systematic investigation of the effects of having several people take part simultaneously in a variety of the then standard psychological experiments.[31] This work was influential in the development of social psychology primarily because Münsterberg called it to the attention of F. H. Allport and encouraged him to repeat and extend it. Allport not only conducted several impressive experiments but also provided a theoretical framework for interpreting the findings.[32] By 1935 Dashiell was able to write a long summary of the work comparing behavior elicited when the subject was working in isolation and in the presence of others.[33] Another important study of this era was that conducted by Moore in which he experimentally demonstrated the influence of "expert" and "majority" opinion upon the moral and aesthetic judgments of individuals.[34] These early experiments not only demonstrated the feasibility of conducting experiments on the influence of groups upon individual behavior; they also developed techniques that are still in use.

   A somewhat different but closely related line of research attempted to compare the performance of individuals and of groups. In these studies, as illustrated by the work of Gordon,[35] Watson,[36] and Shaw,[37] tasks were employed that could be performed either by individuals or by groups of people, and the question was asked whether individuals or groups did the better job. As it turned out, this question is unanswerable unless the conditions are further specified, but much was learned in seeking an answer.

All this work made it much more likely that such a field as group dynamics could develop by bringing groups into the laboratory. Although these early experiments did not, strictly speaking, deal with properties of groups, they made it evident that the influence of groups upon individuals could be studied experimentally, and they made it much easier to conceive of the idea of varying group properties experimentally in the laboratory.

2. *Controlled observation of social interaction.* One might think that the most obvious device for learning about the nature of group functioning would be simply to watch groups in action. Indeed, this procedure has been employed by chroniclers and reporters throughout history and has continued to be a source of data, perhaps most impressively as employed by social anthropologists in their reports of the behavior, culture, and social structure of primitive societies. The major drawback of the procedure as a scientific technique is that the reports given by observers (the scientific data) depend to such a high degree upon the skill, sensitivity, and interpretive predilections of the observer. The first serious attempts to refine methods of observation, so that objective and quantitative data might be obtained, occurred around 1930 in the field of child psychology. A great amount of effort went into the construction of categories of observation that would permit an observer simply to indicate the presence or absence of a particular kind of behavior or social interaction during the period of observation. Typically, reliability was heightened by restricting observation to rather overt interactions whose "meaning" could be revealed in a short span of time and whose classification required little interpretation by the observer. Methods were also developed for sampling the interactions of a large group of people over a long time so that efficient estimates of the total interaction could be made on the basis of more limited observations. By use of such procedures and by careful training of observers quantitative data of high reliability were obtained. The principal researchers responsible for these important advances were Goodenough,[38] Jack,[39] Olson,[40] Parten,[41] and Thomas.[42]

3. *Sociometry.* A somewhat different approach to the study of groups is to ask questions of the members. Data obtained in this manner can, of course, reflect only those things the individual is able, and willing, to report. Nevertheless such subjective reports from the members of a group might be expected to add valuable information to the more objective observations of behavior. Of the many devices for obtaining information from group members one of the earliest and most commonly used is the sociometric test, which was invented by Moreno.[43] During World War I, Moreno had administrative responsibility for a camp of Tyrolese displaced persons, and he observed that the adjustment of people seemed

to be better when they were allowed to form their own groups within the camp. Later, in the United States, he undertook to check this insight by more systematic research on groups of people in such institutions as schools and reformatories. For this purpose, he constructed a simple questionnaire on which each person was to indicate those other people with whom he would prefer to share some specified activity. It quickly became apparent that his device, and modifications of it, could provide valuable information about interpersonal attractions and repulsions among any collection of people. The data concerning "who chooses whom" could be converted into a "sociogram," or a picture in which individuals are represented by circles and choices by lines. Inspection of such sociograms revealed that some groups were more tightly knit than others, that individuals varied greatly in their social expansiveness and in the number of choices they received, and that cliques formed on the basis of characteristics such as age, sex, and race. In short, the sociometric test promised to yield valuable information about both individuals and interpersonal relations in groups. Although based essentially on subjective reports of individuals, the sociometric test provides quantifiable data about patterns of attractions and repulsions existing in a group. The publication by Moreno[44] in 1934 of a major book based on experience with the test and the establishment in 1937 of a journal, *Sociometry*, ushered in a prodigious amount of research employing the sociometric test and numerous variations of it.

The significance of sociometry for group dynamics lay both in the provision of a useful technique for research on groups and in the attention it directed to such features of groups as social position, patterns of friendship, sub-group information, and, more generally, informal structure.

Beginnings of Group Dynamics

By the mid-1930s conditions were ripe within the social sciences for a rapid advance in empirical research on groups. And, in fact, a great burst of such activity did take place in America just prior to the entry of the United States into World War II. This research, moreover, began to display quite clearly the characteristics that are now associated with work in group dynamics. Within a period of approximately five years several important research projects were undertaken, more or less independently of one another but all sharing these distinctive features. We now briefly consider four of the more influential of these.

Experimental Creation of Social Norms

In 1936 Sherif published a book containing a systematic theoretical analysis of the concept *social norm* and an ingenious experimental investigation of the origin of social norms among groups of people.[45] Probably the most important feature of this book was its bringing together of ideas and observations from sociology and anthropology and techniques of laboratory experimentation from experimental psychology.

Sherif began by accepting the existence of customs, traditions, standards, rules, values, fashions, and other criteria of conduct (which he subsumed under the general label, social norm). Further, he agreed with Durkheim that such "collective representations" have, from the point of view of the individual, the properties of exteriority and constraint. At the same time, however, he agreed with F. H. Allport that social norms have been too often treated as something mystical and that scientific progress can be achieved only by subjecting phenomena to acceptable techniques of empirical research. He proposed that social norms should be viewed simultaneously in two ways: (*a*) as the product of social interaction and (*b*) as social stimuli which impinge upon any given individual who is a member of a group having these norms. Conceived in this way, it would be possible to study experimentally the origin of social norms and their influence on individuals.

In formulating his research problem, Sherif drew heavily upon the findings of Gestalt psychology in the field of perception. He noted that this work had established that there need not necessarily be a fixed point-to-point correlation between the physical stimulus and the experience and behavior it arouses. The frame of reference a person brings to a situation influences in no small way how he sees that situation. Sherif proposed that psychologically a social norm functions as such a frame of reference. Thus, if two people with different norms face the same situation (for example, a Mohammedan and a Christian confront a meal of pork chops), they will see it and react to it in widely different ways. For each, however, the norm serves to give meaning and to provide a stable way of reacting to the environment.

Having thus related social norms to the psychology of perception, Sherif proceeded to ask how norms arise. It occurred to him that he might gain insight into this problem by placing people in a situation that had no clear structure and in which they would not be able to bring to bear any previously acquired frame of reference or social norm. Sherif stated the general objective of his research as follows:

> . . . What will an individual do when he is placed in an objectively unstable situation in which all basis of comparison, as far as the external field of stimulation is concerned, is absent? In other words, what will he do when the external frame of reference is eliminated, in so far as the aspect in which we are interested is concerned? Will he give a hodgepodge of erratic judgments? Or will he establish a point of reference of his own? *Consistent* results in this situation may be taken as the index of a subjectively evolved frame of reference. . . .
>
> Coming to the social level we can push our problem further. What will a group of people do in the same unstable situation? Will the different individuals in the group give a hodgepodge of judgments? Or will there be established a common norm peculiar to the particular group situation and depending upon the presence of these individuals together and their influence upon one another? If they in time come to perceive the uncertain and unstable situation which they face in common in such a way as to give it some sort of order, perceiving it as ordered by a frame of reference developed among them in the course of the experiment, and if this frame of reference is peculiar to the group, then we may say that we have at least the prototype of the psychological process involved in the formation of a norm in a group.[46]

In order to subject these questions to experimental investigation, Sherif made use of what is known in psychology as the autokinetic effect. It had previously been shown in perceptual research that if a subject looks at a stationary point of light in an otherwise dark room he will soon see it as moving. Furthermore, there are considerable individual differences in the extent of perceived motion. Sherif's experiment consisted of placing subjects individually in the darkened room and getting judgments of the extent of apparent motion. He found that upon repeated test the subject establishes a range within which his judgments fall and that this range is peculiar to each individual. Sherif then repeated the experiment, but this time having groups of subjects observe the light and report aloud their judgments. Now he found that the individual ranges of judgment converged to a group range that was peculiar to the group. In additional variations Sherif was able to show that.

> When the individual, in whom a range and a norm within that range are first developed in the individual situation, is put into a group situation, together with other individuals who also come into the situation with their own ranges and norms established in their own individual sessions, the ranges and norms tend to converge.[47]

Moreover, "when a member of a group faces the same situation subsequently *alone*, after once the range and norm of his group have been established, he perceives the situation in terms of the range and norm that he brings from the situation."[48]

Sherif's study did much to establish the feasibility of subjecting group phenomena to experimental investigation. It should be noted that he did not choose to study social norms existing in any natural group. Instead, he formed new groups in the laboratory and observed the development of an entirely new social norm. Although Sherif's experimental situation might seem artificial, and even trivial, to the anthropologist or sociologist, this very artificiality gave the findings a generality not ordinarily achieved by naturalistic research. By subjecting a group-level concept, like social norm, to psychological analysis, Sherif helped obliterate what he considered to be the unfortunate categorical separation of individual and group. And his research helped establish among psychologists the view that certain properties of groups have reality, for, as he concluded, "the fact that the norm thus established is peculiar to the group suggests that there is a factual psychological basis in the contentions of social psychologists and sociologists who maintain that new and supra-individual qualities arise in the group situations."[49]

Social Anchorage of Attitudes

During the years 1935–39, Newcomb was conducting an intensive investigation of the same general kind of problem that interested Sherif but with quite different methods.[50] Newcomb selected a "natural" rather than a "laboratory" setting in which to study the operation of social norms and social influence processes, and he relied primarily upon techniques of attitude measurement, sociometry, and interviewing to obtain his data. Bennington College was the site of his study, the entire student body were his subjects, and attitudes toward political affairs provided the content of the social norms.

It was first established that the prevailing political atmosphere of the campus was "liberal" and that entering students, who came predominantly from "conservative" homes, brought with them attitudes that deviated from the college culture. The power of the college community to change attitudes of students was demonstrated by the fact that each year senior students were more liberal than freshmen. The most significant feature of this study, however, was its careful documentation of the ways in which these influences operated. Newcomb showed for example, how the community "rewarded" students for adopting the approved attitudes. Thus, a sociometric-like test, in which students chose those "most worthy to represent the college at an intercollegiate gathering," revealed that the students thus chosen in each class were distinctly less conservative than those not so chosen. And, those students enjoying a reputation for having a close identification with the college, for being "good citizens," were also relatively more liberal in their political attitudes. By means of several ingenious devices Newcomb was able to discover the student's "subjective role," or self-view of his own relationship to the student community. Analysis of these data revealed several different ways in which students accommodated to the social pressures of the community. Of particular interest in this analysis was the evidence of conflicting group loyalties between membership in the college community and membership in the family group and some of the conditions determining the relative influence of each.

Newcomb's study showed that the attitudes of individuals are strongly rooted in the groups to which people belong, that the influence of a group upon an individual's attitudes depends upon the nature of the relationship between the individual and the group, and that groups evaluate members, partially at least, on the basis of their conformity to group norms. Although most of these points had been made in one form or another by writers in the speculative era of social science, this study was especially significant because it provided detailed objective, and quantitative evidence. It thereby demonstrated, as Sherif's study did in a different way, the feasibility of conducting scientific research on important features of group life.

Groups in Street Corner Society

The sociological and anthropological background of group dynamics is most apparent in the third important study of this era. In 1937 W. F. Whyte moved into one of the slums of Boston to begin a three and one-half year study of social clubs, political organizations, and racketeering. His method was that of "the participant observer," which had been most highly developed in anthropological research. More specifically, he drew upon the experience of Warner and Arensberg which was derived from the "Yankee City" studies. In various ways he gained admittance to the social and political life of the community and faithfully kept notes of the various happenings that he observed or heard about. In the resulting book, Whyte reported in vivid detail on the structure, culture, and functioning of the Norton Street gang and the Italian Community Club.[51] The importance of these social groups in the life of their members and in the political structure of the larger society was extensively documented.

In the interpretation and systematization of his findings, Whyte was greatly influenced by the "interactionist" point of view that was then being developed by

Arensberg and Chapple, and that was subsequently presented by such writers as Chapple,[52] Bales,[53] and Homans.[54] The orientation derived by Mayo and his colleagues from the Western Electric studies is also evident in Whyte's analysis of his data. Although he made no effort to quantify the interactions he observed, Whyte's great care for detail lent a strong flavor of objectivity to his account of the interactions among the people he observed. His "higher order" concepts, like social structure, cohesion, leadership, and status, were clearly related to the more directly observable interactions among people, thus giving them a close tie with empirical reality.

The major importance of this study for subsequent work in group dynamics was threefold: (*a*) it dramatized, and described in painstaking detail, the great significance of groups in the lives of individuals and in the functioning of larger social systems. (*b*) It gave impetus to the interpretation of group properties and processes in terms of interactions among individuals. (*c*) It generated a number of hypotheses concerning the relations among such variables as initiation of interaction, leadership, status, mutual obligations, and group cohesion. These hypotheses have served to guide much of Whyte's later work on groups as well as the research of many others.

Experimental Manipulation of Group Atmosphere

By far the most influential work in the emerging study of group dynamics was that of Lewin, Lippitt, and White.[55] Conducted at the Iowa Child Welfare Research Station between 1937 and 1940, these investigations of group atmosphere and styles of leadership accomplished a creative synthesis of the various trends and developments considered above. In describing the background of this research, Lippitt noted that the issue of what constitutes "good" leadership had come to the fore in the professions of social group work, education, and administration, and he observed that, with the exception of the Western Electric studies, remarkably little research had been conducted to help guide practice in these professions. In setting up his theoretical problem, he drew explicitly on the previous work in social, clinical, and child psychology, sociology, cultural anthropology, and political science. And in designing his research, he made use with important modifications, of the available techniques of experimental psychology, controlled observation, and sociometry. This work, then, relied heavily upon previous advances in social science and the professions, but it had an originality and significance which immediately produced a marked impact on all these fields.

The basic objective of this research was to study the influences upon the group as a whole and upon individual members of certain experimentally induced "group atmospheres," or "styles of leadership." Groups of ten- and eleven-year-old children were formed to meet regularly over a period of several weeks under the leadership of an adult, who induced the different group atmospheres. In creating these groups care was taken to assure their initial comparability; by utilizing the sociometric test, playground observations, and teacher interviews, the structural properties of the various groups were made as similar as possible; on the basis of school records and interviews with the children, the backgrounds and individual characteristics of the members were equated for all the groups; and the same group activities and physical setting were employed in every group.

The experimental manipulation consisted of having the adult leaders behave in a prescribed fashion in each experimental treatment, and in order to rule out the differential effects of the personalities of the leaders, each one led a group under each of the experimental conditions. Three types of leadership, or group atmosphere, were investigated: democratic, autocratic, and laissez faire.

In the light of present-day knowledge it is clear that a considerable number of separable variables were combined within each style of leadership. Perhaps for this very reason, however, the effects produced in the behavior of the group members were large and dramatic. For example, rather severe forms of scapegoating occurred in the autocratic groups, and at the end of the experiment the children in some of the autocratic groups proceeded to destroy the things they had constructed. Each group, moreover, developed a characteristic level of aggressiveness, and it was demonstrated that when individual members were transferred from one group to another their aggressiveness changed to approach the new group level. An interesting insight into the dynamics of aggression was provided by the rather violent emotional "explosion" which took place when some of the groups that had reacted submissively to autocratic leadership were given a new, more permissive leader.

As might be expected from the fact that this research was both original and concerned with emotionally loaded matters of political ideology, it was immediately subjected to criticism, both justified and unjustified. But the major effect on the social sciences and relevant professions was to open up new vistas and to raise the level of aspiration. The creation of "miniature political systems" in the laboratory and the demonstration of their power to influence the behavior and social relations of people made it clear that practical problems of group management could be subjected to the experimental method and that social scientists could employ the methods of science to solve problems of vital significance to society.

Of major importance for subsequent research in group dynamics was the way in which Lewin formulated the essential purpose of these experiments. The problem of leadership was chosen for investigation, in part, because of its practical importance in education, social group work, administration, and political affairs. Nevertheless, in creating the different types of leadership in the laboratory the intention was not to mirror or to simulate any "pure types" that might exist in society. The purpose was rather to lay bare some of the more important ways in which leader behavior may vary and to discover how various styles of leadership influence the properties of groups and the behavior of members. As Lewin put it, the purpose "was not to duplicate any given autocracy or democracy or to study an 'ideal' autocracy or democracy, but to create set-ups which would give insight into the underlying group dynamics."[56] This statement, published in 1939, appears to be the earliest use by Lewin of the phrase group dynamics.

It is important to note rather carefully how Lewin generalized the research problem. He might have viewed this research primarily as a contribution to the technology of group management in social work or education. Or he might have placed it in the context of research on leadership. Actually, however, he stated the problem in a most abstract way as one of learning about the underlying dynamics of group life. He believed that it was possible to construct a coherent body of empirical knowledge about the nature of group life that would be meaningful when specified for any particular kind of group. Thus, he envisioned a general theory of groups that could be brought to bear on such apparently diverse matters as family life, work groups, classrooms, committees, military units, and the community. Furthermore, he saw such specific problems as leadership, status, communication, social norms, group atmosphere, and intergroup relations as part of the general problem of understanding the nature of group dynamics. Almost immediately, Lewin and those associated with him began various research projects designed to contribute information relevant to a general theory of group dynamics. Thus, French conducted a laboratory experiment designed to compare the effects of fear and frustration on organized versus unorganized groups. Bavelas undertook an experiment to determine whether the actual behavior of leaders of youth groups could be significantly modified through training.[57] Later, Bavelas suggested to Lewin the cluster of ideas that became known as "group decision." With America's entry into the war, he and French, in association with Marrow, explored group decision and related techniques as a means of improving industrial production;[58] and Margaret Mead interested Lewin in studying problems related to wartime food shortages, with the result that Radke together with others[59] conducted experiments on group decision as a means of changing food habits.

Summary

Group dynamics is a field of inquiry dedicated to advancing knowledge about the nature of groups, the laws of their development, and their interrelations with individuals, other groups, and larger institutions. It may be identified by its reliance upon empirical research for obtaining data of theoretical significance, its emphasis in research and theory upon the dynamic aspects of group life, its broad relevance to all the social sciences, and the potential applicability of its findings to the improvement of social practice.

It became an identifiable field toward the end of the 1930s in the United States and has experienced a rapid growth since that time. Its rise was fostered by certain conditions that were particularly favorable in the United States just prior to World War II. These same conditions have facilitated its growth here and in certain other countries since that time. Of particular importance among these has been the acceptance by significant segments of society of the belief that research on groups is feasible and ultimately useful. This belief was initially encouraged by a strong interest in groups among such professions as social group work, group psychotherapy, education, and administration. It was made feasible because the social sciences had attained sufficient progress, by clarifying basic assumptions about the reality of groups and by designing research techniques for the study of groups, to permit empirical research on the functioning of groups.

By the end of the 1930s several trends converged with the result that a new field of group dynamics began to take shape. The practical and theoretical importance of groups was by then documented empirically. The feasibility of conducting objective and quantitative research on the dynamics of group life was no longer debatable. And the reality of groups had been removed from the realm of mysticism and placed squarely within the domain of empirical social science. Group norms could be objectively measured, even created experimentally in the laboratory, and some of the processes by which they influence the behavior and attitudes of individuals had been determined. The dependence of certain emotional states of individuals upon the prevailing group atmosphere had been established. And different styles of leadership had been created experimentally and shown to produce marked consequences on the functioning of groups. After the interruption imposed by World War II, rapid advances were made in constructing a systematic, and empirically based, body of knowledge concerning the dynamics of group life.

Notes

[1] W. I. Thomas and F. Znaniecki, *The Polish Peasant in Europe and America* (Boston: Badger, 1918).

[2] F. Thrasher, *The Gang* (Chicago: University of Chicago Press, 1927).

[3] C. R. Shaw, *The Jack Roller* (Chicago: University of Chicago Press, 1939).

[4] G. Myrdal, *An American Dilemma* (New York: Harper, 1944).

[5] W. Newstetter, M. Feldstein, and T. M. Newcomb, *Group Adjustment, A Study in Experimental Sociology* (Cleveland: Western Reserve University, School of Applied Social Sciences, 1938).

[6] H. M. Busch, *Leadership in Group Work* (New York: Association Press, 1934).

[7] G. L. Coyle, *Social Process in Organized Groups* (New York: Rinehart, 1930).

[8] G. Wilson and G. Ryland, *Social Group Work Practice* (Boston: Houghton Mifflin, 1949).

[9] F. Redl and D. Wineman, *Children Who Hate* (Glencoe, IL: Free Press, 1951).

[10] S. Scheidlinger, P*sychoanalysis and Group Behavior* (New York: Norton, 1952).

[11] S. R. Slavson, *Analytic Group Psychotherapy* (New York: Columbia University Press, 1950).

[12] W. R. Bion, "Experiences in Groups, I–VI," Human Relations, Vol. 1 (1948): 314–20, 487–96; **2** (1949): 13–22, 295–303; **3** (1950): 3–14, 395–402.

[13] A. T. M. Wilson, "Some Aspects of Social Process," *Journal of Social Issues* (1951, Suppl. Series 5).

[14] J. L. Moreno, *Who Shall Survive?* (Washington, DC: Nervous and Mental Diseases Publishing Co., 1934).

[15] G. R. Bach, *Intensive Group Psychotherapy* (New York: Ronald Press, 1954).

[16] M. P. Follett, *The New State: Group Organization the Solution of Popular Government* (New York: Longmans, Green, 1918). M. P. Follett, *Creative Experience* (New York: Longmans, Green, 1924).

[17] E. Mayo, *The Human Problems of an Industrial Civilization* (New York: Macmillan, 1933). F. J. Roethlisberger and W. J. Dickson, *Management and the Worker* (Cambridge, MA: Harvard University Press, 1939).

[18] M. Haire, "Group Dynamics in the Industrial Situation," in *Industrial Conflict*, eds. A. Kornhauser, R. Dubin, and A. M. Ross (New York: McGraw-Hill, 1954) p. 376.

[19] C. I. Barnard, *The Functions of the Executive* (Cambridge, MA: Harvard University Press, 1938).

[20] For example, at the time Lewin established the Research Center for Group Dynamics at M.I.T., the American Jewish Congress created a related organization known as the Commission on Community Interrelations to undertake "action research" on problems of intergroup relations. And heavy financial support for research in group dynamics has come from the National Institute of Mental Health, the United States Navy and Air Force, and several large business organizations.

[21] W. H. Whyte, Jr., *The Organization Man* (New York: Simon and Schuster, 1956).

[22] F. H. Allport, *Social Psychology* (Boston: Houghton Mifflin, 1924), p. 9.

[23] K. Lewin, *Field Theory in Social Science* (New York: Harper, 1951), p. 190.

[24] *Ibid.*, p. 193.

[25] E. S. Bogardus, "Measuring Social Distance," *Journal of Applied Sociology*, Vol. 9 (1925): 299–308.

[26] L. L. Thurstone, "Attitudes Can Be Measured," *Journal of Sociology*, Vol. 33 (1928): 529–54.

[27] L. L. Thurstone and E. J. Chave, *The Measurement of Attitude* (Chicago: University of Chicago Press, 1929).

[28] R. Likert, "A Technique for the Measurement of Attitudes," *Archives of Psychology* No. 140 (1932).

[29] G. W. Allport, "The Historical Background of Modern Social Psychology," in *Handbook of Social Psychology*, ed. G. Lindzey (Cambridge, MA: Addison-Wesley, 1954), p.46.

[30] N. Triplett, "The Dynamogenic Factors in Pacemaking and Competition," *American Journal of Psychology,* Vol. 9 (1897): 507–33.

[31] W. Moede, *Experimentelle massenpsychologie* (Leipzig: S. Hirzel, 1920).

[32] F. H. Allport, *op cit.*

[33] J. F. Dashiell, "Experimental Studies of the Influence of Social Situations on the Behavior of Individual Human Adults," in *Handbook of Social Psychology*, ed. C. C. Murchison (Worcester, MA: Clark University Press, 1935), pp. 1097–1158.

[34] H. T. Moore, "The Comparative Influence of Majority and Expert Opinion," *American Journal of Psychology*, Vol. 32 (1921): 16–20.

[35] K. Gordon, "Group Judgments in the Field of Lifted Weights," *Journal of Experimental Psychology*, Vol. 7 (1924): 398–400.

[36] G. B. Watson, "Do Groups Think More Effectively than Individuals?," *Journal of Abnormal and Social Psychology*, Vol. 23 (1928): 328–36.

[37] M. E. Shaw, "A Comparison of Individuals and Small Groups in the Rational Solution of Complex Problems," *American Journal of Psychology*, Vol. 44 (1932): 491–504.

[38] F. L. Goodenough, "Measuring Behavior Traits by Means of Repeated Short Samples," *Journal of Juvenile Research*, Vol. 12 (1928): 230–35.

[39] L. M. Jack, "An Experimental Study of Ascendent Behavior in Preschool Children, "*University of Iowa Studies in Child Welfare,* Vol. 9, no. 3 (1934).

[40] W. C. Olson and E. M. Cunningham, "Time-Sampling Techniques," *Child Development*, Vol. 5 (1934): 41–58.

[41] M. B. Parten, "Social Participation among Preschool Children," *Journal of Abnormal and Social Psychology*, Vol. 27 (1932): 243–69.

[42] D. S. Thomas, "An Attempt to Develop Precise Measurement in the Social Behavior Field," *Sociologus*, Vol. 9 (1933): 1–21.

[43] Moreno, *op cit.*

[44] *Ibid.*

[45] M. Sherif, *The Psychology of Social Norms* (New York: Harper, 1936).

[46] *Ibid.*, pp. 90–91.

[47] *Ibid.*, p. 104.

[48] *Ibid.*, p. 105.

[49] *Ibid.*

[50] T. M. Newcomb, *Personality and Social Change* (New York: Dryden, 1943).

[51] W. F. Whyte, Jr., *Street Corner Society* (Chicago: University of Chicago Press, 1943).

[52] E. D. Chapple, "Measuring Human Relations: An Introduction to the Study of Interaction of Individuals," *Genetic Psychology Monographs*, Vol. 22 (1940): 3–147.

[53] R. F. Bales, *Interaction Process Analysis* (Cambridge, MA: Addison-Wesley, 1950).

[54] G. C. Homans, *The Human Group* (New York: Harcourt, Brace, 1950).

[55] K. Lewin, R. Lippitt, and R. White, "Patterns of Aggressive Behavior in Experimentally Created 'Social Climates'," *Journal of Social Psychology* 10 (1939): 271–99. R. Lippitt, "An Experimental Study of Authoritarian and Democratic Group Atmospheres," *University of Iowa Studies in Child Welfare,* Vol. 16, No. 3 (1940): 43–195.

[56] K. Lewin, *Resolving Social Conflicts* (New York: Harper, 1948), p. 74.

[57] A. Bavelas, "Morale and Training of Leaders," in *Civilian Morale*, ed. G. Watson (Boston: Houghton Mifflin, 1942).

[58] A. J. Marrow, *Making Management Human* (New York: McGraw-Hill, 1957).

[59] K. Lewin, "Forces Behind Food Habits and Methods of Change," *Bulletin of the National Research Council*, Vol. 108 (1943): 35–65. M. Radke and D. Klisurich, "Experiments in Changing Food Habits," *Journal of the American Dietetics Association*, Vol. 23 (1947): 403–09.

4

Group and Intergroup Relationships

Edgar H. Schein

Groups in organizations have become the subject of much mythology and the target for strong feelings. Though groups are nearly universal in organizations, some managers who have little faith in teamwork and committees pride themselves on running an operation in which things are done only by individuals, not by groups. Elsewhere, one finds managers saying with equal pride that they make all their major decisions in groups and rely heavily on teamwork. People differ greatly in their stereotypes of what a group is, what a group can and cannot do, and how effective a group can be. A classic joke told by those who are against the use of groups is that "a camel is a horse which was put together by a committee."

What, then, is the "truth" about groups? Why do they exist? What functions do groups fulfill for the organization and for their members? How should one conceptualize a group, and how does one judge the goodness or effectiveness of a group? What kinds of things can groups do and what can they not do? What impact do groups have on their members, on each other, and on the organization within which they exist? What are the pros and cons of intergroup cooperation and intergroup competition? How does one manage and influence groups? These are some of the questions we will discuss in this chapter.

The reason for devoting an entire chapter to groups is that there is ample evidence that they do have a major impact on their members, on other groups, and on the host organization. Their existence ultimately is stimulated by the very concept of organization. An organization divides up its ultimate task into subtasks which are assigned to various subunits. These subunits in turn may divide the task and pass it down further, until a level is reached where several people take a subgoal and divide it among themselves as individuals, but no longer create units. At this level of formal organization, we have the basis for group formation along functional lines. The sales department or some part thereof may come to be a group; the production department may be a single group or a set of groups; and so on. What basically breaks an organization into groups, therefore, is division of labor. The organization itself generates forces toward the formation of various smaller functional task groups within itself.

Definition of a Group

How big is a group and what characterizes it? It has generally been difficult to define a group, independent of some specific purpose or frame of reference. Since we are examining psychological problems in organizations, it would appear most appropriate to define the group in psychological terms.

- A psychological group is any number of people who (1) interact with one another, (2) are psychologically aware of one another, and (3) perceive themselves to be a group.

The size of a group is thus limited by the possibilities of mutual interaction and mutual awareness. Mere aggregates of people do not fit this definition because they do not interact and do not perceive themselves to be a group even if they are aware of each other as, for instance, a crowd on a street corner watching some event. A total department, a union, or a whole organization would not be a group in spite of thinking of themselves as "we," because they generally do not all interact and are not all aware of each other. Work teams, committees, subparts of departments, cliques, and various other informal associations among organizational members would fit this definition of a group.

Having defined a group, and having indicated that the basic force toward group formation arises out of the organizational process itself, let us now examine the kinds of groups which are actually found in organizations and the functions which such groups appear to fulfill for the organization and for its members.

Types of Groups in Organizations

Formal Groups

Formal groups are created in order to fulfill specific goals and carry on specific tasks which are clearly related to the total organizational mission. Formal groups can be of two types, based on their duration. *Permanent* formal groups are bodies such as the top management team, work units in the various departments of the organization, staff groups providing specialized services to the work organization, permanent committees, and so on. *Temporary* formal groups are committees or task forces which may be created to carry out a particular job but which, once the job is carried out, cease to exist unless some other task is found for them or unless they take on informal functions. Thus, an organization may create a committee or study group to review salary policies, to study the relationship between the organization and the community, to try to invent some proposals for improving relations between the union and management, to think of new products and services, and so on. Temporary formal groups may exist for a long time. What makes them temporary is that they are defined as such by the organization and that the members feel themselves to be a part of a group which may at any time go out of existence.

Informal Groups

As I have pointed out, the members of organizations are formally called upon to provide only certain activities to fulfill their organizational role. But, because the whole man actually reports for work or joins the organization and because man has needs beyond the minimum ones of doing his job, he will seek fulfillment of some of these needs through developing a variety of relationships with other members of the organization. If the ecology of the work area and the time schedule of the work permit, these informal relationships will develop into informal groups. In other words, the tendency toward informal groups can almost always be assumed to exist because of the nature of man. How this tendency works itself out in the actual creation of groups, however, depends very much on the physical location of people, the nature of their work, their time schedules, and so on. Informal groups therefore arise out of the particular combination of "formal" factors and human needs.

Some examples may help to clarify this important point. It has been found in a number of studies of friendship and informal association that such relationships can be predicted to a large degree simply from the probability of who would meet whom in the day-to-day routine. In a housing project, this likelihood was largely determined by the actual location and direction of doorways.[1] Those people who met because their doorways faced were more likely to become friends than those whose doorways made meeting less likely. In the bank-wiring room of the Hawthorne studies, the two major informal cliques were the "group in the front" and the "group in the back," this pattern arising out of actual job-related interactions as well as slight differences in the work performed in the two parts of the room. The reason why the men in front considered themselves to be superior was that they were doing more difficult work, though they were not actually paid more for it. Thus, informal groups tend to arise partly out of the formal features of the organization.

If the organization sets itself to *prevent* informal group formation, it can do so by designing the work and its physical layout in such a way that no opportunities for interaction arise, as in the case of the assembly line, or it can systematically rotate leaders and key members to prevent any stable group structure from emerging, as the Chinese Communists did in handling American prisoners of war in Korea.[2]

Assuming that the organization does not set out to limit informal group formation, and that the nature of the work permits it, what kinds of informal groups do we find in organizations? The commonest kinds can be called, to follow Dalton's terminology, *horizontal cliques*.[3] By this, he means an informal association of workers, managers, or organizational members who are more or less of the same rank, and work in more or less the same area. The bank-wiring room had two such cliques in it. Most organizations that have been studied, regardless of their basic function; (that is, mutual benefit, business, commonweal, or service), have an extensive informal organization consisting of many such cliques.

A second type, which can be called a *vertical clique*, is a group composed of members from different levels within a given department. For example, in several organizations that Dalton studied, he found groups that consisted of a number of workers, one or two foremen, and one or more higher-level managers. Some of the members were actually in superior-subordinate relationships to one another. A group such as this apparently comes into being because of earlier acquaintance of the members or because they need each other to accomplish their goals. For example, such groups often serve a key communication function both upward and downward.

A third type of clique can be called a *mixed clique.*[4] This will have in it members of different ranks, from different departments, and from different physical locations. Such cliques may arise to serve common interests or to fulfill functional needs that are not taken care of by the organization. For example, the head of manufacturing may cultivate a relationship with the best worker in the maintenance department in order to be able to short-circuit formal communication channels when a machine breaks down and he needs immediate maintenance work. On the college campus we have seen the growth of informal groups which consist of students, faculty, and high level administrators to work on problems that the formal committee structure cannot handle. Relationships outside of the organizational context may be an important basis for the formation of such cliques. For example, a number of members may live in the same part of town, or attend the same church, or belong to the same social club.

Functions Fulfilled by Groups

Formal, Organizational Functions

By formal, organizational functions, I mean those which pertain to the accomplishment of the organization's basic mission. Thus, by definition, formal groups serve certain formal functions such as getting work out, generating ideas, or serving as liaison. The formal functions are the tasks that are assigned to the group and for which it is officially held responsible.

Psychological, Personal Functions

Because organizational members bring with them a variety of needs, and because group formation can fulfill many of these needs, we can list a number of psychological functions which groups fulfill for their members. Groups can provide:

a. An outlet for *affiliation needs*, that is, needs for friendship, support, and love.

b. A means of *developing, enhancing, or confirming a sense of identity and maintaining self-esteem.*

   Through group membership a person can develop or confirm some feelings of who he is, can gain some status, and thereby enhance his sense of self-esteem.

c. A means of *establishing and testing reality.* Through developing consensus among group members, uncertain parts of the social environment can be made "real" and stable, as when several workers agree that their boss is a slave-driver or when, by mutual agreement, they establish the reality that if they work harder, management will cut the piece rate of whatever they are making. Each person can validate his own perceptions and feelings best by checking them with others.

d. A means of *increasing security and a sense of power* in coping with a common and powerful enemy or threat. Through banding together into bargaining units such as unions or through agreeing to restrict output, groups can offset some of the power that management has over members individually.

e. A means of *getting some job done that members need to have done*, such as gathering information, or helping out when some are sick or tired, or avoiding boredom and providing stimulation to one another, or bringing new members of the organization quickly into the informal structure, and so on.

Multiple or Mixed Functions

One of the commonest findings that comes from the study of groups in organizations—and which incidentally, is a reason why organizations are so much more complex than traditional organization theory envisioned—is that most groups turn out to have both formal and informal functions; they serve the needs of both the organization and the individual members. Psychological groups, therefore, may well be the key unit for facilitating the integration of organizational goals and personal needs.

For example, a formal work crew such as is found in industry or in the Army (say, a platoon) often becomes a psychological group that meets a variety of the psychological needs mentioned. If this process occurs, it often becomes the source of much higher levels of loyalty, commitment, and energy in the service of organizational goals than would be possible if the psychological needs were met in informal groups that did not coincide with the formal one. One key issue for research and for management practice, therefore, is the determination of the conditions which will facilitate the fulfillment of psychological needs in *formal* work groups.

An example of an informal group that begins to serve formal, organizational functions would be the kind of grouping, found by Dalton, that enables top management to use informal channels of communication to obtain information quickly on conditions in various parts of the organization, and which also enables line operators to determine quickly what changes in production policy are in the offing and prepare for them long before they are formally announced. The actual mechanism might be the exchange of information at lunch, at the local meeting of the Rotary Club, over golf at the country club, or through an informal telephone conversation. According to Dalton, these contacts not only meet many psychological needs, but they are clearly *necessary* for the maintenance of organizational effectiveness.

Variables Affecting the Integration in Groups of Organizational Goals and Personal Needs

There are a variety of factors that will determine the kinds of groups which will tend to exist in an organization and whether such groups will tend to fulfill both organizational and personal functions or only one or the other. These variables can be divided up into three classes: environmental factors—the cultural, social, and technological climate in which the group exists; membership factors—the kinds of people, categorized in terms of personal background, values, relative status, and so on, who are in the group; and dynamic factors—how the group is organized, the manner in which the group is led or managed, the amount of training members have received in leadership and membership skills, the kinds of tasks given to the group, its prior history of success or failure, and so on.

Environmental Factors

Environmental factors such as the organization of the work, the physical location of workers, and the time schedule imposed will determine who will interact with whom and therefore which people are likely to form into groups in the first place. If groups are to be encouraged to fulfill organizational tasks, it obviously follows that the work environment must permit and, in fact, promote the emergence of "logical" groups. This end can be accomplished by actually designating certain groups as work teams, or allowing groups to emerge by facilitating interaction and allowing enough free time for it to occur.

In many cases, the nature or location of a job itself requires effective group action, as in bomber, tank, or submarine crews, in groups who work in isolation for long periods of time (say, in a radar station), or in medical teams or ward personnel in a hospital. In other cases, even though the technical requirements do not demand it, an organization often encourages group formation. For example, the Army, rather than replace soldiers one at a time, has begun to use four-man groups who go through basic training together as combat replacements. In the hotel industry, where it is crucial that the top management of a given hotel work well together, one company has begun a conscious program of training the top team together before they take charge of a hotel in order to insure good working relations.

The degree to which such logically designed groups come to serve psychological needs will depend to a large extent on another environmental factor—the managerial climate. The managerial climate is determined primarily by the prevailing assumptions in the organization about the nature of man. If assumptions of *rational-economic man* are favored, it is unlikely that groups will be rationally utilized in the first place. According to those assumptions, groups are at most to be tolerated or, preferably, destroyed in the interest of maximizing individual efficiency. If coordination is required, it is to be supplied by the assembly line or some other mechanical means. Consequently, a climate based on assumptions of rational-economic man is most likely to produce defensive anti-management groups. Such groups will arise to give their members the sense of self-esteem and security that the formal organization denies them.

An organization built on the assumptions and values of *social man* will encourage and foster the growth of groups, but may err in not being logical in creating groupings that will facilitate task performance. This kind of organization often maintains a philosophy of job design and job allocation built on the assumptions of rational-economic man, but then attempts to meet man's affiliative needs by creating various social groups for him *extrinsic* to the immediate work organization—company bowling leagues, baseball teams, picnics, and social activities. The organizational logic then dictates that in exchange for the fulfillment of his social needs, a man should work harder on his individually designed job. This logic does not permit the integration of formal and informal group forces, because the groups have no intrinsic task function in the first place.

An organization built on the assumptions and values of *self-actualizing man* is more likely to create a climate conducive to the emergence of psychologically meaningful groups because of the organization's concern with the meaningfulness of work. However, such organizations—for example, research divisions of industrial concerns or university departments—often fail to see the importance of groups as a means for individuals' self-actualization. So much emphasis is given to challenging each individual and so little emphasis is given to collective effort in which individual contributions are difficult to judge, that groups are not likely to be encouraged to develop.

The effective integration of organizational and personal needs probably requires a climate based on the assumptions of *complex man* because groups are not the right answer to all problems at all times. Those organizations which are able to use groups effectively tend to be very careful in deciding when to make use of a work team or a committee and when to set up conditions which promote or discourage group formation. There are no easy generalizations in this area, hence a diagnostic approach may be the most likely to pay off. The type of task involved, the past history of the organization with regard to the use of groups, the people available and their ability to be effective group members, the kind of group leadership available—these are all critical.

Membership Factors

Whether a group will work effectively on an organizational task and at the same time become psychologically satisfying to its members depends in part on the group composition. For any effective work to occur, there must be a certain amount of *consensus on basic values and on a medium of communication*. If personal backgrounds, values, or status differentials prevent communication, the group cannot perform well. It is particularly important that relative status be carefully assessed in order to avoid the fairly common situation where a lower-ranking member will not give accurate information to a higher-ranking member because he does not wish to be punished for saying possibly unpleasant things or things he believes the other does not wish to hear.

The commonest example is the department staff meeting in which the boss asks his various subordinates how things are going in their units. Often subordinates will respond only with vague statements that everything is all right because they know that the boss wants and expects things that way, and because they do not wish to be embarrassed in front of their peers by admitting failures. Consequently, for problem-solving, such a group is very ineffective.

Another typically difficult group is a committee composed of representatives of various departments of the organization. Each person is likely to be so concerned about the group he came from, wishing to uphold its interests as its representative, that it becomes difficult for the members to become identified with the new committee.

A third kind of problem group, illustrating conflict of values, is the typical labor-management bargaining committee. Even though the mission of the group may be to invent new solutions to chronic problems, the labor members typically cannot establish good communications with the management members because they feel that the latter look down upon them, devalue them as human beings, and do not respect them. These attitudes may be communicated in subtle ways, such as by asking that the meetings be held in management's meeting rooms rather than offering to meet on neutral territory or in a place suggested by the labor group.

For each of the above problems, the only remedy is to provide the group enough common experience to permit a communication system and a climate of trust to emerge. Such common experience can be obtained by holding long meetings away from the place of work, thereby encouraging members to get to know each other in more informal settings, or by going through some common training experience. Thus experience-based training exercises or workshops serve not only to educate people about groups, but also to provide group members a common base of experience from which to build better working relationships.

An inadequate distribution of relevant abilities and skills may be another important membership problem. For any work group to be effective, it must have within it the resources to fulfill the task it is given. If the group fails in accomplishing its task because of lack of resources and thereby develops a psychological sense of failure, it can hardly develop the strength and cohesiveness to serve other psychological needs for its members. All of these points indicate that just bringing a collection of people into interaction does not insure a good working group. It is important to consider the characteristics of the members and to assess the likelihood of their being able to work with one another and serve one another's needs.[5]

Notes

[1] L. Festinger, S. Schachter, and K. Back, *Social Pressures in Informal Groups: A Study of a Housing Project* (New York: Harper & Row, 1950).

[2] E. H. Schein, "The Chinese Indoctrination Program for Prisoners of War," *Psychiatry* 19 (1956): 149–72.

[3] M. Dalton, *Men Who Manage* (New York: John Wiley, 1959).

[4] Dalton has called these "random" cliques.

[5] A number of research studies have attempted to determine whether group effectiveness could be predicted from personality variables. Among these the best example is William Schutz' work reported in *FIRO: A Three-dimensional Theory of Interpersonal Behavior* (New York: Holt, Rinehart, and Winston, 1958).

5

Groupthink

Irving L. Janis

"How could we have been so stupid?" President John F. Kennedy asked after he and a close group of advisers had blundered into the Bay of Pigs invasion. For the last two years I have been studying that question, as it applies not only to the Bay of Pigs decision-makers but also to those who led the United States into such other major fiascoes as the failure to be prepared for the attack on Pearl Harbor, the Korean War stalemate, and the escalation of the Vietnam War.

Stupidity certainly is not the explanation. The men who participated in making the Bay of Pigs decision, for instance, comprised one of the greatest arrays of intellectual talent in the history of American Government—Dean Rusk, Robert McNamara, Douglas Dillon, Robert Kennedy, McGeorge Bundy, Arthur Schlesinger, Jr., Allen Dulles, and others.

It also seemed to me that explanations were incomplete if they concentrated only on disturbances in the behavior of each individual within a decision-making body: temporary emotional states of elation, fear, or anger that reduce a man's mental efficiency, for example, or chronic blind spots arising from a man's social prejudices or idiosyncratic biases.

I preferred to broaden the picture by looking at the fiascoes from the standpoint of group dynamics as it has been explored over the past three decades, first by the great social psychologist Kurt Lewin and later in many experimental situations by myself and other behavioral scientists. My conclusion after poring over hundreds of relevant documents—historical reports about formal group meetings and informal conversations among the members—is that the groups that committed the fiascoes were victims of what I call "groupthink."

"Groupy"

In each case study, I was surprised to discover the extent to which each group displayed the typical phenomena of social conformity that are regularly encountered in studies of group dynamics among ordinary citizens. For example, some of the phenomena appear to be completely in line with findings from social-psychological experiments showing that powerful social pressures are brought to bear by the members of a cohesive group whenever a dissident begins to voice his objections to a group consensus. Other phenomena are reminiscent of the shared illusions observed in encounter groups and friendship cliques when the members simultaneously reach a peak of "groupy" feelings.

Above all, there are numerous indications pointing to the development of group norms that bolster morale at the expense of critical thinking. One of the most common norms appears to be that of remaining loyal to the group by sticking with the policies to which the group has already committed itself, even when those policies are obviously working out badly and have unintended consequences that disturb the conscience of each member. This is one of the key characteristics of groupthink.

1984

I use the term groupthink as a quick and easy way to refer to the mode of thinking that persons engage in when *concurrence-seeking* becomes so dominant in a cohesive ingroup that it tends to override realistic appraisal of alternative courses of action. Groupthink is a term of the same order as the words in the newspeak vocabulary George Orwell used in his dismaying world of *1984*. In that context, groupthink takes on an invidious connotation. Exactly such a connotation is intended, since the term refers to a deterioration in mental efficiency, reality testing and moral judgments as a result of group pressures.

The symptoms of groupthink arise when the members of decision-making groups become motivated to avoid being too harsh in their judgments of their leaders' or their colleagues' ideas. They adopt a soft line of criticism, even in their own thinking. At their meetings, all the members are amiable and seek complete concurrence on every important issue, with no bickering or conflict to spoil the cozy, "we-feeling" atmosphere.

Kill

Paradoxically, soft-headed groups are often hard-hearted when it comes to dealing with outgroups or enemies. They find it relatively easy to resort to dehumanizing solutions—they will readily authorize bombing attacks that kill large numbers of civilians in the name of the noble cause of persuading an unfriendly government to negotiate at the peace table. They are unlikely to pursue the more difficult and controversial issues that arise when alternatives to a harsh military solution come up for discussion. Nor are they inclined to raise ethical issues that carry the implication that *this fine group of ours, with its humanitarianism and its high-minded principles, might be capable of adopting a course of action that is inhumane and immoral.*

Norms

There is evidence from a number of social-psychological studies that as the members of a group feel more accepted by the others, which is a central feature of increased group cohesiveness, they display less overt conformity to group norms. Thus we would expect that the more cohesive a group becomes, the less the members will feel constrained to censor what they say out of fear of being socially punished for antagonizing the leader or any of their fellow members.

In contrast, the groupthink type of conformity tends to increase as group cohesiveness increases. Groupthink involves nondeliberate suppression of critical thoughts as a result of internalization of the group's norms, which is quite different from deliberate suppression on the basis of external threats of social punishment. The more cohesive the group, the greater the inner compulsion on the part of each member to avoid creating disunity, which inclines him to believe in the soundness of whatever proposals are promoted by the leader or by a majority of the group's members.

In a cohesive group, the danger is not so much that each individual will fail to reveal his objections to what the others propose but that he will think the proposal is a good one, without attempting to carry out a careful, critical scrutiny of the pros and cons of the alternatives. When groupthink becomes dominant, there also is considerable suppression of deviant thoughts, but it takes the form of each person's deciding that his misgivings are not relevant and should be set aside, that the benefit of the doubt regarding any lingering uncertainties should be given to the group consensus.

Stress

I do not mean to imply that all cohesive groups necessarily suffer from groupthink. All ingroups may have a mild tendency toward groupthink, displaying one or another of the symptoms from time to time, but it need not be so dominant as to influence the quality of the group's final decision. Neither do I mean to imply that there is anything necessarily inefficient or harmful about group decisions in general. On the contrary, a group whose members have properly defined roles, with traditions concerning the procedures to follow in pursuing a critical inquiry, probably is capable of making better decisions than any individual group member working alone.

The problem is that the advantages of having decisions made by groups are often lost because of powerful psychological pressures that arise when the members work closely together, share the same set of values and, above all, face a crisis situation that puts everyone under intense stress.

The main principle of groupthink, which I offer in the spirit of Parkinson's Law, is this:

> The more amiability and esprit de corps there is among the members of a policy-making ingroup, the greater the danger that independent critical thinking will be replaced by groupthink, which is likely to result in irrational and dehumanizing actions directed against outgroups.

Symptoms

In my studies of high-level governmental decision-makers, both civilian and military, I have found eight main symptoms of groupthink.

1. Invulnerability

Most or all of the members of the ingroup share an *illusion* of invulnerability that provides for them some degree of reassurance about obvious dangers and leads them to become overoptimistic and willing to take extraordinary risks. It also causes them to fail to respond to clear warnings of danger.

The Kennedy ingroup, which uncritically accepted the Central Intelligence Agency's disastrous Bay of Pigs plan, operated on the false assumption that they could keep secret the fact that the United States was responsible for the invasion of Cuba. Even after news of the plan began to leak out, their belief remained unshaken. They failed even to consider the danger that awaited them: a worldwide revulsion against the United States.

A similar attitude appeared among the members of President Lyndon B. Johnson's ingroup, the "Tuesday Cabinet," which kept escalating the Vietnam War despite repeated setbacks and failures. "There was a belief," Bill Moyers commented after he resigned, "that if we indicated a willingness to use our power, they [the North Vietnamese] would get the message and back away from an all-out confrontation. . . . There was a confidence—it was never bragged about, it was just there—that when the chips were really down, the other people would fold."

A most poignant example of an illusion of invulnerability involves the ingroup around Admiral H. E. Kimmel, which failed to prepare for the possibility of a Japanese attack on Pearl Harbor despite repeated warnings. Informed by his intelligence chief that radio contact with Japanese aircraft carriers had been lost, Kimmel joked about it: "What, you don't know where the carriers are? Do you mean to say that they could be rounding Diamond Head (at Honolulu) and you wouldn't know it?" The carriers were in fact moving full-steam toward Kimmel's command post at the time. Laughing together about a danger signal, which labels it as a purely laughing matter, is a characteristic manifestation of groupthink.

2. Rationale

As we see, victims of groupthink ignore warnings; they also collectively construct rationalizations in order to discount warnings and other forms of negative feedback that, taken seriously, might lead the group members to reconsider their assumptions each time they recommit themselves to past decisions. Why did the Johnson ingroup avoid reconsidering its escalation policy when time and again the expectations on which they based their decisions turned out to be wrong? James C. Thompson, Jr., a Harvard historian who spent five years as an observing participant in both the State Department and the White House, tells us that the policymakers avoided critical discussion of their prior decisions and continually invented new rationalizations so that they could sincerely recommit themselves to defeating the North Vietnamese.

In the fall of 1964, before the bombing of North Vietnam began, some of the policymakers predicted that six weeks of air strikes would induce the North Vietnamese to seek peace talks. When someone asked, "What if they don't?" the answer was that another four weeks certainly would do the trick.

Later, after each setback, the ingroup agreed that by investing just a bit more effort (by stepping up the bomb tonnage a bit, for instance), their course of action would prove to be right. *The Pentagon Papers* bear out these observations.

In *The Limits of Intervention*, Townsend Hoopes, who was acting Secretary of the Air Force under Johnson, says that Wait W. Rostow in particular showed a remarkable capacity for what has been called "instant rationalization." According to Hoopes, Rostow buttressed the group's optimism about being on the road to victory by culling selected scraps of evidence from news reports or, if necessary, by inventing "plausible" forecasts that had no basis in evidence at all.

Admiral Kimmel's group rationalized away their warnings, too. Right up to December 7, 1941, they convinced themselves that the Japanese would never dare attempt a full-scale surprise assault against Hawaii because Japan's leaders would realize that it would precipitate an all-out war which the United States would surely win. They made no attempt to look at the situation through the eyes of the Japanese leaders—another manifestation of groupthink.

3. Morality

Victims of groupthink believe unquestioningly in the inherent morality of their ingroup; this belief inclines the members to ignore the ethical or moral consequences of their decisions.

Evidence that this symptom is at work usually is of a negative kind—the things that are left unsaid in group meetings. At least two influential persons had doubts about the morality of the Bay of Pigs adventure. One of them, Arthur Schlesinger, Jr., presented his strong objections in a memorandum to President Kennedy and Secretary of State Rusk but suppressed them when he attended meetings of the Kennedy team. The other, Senator J. William Fulbright, was not a member of the group, but the president invited him to express his misgivings in a speech to the policymakers. However, when Fulbright finished speaking the President moved on to other agenda items without asking for reactions of the group.

David Kraslow and Stuart H. Loory, in *The Secret Search for Peace in Vietnam*, report that during 1966 President Johnson's ingroup was concerned primarily with selecting bomb targets in North Vietnam. They based their selections on four factors—the military advantage, the risk to American aircraft and pilots, the danger of forcing other countries into the fighting, and the danger of heavy civilian casualties. At their regular Tuesday luncheons, they weighed these factors the way schoolteachers grade examination papers, averaging them out. Though evidence on this point is scant, I suspect that the group's ritualistic adherence to a standardized procedure induced the members to feel morally justified in their destructive way of dealing with the Vietnamese people—after all, the danger of heavy civilian casualties from U.S. air strikes was taken into account on their checklists.

4. Stereotypes

Victims of groupthink hold stereotyped views of the leaders of enemy groups: they are so evil that genuine attempts at negotiating differences with them are unwarranted, or they are too weak or too stupid to deal effectively with whatever attempts the ingroup makes to defeat their purposes, no matter how risky the attempts are.

Kennedy's groupthinkers believed that Premier Fidel Castro's air force was so ineffectual that obsolete B-26s could knock it out completely in a surprise attack before the invasion began. They also believed that Castro's army was so weak that a small Cuban-exile brigade could establish a well-protected beachhead at the Bay of Pigs. In addition, they believed that Castro was not smart enough to put down any possible internal uprisings in support of the exiles. They were wrong on all three assumptions. Though much of the blame was attributable to faulty intelligence, the point is that none of Kennedy's advisers even questioned the CIA planners about these assumptions.

The Johnson advisers' sloganistic thinking about "the Communist apparatus" that was "working all around the world" (as Dean Rusk put it) led them to overlook the powerful nationalistic strivings of the North Vietnamese government and its efforts to ward off Chinese domination. The crudest of all stereotypes used by Johnson's inner circle to justify their policies was the domino theory ("If we don't stop the Reds in South Vietnam, tomorrow they will be in Hawaii and next week they will be in San Francisco," Johnson once said). The group so firmly accepted this stereotype that it became almost impossible for any adviser to introduce a more sophisticated viewpoint.

In the documents on Pearl Harbor, it is clear to see that the Navy commanders stationed in Hawaii had a naive image of Japan as a midget that would not dare to strike a blow against a powerful giant.

5. Pressure

Victims of groupthink apply direct pressure to any individual who momentarily expresses doubts about any of the group's shared illusions or who questions the validity of the arguments supporting a policy alternative favored by the majority. This gambit reinforces the concurrence-seeking norm that loyal members are expected to maintain.

President Kennedy probably was more active than anyone else in raising skeptical questions during the Bay of Pigs meetings, and yet he seems to have encouraged the group's docile, uncritical acceptance of defective arguments in favor of the CIA's plan. At every meeting, he allowed the CIA representatives to dominate the discussion. He permitted them to give their immediate refutations in response to each tentative doubt that one of the others expressed, instead of asking whether anyone shared the doubt or wanted to pursue the implications of the new worrisome issue that had just been raised. And at the most crucial meeting, when he was calling on each member to give his vote for or against the plan, he did not call on Arthur Schlesinger, the one man there who was known by the president to have serious misgivings.

Historian Thomson informs us that whenever a member of Johnson's ingroup began to express doubts, the group used subtle social pressures to "domesticate" him. To start with, the dissenter was made to feel at home, provided that he lived up to two restrictions: (1) that he did not voice his doubts to outsiders, which would play into the hands of the opposition; and (2) that he kept his criticisms within the bounds of acceptable deviation, which meant not challenging any of the fundamental assumptions that went into the group's prior commitments. One such "domesticated dissenter" was Bill Moyers. When Moyers arrived at a meeting, Thomson tells us, the President greeted him with, "Well, here comes Mr. Stop-the-Bombing."

6. Self-Censorship

Victims of groupthink avoid deviating from what appears to be group consensus; they keep silent about their misgivings and even minimize to themselves the importance of their doubts.

As we have seen, Schlesinger was not at all hesitant about presenting his strong objections to the Bay of Pigs plan in a memorandum to the President and the Secretary of State. But he became keenly aware of his tendency to suppress objections at the White House meetings. "In the months after the Bay of Pigs I bitterly reproached myself for having kept so silent during those crucial discussions in the cabinet room," Schlesinger writes in *A Thousand Days*. "I can only explain my failure to do more than raise a few timid questions by reporting that one's impulse to blow the whistle on this nonsense was simply undone by the circumstances of the discussion."

7. Unanimity

Victims of groupthink share an *illusion* of unanimity within the group concerning all judgments expressed by members who speak in favor of the majority view. This symptom results partly from the preceding one, whose effects are augmented by the false assumption that any individual who remains silent during any part of the discussion is in full accord with what the others are saying.

When a group of persons who respect each other's opinions arrives at a unanimous view, each member is likely to feel that the belief must be true. This reliance on consensual validation within the group tends to replace individual critical thinking and reality testing unless there are clear-cut disagreements among the members. In contemplating a course of action such as the invasion of Cuba, it is painful for the members to confront disagreements within their group, particularly if it becomes apparent that there are widely divergent views about whether the preferred course of action is too risky to undertake at all. Such disagreements are likely to arouse anxieties about making a serious error. Once the sense of unanimity is shattered, the members no longer can feel complacently confident about the decision they are inclined to make. Each man must then face the annoying realization that there are troublesome uncertainties and he must diligently seek out the best information he can get in order to decide for himself exactly how serious the risks might be. This is one of the unpleasant consequences of being in a group of hard-headed, critical thinkers.

To avoid such an unpleasant state, the members often become inclined, without quite realizing it, to prevent latent disagreements from surfacing when they are about to initiate a risky course of action. The group leader and the members support each other in playing up the areas of convergence in their thinking, at the expense of fully exploring divergencies that might reveal unsettled issues.

"Our meetings took place in a curious atmosphere of assumed consensus," Schlesinger writes. His additional comments clearly show that, curiously, the consensus was an illusion—an illusion that could be maintained only because the major participants did not reveal their own reasoning or discuss their idiosyncratic assumptions and vague reservations. Evidence from several sources makes it clear that even the three principals—President Kennedy, Rusk, and McNamara—had widely differing assumptions about the invasion plan.

8. Mindguards

Victims of groupthink sometimes appoint themselves as mindguards to protect the leader and fellow members from adverse information that might break the complacency they shared about the effectiveness and morality of past decisions. At a large birthday party for his wife, Attorney General Robert F. Kennedy, who had been constantly informed about the Cuban invasion plan, took Schlesinger aside and asked him why he was opposed. Kennedy listened coldly and said, "You may be right or you may be wrong, but the President has made his mind up. Don't push it any further. Now is the time for everyone to help him all they can."

Rusk also functioned as a highly effective mindguard by failing to transmit to the group the strong objections of three "outsiders" who had learned of the invasion plan—Undersecretary of State Chester Bowles, USIA Director Edward K. Murrow, and Rusk's intelligence chief, Roger Hilsman. Had Rusk done so, their warnings might have reinforced Schlesinger's memorandum and jolted some of Kennedy's ingroup, if not the President himself, into reconsidering the decision.

Products

When a group of executives frequently displays most or all of these interrelated symptoms, a detailed study of their deliberations is likely to reveal a number of immediate consequences. These consequences are, in effect, products of poor decision-making practices because they lead to inadequate solutions to the problems under discussion.

First, the group limits its discussions to a few alternative courses of action (often only two) without an initial survey of all the alternatives that might be worthy of consideration.

Second, the group fails to reexamine the course of action initially preferred by the majority after they learn of risks and drawbacks they had not considered originally.

Third, the members spend little or no time discussing whether there are no obvious gains they may have overlooked or ways of reducing the seemingly prohibitive costs that made rejected alternatives appear undesirable to them.

Fourth, members make little or no attempt to obtain information from experts within their own organizations who might be able to supply more precise estimates of potential losses and gains.

Fifth, members show positive interest in facts and opinions that support their preferred policy; they tend to ignore facts and opinions that do not.

Sixth, members spend little time deliberating about how the chosen policy might be hindered by bureaucratic inertia, sabotaged by political opponents, or temporarily derailed by common accidents. Consequently, they fail to work out contingency plans to cope with foreseeable setbacks that could endanger the overall success of their chosen course.

Support

The search for an explanation of why groupthink occurs has led me through a quagmire of complicated theoretical issues in the murky area of human motivation. My belief, based on recent social psychological research, is that we can best understand the various symptoms of groupthink as a mutual effort among the group members to maintain self-esteem and emotional equanimity by providing social support to each other, especially at times when they share responsibility for making vital decisions.

Even when no important decision is pending, the typical administrator will begin to doubt the wisdom and morality of his past decisions each time he receives information about setbacks, particularly if the information is accompanied by negative feedback from prominent men who originally had been his supporters. It should not be surprising, therefore, to find that individual members strive to develop unanimity and esprit de corps that will help bolster each other's morale, to create an optimistic outlook about the success of pending decisions, and to reaffirm the positive value of past policies to which all of them are committed.

Pride

Shared illusions of invulnerability, for example, can reduce anxiety about taking risks. Rationalizations help members believe that the risks are really not so bad after all. The assumption of inherent morality helps the members to avoid feelings of shame or guilt. Negative stereotypes function as stress-reducing devices to enhance a sense of moral righteousness as well as pride in a lofty mission.

The mutual enhancement of self-esteem and morale may have functional value in enabling the members to maintain their capacity to take action, but it has maladaptive consequences insofar as concurrence-seeking tendencies interfere with critical, rational capacities and lead to serious errors of judgment.

While I have limited my study to decision-making bodies in Government, groupthink symptoms appear in business, industry, and any other field where small, cohesive groups make the decisions. It is vital, then, for all sorts of people—and especially group leaders—to know what steps they can take to prevent groupthink.

Remedies

To counterpoint my case studies of the major fiascoes, I have also investigated two highly successful group enterprises, the formulation of the Marshall Plan in the Truman Administration and the handling of the Cuban missile crisis by President Kennedy and his advisers. I have found it instructive to examine the steps Kennedy took to change his group's decision-making processes. These changes ensured that the mistakes made by his Bay of Pigs ingroup were not repeated by the missile-crisis ingroup, even though the membership of both groups was essentially the same.

The following recommendations for preventing groupthink incorporate many of the good practices I discovered to be characteristic of the Marshall Plan and missile-crisis groups:

1. The leader of a policy-forming group should assign the role of critical evaluator to each member, encouraging the group to give high priority to open airing of objections and doubts. This practice needs to be reinforced by the leader's acceptance of criticism of his own judgments in order to discourage members from soft-pedaling their disagreements and from allowing their striving for concurrence to inhibit critical thinking.

2. When the key members of a hierarchy assign a policy-planning mission to any group within their organization, they should adopt an impartial stance instead of stating preferences and expectations at the beginning. This will encourage open inquiry and impartial probing of a wide range of policy alternatives.

3. The organization routinely should set up several outside policy-planning and evaluation groups to work on the same policy question, each deliberating under a different leader. This can prevent the insulation of an ingroup.

4. At intervals before the group reaches a final consensus, the leader should require each member to discuss the group's deliberations with associates in his own unit of the organization—assuming that those associates can be trusted to adhere to the same security regulations that govern the policymakers—and then to report back their reactions to the group.

5. The group should invite one or more outside experts to each meeting on a staggered basis and encourage the experts to challenge the views of the core members.

6. At every general meeting of the group, whenever the agenda calls for an evaluation of policy alternatives, at least one member should play devil's advocate, functioning as a good lawyer in challenging the testimony of those who advocate the majority position.

7. Whenever the policy issue involves relations with a rival nation or organization, the group should devote a sizable block of time, perhaps an entire session, to a survey of all warning signals from the rivals and should write alternative scenarios on the rivals' intentions.

8. When the group is surveying policy alternatives for feasibility and effectiveness, it should from time to time divide into two or more subgroups to meet separately under different chairmen, and then come back together to hammer out differences.

9. After reaching a preliminary consensus about what seems to be the best policy, the group should hold a "second-chance" meeting at which every member expresses as vividly as he can all his residual doubts, and rethinks the entire issue before making a definitive choice.

How

These recommendations have their disadvantages. To encourage the open airing of objections, for instance, might lead to prolonged and costly debates when a rapidly growing crisis requires immediate solution. It also could cause rejection, depression, and anger. A leader's failure to set a norm might create cleavage between leader and members that could develop into a disruptive power struggle if the leader looks on the emerging consensus as anathema. Setting up outside evaluation groups might increase the risk of security leakage. Still, inventive executives who know their way around the organizational maze probably can figure out how to apply one or another of the prescriptions successfully, without harmful side effects.

They also could benefit from the advice of outside experts in the administrative and behavioral sciences. Though these experts have much to offer, they have had few chances to work on policy-making machinery within large organizations. As matters now stand, executives innovate only when they need new procedures to avoid repeating serious errors that have deflated their self-images.

In this era of atomic warheads, urban disorganization, and eco-catastrophes, it seems to me that policymakers should collaborate with behavioral scientists and give top priority to preventing groupthink and its attendant fiascoes.

6

Transactional Analysis

Muriel James and Dorothy Jongeward

The crazy person says, "I am Abraham Lincoln," and the neurotic says, "I wish I were Abraham Lincoln," and the healthy person says, "I am I, and you are you."

—Frederick Perls[1]

Many people come to a time in their lives when they are provoked to define themselves. At such a time transactional analysis offers a frame of reference that most people can understand and put to use in their own lives. This chapter provides a brief overview of TA theory and its applications.[2] Subsequent chapters consider each phase in depth.

Transactional analysis is concerned with four kinds of analysis:

Structural Analysis: the analysis of individual personality.

Transactional Analysis: the analysis of what people do and say to one another.

Game Analysis: the analysis of ulterior transactions leading to a payoff.

Script Analysis: the analysis of specific life dramas that persons compulsively play out.

Introduction to Structural Analysis

Structural analysis offers one way of answering the questions: Who am I? Why do I act the way I do? How did I get this way? It is a method of analyzing a person's thoughts, feelings, and behavior, based on the phenomena of ego states.[3]

Imagine a mother loudly scolding her noisy, quarrelsome children. Her face wears a scowl. Her voice is shrill. Her arm is tense and held high in the air. Suddenly, the phone rings and she hears a friend's voice. The mother's posture, tone, and expression begin to change. Her voice becomes well modulated. Her once tense arm lies quietly in her lap.

Imagine two factory workers angrily arguing with each other about a work problem. Their argument is animated and fierce. They look like two children fighting over a piece of candy. Suddenly, they hear a crash of steel followed by an agonized scream. Their entire demeanor changes. Their argument is dropped. Their angry expressions give way to concern. One hurries to see what's wrong; the other calls an ambulance. According to the theory of structural analysis, the workers, as well as the mother, changed ego states.

Berne defines an ego state as "A consistent pattern of feeling and experience directly related to a corresponding consistent pattern of behavior."[4] Berne writes:

> . . . in this respect the brain functions like a tape recorder to preserve complete experiences in serial sequence, in a form recognizable as "ego states"— indicating that ego states comprise the natural way of experiencing and of recording experiences in their totality. Simultaneously, of course, experiences are recorded in fragmented forms. . . .[5]

The implications are that a person's experiences are recorded in the brain and nervous tissue. This includes everything a person experienced in childhood and incorporated from parent figures, perceptions of events and feelings associated with these events, and the distortions brought to memories. These recordings are stored as though on videotape. They can be replayed, and the event recalled and even re-experienced.

Each person has three ego states which are separate and distinct sources of behavior: the Parent ego state, the Adult ego state, and the Child ego state. These are not abstract concepts but realities. "Parent, Adult, and Child represent real people who now exist or who once existed, who have legal names and civic identities."[6]

The structure of personality is diagrammed on the following page.

Ego states are colloquially termed Parent, Adult, and Child. When capitalized in this book they refer to ego states, not to actual parents, adults, or children.

The three ego states are defined as follows:

The *Parent ego state* contains the attitudes and behavior incorporated from external sources, primarily parents. Outwardly, it often is expressed toward others in prejudicial, critical, and nurturing behavior. Inwardly, it is experienced as old Parental messages which continue to influence the inner Child.

The *Adult ego state* is not related to a person's age. It is oriented to current reality and the objective gathering of information. It is organized, adaptable, intelligent, and functions by testing reality, estimating probabilities, and computing dispassionately.

The *Child ego state* contains all the impulses that come naturally to an infant. It also contains the recordings of the child's early experiences, responses, and the "positions" taken about self and others. It is expressed as "old" (archaic) behavior from childhood.

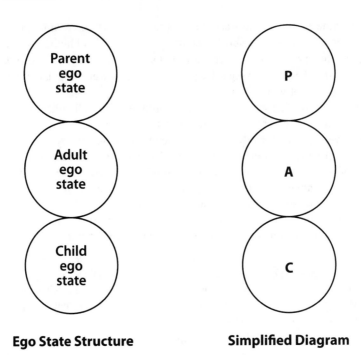

Ego State Structure   **Simplified Diagram**

When you are acting, thinking, or feeling as you observed your parents to be doing, you are in your Parent ego state.

When you are dealing with current reality, gathering facts, and computing objectively, you are in your Adult ego state.

When you are feeling and acting as you did when you were a child, you are in your Child ego state.

Case Illustration

A client was advised to investigate a private school for his son. When he reported his findings about the school where the teaching was informal and creativity encouraged, three distinct reactions were easily observable. First, he scowled and said, "I can't see how anyone could learn anything at that school. There's dirt on the floor!" Leaning back in his chair, his forehead smoothed out as he reflected, "Before I decide, I think I should check on the school's scholastic rating and talk to some of the parents." The next minute, a broad grin crossed his face, and he said, "Gee, I'd love to have gone to a school like that!"

When queried about his responses, the client readily analyzed that his first was the way his father would have responded. His second was his Adult looking for more data. His third was his Child recalling his own unhappy school experience and imagining the fun he might have had at a school such as the one he visited.

Before making a final decision, he pursued his Adult questions. Subsequently, his son attended this school, is currently having a good time there, and is achieving well beyond his former level.

According to structural analysis, each person may respond to a specific stimulus in quite distinct ways from each of the ego states; sometimes these ego states are in concert, sometimes in conflict. Let's look at the following examples.

To a stimulus of a piece of modern art

Parent:	Good grief! What's it supposed to be!
Adult:	That costs $350 according to the price tag.
Child:	Ooo, what pretty color!

To a request for an office report

Parent:	Mr. Brown is not cut out to be a supervisor.
Adult:	I know Mr. Brown needs these by five o'clock.
Child:	No matter what I do, I can't please Mr. Brown.

To an act of violence on the street

Parent:	It serves that girl right for being out so late.
Adult:	I'd better call the police.
Child:	Say, is this ever exciting!

To being offered a piece of chocolate cake when dieting

Parent:	Go ahead, honey, it will keep up your energy.
Adult:	That piece of cake must have at least 400 calories. I think I'll skip it.
Child:	What yummy cake! I could eat the whole thing.

To a crash of rock music

Parent:	That horrible stuff kids listen to today!
Adult:	It's hard for me to think or talk when the music is so loud.
Child:	That makes me want to dance.

To the late arrival of a young woman secretary

Parent:	Poor thing looks as if she hasn't slept a wink.
Adult:	If she doesn't make up her time, the other employees will be dissatisfied.
Child:	I sure wish I could take time off for fun.

To a lecturer using four-letter words

Parent:	Using such expletives only shows a weak vocabulary.
Adult:	I wonder why he chooses those words to use and what their effect is on the audience.
Child:	I wish I dared to talk like that.

To the smell of cabbage

Parent:	Cabbage really keeps the family healthy.
Adult:	Cabbage has high vitamin C content.
Child:	Nobody's going to make me eat that stinky stuff.

To a new male acquaintance putting his arm around you

   Parent: Never let a stranger touch you.

   Adult: I wonder why he's doing it?

   Child: He scares me.

People can feel, smell, touch, speak, listen, look, and act from each ego state. Each ego state has its own programming. Some people respond from one ego state more than from the others. People, for example, who tend to respond most often from their Parent ego state view the world as they observed their parents viewing it. In this case their ability to sense the world for themselves is diminished or distorted.

Development of Ego States

When first born, the infant's awareness is centered on personal needs and comforts. The baby seeks to avoid painful experiences and responds at the feeling level. Almost immediately the infant's unique Child ego state emerges. (Prenatal influences on the Child ego state have not yet been determined.)

The Parent ego state develops next. It is often first observed when the young child plays at parenting, imitating parental behavior. Sometimes it's a shock for parents to see themselves being played back. Sometimes they are very pleased.

The Adult ego state develops as the child tries to make sense out of the world and figures out that other people can be manipulated. The child may ask, "Why do I have to eat when I'm not hungry?" and may try to manipulate others by faking a stomach ache in order to avoid eating.

Case Illustration

Sheri, aged twenty-two months, received a doll-stroller at Christmas. She tried to climb into it saying, "Me, baby." It was too small. She then tried putting her doll in. The doll fit. Sheri squealed, "Me, mommy," and started to push the stroller but soon grew tired of playing this part. Angrily she threw the doll out, pushed over the stroller, righted it, and tried to get in again. Still she could not fit. Frustrated, she put the doll in once more. She tried this switch four times. Then, apparently deciding she was too big, she settled for being mommy and acted toward her doll in ways her mother acted toward her.

Sheri's motherly behavior, an actual imitation of her mother, was from her Parent ego state. Although in her Child ego state Sheri wanted to be a baby, her emerging Adult ego state collected and processed objective data—that she couldn't fit into the stroller.

Any situation may activate a specific ego state and sometimes, as in the case of Sheri, different ego states within a person vie for control. Between two people, one "baby" confronted with another "baby" may try to be a parent or may try to be a "bigger" baby.

Introduction to Analyzing Transactions

Any time one person recognizes another with a smile, a nod, a frown, a verbal greeting, etc., this recognition, in TA language, is called a *stroke*. Two or more strokes make a transaction. All transactions can be classified as complementary, crossed, or ulterior.[7]

Complementary Transactions

A complementary transaction occurs when a message, sent from a specific ego state, gets the predicted response from a specific ego state in the other person. Berne describes a complementary transaction as one which is "appropriate and expected and follows the natural order of healthy human relationships."[8] For example, if a wife who is grieving for her lost friend is comforted by a sympathetic husband, her momentary dependency need is answered appropriately (shown in the diagram below).

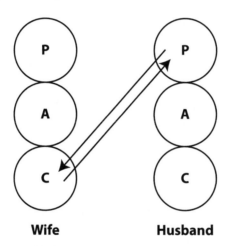

Wife   **Husband**

A complementary transaction can occur between any two ego states. For example, two people may transact Parent-Parent when lamenting their children's leaving home; Adult-Adult when solving a problem; Child-Child or Parent-Child when having fun together. A person can transact from his or her Parent with any of the ego states of another person and can also do this with the Adult and Child ego states. If the response is the expected one, the transaction is complementary. The lines of communication are *open,* and the people can continue transacting with one another.

Gestures, facial expressions, body posture, tone of voice, and so forth, all contribute to the meaning in every transaction. If a verbal message is to be completely understood, the receiver must take into consideration the nonverbal aspects as well as the spoken words.

To better understand the following illustrations, we must assume that the stimulus is straightforward and the verbal and nonverbal messages are congruent.

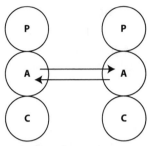

Data Exchange in Adult/Adult transaction (Figure 2)

1. What is the yearly salary for this job?
2. It starts at $10,000.

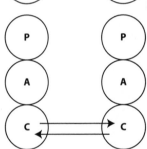

Sympathetic Parent/Parent transaction (Figure 3)

1. Those children really miss their father.
2. Yes, let's take them to the park for a little fun.

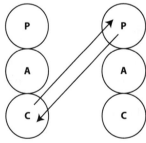

Playful Child/Child transaction (Figure 4)

1. I really like you.
2. I like you, too.

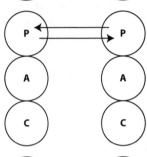

Child/Nurturing Parent transaction (Figure 5)

1. I'm so worried about my son I can't concentrate on this report.
2. You can leave work early to go by the hospital and see him.

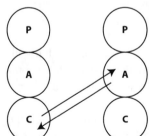

Angry Child/Listening Adult feedback transaction (Figure 6)

1. I'm so mad I could throw this darn typewriter out of the window.
2. Something made you so angry you'd like to throw the equipment around. Is that how it is?

Any illustration is, at best, an educated guess. To be totally accurate, the actual Parent, Adult, and Child ego states of each person would need to be known.

In each of the above transactions communication is open because the responses given were expected responses and were appropriate to the stimulus. This does not always happen. Sometimes a stimulus receives an unexpected or inappropriate response, and the lines of communication become crossed.

Crossed Transactions

When two people stand glaring at each other, turn their backs on each other, are unwilling to continue transacting, or are puzzled by what has just occurred between them, it is likely that they have just experienced a *crossed transaction*. A crossed transaction occurs when an unexpected response is made to the stimulus. An inappropriate ego state is activated, and the lines of transacting between the people are crossed. At this point, people tend to withdraw, turn away from each other, or switch the conversation in another direction. If a husband responds unsympathetically to his grieving wife, "Well, how do you think I feel!" he is likely to cause her to turn away from him (Figure 7).

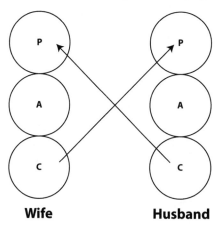

Wife   **Husband**

Crossed transactions are a frequent source of pain between people—parents and children, husband and wife, boss and employee, teacher and student, and so forth. The person who initiates a transaction, expecting a certain response, does not get it. The individual is crossed up and often feels discounted and misunderstood.

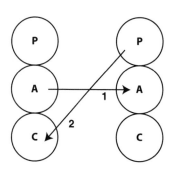

Figure 8

1. Boss: What time is it?
2. Secretary: You're always in such a hurry!

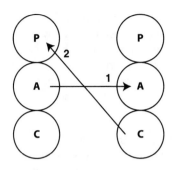

Figure 9

1. Husband: Can you take the car to be serviced this afternoon?

2. Wife: Today I iron. Johnny expects a birthday cake. The cat has to go to the vet, and now you want me to take the car in!

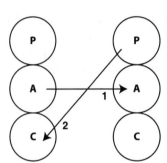

Figure 10

1. Boss: I need 25 copies of this report for the board meeting this afternoon. Can you get them for me?

2. Secretary: Aren't you lucky you've got me around to take care of you?

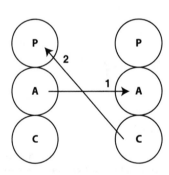

Figure 11

1. Scientist A: There may be some variables we haven't considered for this experiment.

2. Scientist B: So what, who cares around here?

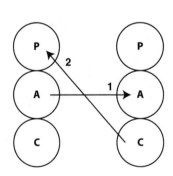

Figure 12

1. Wife: I'd like to use the car on Wednesday night and have a good visit with my sister.

2. Husband: Gee, you never want to talk to me.

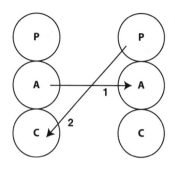

Figure 13

1. Supervisor: Have you seen the Willows contract, Miss Smith?

2. File clerk: If you ran this department the way you're supposed to, you wouldn't have to ask me where the Willows contract is.

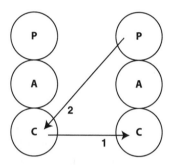

Figure 14

1. John: Let's have fun.

2. Marcia: Can't you ever be serious?

Transactions may be direct or indirect, straightforward or diluted, intense or weak. *Indirect transactions* are three-handed. One person speaks to another while hoping to influence the third who can overhear it. For example, a man may be too fearful to speak directly to his boss, so says something to a co-worker, hoping the boss will "get the message."

Diluted transactions are often half hostile, half affectionate. The message is buried in some form of kidding. For example, one student may say to another, "Hey genius, when are you going to finish that book? I want to read it." The other may toss the book, saying, "Here you are, butterfingers. Catch it if you can."

Weak transactions are those that are superficial, perfunctory, and lack feelings of intensity. Such is the case if a wife says to her husband, "I wonder if we should go out for dinner tonight," and he responds, "I don't care, dear. Whatever you say, dear."

In healthy relationships people transact directly, straightforwardly, and, on occasion, intensely.[9] These transactions are complementary and free from ulterior motives.

Ulterior Transactions

Ulterior transactions are the most complex. They differ from complementary and crossed transactions in that they always involve more than two ego states. When an ulterior message is sent, it is disguised under a socially acceptable transaction. Such is the purpose of the old cliché: "Wouldn't you like to come up to see my etchings?" In this instance the Adult is verbalizing one thing while the Child, with the use of innuendo, is sending a different message (Figure 15).

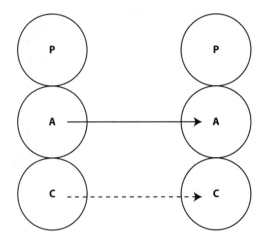

If a car salesman says with a leer to his customer, "This is our finest sports car, but it may be too racy for you," he is sending a message that can be heard by either the customer's Adult or Child ego state (see Figure 16). If the customer's Adult hears, the response may be, "Yes, you're right, considering the requirements of my job." If the customer's Child hears, the response may be, "I'll take it. It's just what I want."

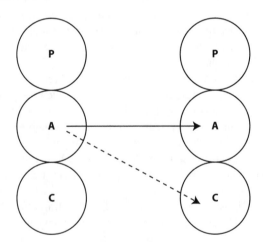

An ulterior message is also given when a secretary submits a letter with several typing errors to the boss. This invites the boss to give the secretary a Parental put-down (see Figure 17). The same happens when a student is continually late with assignments, absent from class, writes illegibly, or in some way provokes the equivalent of parental criticism.

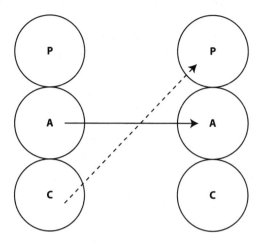

The same kind of ulterior transaction occurs if a man who has been a "reformed" alcoholic comes to work with a hangover, but with a glimmer in his eye, and boasts to his co-worker, "Boy, I really blew it last night and drank myself under the table. What a head I've got today!" On the surface he is giving factual information. However, at the ulterior level, the alcoholic's Child ego state is looking for the Parent in the other to smile indulgently and thus condone his drinking.

Instead of a Parent response he may activate his co-worker's Child ego state, and he may respond by laughing at the tragedy. If the co-worker laughs, from either his Parent or his Child ego state, he reinforces the (parental) injunction, usually given nonverbally to the alcoholic (as a child), "Get lost, you bum." This inappropriate laugh or smile is described by Claude Steiner as the *gallows transaction*.[10] The smile serves to tighten the noose, and destructive behavior is reinforced.

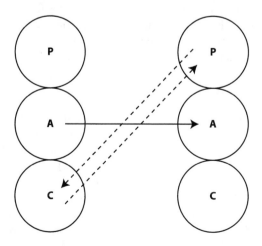

Any smiling response to a person's misfortunes may serve as a gallows transaction. Such is the case when

a teacher acts amused at a pupil's "stupid behavior,"

a mother laughs at her accident-prone three-year-old,

a father beams over the risks his son takes.

These gallows transactions, like other transactions with ulterior motives, are common among losers. Losers use them to promote their psychological games.

The Games People Play

People play psychological games with one another that are similar to games, like Monopoly, bridge, or checkers, that people play at social gatherings. The players must know the game in order to play—after all, if one person enters a card party ready to play bridge, and everyone else is playing pinochle, that person can't very well play bridge.

All games have a beginning, a given set of rules, and a concluding payoff. Psychological games, however, have an ulterior purpose. They are not played for fun. Of course, neither are some poker games.

Berne defines a *psychological game* as "a recurring set of transactions, often repetitive, superficially rational, with a concealed motivation; or, more colloquially, as a series of transactions with a gimmick."[11] Three specific elements must be present to define transactions as games:

1. an ongoing series of complementary transactions which are plausible on the social level,

2. an ulterior transaction which is the underlying message of the game, and

3. a predictable payoff which concludes the game and is the real purpose for playing.

Games prevent honest, intimate, and open relationships between the players. Yet people play them because they fill up time, provoke attention, reinforce early opinions about self and others, and fulfill a sense of destiny.

Psychological games are played to win, but a person who plays games as a way of life is not a winner. Sometimes, a person acts like a loser in order to win the game (Figure 19). For example, in a game of *Kick Me* a player provokes someone else to a put-down response.

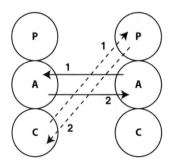

Student: I stayed up too late last night and don't have my assignment ready. (ulterior: I'm a bad boy, kick me.)

Instructor: You're out of luck. This is the last day I can give credit for that assignment (ulterior: Yes, you are a bad boy and here is your kick.)

Though they may deny it, people who are used to this game tend to attract others who can play the complementary hand and are willing to "kick" in response.

Every game has a first move. Some first moves are nonverbal: turning a cold shoulder, batting a flirty eye, shaking an accusative finger, slamming a door, tracking mud in the house, reading someone's mail, looking woebegone, not speaking. Other first moves are verbal statements, such as:

"You look so lonesome over here by yourself. . . ."
"How could you go to school wearing that get-up!"
"He criticized you. Are you going to take that?"
"I have this terrible problem. . . ."
"Isn't it awful that. . . ."

Barbara and Tom's favorite game was *Uproar.* They both knew the first move in the game, so either could start it. Once it was started, a predictable set of transactions occurred which climaxed with a loud fight. The outcome was always the same—hostile withdrawal to avoid closeness. This was their payoff for playing the game, the avoidance of intimacy.

To set up the game either Barbara or Tom provoked the other with nonverbal behavior such as sulking, chain-smoking, withdrawing, or acting irritated. When the partner was "hooked" into playing, the game was under way. As the game continued he/she got a put-off or a put-down. After exchanging many angry words, they finally withdrew from each other.

When Barbara starts the game, the transactions are:

Barbara:	(Begins pouting and chain-smoking with exaggerated gestures)
Tom:	"What's the matter? What's wrong?"
Barbara:	"It's none of your business!"
Tom:	(Goes out to the local bar)
Barbara:	(Explodes in anger when he returns. A long battle ensues, filled with accusations and counteraccusations. The payoff comes when Barbara breaks into tears, runs into the bedroom, and slams the door. Tom retreats to the kitchen for another drink. They make no further contact that evening.)

When Tom initiates the game, the transactions are:

Tom:	(Fixes a drink for himself, goes off to the den, and closes the door.)
Barbara:	"Why didn't you fix a drink for me? Is something wrong?"
Tom:	"Can't I even have a few minutes alone!"
Barbara:	"If you want to be alone, I'll leave!" (Barbara goes shopping, buys things they can't afford, and returns carrying several packages.)
Tom:	(Explodes in anger about the way she spends money. The game comes full circle when she stamps away mad, and he fixes his bed in the den.)

Games tend to be repetitious. People find themselves saying the same words in the same way, only the time and place may change. Perhaps the replay contributes to what is often described as "I feel as if I've done this before."

People play games with different degrees of intensity, from the socially accepted, relaxed level to the criminal homicide/suicide level. Berne writes:

a) A First-Degree Game is one which is socially acceptable in the agent's circle.
b) A Second-Degree Game is one from which no permanent, irremediable damage arises, but which the players would rather conceal from the public.
c) A Third-Degree Game is one which is played for keeps, and which ends in the surgery, the courtroom or the morgue.[12]

Games are individually programmed. They are played from the Parent ego state if the parent's games are imitated. They are played from the Adult ego state if they are consciously calculated. They are played from the Child ego state if they are based on early life experiences, decisions, and the "positions" that a child takes about self and others.

Days of Decision

Before children are eight years old they develop a concept about their own worth. They also formulate ideas about the worth of others. They crystallize their experiences and decide what it all means to them, what parts they are going to play, and how they are going to play them. These are children's days of decision.[13]

When decisions about self and others are made very early in life, they may be quite unrealistic. They are very likely to be somewhat distorted and irrational, because children perceive life through the small peekhole of their existence. These distortions can create some degree of pathology ranging from inconsequential to serious. However, they seem logical and make sense at the time the child makes them. The following story, reported by Betty, a woman of forty-three who had been married to an alcoholic for twenty years, illustrates the effect of early decisions.

Case Illustration

My father was a brutal alcoholic. When he was drunk he would hit me and scream at me. I would try to hide. One day when he came home, the door flew open and he was drunker than usual. He picked up a butcher knife and started running through the house. I hid in a coat closet. I was almost four years old. I was so scared in the closet. It was dark and spooky, and things kept hitting me in the face. That day I decided who men were—beasts, who would only try to hurt me. I was a large child and I remember thinking, "If I were smaller, he'd love me," or "If I were prettier, he'd love me." I always thought I wasn't worth anything.

The "days of decision" lead a person to take psychological positions.[14] In the above case the woman took the positions, "I'm unworthy (I am not-OK)" and "Men are beasts who will hurt me (men are not-OK)." On the basis of these positions she selected people who would play certain roles that fit into her life drama.

She married a "beast" who was also an alcoholic. In addition, she often played the game of *Rapo* at social gatherings. When playing her game, she would engage a man in conversation and lead him on seductively. If he responded to her message, she would turn away in righteous indignation, confident once more that "men are beasts who will hurt me."

Psychological Positions

When taking positions about themselves, people may conclude:

I'm smart.	I'm stupid.
I'm nice.	I'm nasty.
I'm powerful.	I'm inadequate.
I'm an angel.	I'm a devil.
I can't do anything wrong.	I can't do anything right.
I'm as good as anybody else.	I don't deserve to live.

When taking positions about others, people may conclude:

People will give me anything I want.	Nobody will give me anything.
People are wonderful.	People are no damn good.
Someone will help me.	People are out to get me.
Everybody likes me.	Nobody likes me.
People are nice.	Everybody's mean.

In general, the above positions are "I'm OK" or "I'm not-OK," and "You're OK" or "You're not-OK." The psychological positions taken about oneself and about others fit into four basic patterns.[15] The first is the winner's position, but even winners may occasionally have feelings that resemble the other three.

The First Position: I'm OK, You're OK

is potentially a mentally healthy position. If realistic, people with this position about themselves and others can solve their problems constructively. Their expectations are likely to be valid. They accept the significance of people.

The Second or Projective Position: I'm OK, You're not-OK

is the position of persons who feel victimized or persecuted, so victimize and persecute others. They blame others for their miseries. Delinquents and criminals often have this position and take on paranoid behavior which in extreme cases may lead to homicide.

The Third or Introjective Position: I'm not-OK, You're OK

is a common position of persons who feel powerless when they compare themselves to others. This position leads them to withdraw, to experience depression, and, in severe cases, to become suicidal.

The Fourth or Futility Position: I'm not-OK, You're not-OK

is the position of those who lose interest in living, who exhibit schizoid behavior, and who, in extreme cases, commit suicide or homicide.

People with the first position feel "Life is worth living." With the second they feel "Your life is not worth much." With the third they feel "My life is not worth much." With the fourth they feel "Life isn't worth anything at all."

Notes

[1]   Perls, *Gestalt Therapy Verbatim*, p. 40.

[2]   See Dorothy Jongeward, *Transactional Analysis Overview* (Reading, MA: Addison-Wesley, 1973). A cassette.

[3]   Eric Berne, *Transactional Analysis in Psychotherapy* (New York: Grove Press, 1961; Souvenir Press of London), pp. 17–43.

 Cf. Paul McCormick and Leonard Campos, *Introduce Yourself to Transactional Analysis: A TA Handbook* (Stockton, Calif.: San Joaquin TA Study Group, distributed by Transactional Pub., 3155 College Ave., Berkeley, CA, 94705, 1969).

 Also see John M. Dusay, "Transactional Analysis," in *A Layman's Guide to Psychiatry and Psychoanalysis* by Eric Berne (New York: Simon and Schuster, 3rd ed., 1968), pp. 277–306.

[4]   Berne, *Principles of Group Treatment*, p. 364.

[5]   *Ibid.*, p. 281.

[6]   Berne, *Transactional Analysis in Psychotherapy*, p. 3.

[7]   Berne, *Games People Play*, pp. 29–64.

[8]   *Ibid.*, p. 29.

[9]   *See* Eric Berne, *The Structure and Dynamics of Organizations and Groups* (Philadelphia: J. B. Lippincott, 1963).

[10] *See* Claude M. Steiner, *Games Alcoholics Play: The Analysis of Life Scripts* (New York: Grove Press, 1971).

[11] Eric Berne, "Transactional Analysis," in *Active Psychotherapy*, Harold Greenwald, Ed. (New York: Atherton Press, 1967), p. 125.

[12] Berne, *Games People Play*, p. 64.

[13] Berne, *Principles of Group Treatment*, pp. 269–278.

[14] *See* Thomas A. Harris, *I'm OK—You're OK* (New York: Harper & Row, 1969).

[15] Eric Berne, "Standard Nomenclature, Transactional Nomenclature," *Transactional Analysis Bulletin,* Vol. 8, No. 32 (Oct. 1969), p. 11.

 Cf. Zelig Selinger, "The Parental Second Position in Treatment," *Transactional Analysis Bulletin,* Vol. 6. No. 21 (Jan. 1967), p. 29.

7

The Johari Window

Jay Hall

High on the diagnostic checklist of corporate health is communication; and the prognosis is less than encouraging. In a recent cross-cultural study,[1] roughly 74 percent of the managers sampled from companies in Japan, Great Britain, and the United States cited communication breakdown as the single greatest barrier to corporate excellence.

Just what constitutes a problem of communication is not easily agreed upon. Some theorists approach the issue from the vantage point of information bits comprising a message; others speak in terms of organizational roles and positions of centrality or peripherality; still others emphasize the directional flows of corporate data. The result is that more and more people are communicating about communication, while the achievement of clarity, understanding, commitment, and creativity—the goals of communication—becomes more and more limited.

More often than not, the communication dilemmas cited by people are not communication problems at all. They are instead *symptoms* of difficulties at more basic and fundamental levels of corporate life. From a dynamic standpoint, problems of communication in organizations frequently reflect dysfunctions at the level of *corporate climate*. The feelings people have about where or with whom they work—feelings of impotence, distrust, resentment, insecurity, social inconsequence, and all the other very human emotions—not only define the climate which prevails but the manner in which communications will be managed. R. R. Blake and Jane S. Mouton[2] have commented upon an oddity of organizational life: when management is effective and relationships are sound, problems of communication tend not to occur. It is only when relationships among members of the organization are unsound and fraught with unarticulated tensions that one hears complaints of communication breakdown. Thus, the quality of relationships in an organization may dictate to a great extent the level of communication effectiveness achieved.

Originally titled "Communication Revisited" by Jay Hall. Copyright © 1973 by The Regents of the University of California. Reprinted from the *California Management Review,* Vol. 15, No. 3. By permission of The Regents.

Interpersonal Styles and the Quality of Relationships

The critical factor underlying relationship quality in organizations is in need of review. Reduced to its lowest common denominator, the most significant determinant of the quality of relationships is the interpersonal style of the parties to a relationship. The learned, characteristic, and apparently preferred manner in which individuals relate to others in the building of relationships—the manner in which they monitor, control, filter, divert, give, and seek the information germane to a given relationship—will dictate over time the quality of relationships which exist among people, the emotional climate which will characterize their interactions, and whether or not there will be problems of communication. In the final analysis, individuals are the human links in the corporate network, and the styles they employ interpersonally are the ultimate determinants of what information goes where and whether it will be distortion-free or masked by interpersonal constraints.

The concept of interpersonal style is not an easy one to define; yet, if it is to serve as the central mechanism underlying the quality of relationships, the nature of corporate climate, managerial effectiveness, and the level of corporate excellence attainable, it is worthy of analysis. Fortunately, Joseph Luft[3] and Harry Ingham—two behavioral scientists with special interests in interpersonal and group processes—have developed a model of social interaction which affords a way of thinking about interpersonal functioning, while handling much of the data encountered in everyday living. The Johari Window, as their model is called, identifies several interpersonal styles, their salient features and consequences, and suggests a basis for interpreting the significance of style for the quality of relationships. An overview of the Johari model should help to sharpen the perception of interpersonal practices among managers and lend credence to the contention of Blake and Mouton that there are few communication problems as such, only unsound relationships. At the same time, a normative statement regarding effective interpersonal functioning and, by extension, the foundations of corporate excellence may be found in the model as well. Finally, the major tenets of the model are testable under practical conditions, and the latter portion of this discussion will be devoted to research on the managerial profile in interpersonal encounters. The author has taken a number of interpretive liberties with the basic provisions of the Johari Awareness model. While it is anticipated that none of these violate the integrity of the model as originally described by Luft, it should be emphasized that many of the inferences and conclusions discussed are those of the author, and Dr. Luft should not be held accountable for any lapses of logic or misapplications of the model in this paper.

The Johari Window: A Graphic Model of Interpersonal Processes

As treated here, the Johari Window is essentially an information processing model; interpersonal style and individual effectiveness are assessed in terms of information processing tendencies and the performance consequences thought to be associated with such practices. The model employs a four-celled figure as its format and reflects the interaction of two interpersonal sources of information—Self and Others—and the behavioral processes required for utilizing that information. The model, depicted in figure 1, may be thought of as representing the various kinds of data available for use in the establishment of interpersonal relationships. The squared field, in effect, represents a personal space. This in turn is partitioned into four regions, with each representing a particular combination or mix of relevant information and having special significance for the quality of relationships. To fully appreciate the implications that each informational region has for interpersonal effectiveness, one must consider not only the size and shape of each region but also the reasons for its presence in the interpersonal space. In an attempt to "personalize" the model, it is helpful to think of oneself as the *Self* in the relationship for, as will be seen presently, it is what the Self does interpersonally that has the most direct impact on the quality of resulting relationships. In organizational terms, it is how the management-Self behaves that is critical to the quality of corporate relationships.

Figure 1 reveals that the two informational sources, Self and Others, have information which is pertinent to the relationship and, at the same time, each lacks information that is equally germane. Thus, there is relevant and necessary information which is *Known by the Self, Unknown by the Self, Known by Others* and *Unknown by Others*. The Self/Other combinations of known and unknown information make up the four regions within the interpersonal space and, again, characterize the various types and qualities of relationships possible within the Johari framework.

Figure 1
The Johari Window: A Model of Interpersonal Processes

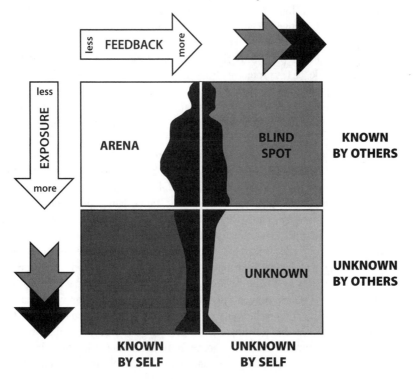

Region I, for example, constitutes that portion of the total interpersonal space which is devoted to mutually held information. This Known by Self-Known by Others facet of the interpersonal space is thought to be the part of the relationship which, because of its shared data characteristics and implied likelihood of mutual understanding, controls interpersonal productivity. That is, the working assumption is that productivity and interpersonal effectiveness are directly related to the amount of mutually held information in a relationship. Therefore, the larger Region I becomes, the more rewarding, effective, and productive the relationship. As the informational context for interpersonal functioning, Region I is called the "Arena."

Region II, using the double classification approach just described, is that portion of the interpersonal space which holds information Known by Others but Unknown by the Self. Thus, this array of data constitutes an interpersonal handicap for the Self, since one can hardly understand the behaviors, decisions, or potentials of others if he doesn't have the data upon which these are based. Others have the advantage of knowing their own reactions, feelings, perceptions, and the like while the Self is unaware of these. Region II, an area of hidden unperceived information, is called the "Blindspot." The Blindspot is, of course, a limiting factor with respect to the size of Region I and may be thought of, therefore, as inhibiting interpersonal effectiveness.

Region III may also be considered to inhibit interpersonal effectiveness, but it is due to an imbalance of information which would seem to favor the Self; as the portion of the relationship which is characterized by information Known by the Self but Unknown by Others, Region III constitutes a protective feature of the relationship for the Self. Data which one perceives as potentially prejudicial to a relationship or which he keeps to himself out of fear, desire for power, or whatever, make up the "Facade." This protective front, in turn, serves a defensive function for the Self. The question is not one of whether a Facade is necessary but rather how much Facade is required realistically; this raises the question of how much conscious defensiveness can be tolerated before the Arena becomes too inhibited and interpersonal effectiveness begins to diminish.

Finally, Region IV constitutes that portion of the relationship which is devoted to material neither known by the self nor by other parties to the relationship. The information in this Unknown by Self-Unknown by Others area is thought to reflect psychodynamic data, hidden potential, unconscious idiosyncrasies, and the data-base of creativity. Thus, Region IV is the "Unknown" area which may become known as interpersonal effectiveness increases.

Summarily, it should be said that the information within all regions can be of any type—feeling data, factual information, assumptions, task skill data, and prejudices—which are relevant to the relationship at hand. Irrelevant data are not the focus of the Johari Window concept: just those pieces of information which have a bearing on the quality and productivity of the relationship should be considered as appropriate targets for the information processing practices prescribed by the model. At the same time, it should be borne in mind that the individuals involved in a relationship, particularly the Self, control what and how information will be processed. Because of this implicit personal control aspect, the model should be viewed as an open system which is *dynamic* and amenable to change as personal decisions regarding interpersonal functioning change.

Basic Interpersonal Processes: Exposure and Feedback

The dynamic character of the model is critical; for it is the movement capability of the horizontal and vertical lines which partition the interpersonal space into regions which gives individuals control over what their relationships will become. The Self can significantly influence the size of his Arena in relating to others by the behavioral processes he employs in establishing relationships. To the extent that one takes the steps necessary to apprise others of relevant information which he has and they do not, he is enlarging his Arena in a downward direction. Within the framework of the model, this enlargement occurs in concert with a reduction of one's Facade. Thus, if one behaves in a non-defensive, trusting, and possibly risk taking manner with others, he may be thought of as contributing to increased mutual awareness and sharing of data. The process one employs toward this end has been called the "Exposure" process. It entails the open and candid disclosure of one's feelings, factual knowledge, wild guesses, and the like in a conscious attempt to share. Frothy, intentionally untrue, diversionary sharing does not constitute exposure; and, as personal experience will attest, it does nothing to help mutual understanding. The Exposure process is under the direct control of the Self and may be used as a mechanism for building trust and for legitimizing mutual exposures.

The need for mutual exposures becomes apparent when one considers the behavioral process required for enlarging the Arena laterally. As a behavior designed to gain reduction in one's Blindspot, the Feedback process entails an active solicitation by the Self of the information he feels others might have which he does not. The active, initiative-taking aspect of this solicitation behavior should be stressed, for again the Self takes the primary role in setting interpersonal norms and in legitimizing certain acts within the relationship. Since the extent to which the Self will actually receive the Feedback he solicits is contingent upon the willingness of others to expose their data, the need for a climate of mutual exposures becomes apparent. Control by the Self of the success of his Feedback-seeking behaviors is less direct therefore than in the case of self-exposure. He will achieve a reduction of his Blindspot only with the cooperation of others; and his own prior willingness to deal openly and candidly may well dictate what level of cooperative and trusting behavior will prevail on the part of other parties to the relationship.

Thus, one can theoretically establish interpersonal relationships characterized by mutual understanding and increased effectiveness (by a dominant Arena) if he will engage in exposing and feedback soliciting behaviors to an optimal degree. This places the determination of productivity and amount of interpersonal reward—and the quality of relationships—directly in the hands of the Self. In theory, this amounts to an issue of interpersonal competence; in practice, it amounts to the conscious and sensitive management of interpersonal processes.

Interpersonal Styles and Managerial Impacts

While one can theoretically employ Exposure and Feedback processes not only to a great but to a similar degree as well, individuals typically fail to achieve such an optimal practice. Indeed, they usually display a significant preference for one or the other of the two processes and tend to overuse one while neglecting the other. This tendency promotes a state of imbalance in interpersonal relationships which, in turn, creates disruptive tensions capable of retarding productivity. Figure 2 presents several commonly used approaches to the employment of Exposure and Feedback processes. Each of these may be thought of as reflecting a basic interpersonal style—that is, fairly consistent and preferred ways of behaving interpersonally. As might be expected, each style has associated with it some fairly predictable consequences.

Figure 2
Interpersonal Styles as Functions of Exposure and Feedback

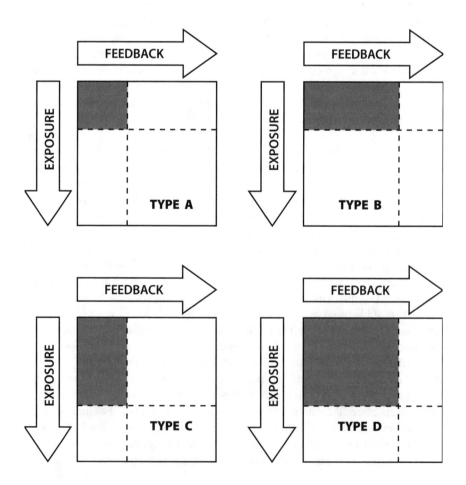

Type A.   This interpersonal style reflects a minimal use of both Exposure and Feedback processes; it is a fairly impersonal approach to interpersonal relationships. The Unknown region dominates under this style; and unrealized potential, untapped creativity, and personal psychodynamics prevail as the salient influences. Such a style would seem to indicate withdrawal and an aversion to risk-taking on the part of its user; interpersonal anxiety and safety-seeking are likely to be prime sources of personal motivation. Persons who characteristically use this style appear to be detached, mechanical, and uncommunicative. They may often be found in bureaucratic highly structured organizations of some type where it is possible, and perhaps profitable, to avoid personal disclosure or involvement. People using this style are likely to be reacted to with more than average hostility, since other parties to the relationship will tend to interpret the lack of Exposure and Feedback solicitation largely according to their own needs and how this interpersonal lack affects need fulfillment.

Subordinates whose manager employs such a style, for example, will often feel that his behavior is consciously aimed at frustrating them in their work. The person in need of support and encouragement will often view a Type A manager as aloof, cold, and indifferent. Another individual in need of firm directions and plenty of order in his work may view the same manager as indecisive and administratively impotent. Yet another person requiring freedom and opportunities to be innovative may see the Type A interpersonal style as hopelessly tradition-bound and as symptomatic of fear and an overriding need for security. The use of Type A behaviors on a large scale in an organization reveals something about the climate and fundamental health of that organization. In many respects, interpersonal relationships founded on Type A uses of exposure and feedback constitute the kind of organizational ennui about which Chris Argyris[4] has written so eloquently. Such practices are, in his opinion, likely to be learned ways of behaving under oppressive policies of the sort which encourage people to act in a submissive and dependent fashion. Organizationally, of course, the result is lack of communication and a loss of human potentials; the Unknown becomes the dominant feature of corporate relationships, and the implications for organizational creativity and growth are obvious.

Type B.   Under this approach, there is also an aversion to Exposure, but aversion is coupled with a desire for relationships not found in Type A. Thus, Feedback is the only process left in promoting relationships, and it is much overused. An aversion to the use of Exposure may typically be interpreted as a sign of basic mistrust of self and others, and it is therefore not surprising that the Facade is the dominant feature of relationships resulting from neglected Exposure coupled with overused Feedback. The style appears to be a probing supportive interpersonal ploy and, once the Facade becomes apparent, it is likely to result in a reciprocal withdrawal of trust by other parties. This may promote feelings of suspicion on the part of others; such feelings may lead to the manager being treated as a rather superficial person without real substance or as a devious sort with many hidden agenda.

Preference for this interpersonal style among managers seems to be of two types. Some managers committed to a quasi-permissive management may employ Type B behaviors in an attempt to avoid appearing directive. Such an approach results in the manager's personal resources never being fully revealed or his opinions being expressed. In contrast—but subject to many of the same inadequacies— is the use of Type B behaviors in an attempt to gain or maintain one's personal power in relationships. Many managers build a facade to maintain personal control and an outward appearance of confidence. As the Johari model would suggest, however, persons who employ such practices tend to become isolated from their subordinates and colleagues alike. Lack of trust predominates and consolidation of power and promotion of an image of confidence may be the least likely results of Type B use in organizations. Very likely, the seeds of distrust and conditions for covert competitiveness—with all the implications for organizational teamwork— will follow from widespread use of Type B interpersonal practices.

Type C.   Based on an overuse of Exposure to the neglect of Feedback, this interpersonal style may reflect ego-striving and/or distrust of others' competence. The person who uses this style usually feels quite confident of his own opinions and is likely to value compliance from others. The fact that he is often unaware of his impact or of the potential of others' contributions is reflected in the dominant Blindspot which results from this style. Others are likely to feel disenfranchised by one who uses this style; they often feel that he has little use for their contributions or concern for their feelings. As a result, this style often triggers feelings of hostility, insecurity, and resentment on the part of others. Frequently, others will learn to perpetuate the manager's Blindspot by withholding important information or giving only selected feedback; as such, this is a reflection of the passive-aggressiveness and unarticulated hostility which this style can cause. Labor-management relations frequently reflect such Blindspot dynamics.

The Type C interpersonal style is probably what has prompted so much interest in "listening" programs around the country. As the Johari model makes apparent, however, the Type C overuse of Exposure and neglect of Feedback is just one of several interpersonal tendencies that may disrupt communications. While hierarchical organizational structure or centrality in communication nets and the like may certainly facilitate the use of individual Type C behaviors, so can fear of failure, authoritarianism, need for control, and over-confidence in one's own opinions; such traits vary from person to person and limit the utility of communication panaceas. Managers who rely on this style often do so to demonstrate competence; many corporate cultures require that the manager be *the* planner, director, and controller and many managers behave accordingly to protect their corporate images. Many others are simply trying to be helpful in a paternalistic kind of way; others are, of course, purely dictatorial. Whatever the reason, those who employ the Type C style have one thing in common: their relationships will be dominated by Blindspots and they are destined for surprise whenever people get enough and decide to force feedback on them, solicited or not.

Type D.   Balanced Exposure and Feedback processes are used to a great extent in this style; candor, openness, and a sensitivity to others' needs to participate are the salient features of the style. The Arena is the dominant characteristic, and productivity increases. In initial stages, this style may promote some defensiveness on the part of others who are not familiar with honest and trusting relationships; but perseverance will tend to promote a norm of reciprocal candor over time in which creative potential can be realized.

Among managers, Type D practices constitute an ideal state from the standpoint of organizational effectiveness. Healthy and creative climates result from its widespread use, and the conditions for growth and corporate excellence may be created through the use of constructive Exposure and Feedback exchanges. Type D practices do not give license to "clobber," as some detractors might claim; and, for optimal results, the data explored should be germane to the relationships and problems at hand, rather than random intimacies designed to overcome self-consciousness. Trust is slowly built, and managers who experiment with Type D processes should be prepared to be patient and flexible in their relationships. Some managers, as they tentatively try out Type D strategies, encounter reluctance and distrust on the part of others, with the result that they frequently give up too soon, assuming that the style doesn't work. The reluctance of others should be assessed against the backdrop of previous management practices and the level of prior trust which characterizes the culture. Other managers may try candor only to discover that they have opened a Pandora's box from which a barrage of hostility and complaints emerges. The temptation of the naive manager is to put the lid back on quickly; but the more enlightened manager knows that when communications are opened up after having been closed for a long time, the most emotionally laden issues—ones which have been the greatest source of frustration, anger, or fear—will be the first to be discussed. If management can resist cutting the dialogue short, the diatribe will run its course as the emotion underlying it is drained off, and exchanges will become more problem centered and future oriented. Management intent will have been tested and found worthy of trust, and creative unrestrained interchanges will occur. Organizations built on such practices are those headed for corporate climates and resource utilization of the type necessary for true corporate excellence. The manager's interpersonal style may well be the catalyst for this reaction to occur.

Summarily, the Johari Window model of interpersonal processes suggests that much more is needed to understand communication in an organization than information about its structure or one's position in a network. People make very critical decisions about what information will be processed, irrespective of structural and network considerations. People bring with them to organizational settings propensities for behaving in certain ways interpersonally. They prefer certain interpersonal styles, sharpened and honed by corporate cultures, which significantly influence—if not dictate entirely—the flow of information in organizations. As such, individuals and their preferred styles of relating one to another amount to the synapses in the corporate network which control and coordinate the human system. Central to an understanding of communication in organizations, therefore, is an appreciation of the complexities of those human interfaces which comprise organizations. The work of Luft and Ingham, when brought to bear on management practices and corporate cultures, may lend much needed insight into the constraints unique to organizational life which either hinder or facilitate the processing of corporate data.

Research on the Managerial Profile:
The Personnel Relations Survey

As treated here, one of the major tenets of the Johari Window model is that one's use of Exposure and Feedback soliciting processes is a matter of personal decision. Whether consciously or unconsciously, when one employs either process or fails to do so he has decided that such practices somehow serve the goals he has set for himself. Rationales for particular behavior are likely to be as varied as the goals people seek; they may be in the best sense of honest intent or they may simply represent evasive logic or systems of self-deception. The *purposeful* nature of interpersonal styles remains nevertheless. A manager's style of relating to other members of the organization is never simply a collection of random, unconsidered acts. Whether he realizes it or not, or admits it or denies it, his interpersonal style *has purpose* and is thought to serve either a personal or interpersonal goal in his relationships.

Because of the element of decision and purposeful intent inherent in one's interpersonal style, the individual's inclination to employ Exposure and Feedback processes may be assessed. That is, his decisions to engage in open and candid behaviors or to actively seek out the information that others are thought to have may be sampled, and his Exposure and Feedback tendencies thus measured. Measurements obtained may be used in determining the manager's or the organization's Johari Window configuration and the particular array of interpersonal predilections which underlie it. Thus, the Luft-Ingham model not only provides a way of conceptualizing what is going on interpersonally, but it affords a rationale for actually assessing practices which may, in turn, be coordinated to practical climate and cultural issues.

Hall and Williams have designed a paper-and-pencil instrument for use with managers which reveals their preferences for Exposure and Feedback in their relationships with subordinates, colleagues, and superiors. The *Personnel Relations Survey*,[5] as the instrument is entitled, has been used extensively by industry as a training aid for providing personal feedback of a type which "personalizes" otherwise didactic theory sessions on the Johari, on one hand, and as a catalyst to evaluation and critique of ongoing relationships, on the other hand. In addition to its essentially training oriented use, however, the *Personnel Relations Survey* has been a basic research tool for assessing current practices among managers. The results obtained from two pieces of research are of particular interest from the standpoint of their implications for corporate climates and managerial styles.

Authority relationships and interpersonal style preferences. Using the *Personnel Relations Survey*, data were collected from 1000 managers. These managers represent a cross-section of those found in organizations today; levels of management ranging from company president to just above first-line supervisor were sampled from all over the United States. Major manufacturers and petroleum and food producers contributed to the research, as well as a major airline, state and federal governmental agencies, and nonprofit service organizations.

Since the *Personnel Relations Survey* addresses the manner in which Exposure and Feedback processes are employed in one's relationships with his subordinates, colleagues, and superiors, the data from the 1000 managers sampled reveal some patterns which prevail in organizations in terms of downward, horizontal, and upward communications. In addition, the shifting and changing of interpersonal tactics as one moves from one authority relationship to another is noteworthy from the standpoint of power dynamics underlying organizational life. A summary of the average tendencies obtained from managers is presented graphically in figure 3.

Of perhaps the greatest significance for organizational climates is the finding regarding the typical manager's use of Exposure. As figure 3 indicates, one's tendency to deal openly and candidly with others is directly influenced by the amount of power he possesses relative to other parties to the relationship. Moving from relationships with subordinates in which the manager obviously enjoys greater formal authority, through colleague relationships characterized by equal authority positions, to relationships with superiors in which the manager is least powerful, the plots of Exposure use steadily decline. Indeed, a straight linear relationship is suggested between amount of authority possessed by the average manager and his use of candor in relationships.

While there are obvious exceptions to this depiction, the average managerial profile on Exposure reveals the most commonly found practices in organizations which, when taken diagnostically, suggest that the average manager in today's organizations has a number of "hang-ups" around authority issues which seriously curtail his interpersonal effectiveness. Consistent with other findings from communication research, these data point to power differences among parties to relation-

Figure 3
Score Plots on Exposure and Feedback for the "Average" Manager
from a Sample of 1000 Managers in the United States

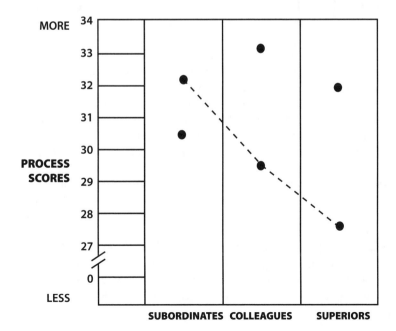

ships as a major disruptive influence on the flow of information in organizations. A more accurate interpretation, however, seems to be that it is not power differences as such which impede communication, but the way people *feel* about these differences and begin to monitor, filter, and control their contributions in response to their own feelings and apprehensions.

Implications for overall corporate climate may become more obvious when the data from the Exposure process are considered with those reflecting the average manager's reliance on Feedback acquisition. As figure 3 reveals, Feedback solicitation proceeds differently. As might be expected, there is less use of the Feedback process in relationships with subordinates than there is of the Exposure process. This variation on the Type C interpersonal style, reflecting an overuse of Exposure to some neglect of Feedback, very likely contributes to subordinate feelings of resentment, lack of social worth, and frustration. These feelings—which are certain to manifest themselves in the quality of subordinate performance if not in production quantity—will likely remain as hidden facets of corporate climate, for a major feature of downward communication revealed in figure 3 is that of managerial Blindspot.

Relationships at the colleague level appear to be of a different sort with a set of dynamics all their own. As reference to the score plots in figure 3 will show, the typical manager reports a significant preference for Feedback seeking behaviors over Exposure in his relationships with his fellow managers. A quick interpretation of the data obtained would be that, at the colleague level, everyone is seeking information but very few are willing to expose any. These findings may bear on a unique feature of organizational life—one which has serious implications for climate among corporate peers. Most research on power and authority relationships suggests that there is the greatest openness and trust among people under conditions of equal power. Since colleague relationships might best be considered to reflect equal if not shared distributions of power, maximum openness coupled with maximum solicitation of others' information might be expected to characterize relationships among management co-workers. The fact that a fairly pure Type B interpersonal style prevails suggests noise in the system. The dominant Facade which results from reported practices with colleagues signifies a lack of trust of the sort which could seriously limit the success of collaborative or cooperative ventures among colleagues. The climate implications of mistrust are obvious, and the present data may shed some light on teamwork difficulties as well as problems of horizontal communication so often encountered during inter-departmental or inter-group contacts.

Interviews with a number of managers revealed that their tendencies to become closed in encounters with colleagues could be traced to a competitive ethic which prevailed in their organizations. The fact was a simple one: "'You don't confide in your 'buddies' because they are bucking for the same job you are! Any worthwhile information you've got, you keep to yourself until a time when it might come in handy." To the extent that this climate prevails in organizations, it is to be expected that more effort goes into facade building and maintenance than is expended on the projects at hand where colleague relationships are concerned.

Superiors are the targets of practices yielding the smallest, and therefore least productive, Arena of the three relationships assessed in the survey. The average manager reports a significant reluctance to deal openly and candidly with his superior while favoring the Feedback process as his major interpersonal gambit; even the use of Feedback, however, is subdued relative to that employed with colleagues. The view from on high in organizations is very likely colored by the interpersonal styles addressed to them; and, based on the data obtained, it would not be surprising if many members of top management felt that lower level management was submissive, in need of direction, and had few creative suggestions of their own. Quite aside from the obvious effect such an expectation might have on performance reviews, a characteristic reaction to the essentially Type B style directed at superiors is, on their part, to invoke Type C behaviors. Thus, the data obtained call attention to what may be the seeds of a self-reinforcing cycle of authority-obedience-authority. The long-range consequences of such a cycle, in terms of relationship quality and interpersonal style, has been found to be corporate-wide adoption of Type A behaviors which serve to depersonalize work and diminish an organization's human resources.

Thus, based on the present research at least, a number of interpersonal practices seem to characterize organizational life which limit not only the effectiveness of communication within, but the attainment of realistic levels of corporate excellence without. As we will see, which style will prevail very much depends upon the individual manager.

Interpersonal practices and managerial styles.   In commenting upon the first of their two major concerns in programs of organization development, Blake and Mouton[6] have stated: "The underlying causes of communication difficulties are to be found in the character of supervision. . . . The solution to the problem of communication is for men to manage by achieving production and excellence through sound utilization of people." To the extent that management style is an important ingredient in the communication process, a second piece of research employing the Johari Window and Managerial Grid models in tandem may be of some interest to those concerned with corporate excellence.

Of the 1000 managers sampled in the *Personnel Relations Survey,* 384 also completed a second instrument, the *Styles of Management Inventory,*[7] based on the Managerial Grid (a two-dimensional model of management styles).[8] Five "anchor" styles are identified relative to one's concern for production vis-a-vis people, and these are expressed in grid notation as follows: 9,9 reflects a high production concern coupled with high people concern; 5,5 reflects a moderate concern for each; 9,1 denotes high production coupled with low people concerns, while 1,9 denotes the opposite orientation; 1,1 reflects a minimal concern for both dimensions. In an attempt to discover the significance of one's interpersonal practices for his overall approach to management, the forty individuals scoring highest on each style of management were selected for an analysis of their interpersonal styles. Thus, 200 managers—forty each who were identified as having dominant managerial styles of either 9,9; 5,5; 9,1; 1,9; or 1,1—were studied relative to their tendencies to employ Exposure and Feedback processes in relationships with their subordinates. The research question addressed was: How do individuals who prefer a given managerial style differ in terms of their interpersonal orientations from other individuals preferring other managerial approaches?

The data were subjected to a discriminant function analysis and statistically significant differences were revealed in terms of the manner in which managers employing a given dominant managerial style also employed the Exposure and Feedback processes. The results of the research findings are presented graphically in figure 4. As the bar graph of Exposure and Feedback scores reveals, those managers identified by a dominant management style of 9,9 displayed the strongest tendencies to employ both Exposure and Feedback in their relationships with subordinates. In addition, the Arena which would result from a Johari plotting of their scores would be in a fairly good state of balance, reflecting about as much use of one process as of the other. The data suggest that the 9,9 style of management—typically described as one which achieves effective production through the sound utilization of people—also entails the sound utilization of personal resources in establishing relationships. The Type D interpersonal style which seems to be associated with the 9,9 management style is fully consistent with the open and unobstructed communication which Blake and Mouton view as essential to the creative resolution of differences and sound relationships.

The 5,5 style of management appears, from the standpoint of Exposure and Feedback employment, to be a truncated version of the 9,9 approach. While the reported scores for both processes hover around the fiftieth percentile, there is a noteworthy preference for Exposure over Feedback. Although a Johari plotting of these scores might also approach a Type D profile, the Arena is less balanced and accounts for only 25 percent of the data available for use in a relationship. Again, such an interpersonal style seems consistent with a managerial approach based on expediency and a search for the middle ground.

As might be expected, the 9,1 managers in the study displayed a marked preference for Exposure over Feedback in their relationships with subordinates. This suggests that managers who are maximally concerned with production issues also are given to an overuse of Exposure—albeit not maximum Exposure—and

Figure 4
A Comparison of Exposure and Feedback Use among Managers with Different Dominant Managerial Styles

this is very likely to maintain personal control. In general, a Type C interpersonal style seems to underlie the 9,1 approach to management; and it is important that such managerial practices may be sustained by enlarged Blindspots.

Considering the opposing dominant concerns of the 1,9 manager as compared to the 9,1, it is not too surprising to find that the major interpersonal process of these managers is Feedback solicitation. As with the 9,1 style, the resulting Arena for 1,9 managers is not balanced; but the resulting tension likely stems from less than desired Exposure, leading to relationships in which the managerial Facade is the dominant feature. The Type B interpersonal style may be said to characterize the 1,9 approach to management, with its attendant effects on corporate climate.

Finally, the use of Exposure and Feedback processes reported by those managers identified as dominantly 1,1 is minimal. A mechanical impersonal approach to interpersonal relationships which is consistent with the low profile approach to management depicted under 1,1 is suggested. The Unknown region apparently dominates relationships, and hidden potential and untapped resources prevail. The consequences of such practices for the quality of relationships, climates, and communication effectiveness have already been described in the discussion of Type A interpersonal behaviors.

In summary, it appears that one's interpersonal style is a critical ingredient in his approach to management. While the uses of Exposure and Feedback reported by managers identified according to management style seem to be quite consistent with what one might expect, it is worthy to mention that the test items comprising the *Personnel Relations Survey* have very little, if anything, to do with production versus people concerns. Rather, one's willingness to engage in risk-taking disclosures of feelings, impressions, and observations coupled with his sensitivity to others' participative needs and a felt responsibility to help them become involved via Feedback solicitation were assessed. The fact that such purposive behaviors coincide with one's treatment of more specific context-bound issues like production and people would seem to raise the question: Which comes first, interpersonal or managerial style? The question is researchable, and management practices and information flow might both be enhanced by the results obtained.

Corporate Climate and Personal Decision

The major thesis of this article has been that interpersonal styles are at the core of a number of corporate dilemmas: communication breakdowns, emotional climates, the quality of relationships, and even managerial practices have been linked to some fairly simple dynamics between people. The fact that the dynamics are simple should not be taken to mean that their management is easy—far from it. But, at the same time, the fact that individuals can and do change their interpersonal style—and thereby set in motion a whole chain of events with corporate significance—should be emphasized. A mere description of one's interpersonal practices has only limited utility, if that is as far as it goes. The value of the Johari Window model lies not so much with its utility for assessing what is but, rather, in its inherent statement of what might be.

Although most people select their interpersonal styles as a *reaction* to what they anticipate from other parties, the key to effective relationships lies in "pro-action"; each manager can be a norm setter in his relationships if he will but honestly review his own interpersonal goals and undertake the risks necessary to their attainment. Organizations can criticize their policies—both formal and unwritten—in search for provisions which serve to punish candor and reward evasiveness while equating solicitation of data from others with personal weakness. In short, the culture of an organization and the personal and corporate philosophies which underlie it may be thought of as little more than a *decision product* of the human system. The quality of this decision will directly reflect the quality of the relationships existing among those who fashion it.

If the model and its derivations make sense, then corporate relationships and managerial practices based on candor and trust, openness and spontaneity, and optimal utilization of interpersonal resources are available options to every member of an organizational family. As we have seen, power distributions among people may adversely influence their interpersonal choices. Management styles apparently constrain individuals, but the choice is still there. Type A practices require breaking away from the corporate womb into which one has retreated; personal experiments with greater Exposure and Feedback, however anxiety producing, may be found in the long-run to be their own greatest reward. For the manager locked into Type B behaviors, the task is more simple; he already solicits Feedback to an excellent degree. Needed is enough additional trust in others—whether genuine or forced—to allow a few experiences with Exposure. Others may be found to be less fragile or reactionary than one imagined. Learning to listen is but part of the task confronting managers inclined toward Type C styles; they must learn to seek out and encourage the exposures of others. This new attention to the Feedback process should not be at the expense of Exposure, however. Revamping Type C does not mean adopting Type B. These are all forms of low-risk, high-potential-yield, personal experiments. Whether they will ever be undertaken and their effects on corporate excellence determined depends upon the individual; the matter is one of personal decision.

Notes

[1] R. R. Blake and Jane S. Mouton, *Corporate Excellence through Grid Organization Development* (Houston, TX: Gulf Publishing Company, 1968), p. 4.

[2] *Ibid.*, pp. 3–5.

[3] Joseph Luft, *Of Human Interaction* (Palo Alto, CA: National Press Books, 1969), *passim.*

[4] C. Argyris, *Interpersonal Competence and Organizational Effectiveness* (Homewood, IL: Dorsey, 1962), *passim.*

[5] J. Hall and Martha S. Williams, *Personnel Relations Survey* (Conroe, TX: Teleometrics International, 1967).

[6] R. R. Blake and Jane S. Mouton. *op. cit.*, p. 5.

[7] J. Hall, J. B. Harvey, and Martha S. Williams, *Styles of Management Inventory* (Conroe, TX: Teleometrics International 1963).

[8] R. R. Blake and Jane S. Mouton, *The Managerial Grid* (Houston, TX: Gulf Publishing Company, 1964), *passim.*

8

The Abilene Paradox
The Management of Agreement

Jerry B. Harvey

The July afternoon in Coleman, Texas (population 5,607) was particularly hot—104 degrees as measured by the Walgreen's Rexall Ex-Lax temperature gauge. In addition, the wind was blowing fine-grained West Texas topsoil through the house. But the afternoon was still tolerable—even potentially enjoyable. There was a fan going on the back porch; there was cold lemonade; and finally, there was entertainment. Dominoes. Perfect for the conditions. The game required little more physical exertion than an occasional mumbled comment. "Shuffle 'em," and an unhurried movement of the arm to place the spots in the appropriate perspective on the table. All in all, it had the makings of an agreeable Sunday afternoon in Coleman—that is, it was until my father-in-law suddenly said, "Let's get in the car and go to Abilene and have dinner at the cafeteria."

I thought, "What, go to Abilene? Fifty-three miles? In this dust storm and heat? And in an un-air-conditioned 1958 Buick?"

But my wife chimed in with, "Sounds like a great idea. I'd like to go. How about you, Jerry?" Since my own preferences were obviously out of step with the rest I replied, "Sounds good to me," and added, "I just hope your mother wants to go."

"Of course I want to go," said my mother-in-law. "I haven't been to Abilene in a long time."

So into the car and off to Abilene we went. My predictions were fulfilled. The heat was brutal. We were coated with a fine layer of dust that was cemented with perspiration by the time we arrived. The food at the cafeteria provided first-rate testimonial material for antacid commercials.

Some four hours and 106 miles later we returned to Coleman, hot and exhausted. We sat in front of the fan for a long time in silence. Then, both to be sociable and to break the silence, I said, "It was a great trip, wasn't it?"

No one spoke. Finally my mother-in-law said, with some irritation, "Well, to tell the truth, I really didn't enjoy it much and would rather have stayed here. I just went along because the three of you were so enthusiastic about going. I wouldn't have gone if you all hadn't pressured me into it."

I couldn't believe it. "What do you mean 'you all'?" I said. "Don't put me in the 'you all' group. I was delighted to be doing what we were doing. I didn't want to go. I only went to satisfy the rest of you. You're the culprits."

My wife looked shocked. "Don't call me a culprit. You and Daddy and Mama were the ones who wanted to go. I just went along to be sociable and to keep you happy. I would have had to be crazy to want to go out in heat like that."

Her father entered the conversation abruptly. "Hell!" he said.

He proceeded to expand on what was already absolutely clear. "Listen, I never wanted to go to Abilene. I just thought you might be bored. You visit so seldom I wanted to be sure you enjoyed it. I would have preferred to play another game of dominoes and eat the leftovers in the icebox."

After the outburst of recrimination we all sat back in silence. Here we were, four reasonably sensible people who, of our own volition, had just taken a 106-mile trip across a godforsaken desert in a furnace-like temperature through a cloud-like dust storm to eat unpalatable food at a hole-in-the-wall cafeteria in Abilene, when none of us had really wanted to go. In fact, to be more accurate, we'd done just the opposite of what we wanted to do. The whole situation simply didn't make sense.

At least it didn't make sense at the time. But since that day in Coleman, I have observed, consulted with, and been a part of more than one organization that has been caught in the same situation. As a result, they have either taken a side-trip, or, occasionally, a terminal journey to Abilene, when Dallas or Houston or Tokyo was where they really wanted to go. And for most of those organizations, the negative consequences of such trips, measured in terms of both human misery and economic loss, have been much greater than for our little Abilene group.

This article is concerned with that paradox—the Abilene Paradox. Stated simply, it is as follows: Organizations frequently take actions in contradiction to what they really want to do and therefore defeat the very purposes they are trying to achieve. It also deals with a major corollary of the paradox, which is that *the inability to manage agreement is a major source of organization dysfunction.* Last, the article is designed to help members of organizations cope more effectively with the paradox's pernicious influence.

As a means of accomplishing the above, I shall: (1) describe the symptoms exhibited by organizations caught in the paradox; (2) describe, in summarized case-study examples, how they occur in a variety of organizations; (3) discuss the underlying causal dynamics; (4) indicate some of the implications of accepting this model for describing organizational behavior; (5) make recommendations for coping with the paradox; and, in conclusion, (6) relate the paradox to a broader existential issue.

Symptoms of the Paradox

The inability to manage agreement, not the inability to manage conflict, is the essential symptom that defines organizations caught in the web of the Abilene Paradox. That inability to manage agreement effectively is expressed by six specific subsymptoms, all of which were present in our family Abilene group.

1. Organization members agree privately, as individuals, as to the nature of the situation or problem facing the organization. For example, members of the Abilene group agreed that they were enjoying themselves sitting in front of the fan, sipping lemonade, and playing dominoes.

2. Organization members agree privately, as individuals, as to the steps that would be required to cope with the situation or problem they face. For members of the Abilene group "more of the same" was a solution that would have adequately satisfied their individual and collective desires.

3. Organization members fail to accurately communicate their desires and/ or beliefs to one another. In fact, they do just the opposite and thereby lead one another into misperceiving the collective reality. Each member of the Abilene group, for example, communicated inaccurate data to other members of the organization. The data, in effect, said, "Yeah, it's a great idea. Let's go to Abilene," when in reality members of the organization individually and collectively preferred to stay in Coleman.

4. With such invalid and inaccurate information, organization members make collective decisions that lead them to take actions contrary to what they want to do, and thereby arrive at results that are counterproductive to the organization's intent and purposes. Thus, the Abilene group went to Abilene when it preferred to do something else.

5. As a result of taking actions that are counterproductive, organization members experience frustration, anger, irritation, and dissatisfaction with their organization. Consequently, they form subgroups with trusted acquaintances and blame other subgroups for the organization's dilemma. Frequently, they also blame authority figures and one another. Such phenomena were illustrated in the Abilene group by the "culprit" argument that occurred when we had returned to the comfort of the fan.

6. Finally, if organization members do not deal with the generic issue—the inability to manage agreement—the cycle repeats itself with greater intensity. The Abilene group, for a variety of reasons, the most important of which was that it became conscious of the process, did not reach that point.

To repeat, the Abilene Paradox reflects a failure to manage agreement. In fact, it is my contention that the inability to cope with (manage) agreement, rather than the inability to cope with (manage) conflict, is the single most pressing issue of modern organizations.

Other Trips to Abilene

The Abilene Paradox is no respecter of individuals, organizations, or institutions. Following are descriptions of two other trips to Abilene that illustrate both the pervasiveness of the paradox and its underlying dynamics.

Case No. 1: The Boardroom

The Ozyx Corporation is a relatively small industrial company that has embarked on a trip to Abilene. The president of Ozyx has hired a consultant to help discover the reasons for the poor profit picture of the company in general and the low morale and productivity of the R&D division in particular. During the process of investigation, the consultant becomes interested in a research project in which the company has invested a sizable proportion of its R&D budget.

When asked about the project by the consultant in the privacy of their offices, the president, the vice-president for research, and the research manager each describes it as an idea that looked great on paper but will ultimately fail because of the unavailability of the technology required to make it work. Each of them also acknowledges that continued support of the project will create cash flow problems that will jeopardize the very existence of the total organization.

Furthermore, each individual indicates he has not told the others about his reservations. When asked why, the president says he can't reveal his "true" feelings because abandoning the project, which has been widely publicized, would make the company look bad in the press and, in addition, would probably cause his vice-president's ulcer to kick up or perhaps even cause him to quit, "because he has staked his professional reputation on the project's success."

Similarly, the vice-president for research says he can't let the president or the research manager know of his reservations because the president is so committed to it that "I would probably get fired for insubordination if I questioned the project."

Finally, the research manager says he can't let the president or vice-president know of his doubts about the project because of their extreme commitment to the project's success.

All indicate that, in meetings with one another, they try to maintain an optimistic facade so the others won't worry unduly about the project. The research director, in particular, admits to writing ambiguous progress reports so the president and the vice-president can "interpret them to suit themselves." In fact, he says he tends to slant them to the "positive" side, "given how committed the brass are."

The scent of the Abilene trail wafts from a paneled conference room where the project research budget is being considered for the following fiscal year. In the meeting itself, praises are heaped on the questionable project and a unanimous decision is made to continue it for yet another year. Symbolically, the organization has boarded a bus to Abilene.

In fact, although the real issue of agreement was confronted approximately eight months after the bus departed, it was nearly too late. The organization failed to meet a payroll and underwent a two-year period of personnel cutbacks, retrenchments, and austerity. Morale suffered, the most competent technical personnel resigned, and the organization's prestige in the industry declined.

Case No. 2: The Watergate

Apart from the grave question of who did what, Watergate presents America with the profound puzzle of why. What is it that led such a wide assortment of men, many of them high public officials, possibly including the President himself, either to instigate or to go along with and later try to hide a pattern of behavior that by now appears not only reprehensible, but stupid? (*The Washington Star and Daily News*, editorial, May 27, 1973.)

One possible answer to the editorial writer's question can be found by probing into the dynamics of the Abilene Paradox. I shall let the reader reach his own conclusions, though, on the basis of the following excerpts from testimony before the Senate investigating committee on "The Watergate Affair."

In one exchange, Senator Howard Baker asked Herbert Porter, then a member of the White House staff, why he (Porter) found himself "in charge of or deeply involved in a dirty tricks operation of the campaign." In response, Porter indicated that he had had qualms about what he was doing, but that he ". . . was not one to stand up in a meeting and say that this should be stopped. . . . I kind of drifted along."

And when asked by Baker why he had "drifted along," Porter replied, "In all honesty, because of the fear of the group pressure that would ensue, of not being a team player," and ". . . I felt a deep sense of loyalty to him [the President] or was appealed to on that basis." (*The Washington Post*, June 8, 1973, p. 20.)

Jeb Magruder gave a similar response to a question posed by committee counsel Dash. Specifically, when asked about his, Mr. Dean's, and Mr. Mitchell's reactions to Mr. Liddy's proposal, which included bugging the Watergate, Mr. Magruder replied, "I think all three of us were appalled. The scope and size of the project were something that at least in my mind were not envisioned. I do not think it was in Mr. Mitchell's mind or Mr. Dean's, although I can't comment on their states of mind at that time."

Mr. Mitchell, in an understated way, which was his way of dealing with difficult problems like this, indicated that this was not an "acceptable project." (*The Washington Post*, June 15, 1973, p. A14.)

Later in his testimony Mr. Magruder said, ". . . I think I can honestly say that no one was particularly overwhelmed with the project. But I think we felt that this information could be useful, and Mr. Mitchell agreed to approve the project, and I then notified the parties of Mr. Mitchell's approval." (*The Washington Post*, June 15, 1973, p. A14.)

Although I obviously was not privy to the private conversations of the principal characters, the data seem to reflect the essential elements of the Abilene Paradox. First, they indicate agreement. Evidently, Mitchell, Porter, Dean, and Magruder agreed that the plan was inappropriate. ("I think I can honestly say that no one was particularly overwhelmed with the project.") Second, the data indicate that the principal figures then proceeded to implement the plan in contradiction to their shared agreement. Third, the data surrounding the case clearly indicate that the plan multiplied the organization's problems rather than solved them. And finally, the organization broke into subgroups with the various principals, such as the President, Mitchell, Porter, Dean, and Magruder, blaming one another for the dilemma in which they found themselves, and internecine warfare ensued.

In summary, it is possible that because of the inability of White House staff members to cope with the fact that they agreed, the organization took a trip to Abilene.

Analyzing the Paradox

The Abilene Paradox can be stated succinctly as follows: Organizations frequently take actions in contradiction to the data they have for dealing with problems and, as a result, compound their problems rather than solve them. Like all paradoxes, the Abilene Paradox deals with absurdity. On the surface, it makes little sense for organizations, whether they are couples or companies, bureaucracies or governments, to take actions that are diametrically opposed to the data they possess for solving crucial organizational problems. Such actions are particularly absurd since they tend to compound the very problems they are designed to solve and thereby defeat the purposes the organization is trying to achieve. However, as Robert Rapaport and others have so cogently expressed it, paradoxes are generally paradoxes only because they are based on a logic or rationale different from what we understand or expect.

Discovering that different logic not only destroys the paradoxical quality but also offers alternative ways for coping with similar situations. Therefore, part of the dilemma facing an Abilene-bound organization may be the lack of a map—a theory or model—that provides rationality to the paradox. The purpose of the following discussion is to provide such a map.

The map will be developed by examining the underlying psychological themes of the profit-making organization and the bureaucracy and it will include the following landmarks: (1) Action Anxiety; (2) Negative Fantasies; (3) Real Risk; (4) Separation Anxiety; and (5) the Psychological Reversal of Risk and Certainty. I hope that the discussion of such landmarks will provide harried organization travelers with a new map that will assist them in arriving at where they really want to go and, in addition, will help them in assessing the risks that are an inevitable part of the journey.

Action Anxiety

Action anxiety provides the first landmark for locating roadways that bypass Abilene. The concept of action anxiety says that the reasons organization members take actions in contradiction to their understanding of the organization's problems lies in the intense anxiety that is created as they think about acting in accordance with what they believe needs to be done. As a result, they opt to endure the professional and economic degradation of pursuing an unworkable research project or the consequences of participating in an illegal activity rather than act in a manner congruent with their beliefs. It is not that organization members do not know what needs to be done—they do know. For example, the various principals in the research organization cited *knew* they were working on a research project that had no real possibility of succeeding. And the central figures of the Watergate episode apparently *knew* that, for a variety of reasons, the plan to bug the Watergate did not make sense.

Such action anxiety experienced by the various protagonists may not make sense, but the dilemma is not a new one. In fact, it is very similar to the anxiety experienced by Hamlet, who expressed it most eloquently in the opening lines of his famous soliloquy:

> To be or not to be; that is the question:
> Whether 'tis nobler in the mind to suffer
> The slings and arrows of outrageous fortune
> Or to take arms against a sea of troubles
> And by opposing, end them? . . .
>
> —(*Hamlet,* Act III, Scene II)

It is easy to translate Hamlet's anxious lament into that of the research manager of our R&D organization as he contemplates his report to the meeting of the budget committee. It might go something like this:

> To maintain my sense of integrity and self-worth or compromise it, that is the question. Whether 'tis nobler in the mind to suffer the ignominy that comes from managing a nonsensical research project, or the fear and anxiety that come from making a report the president and V.P. may not like to hear.

So, the anguish, procrastination, and counterproductive behavior of the research manager or members of the White House staff are not much different from those of Hamlet; all might ask with equal justification Hamlet's subsequent searching question of what it is

> that makes us rather bear those ills we have
> than fly to others we know not of.
>
> —(*Hamlet,* Act III, Scene II)

In short, like the various Abilene protagonists, we are faced with a deeper question: Why does action anxiety occur?

Negative Fantasies

Part of the answer to that question may be found in the negative fantasies organization members have about acting in congruence with what they believe should be done. Hamlet experienced such fantasies.

Specifically, Hamlet's fantasies of the alternatives to the current evils were more evils, and he didn't entertain the possibility that any action he might take could lead to an improvement in the situation. Hamlet's was not an unusual case, though. In fact, the "Hamlet syndrome" clearly occurred in both organizations previously described. All of the organization protagonists had negative fantasies about what would happen if they acted in accordance with what they believed needed to be done.

The various managers in the R&D organization foresaw loss of face, prestige, position, and even health as the outcome of confronting the issues about which they believed, incorrectly, that they disagreed. Similarly, members of the White

House staff feared being made scapegoats, branded as disloyal, or ostracized as non-team players if they acted in accordance with their understanding of reality.

To sum up, action anxiety is supported by the negative fantasies that organization members have about what will happen as a consequence of their acting in accordance with their understanding of what is sensible. The negative fantasies, in turn, serve an important function for the persons who have them. Specifically, they provide the individual with an excuse that releases him psychologically, both in his own eyes and frequently in the eyes of others, from the responsibility of having to act to solve organization problems.

It is not sufficient, though, to stop with the explanation of negative fantasies as the basis for the inability of organizations to cope with agreement. We must look deeper and ask still other questions: What is the source of the negative fantasies? Why do they occur?

Real Risk

Risk is a reality of life, a condition of existence. John Kennedy articulated it in another way when he said at a news conference, "Life is unfair." By that I believe he meant we do not know, nor can we predict or control with certainty, either the events that impinge upon us or the outcomes of actions we undertake in response to those events.

Consequently, in the business environment, the research manager might find that confronting the president and the vice-president with the fact that the project was a "turkey" might result in his being fired. And Mr. Porter's saying that an illegal plan of surveillance should not be carried out could have caused his ostracism as a non-team player. There are too many cases when confrontation of this sort has resulted in such consequences. The real question, though, is not, Are such fantasized consequences possible? but, Are such fantasized consequences likely?

Thus real risk is an existential condition, and all actions do have consequences that, to paraphrase Hamlet, may be worse than the evils of the present. As a result of their unwillingness to accept existential risk as one of life's givens, however, people may opt to take their organizations to Abilene rather than run the risk, no matter how small, of ending up somewhere worse.

Again, though, one must ask, What is the real risk that underlies the decision to opt for Abilene? What is at the core of the paradox?

Fear of Separation

One is tempted to say that the core of the paradox lies in the individual's fear of the unknown. Actually, we do not fear what is unknown, but we are afraid of things we do know about. What do we know about that frightens us into such apparently inexplicable organizational behavior?

Separation, alienation, and loneliness are things we do know about—and fear. Both research and experience indicate that ostracism is one of the most powerful punishments that can be devised. Solitary confinement does not draw its coercive strength from physical deprivation. The evidence is overwhelming that we have a fundamental need to be connected, engaged, and related and a reciprocal need not to be separated or alone. Every one of us, though, has experienced alone-ness. From the time the umbilical cord was cut, we have experienced the real anguish of separation—broken friendships, divorces, deaths, and exclusions. C. P. Snow vividly described the tragic interplay between loneliness and connection:

> Each of us is alone; sometimes we escape from our solitariness, through love and affection or perhaps creative moments, but these triumphs of life are pools of light we make for ourselves while the edge of the road is black. Each of us dies alone.

That fear of taking risks that may result in our separation from others is at the core of the paradox. It finds expression in ways of which we may be unaware, and it is ultimately the cause of the self-defeating, collective deception that leads to self-destructive decisions within organizations.

Concretely, such fear of separation leads research committees to fund projects that none of its members want and, perhaps, White House staff members to engage in illegal activities that they don't really support.

The Psychological Reversal of Risk and Certainty

One piece of the map is still missing. It relates to the peculiar reversal that occurs in our thought processes as we try to cope with the Abilene Paradox. For example, we frequently fail to take action in an organizational setting because we fear that the actions we take may result in our separation from others, or, in the language of Mr. Porter, we are afraid of being tabbed as "disloyal" or are afraid of being ostracized as "non-team players." But therein lies a paradox within a paradox, because our very unwillingness to take such risks virtually ensures the separation and aloneness we so fear. In effect, we reverse "real existential risk" and "fantasized risk"—and by doing so transform what is a probability statement into what, for all practical purposes, becomes a certainty.

Take the R&D organization described earlier. When the project fails, some people will get fired, demoted, or sentenced to the purgatory of a make-work job in an out-of-the-way office. For those who remain, the atmosphere of blame, distrust, suspicion, and backbiting that accompanies such failure will serve only to further alienate and separate those who remain.

The Watergate situation is similar. The principals evidently feared being ostracized as disloyal non-team players. When the illegality of the act surfaced, however, it was nearly inevitable that blaming, self-protective actions, and scape-goating would result in the very emotional separation from both the President and one another that the principals feared. Thus, by reversing real and fantasized risk, they had taken effective action to ensure the outcome they least desired.

One final question remains: Why do we make this peculiar reversal? I sup-port the general thesis of Alvin Toffler and Philip Slater, who contend that our cul-tural emphasis on technology, competition, individualism, temporariness, and mobility has resulted in a population that has frequently experienced the terror of loneliness and seldom the satisfaction of engagement. Consequently, though we have learned of the reality of separation, we have not had the opportunity to learn the reciprocal skills of connection, with the result that, like the ancient dinosaurs, we are breeding organizations with self-destructive decision-making proclivities.

A Possible Abilene Bypass

Existential risk is inherent in living, so it is impossible to provide a map that meets the no-risk criterion, but it may be possible to describe the route in terms that make the landmarks understandable and that will clarify the risks involved. In order to do that, however, some commonly used terms such as victim, victimizer, collusion, responsibility, conflict, conformity, courage, confrontation, reality, and knowledge have to be redefined. In addition, we need to explore the relevance of the redefined concepts for bypassing or getting out of Abilene.

Victim and victimizer.   Blaming and fault-finding behavior is one of the basic symptoms of organizations that have found their way to Abilene, and the target of blame generally doesn't include the one who criticizes. Stated in different terms, executives begin to assign one another to roles of victims and victimizers. Ironic as it may seem, however, this assignment of roles is both irrelevant and dysfunctional, because once a business or a government fails to manage its agreement and arrives in Abilene, all its members are victims. Thus, arguments and accusations that identify victims and victimizers at best become symptoms of the paradox, and, at worst, drain energy from the problem-solving efforts required to redirect the organization along the route it really wants to take.

Collusion.   A basic implication of the Abilene Paradox is that human problems of organization are reciprocal in nature. As Robert Tannenbaum has pointed out, you can't have an autocratic boss unless subordinates are willing to collude with his autocracy, and you can't have obsequious subordinates unless the boss is willing to collude with their obsequiousness.

Thus, in plain terms, each person in a self-defeating, Abilene-bound organization *colludes* with others, including peers, superiors, and subordinates, sometimes consciously and sometimes subconsciously, to create the dilemma in which the organization finds itself. To adopt a cliché of modern organization, "It takes a real team effort to go to Abilene." In that sense each person, in his own collusive manner, shares responsibility for the trip, so searching for a locus of blame outside oneself serves no useful purpose for either the organization or the individual. It neither helps the organization handle its dilemma of unrecognized agreement nor does it provide psychological relief for the individual, because focusing on conflict when agreement is the issue is devoid of reality. In fact, it does just the opposite, for it causes the organization to focus on managing conflict when it should be focusing on managing agreement.

Responsibility for problem-solving action.   A second question is, Who is responsible for getting us out of this place? To that question is frequently appended a third one, generally rhetorical in nature, with "should" overtones, such as, Isn't it the boss (or the ranking government official) who is responsible for doing something about the situation?

The answer to that question is no.

The key to understanding the functionality of the no answer is the knowledge that, when the dynamics of the paradox are in operation, the authority figure—and others—are in unknowing agreement with one another concerning the organization's problems and the steps necessary to solve them. Consequently, the power to destroy the paradox's pernicious influence comes from confronting and speaking to the underlying reality of the situation, and not from one's hierarchical position within the organization. Therefore, any organization member who chooses to risk confronting that reality possesses the necessary leverage to release the organization from the paradox's grip.

In one situation, it may be a research director's saying, "I don't think this project can succeed." In another, it may be Jeb Magruder's response to this question of Senator Baker:

> If you were concerned because the action was known to you to be illegal, because you thought it improper or unethical, you thought the prospects for success were very meager, and you doubted the reliability of Mr. Liddy, what on earth would it have taken to decide against the plan?

Magruder's reply was brief and to the point:

> Not very much, sir. I am sure that if I had fought vigorously against it, I think any of us could have had the plan cancelled. (*Time*, June 25, 1973, p. 12)

Reality, knowledge, confrontation.   Accepting the paradox as a model describing certain kinds of organizational dilemmas also requires rethinking the nature of reality and knowledge, as they are generally described in organizations. In brief, the underlying dynamics of the paradox clearly indicate that organization members generally know more about issues confronting the organization than they don't know. The various principals attending the research budget meeting, for example, knew the research project was doomed to failure. And Jeb Magruder spoke as a true Abilener when he said, "We knew it was illegal, probably, inappropriate." (*The Washington Post,* June 15, 1973, p. A16)

Given this concept of reality and its relationship to knowledge, confrontation becomes the process of facing issues squarely, openly, and directly in an effort to discover whether the nature of the underlying collective reality is agreement or conflict. Accepting such a definition of confrontation has an important implication for change agents interested in making organizations more effective. That is, organization change and effectiveness may be facilitated as much by confronting the organization with what it knows and agrees upon as by confronting it with what it doesn't know or disagrees about.

Real Conflict and Phony Conflict

Conflict is a part of any organization. Couples, R&D divisions, and White House staffs all engage in it. However, analysis of the Abilene Paradox opens up the possibility of two kinds of conflict—real and phony. On the surface, they look alike. But, like headaches, they have different causes and therefore require different treatment.

Real conflict occurs when people have real differences. ("My reading of the research printouts says that we can make the project profitable." "I come to the opposite conclusion.") ("I suggest we 'bug' the Watergate." "I'm not in favor of it.")

Phony conflict, on the other hand, occurs when people agree on the actions they want to take, and then do the opposite. The resulting anger, frustration, and blaming behavior generally termed "conflict" are not based on real differences. Rather, they stem from the protective reactions that occur when a decision that no one believed in or was committed to in the first place goes sour. In fact, as a paradox within a paradox, such conflict is symptomatic of agreement!

Group Tyranny and Conformity

Understanding the dynamics of the Abilene Paradox also requires a "reorientation" in thinking about concepts such as "group tyranny"—the loss of the individual's distinctiveness in a group, and the impact of conformity pressures on individual behavior in organizations. Group tyranny and its result, individual conformity, generally refer to the coercive effect of group pressures on individual behavior. Sometimes referred to as Groupthink, it has been damned as the cause for everything from the lack of creativity in organizations ("A camel is a horse designed by a committee") to antisocial behavior in juveniles ("My Johnny is a good boy. He was just pressured into shoplifting by the kids he runs around with").

However, analysis of the dynamics underlying the Abilene Paradox opens up the possibility that individuals frequently perceive and feel as if they are experiencing the coercive organization conformity pressures when, in actuality, they are responding to the dynamics of mismanaged agreement. Conceptualizing, experiencing, and responding to such experiences as reflecting the tyrannical pressures of a group again serves as an important psychological use for the individual: As was previously said, it releases him from the responsibility of taking action and thus becomes a defense against action. Thus, much behavior within an organization that heretofore has been conceptualized as reflecting the tyranny of conformity pressures is really an expression of collective anxiety and therefore must be reconceptualized as a defense against acting.

A well-known example of such faulty conceptualization comes to mind. It involves the heroic sheriff in the classic Western movies who stands alone in the jailhouse door and singlehandedly protects a suspected (and usually innocent) horse thief or murderer from the irrational, tyrannical forces of group behavior— that is, an armed lynch mob. Generally, as a part of the ritual, he threatens to blow off the head of anyone who takes a step toward the door. Few ever take the challenge, and the reason is not the sheriff's six-shooter. What good would one pistol be against an armed mob of several hundred people who *really* want to hang somebody? Thus, the gun in fact serves as a face-saving measure for people who don't wish to participate in a hanging anyway. ("We had to back off. The sheriff threatened to blow our heads off.")

The situation is one involving agreement management, for a careful investigator canvassing the crowd under conditions in which the anonymity of the interviewees' responses could be guaranteed would probably find: (1) that few of the individuals in the crowd really wanted to take part in the hanging; (2) that each person's participation came about because he perceived, falsely, that others wanted to do so; and (3) that each person was afraid that others in the crowd would ostracize or in some other way punish him if he did not go along.

Diagnosing The Paradox

Most individuals like quick solutions, "clean" solutions, "no risk" solutions to organization problems. Furthermore, they tend to prefer solutions based on mechanics and technology, rather than on attitudes of "being." Unfortunately, the underlying reality of the paradox makes it impossible to provide either no-risk solutions or action technologies divorced from existential attitudes and realities. I do, however, have two sets of suggestions for dealing with these situations. One set of suggestions relates to diagnosing the situation, the other to confronting it.

When faced with the possibility that the paradox is operating, one must first make a diagnosis of the situation, and the key to diagnosis is an answer to the question, Is the organization involved in a conflict-management or an agreement-management situation? As an organization member, I have found it relatively easy to make a preliminary diagnosis as to whether an organization is on the way to Abilene or is involved in legitimate, substantive conflict by responding to the Diagnostic Survey shown in the accompanying figure. If the answer to the first question is "not characteristic," the organization is probably not in Abilene or conflict. If the answer is "characteristic," the organization has a problem of either real or phony conflict, and the answers to the succeeding questions help to determine which it is.

In brief, for reasons that should be apparent from the theory discussed here, the more times "characteristic" is checked, the more likely the organization is on its way to Abilene. In practical terms, a process for managing agreement is called for. And finally, if the answer to the first question falls into the "characteristic" category and most of the other answers fall into the category "not characteristic," one may be relatively sure the organization is in a real conflict situation and some sort of conflict management intervention is in order.

Coping with the Paradox

Assuming a preliminary diagnosis leads one to believe he and/or his organization is on the way to Abilene, the individual may choose to actively confront the situation to determine directly whether the underlying reality is one of agreement or conflict. Although there are, perhaps, a number of ways to do it, I have found one way in particular to be effective—confrontation in a group setting. The basic approach involves gathering organization members who are key figures in the problem and its solution into a group setting. Working within the context of a group is important because the dynamics of the Abilene Paradox involve collusion among group members; therefore, to try to solve the dilemma by working with individuals and small subgroups would involve further collusion with the dynamics leading up to the paradox.

Figure 1: Organization Diagnostic Survey

Instructions: For each of the following statements please indicate whether it *is* or *is not* characteristic of your organization.

1. There is conflict in the organization.
2. Organization members feel frustrated, impotent, and unhappy when trying to deal with it. Many are looking for ways to escape. They may avoid meetings at which the conflict is discussed, they may be looking for other jobs, or they may spend as much time away from the office as possible by taking unneeded trips or vacation or sick leave.
3. Organization members place much of the blame for the dilemma on the boss or other groups. In "back room" conversations among friends the boss is termed incompetent, ineffective, "out of touch," or a candidate for early retirement. To his face, nothing is said, or at best, only oblique references are made concerning his role in the organization's problems. If the boss isn't blamed, some other group, division, or unit is seen as the cause of the trouble: "We would do fine if it were not for the damn fools in Division X."
4. Small subgroups of trusted friends and associates meet informally over coffee, lunch, and so on to discuss organizational problems. There is a lot of agreement among the members of these subgroups as to the cause of the troubles and the solutions that would be effective in solving them. Such conversations are frequently punctuated with statements beginning with, "We should do. . . ."
5. In meetings where those same people meet with members from other subgroups to discuss the problem they "soften their positions," state them in ambiguous language, or even reverse them to suit the apparent positions taken by others.
6. After such meetings, members complain to trusted associates that they really didn't say what they wanted to say, but also provide a list of convincing reasons why the comments, suggestions, and reactions they wanted to make would have been impossible. Trusted associates commiserate and say the same was true for them.
7. Attempts to solve the problem do not seem to work. In fact, such attempts seem to add to the problem or make it worse.
8. Outside the organization individuals seem to get along better, be happier, and operate more effectively than they do within it.

The first step in the meeting is for the individual who "calls" it (that is, the confronter) to own up to his position first and be open to the feedback he gets. The owning up process lets the others know that he is concerned lest the organization may be making a decision contrary to the desires of any of its members. A statement like this demonstrates the beginning of such an approach:

> I want to talk with you about the research project. Although I have previously said things to the contrary, I frankly don't think it will work, and I am very anxious about it. I suspect others may feel the same, but I don't know.

Anyway, I am concerned that I may end up misleading you and that we may end up misleading one another, and if we aren't careful, we may continue to work on a problem that none of us wants and that might even bankrupt us. That's why I need to know where the rest of you stand. I would appreciate any of your thoughts about the project. Do you think it can succeed?

What kinds of results can one expect if he decides to undertake the process of confrontation? I have found that the results can be divided into *two* categories, at the technical level and at the level of existential experience. Of the two, I have found that for the person who undertakes to initiate the process of confrontation, the existential experience takes precedence in his ultimate evaluation of the outcome of the action he takes.

The technical level.   If one is correct in diagnosing the presence of the paradox, I have found the solution to the technical problem may be almost absurdly quick and simple, nearly on the order of this:

"Do you mean that you and I and the rest of us have been dragging along with a research project that none of us has thought would work? It's crazy. I can't believe we would do it, but we did. Let's figure out how we can cancel it and get to doing something productive." In fact, the simplicity and quickness of the solution frequently don't seem possible to most of us, since we have been trained to believe that the solution to conflict requires a long, arduous process of debilitating problem solving.

Also, since existential risk is always present, it is possible that one's diagnosis is incorrect, and the process of confrontation lifts to the level of public examination real, substantive conflict, which may result in heated debate about technology, personalities, and/or administrative approaches. There is evidence that such debates, properly managed, can be the basis for creativity in organizational problem solving. There is also the possibility, however, that such debates cannot be managed, and substantiating the concept of existential risk, the person who initiates the risk may get fired or ostracized. But that again leads to the necessity of evaluating the results of such confrontation at the existential level.

Existential results.   Evaluating the outcome of confrontation from an existential framework is quite different from evaluating it from a set of technical criteria. How do I reach this conclusion? Simply from interviewing a variety of people who have chosen to confront the paradox and listening to their responses. In short, for them, psychological success and failure apparently are divorced from what is traditionally accepted in organizations as criteria for success and failure.

For instance, some examples of success are described when people are asked, "What happened when you confronted the issue?" They may answer this way:

> I was told we had enough boat rockers in the organization, and I got fired. It hurt at first, but in retrospect it was the greatest day of my life. I've got another job and I'm delighted. I'm a free man.

Another description of success might be this:

I said I don't think the research project can succeed and the others looked shocked and quickly agreed. The upshot of the whole deal is that I got a promotion and am now known as a "rising star." It was the high point of my career.

Similarly, those who fail to confront the paradox describe failure in terms divorced from technical results. For example, one may report:

I didn't say anything and we rocked along until the whole thing exploded and Joe got fired. There is still a lot of tension in the organization, and we are still in trouble, but I got a good performance review last time. I still feel lousy about the whole thing, though.

From a different viewpoint, an individual may describe his sense of failure in these words:

I knew I should have said something and I didn't. When the project failed, I was a convenient whipping boy. I got demoted; I still have a job, but my future here is definitely limited. In a way I deserve what I got, but it doesn't make it any easier to accept because of that.

Most important, the act of confrontation apparently provides intrinsic psychological satisfaction, regardless of the technological outcomes for those who attempt it.

The real meaning of that existential experience, and its relevance to a wide variety of organizations, may lie, therefore, not in the scientific analysis of decision making but in the plight of Sisyphus. That is something the reader will have to decide for himself.

The Abilene Paradox and the Myth of Sisyphus

In essence, this paper proposes that there is an underlying organizational reality that includes both agreement and disagreement, cooperation and conflict. However, the decision to confront the possibility of organization agreement is all too difficult and rare, and its opposite, the decision to accept the evils of the present, is all too common. Yet those two decisions may reflect the essence of both our human potential and our human imperfectability. Consequently, the choice to confront reality in the family, the church, the business, or the bureaucracy, though made only occasionally, may reflect those "peak experiences" that provide meaning to the valleys.

In many ways, they may reflect the experience of Sisyphus. As you may remember, Sisyphus was condemned by Pluto to a perpetuity of pushing a large stone to the top of a mountain, only to see it return to its original position when he released it. As Camus suggested in his revision of the myth, Sisyphus's task was absurd and totally devoid of meaning. For most of us, though, the lives we lead pushing papers or hubcaps are no less absurd, and in many ways we probably spend about as much time pushing rocks in our organizations as did Sisyphus.

Camus also points out, though, that on occasion as Sisyphus released his rock and watched it return to its resting place at the bottom of the hill, he was able to recognize the absurdity of his lot and, for brief periods of time, transcend it. So it may be with confronting the Abilene Paradox. Confronting the absurd paradox of agreement may provide, through activity, what Sisyphus gained from his passive but conscious acceptance of his fate. Thus, through the process of active confrontation with reality, we may take respite from pushing our rocks on their endless journeys and, for brief moments, experience what C. P. Snow termed "the triumphs of life we make for ourselves" within those absurdities we call organizations.

Selected Bibliography

Chris Argyris in *Intervention Theory and Method: A Behavioral Science View* (Addison-Wesley, 1970) gives an excellent description of the process of "owning up" and being "open," both of which are major skills required if one is to assist his organization in avoiding or leaving Abilene.

Albert Camus in *The Myth of Sisyphus and Other Essays* (Vintage Books, Random House, 1955) provides an existential viewpoint for coping with absurdity, of which the Abilene Paradox is a clear example.

Jerry B. Harvey and R. Albertson in "Neurotic Organizations; Symptoms, Causes and Treatment," Parts I and II, *Personnel Journal* (September and October 1971) provide a detailed example of a third-party intervention into an organization caught in a variety of agreement-management dilemmas.

Irving Janis in *Victims of Groupthink* (Houghton-Mifflin Company, 1972) offers an alternative viewpoint for understanding and dealing with many of the dilemmas described in "The Abilene Paradox." Specifically, many of the events that Janis describes as examples of conformity pressures (that is, group tyranny) I would conceptualize as mismanaged agreement.

In his *The Pursuit of Loneliness* (Beacon Press, 1970), Philip Slater contributes an in-depth description of the impact of the role of alienation, separation, and loneliness (a major contribution to the Abilene Paradox) in our culture.

Richard Walton in *Interpersonal Peacemaking: Confrontation and Third Party Consultation* (Addison-Wesley, 1969) describes a variety of approaches for dealing with conflict when it is real, rather than phony.

9

Stages of Group Development

Bruce W. Tuckman and Mary Ann C. Jensen

Tuckman (1965) reviewed fifty-five articles dealing with stages of small-group development in an attempt to isolate those concepts common to the various studies and produce a generalizable model of changes in group life over time. He examined studies of (1) therapy groups, (2) human relations training or T-groups, and (3) natural and laboratory-task groups in terms of two realms—task and interpersonal. The way members acted and related to one another was considered group structure or the interpersonal realm; the content of the interaction as related to the task was referred to as the task-activity realm. Both realms represented simultaneous aspects of group functioning because members completed tasks while relating to one another.

The Model

As a result of the literature reviewed, Tuckman proposed a model of developmental stages for various group settings over time, labeled (1) testing and dependence, (2) intragroup conflict, (3) development of group cohesion, and (4) functional role relatedness. The stages of task activity were labeled (1) orientation to task, (2) emotional response to task demands, (3) open exchange of relevant interpretations, and (4) emergence of solutions. An essential correspondence between the group-structure realm and the task-activity realm over time caused Tuckman to summarize the four stages as "forming," "storming," "norming," and "performing." He acknowledged, however, that this was "a conceptual statement suggested by the data presented and subject to further test."

Tuckman cited several limitations of the literature, e.g., that the literature could not be considered truly representative of small-group developmental processes because there was an overrepresentation of therapy and T-group settings and an underrepresentation of natural or laboratory-group settings, making generalizing difficult. He suggested the need for further research on natural and laboratory groups, indicated the need for more rigorous methodological considerations in studying group process, and criticized the use of a single group for observation because it made control and systematic manipulation of independent variables impossible.

Tuckman provided a developmental model of group process by organizing and conceptualizing existing research data and theoretical precepts rather than by presenting original empirical data to support a particular model. He stated, however, that his model was in need of further testing.

Purpose and Methodology of This Review

The purpose of this follow-up study is to discover whether anyone has empirically tested the model of group development proposed by Tuckman in 1965, to investigate any new models in light of Tuckman's hypothesis, and to determine whether any alternative models have been conceived.

To locate any studies referencing the 1965 Tuckman article, the *Science Citation Index* from 1965 and the *Social Science Citation Index* from 1970 were consulted and a list of fifty-seven articles was compiled. Of these, only those studies concerned primarily with empirical research (approximately twenty-two) were reviewed.

Review of the "New" Literature

Only one study could be found that set out to test Tuckman's hypothesis. Runkel et al. (1971) studied three groups of fifteen to twenty college students in a classroom setting. The task of each group was to decide on a project, collect and interpret data, and write a final report. During meetings of the work group, sixteen observers, armed with descriptions of the Tuckman model of stage development, observed the group "until something happened that fitted a behavior described by Tuckman as belonging to one of the four stages of group structure or task activity" (p. 186). The observers rotated among groups in an effort to reduce observer bias. Ratings from observers supported Tuckman's theory of group development.

Although this empirical test of Tuckman's hypothesis supported his suggested developmental sequence, observers were given only descriptions of Tuckman's four stages and asked to "fit" their observations to that model. A methodology less prone to observer bias would have been to have observers record particular behaviors apparent in the group; at a later time, these could have been reviewed in light of particular models. Runkel et al. did, however, provide an empirical base for further testing of the Tuckman model.

Several articles from the literature contained elements of the Tuckman model. Zurcher (1969) offered some explanation of the developmental sequence in natural groups, an area Tuckman described as underrepresented in the literature. Data were obtained from 174 meetings of twelve poverty program neighborhood action committees in Topeka, Kansas, over a nineteen-month period. Results from a team of participant-observers indicated that the stages of development for these neighborhood committees included (1) orientation, (2) catharsis, (3) focus, (4) action, (5) limbo, (6) testing, and (7) purposive. Zurcher stated that these seven stages "could parsimoniously have been reduced to four stages suggested by Tuckman" as shown below.

Orientation	Forming
Catharsis	Storming
Focus, Action, Limbo, Testing	Norming
Purposive	Performing

Although Zurcher's results would serve to support the Tuckman model, he did not specifically set out to test any particular model of group development and did not present any statistical treatment of his data.

Smith (1966) observed, over a period of approximately four months, a group of seven men stationed in Antarctica and collected data on technical-task activities as well as on behavioral dimensions of informal structure. He reported on only two developmental stages rather than the four listed by Tuckman. However, Smith's two developmental *stages* appear to be task-activity behavior and interpersonal behavior, both of which were identified by Tuckman as the *realms* of group behavior. Smith's results serve to reinforce the hypothesis that task and interpersonal dimensions play a substantial role in the way groups develop.

Smith also concluded that the order of development would be different for various groups. Although the interpersonal "stage" seemed most important for therapy or training groups, task activity was stressed by the men in Antarctica. That the content or task activity appeared prior to development of a group structure might be due to the specific nature of the group assignment and to the well-defined roles of the participants, which suggest that those aspects related to the primary purpose of the group develop first. Due to the uniqueness of his group in terms of task and setting, Smith's results might not be applicable to other types of groups.

Shambaugh and Kanter (1969) described the evolution of a therapy group for spouses of patients on hemodialysis machines. A group of six spouses met weekly for a period of eight months. As observed by the group leader/psychiatrist, the stages of group development included (1) initial experience, (2) formation of the group, (3) optimism and partial separation, and (4) final stage.

The authors believed that this group was a "paradigm of the unconscious forces inherent in group structure and process" and that "the overall developmental sequence was that of the usual small group." They did not attempt to "test" any particular model of group development; however, their observations appeared to fit the behaviors characterizing Tuckman's stages of "forming," "storming," "norming," and "performing" (i.e., dependence on leader, criticism among members, optimism, and cohesiveness). Shambaugh and Kanter did not describe behaviors characteristic of each stage clearly, which made it difficult to differentiate among them. The authors did observe, however, that their observations supported Tuckman's four-stage theory.

A second problem with this study was the introduction of new members into the group prior to the final stage, which made identification of the four stages and the characteristic behaviors pertinent to each difficult.

Lacoursiere (1974) observed stage development while using a group method to facilitate learning for student nurses involved in a psychiatric setting. The student nurses, in their twenties, single, and female (except for one male student in each of the three groups observed), worked in a state mental hospital and met as a group for one and one-half hours each week to discuss their concerns. Over a ten-week period, Lacoursiere observed four stages of group development:

1. Orientation, characterized by fears and anxieties and fairly strong positive expectations;

2. Dissatisfaction, characterized by an increasing sense of frustration, along with depression and anger;

3. Production, demonstrated by a more realistic appraisal of what could be accomplished; and

4. Termination, concerned with sadness and some self-evaluation.

Lacoursiere's four stages differed from Tuckman's in three respects. First, in stage 2, dissatisfaction, there was a lack of intragroup conflict among the student nurses. Any anger and hostility present was directed toward the hospital, the staff, and psychiatry in general rather than toward group members. Second, Lacoursiere combined "norming" and "performing" into stage 3, production, at which time students' expectations became more realistic and they desired "to learn what can be learned and to do what they can reasonably do as student nurses" (p. 348). Third, and the major difference between models, was the addition of the termination stage.

Another article dealing with the training of nursing students was one by Spitz and Sadock (1973), who observed twenty-one second-year nursing students, all white females from twenty to forty years old, using techniques such as role playing, videotaping, and analysis of dreams. Spitz and Sadock categorized group life into three phases:

1. Stage One, characterized by anxiety, guardedness, dependency, and a mixture of curiosity and confusion;

2. Stage Two, the period of beginning trust, cohesiveness, interdependence, and group interaction;

3. Stage Three, the final phase of disengagement, anxiety about separation and termination, and positive feelings toward the leader.

Stages one and two contain elements of Tuckman's "forming" and "norming" stages, respectively. Tuckman's second stage, "storming," has for the most part been eliminated. Although Lacoursiere's group demonstrated anger and hostility toward an outside force, Spitz and Sadock's group appeared only to touch on themes of anger and discontent in their group discussions. It is of significance that neither student-nurse group demonstrated noticeable characteristics of intragroup conflict. Possibly the close association experienced by student nurses unites them in a cohesive, personal group. Also, the groups' composition—overwhelmingly female—might be a factor, as women have traditionally been socialized to be more passive and trusting. Spitz and Sadock also observed third-year medical students and found them to be more guarded and more "overtly hostile." Group composition, therefore, may he one of the variables that influence appearance of stages in the developmental process.

A second variation in Spitz and Sadock's model, which also was found in the Lacoursiere model, was the addition of a stage concerned with termination and separation, a significant departure from the Tuckman model.

Braaten (1975) compiled an interesting review of fourteen models of the developmental stages of groups. Several of the more recent models not reviewed in the 1965 Tuckman article demonstrated a resemblance to his four-stage model. For example, Yalom (1970) presented a four-stage model, including an initial phase of orientation and hesitant participation; a second phase of conflict, dominance, and rebellion; a third phase of intimacy, closeness, and cohesiveness; and a final phase of termination (differing from Tuckman).

Braaten presented a composite model of the fourteen theories and also set forth his own model. His composite model utilized the three stages identified by Tuckman as "forming," "storming," and "performing" (which incorporated "norming") and added a final stage of termination. Braaten's own model followed the composite model fairly closely:

1. Initial phase lacking in structure;

2. An early phase characterized by hostility and conflicts between subgroups;

3. The mature work phase in which norms are resolved and interdependency and trust formation are apparent;

4. Termination, concerned with disengagement and ending.

Braaten concluded, as did Tuckman, that there appeared to be substantial agreement among authors on the aspects of a developmental phase model but that systematic research was needed to verify the theoretical concepts. Braaten's review of the literature suggests that empirical research in stages of small-group development is sparse and inconclusive.

Only two of the journal articles reviewed substantially deviated from the four-stage Tuckman model. Dunphy (1968) conducted an empirical study of the developmental process in self-analytic groups (therapy and T-groups). He observed two sections of a Harvard Social Relations 120 course for a period of nine months. Through the use of a computer system of content analysis, Dunphy identified six development phases for the group:

1. Maintenance of external normative standards;

2. Individual rivalry;

3. Aggression;

4. Negativism;

5. Emotional concerns;

6. High affection.

Individual rivalry, aggression, and negativism parallel Tuckman's second stage, "storming." Emotional concerns and high affection might be viewed in terms of the "norming" stage. However, Dunphy's model does not include any stage resembling "performing." Dunphy acknowledged that his results might not be generalizable to all self-analytic groups and that further testing was needed to establish the extent of their validity.

A study by Heckel, Holmes, and Salzberg (1967) examined whether distinct verbal behavioral phases occur in group psychotherapy. Seventeen neuropsychiatric male and female patients were observed over eighteen sessions of group therapy. Verbal responses of participants were recorded and grouped according to type of response and specific category (i.e., therapist-directed response, etc.). Results revealed a significant change between the seventh and eighth and twelfth and thirteenth sessions. Therapist-directed responses were most noticeably affected, going from fifty-nine to twenty-three; group-directed responses went from twenty-one to thirty-nine. On the basis of these results, Heckel et al. believed their findings were "somewhat supportive" of a two-stage hypothesis of group development. The authors did not describe characteristics of the two stages, however, nor did they attempt to propose their own theoretical model for further testing.

A second study by Heckel, Holmes, and Rosecrans (1971) employed a factor-analytic approach for analyzing verbal responses of group-therapy members. Utilizing the theory of two-stage development derived from the 1967 study, the authors rated responses from approximately thirty male neuropsychiatric patients during their second and third sessions and from seventeen of these patients during the twelfth and thirteenth sessions. The authors reported that combined results from sessions two and three indicated low group cohesiveness, high defensiveness and superficial verbal interaction and a pattern of personal and group-building responses. An obvious change had occurred by the twelfth and thirteenth sessions, but the loss of almost half the members of the group by this time also may have had an impact on changes in their verbal responses. Without observing interactions over the life of the group, the suggestion that these four sessions represent the *only* changes taking place seems premature.

Mann (1967) offered a third variation to the four-stage model. Through the use of factor analysis, he categorized five stages of group development: (1) initial complaining, (2) premature enactment, (3) confrontation, (4) internalization, (5) separation and terminal review. This model appears to incorporate characteristics of Tuckman's "forming," "storming," "norming," and "performing" stages, with the addition of stage 5—termination.

Braaten (1975) included an updated version of Mann's (1971) developmental model:

1. Dependency upon trainer;
2. Initial anxiety and/or resistance;
3. Mounting frustration, hostility;
4. Work phase, intimacy, integration, mutual synthesis;
5. Separation.

Discussion

This review of articles was undertaken to discover whether the Tuckman (1965) model of group development had been empirically tested. Only Runkel et al. (1971) set out to test this model. Their conclusions were supportive of Tuckman's four-stage model, but their results may not be reliable because of the researchers' methodology.

The bulk of the literature from 1965 to the present has been theoretical in nature; those articles describing empirical research were not primarily concerned with testing already existing models. Many of the authors described a group's behavior and offered their own models of group development, however similar to models already described in the literature.[1] Two studies and a review did identify termination as an important final stage overlooked by Tuckman. Braaten's (1975) review of fourteen models led to a composite model incorporating "forming," "storming," and "performing" stages and including a termination stage.

Gibbard and Hartman (1973) introduced the concept of a "life cycle" model as developed by Mills (1964). Proponents of a life cycle approach recognize the importance of separation concerns as an issue in group development. Although Tuckman saw performing as the final stage of group evolution, those who agree with a life cycle model view separation as an important issue throughout the life of the group and as a separate and distinct final stage. With a substantial amount of activity taking place in training and therapy groups in which presumably strong interpersonal feelings are developed, the "death of the group" becomes an extremely important issue to many of the group members. As a reflection of the recent appearance of studies postulating a life cycle approach (Mann, 1971; Gibbard & Hartman, 1973; Spitz & Sadock, 1973; Lacoursiere, 1974; Braaten, 1975), the Tuckman model is hereby amended to include a fifth stage: adjourning.

Conclusion

It is noteworthy that since 1965 there have been few studies that report empirical data concerning the stages of group development. It is also of interest that most authors, although writing from a theoretical framework, call for further research to verify their hypotheses. A virtually untapped field is the empirical testing of existing models of group-stage development. There is a need to supply statistical evidence as to the usefulness and applicability of the various models suggested in the literature.

A major outcome of this review has been the discovery that recent research posits the existence of a final discernible and significant stage of group development—termination. Because the 1965 model was a conceptual statement determined by the literature, it is reasonable, therefore, to modify the model to reflect recent literature. The model now stands: forming, storming, norming, performing, and adjourning.

Note

[1] Other studies examined but not cited because of their limited relevance to the discussion are Lundgren (1971), Liebowitz (1972), Tucker (1973), and Adelson (1975).

References

Adelson, J. Feedback and group development. *Small Group Behavior*, 1975 *6*(4), 389–401.

Braaten, L. J. Developmental phases of encounter groups and related intensive groups: A critical review of models and a new proposal. *Interpersonal Development*, 1974–75, *5*, 112–129.

Dunphy, D. Phases, roles and myths in self-analytic groups. *Journal of Applied Behavioral Science*, 1968, *4*(2), 195–225.

Gibbard, G., & Hartman, J. The oedipal paradigm in group development: A clinical and empirical study. *Small Group Behavior*, 1973, *4*(3), 305–349.

Heckel, R., Holmes, G., & Salzberg, H. Emergence of distinct verbal phases in group therapy. *Psychological Reports*, 1967, *21*, 630–632.

Heckel, R. V., Holmes, G. R., & Rosecrans, C. J. A factor analytic study of process variables in group therapy. *Journal of Clinical Psychology*, 1971, *27*(1), 146–150.

Lacoursiere, R. A group method to facilitate learning during the stages of a psychiatric affiliation. *International Journal of Group Psychotherapy*, 1974, *24*, 342, 351.

Liebowitz, B. A method for the analysis of the thematic structure of T-groups. *The Journal of Applied Behavioral Science*, 1972, *8*(2), 149–173.

Lundgren, D. C. Trainer style and patterns of group development. *The Journal of Applied Behavioral Science*, 1971, *7*(6), 689–709.

Lundgren, D. C. Attitudinal and behavioral correlates of emergent status in training groups. *Journal of Social Psychology*, 1973, *90*, 141–153.

Mann, R. D. The development of the member-trainer relationship in self-analytic groups. In C. L. Cooper & I. L. Mangham (Eds.), *T-groups: A survey of research*. London: Wiley-Interscience, 1971.

Mann, R. D. *Interpersonal styles and group development*. New York: John Wiley, 1967.

Mills, T. M. *Group transformation*. Englewood Cliffs, N.J.: Prentice-Hall, 1964.

Runkel, P. J., Lawrence, M., Oldfield, S., Rider, M., Clark, C. Stages of group development: An empirical test of Tuckman's hypothesis. *The Journal of Applied Behavioral Science*, 1971, *7*(2), 180–193.

Shambaugh, P., & Kanter, S. Spouses under stress: Group meetings with spouses of patients on hemodialysis. *American Journal of Psychiatry*, 1969, *125*, 928–936.

Smith, W. M. Observations over the lifetime of a small isolated group; structure, danger, boredom, and vision. *Psychological Reports*, 1966, *19*, 475–514.

Spitz, H., & Sadock, B. Psychiatric training of graduate nursing students. *N. Y. State Journal of Medicine*, June 1, 1973, pp. 1334–1338.

Tucker, D. M. Some relationships between individual and group development. *Human Development*, 1973, *16*, 249–272.

Tuckman, B. W. Developmental sequence in small groups. *Psychological Bulletin*, 1965, *63*(6), 384–399.

Yalom, I. *The theory and practice of group psychotherapy*. New York: Basic Books, 1970.

Zurcher, L. A., Jr. Stages of development in poverty program neighborhood action committees. *The Journal of Applied Behavioral Science*, 1969, *5*(2), 223–258.

10

Self-Directed Work Teams

Ralph Stayer

In 1980, I was the head of a successful family business—Johnsonville Sausage—that was in great shape and required radical change.

Our profits were above the average for our industry, and our financial statements showed every sign of health. We were growing at a rate of about 20% annually, with sales that were strong in our home state of Wisconsin and steadily rising in Minnesota, Michigan, and Indiana. Our quality was high. We were respected in the community. I was making a lot of money.

And I had a knot in my stomach that wouldn't go away. For one thing, I was worried about competition. We were a small, regional producer with national competitors who could outpromote, outadvertise, and underprice us any time they chose.

In addition to our big national competitors, we had a host of local and regional producers small enough to provide superior service to customers who were virtually their neighbors. We were too big to have the small-town advantage and too small to have advantages of national scale. Our business was more vulnerable than it looked.

What worried me more than the competition, however, was the gap between potential and performance. Our people didn't seem to care. Every day I came to work and saw people so bored by their jobs that they made thoughtless, dumb mistakes. They mislabeled products or added the wrong seasonings or failed to mix them into the sausage properly. Someone drove the prongs of a forklift right through a newly built wall. Someone else ruined a big batch of fresh sausage by spraying it with water while cleaning the work area. These were accidents. No one was deliberately wasting money, time, and materials; it was just that people took no responsibility for their work. They showed up in the morning, did halfheartedly what they were told to do, and then went home.

Now, I didn't expect them to be as deeply committed to the company as I was. I owned it, and they didn't. But how could we survive a serious competitive challenge with this low level of attentiveness and involvement?

Getting to Points B and A

In 1980, I began looking for a recipe for change. I started by searching for a book that would tell me how to get people to care about their jobs and their company. Not surprisingly, the search was fruitless. No one could tell me how to wake up my own work force; I would have to figure it out for myself.

And yet, I told myself, why not? I had made the company, so I could fix it. This was an insight filled with pitfalls but it *was* an insight: the fault was not someone else's, the fault was mine.

Of course, I hadn't really built the company all alone, but I had created the management style that kept people from assuming responsibility. Of course, it was counterproductive for me to own all the company's problems by myself, but in 1980 every problem did, in fact, rest squarely on my shoulders, weighing me down and—though I didn't appreciate it at the time—crippling my subordinates and strangling the company. If I was going to fix what I had made, I would have to start by fixing myself. In many ways that was my good luck, or, to put the same thought another way, thank God I was the problem so I could be the solution.

As I thought about what I should do, I first asked myself what I needed to do to achieve the company's goals. But what *were* the company's goals? What did I really want Johnsonville to be? I didn't know.

This realization led me to a second insight: nothing matters more than a goal. The most important question any manager can ask is, "In the best of all possible worlds, what would I really want to happen?"

I tried to picture what Johnsonville would have to be to sell the most expensive sausage in the industry and still have the biggest market share. What I saw in my mind's eye was definitely not an organization where I made all the decisions and owned all the problems. What I saw was an organization where people took responsibility for their own work, for the product, for the company as a whole. If that happened, our product and service quality would improve, our margins would rise, and we could reduce costs and successfully enter new markets. Johnsonville would be much less vulnerable to competition.

The image that best captured the organizational end state I had in mind for Johnsonville was a flock of geese on the wing. I didn't want an organizational chart with traditional lines and boxes, but a "V" of individuals who knew the common goal, took turns leading, and adjusted their structure to the task at hand. Geese fly in a wedge, for instance, but land in waves. Most important, each individual bird is responsible for its own performance.

With that end state in mind as Point B, the goal, I turned to the question of our starting point, Point A. Johnsonville was financially successful, but I was dissatisfied with employee attitudes. So I conducted an attitude survey to find out what people thought about their jobs and the company and to get an idea of how they perceived the company's attitude toward them. I knew there was less commitment than I wanted, but I was startled all the same to find that Johnsonville attitudes were only average—no better than employee attitudes at big, impersonal companies like General Motors.

At first I didn't want to believe the survey, and I looked for all kinds of excuses. The methodology was faulty. The questions were poorly worded. I didn't want to admit that we had an employee motivation problem because I didn't know how to deal with that. But however strong the temptation, the mistakes and poor performance were too glaring to ignore.

The survey told me that people saw nothing for themselves at Johnsonville. It was a job, a means to some end that lay outside the company. I wanted them to commit themselves to a company goal, but they saw little to commit to. And at that stage, I still couldn't see that the biggest obstacle to changing their point of view was me. Everything I had learned and experienced to that point had convinced me that anything I didn't do myself would not be done right. As I saw it, my job was to create the agenda and then motivate "them" to carry it out.

In fact, I expected my people to follow me the way buffalo follow their leader—blindly. Unfortunately, that kind of leadership model almost led to the buffalo's extinction. Buffalo hunters used to slaughter the herd by finding and killing the leader. Once the leader was dead, the rest of the herd stood around waiting for instructions that never came, and the hunters could (and did) exterminate them one by one.

I realized that I had been focused entirely on the financial side of the business—margins, market share, return on assets—and had seen people as dutiful tools to make the business grow. The business *had* grown nicely—and that very success was my biggest obstacle to change. I had made all the decisions about purchasing, scheduling, quality, pricing, marketing, sales, hiring, and all the rest of it. Now the very things that had brought me success—my centralized control, my aggressive behavior, my authoritarian business practices—were creating the environment that made me so unhappy. I had been Johnsonville Sausage, assisted by some hired hands who, to my annoyance, lacked commitment. But why should they make a commitment to Johnsonville? They had no stake in the company and no power to make decisions or control their own work. If I wanted to improve results, I had to increase their involvement in the business.

This was an insight that I immediately misused. Acting on instinct, I ordered a change. "From now on," I announced to my management team, "you're all responsible for making your own decisions." I went from authoritarian control to authoritarian abdication. No one had asked for more responsibility; I forced it down their throats. They were good soldiers, and they did their best, but I had trained them to expect me to solve their problems. I had nurtured their inability by expecting them to be incapable; now they met my expectations with an inability to make decisions unless they knew which decisions I wanted them to make.

After more than two years of working with them, I finally had to replace all three top managers. Worst of all, I now see that in a way they were right. I didn't really *want* them to make independent decisions. I wanted them to make the deci-

JOHNSONVILLE FOODS, INC.
COMPANY PERFORMANCE-SHARE EVALUATION FORM

Please check one: _____ Self _____ Coach

I. PERFORMANCE

A. Customer Satisfaction

How do I rate the quality of the work I do? Do I contribute my best to producing a product to be proud of—one that I would purchase or encourage someone else to purchase?

Score _____

B. Cost-Effectiveness

To what extent do I perform my job in a cost-effective manner? Do I strive to work smarter? To work more productively with fewer errors? To complete my job functions in a timely manner, eliminating overtime when possible? To reduce waste where possible in all departments?

Score _____

C. Attitude

To what extent do I have a positive attitude toward my personal, department, and company goals as expressed by my actions, feelings, and thoughts? Do I like to come to work? Am I thoughtful and considerate toward fellow members? Do I work to promote better attitudes? Do I demonstrate company loyalty?

Score _____

D. Responsibility

To what extent do I take responsibility for my own job? Do I accept a challenge? Do I willingly take on or look for additional responsibilities? Do I work independently of supervision?

Score _____

E. Ideas

To what extent have I offered ideas and suggestions for improvements? Do I suggest better ways of doing things instead of just complaining?

Score _____

F. Problem Solver/Preventer

To what extent have I contributed to solving or preventing problems? Do I anticipate problem situations and try to avoid them? Do I push-pull when necessary? Do I keep an open line of communication?

Score _____

G. Safety

To what extent do my actions show my concern for safety for myself and others? Do I alert coworkers to unsafe procedures? Do I alert my coach to unsafe conditions in my department?

Score _____

H. Quality Image

To what extent have I displayed a high-quality image in my appearance, language, personal hygiene, and working environment?

Score _____

(continued)

II. TEAMWORK

A. Contribution to Groups

How would I rate my contribution to my department's performance? Am I aware of department goals? Do I contribute to a team? Do I communicate with team members?

Score _____

B. Communication

To what extent do I keep others informed to prevent problems from occurring? Do I work to promote communication between plants and departments? Do I relay information to the next shift? Do I speak up at meetings and let my opinions and feelings be known?

Score _____

C. Willingness to Work Together

To what extent am I willing to share the responsibility of getting the work done? Do I voluntarily assist others to obtain results? Do I demonstrate a desire to accomplish department goals? Do I complete paperwork accurately and thoroughly and work toward a smooth flow of information throughout the company? Am I willing to share in any overtime?

Score _____

D. Attendance and Timeliness

Do I contribute to the team by being present and on time for work (including after breaks and lunch)? Do I realize the inconvenience and hardship caused by my absence or tardiness?

Score _____

III. PERSONAL DEVELOPMENT

A. To what extent am I actively involved in lifelong learning? Taking classes is not the only way to learn. Other ways include use of our resource center or libraries for reading books, articles, etc.

Score _____

B. Do I improve my job performance by applying what I have learned?

Score _____

C. Do I ask questions pertaining to my job and other jobs too?

Score _____

D. Do I try to better myself not only through work but in all aspects of my life?

Score _____

E. Do I seek information about our industry?

Score _____

TOTAL POINTS: _____

sions I would have made. Deep down, I was still in love with my own control; I was just making people guess what I wanted instead of telling them. And yet I had to replace those three managers. I needed people who didn't guess so well, people who couldn't read my mind, people strong enough to call my bluff and seize ownership of Johnsonville's problems whether I "really" wanted to give it up or not.

I spent those two years pursuing another mirage as well—detailed strategic and tactical plans that would realize my goal of Johnsonville as the world's greatest sausage maker. We tried to plan organizational structure two to three years before it would be needed—who would be responsible for what and who would report to whom, all carefully diagramed in boxes and lines on charts. Later I realized that these structural changes had to grow from day-to-day working realities; no one could dictate them from above, and certainly not in advance. But at the time, my business training told me this was the way to proceed. The discussions went on at an abstract level for months, the details overwhelmed us, and we got nowhere.

In short, the early 1980s were a disaster. After two years of stewing, it began to dawn on me that my first reactions to most situations were usually dead wrong. After all, my organizational instincts had brought us to Point A to begin with. Pursuing those instincts now would only bring us *back* to Point A. I needed to start thinking before I acted, and the thought I needed to think was, "Will this action help us achieve our new Point B?"

Point B also needed some revision. The early 1980s taught me that I couldn't give responsibility. People had to expect it, want it, even demand it. So my end state needed redefining. The goal was not so much a state of shared responsibility as an environment where people insist on being responsible.

To bring people to that new Point B, I had to learn to be a better coach. It took me additional years to learn the art of coaching, by which, in a nutshell, I mean communicating a vision and then getting people to see their own behavior, harness their own frustrations, and own their own problems.

Early in the change process, for example, I was told that workers in one plant disliked working weekends, which they often had to do to meet deliveries. Suspecting that the weekends weren't really necessary, I pressed plant managers to use the problem as an opportunity. I asked them if they had measured production efficiency, for instance, and if they had tried to get their workers to take responsibility for the overtime problem. The first thing everyone discovered was that machine downtime hovered between 30% and 40%. Then they started coming to terms with the fact that all that downtime had its causes—lateness, absences, sloppy maintenance, slow shift startups. Once the workers began to see that they themselves were the problem, they realized that they could do away with weekend work. In three weeks, they cut downtime to less than 10% and had Saturdays and Sundays off.

Managing the Context

The debacle of ordering change and watching it fail to occur showed me my limitations. I had come to realize that I didn't directly control the performance of the people at Johnsonville, that as a manager I didn't really manage people. They managed themselves. But I did manage the context. I provided and allocated the resources. I designed and implemented the systems. I drew up and executed the organizational structure. The power of any contextual factor lies in its ability to shape the way people think and what they expect. So I worked on two contextual areas: systems and structures.

Systems

I first attacked our quality control system. Quality was central to our business success, one of our key competitive advantages. But even though our quality was better than average, it wasn't yet good enough to be great.

We had the traditional quality control department with the traditional quality control responsibilities—catching errors before they got to the customer. Senior management was a part of the system. Several times a week we evaluated the product—that is to say, we *checked* it—for taste, flavor, color, and texture.

One day it struck me that by checking the product, top management had assumed responsibility for its quality. We were not encouraging people to be responsible for their own performance. We were not helping people commit themselves to making Johnsonville a great company.

This line of reasoning led me to another insight: the first strategic decision I needed to make was who should make decisions. On the theory that those who implement a decision and live with its consequences are the best people to make it, we changed our quality control system. Top management stopped tasting sausage, and the people who made sausage started. We informed line workers that from now on it would be their responsibility to make certain that only top-quality product left the plant. In the future, they would manage quality control.

It surprised me how readily people accepted this ownership. They formed teams of workers to resolve quality problems. For example, one team attacked the problem of leakers—vacuum-packed plastic packages of sausage that leaked air and shortened shelf life. The team gathered data, identified problems, worked with suppliers and with other line workers to develop and implement solutions, even visited retail stores to find out how retailers handled the product so we could make changes that would prevent their problems from occurring. The team took complete responsibility for measuring quality and then used those measurements to improve production processes. They owned and expected to own all the problems of producing top-quality sausage, and they wanted to do the best possible job. The results were amazing. Rejects fell from 5% to less than 0.5%.

Clearly this new quality control system was helping to create the end state we were after. Its success triggered changes in several other systems as well.

Teams of workers in other areas began to taste the product every morning and discuss possible improvements. They asked for information about costs and customer reactions, and we redesigned the information system to give it to them.

We began to forward customer letters directly to line workers. They responded to customer complaints and sent coupons for free Johnsonville sausage when they felt it was warranted. They came to own and expect responsibility for correcting the problems that customers raised in their letters.

People in each section on the shop floor began to collect data about labor costs, efficiency, and yield. They posted the data and discussed it at the daily tasting meeting. Increasingly, people asked for more responsibility, and the information system encouraged them to take it. We were progressing toward our end state, and as we made progress we uncovered deeper and more complex problems.

One of these arose when people on the shop floor began to complain about fellow workers whose performance was still slipshod or indifferent. In fact, they came to senior management and said, "You don't take your own advice. If you did, you wouldn't let these poor performers work here. It's your job to either fix them or fire them."

Our first reaction was to jump in and do something, but by now we had learned to think before acting. We asked ourselves if accepting responsibility for this problem would help us reach Point B. The answer was clearly no. More important, we asked ourselves who was in the best position to own the problem and came to the obvious conclusion that the people on the shop floor knew more about shop-floor performance than we did, so they were the best ones to make these decisions.

We offered to help them set performance standards and to coach them in confronting poor performers, but we insisted that since they were the production-performance experts, it was up to them to deal with the situation. I bit my tongue time and time again, but they took on the responsibility for dealing with performance problems and actually fired individuals who wouldn't perform up to the standards of their teams.

This led to a dramatic change in Johnsonville's human resource system. Convinced that inadequate selection and training of new workers caused performance problems, line workers asked to do the selection and training themselves. Managers helped them set up selection and training procedures, but production workers made them work. Eventually, line workers assumed most of the traditional personnel functions.

The compensation system was another early target for change. We had traditionally given across-the-board annual raises like most other businesses. What mattered was longevity, not performance. That system was also a stumbling block on our way to Point B, so we made two changes.

First, we eliminated the annual across-the-board raise and substituted a pay-for-responsibility system. As people took on new duties—budgeting, for instance, or training—they earned additional base income. Where the old system rewarded people for hanging around, regardless of what they contributed, the new one encouraged people to seek responsibility.

Second, we instituted what we called a "company performance share," a fixed percentage of pretax profits to be divided every six months among our employees. We based individual shares on a performance-appraisal system designed and administered by a volunteer team of line production workers from various departments. The system is explained in the insert "How Johnsonville Shares Profits on the Basis of Performance."

These system changes taught me two more valuable lessons. First, just start. Don't wait until you have all the answers. When I set out to make these changes, I had no clear picture of how these new systems would interact with one another or with other company systems and procedures, but if I had waited until I had all the answers, I'd still be waiting. A grand plan was impossible; there were too many variables. I wasn't certain which systems to change; I just knew I had to change something in order to alter expectations and begin moving toward my goal.

How Johnsonville Shares Profits on the Basis of Performance

Every six months, we evaluate the performance of everyone at Johnsonville to help us compute shares in our profit-sharing program. Except "we" is the wrong word. In practice, performance evaluations are done by the employees themselves. For example, 300 wage earners—salaried employees have a separate profit-sharing pool and a different evaluation system—fill out forms in which they rate themselves on a scale of 1 to 9 in 17 specific areas grouped into three categories: performance, teamwork, and personal development.

Scores of 3, 4, or 5—the average range—are simply entered on the proper line. Low scores of 1 or 2 and high scores of 6 to 9 require a sentence or two of explanation.

Each member's coach fills out an identical form, and later both people sit down together and discuss all 17 areas. In cases of disagreement, the rule is only that their overall point totals must agree within nine points, whereupon the two totals are averaged to reach a final score. If they cannot narrow the gap to nine points, an arbitration group is ready to step in and help, but so far mediation has never been needed.

All final scores, names deleted, are then passed to a profit-sharing team that carves out five categories of performance: a small group of superior performers (about 5% of the total), a larger group of better-than-average workers (roughly 20%), an average group amounting to about 50% of the total work force, a below-average group of 20%, and a small group of poor performers who are often in some danger of losing their jobs.

The total pool of profits to be shared is then divided by the number of workers to find an average share—for the purpose of illustration, let's say $1,000. Members of the top group get a check for 125% of that amount or $1,250. Members of the next group get 110% ($1,100), of the large middle group, 100% or $1,000, and so on down to $900 and $750.

Yes, people do complain from time to time, especially if they think they've missed a higher share by only a point or two. The usual way of dealing with such situations is to help the individual improve his or her performance in enough areas to ensure a higher score the next time. But overall satisfaction with the system is very high, partly because fellow workers invented it, administer it, and constantly revise it in an effort to make it more equitable. The person currently in charge of the Johnsonville profit-sharing team is an hourly worker from the shipping department.

Many forms have been used over the years—a new one is under consideration at this moment—but the questions most recently asked, in a slightly edited version, are reprinted in this article.

Second, start by changing the most visible system you directly control. You want your first effort to succeed. I knew I could control who tasted the product because I was doing the tasting. I also knew it was a highly visible action. Everyone waited to hear my taste-test results. By announcing that I wasn't going to taste the product anymore and that the people who made it were, everyone knew immediately that I was serious about spreading responsibility.

Structures

Along with the system changes, I introduced a number of changes in company structure. Teams gradually took over a number of the functions previously performed by individual managers in the chain of command, with the result that the number of hierarchical layers went from six to three.

Teams had already taken on responsibility for selecting, training, evaluating, and, when necessary, terminating fellow employees. Now they began to make all decisions about schedules, performance standards, assignments, budgets, quality measures, and capital improvements as well. In operations, teams assumed the supervisors' functions, and those jobs disappeared. Those former supervisors who needed authority in order to function left the company, but most went into other jobs at Johnsonville, some of them into technical positions.

The function of the quality control department was redefined. It stopped checking quality—now done by line workers—and began providing technical support to the production people in a cooperative effort to *improve* quality. The department developed systems for continuous on-line monitoring of fat, moisture, and protein content, for example, and it launched a program of outside taste testing among customers.

The traditional personnel department disappeared and was replaced by a learning and personal development team to help individual employees develop their own Points B and A—their destinations and starting points—and figure out how to use Johnsonville to reach their goals. We set up an educational allowance for each person, to be used however the individual saw fit. In the beginning, some took cooking or sewing classes; a few took flying lessons. Over time, however, more and more of the employees focused on job-related learning. Today more than 65% of all the people at Johnsonville are involved in some type of formal education.

The end state we all now envision for Johnsonville is a company that never stops learning. One part of learning is the acquisition of facts and knowledge—about accounting, machine maintenance, marketing, even about sky diving and Italian cooking. But the most important kind of learning teaches us to question our own actions and behavior in order to better understand the ways we perform, work, and live.

Helping human beings fulfill their potential is of course a moral responsibility, but it's also good business. Life is aspiration. Learning, striving people are happy people and good workers. They have initiative and imagination, and the companies they work for are rarely caught napping.

Learning is change, and I keep learning and relearning that change is and needs to be continuous. For example, our system and structural changes were reciprocal. The first led to the second, which then in turn led to new versions of the first.

Initially, I had hoped the journey would be as neat and orderly as it now appears on paper. Fortunately—since original mistakes are an important part of learning—it wasn't. There were lots of obstacles and challenges, much backsliding, and myriad false starts and wrong decisions.

For example, team leaders chosen by their team members were supposed to function as communication links, leaving the traditional management functions of planning and scheduling to the group itself. No sooner had the team leaders been appointed, however, than they began to function as supervisors. In other words, they immediately fell into the familiar roles they had always seen. We had neglected to give them and the plant managers adequate training in the new team model. The structure changed, but mind-sets didn't. It was harder to alter people's expectations than I had realized.

Influencing Expectations

I discovered that change occurs in fits and starts, and that while I could plan individual changes and events, I couldn't plan the whole process. I also learned that expectations have a way of becoming reality, so I tried to use every available means—semantic, symbolic, and behavioral—to send messages that would shape expectations to Johnsonville's advantage.

For example, we wanted to break down the traditional pictures in people's minds of what managers do and how subordinates and employees behave, so we changed the words we used. We dropped the words employee and subordinate. Instead we called everyone a "member" of the organization, and managers became "coordinators" or "coaches."

Our promotion system had always sent a powerful message: to move up the ladder you need to become a manager and solve problems for your people. But this was now the wrong message. I wanted coordinators who could build problem-solving capacities in others rather than solve their problems for them. I recast the job requirements for the people whose work I directly coordinated (formerly known as "my management team"), and they, in turn, did the same for the people whose work they coordinated. I took every opportunity to stress the need for coaching skills, and I continually de-emphasized technical experience. Whenever someone became a coordinator, I made sure word got around that the promotion was for demonstrated abilities as a teacher, coach, and facilitator.

This new promotion standard sent a new message: to get ahead at Johnsonville, you need a talent for cultivating and encouraging problem solvers and responsibility takers.

I discovered that people watched my every action to see if it supported or undermined our vision. They wanted to see if I practiced what I preached. From the outset I did simple things to demonstrate my sincerity. I made a sign for my desk that said THE QUESTION IS THE ANSWER, and when people came to me with questions, I asked myself if they were questions I should answer. Invariably, they weren't. Invariably, people were asking me to make decisions for them. Instead of giving answers, I turned the tables and asked the questions myself, trying to make them repossess their own problems. Owning problems was an important part of the end state I'd envisioned. I wasn't about to let people give theirs to me.

I also discovered that in meetings people waited to hear my opinion before offering their own. In the beginning, I insisted they say what they thought, unaware that I showed my own preferences in subtle ways—my tone of voice, the questions I asked—which, nevertheless, anyone could read and interpret expertly. When I realized what was happening, I began to stay silent to avoid giving any clue to where I stood. The result was that people flatly refused to commit themselves to any decision at all. Some of those meetings would have gone on for days if I hadn't forced people to speak out before they'd read my mind.

In the end, I began scheduling myself out of many meetings, forcing others to make their decisions without me. I also stopped collecting data about production problems. I learned that if I had information about daily shortages and yields, I began to ask questions that put me firmly back in possession of the problems.

Eventually, I came to understand that everything I did and said had a symbolic as well as a literal meaning. I had to anticipate the potential impact of every word and act, ask myself again and again if what I was about to do or say would reinforce the vision or undermine it, bring us closer to Point B or circle us back to Point A, encourage people to own their own problems or palm them off on me. My job, as I had come to see it, was to put myself out of a job.

Watershed

By mid-1985, we had all come a long way. Johnsonville members had started wanting and expecting responsibility for their own performance, and they usually did a good job. Return on assets was up significantly, as were margins and quality. But on the whole, the process of change had been a journey without any major mileposts or station stops.

Then Palmer Sausage (not its real name) came along and gave us our watershed—a golden opportunity and a significant threat to our existence.

Palmer is a much larger sausage company that had contracted with us for private-label products during a strike in the early 1980s. Our quality was so high that they kept us on as a supplier after the strike ended. Now Palmer had decided to consolidate several facilities and offered to let us take over part of the production of a plant they were closing. It represented a huge increase in their order, and the additional business was very tempting: it could be very profitable, and it would justify the cost of a new and more efficient plant of our own. The upside was extremely attractive—if we could handle it.

That was what worried me. To handle an expanded Palmer contract, we'd have to hire and train a large group of people quickly and teach our present people new skills, keep quality high on both the Palmer products and our own, work six and seven days a week for more than a year until our new plant was ready, and run the risk if Palmer cancelled—which it could do on 30-days' notice—of saddling ourselves with big layoffs and new capacity we no longer had a market for. Maybe it wasn't a bet-the-company decision, but it was as close as I'd like to come.

Before 1982, I would have met for days with my senior team to discuss all these issues, and we would probably have turned down the opportunity in the face of such an overwhelming downside. But by 1985, it was clear to me that the executive group was the wrong group to make this decision. The executives would not be responsible for successfully implementing such a move. The only way we could do Palmer successfully was if everyone at Johnsonville was committed to making it work, so everyone had to decide.

Until that moment, my senior team had always made the strategic decisions. We took advice from people in the operating departments, but the senior staff and I had dealt with the ultimate problems and responsibilities. We needed to move to a new level. This was a problem all of our people had to own.

My senior managers and I called a meeting of the entire plant, presented the problem, and posed three questions. What will it take to make it work? Is it possible to reduce the downside? Do we want to do it?

We asked the teams in each area to discuss these questions among themselves and develop a list of pros and cons. Since the group as a whole was too large to work together effectively, each team chose one member to report its findings to a plantwide representative body to develop a plantwide answer.

The small groups met almost immediately, and within days their representatives met. The discussion moved back and forth several times between the representative body and the smaller groups.

To make it work, the members decided we'd have to operate seven days a week, hire and train people to take new shifts, and increase efficiency to get more from current capacity. They also thought about the downside risk. The biggest danger was that we'd lose the added business after making all the investments and sacrifices needed to handle it. They figured the only way to reduce that downside potential was to achieve quality standards so high that we would actually improve the already first-rate Palmer product and, at the same time, maintain standards on our own products to make sure Johnsonville brands didn't fall by the wayside.

Two weeks later, the company decided almost unanimously to take the business. It was one of the proudest moments of my life. Left to our traditional executive decision making, we would have turned Palmer down. The Johnsonville people, believing in themselves, rose to the challenge. They really did want to be great.

The results surpassed our best projections. Learning took place faster than anticipated. Quality rose in our own product line as well as for Palmer. The new plant came on line in 1987. Palmer has come back to us several times since to increase the size of its orders even further.

Success—The Greatest Enemy

The pace of change increased after Palmer. Now that all of Johnsonville's people expected and wanted some degree of responsibility for strategic decisions, we had to redefine Point A, our current situation. The new level of involvement also led us to a more ambitious view of what we could ultimately achieve—Point B, our vision and destination.

We made additional changes in our career-tracking system. In our early enthusiasm, we had played down the technical aspects of our business, encouraging everyone to become a coordinator, even those who were far better suited to technical specialties. We also had some excellent salespeople who became coordinators because they saw it as the only path to advancement, though their talents

---

Ralph Stayer's Guide to Improving Performance

Getting better performance from any group or individual, yourself included, means a permanent change in the way you think and run your business. Change of this kind is not a single transaction but a journey, and the journey has a specific starting point and a clear destination.

The journey is based on six observations about human behavior that I didn't fully grasp when I started, though I'd have made faster progress and fewer mistakes if I had.

1. People want to be great. If they aren't, it's because management won't let them be.

2. Performance begins with each individual's expectations. Influence what people expect and you influence how people perform.

3. Expectations are driven partly by goals, vision, symbols, semantics, and partly by the context in which people work, that is, by such things as compensation systems, production practices, and decision-making structures.

4. The actions of managers shape expectations.

5. Learning is a process, not a goal. Each new insight creates a new layer of potential insights.

6. The organization's results reflect me and my performance. If I want to change the results, I have to change myself first. This is particularly true for me, the owner and CEO, but it is equally true for every employee.

So to make the changes that will lead to great performance, I recommend focusing on goals, expectations, contexts, actions, and learning. Lee Thayer, a humanities professor at the University of Wisconsin, has another way of saying pretty much the same thing. He argues that since performance is the key to organizational success, management's job is to establish the conditions under which superb performance serves both the company's and the individual's best interests.

CEOs need to focus first on changing themselves before they try to change the rest of the company. The process resembles an archaeological dig, or at least it did for me. As I uncovered and solved one problem, I almost invariably exposed another, deeper problem. As I gained one insight and mastered one situation, another situation arose that required new insight and more learning. As I approached one goal, a new, more important, but more distant goal always began to take shape.

and interests lay much more in selling than in coaching. When they became coordinators, we lost in three ways: we lost good salespeople, we created poor coordinators, and we lost sales from other good salespeople because they worked for these poor coordinators.

A career team recommended that Johnsonville set up dual career tracks—one for specialists and one for coordinators—that would enable both to earn recognition, status, and compensation on the basis of performance alone. The team, not the senior coordinators, agreed to own and fix the compensation problem.

Everyone at Johnsonville discovered they could do considerably better and earn considerably more than they had imagined. Since they had little trouble meeting the accelerated production goals that they themselves had set, members raised the minimum acceptable performance criteria and began routinely to expect more of themselves and others.

Right now, teams of Johnsonville members are meeting to discuss next year's capital budget, new product ideas, today's production schedule, and yesterday's quality, cost, and yield. More important, these same teams are redesigning their systems and structures to manage their continuing journey toward Point B, which, along with Point A, they are also continually redefining. Most important of all, their general level of commitment is now as high or higher than my own.

In fact, our greatest enemy now is our success. Our sales, margins, quality, and productivity far exceed anything we could have imagined in 1980. We've been studied and written about, and we've spent a lot of time answering questions and giving advice. We've basked in the limelight, telling other people how we did it. All the time we kept telling ourselves, "We can't let this go to our heads." But of course it had already gone to our heads. We had begun to talk and brag about the past instead of about what we wanted for the future. Once we saw what we were doing, we managed to stop and, in the process, learn a lesson about the hazards of self-congratulation.

When I began this process of change ten years ago, I looked forward to the time when it would all be over and I could get back to my real job. But I've learned that change is the real job of every effective business leader because change is about the present and the future, not about the past. There is no end to change. This story is only an interim report.

Yet another thing I've learned is that the cause of excitement at Johnsonville Sausage is not change itself but the process used in producing change. Learning and responsibility are invigorating, and aspirations make our hearts beat. For the last five years, my own aspiration has been to eliminate *my* job by creating such a crowd of self-starting, problem-solving, responsibility-grabbing, independent thinkers that Johnsonville would run itself.

Two years ago, I hired a new chief operating officer and told him he should lead the company and think of me as his paid consultant. Earlier this year, he invited me to a management retreat, and I enjoyed myself. Other people owned the problems that had once been mine. My whole job was to generate productive conversations about Johnsonville's goals and to communicate its vision.

On the second evening of the retreat, I was given a message from my COO. There was a special session the next morning, he wrote, and added, "I want you there at 8:15." Instinctively, it made me mad. Johnsonville was my company; I built it; I fixed it; he owed me his job. Who the hell did he think he was giving me orders like a hired consultant?

Then, of course, I laughed. It's not always easy giving up control, even when it's what you've worked toward for ten years. He wanted me there at 8:15? Well, good for him. I'd be there.

Leadership

L eadership is generally defined as the process of influencing the activities of others toward the accomplishment of goals. For centuries people have sought methods for becoming effective leaders and the literature of organizational behavior is rich with theories of leadership. This section reviews some of the better-known conceptual models.

In "The Managerial Grid," Robert Blake and Jane Mouton suggest that there are two key dimensions of managerial behavior: the concern for production and the concern for people. Five different combinations of these two dimensions are described:

- 9, 1 high concern for production and low concern for people
- 9, 9 high concern for production and high concern for people
- 1, 9 low concern for production and high concern for people
- 1, 1 low concern for production and low concern for people
- 5, 5 moderate concern for production and moderate concern for people

Blake and Mouton's well-known model suggests that the 9, 9 approach promotes conditions that will lead to high levels of creativity, productivity, and morale.

In their 1973 article, "How to Choose a Leadership Pattern," Robert Tannenbaum and Warren H. Schmidt view leader behavior on a continuum ranging from authoritarian (boss-centered) to democratic (subordinate-centered) and discuss numerous behaviors occurring along this spectrum. The problem facing managers is how to be "democratic" in relationships with subordinates while maintaining adequate authority and control within the organization. In making this decision, managers are asked to examine various forces in themselves, forces in their subordinates, and forces inherent in the situation. The unique circumstances of the situation then determine the appropriate pattern of leader behavior.

It is important to note that the "situational" nature of their analysis was conceived some 15 years before the situational approach became widely popular.

In "Leadership Decision Making," Victor Vroom and Arthur Jago present their model for determining the appropriate form and amount of participation in decision making for different situations. The decision tree model asks a series of questions related to quality requirements, adequacy of information, problem structure, whether acceptance by subordinates is critical to implementation, etc. Depending on the answers, different levels of involvement in decision making are prescribed for individual and group problems. These levels range from the leader solving the problem or making the decision to allowing the individual or group to develop the solution.

The One Minute Manager, coauthored by Kenneth H. Blanchard and Spencer Johnson, became a best seller with its common-sense approach to managing people. The book reveals three "secrets" of effective management: one minute goal setting, one minute praising, and one minute reprimands. *The One Minute Manager* struck a responsive chord among practicing managers who recognized the problems associated with: (a) not clearly communicating goals and expectations to employees, (b) failing to recognize people's positive contributions, and (c) not holding employees accountable for their behavior. In the excerpt provided here, Blanchard describes how to put the three secrets to work.

In "Fundamental Leadership Practices," James Kouzes and Barry Posner describe how they examined thousands of "best leadership experiences" and identified five common denominators among the best leaders:

- They "challenge the process" by not being content with the status quo and search for opportunities to innovate, grow, and improve through experimentation and reasonable risk taking.
- They "inspire a shared vision" by envisioning exciting and worthy possibilities and enlisting others toward the cause.
- They "enable others to act" by fostering collaboration, building trust, and strengthening others' capacity to perform.
- They "model the way" by clarifying values and setting the example.
- They "encourage the heart" by recognizing contributions and celebrating victories.

Central to all of these denominators is developing effective relationships between those who aspire to lead and those who choose to follow.

Harvard Business School Professor John Kotter compares "Management and Leadership." Management is viewed as a set of key processes—planning, budgeting, organizing, staffing, controlling, and problem solving—aimed at producing predictability and order. Leadership, on the other hand, is defined as establishing direction, aligning people, and motivating and inspiring people to produce desirable and often dramatic change. Kotter contends that due to accelerating change and increased complexity, most organizations today require effective management *and* strong leadership to prosper.

In his classic essay, "The Servant as Leader," Robert Greenleaf describes how the role of the servant and the role of a leader can be united into one person.

He suggests that "servant leadership" puts serving others first and strives to ensure that other people's needs are satisfied. By doing so, those being served become healthier, wiser, freer, more autonomous, and more likely to become servant-leaders themselves. Also, Greenleaf suggests that becoming a true servant-leader requires a long, arduous process of learning to listen.

"Situational Leadership" (originally called Life Cycle Theory of Leadership) was developed by Paul Hersey and Ken Blanchard at Ohio University. The key point of Situational Leadership is that the appropriate leadership style for a particular situation depends on the "performance readiness" of the follower. According to Paul Hersey, the three steps in using Situational Leadership are:

- Identify the specific job, task, or activity.
- Assess the follower's current performance readiness.
- Use the matching leadership style.

There are four performance readiness levels:

- R1 = Unable and Insecure or Unable and Unwilling
- R2 = Unable but Confident or Willing
- R3 = Able but Insecure or Able but Unwilling
- R4 = Able and Confident and Willing

Depending on the follower's readiness level, the leader should use the "matching" leadership style. The four leadership styles in this model are:

- S1 = High Task/Low Relationship
- S2 = High Task/High Relationship
- S3 = High Relationship/Low Task
- S4 = Low Relationship/Low Task

Situational Leadership provides practical and useful guidelines for assessing the follower's readiness level and then prescribes the appropriate amount of direction and support to use for that level. Using the appropriate leadership style will have a positive impact on the follower's performance and development.

In "Crucibles of Leadership," authors Warren Bennis and Robert Thomas ponder the question of what makes an effective leader. Some people naturally inspire confidence, loyalty, and hard work, while others stumble again and again. Bennis and Thomas believe that an important success factor is the way people deal with adversity. More specifically, one of the most reliable indicators of true leadership is an individual's ability to find meaning in negative events, to learn from even the most trying circumstances, and to emerge stronger and more committed than ever. The authors call these transformative experiences "crucibles" through which an individual comes to a new or an altered sense of identity. Numerous examples of crucible experiences are provided where leaders were able to grow from their difficult experiences instead of being destroyed by them.

1

The Managerial Grid

Robert Blake and Jane Mouton

A variety of theories regarding managerial behavior can be identified. These theories, or sets of assumptions, are based on the way in which three organization universals are connected to one another.[1] One of the three is *concern for production;* the amount of emphasis supervision places on achieving production. A second is *concern for people;* the productive unit of the organization. The third is hierarchy; the *boss* aspect. Whenever a man acts as a manager, he is in some way making assumptions about how to solve problems of achieving organization purposes of production through people.[2]

Dimensions of the Grid

Before going on let's define exactly what we mean by "concern for." This is not meant to indicate *how much* (such as, how much production, meaning quantity), nor is it intended to reflect the degree that the needs of people actually are met. Rather, emphasis here is on the *degree* of "concern for" which is present in the *boss* because his *actions* are rooted in, and flow out of, his own *basic attitudes.* What is significant is *how* a supervisor is concerned about production and *how* he concerns himself about people, and *how* these concerns intertwine.[3,4]

Concern for Production

The words *production* or *people* cover a range of considerations. Attitudes of concern toward production, for example, may be seen in the quality of policy decisions, the number of creative ideas that applied research turns into useful products, procedures or processes; number of accounts processed; quality and thoroughness of staff services; workload and efficiency measurements; volume of sales or units of physical output. Production as used here is not limited to *things.* Its proper meaning covers whatever it is that organizations engage people to accomplish.

At the lowest level, it is true, concern for production may take the form of the number of units of things that can be counted or of time required to attain a certain production schedule. But at the top of an organization, concern for production may be demonstrated in the kind of policies which are established and the character of direction given to major programs of organization effort. Indeed, the concern for production at the top may be expressed through finding new directions or new products to sustain organization growth and development.

Concern for People

In a similar fashion, concern for people can be expressed in a variety of different ways. Included are concern for degree of personal commitment to completing a job one is responsible for; accountability based on trust; self-esteem or the personal worth of an individual; establishing and maintaining good working conditions; maintaining an equitable salary structure and fringe benefits; desire for security in work; social relations or friendships with associates; etc.

As will be seen, *concern for production* and *concern for people* are expressed in vastly different ways, depending on the specific manner in which these two concerns are joined.[5]

"Pure" Theories

The *Managerial Grid,* depicted in Figure 1, shows these two concerns and a range of possible interactions between them. The horizontal axis indicates concern for production while the vertical axis indicates concern for people. Each is expressed as a nine-point scale of concern. The number 1 in each instance represents minimum concern. The 9 stands for maximum concern.

At the lower left corner of the grid is the 1, 1 style. This has a minimum of both concerns; that is, of concern for production and concern for people. Going up the grid from the 1, 1 style to the upper left corner is found the 1, 9 style. Here there is a minimum of concern for production but maximum concern for people. In the lower right corner is 9, 1. This style has a maximum concern for production and a minimum for human aspects. In the upper right corner is the 9, 9 style, where concern for both people and production reaches maximum. Then, in the center is the 5, 5 style, which is a "middle of the road" or an intermediate amount of both kinds of concerns.

It should be emphasized that the manner in which these two concerns are linked together by a manager defines how he uses hierarchy. In addition, the character of *concern for* at different grid positions differs, even though the *degree* may be the same. For example, when high concern for people is coupled with a low concern for production, the type of people concern expressed (*i.e.,* that people be "happy") is far different from the type of high concern for people shown when a high concern for production is also evident (*i.e.,* that people be involved in the work and strive to contribute to organization purpose).

A number of additional managerial theories may be shown on this grid. Indeed, in a 9-point system such as is employed here, 81 "mixtures" of these two

Figure 1
The Managerial Grid

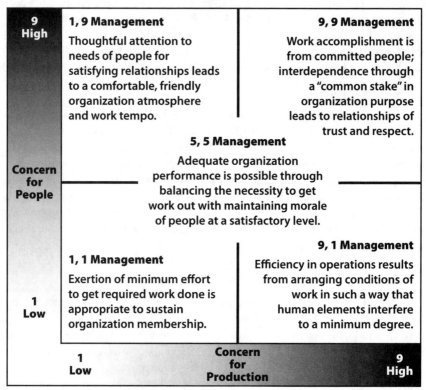

concerns might be pictured. However, emphasis first will be placed on analyzing the assumptions at the corners and midpoint. Each of these five theories defines a definite but different set of assumptions regarding how individuals, in fact, do orient themselves for managing situations of production that involve people. The important point here is that when a manager confronts a situation in which work is to be accomplished through people, there are, indeed, alternative ways for him to go about supervising. To increase his managerial competence he needs to know them and to be able to select the best course of action for any given situation from among a number of possibilities.[6]

As in any field of applied endeavor, disagreement can arise between what is the best theory and what theory is most realistic for practical application in a "live" situation. However, as in any applied setting, the answer regarding what is best can only be given in the light of existing realities. There is no ideological way of saying what is best without reference to actual circumstances. But the choice is neither arbitrary nor random. The *results* a manager obtains will reflect, in predictable ways, the kinds of assumptions he applied in that situation.[7] If the assumptions do not "fit" the situation well, poorer results will be obtained than if they do.

Significance and Interpretation of Grid Positions

Should the five "pure" theories be viewed as defining a set of personality characteristics? If not, then in what manner should they be considered? One answer is that these positions constitute anchorages for managerial attitudes and practices. Conceived of in this manner, aspects of the grid are more accurately regarded as describing systems of pressures acting on an individual to manage in a certain fashion. Such pressures arise:

1. from inside himself,

2. from the immediate external situation, and/or

3. from characteristics of the organizational system including traditions, established practices and procedures.

Though most people seem to be predisposed to manage in one way or another, points on the grid are *not* to be thought of as personality types that isolate a given individual's behavior. They do not slot him in a rigid and inflexible way into a certain place. Behavior is more changing and flexible than that.

In comparison with a mechanical explanation of managerial behavior, the grid pictures a number of different sets of assumptions about how an individual *can* manage. Any set of assumptions is subject to change. Whenever a person changes his underlying managerial assumptions, his actual managerial practices shift accordingly, or else a gross discrepancy is present between the attitudes he expresses and the actions he takes. A given individual's style, then, may be viewed as a dominant set of assumptions.[8] These assumptions orient his thinking and his behavior in dealing with production/people relationships. Furthermore, he may or may not be aware of the assumptions that are guiding his actions.[9] The purpose of this effort, and of much management training, is to aid an individual to become more knowledgeable regarding his own assumptions about how to manage.

Observe an individual's behavior in a variety of situations. It becomes clear that even the notion of one dominant style, a single set of managerial assumptions, is not sufficient to catch the full implication of a person's managerial approach. In addition to a dominant set of managerial assumptions, which are the most characteristic of the managerial style a person has adopted, the concept of a *backup* set of assumptions is a useful one. An individual's backup theory is the one he uses when his dominant theory fails to get the desired results. It is the style he falls back on. Any style may be a backup to any other theory as a dominant style.

Which managerial style is dominant for any given person in any particular situation can be determined by any one or several sets of conditions in combination.

Organization

Managerial behavior frequently is determined by situational factors, such as the organization in which a person operates. Thus, when organizational practices are so fixed or rigid as to permit only small variations in individual behavior, the managerial style exhibited may reflect little of a man's personal thinking and much of his organization beliefs about "the right way to manage." Therefore, one section within each of the anchor positions is concerned with organization or situational requirements which are likely to call forth various managerial styles.

Situation

The situation itself may be the determining or overriding factor dictating which set of managerial assumptions are employed to deal with it. Management of people in the crisis of an explosive situation is likely to be different than it would be under circumstances that are routine.

Values

Any individual's choice of managerial assumptions may be based on values or beliefs he holds concerning the "right" way to treat people, or the way to manage to achieve "best" results. Any given set of assumptions can have a personal value attached to them which represents an individual's private conviction concerning the desirability of any managerial style as a dominant one.

Personality

The dominant managerial style may, to an important degree, result from deep-rooted personality characteristics which predispose an individual to prefer one approach over another. Thus, in the sections concerned with the five anchor positions (Figure 1), the personality dispositions likely to be found in conjunction with a given managerial style are presented.

Chance

Finally, a set of managerial assumptions may guide a person's behavior because he has not been confronted with, nor has discovered in his own experience, that other sets of assumptions about how to manage are available. "Chance," so to speak, has not helped him learn. But many managers, upon learning the variety of managerial styles available to them, do shift, sometimes rather dramatically, from one style to another, as they seek to integrate people into production. Seeing alternatives, they embrace a different set of assumptions.

The point to be emphasized here is that managerial styles are *not* fixed. They are not unchanging. They are determined by a range of factors. . . .

The 9, 1 Managerial Style

In the lower right-hand corner of the grid is 9, 1. At this position a high concern for production, 9, is coupled with a low concern for people, 1. In the 9, 1 managerial style, the assumption is made that, somehow, there is an inevitable contradiction between organizational needs of production and personal needs of people. If one is met, the other must be sacrificed. Yet, people must be used to attain the production for which the manager feels responsible. If he acts from a 9, 1 orientation, he seeks to resolve the dilemma by arranging conditions of work which minimize feelings and attitudes.[10] He does so in a way that prevents the "human elements from interfering with efficiency and output."

A manager operating at a 9, 1 level, in the extreme, might be characterized as an exacting taskmaster. He drives himself and his people alike. One thought monopolizes his concern and action—*production*. 9, 1 personifies the entrepreneurial spirit.[11]

9, 1 is one of the positions on the grid where concern for people is low. Thus, it is not surprising that topics such as conflict, creativity, and commitment receive little attention. This does not indicate that topics such as conflict, creativity and commitment do not contain managerial assumptions under 9, 1. Indeed, they do. The point is that they are weighted unevenly. Far more attention is given to how to organize work than to the conditions of organizing people in order to make it possible for them to work with maximum productivity.[12]

Management under 9, 1

Under a 9, 1 theory, a manager has a position of authority in the hierarchy and he knows it. He feels his responsibilities are to plan, direct, and control the actions of his subordinates in whatever way is necessary to reach the production objectives of the enterprise. The boss plans, subordinates execute. They carry out the various plans, directions and schedules placed upon them. The aim under this approach is to get production! Schedules are to be met! People are expected to do what they are told to do—no more, no less.[13] A 9, 1 managerial orientation is typified in the following quotations:

Planning. "I do planning by setting the production quotas and schedules to be followed by each subordinate. Then, I work out the procedures and operating ground rules and I make individual assignments. I also establish check points so I can ascertain that actions I have authorized are being taken as I intended them to be done."

Work Execution. "I watch the work closely. I criticize as I see the necessity for it and authorize changes as needs for them arise."

Follow-up. "I have plans laid for the next assignments and move people on to them as operations dictate. Recognition and corrective actions are extended to individuals on a one-by-one basis."

These three statements contain a number of 9, 1 assumptions concerning how to manage performance. The above orientations to managerial responsibilities are, in themselves, keys to understanding the 9, 1 style. The success of 9, 1 management is measured solely in terms of production and profit.[14] Personal managerial success in this context, then, has its reward in achieving production goals. *Achievement* becomes the watchword of the 9, 1 approach.[15] Here organization is like a competitive hurdle race. Victory goes to the swiftest, the one able to surmount each hurdle he confronts—without help. To the victor belong the spoils of organization. . . .

The 1, 9 Managerial Style

In the upper left-hand corner of the grid is the 1, 9 managerial orientation. Here a low functional concern for production, 1, is coupled with high concern for people. As with 9, 1, the 1, 9 managerial orientation also is rooted in the assumption that production requirements are contrary to the needs of people.[16] To a manager with a 1, 9 style, however, the attitudes and feelings of people *are* important. They are valuable in their own right. They come first. Within this context, conditions are arranged that personal, social and welfare needs can be met.[17]

Management under 1, 9

When asked to describe his hierarchical responsibilities, a person operating under 1, 9 assumptions is likely to use the same *words* as those the manager operating under 9, 1 might use. He would say that his job is to plan, direct and control the activities of *his* subordinates. His aim as a manager, however, is to avoid pressuring for production at a rate higher than that which would win acceptance from organizational members. He leads by following. By deemphasizing production, the 1, 9 approach avoids some of the conflict that arises from production decisions that disturb people. A deeper 1, 9 attitude is seen in the feeling that, "You can't *push* people for production because if you do, they balk and resist," or "You can lead a horse to water, but you can't make him drink." "When people have turned against you, they are in trouble and you are, too." How he plans and directs subordinates and the way in which follow-up takes place are briefly outlined below.[18]

Planning.   "I give broad assignments to my subordinates and convey my confidence by saying, 'I'm sure you know how to do this and that you will do it well.'"

Work Execution.   "I see my people frequently and encourage them to visit with me as their time permits. My door is always open. My goal is to see to it that they are able to get the things they want. That's the way to encourage people."

Follow-up.   "I hold a meeting with those who are on the job where I place emphasis on congratulating the group as well as individuals. We have fun and when we get down to business our wrap-up sessions usually revolve around why we did as well as we did do and how we can help things to go as smoothly or more so in the future. Criticism rarely helps. My motto is 'don't say anything if you can't say something nice.'"

The 1, 9 managerial style, in other words, focuses on how to arrange conditions of work which will permit people to fit them with comfort, ease and security.[19] Under the 1, 9 set of assumptions, it is felt that organizational demands for production often are harsh, overdemanding and unnecessary. When his people become disturbed, the manager with a 1, 9 orientation also becomes disturbed. To counterbalance the demands of the organization, the manager can lighten work conditions by emphasizing the positive aspects of work, or by giving a bonus of some sort.[20] Informal conversation, a joke, an understanding pat on the back, a smile, coffee together—all help the task to pass a little easier and to make life a little more enjoyable. . . .[21]

The 1, 1 Managerial Style

Low concern for production, 1, is coupled with low concern for people, 1, in the lower left-hand corner of the grid, where the 1, 1 managerial pattern is located. Like 9, 1 or 1, 9, an incompatibility is assumed to exist between production requirements and needs of people. However, since concern for both is low, the manager with a 1, 1 orientation experiences little or no dilemma between production and people—he is more or less "out of it." But, the person managing 1, 1 has learned to "be out of it," while remaining in the organization. Little is expected of him, and little is given by him in return.[22] 1, 1 as an approach is rare in organization situations of nonrepetitive action where each situation presents a different set of problems to be solved. It is far more common in routine operations, and in various staff functions.[23]

The phrase "1, 1 management" of people is an anomaly. A person who has adopted a 1, 1 orientation might better be described as "lost among," rather than "managing" people. Anomalous though it may seem, there are, today, many persons in managerial ranks whose supervision is best pictured as 1, 1.

The 1, 1 approach is unnatural. It comes to those who accepted defeat. To permit oneself again to become involved and concerned over what happens in the work situation can only lead to deeper frustration and discouragement.[24] It is an approach characterized, then, by low involvement with people and the contribution of minimum effort toward organization purpose.[25]

Management under 1, 1

The supervisory approach under 1, 1 is to put people on jobs and to leave them alone. He does this by letting people do their work as they see fit. He does not pester them. "Don't put your hand in a hornet's nest," is a motto characteristic of a manager who operates in the 1, 1 direction. His administrative responses are of minimum movement, enough to get the pressure off his back, but little more. The following show how a 1, 1 supervisor views his managerial responsibilities.[26]

Planning.   "I give broad assignments though I don't think in terms of goals or schedules. I do little planning. A way that you might describe my job is I'm a message carrier. I carry the story from those one level above to those one level below me. I put as little 'embroidery' or interpretation on what I pass as possible. I do what my job description requires."

Work Execution.   "If I make the rounds, I take little on-the-spot action. People are free to solve their own problems. They like it that way. I do, too."

Follow-up.   "If he inquires, I talk to my boss who tells me what is to be done next and to find out how he wants it done and who he wants to do it."

With a 1, 1 orientation, a person takes responsibility for filling his position, but only in a superficial way. His imprint is like a shadow on the sand. It passes over the ground, but leaves no permanent mark. Before judging whether such a prospect is unattractive, however, consider first what this can mean. A person may leave no mark in the organization of which he is a member, but neither does the organization leave its mark on him—a mark which, otherwise, could inflict the pain of anxiety and the frustration of failure. . . .[27]

The 5, 5 Managerial Style

The middle of the grid identifies 5, 5. It is where intermediate concern for production, 5, is linked with moderate concern for people. 5, 5 also assumes conflict between organization purpose of production and needs of people.[28] Rather than resolving the issue in the direction of production as in 9, 1, or of people as in 1, 9, or "leaving the field" as in 1, 1, satisfactory or workable solutions are found through equilibrium or compromise processes.[29] Acceptable, even though not sound, production is possible from this approach without unduly disturbing people.[30] The 5, 5 orientation assumes that people are practical, that they realize *some* effort will have to be exerted on the job. Also, by yielding some push for production and considering attitudes and feelings, people accept the situation and are more or less "satisfied."

The 5, 5 approach is based on a persuasive logic. It says; "What person or movement has ever had its exclusive way? Extreme positions are to be avoided. Doesn't experience show, again and again, that steady progress comes from compromise, trading out, and a willingness to yield some advantages in order to gain others? Democracy, as it has come to be interpreted by many today, operates quite well by yielding to the many and mollifying the few." Realistically, then, the guiding assumption of 5, 5 is *not to seek the best position for either production or people* ("that would be too 'ideal'"), but to find the position that is in between both, about half-way.[31]

Management under 5, 5

The key to 5, 5 is found in placing some emphasis on production. Since recognition is given to the fact that, realistically, people cannot be ignored or disregarded, some deliberate consideration is given to the people side. Yet, this is different than 9, 1, as can be seen in the managerial examples that will follow; the 5, 5 approach holds to the responsibility to plan, direct and control, typical of 9, 1.[32] However, just as important, a major part of this responsibility is seen to be coupled with a need to communicate, to get understanding, and to elicit suggestions from subordinates.[33] This aspect is different from 1, 9. In other ways the 5, 5 style is designed to open up the possibility of subordinates' thinking about their job in more than a 1, 9 social manner.[34] The way in which combining and splitting is done in a 5, 5 orientation can be seen in the following descriptions.[35]

Planning.
"I plan work for each subordinate, more in a general way than down to details. After explaining aims and schedules, I make individual assign-

ments. I insure that subordinates are agreeable with what is expected of them and that they feel free to come back if they need help in carrying my assignments out."

Work Execution. "I keep up with each man's job and review his progress with him from time to time or when he asks for it. I give positive suggestions if a subordinate is having difficulty."

Follow-up. "I meet with those involved in the job on a carrot-and-stick approach. I try to get discussion in order to point out good points as well as mistakes and to indicate how people can improve without *telling them*. Each individual gets the opportunity to discuss any reasonable suggestions he might have for improvement before I describe the next assignment."

In other words, there is a mixture, or balance, between taking people into consideration while still emphasizing the relevant aspects of work. In day-by-day activities, if either production or people are suffering, the 5, 5 approach is to fix it by finding a new position that can eliminate the imbalance. The flow of work through people under conditions of 5, 5 is a delicate one. The 5, 5 approach requires constant attention. It demands a delicate "balancing act," combined with the skills of a go-between. . . .

The 9, 9 Managerial Style

In the upper right-hand corner is located 9, 9, where a high concern for production, 9, is coupled with a 9 of high concern for people. Unlike the other basic approaches, it is assumed in the 9, 9 managerial style that there is no necessary and inherent conflict between organization purpose of production requirements and the needs of people. Under 9, 9 effective integration of people with production is possible by involving them and their ideas in determining the conditions and strategies of work.[36,37] Needs of people to think, to apply mental effort in productive work and to establish sound and mature relationships with one another are utilized to accomplish organizational requirements.[38] A basic aim of 9, 9 management, then, is to promote the conditions that integrate creativity, high productivity, and high morale through concerted team action.[39]

The 9, 9 orientation views the integration of people into work from a different perspective than other approaches. In contrast with 9, 1, the solution for a given problem is not necessarily defined by the boss' authority.[40] Unlike 5, 5, the 9, 9 approach is oriented toward discovering the best and most effective solution in a given situation, not the one defined by tradition, etc.[41] By utilizing the mental *and* execution skills of people, this approach aims at the highest attainable level of production. This highest level is only possible through work situations that meet mature needs of people. Sociability for the sake of togetherness, status based on aspects unrelated to work, or power exercised for its own sake, or out of frustration, are not viewed as mature needs. Rather, *accomplishment* and *contribution* are seen as the critical aspect of organization performance and individual motivation. When one is met, the other is gratified automatically.

Management under 9, 9

Mutual understanding and agreement as to what the organizational goals are and of the means by which they are to be attained is at the core of work direction.[42,43] In a real sense people and production *are* interconnected.[44] The manager with a 9, 9 orientation views his responsibility as seeing to it (but not necessarily doing it by himself) that planning, directing and controlling *are* accomplished soundly. Who are best qualified to do it? Those with the most stake in the outcome, regardless of level.

As in the examples following, a boss with a 9, 9 orientation still retains the responsibility for such aspects of work direction as planning. There is no abdication of the 1, 1 variety, nor is there tolerance with "least common denominator" solutions of the kind that crop up under 1, 9, nor of middle-road compromises of divergent interests as in 5, 5. But in the 9, 9 approach others, where indicated, are drawn in on the actual planning of work activities. He might say that, "My job is not necessarily to *make* sound decisions, but it surely is my job to *see* to it that sound decisions are made." The 9, 9 style is seen in the following.[45]

Planning. "I get the people who have relevant facts and/or stakes in the outcome to review the whole picture and to get their reaction and ideas. Then, I, with them, establish goals and flexible schedules as well as procedures and ground rules, and set up individual responsibilities."

Work Execution. "I keep familiar with major points of progress and exert influence on subordinates through identifying problems and revising goals and schedules *with* them as necessary. I lend assistance when needed by helping to remove road blocks."

Follow-up. "I conduct a 'wrap-up' with those responsible. We evaluate how a job went and probe what can be learned from it and how what we learned can be applied in future work. If appropriate, I give recognition on a team basis as well as recognizing outstanding individual contributions."

A general theme in the three excerpts above is that of *creating* conditions of work where people understand the problem, have stakes in the outcome, and where their ideas make a real contribution to the result obtained. This concept of participation is based on the notion that when people can think, when they have influence on outcomes, they *support* rather than comply or resist. Furthermore, with effective leadership, which can arouse *sound* participation, the probability is increased that solutions achieved will be sound and fundamental, not needing constant review and revision. People are able to give the best *of* themselves rather than seeking the best *for* themselves, as is often true when one's contributions are not sought.

Notes

[1] The line of thinking that leads to the generalized version of the Managerial Grid is consistent with work by C. Argyris, *Personality and Organization.* New York: Harper, 1957; K. D. Benne and P. Sheats, Functional Roles of Group Members. *Journal of Social Issues,* 2, 1948, 42–47; E. A. Fleishman, E. F. Harris, & H. E. Burtt, *Leadership and Supervision in Industry.* Columbus, Ohio: Bureau of Educational Research, Ohio State University, 1955; R. Likert, *New Patterns of Management.* New York: McGraw-Hill, 1961; D. McGregor, *The Human Side of Enterprise.* New York: McGraw-Hill, 1960; D. Moment & A. Zaleznik, *Role Development and Interpersonal Competence.* Boston: Harvard University, 1963; and T. Parsons, R. F. Bales & E. A. Shils, *Working Papers in the Theory of Action.* Glencoe, Ill: Free Press, 1953.

[2] Sherif, M. & Sherif, C. *An Outline of Social Psychology.* (Rev.) New York: Harper & Bros., 1956, 143–180.

[3] Simon, H. A. Recent Advances in Organization Theory. *Research Frontiers in Politics and Government,* 1955. Washington, D.C.: Brookings.

[4] Allen, L. A. *Management and Organization.* New York: McGraw, 1958, 58.

[5] Bavelas, A. Communication Patterns in Task-Oriented Groups. *Journal of the Acoustical Society of America,* 22, 1950, 725–730. Also in D. Cartwright & A. Zander, (Eds.), *Group Dynamics: Research and Theory.* Evanston, Ill.: Row, Peterson, 1956, 493–506. Pfeffer, J. M. & Sherwood, F. P. *Administrative Organization.* Englewood Cliffs, N. J.: Prentice-Hall, 1960, 52–73. Kelley, H. H. Communication in Experimentally Created Hierarchies. *Human Relations,* 4, 1951, 39–56.

[6] Appley, L. A. *Management in Action.* New York: American Management Association, 1956, 20–22.

[7] Likert, R. A Motivational Approach to a Modified Theory of Organization and Management. In M. Haire (Ed.), *Modern Organization Theory.* New York: Wiley, 1959, 184–217. Stanton, E. S. Company Policies and Supervisors' Attitudes toward Supervision. *Journal of Applied Psychology,* 44, 1960, 22–26.

[8] In this book, attention is not focused on organization and managerial principles and functions *per se;* such as unity of direction, span of control, delegation of authority, etc. Rather, consideration is limited to the assumptions a manager operates under when, for example, he delegates authority, or plans a given work activity. Organization principles and management functions are treated as neutral or as givens, whereas the *ways* in which they are applied under different managerial styles *are* subject to examination.

[9] Blake, R. R., Mouton, J. S. & Bidwell, A. C. "The Managerial Grid," *Advanced Management-Office Executive,* 1, 1962, 12–15, 36. Blake, R. R., and Mouton, J. S. The Developing Revolution in Management Practices. *ASTD Journal,* 16, 1962, 29–50.

[10] In their early work with small groups, Bales and others identified two distinct roles assumed by various members in problem-solving groups—"task" role and "social" role. Both sets of role behavior are rarely observed in the actions of any one individual, i.e., a person is either concerned for the task (production) or his concern is for the social (people) aspects of a group's activities— seldom both *at the same time.* Representative experimental work and discussion of theory is contained in R. F. Bales, The Equilibrium Problem in Small Groups. In T. Parsons, R. F. Bales & E. A. Shils, *Working Papers in the Theory of Action.* Glencoe, Ill.: Free Press, 1953, 111–161. (Also abridged in A. P. Hare, E. F. Borgatta & R. F. Bales (Eds.), *Small Groups.* New York: Knopf, 1955, 424–456.) Also, see Slater, P. E. Role Differentiations in Small Groups. *American Sociological Review,* 20, 1955, 300–310; Bales, R. F. & Slater, P. Role Differentiation. In T. Parsons, R. F. Bales, et al. *Family, Socialization, and Interaction Process.* Glencoe, Ill.: Free Press, 1955; Slater, P. E. Role Differentiations in Small Groups. *American Sociological Review,* 20, 1955, 300–310.

[11] A recent study by Moment and Zaleznik is in line with the early work of Bales, *et al.* In addition to Task (Technical) and Social roles, Moment and Zaleznik identify a detached, sometimes passive, sometimes hostile and competitive role (Underchosen) and a Fusion role (Star), the latter being high on both task and "congeniality." *Stars* demonstrated a higher combination of task *and* socially relevant behavior. However, a partial dichotomy rather than integration (Fusion) in the two concerns is suggested in some aspects for the roles of the Stars: "Satisfaction comes from engagement in the social-technical process in a way that *balances* progress toward improvement with the dis-

ruptions of change." p. 121. Moment, D. & Zaleznik, A. *Role Development and Interpersonal Competence.* Boston: Harvard University, 1963. (Italics, i.e., *balances,* ours). A split between production and people concerns is still assumed under 5, 5 and is contrasted with an *integration* of these two concerns under 9, 9. Since 5, 5 (balancing), *per se,* is not treated by Moment and Zaleznik, it appears that both 5, 5 and 9, 9 (integration) fall into the category of "Stars."

[12] Maier, N. R. F. *Psychology in Industry.* (2nd Ed.). Boston: Houghton, 1955, 139–140.

[13] Marrow, A. J. *Making Management Human.* New York: McGraw-Hill, 1957, 73.

[14] Barnard, C. I. *The Functions of the Executive.* Cambridge: Harvard University, 1938, 67; Urwick, L. *The Elements of Administration.* New York: Harper, 1953, 36–39.

[15] Davis, R. C. *The Fundamentals of Top Management.* New York: Harper and Brothers, 1951. *Working Papers in the Theory of Action.* Glencoe, Ill.: Free Press, 1953, 111–161. Some Philosophies of Management. *Advanced Management,* 24, (7), 1959, 6–8.

[16] McNair, M. P. Thinking Ahead: What Price Human Relations? *Harvard Business Review,* 35, March-April, 1957, 15–39.

[17] Walker, C. R. & Guest, R. H. *The Man on the Assembly Line.* Cambridge: Harvard University Press, 1952, 141–163.

[18] Mayfield, H. The Counseling Function in Management. *The Personnel Administrator,* 3, (1), 1958, 23–24. Also in I. L. Heckmann, Jr., & S. G. Huneryager (Eds.), *Human Relations in Management.* Cincinnati: South-Western, 1960, 513–519.

[19] *The Managerial Grid: A Self-Examination of Managerial Styles.* Austin, Tex.: Scientific Methods, Inc., 1962.

[20] Gellerman, S. W. *People, Problems and Profits.* New York: McGraw-Hill, 1960, 165; Cleeton, G. U. The Human Factor in Industry. *The Annals of the American Academy of Political and Social Sciences,* 274, March, 1951, 17–24. Also in I. L. Heckmann, Jr., & S. G. Huneryager (Eds.), *op. cit.,* 17–26.

[21] Stagner, R. *Psychology of Industrial Conflict.* New York: Wiley, 1956, 327–329.

[22] Shaw, D. M. Size and Share in Task and Motivation in Work Groups. *Sociometry,* 23, 1960, 203–208.

[23] Blau, P. M. *The Dynamics of Bureaucracy.* Chicago: University of Chicago, 1955, 172–179, 184–88; Collins, O., Dalton, M. & Roy, D. Restriction of Output and Social Cleavage in Industry. *Applied Anthropology,* 5, (8), 1946, 1–14; Whyte, W. F. *Money and Motivation.* New York: Harper, 1955; Argyris, C. *Personality and Organization.* New York: Harper, 1957.

[24] McGee, R. *Social Disorganization in America.* San Francisco: Chandler, 1962, 66–78.

[25] Experimental studies and observations of children and adults have demonstrated the reactive and accommodative behavior of individuals to situations of prolonged frustration. The adaptive behavior described in these studies is most like the 1, 1 orientation. Representative studies include: Eisenberg, P. & Lazarsfeld, P. F. The Psychological Effects of Unemployment. *Psychological Bulletin,* 35, 1938, 358–390; Lewin, K., Lippitt, R., & White, R. K. Patterns of Aggressive Behavior in Experimentally Created "Social Climates." *Journal of Social Psychology,* 10, 1939, 271–299; Dollard, J., Doob, L. W., Miller, N. E., Mowrer, O. H., & Sears, R. R. *Frustration and Aggression.* New Haven: Yale University, 1939; Barker, R. G., Dembo, T., & Lewin, K. Frustration and Regression: An Experiment with Young Children. *University of Iowa Studies in Child Welfare,* 18, I, 1941; Merrill, M. A. *Problems of Child Delinquency.* Boston: Houghton, 1947; Marquart, D. I. The Pattern of Punishment and Its Relation to Abnormal Fixation in Adult Human Subjects. *Journal of Genetic Psychology,* 39, 1948, 107–144; Wright, M. E. The Influence of Frustration Upon the Social Relations of Young Children. *Character & Personality,* 12, 1943, 111–112; Maier, N. R. F. *Pruetration: The Study of Behavior Without a Goal.* Ann Arbor: University of Michigan, 1949; Heber, R. F. & Heber, M. E. The Effect of Group Failure and Success on Social Status. *Journal of Educational Psychology,* 48, 1957, 129–134; Pepitone, A. & Kleiner, R. The Effects of Threat and Frustration on Group Cohesiveness. *Journal of Abnormal & Social Psychology,* 54, 1957, 192–199; Moment, D. & Zaleznik, A. *Role Development and Interpersonal Competence.* Boston: Harvard University, 1963, 124–125. (Lewin, et al., speak of "laissez faire" leadership and Moment and Zaleznik speak of an "Underchosen" role.)

[26] Drucker, P. F. *The New Society.* New York: Harper, 1950, 83; Vitalis, M. *Motivation and Morale in Industry.* New York: Norton, 1953, 51; Argyris, C., *op. cit.,* 89–95; Schutz, W. C. The Interpersonal Underworld. *Harvard Business Review,* 36, (4), 1958, 123–135.

[27] *The Managerial Grid: A Self-Examination of Managerial Styles.* Austin, Tex.: Scientific Methods, Inc., 1962.

[28] Shull, F. A. Administrative Perspectives of Human Relations. *Advanced Management,* March, 1960, 18–22; Roethlisberger, F. J. The Foreman: Master and Victim of Double Talk. *Harvard Business Review,* 23, 1945, 283–298.

[29] Shull, F. A., *op. cit.*

[30] Pfeffer, J. M. & Presthus, R. V. The Role of Human Relations. In K. Davis & W. Scott (Eds.), *Readings in Human Relations.* New York: McGraw-Hill, 1959, 253; Davis, R. C., *op. cit.*

[31] Drucker, P. F. Integration of People and Planning. *Harvard Business Review,* 33, 1955, 35–40; Urwick, L. F. The Purpose of a Business. In K. Davis & W. Scott (Eds.), *op. cit.,* 85–91.

[32] Katz, R. L. Skills of an Effective Administrator. *Harvard Business Review,* 31, 1955, 33–42; Allen, L. A. *Management and Organization.* New York: McGraw-Hill, 1958, 43–44; Tannenbaum, R. & Schmidt, W. H. How to Choose a Leadership Pattern. *Harvard Business Review,* 36, 1958, 95–101.

[33] McCauley, B. G. Accent the Man in Management. *Advanced Management,* August, 1960, 24–27.

[34] *The Managerial Grid: A Self-Examination of Managerial Styles.* Austin, Tex.: Scientific Methods, Inc., 1962.

[35] Allen, L. A., *op. cit.*

[36] Lawrence, P. R., Bailey, J. C., Katz, R. L., Seiler, J. A., Orth, C. D., Clark, J. V., Barnes, L. B. & Turner, A. N. *Organizational Behavior and Administration: Cases, Concepts, and Research Findings.* Homewood, Ill.: Dorsey, 1961, 185; Strauss, G. & Sayles, L. R. *Personnel: The Human Problems of Management.* Englewood Cliffs, N. J.: Prentice-Hall, 1960, 36–41.

[37] The theory and concepts of 9, 9 management find life in the pioneering work of Kurt Lewin and his associates, particularly the concepts of *participation, goal-setting, involvement and commitment, interpersonal relations,* and *strategies for individual and organizational change.* See especially, Lewin, K. *Field Theory in Social Science.* New York: Harper, 1951. Also see Lewin, K. Forces Behind Food Habits and Methods of Change. *Bulletin of National Research Council,* 108, 1943, 35–65; Lewin, K. Frontiers in Group Dynamics: Concept, Method and Reality in Social Science: Social Equilibrium and Social Change. *Human Relations,* 1, 1947, 5–41; Lewin, K. Group Decision and Social Change. In T. M. Newcomb & E. L. Hartley (Eds.), *Readings in Social Psychology.* New York: Holt, 1947, 330–344; Lewin, K. Frontiers in Group Dynamics: II. Channels of Group Life: Social Planning and Action Research. *Human Relations,* 1, 1947, 143–153; Lewin, K. *Resolving Social Conflicts: Selected Papers on Group Dynamics.* New York: Harper, 1948; Lewin, K. Behavior and Development as a Function of the Total Situation. In L. Carmichael (Ed.), *Manual of Child Psychology.* New York: Wiley, 1946, 791–844. (Also see references in Ch. 3.) For a discussion of and additional relevant references to Lewin's work, see Deutsch, M. Field Theory in Social Psychology. In G. Lindsey (Ed.), *Handbook of Social Psychology. Vol. I.* Reading, Mass.: Addison-Wesley, 1954, 181–222.

[38] Wolfe, D. M. Power and Authority in the Family. In D. Cartwright (Ed.), *Studies in Social Power.* Ann Arbor: Institute for Social Research, 1959, 100–101; Vroom, V. H. *Some Personality Determinants of the Effects of Participation.* Englewood Cliffs, NJ: Prentice-Hall, 1960, 1–18.

[39] Guest, R. H. *Organizational Change: The Effect of Successful Leadership.* Homewood, Ill.: Dorsey, 1962, 40–81. (This work of Guest is one of the best descriptions in the literature of the managerial actions of a 9, 9 manager. See esp. "Plant Y," post-1953.)

[40] See Ch. 3 of *The Managerial Grid* by Blake and Mouton. Also see Ch. 1 and 36–38 of Strauss, G. & Sayles, L. R., *op. cit.*

[41] See Ch. 6 of *The Managerial Grid* by Blake and Mouton.

[42] The work of Argyris and McGregor has crystallized and put into perspective the more mature needs of individuals in the work situation. See Argyris, C., *Personality and Organization,* Harper & Bros., New York, 1957, esp. pp. 20–53. McGregor, D. *The Human Side of Enterprise.* McGraw-Hill, New York, 1960, esp. pp. 45–58.

[43] The work of Herzberg, *et al.,* demonstrates that motivation of a more fundamental and long-lasting character is embedded in the work itself *i.e.,* responsibility, achievement, advancement, and other factors that create a sense of significant accomplishment. Factors not directly related to work, *i.e. hygienic,* take on more importance as work becomes less challenging and meaningful. See Herzberg, F., Mausner, B., & Snyderman, B. B., *The Motivation to Work.* New York: Wiley, 1959, pp. 64, 70, 132, 144. Also see White, R. W., Motivation Reconsidered: The Concept of Competence. *Psychological Review,* 66, 1959, 297–334.

[44] Hare, A. P. Small Group Discussions with Participatory and Supervisory Leadership. *Journal of Abnormal & Social Psychology, 48,* 1953, 273–275.

[45] Marrow, A. J. *Making Management Human.* New York: McGraw-Hill, 1957, 29. (The work of Marrow, Bavelas and others at Harwood represents the successful attempt of one management group to apply 9, 9 concepts in its organization improvement efforts.)

2

How to Choose a Leadership Pattern

Robert Tannenbaum and Warren H. Schmidt

- I put most problems into my group's hands and leave it to them to carry the ball from there. I serve merely as a catalyst, mirroring back the people's thoughts and feelings so that they can better understand them.

- It's foolish to make decisions oneself on matters that affect people. I always talk things over with my subordinates, but I make it clear to them that I'm the one who has to have the final say.

- Once I have decided on a course of action, I do my best to sell my ideas to my employees.

- I'm being paid to lead. If I let a lot of other people make the decisions I should be making, then I'm not worth my salt.

- I believe in getting things done. I can't waste time calling meetings. Someone has to call the shots around here, and I think it should be me.

Each of these statements represents a point of view about "good leadership." Considerable experience, factual data, and theoretical principles could be cited to support each statement, even though they seem to be inconsistent when placed together. Such contradictions point up the dilemma in which the modern manager frequently finds himself.

New Problem

The problem of how the modern manager can be "democratic" in his relations with subordinates and at the same time maintain the necessary authority and control in the organization for which he is responsible has come into focus increasingly in recent years.

Earlier in the century this problem was not so acutely felt. The successful executive was generally pictured as possessing intelligence, imagination, initiative, the capacity to make rapid (and generally wise) decisions, and the ability to inspire subordinates. People tended to think of the world as being divided into "leaders" and "followers."

New Focus

Gradually, however, from the social sciences emerged the concept of "group dynamics" with its focus on *members* of the group rather than solely on the leader. Research efforts of social scientists underscored the importance of employee involvement and participation in decision making. Evidence began to challenge the efficiency of highly directive leadership, and increasing attention was paid to problems of motivation and human relations.

Through training laboratories in group development that sprang up across the country, many of the newer notions of leadership began to exert an impact. These training laboratories were carefully designed to give people a firsthand experience in full participation and decision making. The designated "leaders" deliberately attempted to reduce their own power and to make group members as responsible as possible for setting their own goals and methods within the laboratory experience.

It was perhaps inevitable that some of the people who attended the training laboratories regarded this kind of leadership as being truly "democratic" and went home with the determination to build fully participative decision making into their own organizations. Whenever their bosses made a decision without convening a staff meeting, they tended to perceive this as authoritarian behavior. The true symbol of democratic leadership to some was the meeting—and the less directed from the top, the more democratic it was.

Some of the more enthusiastic alumni of these training laboratories began to get the habit of categorizing leader behavior as "democratic" *or* "authoritarian." The boss who made too many decisions himself was thought of as an authoritarian, and his directive behavior was often attributed solely to his personality.

New Need

The net result of the research findings and of the human relations training based upon them has been to call into question the stereotype of an effective leader. Consequently, the modern manager often finds himself in an uncomfortable state of mind.

Often he is not quite sure how to behave; there are times when he is torn between exerting "strong" leadership and "permissive" leadership. Sometimes new knowledge pushes him in one direction ("I should really get the group to help make this decision"), but at the same time his experience pushes him in another direction ("I really understand the problem better than the group and therefore I should make the decision"). He is not sure when a group decision is really appropriate or when holding a staff meeting serves merely as a device for avoiding his own decision-making responsibility.

The purpose of our article is to suggest a framework which managers may find useful in grappling with this dilemma. First, we shall look at the different patterns of leadership behavior that the manager can choose from in relating himself to his subordinates. Then, we shall turn to some of the questions suggested by this range of patterns. For instance, how important is it for a manager's subordinates to know what type of leadership he is using in a situation? What factors should he consider in deciding on a leadership pattern? What difference do his long-run objectives make as compared to his immediate objectives?

Range of Behavior

Figure 1 presents the continuum or range of possible leadership behavior available to a manager. Each type of action is related to the degree of authority used by the boss and to the amount of freedom available to his subordinates in reaching decisions. The actions seen on the extreme left characterize the manager who maintains a high degree of control while those seen on the extreme right characterize the manager who releases a high degree of control. Neither extreme is absolute; authority and freedom are never without their limitations.

Now let us look more closely at each of the behavior points occurring along this continuum.

The Manager Makes the Decision and Announces It

In this case the boss identifies a problem, considers alternative solutions, chooses one of them, and then reports this decision to his subordinates for implementation. He may or may not give consideration to what he believes his subordinates will think or feel about his decision; in any case, he provides no opportunity for them to participate directly in the decision-making process. Coercion may or may not be used or implied.

Figure 1
Continuum of Leadership Behavior

The Manager "Sells" His Decision

Here the manager, as before, takes responsibility for identifying the problem and arriving at a decision. However, rather than simply announcing it, he takes the additional step of persuading his subordinates to accept it. In doing so, he recognizes the possibility of some resistance among those who will be faced with the decision and seeks to reduce this resistance by indicating, for example, what the employees have to gain from his decision.

The Manager Presents His Ideas, Invites Questions

Here the boss who has arrived at a decision and who seeks acceptance of his ideas provides an opportunity for his subordinates to get a fuller explanation of his thinking and his intentions. After presenting the ideas, he invites questions so that his associates can better understand what he is trying to accomplish. This "give and take" also enables the manager and the subordinates to explore more fully the implications of the decision.

The Manager Presents a Tentative Decision Subject to Change

This kind of behavior permits the subordinates to exert some influence on the decision. The initiative for identifying and diagnosing the problem remains with the boss. Before meeting with his staff, he has thought the problem through and arrived at a decision—but only a tentative one. Before finalizing it, he presents his proposed solution for the reaction of those who will be affected by it. He says in effect, "I'd like to hear what you have to say about this plan that I have developed. I'll appreciate your frank reactions, but will reserve for myself the final decision."

The Manager Presents the Problem, Gets Suggestions, and Then Makes His Decision

Up to this point the boss has come before the group with a solution of his own. Not so in this case. The subordinates now get the first chance to suggest solutions. The manager's initial role involves identifying the problem. He might, for example, say something of this sort: "We are faced with a number of complaints from newspapers and the general public on our service policy. What is wrong here? What ideas do you have for coming to grips with this problem?"

The function of the group becomes one of increasing the manager's repertory of possible solutions to the problem. The purpose is to capitalize on the knowledge and experience of those who are on the "firing line." From the expanded list of alternatives developed by the manager and his subordinates, the manager then selects the solution that he regards as most promising.[1]

The Manager Defines the Limits and Requests the Group to Make a Decision

At this point the manager passes to the group (possibly including himself as a member) the right to make decisions. Before doing so, however, he defines the problem to be solved and the boundaries within which the decision must be made.

An example might be the handling of a parking problem at a plant. The boss decides that this is something that should be worked on by the people involved, so he calls them together and points up the existence of the problem. Then he tells them:

> There is the open field just north of the main plant which has been designated for additional employee parking. We can build underground or surface multi-level facilities as long as the cost does not exceed $100,000. Within these limits we are free to work out whatever solution makes sense to us. After we decide on a specific plan, the company will spend the available money in whatever way we indicate.

The Manager Permits the Group to Make Decisions within Prescribed Limits

This represents an extreme degree of group freedom only occasionally encountered in formal organizations, as, for instance, in many research groups. Here the team of managers or engineers undertakes the identification and diagnosis of the problem, develops alternative procedures for solving it, and decides on one or more of these alternative solutions. The only limits directly imposed on the group by the organization are those specified by the superior of the team's boss. If the boss participates in the decision-making process, he attempts to do so with no more authority than any other member of the group. He commits himself in advance to assist in implementing whatever decision the group makes.

Key Questions

As the continuum in figure 1 demonstrates, there are a number of alternative ways in which a manager can relate himself to the group or individuals he is supervising. At the extreme left of the range, the emphasis is on the manager—on what *he* is interested in, how *he* sees things, how *he* feels about them. As we move toward the subordinate-centered end of the continuum, however, the focus is increasingly on the subordinates—on what *they* are interested in, how *they* look at things, how *they* feel about them.

When business leadership is regarded in this way, a number of questions arise. Let us take four of especial importance:

Can a boss ever relinquish his responsibility by delegating it to someone else?   Our view is that the manager must expect to be held responsible by his superior for the quality of the decisions made, even though operationally these decisions may have been made on a group basis. He should, therefore, be ready to accept whatever risk is involved whenever he delegates decision-making power to his subordinates. Delegation is not a way of "passing the buck." Also, it should be emphasized that the amount of freedom the boss gives to his subordinates cannot be greater than the freedom which he himself has been given by his own superior.

Should the manager participate with his subordinates once he has delegated responsibility to them?   The manager should carefully think over this question and decide on his role prior to involving the subordinate group. He should ask if his presence will inhibit or facilitate the problem-solving process. There may

Figure 2
Continuum of Manager-Nonmanager Behavior

Manager power and influence

Nonmanager power and influence

Area of freedom for manager

Area of freedom for nonmanagers

| Manager able to make decision which nonmanagers accept. | Manager must "sell" his decision before gaining acceptance. | Manager presents decision but must respond to questions from nonmanagers. | Manager presents tentative decision subject to change after nonmanager inputs. | Manager presents problem, gets inputs from nonmanagers, then decides. | Manager defines limits within which nonmanagers make decision. | Manager and nonmanagers jointly make decision within limits defined by organizational constraints. |

Resultant manager and nonmanager behavior

The Organizational Environment

be some instances when he should leave the group to let it solve the problem for itself. Typically, however, the boss has useful ideas to contribute, and should function as an additional member of the group. In the latter instance, it is important that he indicate clearly to the group that he sees himself in a member role rather than in an authority role.

How important is it for the group to recognize what kind of leadership behavior the boss is using? It makes a great deal of difference. Many relationship problems between boss and subordinate occur because the boss fails to make clear how he plans to use his authority. If, for example, he actually intends to make a certain decision himself, but the subordinate group gets the impression that he has delegated this authority, considerable confusion and resentment are likely to follow. Problems may also occur when the boss uses a "democratic" facade to conceal the fact that he has already made a decision which he hopes the group will accept as its own. The attempt to "make them think it was their idea in the first place" is a risky one. We believe that it is highly important for the manager to be honest and clear in describing what authority he is keeping and what role he is asking his subordinates to assume in solving a particular problem.

Can you tell how "democratic" a manager is by the number of decisions his subordinates make? The sheer number of decisions is not an accurate index of the amount of freedom that subordinate group enjoys. More important is the *significance* of the decisions which the boss entrusts to his subordinates. Obviously a decision on how to arrange desks is of an entirely different order from a decision involving the introduction of new electronic data-processing equipment. Even though the widest possible limits are given in dealing with the first issue, the group will sense no particular degree of responsibility. For a boss to permit the group to decide equipment policy, even within rather narrow limits, would reflect a greater degree of confidence in them on his part.

Deciding How to Lead

Now let us turn from the types of leadership which are possible in a company situation to the question of what types are *practical* and *desirable*. What factors or forces should a manager consider in deciding how to manage? Three are of particular importance: forces in the manager, forces in the subordinates, and forces in the situation.

We should like briefly to describe these elements and indicate how they might influence a manager's action in a decision-making situation.[2] The strength of each of them will, of course, vary from instance to instance, but the manager who is sensitive to them can better assess the problems which face him and determine which mode of leadership behavior is most appropriate for him.

Forces in the manager. The manager's behavior in any given instance will be influenced greatly by the many forces operating within his own personality. He will, of course, perceive his leadership problems in a unique way on the basis of his background knowledge, and experience. Among the important internal forces affecting him will be the following:

1. *His value system.* How strongly does he feel that individuals should have a share in making the decisions which affect them? Or how convinced is he that the official who is paid to assume responsibility should personally carry the burden of decision making? The strength of his convictions on questions like these will tend to move the manager to one end or the other of the continuum shown in figure 1. His behavior will also be influenced by the relative importance that he attaches to organizational efficiency, personal growth of subordinates, and company profits.[3]

2. *His confidence in his subordinates.* Managers differ greatly in the amount of trust they have in other people generally, and this carries over to the particular employees they supervise at a given time. In viewing his particular group of subordinates, the manager is likely to consider their knowledge and competence with respect to the problem. A central question he might ask himself is: "Who is best qualified to deal with this problem?" Often he may, justifiably or not, have more confidence in his own capabilities than in those of his subordinates.

3. *His own leadership inclinations.* There are some managers who seem to function more comfortably and naturally as highly directive leaders. Resolving problems and issuing orders come easily to them. Other

managers seem to operate more comfortably in a team role, where they are continually sharing many of their functions with their subordinates.

4. *His feelings of security in an uncertain situation.* The manager who releases control over the decision-making process thereby reduces the predictability of the outcome. Some managers have a greater need than others for predictability and stability in their environment. This "tolerance for ambiguity" is being viewed increasingly by psychologists as a key variable in a person's manner of dealing with problems.

The manager brings these and other highly personal variables to each situation he faces. If he can see them as forces which, consciously or unconsciously, influence his behavior, he can better understand what makes him prefer to act in a given way. And understanding this, he can often make himself more effective.

Forces in the subordinate.   Before deciding how to lead a certain group, the manager will also want to consider a number of forces affecting his subordinates' behavior. He will want to remember that each employee, like himself, is influenced by many personality variables. In addition, each subordinate has a set of expectations about how the boss should act in relation to him (the phrase "expected behavior" is one we hear more and more often these days at discussions of leadership and teaching). The better the manager understands these factors, the more accurately he can determine what kind of behavior on his part will enable his subordinates to act most effectively.

Generally speaking, the manager can permit his subordinates greater freedom if the following essential conditions exist:

- If the subordinates have relatively high needs for independence. (As we all know, people differ greatly in the amount of direction that they desire.)
- If the subordinates have a readiness to assume responsibility for decision making. (Some see additional responsibility as a tribute to their ability; others see it as "passing the buck.")
- If they have a relatively high tolerance for ambiguity. (Some employees prefer to have clear-cut directives given to them; others prefer a wider area of freedom.)
- If they are interested in the problem and feel that it is important.
- If they understand and identify with the goals of the organization.
- If they have the necessary knowledge and experience to deal with the problem.
- If they have learned to expect to share in decision making. (Persons who have come to expect strong leadership and are then suddenly confronted with the request to share more fully in decision making are often upset by this new experience. On the other hand, persons who have enjoyed a considerable amount of freedom resent the boss who begins to make all the decisions himself.)

The manager will probably tend to make fuller use of his own authority if the above conditions do *not* exist; at times there may be no realistic alternative to running a "one-man show."

The restrictive effect of many of the forces will, of course, be greatly modified by the general feeling of confidence which subordinates have in the boss. Where they have learned to respect and trust him, he is free to vary his behavior. He will feel certain that he will not be perceived as an authoritarian boss on those occasions when he makes decisions by himself. Similarly, he will not be seen as using staff meetings to avoid his decision-making responsibility. In a climate of mutual confidence and respect, people tend to feel less threatened by deviations from normal practice, which in turn makes possible a higher degree of flexibility in the whole relationship.

Forces in the situation.   In addition to the forces which exist in the manager himself and in his subordinates, certain characteristics of the general situation will also affect the manager's behavior. Among the more critical environmental pressures that surround him are those which stem from the organization, the work group, the nature of the problem, and the pressures of time. Let us look briefly at each of these:

1. *Type of organization.* Like individuals, organizations have values and traditions which inevitably influence the behavior of the people who work in them. The manager who is a newcomer to a company quickly discovers that certain kinds of behavior are approved while others are not. He also discovers that to deviate radically from what is generally accepted is likely to create problems for him.

   These values and traditions are communicated in numerous ways— through job descriptions, policy pronouncements, and public statements by top executives. Some organizations, for example, hold to the notion that the desirable executive is one who is dynamic, imaginative, decisive, and persuasive. Other organizations put more emphasis upon the importance of the executive's ability to work effectively with people— his human relations skills. The fact that his superiors have a defined concept of what the good executive should be will very likely push the manager toward one end or the other of the behavioral range.

   In addition to the above, the amount of employee participation is influenced by such variables as the size of the working units, their geographical distribution, and the degree of inter- and intraorganizational security required to attain company goals. For example, the wide geographical dispersion of an organization may preclude a practical system of participative decision making, even though this would otherwise be desirable. Similarly, the size of the working units or the need for keeping plans confidential may make it necessary for the boss to exercise more control than would otherwise be the case. Factors like these may limit considerably the manager's ability to function flexibly on the continuum.

2. *Group effectiveness.* Before turning decision-making responsibility over to a subordinate group, the boss should consider how effectively its members work together as a unit.

One of the relevant factors here is the experience the group has had in working together. It can generally be expected that a group which has functioned for some time will have developed habits of cooperation and thus be able to tackle a problem more effectively than a new group. It can also be expected that a group of people with similar backgrounds and interests will work more quickly and easily than people with dissimilar backgrounds, because the communication problems are likely to be less complex.

The degree of confidence that the members have in their ability to solve problems as a group is also a key consideration. Finally, such group variables as cohesiveness, permissiveness, mutual acceptance, and commonality of purpose will exert subtle but powerful influence on the group's functioning.

3. *The problem itself.* The nature of the problem may determine what degree of authority should be delegated by the manager to his subordinates. Obviously he will ask himself whether they have the kind of knowledge which is needed. It is possible to do them a real disservice by assigning a problem that their experience does not equip them to handle.

Since the problems faced in large or growing industries increasingly require knowledge of specialists from many different fields, it might be inferred that the more complex a problem, the more anxious a manager will be to get some assistance in solving it. However, this is not always the case. There will be times when the very complexity of the problem calls for one person to work it out. For example, if the manager has most of the background and factual data relevant to a given issue, it may be easier for him to think it through himself than to take the time to fill in his staff on all the pertinent background information.

The key question to ask, of course, is: "Have I heard the ideas of everyone who has the necessary knowledge to make a significant contribution to the solution of this problem?"

4. *The pressure of time.* This is perhaps the most clearly felt pressure on the manager (in spite of the fact that it may sometimes be imagined). The more that he feels the need for an immediate decision, the more difficult it is to involve other people. In organizations which are in a constant state of "crisis" and "crash programming" one is likely to find managers personally using a high degree of authority with relatively little delegation to subordinates. When the time pressure is less intense, however, it becomes much more possible to bring subordinates in on the decision-making process.

These, then, are the principal forces that impinge on the manager in any given instance and that tend to determine his tactical behavior in relation to his subordinates. In each case his behavior ideally will be that which makes possible the most effective attainment of his immediate goal within the limits facing him.

Long-Run Strategy

As the manager works with his organization on the problems that come up day by day, his choice of a leadership pattern is usually limited. He must take account of the forces just described and, within the restrictions they impose on him, do the best that he can. But as he looks ahead months or even years, he can shift his thinking from tactic to large-scale strategy. No longer need he be fettered by all of the forces mentioned, for he can view many of them as variables over which he has some control. He can, for example, gain new insights or skills for himself, supply training for individual subordinates, and provide participative experiences for his employee group.

In trying to bring about a change in these variables, however, he is faced with a challenging question: At which point along the continuum should he act? The answer depends largely on what he wants to accomplish. Let us suppose that he is interested in the same objectives that most modern managers seek to attain when they can shift their attention from the pressure of immediate assignments:

1. To raise the level of employee motivation.
2. To increase the readiness of subordinates to accept change.
3. To improve the quality of all managerial decisions.
4. To develop teamwork and morale.
5. To further the individual development of employees.

In recent years the manager has been deluged with a flow of advice on how best to achieve these longer-run objectives. It is little wonder that he is often both bewildered and annoyed. However, there are some guidelines which he can usefully follow in making a decision.

Most research and much of the experience of recent years give a strong factual basis to the theory that a fairly high degree of subordinate-centered behavior is associated with the accomplishment of the five purposes mentioned.[4] This does not mean that a manager should always leave all decisions to his assistants. To provide the individual or the group with greater freedom than they are ready for at any given time may very well tend to generate anxieties and therefore inhibit rather than facilitate the attainment of desired objectives. But this should not keep the manager from making a continuing effort to confront his subordinates with the challenge of freedom.

Conclusion

In summary, there are two implications in the basic thesis that we have been developing. The first is that the successful leader is one who is keenly aware of those forces which are most relevant to his behavior at any given time. He accurately understands himself, the individuals and group he is dealing with, and the company and broader social environment in which he operates. And certainly he is able to assess the present readiness for growth of his subordinates.

But this sensitivity or understanding is not enough, which brings us to the second implication. The successful leader is one who is able to behave appropriately in the light of these perceptions. If direction is in order, he is able to direct; if considerable participative freedom is called for, he is able to provide such freedom.

Thus, the successful manager of men can be primarily characterized neither as a strong leader nor as a permissive one. Rather, he is one who maintains a high batting average in accurately assessing the forces that determine what his most appropriate behavior at any given time should be and in actually being able to behave accordingly. Being both insightful and flexible, he is less likely to see the problems of leadership as a dilemma.

Notes

[1] For a fuller explanation of this approach, see Leo Moore, "Too Much Management, Too Little Change," *Harvard Business Review* (January–February 1956), p. 41.

[2] "See also Robert Tannenbaum and Fred Massarik, "Participation by Subordinates in the Managerial Decision-Making Process," *Canadian Journal of Economics and Political Science* (August 1950), p. 413.

[3] See Chris Argyris, "Top Management Dilemma: Company Needs vs. Individual Development," *Personnel* (September 1955), pp. 123–134.

[4] For example, see Warren H. Schmidt and Paul C. Buchanan, *Techniques That Produce Teamwork* (New London: Arthur C. Croft Publications, 1954) and Morris S. Viteles, *Motivation and Morale in Industry* (New York: W. W. Norton & Company, Inc., 1953).

3

Leadership Decision Making

Victor H. Vroom and Arthur G. Jago

Introduction

Several scholarly disciplines share an interest in the decision-making process. On one hand, there are related fields of operations research and management science, both concerned with how to improve the decisions which are made. Their models of decision making, aimed at providing a rational basis for selecting among alternative courses of action, are termed *normative* or *prescriptive* models. On the other hand, there have been attempts by psychologists, sociologists, and political scientists to understand the decisions and choices that people do make. March and Simon (1958) were among the first to suggest that an understanding of the decision-making process could be central to an understanding of the behavior of organizations—a point of view that was later amplified by Cyert and March (1963) in their behavioral theory of the firm. In this tradition, the goal is understanding rather than improvement, and the models are descriptive rather than normative.

Whether the models are normative or descriptive, the common ingredient is a conception of decision making as an information-processing activity, frequently one which takes place within a single manager. Both sets of models focus on the set of alternative decisions or problem solutions from which the choice is, or should be, made. The normative models are based on the consequences of choices among these alternatives, the descriptive models on the determinants of these choices.

In this article, the authors take a somewhat different, although complementary, view of managerial decision making. They view decision making as a social process, with the elements of the process presented in terms of events between people, rather than events that occur within a person. When a problem or occasion for decision making occurs within an organization, there are typically several alternative social mechanisms available for determining what solution is chosen or deci-

Originally titled "Decision Making as a Social Process: Normative and Descriptive Models of Leader Behavior." Reprinted with permission from *Decision Sciences,* Vol. 5, 1974, pp. 743–755. *Decision Sciences Journal* is a publication of the Decision Sciences Institute located at Georgia State University, Atlanta, GA, USA.

sion reached. These alternatives vary in the person or persons participating in the problem-solving and decision-making process, and in the relative amounts of influence that each has on the final solution or decision reached.

There are both descriptive and normative questions to be answered about the social processes used for decision making in organizations. The normative questions hinge on knowledge concerning the consequences of alternatives for the effective performance of the system. The dimensions on which social processes can vary constitute the independent variables, and criteria of the effectiveness of the decisions constitute dependent variables. Ultimately, such knowledge could provide the foundation for a specification of the social and interpersonal aspects of how decisions *should be* made within organizations.

Similarly, the descriptive questions concern the circumstances under which alternative social processes for decision making *are* used in organizations. The dimensions on which social processes vary become the dependent variables, and characteristics of the manager who controls the process and the nature of the decision itself provide the basis for the specification of independent variables.

Vroom and Yetton (1973) provided a start to an examination of both normative and descriptive questions through an examination of one dimension of decision making—the extent to which a leader encourages the participation of his subordinates in decision making. Participation in decision making was a logical place to start since there is substantial evidence of its importance and of the circumstances surrounding different consequences of it (Lowin, 1968; Vroom, 1970; Wood, 1973).

The purpose of this article is twofold: (1) to provide a brief summary of the objectives, methods, and results of the research pertaining to both normative and descriptive models of decision processes used in organizations (described in detail in Vroom and Yetton, 1973); (2) to describe some recent extensions of the previous work, including an empirical investigation designed to explore facets of decision making not previously studied.

Vroom and Yetton concern themselves primarily with problems or decisions to be made by managers with a formally defined set of subordinates reporting to them. In each problem or decision, the manager must have some area of freedom or discretion in determining the solution adopted, and the solution must affect at least one of the manager's subordinates. Following Maier, Solem, and Maier (1957), they further make a distinction between group problems and individual problems. If the solution adopted has potential effects on all immediate subordinates or some readily identifiable subset of them, it is classified as a group problem. If the solution affects only one of the subordinates, it is called an *individual problem*. This distinction is an important one because it determines the range of decision-making processes available to the manager. Table 1 shows a taxonomy of decision processes for both types of problems. Each process is represented by a symbol (e.g., AI, CI, GII, DI), which provides a convenient method of referring to each process. The letters in the code signify the basic properties of the process (A stands for autocratic; C for consultative; G for group; and D for delegated). The roman numerals that follow the letters constitute variants on that process. Thus, AI represents the first variant on an autocratic process; AII the second variant, and so on.

The processes shown in table 1 are arranged in columns corresponding to their presumed applicability to either group or individual problems and are arranged within columns in order of increasing opportunity for the subordinate to influence the solution to the problem.

The discrete alternative processes shown in table 1 can be used both normatively and descriptively. In the former use, they constitute discrete alternatives available to the manager or decision maker, who presumably is motivated to choose that alternative which has the greatest likelihood of producing effective results for his organization. In the latter use, the processes constitute forms of behavior on the part of individuals which require explanation. In the balance of this paper, we will attempt to keep in mind these two uses of the taxonomy and will discuss them separately.

Table 1
Decision-Making Processes

For Individual Problems

AI You solve the problem or make the decision yourself, using information available to you at that time.

AII You obtain any necessary information from the subordinate, then decide on the solution to the problem yourself. You may or may not tell the subordinate what the problem is, in getting the information from him. The role played by your subordinate in making the decision is clearly one of providing specific information which you request, rather than generating or evaluating alternative solutions.

CI You share the problem with the relevant subordinate, getting his ideas and suggestions. Then *you* make the decision. The decision may or may not reflect your subordinate's influence.

GI You share the problem with one of your subordinates and together you analyze the problem and arrive at a mutually satisfactory solution in an atmosphere of free and open exchange of information and ideas. You both contribute to the resolution of the problem with the relative contribution of each being dependent on knowledge, rather than formal authority.

DI You delegate the problem to one of your subordinates, providing him with any relevant information that you possess, but giving him responsibility for solving the problem by himself. Any solution which the person reaches will receive your support.

For Group Problems

AI You solve the problem or make the decision yourself, using information available to you at that time.

AII You obtain any necessary information from subordinates, then decide on the solution to the problem yourself. You may or may not tell subordinates what the problem is, in getting the information from them. The role played by your subordinates in making the decision is clearly one of providing specific information which you request, rather than generating or evaluating solutions.

CI You share the problem with the relevant subordinates individually, getting their ideas and suggestions without bringing them together as a group. Then *you* make the decision. This decision may or may not reflect your subordinates' influence.

CII You share the problem with your subordinates in a group meeting. In this meeting you obtain their ideas and suggestions. Then *you* make the decision which may or may not reflect your subordinates' influence.

GII You share the problem with your subordinates as a group. Together you generate and evaluate alternatives and attempt to reach agreement (consensus) on a solution. Your role is much like that of chairman; coordinating the discussion, keeping it focused on the problem, and making sure that the critical issues are discussed. You do not try to influence the group to adopt "your" solution and are willing to accept and implement any solution which has the support of the entire group.

A Normative Model of Decision Processes

What would be a rational way of deciding on the form and amount of participation in decision making to be used in different situations? Neither debates over the relative merits of Theory X and Theory Y (McGregor, 1960) nor the apparent truism that leadership depends on the situation are of much help here. The aim in this portion of the research is to develop a framework for matching a leader's behavior, as expressed in the alternatives presented in table 1, to the demands of his situation. Any framework developed must be consistent with empirical evidence concerning the consequences of participation and be so operational that a trained leader could use it to determine how he should act in a given situation.

The normative model should provide a basis for effective problem solving and decision making by matching the desired decision process with relevant properties of particular problems or decisions to be made. Following Maier (1963), the effectiveness of a decision is thought to be a function of three classes of outcomes, each of which may be expected to be affected by the decision process used. These are:

1. The quality or rationality of the decision.

2. The acceptance or commitment on the part of subordinates to execute the decision effectively.

3. The amount of time required to make the decision.

Space prevents an exposition of the empirical evidence concerning the consequences of participation, but the reader interested in these questions is referred to Vroom (1970) and to Vroom and Yetton (1973, pp. 20–31) for a presentation of that evidence. Since the research program began, a number of normative models for choosing among alternative decision processes have been developed. Each revision is slightly more complex than its predecessor but, in the minds of both developers and users, also is more accurate in forecasting the consequences of alternatives. Most of these models have been concerned solely with group problems (the right-hand column in table 1). In Vroom and Yetton (1973) virtually all of the discussion of normative models is oriented toward group problems; although, in their discussion of further revisions and extensions of the model, they discuss the possibility of a model for both individual and group problems and present a tentative model which governs choice of decision processes for both types.

Figure 1 shows the latest version of a model intended to deal with both types of problems. Like previous models, it is expressed in the form of a decision tree. Arranged along the top of the tree are a set of eight problem attributes, expressed here in the form of simple yes–no questions that a leader could ask himself about the decision-making situation he is presently confronting.[1] To use the model, one starts at the left-hand side of the tree and works toward the right-hand side, asking oneself the questions pertaining to any box that is encountered. When a terminal node is reached, a number will be found designating the problem type and one or more decision-making processes considered appropriate for that problem. Within each problem type there are both individual and group problems, and the feasible set of methods is different for each.

Figure 1
Decision-Process Flow Chart for Both Individual and Group Problems

A. Is there a quality requirement such that one solution is likely to be more rational than another?

B. Do I have sufficient info to make a high-quality decision?

C. Is the problem structured?

D. Is acceptance of decision by subordinates critical to effective implementation?

E. If I were to make the decision by myself, is it reasonably certain that it would be accepted by my subordinates?

F. Do subordinates share the organizational goals to be attained in solving this problem?

G. Is conflict among subordinates likely in preferred solutions? (This question is irrelevant to individual problems.)

H. Do subordinates have sufficient info to make a high-quality decision?

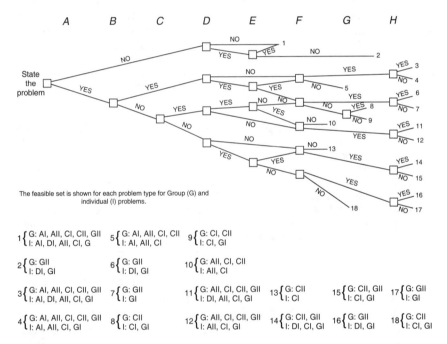

The feasible set is shown for each problem type for Group (G) and individual (I) problems.

$1\begin{cases} \text{G: AI, AII, CI, CII, GII} \\ \text{I: AI, DI, AII, CI, G} \end{cases}$ $5\begin{cases} \text{G: AI, AII, CI, CII} \\ \text{I: AI, AII, CI} \end{cases}$ $9\begin{cases} \text{G: CI, CII} \\ \text{I: CI, GI} \end{cases}$

$2\begin{cases} \text{G: GII} \\ \text{I: DI, GI} \end{cases}$ $6\begin{cases} \text{G: GII} \\ \text{I: DI, GI} \end{cases}$ $10\begin{cases} \text{G: AII, CI, CII} \\ \text{I: AII, CI} \end{cases}$

$3\begin{cases} \text{G: AI, AII, CI, CII, GII} \\ \text{I: AI, DI, AII, CI, GI} \end{cases}$ $7\begin{cases} \text{G: GII} \\ \text{I: GI} \end{cases}$ $11\begin{cases} \text{G: AII, CI, CII, GII} \\ \text{I: DI, AII, CI, GI} \end{cases}$ $13\begin{cases} \text{G: CII} \\ \text{I: CI} \end{cases}$ $15\begin{cases} \text{G: CII, GII} \\ \text{I: CI, GI} \end{cases}$ $17\begin{cases} \text{G: GII} \\ \text{I: GI} \end{cases}$

$4\begin{cases} \text{G: AI, AII, CI, CII, GII} \\ \text{I: AI, AII, CI, GI} \end{cases}$ $8\begin{cases} \text{G: CII} \\ \text{I: CI, GI} \end{cases}$ $12\begin{cases} \text{G: AII, CI, CII, GII} \\ \text{I: AII, CI, GI} \end{cases}$ $14\begin{cases} \text{G: CII, GII} \\ \text{I: DI, CI, GI} \end{cases}$ $16\begin{cases} \text{G: GII} \\ \text{I: DI, GI} \end{cases}$ $18\begin{cases} \text{G: CII} \\ \text{I: CI, GI} \end{cases}$

The decision processes specified for each problem type are not arbitrary. The specification of the feasible set of decision processes for each problem type is governed by a set of 10 rules that serve to protect the quality and acceptance of the decision by eliminating alternatives that risk one or the other of these decision outcomes. These rules, consistent with existing empirical evidence concerning the consequences of participation, are shown in table 2 in both verbal and set-theoretic form. It should be noted that the rules are of three distinct types. Rules 1 through 4 are designed to protect the quality or rationality of the decision; Rules 5 through 8 are designed to protect the acceptance of or commitment to the decision; and Rules

Table 2
Rules Underlying the Normative Model

1. *The Leader Information Rule:* $A \cap \bar{B} \rightarrow \bar{A}I$
If the quality of the decision is important and the leader does not possess enough information or expertise to solve the problem by himself, then AI is eliminated from the feasible set.

2. *The Subordinate Information Rule:*
$A \cap \bar{H} \rightarrow \bar{D}I$
(applicable to individual problems only)
If the quality of the decision is important and the subordinate does not possess enough information or expertise to solve the problem himself, then DI is eliminated from the feasible set.

3a. *The Goal Congruence Rule:*
$A \cap \bar{F} \rightarrow \bar{G}II, \bar{D}I$
If the quality of the decision is important and the subordinates are not likely to pursue organization goals in their efforts to solve this problem, then GII and DI are eliminated from the feasible set.

3b. *The Augmented Goal Congruence Rule:*
$A \cap (\bar{D} \cap E) \cap \bar{F} \rightarrow \bar{G}I$
(applicable to individual problems only)
Under the conditions specified in the previous rule (i.e., quality of decision is important, and the subordinate does not share the organizational goals to be attained in solving the problem) GI may also constitute a risk to the quality of the decision taken in response to an individual problem. Such a risk is a reasonable one to take only if the nature of the problem is such that the acceptance of the subordinate is critical to the effective implementation and prior probability of acceptance of an autocratic solution is low.

4a. *The Unstructured Problem Rule (Group):*
$A \cap \bar{B} \cap \bar{C} \rightarrow \bar{A}I, \bar{A}II, \bar{C}I$
In decisions in which the quality of the decision is important, if the leader lacks the necessary information or expertise to solve the problem by himself and if the problem is unstructured, the method of solving the problem should provide for interaction among subordinates. Accordingly, AI, AII, and CI are eliminated from the feasible set.

4b. *The Unstructured Problem Role (Individual):* $A \cap \bar{B} \cap \bar{C} \rightarrow \bar{A}I, \bar{A}II$
In decisions in which the quality of the decision is important, if the leader lacks the necessary information to solve the problem by himself and if the problem is unstructured, the method of solving the problem should permit the subordinate to generate solutions to the problem. Accordingly, AI and AII are eliminated from the feasible set.

5. *The Acceptance Rule:* $D \cap \bar{E} \rightarrow \bar{A}I, \bar{A}II$
If the acceptance of the decision by subordinates is critical to effective implementation and if it is not certain that an autocratic decision will be accepted, AI and AII are eliminated from the feasible set.

9 through 10 eliminate the use of group methods for individual problems and vice versa. The decision tree is merely a convenient structure for applying these rules, and, once the problem type has been determined, the rules have all been applied. It can be seen that there are some problem types for which only one method remains in the feasible set, and others for which two, three, four, or even five methods remain in the feasible set.

When more than one method remains in the feasible set, there are a number of ways in which one might choose among them. One method, called Model A and discussed at length by Vroom and Yetton, uses the number of man-hours required by the process of decision making. They argue that if the alternatives within the feasible set are equal in the probability of generating a rational decision which subordinates will accept, a choice among them based on the time requirement of each will be of maximum short-run benefit to the organization.

The basis for estimating the relative requirements in man-hours for the alternatives given for group problems is simple. Vroom and Yetton argue that

Table 2 *(cont'd).*

6. *The Conflict Rule:* $D \cap \bar{E} \cap G \rightarrow \bar{AI}, \bar{AII}, \bar{CI}$
   (applicable to group problems only)

If the acceptance of the decision is critical, an autocratic decision is not certain to be accepted, and disagreement among subordinates in methods of attaining the organizational goal is likely, the methods used in solving the problem should enable those in disagreement to resolve their differences with full knowledge of the problem. Accordingly, AI, AII, and CI, which permit no interaction among subordinates, are eliminated from the feasible set.

7. *The Fairness Rule:*
   $\bar{A} \cap D \cap \bar{E} \rightarrow \bar{AI}, \bar{AII}, \bar{CI}, \bar{CII}$

If the quality of the decision is unimportant, but acceptance of the decision is critical and not certain to result from an autocratic decision, the decision process used should permit the subordinates to interact with one another and negotiate over the fair method of resolving any differences with full responsibility on them for determining what is equitable. Accordingly, AI, AII, CI, and CII are eliminated from the feasible set.

8. *The Acceptance Priority Rule:*
   $D \cap \bar{E} \cap F \rightarrow \bar{AI}, \bar{AII}, \bar{CI}, \bar{CII}$

If acceptance is critical, not certain to result from an autocratic decision and if (the) subordinate(s) is (are) motivated to pursue the organizational goals represented in the problem, then methods which provide equal partnership in the decision-making process can provide greater acceptance without risking decision quality. Accordingly, AI, AII, CI, and CII are eliminated from the feasible set.

9. *The Group Problem Rule:* Group $\rightarrow \bar{GI}, \bar{DI}$

If a problem has approximately equal effects on each of a number of subordinates (i.e., is a group problem) the decision process used should provide them with equal opportunities to influence that decision. Use of a decision process, such as GI or DI, which provides opportunities for only one of the affected subordinates to influence that decision, may in the short run produce feelings of inequity reflected in lessened commitment to the decision on the part of those "left out" of the decision process and, in the long run, be a source of conflict and divisiveness.

10. *The Individual Problem Rule:*
    Individual $\rightarrow \bar{CII}, \bar{GII}$

If a problem affects only one subordinate, decision processes which *unilaterally* introduce other (unaffected) subordinates as equal partners constitute an unnecessary use of time of the unaffected subordinates and can reduce the amount of commitment of the affected subordinate to the decision by reducing the amount of his opportunity to influence the decision. Thus, CII and GII are eliminated from the feasible set.

more participative processes require more time. Therefore, the ordering of the methods shown for group problems in terms of man-hours is perfectly correlated with the degree of participation they permit (AI<AII<CICII<G<II). However, the extension of the model to cover individual problems complicates this picture, since the decision process which provides greatest opportunity for subordinate influence, DI, is certainly less time consuming than GI, which requires reaching a solution that has the agreement of both superior and subordinate. While the differences in time requirements of the alternatives for individual problems is not nearly so great as the differences in the alternatives for group problems, we have assumed an ordering such that AI<DI<AII<CI<GI. The reader will note that the ordering of alternatives from left to right within the feasible sets for each problem type in figure 1 reflects this assumption. Thus, for both group and individual problems, the minimum-man-hours solution is assumed to be the alternative furthest to the left within the feasible set.

There are, however, other bases for choice within the feasible set. A manager may wish to choose the most participative alternative that can be used while still producing rational and acceptable solutions to organizational problems. Such a position could be grounded in humanistic considerations, emphasizing the intrinsic value of participation, or on pragmatic considerations, such as the utility of participation in developing informed and responsible behavior (Vroom and Yetton, 1973). A model based on these considerations is termed *Model B*.

The reader should note that both Models A and B are consistent with the rules which generate the feasible set. They merely represent different bases for choice within it. Model A chooses the method within the feasible set which is the most economical method in terms of man-hours. Its choice is always the method furthest to the left in the set shown in figure 1. Model B chooses the most participative method available within the feasible set, which is that method closest to the bottom of table 1. Model A seeks to minimize man-hours, subject to quality and acceptance constraints, while Model B seeks to maximize participation, subject to quality and acceptance constraints. Of course, when only one process exists within the feasible set, the choices of Model A and B are identical. Perhaps the best way of illustrating the model is to show how it works in sample situations. Following are a set of actual leadership problems,[2] each based on a retrospective account by a manager who experienced the problem. The reader may wish, after reading each case, to analyze it himself using the model and then to compare his analysis with that of the authors.

Case I. You are president of a small but growing midwestern bank, with its head office in the state's capital and branches in several nearby market towns. The location and type of business are factors which contribute to the emphasis on traditional . . . and conservative banking practices at all levels.

When you bought the bank five years ago, it was in poor financial shape. Under your leadership, much progress has been made. This progress has been achieved while the economy has moved into a mild recession, and, as a result, your prestige among your bank managers is very high. Your success, which you are inclined to attribute principally to good luck and to a few timely decisions on your part, has, in your judgment, one unfortunate by-product. It has caused your subordinates to look to you for leadership and guidance in decision making beyond what you consider necessary. You have no doubts about the fundamental capabilities of these men but wish that they were not quite so willing to accede to your judgment.

You have recently acquired funds to permit opening a new branch. Your problem is to decide on a suitable location. You believe that there is no "magic formula" by which it is possible to select an optimal site. The choice will be made by a combination of some simple common-sense criteria and "what feels right." You have asked your managers to keep their eyes open for commercial real estate sites that might be suitable. Their knowledge about the communities in which they operate should be extremely useful in making a wise choice.

Their support is important because the success of the new branch will be highly dependent on your managers' willingness to supply staff and technical assistance during its early days. Your bank is small enough for everyone to feel like part of a team, and you feel that this has been and will be critical to the bank's prosperity.

The success of this project will benefit everybody. Directly, they will benefit from the increased base of operations, and, indirectly, they will reap the personal and business advantages of being part of a successful and expanding business.

Analysis:

A (Quality?) = Yes
B (Leader's information?) = No
C (Structured?) = No
D (Acceptance?) = Yes
E (Prior probability of
   acceptance?) = Yes
F (Goal congruence?) = Yes
G^3 (Conflict?) = No
H^3 (Subordinate information?) = Yes

Synthesis:

Problem type	14-Group
Feasible set	CII, GII
Model A behavior	CII
Model B behavior	GII

Case II: You are regional manager of an international management consulting company. You have a staff of six consultants reporting to you, each of whom enjoys a considerable amount of autonomy with clients in the field.

Yesterday you received a complaint from one of your major clients to the effect that the consultant whom you assigned to work on the contract with them was not doing his job effectively. They were not very explicit about the nature of the problem, but it was clear that they were dissatisfied and that something would have to be done if you were to restore the client's faith in your company.

The consultant assigned to work on that contract has been with the company for six years. He is a systems analyst and is one of the best in that profession. For the first four or five years his performance was superb, and he was a model for the other more junior consultants. However, recently he has seemed to have a "chip on his shoulder," and his previous identification with the company and its objectives has been replaced with indifference. His negative attitude has been noticed by other consultants, as well as by clients. This is not the first such complaint that you have had from a client this year about his performance. A previous client even reported to you that the consultant reported to work several times obviously suffering from a hangover and that he had been seen around town in the company of "fast" women.

It is important to get to the root of this problem quickly if that client is to be retained. The consultant obviously has the skill necessary to work with the clients effectively. If only he were willing to use it!

Analysis:

A (Quality?) = Yes
B (Leader's information?) = No
C (Structured?) = No
D (Acceptance?) = Yes
E (Prior probability of
   acceptance?) = No
F (Goal congruence?) = No
H^3 (Subordinate information?) = Yes

Synthesis:

Problem type	18-Individual
Feasible set	CI, GI
Model A behavior	CI
Model B behavior	GI

Case III: You have recently been appointed manager of a new plant which is presently under construction. Your team of five department heads has been selected, and they are now working with you in selecting their own staffs, purchasing equipment, and generally anticipating the problems that are likely to arise when you move into the plant in three months.

Yesterday, you received from the architect a final set of plans for the building, and, for the first time, you examined the parking facilities that are available. There is a large lot across the road from the plant intended primarily for hourly workers and lower-level supervisory personnel. In addition, there are seven spaces immediately adjacent to the administrative offices, intended for visitor and reserved parking. Company policy requires that a minimum of three spaces be made available for visitor parking, leaving you only four spaces to allocate among yourself and your five department heads. There is no way of increasing the total number of such spaces without changing the structure of the building.

Up to now, there have been no obvious status differences among your team, who have worked together very well in the planning phase of the operation. To be sure, there are salary differences, with your administrative, manufacturing, and engineering managers receiving slightly more than the quality control and industrial relations managers. Each has recently been promoted to his new position and expects reserved parking privileges as a consequence of his new status. From past experience, you know that people feel strongly about things which would be indicative of their status. So you and your subordinates have been working together as a team, and you are reluctant to do anything which might jeopardize the team relationship.

Analysis:		**Synthesis:**	
A	(Quality?) = No	Problem type	2-Group
D	(Acceptance?) = Yes	Feasible set	GII
E	(Prior probability of	Model A behavior	GII
	acceptance?) = No	Model B behavior	GII
G^3	(Conflict?) = Yes		

Case IV: You are executive vice president for a small pharmaceutical manufacturer. You have the opportunity to bid on a contract for the Defense Department pertaining to biological warfare. The contract is outside the mainstream of your business; however, it could make economic sense since you do have unused capacity in one of your plants, and the manufacturing processes are not dissimilar.

You have written the document to accompany the bid and now have the problem of determining the dollar value of the quotation which you think will win the job for your company. If the bid is too high, you will undoubtedly lose to one of your competitors; if it is too low, you would stand to lose money on the program.

There are many factors to be considered in making this decision, including the cost of the new raw materials and the additional administrative burden of relationships with a new client, not to speak of factors which are likely to influence the bids of your competitors, such as how much they *need* this particular contract. You have been busy assembling the necessary data to make this decision but there remain several "unknowns," one of which involves the manager of the plant in which the new products will be manufactured. Of all your subordinates, only he is in the position to estimate the costs of adapting the present equipment to their new purpose, and his cooperation and support will be necessary in ensuring that the specifications of the contract will be met.

However, in an initial discussion with him when you first learned of the possibility of the contract, he seemed adamantly opposed to the idea. His previous experience has not particularly equipped him with the ability to evaluate projects like this one, so you were not overly influenced by his opinions. From the nature of his arguments, you inferred that his opposition was ideological, rather than economic. You recall that he was actively involved in a local "peace organization" and, within the company, was one of the most vocal opponents to the war in Vietnam.

Analysis:

A (Quality?) = Yes
B (Leader's information?) = No
C (Structured?) = Yes
D (Acceptance?) = Yes
E (Prior probability of
      acceptance?) = No
F (Goal congruence?) = No
H^3 (Subordinate information?) = No

Synthesis:

Problem type	8- or 9-Individual
Feasible set	CI, GI
Model A behavior	CI
Model B behavior	GI

Toward a Descriptive Model

So far, we have been concerned only with normative or prescriptive questions. But, how do managers really behave? What decision rules underlie their willingness to share their decision-making power with their subordinates? In what respects are these decision rules similar to or different from those employed in the normative model?

The manner in which these questions are posed is at variance with much of the conventional treatment of such issues. Frequently, leaders are typed as autocratic or participative or as varying on a continuum between these extremes. In effect, autocratic or participative behavior is assumed to be controlled by a personality trait, the amount of which varies from one person to another. The trait concept is a useful one for summarizing differences among people but allows no room for the analysis of intra-individual differences in behavior. Following Lewin's (1951) classic formation $B = f(P, E)$, we assumed that a leader's behavior in a given situation reflects characteristics of that leader, properties of the situation, and the interaction of the two.

Two somewhat different research methods have been used in studying the situational determinants of participative behavior. The first method (Vroom and Yetton, 1973, chapter 4) utilized what we have come to refer to as "recalled problems." Over 500 managers, all of whom were participants in management development programs, provided written descriptions of a group problem which they encountered recently. These descriptions ranged in length from one paragraph to several pages and covered virtually every facet of managerial decision making.

Each manager was then asked to indicate which of the methods shown on the right-hand side of table 1 (AI, AII, CI, CII, GII) he had used in solving the problem. Finally, each manager was asked a set of questions concerning the problem he had selected. These questions corresponded to attributes in the normative model.

Preliminary investigation revealed that managers perceived the five alternatives as varying (in the order shown in table 1) on a scale of participation, but that the four intervals separating adjacent processes were not seen as equal. On the basis of the application of several scaling methods (Vroom and Yetton, 1973, pp. 65–71), the following values on a scale of participation were assigned to each process: AI = 0; AII = .625; CI = 5.0; CII = 8.125; GII = 10.

Using the managers' judgments of the status of the problems they described on the problem attributes as independent variables and the scale values of their behavior on the problem as a dependent variable, it is possible to use the method of multiple regression to determine the properties of situations (i.e., problems), which are associated with autocratic or participative behavior. It is also possible to insert the managers' judgments concerning their problems into the normative model and to determine the degree of correspondence between managerial and model behavior.

Several investigations have been conducted using this method—all of which have been restricted to group problems and the decision processes corresponding to them. The results are consistent with the view that there are important differences in the processes used for different kinds of problems. Specifically, managers were more likely to exhibit autocratic behavior on structured problems in which they believed that they had enough information, their subordinates lacked information, their subordinates' goals were incongruent with the organizational goals, their subordinates' acceptance of the decision was not critical to its effective implementation, and the prior probability that an autocratic decision would be accepted was high. Thus, many (but not all) of the attributes contained in the normative model had an effect on the decision processes which managers employed, and the directions of these effects are similar to those found in the model. However, it would be a mistake to conclude that the managers' behavior was always identical to that of the model. In approximately two-thirds of the problems, nevertheless, the behavior which the manager reported was within the feasible set of methods prescribed for that problem, and in about 40 percent of the cases it corresponded exactly to the minimum man-hours (Model A) solution.

Several observations help to account for differences between the model and the typical manager in the sample. First, as is apparent from an inspection of figure 1, the normative model incorporates a substantial number of interactions among attributes, whereas no such interactions appeared in the results of the regression analysis. Second, the magnitude of the effects of two attributes pertaining to the acceptance or commitment of subordinates to decisions was considerably weaker in the descriptive than in the normative model, suggesting that these considerations play less of a role in determining how people behave. This inference was further supported by the fact that rules designed to protect the acceptance of the decision in the normative model were violated far more frequently than rules designed to protect decision quality.

The results of this research were supportive of the concept of intrapersonal variance in leadership style and helped to identify some of the situational factors influencing leaders' choices of decision processes. There were, however, some key methodological weaknesses to this research. Limited variance in and inter-correlations among the problem attributes restricted the extent to which situational effects could be determined with precision. Furthermore, the fact that subjects selected and scored their own problems may have led to confounding of individual differences and situational effects. Finally, since only one problem was obtained from each manager, it was impossible to identify interactions between person and situational variables (i.e., idiosyncratic rules for deciding when and to what extent to encourage participation by subordinates).

The methodological problems inherent in the use of "recalled problems" dictated a search for another method with which to explore the same phenomenon. The technique selected involved the development of a standardized set of administrative problems or cases, each of which depicted a leader faced with some organizational requirement for action or decision making. Managers were asked to assume the role of leader in each situation and to indicate which decision process they would employ.

Several standardized sets of cases were developed, using rewritten accounts of actual managerial problems obtained from the previous method. These sets of cases, or problem sets, were developed in accordance with a multi-factorial experimental design, within which the problem attributes were varied orthogonally. Each case corresponded to a particular combination of problem characteristics, and the entire set of cases permitted the simultaneous variation of each problem attribute. To ensure conformity of a given case or problem with the specifications of a cell in the experimental design, an elaborate procedure for testing cases was developed (Vroom and Yetton, 1973, pp. 97–101), involving coding of problems by expert judges and practicing managers.

This method showed promise of permitting the replication of the results using recalled problems with a method that avoided spurious effects stemming from the influence of uncontrolled variables on problem selection. Since the use of a "repeated measures design" permitted a complete experiment to be performed on each subject, the main effects of each of the problem attributes on the decision processes used by the subject could be identified. By comparing the results for different subjects, the similarities and differences in these main effects and the relative importance of individual differences and of situational variables could be ascertained.

Vroom and Yetton worked exclusively with group problems and with an experimental design which called for 30 cases. The results, obtained from investigations of eight distinct populations comprising over 500 managers, strongly support the major findings from the use of recalled problems, both in terms of the amount of correspondence with the normative model and the specific attributes of situations which tended to induce autocratic and participative decision processes. Moreover, the nature of the methods used made it possible also to obtain precise estimates of the amount of variance attributable to situational factors and individual differences. Only 10 percent of the total variance could be accounted for in terms of general tendencies to be autocratic or participative (as expressed in differences among individuals in mean behavior on all 30 problems), while about 30 percent was attributable to situational effects (as expressed in differences in mean behavior among situations).

What about the remaining 60 percent of the variance? Undoubtedly, some of it can be attributed to errors of measurement, but Vroom and Yetton were able to show that a significant portion of that variance can be explained in terms of another form of individual differences (i.e., differences among managers in ways of "tailoring" their approach to the situation). Theoretically, these can be thought of as differences in decision rules that they employ concerning when to encourage participation.

Notes

[1] For a detailed definition of these attributes and of criteria to be used in making Yes-No judgments, see Vroom and Yetton (1973, pp. 21–31).

[2] For additional problems and their analysis, see Vroom and Yetton (1973, pp. 40–44).

[3] The question pertaining to this attribute is asked in the decision tree but is irrelevant to the prescribed behavior.

References

Cyert, R. M., and J. G. March. *A Behavioral Theory of the Firm.* Englewood Cliffs, NJ: Prentice-Hall, 1963.

Lewin, K. "Frontiers in Group Dynamics." *Field Theory in Social Science*, ed. D. Cartwright. New York: Harper & Row, 1951, pp. 188–237.

Lowin, A. "Participative Decision Making: A Model, Literature Critique, and Prescriptions for Research." *Organizational Behavior and Human Performance* 3 (1968), pp. 68–106.

Maier, N. R. F., A. R. Solem, and A. A. Maier. *Supervisory and Executive Development: A Manual for Role Playing.* New York: John Wiley & Sons, 1957.

Maier, N. R. F. "Problem-Solving Discussions and Conferences." *Leadership Methods and Skills.* New York: McGraw-Hill, 1963.

March, J. G., and H. A. Simon. *Organizations.* New York: John Wiley & Sons, 1958.

McGregor, D. *The Human Side of Enterprise.* New York: McGraw-Hill, 1960.

Overall, J. E., and D. K. Spiegel. "Concerning Least Squares Analysis of Experimental Data." *Psychological Bulletin* 72 (1969), pp. 311–22.

Vroom, V. H. "Industrial Social Psychology." *Handbook of Social Psychology*, ed. L. G. Lindzey and E. Aronson. Reading, MA: Addison-Wesley, 1970, chap. 5, pp. 196–268.

Vroom, V. H., and P. W. Yetton. *Leadership and Decision-Making.* Pittsburgh: University of Pittsburgh Press, 1973.

Wood, M. T. "Power Relationships and Group Decision Making in Organizations." *Psychological Bulletin* 79 (1973), pp. 280–93.

4

One Minute Management

Kenneth H. Blanchard

While managers all over the world feel the three secrets of One Minute Management are common sense, they are quick to admit that they are not common practice. Recognizing that fact, I make the following suggestions and comments about putting the three secrets—One Minute Goal Setting, One Minute Praising, and One Minute Reprimands—to work.

One Minute Goal Setting

The first secret to being a One Minute Manager is One Minute Goal Setting. This involves making sure that every one of your staff is clear on two things: what they [*sic*] are being asked to do (areas of accountability) and what good behavior looks like (performance standards).

In our organization, we do a great deal of diagnostic work. And when we go into companies to help improve productivity, we begin by asking people to tell us what they do. Next we go to their managers and ask them to tell us what their people do. When we compare the responses, we often find two different lists, particularly if we ask these people to prioritize their duties.

One of the biggest obstacles to productivity improvement is that people who are most closely tied to a productivity issue do not even know it is their responsibility. For example, we once worked with a group of restaurant managers who were concerned about sales. We asked the managers, "Who is responsible for generating sales?" They replied, "The waiters." But when we asked the waiters what their job was, they said, "Serving food and taking orders." I was in one of these restaurants recently and the menu said, "Soup of the day." I asked the waiter what the soup of the day was, and he said, "Lentil, but it looks awful!"

Again, the first part of effective One Minute Goal Setting is to make sure people know what they are being asked to do. The second part is letting people know what doing a good job means.

Reprinted by permission of the publisher from *Executive Excellence* (June 1984), pp. 7–8.

We ask people, "Are you doing a good job?" Most people say, "Yes, I think so." Then we ask the tough question: "How do you know?" The primary response we receive is, "I haven't been chewed out lately by my boss," as if the number one motivator of people was non-punishment. That is not very motivating. And it leads to the most commonly used management style in America. When our people perform well we do nothing, but if they "screw up" we hit them. We call this the "leave-alone-zap" style of management. And believe me, it's not a very motivating style.

A number of years ago, researchers conducted a study to find out what unmotivated workers do in their free time. They assumed that unmotivated workers would also be unmotivated after work but, upon observation, soon found that was not true. In fact, they were amazed at how motivated these workers got at 5:00 P.M. when they headed out the door to hunt, fish, golf, coach, construct, sew, or cook.

What is different about what people do at work versus after work that makes such a motivational difference? I once heard Scott Myers, a top management consultant, use an example of bowling to give the answer. Imagine an unmotivated worker bowling. What do you think this person would do when he or she threw a strike? Jump up and down and yell like anyone else. If that's true, then why aren't people jumping up and yelling in your company? Why don't your kids come down to breakfast in the morning yelling, "I cleaned up my room again—all right!"

The reason people are not yelling in organizations, following our bowling example, is that when they approach the alley, they notice there are no pins at the other end. How long would you want to bowl without any pins? And yet every day in the world of work people are literally bowling without any pins—they don't know what their goals are. That is why we work hard to get managers to set goals with their people. Without any "pins," people cannot get any feedback on performance. And the number one motivator of people is feedback on performance. In fact, the One Minute Manager has a saying that is worth remembering: "Feedback is the Breakfast of Champions." And you obtain feedback through information on performance.

I think it's vital to put information on the performance of people into the hands of managers. Many organizations have elaborate systems for getting information to accountants and top executives, but never to anyone who can use it on a day-to-day basis. Managers need information—it's the most important tool they have. How can they know what to do if they don't know how well they are doing? Can you imagine training for the Olympics and not knowing how fast you ran or how high you jumped?

The first secret of the One Minute Manager is setting clear goals that are observable and measurable. Be careful, though, not to set too many goals. People can handle three to five goals at a time. Before you fill notebooks with goals, remember the 80/20 rule: 80 percent of the results you want to obtain from people comes from 20 percent of their activities. Therefore, you want to set goals toward accomplishing the few key activities that will yield the 80 percent of the desired result.

One Minute Praising

Once you make your people clear on what you are asking them to do and what good behavior looks like, you are ready for the second secret: One Minute Praising. Sneak around your organization and see if you can catch people doing anything right. When you do, give them a One Minute Praising. In order for your praising to be effective, you must be specific. Tell people what they did right. Say, "You submitted your report on time Friday and it was well written; in fact, I used it in a meeting today, and that report made you and me and our whole department look good."

After you praise people, tell them how you feel about what they did. Don't intellectualize. People want to know your gut feelings. "Let me tell you how I feel about that," you begin. "I feel super. You know I was so proud at the meeting that I want you to know I really feel good about you being on our team. Thanks a lot." Did that take very long? No. But did it last? Yes. People love it, and they remember it.

To help managers in catching their people doing things right, I often suggest that they schedule at least two hours each week for praising. But I warn them to do their homework *first* before they begin to wander around and praise people; otherwise, they will get themselves into trouble. For instance, one manager called me and said, "I'm doing what you told me to do—praising people from 1:30 to 2:30 on Wednesdays and Fridays—but it's not working." I said, "Why not?" He said, "I don't know." So I went over and had lunch with him one Wednesday. At 1:30 he said, "It's praising time." The moment he went out among his people I knew why it wasn't working. He was going up to people and saying things like, "Appreciate your efforts; thank you very much; I don't know what I'd do without you; keep up the good work." His staff thought he was running for political office.

Instead of praising people at random, first find out what they have done right. Use examples like, "I see productivity in your department is up ten percent"; or "Your report helped us win the contract with the Jones Company." To be effective, praising must be specific.

Praising is the most powerful asset a manager has. In fact, it is the key to training people and making "winners" of everyone working for you. When you can't find winners—people who have proven that they can do the job, who have a good track record—you have to find potential winners and train them.

There are five steps to this training: 1) tell them what to do; 2) show them what to do; 3) let them try; 4) observe their performance (don't disappear and leave them alone); 5) praise progress and go back to show and tell again. You'll notice there is no mention of punishment here. Yelling at people does not teach them skills. Forget punishment as a training technique. Punishing people who are not yet winners will only immobilize them or teach them to avoid the punisher. If you do not see any progress, you cannot praise the person, but neither should you punish the performance. Go back to show and tell and redirect. If no progress is made after a while, you should talk to the person about career planning.

One Minute Reprimand

At this point people often say One Minute Management is not a tough enough management system. They say, "In the real world you have to be tough." Well, the third secret usually satisfies those people. It is called the One Minute Reprimand.

The "secret" is to reprimand only those people who know how to do the job, who have the skills, and you only reprimand them so they will start using their skills again.

There are four things to remember about a reprimand. First, do it immediately. Don't be one of those great "gunnysack" managers who see people doing something wrong but don't say anything; instead, they store up their feelings of disappointment or anger in an imaginary sack until one dark day, they dump their full load on a person. They let him "have it," telling him everything he has done wrong in the last six months. Second, be specific. Let people know exactly why you are angry or disappointed in them. Third, show and tell them how you feel about what they did wrong. Remember you have thoughts in your head but feelings in your stomach; what people really want to know is what you feel about what they did wrong. After you tell them how you feel, take a deep breath and give them the fourth part of the reprimand, which is the most important. End the reprimand with a praise. "Let me tell you one other thing. You are good, you are one of my best people. That is why I am annoyed with you. Normally, you get your reports in on time—this isn't anything like you. I want to tell you I am not going to let you get away with it because I count on you; you are one of my best people." I praise at the end of the reprimand for an important reason. When we part ways, I want them thinking about what they did wrong, not how I treated them.

Let me explain the difference between reprimanding someone who is good and redirecting someone who is learning. This example involves two college basketball players—Roger and John—whom I coached when I was in graduate school.

Roger could do it all. He could jump, shoot, rebound, and run like a deer. He was one of the best players the school had recruited in ten years, but he only wanted to play one end of the court—offense. Again and again, we asked him why he wouldn't play defense, but nothing seemed to work. Finally, we hauled the kid out of the game, put our nose against his nose, and screamed and yelled at him how we felt about his not playing defense. The first time we did this he said, "Why are you always yelling at me?" We yelled back, "Because you are good. You are the best player we've recruited in ten years." Then we put him back in the game.

Now John was a different story. If we put him in the game and he caught the ball, it was progress. If we were to treat him the same way when he made a mistake it would destroy him—or he would destroy us—because it would be unfair. So we would bench him and talk with him carefully. We had to teach him, and we could not teach him by yelling at him every time he made a mistake. The same reprimand behavior that was effective with Roger was ineffective with John.

So, remember to set clear goals in the beginning and then praise and reprimand according to people's performance and skills. If people do something right, praise them. If they make a mistake and they know better, give them a reprimand.

When you reprimand, though, show them you are angry or disappointed with their behavior, but reaffirm their value as a person.

When you apply these three "secrets" to your work, let your staff know what you are trying to do. If you try practicing this without involving them, they will think you are out of your mind. But once they know the three steps too, they will help you become a One Minute Manager.

5

Fundamental Leadership Practices

James M. Kouzes and Barry Z. Posner

The Five Fundamental Practices of Exemplary Leadership

As we looked deeper into the dynamic process of leadership, through case analyses and survey questionnaires, we uncovered five fundamental practices that enable leaders to get extraordinary things done. The individual stories of how ordinary people got extraordinary things done brought the leadership model to life for us, giving it character and color. When they were at their personal best, the leaders we studied were able to

- Challenge the process
- Inspire a shared vision
- Enable others to act
- Model the way
- Encourage the heart

These practices, which we discuss briefly in this chapter and elaborate on in later chapters, aren't the private property of the people we studied or of a few select shining stars. They've stood the test of time, and they're available to anyone, in any organization or situation, who accepts the leadership challenge.

Challenging the Process

Leaders venture out. While many people in our studies attributed their success to "luck" or "being in the right place at the right time," none of them sat idly by waiting for fate to smile upon them. Those who lead others to greatness seek and accept challenge. Jean Campbell, for instance, rose to the occasion when nature jolted SSI off its foundations. In the process, she also found innovative ways to run the business. Antonio Zárate caused a quake of his own by confronting a traditional culture with some radical new ideas.

Reprinted with permission of John Wiley & Sons from *The Leadership Challenge* by James M. Kouzes and Barry Z. Posner, pp. 8–14 and 17–18. Copyright 1987, 1995.

Every single personal-best leadership case we collected involved some kind of challenge. The challenge may have been an innovative new product, a cutting-edge service, a groundbreaking piece of legislation, an invigorating campaign to get adolescents to join an environmental program, a revolutionary turnaround of a bureaucratic military program, or the start-up of a new plant or business. Whatever the challenge, all the cases involved a change from the status quo. Not one person claimed to have done his or her personal best by keeping things the same. *In short, all leaders challenge the process.*

Leaders are pioneers—people who are willing to step out into the unknown. They're willing to take risks, to innovate and experiment in order to find new and better ways of doing things. But leaders need not always be the creators or originators of new products, services, or processes. In fact, it's just as likely that they're not. Product and service innovations tend to come from customers, clients, vendors, people in the labs, and people on the front lines, while process innovations tend to come from the people doing the work. Sometimes a dramatic external event thrusts us into a radically new condition.

The leader's primary contribution is in the recognition of good ideas, the support of those ideas, and the willingness to challenge the system in order to get new products, processes, services, and systems adopted. It might be more accurate, then, to say that leaders are early *adopters* of innovation. Leaders know well that experimentation, innovation, and change all involve risk and failure, but they proceed anyway.

It would be ridiculous to assert that those who fail over and over again eventually succeed as leaders. Success in any endeavor isn't a process of simply buying enough lottery tickets. The key that unlocks the door to opportunity is learning. In his own study of exemplary leadership practices, University of Southern California professor Warren Bennis writes [in *On Becoming a Leader*] that "leaders learn by leading, and they learn best by leading in the face of obstacles. As weather shapes mountains, so problems shape leaders. Difficult bosses, lack of vision and virtue in the executive suite, circumstances beyond their control, and their own mistakes have been the leaders' basic curriculum." In other words, leaders are learners. They learn from their failures as well as their successes.

Inspiring a Shared Vision

When people described to us their personal-best leadership experiences, they told of times when they imagined an exciting, highly attractive future for their organization. They had visions and dreams of what *could* be. They had absolute and total personal belief in those dreams, and they were confident in their abilities to make extraordinary things happen. Every organization, every social movement, begins with a dream. The dream or vision is the force that invents the future. In the rubble, Campbell saw a new and even more responsive Synergistic Systems; Zárate imagined a company of total quality people producing total quality products.

Leaders inspire a shared vision. They gaze across the horizon of time, imagining the attractive opportunities that are in store when they and their constituents arrive at a distant destination. Leaders have a desire to make something happen, to change the way things are, to create something that no one else has ever created before.

In some ways, leaders live their lives backward. They see pictures in their mind's eye of what the results will look like even before they've started their project, much as an architect draws a blueprint or an engineer builds a model. Their clear image of the future pulls them forward. Yet visions seen only by leaders are insufficient to create an organized movement or a significant change in a company. A person with no constituents is *not* a leader, and people will not follow until they accept a vision as their own. Leaders cannot command commitment, only inspire it.

To enlist people in a vision, leaders must know their constituents and speak their language. People must believe that leaders understand their needs and have their interests at heart. Only through an intimate knowledge of their dreams, their hopes, their aspirations, their visions, their values is the leader able to enlist support. Leadership is a dialogue, not a monologue.

Leaders breathe life into the hopes and dreams of others and enable them to see the exciting possibilities that the future holds. Leaders forge a unity of purpose by showing constituents how the dream is for the common good.

Leaders can't ignite the flame of passion in others if they don't express enthusiasm for the compelling vision of their group. Leaders communicate their passion through vivid language and an expressive style.

Without exception, the people in our study reported that they were incredibly enthusiastic about their personal-best projects. Their own enthusiasm was catching; it spread from leader to constituents. Their belief in and enthusiasm for the vision were the sparks that ignited the flame of inspiration.

Enabling Others to Act

The individuals in our study recognized that grand dreams don't become significant realities through the actions of a single leader. Leadership is a team effort. After reviewing over 2,500 personal-best cases, we developed a simple test to detect whether someone is on the road to becoming a leader. That test is the frequency of the use of the word *we*.

Exemplary leaders enlist the support and assistance of all those who must make the project work. This sense of teamwork goes far beyond a few direct reports or close confidants. In today's "virtual" organization, cooperation can't be restricted to a small group of loyalists; it must include peers, managers, customers and clients, suppliers, citizens—all those who have a stake in the vision. Leaders involve, in some way, all those who must live with the results, and they make it possible for others to do good work. *They enable others to act.* Leaders know that no one does his or her best when feeling weak, incompetent, or alienated; they know that those who are expected to produce the results must feel a sense of ownership.

David Butler, controller at Plextor, told us the following: "As a society and global economy, we've progressed beyond the industrial revolution. The control-oriented structures and management techniques of that era don't apply any-more. . . . You need to give people on the front lines proper vision and proper training, and then follow that up with responsibility so they can act on decisions." Leaders recognize the validity of Butler's statement and work to make people feel strong, capable, and committed. Leaders enable others to act not by hoarding the power they have but by giving it away. When people have more discretion, more authority, and more information, they're much more likely to use their ener-gies to produce extraordinary results.

In the cases we analyzed, leaders proudly discussed teamwork, trust, and empowerment as essential elements of their efforts. For constituents, too, a leader's ability to enable others to act is essential; in fact, from the constituents' vantage point, this is the most significant of the five practices. Leadership is a relationship, founded on trust and confidence. Without trust and confidence, peo-ple don't take risks. Without risks, there's no change. Without change, organiza-tions and movements die.

Modeling the Way

Titles are granted, but it's your behavior that wins you respect. As Gayle Hamilton, a division manager with Pacific Gas & Electric Company, told us, "I would never ask anyone to do anything I was unwilling to do first." Leaders go first. They set an example and build commitment through simple, daily acts that create progress and momentum. *Leaders model the way through personal exam-ple and dedicated execution.*

To model effectively, leaders must first be clear about their guiding princi-ples. Leaders are supposed to stand up for their beliefs, so they better have some beliefs to stand up for. Eloquent speeches about common values aren't nearly enough. Leaders' deeds are far more important than their words and must be con-sistent with them. Toni-Ann Lueddecke knows that there are no unimportant tasks in an organization's efforts at excellence. She demonstrates this to her asso-ciates in her seven Gymboree Play Centers in New Jersey by her daily actions. As just one example, she scrubs floors just as often as she teaches classes.

At a faculty convocation at Santa Clara University several years ago, the Reverend William J. Rewak, S.J., then president, spoke eloquently about changes anticipated for the campus. After showing slides of the planned new buildings and gardens, he said, "Vision needs management, electricity, and concrete." Grand dreams, he reminded us, can't become significant realities with élan alone. New tomorrows aren't realized without hard work and persistence. The personal-best projects we heard about in our research were all distinguished by relentless effort, steadfastness, competence, and attention to detail.

Leaders need operational plans. They must steer projects along a predeter-mined course, measure performance, give feedback, meet budgets and schedules, and take corrective action. Yet the personal-best cases we examined included very little about grand strategic plans and massive organizational changes; they sounded more like action adventure stories. They were about the power of little things piled one on top of the other until they added up to something big. Concentrating on producing small wins, leaders build confidence that even the biggest challenges can be met. In so doing, they strengthen commitment to the long-term future.

Encouraging the Heart

The climb to the top is arduous and long. People become exhausted, frustrated, and disenchanted. They're often tempted to give up. *Leaders encourage the heart of their constituents to carry on.* If people observe a charlatan making noisy pretenses, they turn away. But genuine acts of caring can uplift the spirits and draw people forward. Jean Campbell held a Town Hall meeting when reconstruction was complete to "celebrate victory," you'll remember; at Metalsa, Antonio Zárate "encourages self-esteem."

Encouragement can come from dramatic gestures or simple actions. When he was plant manager of the Wire and Cable Division of Raychem Corporation, Phil Turner would occasionally put on a clown costume and give out balloons to employees. He still enjoys celebrating milestones in various ways, and people get a good laugh from his playful acts. Heather Gioia, president of TPG/Learning Systems, is a master of recognition. She gives out stickers, stuffed animals, masks, buttons, toys, and every other conceivable award to people when they achieve a milestone.

It's part of the leader's job to show people that they can win. In the cases we collected, there were thousands of examples of individual recognition and group celebration. You can use marching bands, bells, T-shirts, note-cards, personal thank-yous, and a host of other awards to offer visible signs of encouragement to keep on winning. Recognition and celebration aren't about fun and games, however. Encouragement is curiously serious business. It's how leaders visibly and behaviorally link rewards with performance. When striving to raise quality, recover from disaster, start up a new service, or make dramatic change of any kind, leaders make sure people benefit when behavior is aligned with cherished values.

In the cases we examined, we saw evidence not only of the encouragement leaders give to others but of the encouragement that leaders give themselves. When we asked George Gananian, owner of Star Graphics, why he worked so hard, he said, "I love to turn the key in the door and put on the coffee pot." Love—of their products, their services, their constituents, their clients and customers, and their work—may be the best-kept leadership secret of all. . . .

The Ten Commitments of Leadership

Embedded in the five fundamental practices of exemplary leadership discussed above are behaviors that can serve as the basis for learning to lead. We call these the Ten Commitments of Leadership. These ten commitments, as shown on the following page, serve as the guide for our discussion of how leaders get extraordinary things done in organizations and as the structure for what's to follow.

Ten Commitments of Leadership

Practices	*Commitments*
Challenging the Process	1. *Search out* challenging opportunities to change, grow, innovate, and improve.
	2. *Experiment,* take risks, and learn from the accompanying mistakes.
Inspiring a Shared Vision	3. *Envision* an uplifting and ennobling future.
	4. *Enlist* others in a common vision by appealing to their values, interests, hopes, and dreams.
Enabling Others to Act	5. *Foster* collaboration by promoting cooperative goals and building trust.
	6. *Strengthen* people by giving power away, providing choice, developing competence, assigning critical tasks, and offering visible support.
Modeling the Way	7. *Set* the example by behaving in ways that are consistent with shared values.
	8. *Achieve* small wins that promote consistent progress and build commitment.
Encouraging the Heart	9. *Recognize* individual contributions to the success of every project.
	10. *Celebrate* team accomplishments regularly.

Source: *The Leadership Challenge* by James M. Kouzes and Barry Z. Posner. Copyright © 1995.

6

Management and Leadership

John P. Kotter

The word leadership is used in two very different ways in everyday conversation. Sometimes it refers to a process that helps direct and mobilize people and/or their ideas; we say, for example, that Fred is providing leadership on the such and such project. At other times it refers to a group of people in formal positions where leadership, in the first sense of the word, is expected; we say that the leadership of the firm is made up of ten people, including George, Alice, etc.

In this chapter, I will use the word almost exclusively in the first sense. The second usage contributes greatly to the confusion surrounding this subject because it subtly suggests that everyone in a leadership position actually provides leadership.[1] This is obviously not true; some such people lead well, some lead poorly, and some do not lead at all. Since most of the people who are in positions of leadership today are called managers, the second usage also suggests that leadership and management are the same thing, or at least closely related. They are not.

Leadership is an ageless topic. That which we call management is largely the product of the last 100 years,[2] a response to one of the most significant developments of the twentieth century: the emergence of large numbers of complex organizations.[3] Modern management was invented, in a sense, to help the new railroads, steel mills, and auto companies achieve what legendary entrepreneurs created them for. Without such management, these complex enterprises tended to become chaotic in ways that threatened their very existence. Good management brought a degree of order and consistency to key dimensions like the quality and profitability of products.

In the past century, literally thousands of managers, consultants, and management educators have developed and refined the processes which make up the core of modern management. These processes, summarized briefly, involve:[4]

1. Planning and budgeting—setting targets or goals for the future, typically for the next month or year; establishing detailed steps for achieving

those targets, steps that might include timetables and guidelines; and then allocating resources to accomplish those plans

2. Organizing and staffing—establishing an organizational structure and set of jobs for accomplishing plan requirements, staffing the jobs with qualified individuals, communicating the plan to those people, delegating responsibility for carrying out the plan, and establishing systems to monitor implementation

3. Controlling and problem solving—monitoring results versus plan in some detail, both formally and informally, by means of reports, meetings, etc.; identifying deviations, which are usually called "problems"; and then planning and organizing to solve the problems

These processes produce a degree of consistency and order. Unfortunately, as we have witnessed all too frequently in the last half century, they can produce order on dimensions as meaningless as the size of the typeface on executive memoranda. But that was never the intent of the pioneers who invented modern management. They were trying to produce consistent results on key dimensions expected by customers, stockholders, employees, and other organizational constituencies, despite the complexity caused by large size, modern technologies, and geographic dispersion. They created management to help keep a complex organization on time and on budget. That has been, and still is, its primary function.[5]

Leadership is very different. It does not produce consistency and order, as the word itself implies; it produces movement. Throughout the ages, individuals who have been seen as leaders have created change, sometimes for the better and sometimes not.[6, 7] They have done so in a variety of ways, though their actions often seem to boil down to establishing where a group of people should go, getting them lined up in that direction and committed to movement, and then energizing them to overcome the inevitable obstacles they will encounter along the way.

What constitutes good leadership has been a subject of debate for centuries. In general, we usually label leadership "good" or "effective" when it moves people to a place in which both they and those who depend upon them are genuinely better off, and when it does so without trampling on the rights of others.[8] The function implicit in this belief is *constructive or adaptive change.*

Leadership within a complex organization achieves this function through three subprocesses which can briefly be described as such:[9]

1. Establishing direction—developing a vision of the future, often the distant future, along with strategies for producing the changes needed to achieve that vision

2. Aligning people—communicating the direction to those whose cooperation may be needed so as to create coalitions that understand the vision and that are committed to its achievement

3. Motivating and inspiring—keeping people moving in the right direction despite major political, bureaucratic, and resource barriers to change by appealing to very basic, but often untapped, human needs, values, and emotions

Figure 1 compares these summaries of both management and leadership within complex organizations.[10]

Figure 1
Comparing Management and Leadership

	Management	Leadership
Creating an agenda	Planning and Budgeting—establishing detailed steps and timetables for achieving needed results, and then allocating the resources necessary to make that happen	Establishing Direction—developing a vision of the future, often the distant future, and strategies for producing the changes needed to achieve that vision
Developing a human network for achieving the agenda	Organizing and Staffing—establishing some structure for accomplishing plan requirements, staffing that structure with individuals, delegating responsibility and authority for carrying out the plan, providing policies and procedures to help guide people, and creating methods or systems to monitor implementation	Aligning People—communicating the direction by words and deeds to all those whose cooperation may be needed so as to influence the creation of teams and coalitions that understand the vision and strategies, and accept their validity
Execution	Controlling and Problem Solving—monitoring results vs. plan in some detail, identifying deviations, and then planning and organizing to solve these problems	Motivating and Inspiring—energizing people to overcome major political, bureaucratic, and resource barriers to change by satisfying very basic, but often unfulfilled, human needs
Outcomes	Produces a degree of predictability and order, and has the potential of consistently producing key results expected by various stakeholders (e.g., for customers, always being on time; for stockholders, being on budget)	Produces change, often to a dramatic degree, and has the potential of producing extremely useful change (e.g., new products that customers want, new approaches to labor relations that help make a firm more competitive)

Management and leadership, so defined, are clearly in some ways similar. They both involve deciding what needs to be done, creating networks of people and relationships that can accomplish an agenda, and then trying to ensure that those people actually get the job done. They are both, in this sense, complete action systems; neither is simply one aspect of the other. People who think of management as being only the implementation part of leadership ignore the fact that leadership has its own implementation processes: aligning people to new directions and then inspiring them to make it happen. Similarly, people who think of leadership as only part of the implementation aspect of management (the motivational part) ignore the direction-setting aspect of leadership.

But despite some similarities, differences exist which make management and leadership very distinct. The planning and budgeting processes of management tend to focus on time frames ranging from a few months to a few years, on details, on eliminating risks, and on instrumental rationality. By contrast, that part of the leadership process which establishes a direction often focuses on longer time frames, the big picture, strategies that take calculated risks, and people's values. In a similar way, organizing and staffing tend to focus on specialization, getting the right person into or trained for the right job, and compliance; while aligning people tends to focus on integration, getting the whole group lined up in the right direction, and commitment. Controlling and problem solving usually focus on containment, control, and predictability; while motivating and inspiring focus on empowerment, expansion, and creating that occasional surprise that energizes people.

But even more fundamentally, leadership and management differ in terms of their primary function. The first can produce useful change, the second can create orderly results which keep something working efficiently. This does not mean that management is never associated with change; in tandem with effective leadership, it can help produce a more orderly change process. Nor does this mean that leadership is never associated with order; to the contrary, in tandem with effective management, an effective leadership process can help produce the changes necessary to bring a chaotic situation under control. But leadership by itself never keeps an operation on time and on budget year after year. And management by itself never creates significant useful change.

Taken together, all of these differences in function and form create the potential for conflict. Strong leadership, for example, can disrupt an orderly planning system and undermine the management hierarchy, while strong management can discourage the risk taking and enthusiasm needed for leadership. Examples of such conflict have been reported many times over the years, usually between individuals who personify only one of the two sets of processes: "pure managers" fighting it out with "pure leaders."[11]

But despite this potential for conflict, the only logical conclusion one can draw from an analysis of the processes summarized in figure 1 is that they are both needed if organizations are to prosper. To be successful, organizations not only must consistently meet their current commitments to customers, stockholders, employees, and others, they must also identify and adapt to the changing needs of these key constituencies over time. To do so, they must not only plan, budget, organize, staff, control, and problem solve in a competent, systematic, and rational manner so as to achieve the results expected on a daily basis, they also must establish, and reestablish, when necessary, an appropriate direction for the future, align people to it, and motivate employees to create change even when painful sacrifices are required.

Indeed, any combination other than strong management and strong leadership has the potential for producing highly unsatisfactory results. When both are weak or nonexistent, it is like a rudderless ship with a hole in the hull. But adding just one of the two does not necessarily make the situation much better. Strong management without much leadership can turn bureaucratic and stifling, producing order for order's sake. Strong leadership without much management can become messianic and cult-like, producing change for change's sake—even if movement is in a totally insane direction. The latter is more often found in political movements than in corporations,[12] although it does occur sometimes in relatively small, entre-preneurial businesses.[13] The former, however, is all too often seen in corporations today, especially in large and mature ones.

With more than enough management but insufficient leadership, one would logically expect to see the following: 1) a strong emphasis on shorter time frames, details, and eliminating risks, with relatively little focus on the long term, the big picture, and strategies that take calculated risks; 2) a strong focus on specialization, fitting people to jobs, and compliance to rules, without much focus on integration, alignment, and commitment; 3) a strong focus on containment, control, and predictability, with insufficient emphasis on expansion, empowerment, and inspiration. Taken together, it is logical to expect this to produce a firm that is somewhat rigid, not very innovative, and thus incapable of dealing with important changes in its market, competitive, or technological environment. Under these circumstances, one would predict that performance would deteriorate over time, although slowly if the firm is large and has a strong market position. Customers would be served less well because innovative products and lower prices from innovative manufacturing would be rare. As performance sinks, the cash squeeze would logically be felt more by investors who get meager or no returns and by employees who eventually are forced to make more sacrifices, including the ultimate sacrifice of their jobs.

This scenario should sound familiar to nearly everyone. Since 1970, literally hundreds of firms have had experiences that are consistent with it. No one can measure the overall impact of all this. But in the United States this problem has surely contributed to the fact that real wages were basically flat from 1973 to 1989, that stock prices when adjusted for inflation were less in late 1988 than in 1969, and that consumers have turned increasingly to less expensive or innovative foreign goods, leaving the country with a crippling trade deficit. And recent evidence suggests that the problem is still a long way from solved.

During 1988, senior executives in a dozen successful U.S. corporations were asked to rate all the people in their managerial hierarchies on the dimensions of both leadership and management.[14] The scale they were given ranged from "weak" to "strong," and their responses were grouped into four categories: people who are weak at providing leadership but strong at management, those who are strong at leadership but not at management, those who are relatively strong at both, and those who do not do either well. The executives were then asked if the specific mix of talent their companies had in each of these four categories was what they needed to prosper over the next five to ten years. They could respond: we have about what we need; we have too few people in this category; or we have too many people like this. A summary of their responses is shown in figure 2.

Half of those polled reported having too many people who provide little if any management or leadership. Executives in professional service businesses such as investment banking and consulting were particularly likely to say this. The other half reported having very few people in this category, which, as one would expect, they said was just fine.

Nearly half reported having too few people who provide strong leadership but weak management. However, those who answered this way typically noted that such people were very valuable as long as they could work closely with others who were strong at management. Most of the remaining respondents reported having about the right number of people in this category for future needs, sometimes commenting that this "right number" was "very few." These respondents tended to be pessimistic about strong leaders/weak managers; they felt such people usually created more problems than they solved.

Figure 2
How Executives in a Dozen Successful U.S. Firms
Rate the People in Their Managerial Hierarchies

		Weak (Management)	Strong (Management)
LEADERSHIP	Strong	Nearly half say they have "too few"* people like this	Virtually all report "too few" people in this quadrant
	Weak	Half say they have "too many" people like this	Nearly two-thirds report "too many" people here

MANAGEMENT

*Respondents were given three choices: (1) too few, (2) too many, (3) about right. The category having the largest number of responses is shown in the chart.

Nearly two-thirds of those surveyed said they had too many people who are strong at management but not at leadership. Some even reported having "far too many." The other third split their responses between "too few" and "about right." Those saying too few usually worked for professional service firms.

Over 95 percent reported having too few people who are strong at both leadership and management. Everyone thought they had some people like that: not super humans who provide outstanding management and excellent leadership but mortals who are moderately strong on one of the two dimensions, and strong or very strong on the other. But the respondents felt they needed more, often many more, to do well over the next decade.

This survey is interesting, not because it proves anything by itself, but because the results are so consistent with a variety of other evidence. As a whole, the data strongly suggests that most firms today have insufficient leadership, and that many corporations are "over-managed" and "under-led."

An even larger survey conducted a few years earlier provides some insight as to why this leadership problem exists.[15] Nearly 80 percent of the 1,000 executives responding to that survey questionnaire said they felt their firms did less than a very good job of recruiting, developing, retaining, and motivating people with leadership potential (see figure 3). These same executives also reported that their companies were not successful in this regard because of a large number of inappropriate practices (see figure 4). For example, 82 percent of the respondents said that "the quality of career planning discussions in their firms" was less than adequate to support the objective of attracting, retaining, and motivating a sufficient number of people who could help with the leadership challenges. Seventy-seven percent said the same thing about "the developmental job opportunities available" and "the information available to high potentials on job openings in the company." Fully 93 percent indicated that "the way managers are rewarded for developing subordinates" with leadership potential was less than adequate to support the need for spotting high-potential people, identifying their development needs, and then meeting those needs. Eighty-seven percent reported the same problem with "the number and type of lateral transfers made for developmental reasons across divisions." Seventy-nine percent said same thing about "the mentoring, role modeling, and coaching provided," 75 percent about "the way feedback is given to subordinates regarding developmental progress," 69 percent about "the way responsibilities are added to the current job of high potentials for development purposes," 66 percent about "formal

Figure 3
Attracting, Developing, Retaining, and Motivating People with Leadership Potential: Results from a Questionnaire of 1,000 Executives

I.   How good a job is your company doing with respect to recruiting and hiring a sufficient number of people into the firm who have the potential of someday providing leadership in important management positions?
very good or excellent   27%
poor or fair   30%

II. How good a job is your firm doing with respect to developing these high-potential employees?
very good or excellent   19%
poor or fair   42%

III. How good a job is your company doing with respect to retaining and motivating these high-potential people?
very good or excellent   20%
poor or fair   43%

Figure 4
Adequacy of Practices Affecting a Firm's Leadership Capacity: Results from the Questionnaire

The questionnaire asks 46 questions about practices that affect the firm's capacity to develop, retain, and motivate sufficient leadership. In summary, people responded:

I.   The vast majority of practices (80%) are more than adequate*
% answering this way = 0.2

II. The vast majority of practices (80%) are adequate**
% answering this way = 3.3

III. A bare majority of the practices (51%) are adequate**
% answering this way = 23.7

*A response of 1 on a 4-point scale.   **A response of 1 or 2 on a 4-point scale.

succession planning reviews," 65 percent about "the firm's participation in outside management training programs," and 60 percent about "the opportunities offered to people to give them exposure to higher levels of management."[16]

Equally interesting is what was not said. Those surveyed did not say their firms had insufficient leadership because there are not enough people on earth with leadership potential. Instead, they put the blame on themselves for not finding, retaining, developing, or supporting people with such potential. Some of those surveyed readily admitted that their firms often scared off such individuals, while others believed that they took talented young people with leadership potential and systematically turned them into cautious managers. These rather critical results would not be particularly surprising if they came from a disenfranchised group of lower- or middle-level managers. But this was not a survey of those groups. It was a poll of senior executives.

There are probably a variety of reasons why so many firms do not appear to have the practices needed to attract, develop, retain, and motivate enough people with leadership potential. But the most basic reason is simply this: until recently, most organizations did not need that many people to handle their leadership challenges.

Modern business organizations are the product of the last century. They were created, for the most part, by strong entrepreneurial leaders[17] like Andrew Carnegie, Pierre Du Pont, and Edward Filene. As these enterprises grew and became more complex, that which we now call management was invented to make them function on time and on budget. As the most successful of these enterprises became larger, more geographically dispersed, and more technologically complicated, especially after World War II, they demanded many more people who could help provide that management.

A huge educational system emerged in response to this need, offering seminars, undergraduate degrees in management, and MBAs.[18] But the favorable economic climate for U.S. businesses after World War II allowed such a degree of stability that most firms didn't need much leadership—until the 1970s. Then suddenly, after twenty-five to thirty years of relatively easy growth, especially in the United States, the business world became more competitive, more volatile, and tougher. A combination of faster technological change, greater international competition, market deregulation, overcapacity in capital-intensive industries, an unstable oil cartel, raiders with junk bonds, and a demographically changing workforce all contributed to this shift. The net result is that doing what was done yesterday, or doing it 5 percent better, is no longer a formula for success. Major changes are more and more necessary to survive and compete effectively in this new environment. More change always demands more leadership (see figure 5). But firms are having difficulty adapting their practices to this new reality.

Examples of this shift can be found nearly everywhere. Consider the case of a small- to medium-sized plant owned by a successful U.S. firm like Honeywell. In 1970, this facility employed 100 people, was 20 years old, and produced control systems for manufacturing settings. Although the facility made nearly two dozen products, one of these accounted for half the volume. That product, relatively unique in the marketplace, was protected by a number of patents. Although

Figure 5
**The Relationship of Change and Complexity to the Amount of
Leadership and Management Needed in a Firm**

Amount of change needed in the operation (due to environmental instability, rapid growth, etc.)

High — Low

Considerable leadership but not much management required (start-up businesses)	Considerable leadership and management required (most businesses and other organizations today)
Little management or leadership required (most organizations until this century)	Considerable management but little leadership required (many successful corporations in the 1950s and 1960s)

Low ◄————————————————► High

The complexity of the operation (due to size, technology, geographical dispersion, the number of products or services, etc.)

the plant's products were sold in over fifty countries, U.S. sales accounted for 70 percent of total volume. In the U.S. market, the plant's main product line held a 34 percent market share in its specific niche; the number two competitor controlled about 24 percent.

An examination of the demands placed on the plant manager back in 1970 reveals the following. First and foremost, he was expected to meet monthly, quarterly, and yearly targets for production, costs, and a number of other quantifiable measures. These targets were established after some negotiation by his boss and were based heavily on historical data. To meet these targets, he allocated his time over the course of the year in roughly the following way:

- 5–10%—working with his staff to produce the monthly, quarterly, and yearly plans to meet the targets
- 20–30%—working with his staff to make sure he had the appropriate organization in place to implement the plans, which in turn involved hiring, firing, performance appraisals, coaching, etc.
- 40–50%—having daily production meetings, weekly budget review meetings, and the like to spot deviations from plan as quickly as possible and to solve them
- 20–25%—all other activities, such as assisting the sales force by meeting an important customer, or deciding if a new technology should be used in one part of the manufacturing process

In other words, he spent the vast majority (75 to 80 percent) of his time *managing* the plant, with a heavy emphasis on the control aspects of management.

If a visitor to this plant in 1970 returned fifteen years later, he would have found a very different facility. In 1985, the plant had more engineers and technicians and fewer foremen and middle managers. Although the number of employees was almost the same, the output was double the 1970 levels. The plant's product line was much more volatile; products introduced within the past five years accounted for nearly 35 percent of its volume versus 15 percent in 1970. The products themselves were more technologically complex, and the technology was changing faster than it had fifteen years earlier. The plant's products were being sold in even more countries, and a greater volume was sold outside the United States. Worldwide market share for the plant's niche was about 14 percent, versus 29 percent in the United States, and its number one competitor, with nearly 22 percent of the world market, was now a Japanese company.

In this environment, the demands placed on the 1985 plant manager were in some ways similar to, but in many ways different from, those found in 1970. The head of this facility in 1985 was still being asked to meet certain quantifiable targets on a monthly, quarterly, and yearly basis. That, in turn, still required producing plans, maintaining an organization, and many controlling efforts to keep things "on track." But the targets themselves were more complex and volatile due to market conditions; thus the process of achieving them was more complicated. More importantly, in addition to all these activities, there was a whole new dimension to the job, one that was time-consuming and difficult, yet essential.

In 1985, the plant manager was being asked to match his Japanese rival by finding a way to increase certain quality measures not by 1 or 5 or 10 percent, but by 100 percent. He was also asked to help the corporate manufacturing staff evaluate a number of options for moving some production out of the country, to find a way to incorporate a completely new technology into the heart of the manufacturing process, to reduce the time required to introduce new products by 50 percent, and to shrink inventories by at least a third. All of this, in turn, required much more from his staff—in terms of time, energy, creativity, and the willingness to make sacrifices and take risks. That created a huge challenge: to somehow get his people energized and committed to helping with the big cost and quality and technology issues. And all of this created change, far more than in 1970, which in turn was bumping up against a corporate bureaucracy designed for a more stable environment. It also led to the sorts of uncertainties that threatened vested interests.

The 1985 plant manager coped with these demands by allocating his time in the following way:

- 30–50%—Engaging in the same types of planning, organizing, and controlling activities as did his predecessor fifteen years earlier, but using a less authoritarian style and delegating more (i.e., managing)
- 50–60%—(a) trying to establish a clear sense of direction for the changes needed in quality, costs, inventories, technologies, and new product introductions, (b) trying to communicate that direction to all his people and to get them to believe that the changes are necessary, and, (c) finally, trying to energize and motivate his people to overcome all the bureaucratic, political, and resource barriers to change (i.e., leading)
- 0–10%—participating in other activities

By almost all standards, the plant manager's job in 1985 was more difficult than it was in 1970, primarily because the firm's business environment was more difficult. In 1985, this person not only had to manage the plant by planning, budgeting, organizing, staffing, and controlling, he also had to provide substantial leadership on dozens of critical business issues. And he was not alone in this respect.

In 1970, in a business environment that was both favorable and changing relatively slowly, sufficient leadership could be supplied by the CEO and several other people. By 1985, in a much tougher and rapidly changing environment, hundreds of individuals, both above and below the plant manager level, were also needed to provide leadership for developing and implementing new marketing programs, new approaches to financing the business, new MIS systems, new labor relations practices, and much more. Doing all this well required skills and strategies that most people did not need in the relatively benign 1950s, 1960s, and early 1970s. It required more than technical and managerial ability. Some of these people had these new skills, but many did not.

This story is interesting because the type of environmental changes involved is not at all unusual. These same kinds of changes can be found in a wide variety of industries and in a large number of countries in addition to the United States (see figure 6).

A simple military analogy sums all this up well. A peacetime army can usually survive with good administration and management up and down the hierarchy, coupled with good leadership concentrated at the very top. A wartime army, however, needs competent leadership at all levels. No one yet has figured out how to manage people effectively into battle. From 1946 into the 1970s, the world economy was, for the most part, at peace. It is no longer. But precious few corporations now have the leadership necessary to win the battles they face in this economic war.

Figure 6
Results of a Poll of Mid-Level Executives from 42 Countries and 31 Industries*

I. For the industry you know best, how different is the business environment today (1988) versus that of 25 years ago (1963)?

1	2	3	4		5
Not Different					Extremely Different

Mean Response:
4.4

II. If the business environment in the industry you know best is significantly different today than it was 25 years ago, how is it different?

Nearly 90 percent report:

• More competitive
• More technological change
• Faster changing

*Survey of 135 people conducted in September 1988.

There are a number of reasons why firms, even some very good ones, have had difficulty adapting to the new business environment. The most obvious relates to the inherent difficulty of the task. All available evidence suggests that finding people with leadership potential and then nurturing that potential is much tougher than finding people with managerial potential and then developing those skills.[19]

Experts have been of limited help, even though a few predicted the environmental changes before the fact, usually in the mid to late 1960s.[20] The biggest recommendation to evolve from this work has been a vague notion that we need to *manage* differently in the future. Individuals have stressed long-term planning, matrix structures, motivational systems and much more. None of the ideas has worked well, and for reasons that are predictable in light of the real difference between management and leadership.

Starting in the early 1980s some people reacted to all this by emphasizing leadership. What is needed to cope with major change, they argued correctly, is not management, but something else. Their descriptions of this "something else" were often vague. But worse yet, most suggested that this other thing—leadership—was needed instead of management. That is, they offered a prescription that was not only wrong, but dangerous.

Strong leadership with weak management is no better, and sometimes actually worse, than the reverse. In such a situation 1) an emphasis on long-term vision but little short-term planning and budgeting, plus 2) a strong group culture without much specialization, structure, and rules, plus 3) inspired people who are not inclined to use control systems and problem-solving disciplines, all conspire to create a situation that can eventually get out of control, even wildly out of control. Under such circumstances, as many small entrepreneurial firms have learned the hard way, critical deadlines, budgets, and promises can go unmet, threatening the very existence of the organization.

The most extreme, and dangerous, examples of this phenomenon are of the Jim Jones variety. In such cases, a charismatic person emerges when a group of people are experiencing considerable pain. This person is not a good manager and, in fact, does not like good managers because they are too rational and controlling. The charismatic has a flawed vision, one that does not try to create real value for both the group and its key outside constituencies. But the lack of a rational management process—that is as powerful as the leadership—means the bad vision is not publicly discussed and discredited. The strong charisma creates commitment and great motivation to move in the direction of the vision. Eventually, this movement leads to tragedy; followers trample other people and then walk off a cliff.

Seeking out, canonizing, and turning over the reigns of power to this type of charismatic non-manager is never the solution to a leadership crisis. But to move beyond this seductively dangerous prescription will require a much clearer sense of what leadership really means in complex organizations, what it looks like, and where it comes from. Given the inherent complexity of the subject matter and the barriers prohibiting rigorous empirical work on such a broad topic, satisfying such a purpose is an extraordinarily difficult task. Nevertheless, that task sets the agenda for this book, and the comparative analysis of leadership vis-à-vis the more clearly understood process of management will be the primary vehicle for achieving that agenda.

Notes

[1] A sizable amount of the literature on leadership is based on studies of people in supervisory or managerial jobs, people who may or may not have been providing effective leadership. See Bass (*Handbook of Leadership: A Survey of Theory and Research*, Free Press, 1981) and Yukl (*Leadership in Organizations*, Prentice-Hall, 1989).

[2] This is not to suggest that management, at least in an elementary form, did not exist centuries earlier. It surely did, and generals, kings, and high priests undoubtedly knew something about it. But the management they knew and used was the product of a vastly less complicated age. Compared to today, the organizations they managed were technologically simple and usually small—in other words, not very complex.

[3] Chandler, *The Visible Hand*, Belknap Press of Harvard University Press, 1977.

[4] Summarized here are the elements of management most commonly included in both a) the many books on that subject published in this century, and b) a 1987 survey conducted by this author which asked 200 executives to describe the actions of someone they knew who was effectively managing whatever he or she was responsible for.

[5] Although not the only function, that seems to be the most common one mentioned in the hundreds of books on management that have been published in the past 60 to 70 years.

[6] Burns, *Leadership*, Harper & Row, 1978.

[7] Levinson and Rosenthal end their study of CEO's with the following conclusion; "Strong leaders are necessary, particularly for organizations that must undergo significant change. Not good managers or executives, but strong leaders." (*CEO: Corporate Leadership in Action*, Basic Books, 1984, p. 289.)

[8] Determining what "generally better off" and "trampling on the rights of others" mean, in practice, can be most difficult and has led to endless philosophical discussions. For the purposes of this book, effectiveness is measured by the cumulative after-the-fact opinions of all those affected by a leadership process.

[9] The list is generally consistent with other important works on leadership in modern organizations—books by Bennis and Nanus (*Leaders: The Strategies for Taking Charge*, Harper & Row, 1985) and Peters and Austin (*A Passion for Excellence: The Leadership Difference*, Random House, 1985), for example. But this specific way of thinking about leadership comes from the studies upon which the book is based (see the Preface).

[10] The distinction between leadership and management is similar in some ways to what Burns (*op. cit.*) and Bass (*Leadership and Performance Beyond Expectations*, Free Press, 1985) have called transformational leadership versus transactional leadership. The book by Burns and a 1977 article by Zaleznik ("Managers and Leaders: Are They Different," *Harvard Business Review*, 55, 5, pp. 67–87) are the first two works of which I am aware that begin to explore these differences.

[11] For a fascinating analysis of the pure types and their potential for conflict, see Zaleznik, *op. cit.*, pp. 67–80.

[12] This occurred in China during the "Cultural Revolution."

[13] Very visible examples, although not extreme ones, include Apple before John Sculley became CEO and People Express during its final year of operation.

[14] Approximately 200 executives were polled during 1987 either with a questionnaire or in an hour-long interview (see Appendix). The dimensions of "management" and "leadership" were not defined for them, but before they were asked to rate their fellow managers on those dimensions, they were first asked to describe in detail the actions of someone they knew who provided effective management and then to describe likewise the actions of someone who has provided effective leadership.

[15] Further details on this survey can be found in Kotter, *The Leadership Factor*, Free Press, 1988.

[16] *Ibid.* Chapter 6.

[17] By "entrepreneurial" I mean leaders who focused on their energies on taking advantage of opportunities to build businesses.

[18] The sheer amount of management education offered today is at least thirty times greater than that offered fifty years ago.

[19] Kotter, *op. cit.*, Chapter 3.

[20] Beckhard, *Organizational Development*, Addison-Wesley, 1969.

7

Servant Leadership

Robert K. Greenleaf

Servant and leader. Can these two roles be fused in one real person, in all levels of status or calling? If so, can that person live and be productive in the real world of the present? My sense of the present leads me to say yes to both questions. This paper is an attempt to explain why and to suggest how.

The idea of *The Servant as Leader* came out of reading Herman Hesse's *Journey to the East.* In this story we see a band of men on a mythical journey, probably also Hesse's own journey. The central figure of the story is Leo who accompanies the party as the *servant* who does their menial chores, but who also sustains them with his spirit and his song. He is a person of extraordinary presence. All goes well until Leo disappears. Then the group falls into disarray and the journey is abandoned. They cannot make it without the servant Leo. The narrator, one of the party, after some years of wandering finds Leo and is taken into the Order that had sponsored the journey. There he discovers that Leo, whom he had known first as *servant,* was in fact the titular head of the Order, its guiding spirit, a great and noble *leader.*

One can muse on what Hesse was trying to say when he wrote this story. We know that most of his fiction was autobiographical, that he led a tortured life, and that *Journey to the East* suggests a turn toward the serenity he achieved in his old age. There has been much speculation by critics on Hesse's life and work, some of it centering on this story which they find the most puzzling. But to me, this story clearly says—*the great leader is seen as servant first,* and that simple fact is the key to his greatness. Leo was actually the leader all of the time, but he was servant first because that was what he was, *deep down inside.* Leadership was bestowed upon a man who was by nature a servant. It was something given, or assumed, that could be taken away. His servant nature was the real man, not bestowed, not assumed, and not to be taken away. He was servant first.

Reprinted from *The Servant as Leader* by Robert K. Greenleaf, pp. 9 and 15–19. Reprinted with permission, The Robert K. Greenleaf Center, Inc. Copyright 1991, 2008.

Who is the Servant-Leader?

The servant-leader *is* servant first—as Leo was portrayed. It begins with the natural feeling that one wants to serve, to serve *first.* Then conscious choice brings one to aspire to lead. He is sharply different from the person who is *leader* first, perhaps because of the need to assuage an unusual power drive or to acquire material possessions. For such it will be a later choice to serve—after leadership is established. The leader-first and the servant-first are two extreme types. Between them there are shadings and blends that are part of the infinite variety of human nature.

The difference manifests itself in the care taken by the servant-first to make sure that other people's highest priority needs are being served. The best test, and difficult to administer, is: do those served grow as persons; do they, *while being served,* become healthier, wiser, freer, more autonomous, more likely themselves to become servants? *And,* what is the effect on the least privileged in society; will he benefit, or, at least, will he not be further deprived?

As one sets out to serve, how can one know that this will be the result? This is part of the human dilemma; one cannot know for sure. One must, after some study and experience, hypothesize—but leave the hypothesis under a shadow of doubt. Then one acts on the hypothesis and examines the result. One continues to study and learn and periodically one re-examines the hypothesis itself.

Finally, one chooses again. Perhaps one chooses the same hypothesis again and again. But it is always a fresh open choice. And it is always an hypothesis under a shadow of doubt. "Faith is the choice of the nobler hypothesis." Not the *noblest,* one never knows what that is. But the *nobler,* the best one can see when the choice is made. Since the test of results of one's actions is usually long delayed, the faith that sustains the choice of the nobler hypothesis is psychological self-insight. This is the most dependable part of the true servant.

The natural servant, the person who is *servant first,* is more likely to persevere and refine his hypothesis on what serves another's highest priority needs than is the person who is *leader first* and who later serves out of promptings of conscience or in conformity with normative expectations.

My hope for the future rests in part on my belief that among the legions of deprived and unsophisticated people are many true servants who will lead, and that most of them can learn to discriminate among those who presume to serve them and identify the true servants.

Everything Begins with the Initiative of an Individual

The forces for good and evil in the world are propelled by the thoughts, attitudes, and actions of individual beings. What happens to our values, and therefore to the quality of our civilization in the future, will be shaped by the conceptions of individuals that are born of inspiration. Perhaps only a few will receive this inspiration (insight) and the rest will learn from them. The very essence of leadership, going out ahead to show the way, derives from more than usual openness to inspiration. Why would anybody accept the leadership of another except that the other sees more clearly where it is best to go? Perhaps this is the current problem: too many who presume to lead do not see more clearly and, in defense of their inadequacy, they all the more strongly argue that the "system" must be preserved—a fatal error in this day of candor.

But the leader needs more than inspiration. He ventures to say, "I will go; come with me!" He initiates, provides the ideas and the structure, and takes the risk of failure along with the chance of success. He says, "I will go, follow me!" when he knows that the path is uncertain, even dangerous. And he trusts those who go with him.

Paul Goodman, speaking through a character in *Making Do,* has said, "If there is no community for you, young man, young man, make it yourself."

What Are You Trying To Do?

What are you trying to do?—one of the easiest to ask and most difficult to answer of questions.

A mark of a leader, an attribute that puts him in a position to show the way for others, is that he is better than most at pointing the direction. As long as he is leading, he always has a goal. It may be a goal arrived at by group consensus; or the leader, acting on inspiration, may simply have said, "Let's go this way." But the leader always knows what it is and can articulate it for any who are unsure. By clearly stating and restating the goal the leader gives certainty and purpose to others who may have difficulty in achieving it for themselves.

The word *goal* is used here in the special sense of the overarching purpose, the big dream, the visionary concept, the ultimate consummation which one approaches but never really achieves. It is something presently out of reach; it is something to strive for, to move toward, or become. It is so stated that it excites the imagination and challenges people to work for something they do not yet know how to do, something they can be proud of as they move toward it.

Every achievement starts with a goal. But not just any goal and not just anybody stating it. The one who states the goal must elicit trust, especially if it is a high risk or visionary goal, because those who follow are asked to accept the risk along with the leader. A leader does not elicit trust unless one has confidence in his values and his competence (including judgment) and unless he has a sustaining spirit (entheos) that will support the tenacious pursuit of a goal.

Not much happens without a dream. And for something great to happen, there must be a great dream. Behind every great achievement is a dreamer of great dreams. Much more than a dreamer is required to bring it to reality; but the dream must be there first.

Listening and Understanding

One of our very able leaders recently was made the head of a large, important, and difficult-to-administer public institution. After a short time he realized that he was not happy with the way things were going. His approach to the problem was a bit unusual. For three months he stopped reading newspapers and listening to news broadcasts; and for this period he relied wholly upon those he met in the course of his work to tell him what was going on. In three months his administrative problems were resolved. No miracles were wrought; but out of a sustained intentness of listening that was produced by this unusual decision, this able man learned and received the insights needed to set the right course. And he strengthened his team by so doing.

Why is there so little listening? What makes this example so exceptional? Part of it, I believe, with those who lead, is that the usual leader in the face of a difficulty tends to react by trying to find someone else on whom to pin the problem, rather than his automatic response being, "I have a problem. What is it? What can *I* do about *my* problem?" The sensible man who takes the latter course will probably react by listening, and somebody in the situation is likely to tell him what his problem is and what he should do about it. Or, he will hear enough that he will get an intuitive insight that resolves it.

I have a bias about this which suggests that only a true natural servant automatically responds to any problem by listening *first*. When he is a leader, this disposition causes him to be *seen* as servant first. This suggests that a non-servant who wants to be a servant might become a *natural* servant through a long arduous discipline of learning to listen, a discipline sufficiently sustained that the automatic response to any problem is to listen first. I have seen enough remarkable transformations in people who have been trained to listen to have some confidence in this approach. It is because true listening builds strength in other people.

Most of us at one time or another, some of us a good deal of the time, would really like to communicate, really get through to a significant level of meaning in the hearer's experience. It can be terribly important. The best test of whether we are communicating at this depth is to ask ourselves, first, are we really listening? Are we listening to the one we want to communicate to? Is our basic attitude, as we approach the confrontation, one of wanting to understand? Remember that great line from the prayer of St. Francis, "Lord, grant that I may not seek so much to be understood as to understand."

8

Situational Leadership

Paul Hersey

Situational Leadership® Model

After years of extensive research, the Situational Leadership® Model was developed to guide a leader in diagnosing a particular situation. The model is based on the amount of direction (task behavior) and socioemotional support (relationship behavior) a leader must provide an individual, or group of people. The appropriate amount of these types of behaviors is determined by the "performance readiness" level the individual is displaying.

There are three steps to using the Situational Leadership® Model:

1. Identify the specific job, task or activity.

2. Assess current performance readiness.

3. Match leader response.

Step 1: Identify the Specific Job, Task or Activity

There is a legal premise that no contract exists unless there is a meeting of the minds. In performance contracting, and that is what leadership is all about, the same basic premise holds true. There needs to be a meeting of the minds. Specifically, what job, task or activity is the focus or purpose of the leader/individual intervention?

The key determinate here is the person's understanding of what the leader wants accomplished. Is there a clear picture of performance in both the leader's and individual's mind? What is to be done? How specific does the leader need to be? For one individual a high degree of specificity may be just what is needed. For another individual that same specificity might be perceived as micromanaging. Once the task or activity has been identified, an effective leader moves to diagnosing the performance readiness level of the person.

Step 2: Assess Current Performance Readiness

How ready, willing and able is the individual? Performance readiness is the interplay between ability and willingness that a person demonstrates for a specific task. The key word here is interplay. These two components, ability and willingness, are an interacting influence system. This means one component has an impact on the other.

Ability is composed of three key variables. It is the amount of knowledge, experience and skill a person is currently and consistently demonstrating for a task.

Willingness is the amount of confidence, commitment and motivation being demonstrated. A strong amount of motivation can make an individual appear very willing. The interplay between ability and willingness determines four general levels of performance readiness.

Figure 1
The Components of Performance Readiness

"knowledge, experience, skill"
(knows how)   (has done)   (is doing)

Performance
Readiness: **Ability**
              —————
              Willingness

"confidence, commitment, motivation"
(can do)   (will do)   (wants to do)

Performance Readiness Level R1: "Unable and Insecure" or "Unable and Unwilling." Unable and Insecure is low skill demonstration and the issue is driven by insecurity. The individual could be intimidated by the task, overwhelmed, unclear or uncertain about what is expected and how to perform. Unable and Unwilling means levels of demonstrated skill are low and the motivation and willingness to perform is also low.

Performance Readiness Level R2: "Unable but Confident or Willing." R2 is often referred to as "not ready yet," sometimes known as the "Enthusiastic Incompetent." In fact, when introducing a new task, this is the performance readiness level where most people start. The confidence and willingness can come from within, from others, or by working in a healthy, safe environment. A person may be "unable" simply because they have not previously performed the task and haven't had the opportunity to demonstrate ability.

Performance Readiness Level R3: "Able but Insecure" or "Able but Unwilling." At this performance readiness level, ability is now being demonstrated, and fairly consistently at moderate to high levels. The individual may be "insecure" when just beginning to perform with less involvement from the leader. The person may be "unwilling" when the task may be less rewarding than expected, problems won't go away, or performing is punishing.

Performance Readiness Level R4: "Able and Confident and Willing."
Once a person reaches R4, consistent high levels of ability blend with confidence, commitment or a sense of ownership. Motivation and desire for accomplishment are also high.

Figure 2
Performance Readiness Level Cues

Able but Insecure or Unwilling
Indicators:
- First time "solo" performance
- Lacks confidence
- Needs feedback and encouragement
- Previously demonstrated knowledge and skill
- Performance slipping – upset about things on or off the job

Unable but Confident or Willing
Indicators:
- Anxious or excited
- Interested and responsive
- Demonstrating moderate ability
- Receptive to input
- Attentive
- Enthusiastic
- New task – no experience

HIGH	MODERATE		LOW
R4	**R3**	**R2**	**R1**
Able and Confident and Willing	Able but Insecure or Unwilling	Unable but Confident or Willing	Unable and Insecure or Unwilling

Able and Confident and Willing
Indicators:
- Consistently performs at high standards
- Can operate autonomously
- Committed to, and enjoys the task
- Keeps boss informed of task progress
- Shares both good and bad news

Unable and Insecure or Unwilling
Indicators:
- Not performing task to acceptable level
- Intimidated by task
- Unclear about directions
- Procrastinating
- Unfinished tasks
- Questioning task
- Avoidance or "passing the buck"
- Defensiveness or discomfort

Step 3: Match Leader Response

Leadership style is composed of two distinct sets of behaviors: relationship behavior and task behavior.

Relationship behavior is the extent to which a leader engages in two-way communication with a person. This type of communication provides socioemotional support or "psychological strokes" for those involved. Explanation of why something should be done is given to the individual. Facilitating, participating or involving behaviors come from the leader.

Task behavior is the amount of guidance or direction provided. It is the extent the leader engages in defining the who, what, when, where and how the task is to be performed.

These observed patterns of influence behavior can be plotted on two separate and distinct axes as shown below.

Figure 3
Influence Behaviors

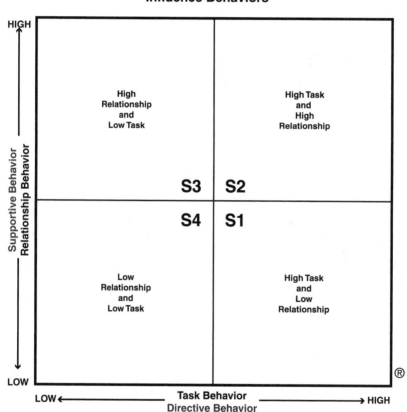

Four combinations of relationship and task behavior are identified. Leadership styles are based on the interaction of the amount of socioemotional support (relationship behavior) leaders provide and the amount of direction (task behavior).

Leadership Style S1: "High Task/Low Relationship."   S1 is categorized as "telling" because this style is characterized by mostly one-way communication. The leader defines the role of the individual and tells the details of who, what, where, when and how in relation to a specific task. *Informing* or *guiding* are also examples of how a style S1 may come across effectively to a person.

Figure 4
Influence Behavior Cues

<table>
<tr>
<td>

High Relationship Low Task

- Encourage input
- Actively listen
- Individual-made decision
- Two-way communications and involvement
- Support risk-taking
- Compliment work
- Praise and build confidence

</td>
<td>

High Task High Relationship

- Providing – who, what, when, where, how and why
- Explain decisions and allow opportunity for clarification
- Two-way dialogue
- Leader-made decisions
- Explain individual's role
- Ask questions to clarify ability level
- Reinforce small improvements

</td>
</tr>
</table>

S4	S3	S2	S1
Low Relationship Low Task	High Relationship Low Task	High Task High Relationship	High Task Low Relationship
Delegating Observing Monitoring Tracking	Participating Encouraging Problem Solving Involving	Selling Explaining Persuading Clarifying	Telling Guiding Directing Instructing

<table>
<tr>
<td>

Low Relationship Low Task

- Delegating tasks
- Big picture
- Individual-made decisions
- Relatively light supervision
- Monitor activities
- Reinforce results
- Remain accessible

</td>
<td>

High Task Low Relationship

- Providing specifics – who, what, when, where, and how
- Role definition
- Predominantly one-way communications
- Leader-made decisions
- Close supervision and accountability
- Incremental instructions
- KISS – Keep it simple and specific

</td>
</tr>
</table>

Leadership Style S2: "High Task/High Relationship." S2 is referred to as "selling" because with this style the individual receives more two-way communication and socioemotional support in an attempt to gain "buy in" to the decisions which have to be made. As the leader works on "selling" the person they focus on *explaining* and *mentoring* in order to increase individual understanding of the task at hand.

Leadership Style S3: "High Relationship/Low Task." S3 is called "participating" because with this leadership style, the leader and individual share in decision making. Two-way communication and facilitating behavior from the leader allow the person to increase their willingness/security, since they already demonstrate the ability to complete the task. *Support* and *encouragement* characterize an effective use of the style S3. This style begins to empower and instill ownership by the individual in the decision making process.

Leadership Style S4: "Low Relationship/Low Task." S4 is referred to as "delegating" since this style involves letting an individual "run their own show." The leader delegates tasks since the person has demonstrated they are able and willing to accomplish the task at hand. A leader using a style S4 spends more time *tracking* and *monitoring* the individual's progress while the person gets the job done.

Figure 5
Situational Leadership®

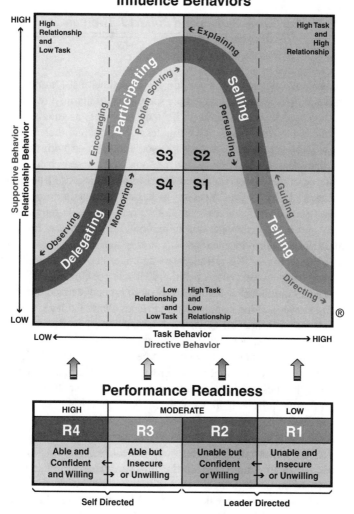

9

Crucibles of Leadership

Warren G. Bennis and Robert J. Thomas

As lifelong students of leadership, we are fascinated with the notion of what makes a leader. Why is it that certain people seem to naturally inspire confidence, loyalty, and hard work, while others (who may have just as much vision and smarts) stumble, again and again? It's a timeless question, and there's no simple answer. But we have come to believe it has something to do with the different ways that people deal with adversity. Indeed, our recent research has led us to conclude that one of the most reliable indicators and predictors of true leadership is an individual's ability to find meaning in negative events and to learn from even the most trying circumstances. Put another way, the skills required to conquer adversity and emerge stronger and more committed than ever are the same ones that make for extraordinary leaders.

Take Sidney Harman. Thirty-four years ago, the then-48-year-old businessman was holding down two executive positions. He was the chief executive of Harman Kardon (now Harman International), the audio components company he had cofounded, and he was serving as president of Friends World College, now Friends World Program, an experimental Quaker school on Long Island whose essential philosophy is that students, not their teachers, are responsible for their education. Juggling the two jobs, Harman was living what he calls a "bifurcated life," changing clothes in his car and eating lunch as he drove between Harman Kardon offices and plants and the Friends World campus. One day while at the college, he was told his company's factory in Bolivar, Tennessee, was having a crisis.

He immediately rushed to the Bolivar factory, a facility that was, as Harman now recalls, "raw, ugly, and, in many ways, demeaning." The problem, he found, had erupted in the polish and buff department, where a crew of a dozen workers, mostly African Americans, did the dull, hard work of polishing mirrors and other parts, often under unhealthy conditions. The men on the night shift were supposed to get a coffee break at 10 PM. When the buzzer that announced the workers' break went on the fritz, management arbitrarily decided to postpone the break for ten minutes, when another buzzer was scheduled to sound. But one worker, "an old black man with an almost biblical name, Noah B. Cross," had "an epiphany," as Harman describes it. "He said, literally, to his fellow workers, 'I don't work for no buzzer. The buzzer works for me. It's my job to tell me when it's ten o'clock. I got me a watch. I'm not waiting another ten minutes. I'm going on my coffee break.' And all 12 guys took their coffee break, and, of course, all hell broke loose."

The worker's principled rebellion—his refusal to be cowed by management's senseless rule—was, in turn, a revelation to Harman: "The technology is there to serve the men, not the reverse," he remembers realizing. "I suddenly had this awakening that everything I was doing at the college had appropriate applications in business." In the ensuing years, Harman revamped the factory and its workings, turning it into a kind of campus—offering classes on the premises, including piano lessons, and encouraging the workers to take most of the responsibility for running their workplace. Further, he created an environment where dissent was not only tolerated but also encouraged. The plant's lively independent newspaper, the *Bolivar Mirror,* gave workers a creative and emotional outlet—and they enthusiastically skewered Harman in its pages.

Harman had, unexpectedly, become a pioneer of participative management, a movement that continues to influence the shape of workplaces around the world. The concept wasn't a grand idea conceived in the CEO's office and imposed on the plant, Harman says. It grew organically out of his going down to Bolivar to, in his words, "put out this fire." Harman's transformation was, above all, a creative one. He had connected two seemingly unrelated ideas and created a radically different approach to management that recognized both the economic and humane benefits of a more collegial workplace. Harman went on to accomplish far more during his career. In addition to founding Harman International, he served as the deputy secretary of commerce under Jimmy Carter. But he always looked back on the incident in Bolivar as the formative event in his professional life, the moment he came into his own as a leader.

The details of Harman's story are unique, but their significance is not. In interviewing more than 40 top leaders in business and the public sector over the past three years, we were surprised to find that all of them—young and old— were able to point to intense, often traumatic, always unplanned experiences that had transformed them and had become the sources of their distinctive leadership abilities.

We came to call the experiences that shape leaders "crucibles," after the vessels medieval alchemists used in their attempts to turn base metals into gold. For the leaders we interviewed, the crucible experience was a trial and a test, a point of deep self-reflection that forced them to question who they were and what mattered to them. It required them to examine their values, question their assumptions, hone their judgment. And, invariably, they emerged from the crucible stronger and more sure of themselves and their purpose—changed in some fundamental way.

Leadership crucibles can take many forms. Some are violent, life-threatening events. Others are more prosaic episodes of self-doubt. But whatever the crucible's nature, the people we spoke with were able, like Harman, to create a narrative around it, a story of how they were challenged, met the challenge, and became better leaders. As we studied these stories, we found that they not only told us how individual leaders are shaped but also pointed to some characteristics that seem common to all leaders—characteristics that were formed, or at least exposed, in the crucible.

Learning from Difference

A crucible is, by definition, a transformative experience through which an individual comes to a new or an altered sense of identity. It is perhaps not surprising then that one of the most common types of crucibles we documented involves the experience of prejudice. Being a victim of prejudice is particularly traumatic because it forces an individual to confront a distorted picture of him- or herself, and it often unleashes profound feelings of anger, bewilderment, and even withdrawal. For all its trauma, however, the experience of prejudice is for some a clarifying event. Through it, they gain a clearer vision of who they are, the role they play, and their place in the world.

Consider, for example, Liz Altman, now a Motorola vice president, who was transformed by the year she spent at a Sony camcorder factory in rural Japan, where she faced both estrangement and sexism. It was, says Altman, "by far, the hardest thing I've ever done." The foreign culture—particularly its emphasis on groups over individuals—was both a shock and a challenge to a young American woman. It wasn't just that she felt lonely in an alien world. She had to face the daunting prospect of carving out a place for herself as the only woman engineer in a plant, and nation, where women usually serve as low-level assistants and clerks known as "office ladies."

Another woman who had come to Japan under similar circumstances had warned Altman that the only way to win the men's respect was to avoid becoming allied with the office ladies. But on her very first morning, when the bell rang for a coffee break, the men headed in one direction and the women in another—and the women saved her a place at their table, while the men ignored her. Instinct told Altman to ignore the warning rather than insult the women by rebuffing their invitation.

Over the next few days, she continued to join the women during breaks, a choice that gave her a comfortable haven from which to observe the unfamiliar office culture. But it didn't take her long to notice that some of the men spent the break at their desks reading magazines, and Altman determined that she could do the same on occasion. Finally, after paying close attention to the conversations around her, she learned that several of the men were interested in mountain biking. Because Altman wanted to buy a mountain bike, she approached them for advice. Thus, over time, she established herself as something of a free agent, sometimes sitting with the women and other times engaging with the men.

And as it happened, one of the women she'd sat with on her very first day, the department secretary, was married to one of the engineers. The secretary took it upon herself to include Altman in social gatherings, a turn of events that probably wouldn't have occurred if Altman had alienated her female coworkers on that first day. "Had I just gone to try to break in with [the men] and not had her as an ally, it would never have happened," she says.

Looking back, Altman believes the experience greatly helped her gain a clearer sense of her personal strengths and capabilities, preparing her for other difficult situations. Her tenure in Japan taught her to observe closely and to avoid jumping to conclusions based on cultural assumptions—invaluable skills in her current position at Motorola, where she leads efforts to smooth alliances with other corporate cultures, including those of Motorola's different regional operations.

Altman has come to believe that she wouldn't have been as able to do the Motorola job if she hadn't lived in a foreign country and experienced the dissonance of cultures: "... even if you're sitting in the same room, ostensibly agreeing ... unless you understand the frame of reference, you're probably missing a bunch of what's going on." Altman also credits her crucible with building her confidence—she feels that she can cope with just about anything that comes her way.

People can feel the stigma of cultural differences much closer to home, as well. Muriel ("Mickie") Siebert, the first woman to own a seat on the New York Stock Exchange, found her crucible on the Wall Street of the 1950s and 1960s, an arena so sexist that she couldn't get a job as a stockbroker until she took her first name off her résumé and substituted a genderless initial. Other than the secretaries and the occasional analyst, women were few and far between. That she was Jewish was another strike against her at a time, she points out, when most of big business was "not nice" to either women or Jews. But Siebert wasn't broken or defeated. Instead, she emerged stronger, more focused, and more determined to change the status quo that excluded her.

When we interviewed Siebert, she described her way of addressing anti-Semitism—a technique that quieted the offensive comments of her peers without destroying the relationships she needed to do her job effectively. According to Siebert, at the time it was part of doing business to have a few drinks at lunch. She remembers, "Give somebody a couple of drinks, and they would talk about the Jews." She had a greeting card she used for those occasions that went like this:

Roses are reddish,
Violets are bluish,
In case you don't know,
I am Jewish.

Siebert would have the card hand-delivered to the person who had made the anti-Semitic remarks, and on the card she had written, "Enjoyed lunch." As she recounts, "They got that card in the afternoon, and I never had to take any of that nonsense again. And I never embarrassed anyone, either." It was because she was unable to get credit for the business she was bringing in at any of the large Wall Street firms that she bought a seat on the New York Stock Exchange and started working for herself.

In subsequent years, she went on to found Muriel Siebert & Company (now Siebert Financial Corporation) and has dedicated herself to helping other people avoid some of the difficulties she faced as a young professional. A prominent advocate for women in business and a leader in developing financial products directed at women, she's also devoted to educating children about financial opportunities and responsibility.

We didn't interview lawyer and presidential adviser Vernon Jordan for this article, but he, too, offers a powerful reminder of how prejudice can prove transformational rather than debilitating. In *Vernon Can Read! A Memoir* (Public Affairs, 2001), Jordan describes the vicious baiting he was subjected to as a young man. The man who treated him in this offensive way was his employer, Robert F. Maddox. Jordan served the racist former mayor of Atlanta at dinner, in a white jacket, with a napkin over his arm. He also functioned as Maddox's chauffeur. Whenever Maddox could, he would derisively announce, "Vernon can read!" as if the literacy of a young African American were a source of wonderment.

Subjected to this type of abuse, a lesser man might have allowed Maddox to destroy him. But in his memoir, Jordan gives his own interpretation of Maddox's sadistic heckling, a tale that empowered Jordan instead of embittering him. When he looked at Maddox through the rearview mirror, Jordan did not see a powerful member of Georgia's ruling class. He saw a desperate anachronism, a person who lashed out because he knew his time was up. As Jordan writes about Maddox,

> His half-mocking, half-serious comments about my education were the death rattle of his culture. When he saw that I was . . . crafting a life for

---

Geeks and Geezers

We didn't set out to learn about crucibles. Our research for this article and for our new book, *Geeks and Geezers*, was actually designed to uncover the ways that *era* influences a leader's motivation and aspirations. We interviewed 43 of today's top leaders in business and the public sector, limiting our subjects to people born in or before 1925, or in or after 1970. To our delight, we learned a lot about how age and era affect leadership style.

Our geeks and geezers (the affectionate shorthand we eventually used to describe the two groups) had very different ideas about paying your dues, work-life balance, the role of heroes, and more. But they also shared some striking similarities—among them a love of learning and strong sense of values. Most intriguing, though, both our geeks and our geezers told us again and again how certain experiences inspired them, shaped them, and, indeed, taught them to lead. And so, as the best research often does, our work turned out to be even more interesting than we thought it would be. We continued to explore the influences of era—our findings are described in our book—but at the same time we probed for stories of these crucible experiences. These are the stories we share with you here.

myself that would make me a man in . . . ways he thought of as being a man, he was deeply unnerved.

Maddox's cruelty was the crucible that, consciously or not, Jordan imbued with redemptive meaning. Instead of lashing out or being paralyzed with hatred, Jordan saw the fall of the Old South and imagined his own future freed of the historical shackles of racism. His ability to organize meaning around a potential crisis turned it into the crucible around which his leadership was forged.

Prevailing over Darkness

Some crucible experiences illuminate a hidden and suppressed area of the soul. These are often among the harshest of crucibles, involving, for instance, episodes of illness or violence. In the case of Sidney Rittenberg, now 79, the crucible took the form of 16 years of unjust imprisonment, in solitary confinement, in Communist China. In 1949 Rittenberg was initially jailed, without explanation, by former friends in Chairman Mao Zedong's government and spent his first year in total darkness when he wasn't being interrogated. (Rittenberg later learned that his arrest came at the behest of Communist Party officials in Moscow, who had wrongly identified him as a CIA agent.) Thrown into jail, confined to a tiny, pitch-dark cell, Rittenberg did not rail or panic. Instead, within minutes, he remembered a stanza of verse, four lines recited to him when he was a small child:

> They drew a circle that shut me out,
> Heretic, rebel, a thing to flout.
> But love and I had the wit to win,
> We drew a circle that took them in!

That bit of verse (adapted from "Outwitted," a poem by Edwin Markham) was the key to Rittenberg's survival. "My God," he thought, "there's my strategy." He drew the prison guards into his circle, developing relationships that would help him adapt to his confinement. Fluent in Chinese, he persuaded the guards to deliver him books and, eventually, provide a candle so that he could read. He also decided, after his first year, to devote himself to improving his mind—making it more scientific, more pure, and more dedicated to socialism. He believed that if he raised his consciousness, his captors would understand him better. And when, over time, the years in the dark began to take an intellectual toll on him and he found his reason faltering, he could still summon fairy tales and childhood stories such as *The Little Engine That Could* and take comfort from their simple messages.

By contrast, many of Rittenberg's fellow prisoners either lashed out in anger or withdrew. "They tended to go up the wall. . . . They couldn't make it. And I think the reason was that they didn't understand . . . that happiness . . . is not a function of your circumstances; it's a function of your outlook on life."

Rittenberg's commitment to his ideals continued upon his release. His cell door opened suddenly in 1955, after his first six-year term in prison. He recounts, "Here was a representative of the central government telling me that I had been wronged, that the government was making a formal apology to me . . . and that they would do everything possible to make restitution." When his captors offered him money to start a new life in the United States or to travel in Europe, Rittenberg declined, choosing instead to stay in China and continue his work for the Communist Party.

And even after a second arrest, which put him into solitary confinement for ten years as retaliation for his support of open democracy during the Cultural Revolution, Rittenberg did not allow his spirit to be broken. Instead, he used his time in prison as an opportunity to question his belief system—in particular, his commitment to Marxism and Chairman Mao. "In that sense, prison emancipated me," he says.

Rittenberg studied, read, wrote, and thought, and he learned something about himself in the process: "I realized I had this great fear of being a turncoat, which . . . was so powerful that it prevented me from even looking at [my assumptions]. . . . Even to question was an act of betrayal. After I got out . . . the scales fell away from my eyes and I understood that . . . the basic doctrine of arriving at democracy through dictatorship was wrong."

What's more, Rittenberg emerged from prison certain that absolutely nothing in his professional life could break him and went on to start a company with his wife. Rittenberg Associates is a consulting firm dedicated to developing business ties between the United States and China. Today, Rittenberg is as committed to his ideals—if not to his view of the best way to get there—as he was 50 years ago, when he was so severely tested.

Meeting Great Expectations

Fortunately, not all crucible experiences are traumatic. In fact, they can involve a positive, if deeply challenging, experience such as having a demanding boss or mentor. Judge Nathaniel R. Jones of the U.S. Court of Appeals for the Sixth Circuit, for instance, attributes much of his success to his interaction with a splendid mentor. That mentor was J. Maynard Dickerson, a successful attorney— the first black city prosecutor in the United States—and editor of a local African-American newspaper.

Dickerson influenced Jones at many levels. For instance, the older man brought Jones behind the scenes to witness firsthand the great civil rights struggle of the 1950s, inviting him to sit in on conversations with activists like Thurgood Marshall, Walter White, Roy Wilkins, and Robert C. Weaver. Says Jones, "I was struck by their resolve, their humor . . . and their determination not to let the system define them. Rather than just feel beaten down, they turned it around." The experience no doubt influenced the many important opinions Judge Jones has written in regard to civil rights.

Dickerson was both model and coach. His lessons covered every aspect of Jones's intellectual growth and presentation of self, including schooling in what we now call "emotional intelligence." Dickerson set the highest standards for Jones, especially in the area of communication skills—a facility we've found essential to leadership. Dickerson edited Jones's early attempts at writing a sports column with respectful ruthlessness, in red ink, as Jones remembers to this day—marking up the copy so that it looked, as Jones says, "like something chickens had a fight over." But Dickerson also took the time to explain every single mistake and why it mattered.

His mentor also expected the teenage Jones to speak correctly at all times and would hiss discreetly in his direction if he stumbled. Great expectations are evidence of great respect, and as Jones learned all the complex, often subtle lessons of how to succeed, he was motivated in no small measure by his desire not to disappoint the man he still calls "Mr. Dickerson." Dickerson gave Jones the kind of intensive mentoring that was tantamount to grooming him for a kind of professional and moral succession—and Jones has indeed become an instrument for the profound societal change for which Dickerson fought so courageously as well. Jones found life-changing meaning in the attention Dickerson paid to him—attention fueled by a conviction that he, too, though only a teenager, had a vital role to play in society and an important destiny.

Another story of a powerful mentor came to us from Michael Klein, a young man who made millions in Southern California real estate while still in his teens, only to lose it by the time he turned 20 and then go on to start several other businesses. His mentor was his grandfather Max S. Klein, who created the paint-by-numbers fad that swept the United States in the 1950s and 1960s. Klein was only four or five years old when his grandfather approached him and offered to share his business expertise. Over the years, Michael Klein's grandfather taught him to learn from and to cope with change, and the two spoke by phone for an hour every day until shortly before Max Klein's death.

The Essentials of Leadership

In our interviews, we heard many other stories of crucible experiences. Take Jack Coleman, 78-year-old former president of Haverford College in Pennsylvania. He told us of one day, during the Vietnam War, when he heard that a group of students was planning to pull down the American flag and burn it—and that former members of the school's football team were going to make sure the students didn't succeed. Seemingly out of nowhere, Coleman had the idea to preempt the violence by suggesting that the protesting students take down the flag, wash it, and then put it back up—a crucible moment that even now elicits tremendous emotion in Coleman as he describes that day.

There's also Common Cause founder John W. Gardner, who died earlier this year at 89. He identified his arduous training as a Marine during World War II as the crucible in which his leadership abilities emerged. Architect Frank Gehry spoke of the biases he experienced as a Jew in college. Jeff Wilke, a general manager at a major manufacturer, told us of the day he learned that an employee had been killed in his plant—an experience that taught him that leadership was about much more than making quarterly numbers.

So, what allowed these people to not only cope with these difficult situations but also learn from them? We believe that great leaders possess four essential skills, and, we were surprised to learn, these happen to be the same skills that allow a person to find meaning in what could be a debilitating experience. First is the ability to engage others in shared meaning. Consider Sidney Harman, who dived into a chaotic work environment to mobilize employees around an entirely new approach to management. Second is a distinctive and compelling voice. Look at Jack Coleman's ability to defuse a potentially violent situation with only his words. Third is a sense of integrity (including a strong set of values). Here, we point again to Coleman, whose values prevailed even during the emotionally charged clash between peace demonstrators and the angry (and strong) former football team members.

But by far the most critical skill of the four is what we call "adaptive capacity." This is, in essence, applied creativity—an almost magical ability to transcend adversity, with all its attendant stresses, and to emerge stronger than before. It's composed of two primary qualities: the ability to grasp context, and hardiness. The ability to grasp context implies an ability to weigh a welter of factors, ranging from how very different groups of people will interpret a gesture to being able to put a situation in perspective. Without this, leaders are utterly lost, because they cannot connect with their constituents. M. Douglas Ivester, who succeeded Roberto Goizueta at Coca-Cola, exhibited a woeful inability to grasp context, lasting just 28 months on the job. For example, he demoted his highest-ranked African-American employee even as the company was losing a $200 million class-action suit brought by black employees—and this in Atlanta, a city with a powerful African-American majority. Contrast Ivester with Vernon Jordan. Jordan realized his boss's time was up—not just his time in power, but the era that formed him. And so Jordan was able to see past the insults and recognize his boss's bitterness for what it was—desperate lashing out.

Hardiness is just what it sounds like—the perseverance and toughness that enable people to emerge from devastating circumstances without losing hope. Look at Michael Klein, who experienced failure but didn't let it defeat him. He found himself with a single asset—a tiny software company he'd acquired. Klein built it into Transoft Networks, which Hewlett-Packard acquired in 1999. Consider, too, Mickie Siebert, who used her sense of humor to curtail offensive conversations. Or Sidney Rittenberg's strength during his imprisonment. He drew on his personal memories and inner strength to emerge from his lengthy prison term without bitterness.

It is the combination of hardiness and ability to grasp context that, above all, allows a person to not only survive an ordeal, but to learn from it, and to emerge stronger, more engaged, and more committed than ever. These attributes allow leaders to grow from their crucibles, instead of being destroyed by them—to find opportunity where others might find only despair. This is the stuff of true leadership.

Power and Influence

L eadership is typically defined as the process of influence. Power is defined as the potential for influence. Power is the resource that enables leaders to influence people to do things they otherwise would not do. This section includes six of the most important ideas on the topic of power and influence.

The first selection is from Niccolo Machiavelli's sixteenth-century treatise *The Prince*. Machiavelli raises the question of whether it is better to have a relationship based on love or fear. Machiavelli contends that it is best to be both loved and feared. If, however, one cannot have both, he suggests that a relationship based on love alone tends to be volatile, short lived, and easily terminated when there is no fear of retaliation. On the other hand, a relationship based on fear tends to be longer lasting because the individual must be ready to incur the sanction (pay the price) before terminating the relationship. Machiavelli warned, however, that one should be careful that this fear does not lead to hatred. Hatred often evokes overt behavior in terms of retaliation, undermining, and attempts to overthrow.

Power enables leaders to exercise influence over other people. John R. P. French Jr. and Bertram Raven, in "The Bases of Social Power," suggest that there are five major bases of power: (1) *expert power,* based on the perception that the leader possesses some special knowledge or expertise; (2) *referent power,* based on the follower's liking, admiring, or identifying with the leader; (3) *reward power,* based on the leader's ability to provide rewards for the follower; (4) *legitimate power,* based on the follower's perception that the leader has the legitimate right or authority to exercise influence over him or her; and (5) *coercive power,* based on the follower's fear that noncompliance with the leader's wishes will lead to punishment. Subsequent research on these power bases has indicated that emphasis on expert and referent power is more positively related to subordinate performance and satisfaction than utilization of reward, legitimate, or coercive power.

In "Position Power and Personal Power" from the classic book, *A Comparative Analysis of Complex Organizations,* Amitai Etzioni contends that leaders derive their power from their organizational offices or positions, their personal characteristics, or both. Position power may be coercive, remunerative, or legitimate. Personal power depends on the positive personal characteristics of the leader. Etzioni classifies leaders according to the type of power they possess and concludes by suggesting that different situations require different types of power.

Gerald R. Salancik and Jeffrey Pfeffer advance a model that contends that power is one of the few institutional mechanisms organizations can use to successfully cope with change. In the selection "Who Gets Power—and How They Hold on to It," Salancik and Pfeffer argue that power helps organizations become "aligned" with external realities to the extent that power is acquired by those subunits of the organization most able to cope with the organization's critical problems and uncertainties. These critical "contingencies" in the external environment change over time. Hence, organizations with mechanisms for sharing and redistributing power in a timely fashion have an increased capacity to be attuned with the needs and demands emanating from their environment.

James MacGregor Burns addresses the power of leadership in his Pulitzer Prize-winning book entitled *Leadership.* In the excerpt included here, he discusses why power is such a fascinating topic, and suggests that we must analyze power in the context of human interactions and relationships. Burns suggests that the two essentials of power are the motivation to utilize one's power and the resources to succeed in one's influence attempts. Also, he asserts that power is a relationship that involves the intention or purpose of both the power holder and the power recipient. Burns concludes by suggesting that the leader's power base must be relevant to those whom the leader is attempting to influence.

In "Situational Leadership and Power," Paul Hersey and Walter E. Natemeyer define power as the potential for influence. They discuss the difference between position power and personal power. Also, seven different power bases are identified and discussed:

- Coercive power
- Connection power
- Reward power
- Legitimate power
- Referent power
- Information power
- Expert power

The remainder of the article contends that there is no single best way to use power. Rather, the appropriate power bases depend on the "readiness level" of the follower. A "situational power" framework is suggested and integrated with the Situational Leadership® Model presented in section IV.

1

Is It Better to Be Loved or Feared?

Niccolo Machiavelli

. . . Every prince ought to wish to be considered kind rather than cruel. Nevertheless, he must take care to avoid misusing his kindness. Cesare Borgia was considered cruel; yet his cruelty restored Romagna, uniting it in peace and loyalty. If
this result is considered good, then he must be judged much kinder than the Florentines who, to avoid being called cruel, allowed Pistoia to be destroyed.[1] A
prince, therefore, must be indifferent to the charge of cruelty if he is to keep his
subjects loyal and united. Having set an example once or twice, he may thereafter
act far more mercifully than the princes who, through excessive kindness, allow
disorders to arise from which murder and rapine ensue. Disorders harm the entire
citizenry, while the executions ordered by a prince harm only a few individuals.
Indeed, of all princes, the newly established one can least of all escape the charge
of cruelty, for new states are encumbered with dangers. As Virgil has Dido say,

> *Res dura, et regni novitas me talia cogunt*
> *Moliri, et late fines custode tueri.*[2]

Nevertheless, he ought to be slow to believe what he hears and slow to act.
Nor should he fear imaginary dangers, but proceed with moderation, prudence,
and humanity, avoiding carelessness born of overconfidence and unbearable
harshness born of excessive distrust.

Here a question arises: whether it is better to be loved than feared, or the
reverse. The answer is, of course, that it would be best to be both loved and
feared. But since the two rarely come together, anyone compelled to choose will
find greater security in being feared than in being loved. For this can be said
about the generality of men: that they are ungrateful, fickle, dissembling, anxious

Reprinted from *The Prince,* by Niccolo Machiavelli, 1513. Bantam Classics edition, 1984.
Taken from chapter 17, "Concerning Cruelty: Whether It Is Better to Be Loved Than to Be
Feared, or the Reverse," pp. 65–67.

to flee danger, and covetous of gain. So long as you promote their advantage, they are all yours, . . . and will offer you their blood, their goods, their lives, and their children when the need for these is remote. When the need arises, however, they will turn against you. The prince who bases his security upon their word, lacking other provision, is doomed; for friendships that are gained by money, not by greatness and nobility of spirit, may well be earned, but cannot be kept; and in time of need, they will have fled your purse. Men are less concerned about offending someone they have cause to love than someone they have cause to fear. Love endures by a bond which men, being scoundrels, may break whenever it serves their advantage to do so; but fear is supported by the dread of pain, which is ever present.

Still a prince should make himself feared in such a way that, though he does not gain love, he escapes hatred; for being feared but not hated go readily together. Such a condition he may always attain if he will not touch the property of his citizens and subjects, nor their women. And if he finds it necessary to take someone's life, he should do so when there is suitable justification and manifest cause; but above all, he should refrain from the property of others, for men are quicker to forget the death of a father than the loss of a patrimony. Furthermore, excuses for seizing property are never lacking and, indeed, anyone who begins to live by plunder will always find pretexts for taking over what belongs to someone else. On the other hand, pretexts for taking someone's life arise more rarely and last a shorter time.

But when a prince is at the head of his armies and must command multitudes of soldiers, then more than ever must he be indifferent to a reputation for cruelty, for without such a reputation no army was ever held together, nor was it ever fit for combat. Among the marvelous deeds of Hannibal is numbered this one: that though he had an enormous army composed of a great variety of races fighting in a foreign land, no dissension ever arose among the troops or between the troops and their leader, either in good times or in bad. This could have had no other source but his inhuman cruelty which, together with his extraordinary qualities of leadership, made him an object of constant reverence and terror to his soldiers. To produce such an effect without this cruelty, his other qualities would have been insufficient. Writers of scant judgment in this matter have, on the one hand, admired his accomplishments and, on the other, condemned their chief source.

The proof that his other qualities would have been insufficient may be seen in the case of Scipio—a most exceptional man not only in his own times but in all remembered history—whose soldiers mutinied in Spain for no reason other than his excessive leniency, which allowed them more freedom than was consonant with military discipline.[3] Fabius Maximus reproved him for it in the Senate and called him the corrupter of Roman arms.[4] When one of his lieutenants ravaged the Locrians, Scipio neither avenged them nor took action to correct his lieutenant's insolence. This too grew out of his mild nature, so much so, in fact, that someone seeking to excuse Scipio's conduct before the Senate observed that many men have more skill in avoiding errors than in correcting them. This propensity would in time have damaged Scipio's fame and glory if he had perse-vered in it, but since he was ruled by the Senate, its potential harmfulness remained hidden, and it redounded to his glory.

Returning to the question, then, of being loved or feared, I conclude that since men love as they themselves determine but fear as their ruler determines, a wise prince must rely upon what he and not others can control. He need only strive to avoid being hated, as I said.

Notes

[1] At Pistoia in 1501 and 1502 a long smoldering rivalry between two factions, which had been encouraged by the Florentines in order to gain control of the city, broke out into rioting. The Florentine government then sent Machiavelli to settle the difficulties. At first, efforts were made to pacify the leaders of the opposing factions. When these failed, the leaders were banished from the city, but only after much bloodshed. Machiavelli had favored banishing them or executing them at the very outset.

[2] "Sore need and my new reign compel these/Deeds, to guard my borders on all sides." *Aeneid* I, 563–64.

[3] For a detailed discussion of the conduct of Hannibal and Scipio, *see The Discourses* Three, XXI.

[4] Fabius Maximus: Roman Consul and dictator, called "the Delayer" for his fight-and-run tactics against Hannibal after the Battle of Lake Trasimene (217 B.C.). Later he opposed Scipio's aggressive policy.

2

The Bases of Social Power

John R. P. French Jr. and Bertram Raven

The processes of power are pervasive, complex, and often disguised in our society. Accordingly one finds in political science, in sociology, and in social psychology a variety of distinctions among different types of social power or among qualitatively different processes of social influence.[1] Our main purpose is to identify the major types of power and to define them systematically so that we may compare them according to the changes which they produce and the other effects which accompany the use of power. The phenomena of power and influence involve a dyadic relation between two agents which may be viewed from two points of view: (a) What determines the behavior of the agent who exerts power? (b) What determines the reactions of the recipient of this behavior? We take this second point of view and formulate our theory in terms of the life space of P, the person upon whom the power is exerted. In this way we hope to define basic concepts of power which will be adequate to explain many of the phenomena of social influence, including some which have been described in other less genotypic terms.

Recent empirical work, especially on small groups, has demonstrated the necessity of distinguishing different types of power in order to account for the different effects found in studies of social influence. Yet there is no doubt that more empirical knowledge will be needed to make final decisions concerning the necessary differentiations, but this knowledge will be obtained only by research based on some preliminary theoretical distinctions. We present such preliminary concepts and some of the hypotheses they suggest.

Power, Influence, and Change

Psychological Change

Since we shall define power in terms of influence, and influence in terms of psychological change, we begin with a discussion of change. We want to define

Reprinted by permission from *Studies in Social Power*, Dorwin Cartwright, ed., 1959, pp. 150–165. Copyright © 1959, Institute for Social Research.

change at a level of generality which includes changes in behavior, opinions, attitudes, goals, needs, values and all other aspects of the person's psychological field. We shall use the word "system" to refer to any such part of the life space.[2] Following Lewin the state of a system at time 1 will be denoted $s_1(a)$.[3]

Psychological change is defined as any alteration of the state of some system a over time. The amount of change is measured by the size of the difference between the states of the system a at time 1 and at time 2: $ch(a) = s_2(a) - s_1(a)$.

Change in any psychological system may be conceptualized in terms of psychological forces. But it is important to note that the change must be coordinated to the resultant force of all the forces operating at the moment. Change in an opinion, for example, may be determined jointly by a driving force induced by another person, a restraining force corresponding to anchorage in a group opinion, and an own force stemming from the person's needs.

Social Influence

Our theory of social influence and power is limited to influence on the person, P, produced by a social agent, O, where O can be either another person, a role, a norm, a group or a part of a group. We do not consider social influence exerted on a group.

The influence of O on system a in the life space of P is defined as the resultant force on system a which has its source in an act of O. This resultant force induced by O consists of two components: a force to change the system in the direction induced by O and an opposing resistance set up by the same act of O.

By this definition the influence of O does not include P's own forces nor the forces induced by other social agents. Accordingly the "influence" of O must be clearly distinguished from O's "control" of P. O may be able to induce strong forces on P to carry out an activity (*i.e.*, O exerts strong influence on P); but if the opposing forces induced by another person or by P's own needs are stronger, then P will locomote in an opposite direction (*i.e.*, O does not have control over P). Thus psychological change in P can be taken as an operational definition of the social influence of O on P only when the effects of other forces have been eliminated.

It is assumed that any system is interdependent with other parts of the life space so that a change in one may produce changes in others. However, this theory focuses on the primary changes in a system which are produced directly by social influence; it is less concerned with secondary changes which are indirectly effected in the other systems or with primary changes produced by nonsocial influences.

Commonly social influence takes place through an intentional act on the part of O. However, we do not want to limit our definition of "act" to such conscious behavior. Indeed, influence might result from the passive presence of O, with no evidence of speech or overt movement. A policeman's standing on a corner may be considered an act of an agent for the speeding motorist. Such acts of the inducing agent will vary in strength, for O may not always utilize all of his power. The policeman, for example, may merely stand and watch or act more strongly by blowing his whistle at the motorist.

The influence exerted by an act need not be in the direction intended by O. The direction of the resultant force on P will depend on the relative magnitude of the induced force set up by the act of O and the resisting force in the opposite direction which is generated by that same act. In cases where O intends to influence P in a given direction, a resultant force in the same direction may be termed positive influence whereas a resultant force in the opposite direction may be termed negative influence.

If O produces the intended change, he has exerted positive control; but if he produces a change in the opposite direction, as for example in the negativism of young children or in the phenomena of negative reference groups, he has exerted negative control.

Social Power

The *strength of power* of O/P in some system *a* is defined as the maximum potential ability of O to influence P in *a*.

By this definition influence is kinetic power, just as power is potential influence. It is assumed that O is capable of various acts which, because of some more or less enduring relation to P, are able to exert influence on P.[4] O's power is measured by his maximum possible influence, though he may often choose to exert less than his full power.

An equivalent definition of power may be stated in terms of the resultant of two forces set up by the act of O: one in the direction of O's influence attempt and another resisting force in the opposite direction. Power is the maximum resultant of these two forces:

$$\text{Power of O / P}(a) = \left(f_{a,x} - f_{\overline{a,x}} \right)^{\max}$$

where the source of both forces is an act of O.

Thus the power of O with respect to system *a* of P is equal to the maximum resultant force of two forces set up by any possible act of O: (a) the force which O can set up on the system *a* to change in the direction x, (b) the resisting force[5] in the opposite direction. Whenever the first component force is greater than the second, positive power exists; but if the second component force is greater than the first, then O has negative power over P.

It is necessary to define power with respect to a specified system because the power of O/P may vary greatly from one system to another. O may have great power to control the behavior of P but little power to control his opinions. Of course a high power of O/P does not imply a low power of P/O; the two variables are conceptually independent.

For certain purposes it is convenient to define the range of power as the set of all systems within which O has power of strength greater than zero. A husband may have a broad range of power over his wife, but a narrow range of power over his employer. We shall use the term "magnitude of power" to denote the summation of O's power over P in all systems of his range.

The Dependence of s(a) on O

Several investigators have been concerned with differences between super-ficial conformity and "deeper" changes produced by social influence.[6] The kinds of systems which are changed and the stability of these changes have been han-dled by distinctions such as "public vs. private attitudes," "overt vs. covert behavior," "compliance vs. internalization," and "own vs. induced forces." Though stated as dichotomies, all of these distinctions suggest an underlying dimension of the degree of dependence of the state of a system on O.

We assume that any change in the state of a system is produced by a change in some factor upon which it is functionally dependent. The state of an opinion, for example, may change because of a change either in some internal factor such as a need or in some external factor such as the arguments of O. Likewise the maintenance of the same state of a system is produced by the stability or lack of change in the internal and external factors. In general, then, psychological change and stability can be conceptualized in terms of dynamic dependence. Our interest is focused on the special case of dependence on an external agent, O.[7]

In many cases the initial state of the system has the character of a quasi-sta-tionary equilibrium with a central force held around $s_1(a)$.[8] In such cases we may derive a tendency toward retrogression to the original state as soon as the force induced by O is removed.[9] Let us suppose that O exerts influence producing a new state of the system, $s_2(a)$. Is $s_2(a)$ now dependent on the continued presence of O? In principle we could answer this question by removing any traces of O from the life space of P and by observing the consequent state of the system at time 3. If $s_3(a)$ retrogresses completely back to $s_1(a)$, then we may conclude that maintenance of $s_2(a)$ was completely dependent on O; but if $s_3(a)$ equals $s_2(a)$, this lack of change shows that $s_2(a)$ has become completely independent of O. In general the degree of dependence of $s_2(a)$ on O, following O's influence, may be defined as equal to the amount of retrogression following the removal of O from the life space of P:

$$\text{Degree of dependence of } s_2(a) \text{ on } O = s_2(a) - s_3(a).$$

A given degree of dependence at time 2 may later change, for example, through the gradual weakening of O's influence. At this later time, the degree of dependence of $s_4(a)$ on O, would still be equal to the amount of retrogression toward the initial state of equilibrium $s_1(a)$. Operational measures of the degree of dependence on O will, of course, have to be taken under conditions where all other factors are held constant.

Consider the example of three separated employees who have been work-ing at the same steady level of production despite normal, small fluctuations in the work environment. The supervisor orders each to increase his production, and the level of each goes up from 100 to 115 pieces per day. After a week of produc-ing at the new rate of 115 pieces per day, the supervisor is removed for a week. The production of employee A immediately returns to 100 but B and C return to only 110 pieces per day. Other things being equal, we can infer that A's new rate was completely dependent on his supervisor whereas the new rate of B and C was dependent on the supervisor only to the extent of 5 pieces. Let us further assume that when the supervisor returned, the production of B and of C returned to 115 without further orders from the supervisor. Now another month goes by during which B and C maintain a steady 115 pieces per day. However, there is a difference between them: B's level of production still depends on O to the extent of 5 pieces whereas C has come to rely on his own sense of obligation to obey the order of his legitimate supervisor rather than on the supervisor's external pressure for the maintenance of his 115 pieces per day. Accordingly, the next time the supervisor departs, B's production again drops to 110 but C's remains at 115 pieces per day. In cases like employee B, the degree of dependence is contingent on the perceived probability that O will observe the state of the system and note P's conformity.[10] The level of observability will in turn depend on both the nature of the system (*e.g.*, the difference between a covert opinion and overt behavior) and on the environmental barriers to observation (*e.g.*, O is too far away from P). In other cases, for example that of employee C, the new behavior pattern is highly dependent on his supervisor, but the degree of dependence of the new state will be related not to the level of observability but rather to factors inside P, in this case a sense of duty to perform an act legitimately prescribed by O. The internalization of social norms is a related process of decreasing degree of dependence of behavior on an external O and increasing dependence on an internal value; it is usually assumed that internalization is accompanied by a decrease in the effects of level of observability.[11]

The concepts "dependence of a system on O" and "observability as a basis for dependence" will be useful in understanding the stability of conformity. In the next section we shall discuss various types of power and the types of conformity which they are likely to produce.

The Bases of Power

By the basis of power we mean the relationship between O and P which is the source of that power. It is rare that we can say with certainty that a given empirical case of power is limited to one source. Normally, the relation between O and P will be characterized by several qualitatively different variables which are bases of power.[12] Although there are undoubtedly many possible bases of power which may be distinguished, we shall here define five which seem especially common and important. These five bases of O's power are: (1) reward power, based on P's perception that O has the ability to mediate rewards for him; (2) coercive power, based on P's perception that O has the ability to mediate punishments for him; (3) legitimate power, based on the perception by P that O has a legitimate right to prescribe behavior for him; (4) referent power, based on P's identification with O; (5) expert power, based on the perception that O has some special knowledge or expertness.

Our first concern is to define the bases which give rise to a given type of power. Next, we describe each type of power according to its strength, range, and the degree of dependence of the new state of the system which is most likely to occur with each type of power. We shall also examine the other effects which the exercise of a given type of power may have upon P and his relationship to O. Finally, we shall point out the interrelationships between different types of power, and the effects of use of one type of power by O upon other bases of power which he might have over P. Thus we shall both define a set of concepts and propose a series of hypotheses. Most of these hypotheses have not been systematically tested, although there is a good deal of evidence in favor of several. No attempt will be made to summarize that evidence here.

Reward Power

Reward power is defined as power whose basis is the ability to reward. The strength of the reward power of O/P increases with the magnitude of the rewards which P perceives that O can mediate for him. Reward power depends on O's ability to administer positive valences and to remove or decrease negative valences. The strength of reward power also depends upon the probability that O can mediate the reward, as perceived by P. A common example of reward power is the addition of piece-work rate in the factory as an incentive to increase production.

The new state of the system induced by a promise of reward (for example the factory worker's increased level of production) will be highly dependent on O. Since O mediates the reward, he controls the probability that P will receive it. Thus P's new rate of production will be dependent on his subjective probability that O will reward him for conformity minus his subjective probability that O will reward him even if he returns to his old level. Both probabilities will be greatly affected by the level of observability of P's behavior. Incidentally, a piece rate often seems to have more effect on production than a merit rating system because it yields a higher probability of reward for conformity and a much lower probability of reward for nonconformity.

The utilization of actual rewards (instead of promises) by O will tend over time to increase the attraction of P toward O and therefore the referent power of O over P. As we shall note later, such referent power will permit O to induce changes which are relatively independent. Neither rewards nor promises will arouse resistance in P, provided P considers it legitimate for O to offer rewards.

The range of reward power is specific to those regions within which O can reward P for conforming. The use of rewards to change systems within the range of reward power tends to increase reward power by increasing the probability attached to future promises. However, unsuccessful attempts to exert reward power outside the range of power would tend to decrease the power; for example if O offers to reward P for performing an impossible act, this will reduce for P the probability of receiving future rewards promised by O.

Coercive Power

Coercive power is similar to reward power in that it also involves O's ability to manipulate the attainment of valences. Coercive power of O/P stems from the expectation on the part of P that he will be punished by O if he fails to conform to the influence attempt. Thus negative valences will exist in given regions of P's life space, corresponding to the threatened punishment by O. The strength of coercive power depends on the magnitude of the negative valence of the threatened punishment multiplied by the perceived probability that P can avoid the punishment by conformity, *i.e.*, the probability of punishment for nonconformity minus the probability of punishment for conformity.[13] Just as an offer of a piece-rate bonus in a factory can serve as a basis for reward power, so the ability to fire a worker if he falls below a given level of production will result in coercive power.

Coercive power leads to dependent change also; and the degree of dependence varies with the level of observability of P's conformity. An excellent illustration of coercive power leading to dependent change is provided by a clothes presser in a factory observed by Coch and French.[14] As her efficiency rating climbed above average for the group the other workers began to "scapegoat" her. That the resulting plateau in her production was not independent of the group was evident once she was removed from the presence of the other workers. Her production immediately climbed to new heights.[15]

At times, there is some difficulty in distinguishing between reward power and coercive power. Is the withholding of a reward really equivalent to a punishment? Is the withdrawal of punishment equivalent to a reward? The answer must be a psychological one—it depends upon the situation as it exists for P. But ordinarily we would answer these questions in the affirmative; for P, receiving a reward is a positive valence as is the relief of suffering. There is some evidence that conformity to group norms in order to gain acceptance (reward power) should be distinguished from conformity as a means of forestalling rejection (coercive power).[16]

The distinction between these two types of power is important because the dynamics are different. The concept of "sanctions" sometimes lumps the two together despite their opposite effects. While reward power may eventually result in an independent system, the effects of coercive power will continue to be dependent. Reward power will tend to increase the attraction of P toward O; coercive power will decrease this attraction.[17] The valence of the region of behavior will become more negative, acquiring some negative valence from the threatened punishment. The negative valence of punishment would also spread to other regions of the life space. Lewin has pointed out this distinction between the effects of rewards and punishment.[18] In the case of threatened punishment, there will be a resultant force on P to leave the field entirely. Thus, to achieve conformity, O must not only place a strong negative valence in certain regions through threat of punishment, but O must also introduce restraining forces, or other strong valences, so as to prevent P from withdrawing completely from O's range of coercive power. Otherwise the probability of receiving the punishment, if P does not conform, will be too low to be effective.

Legitimate Power

Legitimate power is probably the most complex of those treated here, embodying notions from the structural sociologist, the group-norm and role oriented social psychologist, and the clinical psychologist.

There has been considerable investigation and speculation about socially prescribed behavior, particularly that which is specified to a given role or position. Linton distinguishes group norms according to whether they are universals for everyone in the culture, alternatives (the individual having a choice as to whether or not to accept them), or specialties (specific to given positions).[19] Whether we speak of internalized norms, role prescriptions and expectations,[20] or internalized pressures,[21] the fact remains that each individual sees certain regions toward which he should locomote, some regions toward which he should not locomote, and some regions toward which he may locomote if they are generally attractive for him. This applies to specific behaviors in which he may, should, or should not engage; it applies to certain attitudes or beliefs which he may, should, or should not hold. The feeling of "oughtness" may be an internalization from his parents, from his teachers, from his religion, or may have been logically developed from some idiosyncratic system of ethics. He will speak of such behaviors with expressions like "should," "ought to," or "has a right to." In many cases, the original source of the requirement is not recalled.

Though we have oversimplified such evaluations of behavior with a positive-neutral-negative trichotomy, the evaluation of behaviors by the person is really more one of degree. This dimension of evaluation we shall call "legitimacy." Conceptually, we may think of legitimacy as a valence in a region which is induced by some internalized norm or value. This value has the same conceptual property as power, namely an ability to induce force fields.[22] It may or may not be correct that values (or the super-ego) are internalized parents, but at least they can set up force fields which have a phenomenal "oughtness" similar to a parent's prescription. Like a value, a need can also induce valences (*i.e.*, force fields) in P's psychological environment, but these valences have more the phenomenal character of noxious or attractive properties of the object or activity. When a need induces a valence in P, for example, when a need makes an object attractive to P, this attraction applies to P but not to other persons. When a value induces a valence, on the other hand, it not only sets up forces on P to engage in the activity, but P may feel that all others ought to behave in the same way. Among other things, this evaluation applies to the legitimate right of some other individual or group to prescribe behavior or beliefs for a person even though the other cannot apply sanctions.

Legitimate power of O/P is here defined as that power which stems from internalized values in P which dictate that O has a legitimate right to influence P and that P has an obligation to accept this influence. We note that legitimate power is very similar to the notion of legitimacy of authority which has long been explored by sociologists, particularly by Weber,[23] and more recently by Goldhammer and Shils.[24] However, legitimate power is not always a role relation: P may accept an induction from O simply because he had previously promised to help O and he values his work too much to break the promise. In all cases, the notion of legitimacy involves some sort of code or standard, accepted by the individual, by virtue of which the external agent can assert his power. We shall attempt to describe a few of these values here.

Bases for legitimate power. Cultural values constitute one common basis for the legitimate power of one individual over another. O has characteristics which are specified by the culture as giving him the right to prescribe behavior for P, who may not have these characteristics. These bases, which Weber has called the authority of the "eternal yesterday," include such things as age, intelligence, caste, and physical characteristics.[25] In some cultures, the aged are granted the right to prescribe behavior for others in practically all behavior areas. In most cultures, there are certain areas of behavior in which a person of one sex is granted the right to prescribe behavior for the other sex.

Acceptance of the social structure is another basis for legitimate power. If P accepts as right the social structure of his group, organization, or society, especially the social structure involving a hierarchy of authority, P will accept the legitimate authority of O who occupies a superior office in the hierarchy. Thus legitimate power in a formal organization is largely a relationship between offices rather than between persons. And the acceptance of an office as *right* is a basis for legitimate power—a judge has a right to levy fines, a foreman should assign work, a priest is justified in prescribing religious beliefs, and it is the management's prerogative to make certain decisions.[26] However, legitimate power also involves the perceived right of the person to hold the office.

Designation by a legitimizing agent is a third basis for legitimate power. An influencer O may be seen as legitimate in prescribing behavior for P because he has been granted such power by a legitimizing agent whom P accepts. Thus a department head may accept the authority of his vice-president in a certain area because that authority has been specifically delegated by the president. An election is perhaps the most common example of a group's serving to legitimize the authority of one individual or office for other individuals in the group. The success of such legitimizing depends upon the acceptance of the legitimizing agent and procedure. In this case it depends ultimately on certain democratic values concerning election procedures. The election process is one of legitimizing a person's right to an office which already has a legitimate range of power associated with it.

Range of legitimate power of O/P. The areas in which legitimate power may be exercised are generally specified along with the designation of that power. A job description, for example, usually specifies supervisory activities and also designates the person to whom the job-holder is responsible for the duties described. Some bases for legitimate authority carry with them a very broad range. Culturally derived bases for legitimate power are often especially broad. It is not uncommon to find cultures in which a member of a given caste can legitimately prescribe behavior for all members of lower castes in practically all regions. More common, however, are instances of legitimate power where the range is specifically and narrowly prescribed. A sergeant in the army is given a specific set of regions within which he can legitimately prescribe behavior for his men.

The attempted use of legitimate power which is outside of the range of legitimate power will decrease the legitimate power of the authority figure. Such use of power which is not legitimate will also decrease the attractiveness of O.[27]

Legitimate power and influence. The new state of the system which results from legitimate power usually has high dependence on O though it may become independent. Here, however, the degree of dependence is not related to the level of observability. Since legitimate power is based on P's values, the source of the forces induced by O include both these internal values and O. O's induction serves to activate the values and to relate them to the system which is influenced, but thereafter the new state of the system may become directly dependent on the values with no mediation by O. Accordingly this new state will be relatively stable and consistent across varying environmental situations since P's values are more stable than his psychological environment.

We have used the term legitimate not only as a basis for the power of an agent, but also to describe the general behaviors of a person. Thus, the individual P may also consider the legitimacy of the attempts to use other types of power by O. In certain cases, P will consider that O has a legitimate right to threaten punishment for nonconformity; in other cases, such use of coercion would not be seen as legitimate. P might change in response to coercive power of O, but it will make a considerable difference in his attitude and conformity if O is not seen as having a legitimate right to use such coercion. In such cases, the attraction of P for O will be particularly diminished, and the influence attempt will arouse more resistance.[28] Similarly the utilization of reward power may vary in legitimacy; the word "bribe," for example, denotes an illegitimate reward.

Referent Power

The referent power of O/P has its basis in the identification of P with O. By identification, we mean a feeling of oneness of P with O, or a desire for such an identity. If O is a person toward whom P is highly attracted, P will have a desire to become closely associated with O. If O is an attractive group, P will have a feeling of membership or a desire to join. If P is already closely associated with O, he will want to maintain this relationship.[29] P's identification with O can be established or maintained if P behaves, believes, and perceives as O does. Accordingly O has the ability to influence P, even though P may be unaware of this referent power. A verbalization of such power by P might be, "I am like O, and therefore I shall behave or believe as O does," or "I want to be like O, and I will be more like O if I behave or believe as O does." The stronger the identification of P with O, the greater the referent power of O/P.

Similar types of power have already been investigated under a number of different formulations. Festinger points out that in an ambiguous situation, the individual seeks some sort of "social reality" and may adopt the cognitive structure of the individual or group with which he identifies.[30] In such a case, the lack of clear structure may be threatening to the individual and the agreement of his beliefs with those of a reference group will both satisfy his need for structure and give him added security through increased identification with his group.[31]

We must try to distinguish between referent power and other types of power which might be operative at the same time. If a member is attracted to a group and he conforms to its norms only because he fears ridicule or expulsion from the group for nonconformity, we would call this coercive power. On the other hand if he conforms in order to obtain praise for conformity, it is a case of reward power. The basic criterion for distinguishing referent power from both coercive and reward power is the mediation of the punishment and the reward by O: to the extent that O mediates the sanctions (*i.e.*, has means control over P) we are dealing with coercive and reward power; but to the extent that P avoids discomfort or gains satisfaction by conformity based on identification, regardless of O's responses, we are dealing with referent power. Conformity with majority opinion is sometimes based on a respect for the collective wisdom of the group, in which case it is expert power. It is important to distinguish these phenomena, all grouped together elsewhere as "pressures toward uniformity," since the type of change which occurs will be different for different bases of power.

The concepts of "reference group"[32] and "prestige suggestion" may be treated as instances of referent power. In this case, O, the prestigious person or group, is valued by P; because P desires to be associated or identified with O, he will assume attitudes or beliefs held by O. Similarly a negative reference group which O dislikes and evaluates negatively may exert negative influence on P as a result of negative referent power.

It has been demonstrated that the power which we designate as referent power is especially great when P is attracted to O.[33] In our terms, this would mean that the greater the attraction, the greater the identification, and consequently the greater the referent power. In some cases, attraction or prestige may have a specific basis, and the range of referent power will be limited accordingly: a group of campers may have great referent power over a member regarding campcraft, but considerably less effect on other regions.[34] However, we hypothesize that the greater the attraction of P toward O, the broader the range of referent power of O/P.

The new state of a system produced by referent power may be dependent on or independent of O; but the degree of dependence is not affected by the level of observability to O.[35] In fact, P is often not consciously aware of the referent power which O exerts over him. There is probably a tendency for some of these dependent changes to become independent of O quite rapidly.

Expert Power

The strength of the expert power of O/P varies with the extent of the knowledge or perception which P attributes to O within a given area. Probably P evaluates O's expertness in relation to his own knowledge as well as against an absolute standard. In any case expert power results in primary social influence on

P's cognitive structure and probably not on other types of systems. Of course changes in the cognitive structure can change the direction of forces and hence of locomotion, but such a change of behavior is secondary social influence. Expert power has been demonstrated experimentally.[36] Accepting an attorney's advice in legal matters is a common example of expert influence; but there are many instances based on much less knowledge, such as the acceptance by a stranger of directions given by a native villager.

Expert power, where O need not be a member of P's group, is called "informational power" by Deutsch and Gerard.[37] This type of expert power must be distinguished from influence based on the content of communication as described by Hovland et al.[38] The influence of the content of a communication upon an opinion is presumably a secondary influence produced after the *primary* influence (*i.e.*, the acceptance of the information). Since power is here defined in terms of the primary changes, the influence of the content on a related opinion is not a case of expert power as we have defined it, but the initial acceptance of the validity of the content does seem to be based on expert power or referent power. In other cases, however, so-called facts may be accepted as self-evident because they fit into P's cognitive structure; if this impersonal acceptance of the truth of the fact is independent of the more or less enduring relationship between O and P, then P's acceptance of the fact is not an actualization of expert power. Thus we distinguish between expert power based on the credibility of O and informational influence which is based on characteristics of the stimulus such as the logic of the argument or the "self-evident facts."

Wherever expert influence occurs it seems to be necessary both for P to think that O knows and for P to trust that O is telling the truth (rather than trying to deceive him).

Expert power will produce a new cognitive structure which is initially relatively dependent on O, but informational influence will produce a more independent structure. The former is likely to become more independent with the passage of time. In both cases the degree of dependence on O is not affected by the level of observability.

The "sleeper effect"[39] is an interesting case of a change in the degree of dependence of an opinion on O. An unreliable O (who probably had negative referent power but some positive expert power) presented "facts" which were accepted by the subjects and which would normally produce secondary influence on their opinions and beliefs. However, the negative referent power aroused resistance and resulted in negative social influence on their beliefs (*i.e.*, set up a force in the direction opposite to the influence attempt), so that there was little change in the subjects' opinions. With the passage of time, however, the subjects tended to forget the identity of the negative communicator faster than they forgot the contents of his communication, so there was a weakening of the negative referent influence and a consequent delayed positive change in the subjects' beliefs in the direction of the influence attempt ("sleeper effect"). Later, when the identity of the negative communicator was experimentally reinstated, these resisting forces were reinstated, and there was another negative change in belief in a direction opposite to the influence attempt.[40]

The range of expert power, we assume, is more delimited than that of referent power. Not only is it restricted to cognitive systems but the expert is seen as having superior knowledge or ability in very specific areas, and his power will be limited to these areas, though some "halo effect" might occur. Recently, some of our renowned physical scientists have found quite painfully that their expert power in physical sciences does not extend to regions involving international politics. Indeed, there is some evidence that the attempted exertion of expert power outside of the range of expert power will reduce that expert power. An undermining of confidence seems to take place.

Summary

We have distinguished five types of power: referent power, expert power, reward power, coercive power, and legitimate power. These distinctions led to the following hypotheses:

1. For all five types, the stronger the basis of power the greater the power.

2. For any type of power the size of the range may vary greatly, but in general referent power will have the broadest range.

3. Any attempt to utilize power outside the range of power will tend to reduce the power.

4. A new state of a system produced by reward power or coercive power will be highly dependent on O, and the more observable P's conformity the more dependent the state. For the other three types of power, the new state is usually dependent, at least in the beginning, but in any case the level of observability has no effect on the degree of dependence.

5. Coercion results in decreased attraction of P toward O and high resistance; reward power results in increased attraction and low resistance.

6. The more legitimate the coercion the less it will produce resistance and decreased attraction.

Notes

[1] S. E. Asch, *Social Psychology* (New York: Prentice-Hall, 1952). L. Festinger, "An Analysis of Compliant Behavior," in *Group Relations at the Crossroads*, eds. M. Sherif and M. O. Wilson (New York: Harper, 1953), pp. 232–56. H. Goldhammer and E. A. Shils, "Types of Power and Status," *Amer. J. Sociol.*, Vol. 45 (1939): 171–78. M. Jahoda, "Psychological Issues in Civil Liberties," *Amer. Psychologist*, Vol. 11 (1956): 234–40. H. Kelman, "Three Processes of Acceptance of Social Influence: Compliance, Identification and Internalization" (Paper read at the meetings of the American Psychological Association, August 1956). R. Linton, *The Cultural Background of Personality* (New York: Appleton-Century-Crofts, 1945). R. Lippitt *et al.*, "The Dynamics of Power," *Hum. Relat.*, Vol. 5 (1952): 37–64. B. Russell, *Power: A New Social Analysis* (New York: Norton, 1938). E. P. Torrance and R. Mason, "Instructor Effort to Influence: An Experimental Evaluation of Six Approaches" (Paper presented at USAF-NRC Symposium on Personnel, Training, and Human Engineering, Washington, DC, 1956).

[2] The word "system" is here used to refer to a whole or to a part of the whole.

[3] K. Lewin, *Field Theory in Social Science* (New York: Harper, 1951).

[4] The concept of power has the conceptual property of *potentiality*; but it seems useful to restrict this potential influence to more or less enduring power relations between O and P by excluding from the definition of power those cases where the potential influence is so momentary or so changing that it cannot be predicted from the existing relationship. Power is a useful concept for describing social structure only if it has a certain stability over time; it is useless if every momentary social stimulus is viewed as actualizing social power.

[5] We define resistance to an attempted induction as a force in the opposite direction which is set up by the same act of O. It must be distinguished from opposition which is defined as existing opposing forces which do not have their source in the same act of O. For example, a boy might resist his mother's order to eat spinach because of the manner of the induction attempt, and at the same time he might oppose it because he didn't like spinach.

[6] Asch, *op. cit.* J. E. Dittes and H. H. Kelley, "Effects of Different Conditions of Acceptance upon Conformity to Group Norms," *J. Abnorm. Soc. Psychol.*, Vol. 53 (1956): 100–107. Festinger, "An Analysis . . . ," *op. cit.* J. R. P. French, Jr., G. Levinger, and H. W. Morrison, "The Legitimacy of Coercive Power" (In preparation). J. R. P. French, Jr. and B. H. Raven, "An Experiment in Legitimate and Coercive Power" (In preparation). Jahoda, *op. cit.* D. Katz and R. L. Schank, *Social Psychology* (New York: Wiley, 1938). H. H. Kelley and E. H. Volkart, "The Resistance to Change of Group-Anchored Attitudes," *Amer. Soc. Rev.*, Vol. 17 (1952): 453–65. Kelman, *op. cit.* Lewin, *Field . . . op. cit.* B. H. Raven and J. R. P. French, Jr., "Group Support, Legitimate Power, and Social Influence," *J. Person.*, Vol. 26 (1958): 400–409. R. Rommetveit, *Social Norms and Roles* (Minneapolis: University of Minnesota Press, 1953).

[7] J. G. March, "An Introduction to the Theory and Measurement of Influence," *Amer. Polit. Sci. Rev.*, Vol. 49 (1955): 431–51.

[8] Lewin, *Field . . . op. cit.*, p. 106.

[9] J. G. Miller, "Toward a General Theory for the Behavioral Sciences," *Amer. Psychologist*, Vol. 10 (1955): 513–31 assumes that all living systems have this character. However, it may be that some systems in the life space do not have this elasticity.

[10] Dittes and Kelley, *op. cit.* Festinger, "An Analysis . . ." *op. cit.* French, Levinger, and Morrison, *op. cit.* French and Raven, *op. cit.* Kelman, *op. cit.*

[11] Rommetveit, *op. cit.*

[12] Lippitt *et al.*, *op. cit.*, chapter 11.

[13] French, Levinger, and Morrison, *op. cit.*

[14] L. Coch and J. R. P. French, Jr., "Overcoming Resistance to Change," *Hum. Relat.*, Vol. 1 (1948): 512–32.

[15] Though the primary influence of coercive power is dependent, it often produces secondary changes which are independent. Brainwashing, for example, utilizes coercive power to produce many primary changes in the life space of the prisoner, but these dependent changes can lead to identification with the aggressor and hence to secondary changes in ideology which are independent.

[16] Dittes and Kelley, *op. cit.*

[17] French, Levinger, and Morrison, *op. cit.* French and Raven, *op. cit.*

[18] K. Lewin, *Dynamic Theory of Personality* (New York: McGraw-Hill, 1935), pp. 114–70.

[19] Linton, *op. cit.*

[20] T. M. Newcomb, *Social Psychology* (New York: Dryden, 1950).

[21] P. G. Herbst, "Analysis and Measurement of a Situation," *Hum. Relat.*, Vol. 2 (1953): 113–40.

[22] Lewin, *Field . . . op cit.*, pp. 40–41.

[23] M. Weber, *The Theory of Social and Economic Organization* (Oxford: Oxford University Press, 1947).

[24] Goldhammer and Shils, *op. cit.*

[25] Weber, *op. cit.*

[26] J. R. P. French, Jr., Joachim Israel, and Dagfinn Ås, "Arbeidernes Medvirkning i Industribedriften. En Eksperimentell Undersrkelse." Oslo, Norway: Institute for Social Research, 1957).

[27] French, Levinger, and Morrison, *op. cit.* French and Raven, *op. cit.* Raven and French, *op. cit.*

[28] French, Levinger, and Morrison, *op. cit.*

[29] E. Stotland *et al.*, "Studies on the Effects of Identification" (Forthcoming, University of Michigan, Institute for Social Research). Torrance and Mason, *op. cit.*

[30] L. Festinger, "Informal Social Communication," *Psychol. Rev.*, Vol. 57 (1950): 271–82.

[31] G. M. Hochbaum, "Self-Confidence and Reactions to Group Pressures," *Amer. Soc. Rev.*, Vol. 19 (1954): 678–87. J. M. Jackson and H. D. Saltzstein, "The Effect of Person-Group Relationships on Conformity Processes," *J. Abnorm. Soc. Psychol.*, Vol. 57 (1959): 17–24.

[32] G. E. Swanson, T. M. Newcomb, and E. L. Hartley, *Readings in Social Psychology* (New York: Henry Holt, 1952).

[33] K. W. Back, "Influence through Social Communication," *J. Abnorm. Soc. Psychol.*, Vol. 46 (1951): 9–23. Festinger, *op. cit.* L. Festinger *et al.*, "The Influence Process in the Presence of Extreme Deviates," *Hum. Relat.*, Vol. 5 (1952): 327–46. L. Festinger, S. Schachter, and K. Back, "The Operation of Group Standards," in *Group Dynamics: Research and Theory*, eds. D. Cartwright and A. Zander (Evanston, IL: Row, Peterson, 1953), pp. 204–23. H. B. Gerard, "The Anchorage of Opinions in Face-to-Face Groups," *Hum. Relat.*, Vol. 7 (1954): 313–25. Kelman, *op. cit.* Lippitt, *et al.*, *op. cit.*

[34] Lippitt *et al.*, *op. cit.*

[35] Festinger, "An Analysis . . ." *op. cit.* Kelman, *op. cit.*

[36] Festinger *et al.*, *op. cit.* H. T. Moore, "The Comparative Influence of Majority and Expert Opinion," *Amer. J. Psychol.*, Vol. 32 (1921): 16–20.

[37] M. Deutsch and H. B. Gerard, "A Study of Normative and Informational Influences upon Individual Judgment," *J. Abnorm. Soc. Psychol.*, Vol. 51 (1955): 629–36.

[38] C. I. Hovland, A. A. Lumsdaine, and F. D. Sheffield, *Experiments on Mass Communication* (Princeton, NJ: Princeton University Press, 1949). C. I. Hovland and W. Weiss, "The Influence of Source Credibility on Communication Effectiveness," *Public Opinion Quarterly*, Vol. 15 (1951): 635–50. Kelman, *op. cit.* H. Kelman and C. I. Hovland, "'Reinstatement' of the Communicator in Delayed Measurement of Opinion Change," *J. Abnorm. Soc. Psychol.*, Vol. 48 (1953): 327–35.

[39] Hovland and Weiss, *op. cit.* Kelman and Hovland, *op. cit.*

[40] Kelman and Hovland, *op. cit.*

3

Position Power and Personal Power

Amitai Etzioni

Sources of Power

Elites are groups of people who have direct power over lower organizational participants. Elites differ according to the *source of their power,* which may be derived from their organizational offices *(position power),* personal characteristics *(personal power),* or both.

Power derived from the person's office *(position power)* may be coercive (e.g., the guard's right to use a gun), remunerative (e.g., the foreman's right to recommend a pay increase), or normative (e.g., the pastor's right to administer the sacrament). People whose power is derived mainly from their position in the organization are referred to as *officers.* People whose power is derived from their personal characteristics *(personal power)* are referred to as *leaders* as long as the kind of power involved is normative.

People who occupy organizational offices which entail power, and who also have personal power over their subordinates, are referred to as *formal leaders.* Thus, in the terms used here, it makes sense to state that a formal leader leads an informal group. People within the organization who have personal but not official power over lower participants are referred to as *informal leaders.*

The same person may have official power over some subordinates and personal influence as well over others. Moreover, he may be an "officer" to some of his subordinates, a formal leader for some others, and an informal leader of participants of his own rank over whom he has no official power. In the following discussion elite members are classified by their relationship to the majority of their subordinates.

Excerpt adapted from *A Comparative Analysis of Complex Organizations*, pp. 153–155 by Amitai Etzioni. Reprinted with the permission of The Free Press, a Division of Simon & Schuster, Inc. Copyright © 1961 by The Free Press. Copyright © 1975 by Amitai Etzioni. All rights reserved.

Types of Elites

We shall, for the sake of convenience, refer here to the formal leaders and officers on the lower organizational level simply as "organizational elites." The informal leaders constitute a nonorganizational elite, since their power is not derived from the organization.

The difference among the three types of elites becomes evident in uninstitutionalized change or crisis situations. Only leaders—formal or informal—succeed in maintaining compliance in such situations, when compliance beyond the boundaries of the bureaucratic "zone of indifference" is required. Informal leaders have only personal power to rely on; hence their power tends to be less stable and their influence less institutionalized than that of officers or formal leaders. Therefore, it is difficult to rely on informal leaders for control of routine and continuous performance, or in any situations in which personal, particularistic bonds are constantly undermined—for example, in a military replacement system with high turnover. In such situations officers are most effective.

Personal Power	Position Power	
	+	**–**
+	Formal Leaders	Informal Leaders
–	Officers	Non-Elite

4

Who Gets Power—and How They Hold on to It

Gerald R. Salancik and Jeffrey Pfeffer

Power is held by many people to be a dirty word or, as Warren Bennis has said, "It is the organization's last dirty secret."

This article will argue that traditional "political" power, far from being a dirty business, is, in its most naked form, one of the few mechanisms available for aligning an organization with its own reality. However, institutionalized forms of power—what we prefer to call the cleaner forms of power: authority, legitimization, centralized control, regulations, and the more modern "management information systems"—tend to buffer the organization from reality and obscure the demands of its environment. Most great states and institutions declined, not because they played politics, but because they failed to accommodate to the political realities they faced. Political processes, rather than being mechanisms for unfair and unjust allocations and appointments, tend toward the realistic resolution of conflicts among interests. And power, while it eludes definition, is easy enough to recognize by its consequences—the ability of those who possess power to bring about the outcomes they desire.

The model of power we advance is an elaboration of what has been called strategic-contingency theory, a view that sees power as something that accrues to organizational subunits (individuals, departments) that cope with critical organizational problems. Power is used by subunits, indeed, used by all who have it, to enhance their own survival through control of scarce critical resources, through the placement of allies in key positions, and through the definition of organizational problems and policies. Because of the processes by which power develops and is used, organizations become both more aligned and more misaligned with their environments. This contradiction is the most interesting aspect of organizational power, and one that makes administration one of the most precarious of occupations.

Reprinted from *Organizational Dynamics,* Winter 1977, by Gerald Salancik and Jeffrey Pfeffer. Copyright 1977 by Elsevier Science and Technology Journals. Reproduced with permission of Elsevier Science and Technology Journals in the format other book via Copyright Clearance Center.

What Is Organizational Power?

You can walk into most organizations and ask without fear of being misunderstood, "Which are the powerful groups or people in this organization?" Although many organizational informants may be *unwilling* to tell you, it is unlikely they will be *unable* to tell you. Most people do not require explicit definitions to know what power is.

Power is simply the ability to get things done the way one wants them to be done. For a manager who wants an increased budget to launch a project that he thinks is important, his power is measured by his ability to get that budget. For an executive vice-president who wants to be chairman, his power is evidenced by his advancement toward his goal.

People in organizations not only know what you are talking about when you ask who is influential but they are likely to agree with one another to an amazing extent. Recently, we had a chance to observe this in a regional office of an insurance company. The office had 21 department managers; we asked ten of these managers to rank all 21 according to the influence each one had in the organization. Despite the fact that ranking 21 things is a difficult task, the managers sat down and began arranging the names of their colleagues and themselves in a column. Only one person bothered to ask, "What do you mean by influence?" When told "power," he responded, "Oh," and went on. We compared the rankings of all ten managers and found virtually no disagreement among them in the managers ranked among the top five or the bottom five. Differences in the rankings came from department heads claiming more influence for themselves than their colleagues attributed to them.

Such agreement on those who have influence, and those who do not, was not unique to this insurance company. So far we have studied over 20 very different organizations—universities, research firms, factories, banks, retailers, to name a few. In each one we found individuals able to rate themselves and their peers on a scale of influence or power. We have done this both for specific decisions and for general impact on organizational policies. Their agreement was unusually high, which suggests that distributions of influence exist well enough in everyone's mind to be referred to with ease—and, we assume, with accuracy.

Where Does Organizational Power Come From?

Earlier we stated that power helps organizations become aligned with their realities. This hopeful prospect follows from what we have dubbed the strategic-contingencies theory of organizational power. Briefly, those subunits most able to cope with the organization's critical problems and uncertainties acquire power. In its simplest form, the strategic-contingencies theory implies that when an organization faces a number of lawsuits that threaten its existence, the legal department will gain power and influence over organizational decisions. Somehow other organizational interest groups will recognize its critical importance and confer upon it a status and power never before enjoyed. This influence may extend beyond handling legal matters and into decisions about product design, advertising production, and so on. Such extensions undoubtedly would be accompanied by appropriate, or acceptable, verbal justifications. In time, the head of the legal department may become the head of the corporation, just as in times past the vice-president for marketing had become the president when market shares were a worrisome problem and, before him, the chief engineer, who had made the production line run as smooth as silk.

Stated in this way, the strategic-contingencies theory of power paints an appealing picture of power. To the extent that power is determined by the critical uncertainties and problems facing the organization and, in turn, influences decisions in the organization, the organization is aligned with the realities it faces. In short, power facilitates the organization's adaptation to its environment—or its problems.

We can cite many illustrations of how influence derives from a subunit's ability to deal with critical contingencies. Michael Crozier described a French cigarette factory in which the maintenance engineers had a considerable say in the plantwide operation. After some probing he discovered that the group possessed the solution to one of the major problems faced by the company, that of troubleshooting the elaborate, expensive, and irascible automated machines that kept breaking down and dumbfounding everyone else. It was the one problem that the plant manager could in no way control.

The production workers, while troublesome from time to time, created no insurmountable problems; the manager could reasonably predict their absenteeism or replace them when necessary. Production scheduling was something he could deal with since, by watching inventories and sales, the demand for cigarettes was known long in advance. Changes in demand could be accommodated by slowing down or speeding up the line. Supplies of tobacco and paper were also easily dealt with through stockpiles and advance orders.

The one thing that management could neither control nor accommodate to, however, was the seemingly happenstance breakdowns. And the foreman couldn't instruct the workers what to do when emergencies developed since the maintenance department kept its records of problems and solutions locked up in a cabinet or in its members' heads. The breakdowns were, in truth, a critical source of uncertainty for the organization, and the maintenance engineers were the only ones who could cope with the problem.

The engineers' strategic role in coping with breakdowns afforded them a considerable say on plant decisions. Schedules and production quotas were set in consultation with them. And the plant manager, while formally their boss, accepted their decisions about personnel in their operation. His submission was to his credit, for without their cooperation he would have had an even more difficult time in running the plant.

Ignoring Critical Consequences

In this cigarette factory, sharing influence with the maintenance workers reflected the plant manager's awareness of the critical contingencies. However, when organizational members are not aware of the critical contingencies they face, and do not share influence accordingly, the failure to do so can create havoc. In one case, an insurance company's regional office was having problems with the performance of one of its departments, the coding department. From the outside, the department looked like a disaster area. The clerks who worked in it were somewhat dissatisfied; their supervisors paid little attention to them, and they resented the hard work. Several other departments were critical of this manager, claiming that she was inconsistent in meeting deadlines. The person most critical was the claims manager. He resented having to wait for work that was handled by her department, claiming that it held up his claims adjusters. Having heard the rumors about dissatisfaction among her subordinates, he attributed the situation to poor supervision. He was second in command in the office and therefore took up the issue with her immediate boss, the head of administrative services. They consulted with the personnel manager and the three of them concluded that the manager needed leadership training to improve her relations with her subordinates. The coding manager objected, saying it was a waste of time, but agreed to go along with the training and also agreed to give more priority to the claims department's work. Within a week after the training, the results showed that her workers were happier but that the performance of her department had decreased, save for the people serving the claims department.

About this time, we began, quite independently, a study of influence in this organization. We asked the administrative services director to draw up flow charts of how the work of one department moved on to the next department. In the course of the interview, we noticed that the coding department began or interceded in the work flow of most of the other departments and casually mentioned to him, "The coding manager must be very influential." He said, "No, not really. Why would you think so?" Before we could reply he recounted the story of her leadership training and the fact that things were worse. We then told him that it seemed obvious that the coding department would be influential from the fact that all the other departments depended on it. It was also clear why productivity had fallen. The coding manager took the training seriously and began spending more time raising her workers' spirits than she did worrying about the problems of all the departments that depended on her. Giving priority to the claims area only exaggerated the problem, for their work was getting done at the expense of the work of the other departments. Eventually the company hired a few more clerks to relieve the pressure in the coding department and performance returned to a more satisfactory level.

Originally we got involved with this insurance company to examine how the influence of each manager evolved from his or her department's handling of critical organizational contingencies. We reasoned that one of the most important contingencies faced by all profit-making organizations was that of generating income. Thus we expected managers would be influential to the extent to which they contributed to this function. Such was the case. The underwriting managers, who wrote the policies that committed the premiums, were the most influential; the claims managers, who kept a lid on the funds flowing out, were a close second. Least influential were the managers of functions unrelated to revenue, such as mailroom and payroll managers. And contrary to what the administrative services manager believed, the third most powerful department head (out of 21) was the woman in charge of the coding function, which consisted of rating, recording, and keeping track of the codes of all policy applications and contracts. Her peers attributed more influence to her than could have been inferred from her place on the organization chart. And it was not surprising, since they all depended on her department. The coding department's records, their accuracy and the speed with which they could be retrieved, affected virtually every other operating department in the insurance office. The underwriters depended on them in getting the contracts straight; the typing department depended on them in preparing the formal contract document; the claims department depended on them in adjusting claims; and accounting depended on them for billing. Unfortunately, the "bosses" were not aware of these dependencies, for unlike the cigarette factory, there were no massive breakdowns that made them obvious, while the coding manager, who was a hard-working but quiet person, did little to announce her importance.

The cases of this plant and office illustrate nicely a basic point about the source of power in organizations. The basis for power in an organization derives from the ability of a person or subunit to take or not take actions that are desired by others. The coding manager was seen as influential by those who depended on her department, but not by the people at the top. The engineers were influential because of their role in keeping the plant operating. The two cases differ in these respects: The coding supervisor's source of power was not as widely recognized as that of the maintenance engineers, and she did not use her source of power to influence decisions; the maintenance engineers did. Whether power is used to influence anything is a separate issue. We should not confuse this issue with the fact that power derives from a social situation in which one person has a capacity to do something and another person does not, but wants it done.

Power Sharing in Organizations

Power is shared in organizations; and it is shared out of necessity more than out of concern for principles of organizational development or participatory democracy. Power is shared because no one person controls all the desired activities in the organization. While the factory owner may hire people to operate his noisy machines, once hired they have some control over the use of the machinery. And thus they have power over him in the same way he has power over them. Who has more power over whom is a mooter point than that of recognizing the inherent nature of organizing as a sharing of power.

Let's expand on the concept that power derives from the activities desired in an organization. A major way of managing influence in organizations is through the designation of activities. In a bank we studied, we saw this principle in action. This bank was planning to install a computer system for routine credit evaluation. The bank, rather progressive-minded, was concerned that the change would have adverse effects on employees and therefore surveyed their attitudes.

The principal opposition to the new system came, interestingly, not from the employees who performed the routine credit checks, some of whom would be relocated because of the change, but from the manager of the credit department. His reason was quite simple. The manager's primary function was to give official approval to the applications, catch any employee mistakes before giving approval, and arbitrate any difficulties the clerks had in deciding what to do. As a consequence of his role, others in the organization, including his superiors, subordinates, and colleagues, attributed considerable importance to him. He, in turn, for example, could point to the low proportion of credit approvals, compared with other financial institutions, that resulted in bad debts. Now, to his mind, a wretched machine threatened to transfer his role to a computer programmer, a man who knew nothing of finance and who, in addition, had ten years less seniority. The credit manager eventually quit for a position at a smaller firm with lower pay, but one in which he would have more influence than his redefined job would have left him with.

Because power derives from activities rather than individuals, an individual's or subgroup's power is never absolute and derives ultimately from the context of the situation. The amount of power an individual has at any one time depends not only on the activities he or she controls, but also on the existence of other persons or means by which the activities can be achieved and on those who determine what ends are desired and, hence, on what activities are desired and critical for the organization. One's own power always depends on other people for these two reasons. Other people, or groups or organizations, can determine the definition of what is a critical contingency for the organization and can also undercut the uniqueness of the individual's personal contribution to the critical contingencies of the organization.

Perhaps one can best appreciate how situationally dependent power is by examining how it is distributed. In most societies, power organizes around scarce and critical resources. Rarely does power organize around abundant resources. In the United States, a person doesn't become powerful because he or she can drive a car. There are simply too many others who can drive with equal facility. In certain villages in Mexico, on the other hand, a person with a car is accredited with enormous social status and plays a key role in the community. In addition to scarcity, power is also limited by the need for one's capacities in a social system. While a racer's ability to drive a car around a 90° turn at 80 m.p.h. may be sparsely distributed in a society, it is not likely to lend the driver much power in the society. The ability simply does not play a central role in the activities of the society.

The fact that power revolves around scarce and critical activities, of course, makes the control and organization of those activities a major battleground in struggles for power. Even relatively abundant or trivial resources can become the bases for power if one can organize and control their allocation and the definition of what is critical. Many occupational and professional groups attempt to do just this in modern economies. Lawyers organize themselves into associations, regulate the entrance requirements for novitiates, and then get laws passed specifying situations that require the services of an attorney. Workers had little power in the conduct of industrial affairs until they organized themselves into closed and controlled systems. In recent years, women and blacks have tried to define themselves as important and critical to the social system, using law to reify their status.

In organizations there are obviously opportunities for defining certain activities as more critical than others. Indeed, the growth of managerial thinking to include defining organizational objectives and goals has done much to foster these opportunities. One sure way to liquidate the power of groups in the organization is to define the need for their services out of existence. David Halberstam presents a description of how just such a thing happened to the group of correspondents that evolved around Edward R. Murrow, the brilliant journalist, interviewer, and war correspondent of CBS News. A close friend of CBS chairman and controlling stockholder William S. Paley, Murrow, and the news department he directed, were endowed with freedom to do what they felt was right. He used it to create some of the best documentaries and commentaries ever seen on television. Unfortunately, television became too large, too powerful, and too suspect in the eyes of the federal government that licensed it. It thus became, or at least the top executives believed it had become, too dangerous to have in-depth, probing commentary on the news. Crisp, dry uneditorializing headliners were considered safer. Murrow was out and Walter Cronkite was in.

The power to define what is critical in an organization is no small power. Moreover, it is the key to understanding why organizations are either aligned with their environments or misaligned. If an organization defines certain activities as critical when in fact they are not critical, given the flow of resources coming into the organization, it is not likely to survive, at least in its present form.

Most organizations manage to evolve a distribution of power and influence that is aligned with the critical realities they face in the environment. The environment, in turn, includes both the internal environment, the shifting situational contexts in which particular decisions get made, and the external environment that it can hope to influence but is unlikely to control.

The Critical Contingencies

The critical contingencies facing most organizations derive from the environmental context within which they operate. This determines the available needed resources and thus determines the problems to be dealt with. That power organizes around handling these problems suggests an important mechanism by which organizations keep in tune with their external environments. The strategic contingencies model implies that subunits that contribute to the critical resources of the organization will gain influence in the organization. Their influence presumably is then used to bend the organization's activities to the contingencies that determine its resources. This idea may strike one as obvious. But its obviousness in no way diminishes its importance. Indeed, despite its obviousness, it escapes the notice of many organizational analysts and managers, who all too frequently think of the organization in terms of a descending pyramid, in which all the departments in one tier hold equal power and status. This presumption denies the reality that departments differ in the contributions they are believed to make to the overall organization's resources, as well as to the fact that some are more equal than others.

Because of the importance of this idea to organizational effectiveness, we decided to examine it carefully in a large midwestern university. A university offers an excellent site for studying power. It is composed of departments with nominally equal power and is administered by a central executive structure much like other bureaucracies. However, at the same time it is a situation in which the departments have clearly defined identities and face diverse external environments. Each department has its own bodies of knowledge, its own institutions, its own sources of prestige and resources. Because the departments operate in different external environments, they are likely to contribute differentially to the resources of the overall organization. Thus a physics department with close ties to NASA may contribute substantially to the funds of the university; and a history department with a renowned historian in residence may contribute to the intellectual credibility or prestige of the whole university. Such variations permit one to examine how these various contributions lead to obtaining power within the university.

We analyzed the influence of 29 university departments throughout an 18-month period in their history. Our chief interest was to determine whether departments that brought more critical resources to the university would be more powerful than departments that contributed fewer or less critical resources.

To identify the critical resources each department contributed, the heads of all departments were interviewed about the importance of seven different resources to the university's success. The seven included undergraduate students (the factor determining size of the state allocations by the university), national prestige, administrative expertise, and so on. The most critical resource was found to be contract and grant monies received by a department's faculty for research or consulting services. At this university, contract and grants contributed somewhat less than 50 percent of the overall budget, with the remainder primarily coming from state appropriations. The importance attributed to contract and grant monies, and the rather minor importance of undergraduate students, was not surprising for this particular university. The university was a major center for graduate education; many of its departments ranked in the top ten of their respective fields.

Grant and contract monies were the primary source of discretionary funding available for maintaining these programs of graduate education, and hence for maintaining the university's prestige. The prestige of the university itself was critical both in recruiting able students and attracting top-notch faculty.

From university records it was determined what relative contributions each of the 29 departments made to the various needs of the university (national prestige, outside grants, teaching). Thus, for instance, one department may have contributed to the university by teaching 7 percent of the instructional units, bringing in 2 percent of the outside contracts and grants, and having a national ranking of 20. Another department, on the other hand, may have taught 1 percent of the instructional units, contributed 12 percent to the grants, and be ranked the third best department in its field within the country.

The question was: Do these different contributions determine the relative power of the departments within the university? Power was measured in several ways; but regardless of how measured, the answer was Yes. Those three resources together accounted for about 70 percent of the variance in subunit power in the university.

But the most important predictor of departmental power was the department's contribution to the contracts and grants of the university. Sixty percent of the variance in power was due to this one factor, suggesting that the power of departments derived primarily from the dollars they provided for graduate education, the activity believed to be the most important for the organization.

The Impact of Organizational Power on Decision Making

The measure of power we used in studying this university was an analysis of the responses of the department heads we interviewed. While such perceptions of power might be of interest in their own right, they contribute little to our understanding of how the distribution of power might serve to align an organization with its critical realities. For this we must look to how power actually influences the decisions and policies of organizations.

While it is perhaps not absolutely valid, we can generally gauge the relative importance of a department of an organization by the size of the budget allocated to it relative to other departments. Clearly it is of importance to the administrators of those departments whether they get squeezed in a budget crunch or are given more funds to strike out after new opportunities. And it should also be clear that when those decisions are made and one department can go ahead and try new approaches while another must cut back on the old, then the deployment of the resources of the organization in meeting its problem is most directly affected.

Thus our study of the university led us to ask the following question: Does power lead to influence in the organization? To answer this question, we found it useful first to ask another one, namely: Why should department heads try to influence organizational decisions to favor their own departments to the exclusion of other departments? While this second question may seem a bit naive to anyone who has witnessed the political realities of organizations, we posed it in a context of research on organizations that sees power as an illegitimate threat to the neater rational authority of modern bureaucracies. In this context, decisions are not believed to be made because of the dirty business of politics but because of the overall goals and purposes of the organization. In a university, one reasonable basis for decision making is the teaching workload of departments and the demands that follow from that workload. We would expect, therefore, that departments with heavy student demands for courses would be able to obtain funds for teaching. Another reasonable basis for decision making is quality. We would expect, for that reason, that departments with esteemed reputations would be able to obtain funds both because their quality suggests they might use such funds effectively and because such funds would allow them to maintain their quality. A rational model of bureaucracy intimates, then, that the organizational decisions taken would favor those who perform the stated purposes of the organization— teaching undergraduates and training professional and scientific talent—well.

The problem with rational models of decision making, however, is that what is rational to one person may strike another as irrational. For most departments, resources are a question of survival. While teaching undergraduates may seem to be a major goal for some members of the university, developing knowledge may seem so to others; and to still others, advising governments and other institutions about policies may seem to be the crucial business. Everyone has his own idea of the proper priorities in a just world. Thus goals, rather than being clearly defined and universally agreed upon, are blurred and contested throughout the organization. If such is the case, then the decisions taken on behalf of the organization as a whole are likely to reflect the goals of those who prevail in political contests, namely, those with power in the organization.

Will organizational decisions always reflect the distribution of power in the organization? Probably not. Using power for influence requires a certain expenditure of effort, time, and resources. Prudent and judicious persons are not likely to use their power needlessly or wastefully. And it is likely that power will be used to influence organizational decisions primarily under circumstances that both require and favor its use. We have examined three conditions that are likely to affect the use of power in organizations: scarcity, criticality, and uncertainty. The first suggests that subunits will try to exert influence when the resources of the organization are scarce. If there is an abundance of resources, then a particular department or a particular individual has little need to attempt influence. With little effort, he can get all he wants anyway.

The second condition, criticality, suggests that a subunit will attempt to influence decisions to obtain resources that are critical to its own survival and activities. Criticality implies that one would not waste effort, or risk being labeled obstinate, by fighting over trivial decisions affecting one's operations.

An office manager would probably balk less about a threatened cutback in copying machine usage than about a reduction in typing staff. An advertising department head would probably worry less about losing his lettering artist than his illustrator. Criticality is difficult to define because what is critical depends on people's beliefs about what is critical. Such beliefs may or may not be based on experience and knowledge and may or may not be agreed upon by all. Scarcity, for instance, may itself affect conceptions of criticality. When slack resources drop off, cutbacks have to be made—those "hard decisions," as congressmen and resplendent administrators like to call them. Managers then find themselves scrapping projects they once held dear.

The third condition that we believe affects the use of power is uncertainty: When individuals do not agree about what the organization should do or how to do it, power and other social processes will affect decisions. The reason for this is simply that, if there are no clear-cut criteria available for resolving conflicts of interest, then the only means for resolution is some form of social process, including power, status, social ties, or some arbitrary process like flipping a coin or drawing straws. Under conditions of uncertainty, the powerful manager can argue his case on any grounds and usually win it. Since there is no real consensus, other contestants are not likely to develop counter arguments or amass sufficient opposition. Moreover, because of his power and their need for access to the resources he controls, they are more likely to defer to his arguments.

Although the evidence is slight, we have found that power will influence the allocations of scarce and critical resources. In the analysis of power in the university, for instance, one of the most critical resources needed by departments is the general budget. First granted by the state legislature, the general budget is later allocated to individual departments by the university administration in response to requests from the department heads. Our analysis of the factors that contribute to a department getting more or less of this budget indicated that sub-unit power was the major predictor, overriding such factors as student demand for courses, national reputations of departments, or even the size of a department's faculty. Moreover, other research has shown that when the general budget has been cut back or held below previous uninflated levels, leading to monies becoming more scarce, budget allocations mirror departmental powers even more closely.

Student enrollment and faculty size, of course, do themselves relate to budget allocations, as we would expect since they determine a department's need for resources, or at least offer visible testimony of needs. But departments are not always able to get what they need by the mere fact of needing. In one analysis it was found that high-power departments were able to obtain budget without regard to their teaching loads and, in some cases, actually in inverse relation to their teaching loads. In contrast, low-power departments could get increases in budget only when they could justify the increases by a recent growth in teaching load, and then only when it was far in excess of norms for other departments.

General budget is only one form of resource that is allocated to departments. There are others such as special grants for student fellowships or faculty research. These are critical to departments because they affect the ability to attract other resources, such as outstanding faculty or students. We examined how power influenced the allocations of four resources department heads had described as critical and scarce.

When the four resources were arrayed from the most to the least critical and scarce, we found that departmental power best predicted the allocations of the most critical and scarce resources. In other words, the analysis of how power influences organizational allocations leads to this conclusion: Those subunits most likely to survive in times of strife are those that are most critical to the organization. Their importance to the organization gives them power to influence resource allocations that enhance their own survival.

How External Environment Influences Executive Selection

Power not only influences the survival of key groups in an organization, it also influences the selection of individuals to key leadership positions, and by such a process further aligns the organization with its environmental context.

We can illustrate this with a recent study of the selection and tenure of chief administrators in 57 hospitals in Illinois. We assumed that since the critical problems facing the organization would enhance the power of certain groups at the expense of others, then the leaders to emerge should be those most relevant to the context of the hospitals. To assess this we asked each chief administrator about his professional background and how long he had been in office. The replies were then related to the hospital's funding, ownership, and competitive conditions for patients and staff.

One aspect of a hospital's context is the source of its budget. Some hospitals, for instance, are run much like other businesses. They sell bed space, patient care, and treatment services. They charge fees sufficient both to cover their costs and to provide capital for expansion. The main source of both their operating and capital funds is patient billings. Increasingly, patient billings are paid for, not by patients, but by private insurance companies. Insurers like Blue Cross dominate and represent a potent interest group outside a hospital's control but critical to its income. The insurance companies, in order to limit their own costs, attempt to hold down the fees allowable to hospitals, which they do effectively from their positions on state rate boards. The squeeze on hospitals that results from fees increasing slowly while costs climb rapidly more and more demands the talents of cost accountants or people trained in the technical expertise of hospital administration.

By contrast, other hospitals operate more like social service institutions, either as government health-care units (Bellevue Hospital in New York City and Cook County Hospital in Chicago, for example) or as charitable institutions. These hospitals obtain a large proportion of their operating and capital funds not from privately insured patients, but from government subsidies or private donations. Such institutions rather than requiring the talents of a technically efficient administrator are likely to require the savvy of someone who is well integrated into the social and political power structure of the community.

Not surprisingly, the characteristics of administrators predictably reflect the funding context of the hospitals with which they are associated. Those hospitals with larger proportions of their budget obtained from private insurance companies were most likely to have administrators with backgrounds in accounting and least likely to have administrators whose professions were business or medicine. In contrast, those hospitals with larger proportions of their budget derived from private donations and local governments were most likely to have administrators with business or professional backgrounds and least likely to have accountants. The same held for formal training in hospital management. Professional hospital administrators could easily be found in hospitals drawing their incomes from private insurance and rarely in hospitals dependent on donations or legislative appropriations.

As with the selection of administrators, the context of organizations has also been found to affect the removal of executives. The environment, as a source of organizational problems, can make it more or less difficult for executives to demonstrate their value to the organization. In the hospitals we studied, long-term administrators came from hospitals with few problems. They enjoyed amicable and stable relations with their local business and social communities and suffered little competition for funding and staff. The small city hospital director who attended civic and Elks meetings while running the only hospital within a 100-mile radius, for example, had little difficulty holding on to his job. Turnover was highest in hospitals with the most problems, a phenomenon similar to that observed in a study of industrial organizations in which turnover was highest among executives in industries with competitive environments and unstable market conditions. The interesting thing is that instability characterized the industries rather than the individual firms in them. The troublesome conditions in the individual firms were attributed, or rather misattributed, to the executives themselves.

It takes more than problems, however, to terminate a manager's leadership. The problems themselves must be relevant and critical. This is clear from the way in which an administrator's tenure is affected by the status of the hospital's operating budget. Naively we might assume that all administrators would need to show a surplus. Not necessarily so. Again, we must distinguish between those hospitals that depend on private donations for funds and those that do not. Whether an endowed budget shows a surplus or deficit is less important than the hospital's relations with benefactors. On the other hand, with a budget dependent on patient billing, a surplus is almost essential; monies for new equipment or expansion must be drawn from it, and without them quality care becomes more difficult and patients scarcer. An administrator's tenure reflected just these considerations. For those hospitals dependent upon private donations, the length of an administrator's term depended not at all on the status of the operating budget but was fairly predictable from the hospital's relations with the business community. On the other hand, in hospitals dependent on the operating budget for capital financing, the greater the deficit the shorter was the tenure of the hospital's principal administrators.

Changing Contingencies and Eroding Power Bases

The critical contingencies facing the organization may change. When they do, it is reasonable to expect that the power of individuals and subgroups will change in turn. At times the shift can be swift and shattering, as it was recently for powerholders in New York City. A few years ago it was believed that David Rockefeller was one of the ten most powerful people in the city, as tallied by *New York* magazine, which annually sniffs out power for the delectation of its readers. But that was before it was revealed that the city was in financial trouble, before Rockefeller's Chase Manhattan Bank lost some of its own financial luster, and before brother Nelson lost some of his political influence in Washington. Obviously David Rockefeller was no longer as well positioned to help bail the city out. Another loser was an attorney with considerable personal connections to the political and religious leaders of the city. His talents were no longer in much demand. The persons with more influence were the bankers and union pension fund executors who fed money to the city; community leaders who represent blacks and Spanish-Americans, in contrast, witnessed the erosion of their power bases.

One implication of the idea that power shifts with changes in organizational environments is that the dominant coalition will tend to be that group that is most appropriate for the organization's environment, as also will the leaders of an organization. One can observe this historically in the top executives of industrial firms in the United States. Up until the early 1950s, many top corporations were headed by former production line managers or engineers who gained prominence because of their abilities to cope with the problems of production. Their success, however, only spelled their demise. As production became routinized and mechanized, the problem of most firms became one of selling all those goods they so efficiently produced. Marketing executives were more frequently found in corporate boardrooms. Success outdid itself again, for keeping markets and production steady and stable requires the kind of control that can only come from acquiring competitors and suppliers or the invention of more and more appealing products—ventures that typically require enormous amounts of capital. During the 1960s, financial executives assumed the seats of power. And they, too, will give way to others. Edging over the horizon are legal experts, as regulation and antitrust suits are becoming more and more frequent in the 1970s, suits that had their beginnings in the success of the expansion generated by prior executives. The more distant future, which is likely to be dominated by multinational corporations, may see former secretaries of state and their minions increasingly serving as corporate figureheads.

The Nonadaptive Consequences of Adaptation

From what we have said thus far about power aligning the organization with its own realities, an intelligent person might react with a resounding ho-hum, for it all seems too obvious: Those with the ability to get the job done are given the job to do.

However, there are two aspects of power that make it more useful for understanding organizations and their effectiveness. First, the "job" to be done has a way of expanding itself until it becomes less and less clear what the job is. Napoleon began by doing a job for France in the war with Austria and ended up emperor, convincing many that only he could keep the peace. Hitler began by promising an end to Germany's troubling postwar depression and ended up convincing more people than is comfortable to remember that he was destined to be the savior of the world. In short, power is a capacity for influence that extends far beyond the original bases that created it. Second, power tends to take on institutionalized forms that enable it to endure well beyond its usefulness to an organization.

There is an important contradiction in what we have observed about organizational power. On the one hand we have said that power derives from the contingencies facing an organization and that when those contingencies change so do the bases for power. On the other hand we have asserted that subunits will tend to use their power to influence organizational decisions in their own favor, particularly when their own survival is threatened by the scarcity of critical resources. The first statement implies that an organization will tend to be aligned with its environment since power will tend to bring to key positions those with capabilities relevant to the context. The second implies that those in power will not give up their positions so easily; they will pursue policies that guarantee their continued domination. In short, change and stability operate through the same mechanism, and, as a result, the organization will never be completely in phase with its environment or its needs.

The study of hospital administrators illustrates how leadership can be out of phase with reality. We argued that privately funded hospitals needed trained technical administrators more so than did hospitals funded by donations. The need as we perceived it was matched in most hospitals, but by no means in all. Some organizations did not conform with our predictions. These deviations imply that some administrators were able to maintain their positions independent of their suitability for those positions. By dividing administrators into those with long and short terms of office, one finds that the characteristics of longer-termed administrators were virtually unrelated to the hospital's context. The shorter-termed chiefs, on the other hand, had characteristics more appropriate for the hospital's problems. For a hospital to have a recently appointed head implies that the previous administrator had been unable to endure by institutionalizing himself.

One obvious feature of hospitals that allowed some administrators to enjoy a long tenure was a hospital's ownership. Administrators were less entrenched when their hospitals were affiliated with and dependent upon larger organizations, such as governments or churches. Private hospitals offered more secure positions for administrators. Like private corporations, they tend to have more diffused ownership, leaving the administrator unopposed as he institutionalizes his reign. Thus he endures, sometimes at the expense of the performance of the organization. Other research has demonstrated that corporations with diffuse ownership have poorer earnings than those in which the control of the manager is checked by a dominant shareholder. Firms that overload their boardrooms with more insiders than are appropriate for their context have also been found to be less profitable.

A word of caution is required about our judgment of "appropriateness." When we argue some capabilities are more appropriate for one context than another, we do so from the perspective of an outsider and on the basis of reasonable assumptions as to the problems the organization will face and the capabilities they will need. The fact that we have been able to predict the distribution of influence and the characteristics of leaders suggests that our reasoning is not incorrect. However, we do not think that all organizations follow the same pattern. The fact that we have not been able to predict outcomes with 100 percent accuracy indicates they do not.

Mistaking Critical Contingencies

One thing that allows subunits to retain their power is their ability to name their functions as critical to the organization when they may not be. Consider again our discussion of power in the university. One might wonder why the most critical tasks were defined as graduate education and scholarly research, the effect of which was to lend power to those who brought in grants and contracts. Why not something else? The reason is that the most powerful departments argued for those criteria and won their case, partly because they were more powerful.

In another analysis of this university, we found that all departments advocate self-serving criteria for budget allocation. Thus a department with large undergraduate enrollments argued that enrollments should determine budget allocations, a department with a strong national reputation saw prestige as the most reasonable basis for distributing funds, and so on. We further found that advocating such self-serving criteria actually benefited a department's budget allotments but, also, it paid off more for departments that were already powerful.

Organizational needs are consistent with a current distribution of power also because of a human tendency to categorize problems in familiar ways. An accountant sees problems with organizational performance as cost accountancy problems or inventory flow problems. A sales manager sees them as problems with markets, promotional strategies, or just unaggressive salespeople. But what is the truth? Since it does not automatically announce itself, it is likely that those with prior credibility, or those with power, will be favored as the enlightened. This bias, while not intentionally self-serving, further concentrates power among those who already possess it, independent of changes in the organization's context.

Institutionalizing Power

A third reason for expecting organizational contingencies to be defined in familiar ways is that the current holders of power can structure the organization in ways that institutionalize themselves. By institutionalization we mean the establishment of relatively permanent structures and policies that favor the influence of a particular subunit. While in power, a dominant coalition has the ability to institute constitutions, rules, procedures, and information systems that limit the potential power of others while continuing their own.

The key to institutionalizing power always is to create a device that legitimates one's own authority and diminishes the legitimacy of others. When the "Divine Right of Kings" was envisioned centuries ago it was to provide an unquestionable foundation for the supremacy of royal authority. There is generally a need to root the exercise of authority in some higher power. Modern leaders are no less affected by this need. Richard Nixon, with the aid of John Dean, reified the concept of executive privilege, which meant in effect that what the president wished not to be discussed need not be discussed.

In its simpler form, institutionalization is achieved by designating positions or roles for organizational activities. The creation of a new post legitimizes a function and forces organization members to orient to it. By designating how this new post relates to older, more established posts, moreover, one can structure an organization to enhance the importance of the function in the organization. Equally, one can diminish the importance of traditional functions. This is what happened in the end with the insurance company we mentioned that was having trouble with its coding department. As the situation unfolded, the claims director continued to feel dissatisfied about the dependency of his functions on the coding manager. Thus he instituted a reorganization that resulted in two coding departments. In so doing, of course, he placed activities that affected his department under his direct control, presumably to make the operation more effective. Similarly, consumer-product firms enhance the power of marketing by setting up a coordinating role to interface production and marketing functions and then appoint a marketing manager to fill the role.

The structures created by dominant powers sooner or later become fixed and unquestioned features of the organization. Eventually, this can be devastating. It is said that the battle of Jena in 1806 was lost by Frederick the Great, who died in 1786. Though the great Prussian leader had no direct hand in the disaster, his imprint on the army was so thorough, so embedded in its skeletal underpinnings, that the organization was inappropriate for others to lead in different times.

Another important source of institutionalized power lies in the ability to structure information systems. Setting up committees to investigate particular organizational issues and having them report only to particular individuals or groups facilitates their awareness of problems by members of those groups while limiting the awareness of problems by the members of other groups. Obviously, those who have information are in a better position to interpret the problems of an organization, regardless of how realistically they may, in fact, do so.

Still another way to institutionalize power is to distribute rewards and resources. The dominant group may quiet competing interest groups with small favors and rewards. The credit for this artful form of cooptation belongs to Louis XIV. To avoid usurpation of his power by the nobles of France and the Fronde that had so troubled his father's reign, he built the palace at Versailles to occupy them with hunting and gossip. Awed, the courtiers basked in the reflected glories of the "Sun King" and the overwhelming setting he had created for his court.

At this point, we have not systematically studied the institutionalization of power. But we suspect it is an important condition that mediates between the environment of the organization and the capabilities of the organization for dealing with that environment. The more institutionalized power is within an organization, the more likely an organization will be out of phase with the realities it faces. President Richard Nixon's structuring of his White House is one of the better documented illustrations. If we go back to newspaper and magazine descriptions of how he organized his office from the beginning in 1968, most of what occurred subsequently follows almost as an afterthought. Decisions flowed through virtually only the small White House staff; rewards, small presidential favors of recognition, and perquisites were distributed by this staff to the loyal; and information from the outside world—the press, Congress, the people on the streets—was filtered by the staff and passed along only if initialed "bh." Thus it was not surprising that when Nixon met war protestors in the early dawn, the only thing he could think to talk about was the latest football game, so insulated had he become from their grief and anger.

One of the more interesting implications of institutionalized power is that executive turnover among the executives who have structured the organization is likely to be a rare event that occurs only under the most pressing crisis. If a dominant coalition is able to structure the organization and interpret the meaning of ambiguous events like declining sales and profits or lawsuits, then the "real" problems to emerge will easily be incorporated into traditional modes of thinking and acting. If opposition is designed out of the organization, the interpretations will go unquestioned. Conditions will remain stable until a crisis develops, so overwhelming and visible that even the most adroit rhetorician would be silenced.

Implications for the Management of Power in Organizations

While we could derive numerous implications from this discussion of power, our selection would have to depend largely on whether one wanted to increase one's power, decrease the power of others, or merely maintain one's position. More important, the real implications depend on the particulars of an organizational situation. To understand power in an organization one must begin by looking outside it—into the environment—for those groups that mediate the organization's outcomes but are not themselves within its control.

Instead of ending with homilies, we will end with a reversal of where we began. Power, rather than being the dirty business it is often made out to be, is probably one of the few mechanisms for reality testing in organizations. And the cleaner forms of power, the institutional forms, rather than having the virtues they are often credited with, can lead the organization to become out of touch. The real trick to managing power in organizations is to ensure somehow that leaders cannot be unaware of the realities of their environments and cannot avoid changing to deal with those realities. That, however, would be like designing the "self-liquidating organization," an unlikely event since anyone capable of designing such an instrument would be obviously in control of the liquidations.

Management would do well to devote more attention to determining the critical contingencies of their environments. For if you conclude, as we do, that the environment sets most of the structure influencing organizational outcomes and problems, and that power derives from the organization's activities that deal with those contingencies, then it is the environment that needs managing, not power. The first step is to construct an accurate model of the environment, a process that is quite difficult for most organizations. We have recently started a project to aid administrators in systematically understanding their environments. From this experience, we have learned that the most critical blockage to perceiving an organization's reality accurately is a failure to incorporate those with the relevant expertise into the process. Most organizations have the requisite experts on hand but they are positioned so that they can be comfortably ignored.

One conclusion you can, and probably should, derive from our discussion is that power—because of the way it develops and the way it is used—will always result in the organization suboptimizing its performance. However, to this grim absolute, we add a comforting caveat: If any criteria other than power were the basis for determining an organization's decisions, the results would be even worse.

5

The Power of Leadership

James MacGregor Burns

We search eagerly for leadership yet seek to cage and tame it. We recoil from power yet we are bewitched or titillated by it. We devour books on power—power in the office, power in the bedroom, power in the corridors. Connoisseurs of power purport to teach about it—what it is, how to get it, how to use it, how to "gain total control" over "everything around you." We think up new terms for power: clout, wallop, muscle. We measure the power of the aides of Great Men by the number of yards between their offices and that of Number One. If authority made the powerful "giddy, proud, and vain," as Samuel Butler wrote, today it entrances both the seekers of power and the powerless.

Why this preoccupation, this near-obsession, with power? In part because we in this century cannot escape the horror of it. Stalin controlled an apparatus that, year after year and in prison after prison, quietly put to death millions of persons, some of them old comrades and leading Bolsheviks, with hardly a ripple of protest from others. Between teatime and dinner Adolf Hitler could decide whether to release a holocaust of terror and death in an easterly or westerly direction, with stupendous impact on the fate of a continent and a world.

Sheer evil and brute power always seem more fascinating than complex human relationships. Sinners usually outsell saints, at least in Western cultures, and the ruthless exercise of power somehow seems more realistic, moral influence more naive. Above all, sheer massed power seems to have the most impact on history. Such, at least, is this century's bias. Perhaps I exemplify the problem of this distorted perception in my own intellectual development. Growing up in the aftermath of one world war, taking part in a second, studying the records of these and later wars, I have been struck by the sheer physical impact of men's armaments. Living in the age of political titans, I too have assumed that their actual power equaled their reputed power. As a political scientist I have belonged

Reprinted from *Leadership,* pp. 9–17, by James MacGregor Burns. Copyright © 1978 by James MacGregor Burns. Reprinted by permission of HarperCollins Publishers.

to a "power school" that analyzed the interrelationships of persons on the basis only of power. Perhaps this was fitting for an era of two world wars and scores of lesser ones, the murder of entire cities, bloody revolutions, the unleashing of the inhuman force of the atom.

I fear, however, that we are paying a steep intellectual and political price for our preoccupation with power. Viewing politics *as* power has blinded us to the role of power *in* politics and hence to the pivotal role of leadership.

Our main hope for disenthralling ourselves from our overemphasis on power lies more in a theoretical, or at least conceptual, effort, than in an empirical one. It lies not only in recognizing that not all human influences are necessarily coercive and exploitative, that not all transactions among persons are mechanical, impersonal, ephemeral. It lies in seeing that the most powerful influences consist of deeply human relationships in which two or more persons *engage* with one another. It lies in a more realistic, a more sophisticated understanding of power, and of the often far more consequential exercise of mutual persuasion, exchange, elevation, and transformation—in short, of leadership. This is not to exorcise power from its pervasive influence in our daily lives; recognizing this kind of power is absolutely indispensable to understanding leadership. But we must recognize the limited reach of "total" or "coercive" power. We must see power—and leadership—as not things but as *relationships*. We must analyze power in a context of human motives and physical constraints. If we can come to grips with these aspects of power, we can hope to comprehend the true nature of leadership—a venture far more intellectually daunting than the study of naked power.

The Two Essentials of Power

We all have *power* to do acts we lack the *motive* to do—to buy a gun and slaughter people, to crush the feelings of loved ones who cannot defend themselves, to drive a car down a crowded city sidewalk, to torture an animal.

We all have the *motives* to do things we do not have the resources to do—to be President or senator, to buy a luxurious yacht, to give away millions to charity, to travel for months on end, to right injustices, to tell off the boss.

The two essentials of power are motive and resource. The two are interrelated. Lacking motive, resource diminishes; lacking resource, motive lies idle. Lacking either one, power collapses. Because both resource and motive are needed, and because both may be in short supply, power is an elusive and limited thing. Human beings, both the agents and the victims of power, for two thousand years or more have tried to penetrate its mysteries, but the nature of power remains elusive. Certainly no one has mastered the secrets of personal power as physicists have penetrated the atom. It is probably just as well.

To understand the nature of leadership requires understanding of the essence of power, for leadership is a special form of power. Forty years ago Bertrand Russell called power the fundamental concept in social science, "in the same sense in which Energy is a fundamental concept in physics." This is a compelling metaphor; it suggests that the source of power may lie in immense reserves of the wants and needs of the wielders and objects of power, just as the winds and the tides, oil and coal, the atom and the sun have been harnessed to supply physical energy. But it is still only a metaphor.

What is power? The "power of A over B," we are told, "is equal to maximum force which A can induce on B minus the maximum resisting force which B can mobilize in the opposite direction." One wonders about the As and the Bs, the Xs and the Ys, in the equations of power. Are they mere croquet balls, knocking other balls and being knocked, in some game of the gods? Or do these As and Xs and the others have wants and needs, ambitions and aspirations, of their own? And what if a ball does not obey a god, just as the children's nurse stood in the autocrat's way? Surely this formula is more physics than power. But the formula offers one vital clue to power: power is a *relationship* among persons.

Power, says Max Weber—he uses the term *Macht*—"is the probability that one actor within a social relationship will be in a position to carry out his own will despite resistance, regardless of the basis on which this probability rests." This formula helps the search for power, since it reminds us that there is no certain relationship between what P (power holder) does and how R (power recipient) responds. Those who have pressed a button and found no light turned on, or who have admonished a child with no palpable effect, welcome the factor of probability. But what controls the *degree* of probability? Motive? Intention? Power resources? Skill? Is P acting on his own, or is he the agent of some other power holder? And what if P orders R to do something to someone else—who then is the *real* power recipient? To answer such questions, P and R and all the other croquet players, mallets, and balls must be put into a broader universe of power relationships—that is, viewed as a *collective* act. Power and leadership become part of a system of social causation.

Essential in a concept of power is the role of *purpose*. This absolutely central value has been inadequately recognized in most theories of power. Power has been defined as the production of intended effects, but the crux of the matter lies in the dimensions of "intent." What is the nature (intensity, persistence, scope) of purpose? How is P's purpose communicated to R—and to what degree is that intent perceived by R as it is by P? Assuming an intent of P, to what extent is there a power relation if P's intent is influenced by P's prior knowledge and anticipation of R's intent? To what extent is intent part of a wider interaction among wants, needs, and values of P and R, before any overt behavior takes place? Few persons have a single intent; if P has more than one, are these intentions deemed equal, hierarchical, or unrelated? These relationships also define the exercise of power as a collective act.

A *psychological* conception of power will help us cut through some of these complexities and provide a basis for understanding the relation of power to leadership. This approach carries on the assumptions above: that power is first of all a *relationship* and not merely an entity to be passed around like a baton or hand grenade; that it involves the *intention* or *purpose* of both power holder and power recipient; and hence that it is *collective,* not merely the behavior of one person. On these assumptions I view the power process as one *in which power holders (P), possessing certain motives and goals, have the capacity to secure changes in the behavior of a respondent (R), human or animal, and in the environment, by utilizing resources in their power base, including factors of skill, relative to the targets of their power-wielding and necessary to secure such changes.* This view of power deals with three elements in the process: the motives and resources of power holders; the motives and resources of power recipients; and the relationship among all these.

The power holder may be the person whose "private motives are displaced onto public objects and rationalized in terms of public interest," to quote Harold Lasswell's classic formula. So accustomed are we to observing persons with power drives or complexes, so sensitive to leaders with the "will to power," so exposed to studies finding the source of the power urge in early deprivation, that we tend to assume the power motive to be exclusively that of seeking to dominate the behavior of others. "But must *all* experiences of power have as their ultimate goal the exercise of power over others?" David McClelland demands. He and other psychologists find that persons with high need for power (*"n Power"*) may derive that need for power not only from deprivation but from other experiences. One study indicated that young men watching a film of John F. Kennedy's Inaugural felt strengthened and inspirited by this exposure to an admired leader. Other persons may draw on internal resources as they grow older and learn to exert power against those who constrain them, like children who self-consciously recognize their exercise of power as they resist their mothers' directives. They find "sources of strength in the self to develop the self."

These and other findings remind us that the power holder has a variety of motives besides that of wielding power over others. They help us correct the traditional picture of single-minded power wielders bent on exerting control over respondents. (Their main motive may be to institute power over *themselves*.) In fact power holders may have as varied motives—of wants, needs, expectations, etc.—as their targets. Some may pursue not power but status, recognition, prestige, and glory, or they may seek power as an intermediate value instrumental to realizing those loftier goals. Some psychologists consider the need to achieve (*"n Achievement"*) a powerful motive, especially in western cultures, and one whose results may be prized more as an *attainment* than as a means of social control. Some use power to collect possessions such as paintings, cars, or jewelry; they may collect wives or mistresses less to dominate them than to love or to display them. Others will use power to seek novelty and excitement. Still others may enjoy the exercise of power mainly because it enables them to exhibit—if only to themselves—their skill and knowledge, their ability to stimulate their own capacities and to master their environment. Those skilled in athletics may enjoy riding horseback or skiing as solitary pastimes, with no one but themselves to admire their skills. The motivational base of this kind of competence has been labeled "effectance" by Robert White.

Still, there *are* the single-minded power wielders who fit the classical images of Machiavelli or Hobbes or Nietzsche, or at least the portraits of the modern power theorists. They consciously exploit their external resources (economic, social, psychological, and institutional) and their "effectance," their training, skill, and competence, to make persons and things do what they want done. The key factor here is indeed "what they want done." The motives of power wielders may or may not coincide with what the respondent wants done; it is P's intention that controls. Power wielders may or may not recognize respondents' wants and needs; if they do, they may recognize them only to the degree necessary to achieve their goals; and if they must make a choice between satisfying their own purposes and satisfying respondents' needs, they will choose the former. Power wielders are not free agents. They are subject—even slaves—to pressures working on them and in them. But once their will and purpose is forged, it may be controlling. If P wants circuses and R wants bread, the power wielder may manipulate popular demand for bread only to the degree that it helps P achieve circuses. At the "naked power" extremity on the continuum of types of power holders are the practitioners of virtually unbridled power—Hitler, Stalin, and the like—subject always, of course, to empowering and constraining circumstances.

The foundation of this kind of control lies in P's "power base" *as it is relevant to those at the receiving end of power.* The composition of the power base will vary from culture to culture, from situation to situation. Some power holders will have such pervasive control over factors influencing behavior that the imbalance between P's and R's power bases, and between the possibility of realizing P's and R's purposes, will be overwhelming. Nazi death camps and communist "re-education" camps are examples of such overwhelming imbalances. A dictator can put respondents physically in such isolation and under such constraint that they cannot even appeal to the dictator's conscience, if he has one, or to sympathetic opinion outside the camp or outside the country, if such exists. More typical, in most cultures, is the less asymmetric relationship in which P's power base supplies P with extensive control over R but leaves R with various resources for resisting. Prisons, armies, authoritarian families, concentration camps such as the United States relocation centers for Japanese-Americans during World War II, exemplify this kind of imbalance. There is a multitude of power balances in villages, tribes, schools, homes, collectives, businesses, trade unions, cities, in which most persons spend most of their lives.

To define power not as a property or entity or possession but as a *relationship* in which two or more persons tap motivational bases in one another and bring varying resources to bear in the process is to perceive power as drawing a vast range of human behavior into its orbit. The arena of power is no longer the exclusive preserve of a power elite or an establishment or persons clothed with legitimacy. Power is ubiquitous; it permeates human relationships. It exists whether or not it is quested for. It is the glory and the burden of most of humanity. A common, highly asymmetric, and sometimes cruel power relation can exist, for example, when one person is in love with another but the other does not reciprocate. The wants and needs and expectations of the person in love are aroused and engaged by a partner whose resources of attractiveness or desirability are high and whose own cluster of motives is less vulnerable. The person possessed by love can maneuver and struggle but still is a slave to the one loved, as the plight of Philip in Somerset Maugham's marvelously titled *Of Human Bondage* illustrates.

Because power can take such multifarious, ubiquitous, and subtle forms, it is reflected in an infinite number of combinations and particularities in specific contexts. Even so, observers *in* those contexts may perceive their particular "power mix" as the basic and universal type, and they will base elaborate descriptions and theories of power on one model—their own. Even Machiavelli's celebrated portrait of the uses and abuses of power, while relevant to a few other cultures and eras, is essentially culture-bound and irrelevant to a host of other power situations and systems. Thus popular tracts on power—how to win power and influence people—typically are useful only for particular situations and may disable the student of power coping with quite different power constellations.

Still there are ways of breaking power down into certain attributes that allow for some generalization and even theory-building. Robert Dahl's breakdown of the reach and magnitude of power is useful and parsimonious. One dimension is *distribution*—the concentration and dispersion of power among persons of diverse influence in various political, social, and economic locations such as geographical areas, castes and classes, status positions, skill groups, communications centers, and the like. Another dimension is *scope*—the extent to which power is generalized over a wide range or is specialized. Persons who are relatively powerful in relation to one kind of activity, Dahl notes, may be relatively weak in other power relationships. Still another dimension is *domain*—the number and nature of power respondents influenced by power wielders compared to those who are not. These dimensions are not greatly different from Lasswell and Abraham Kaplan's conception of the weight, scope, and domain of power.

A more common way to organize the data of power is in terms of the *size* of the *arena* in which power is exercised. The relation of P and R is, in many studies, typically one of micropower, as Edward Lehman calls it. Most power relations embrace a multiplicity of power holders; the relation is one among many Ps and many Rs. As power holders and respondents multiply, the number of relationships increases geometrically. Macropower, as Lehman contends, has distinct attributes of its own; the complex relations involved in the aggregate are not simply those of micropower extended to a higher plane. Causal interrelations become vastly more complex as a greater number of power actors and power components come into play. Paradoxically, we may, with modern techniques of fact-gathering and of empirical analysis, gain a better understanding of mass phenomena of power and leadership than of the more intricate and elusive interactions in micropower situations.

Whatever the dimensions or context, the fundamental process remains the same. *Power wielders draw from their power base's resources relevant to their own motives and the motives and resources of others upon whom they exercise power.* The power base may be narrow and weak, or it may consist of ample and multiple resources useful for vast and long-term exercises of power, but the process is the same. Dominated by personal motives, P draws on supporters, on funds, on ideology, on institutions, on old friendships, on political credits, on status, and on his own skills of calculation, judgment, communication, and timing, to mobilize those elements that relate to the motives of the persons P wishes to control—even if in the end P overrides their values and goals—just as P mobilizes machines and fuel and manpower and engineering expertise relevant to the tasks of building dams or clearing forests.

Power shows many faces and takes many forms. It may be as visible as the policeman's badge or billy or as veiled as the politician's whisper in the back room. It may exist as an overwhelming presence or as a potential that can be drawn on at will. It may appear in the form of money, sex appeal, authority, administrative regulation, charisma, munitions, staff resources, or instruments for torture. But all these resources must have this in common: *they must be relevant to the motivations of the power recipients.* Even the most fearsome of power devices, such as imprisonment or torture or denial of food or water, may not affect the behavior of a masochist or a martyr.

The exception to this qualification is the appalling power totally to dominate a power object physically or mentally through slavery, imprisonment, deportation, or hypnotism. This kind of power has two significant implications. One is the expenditure of effort and resources by P to exercise this kind of control; unless power has been inherited, P has invested, over a period of time and through many power-related acts, in power resources that permit exertion of "total" power. The other is the constraint that may tighten when P exercises total psychological or physical control; P may gain power over a limited number of persons or goods at the expense of antagonizing other persons—perhaps millions of them—by threatening and attacking their values. Power can be fully analyzed and measured only by viewing it in the context of multiple human interactions and broad causal relationships.

6

Situational Leadership and Power

Paul Hersey and Walter E. Natemeyer

The concepts of leadership and power have generated lively interest, debate, and occasionally confusion throughout the evolution of management thought. In fact, power is closely related to leadership, for power is one of the means by which a leader influences the behavior of followers.[1] Given this integral relationship between leadership and power, leaders must not only assess their leader behavior in order to understand how they actually influence other people, but they must also examine their possession and use of power.[2]

Power Defined

We earlier defined leadership as an attempt to influence another individual or group and concluded that leadership is an influence process. *Power is influence potential*—the resource that enables a leader to gain compliance or commitment from others. Despite its critical importance, power is a subject that is often avoided, for power can have an unpleasant side, and many people may want to wish it away and pretend it is not there. But power is a real-world issue. Leaders who understand and know how to use power are more effective than those who do not or will not use power. To successfully influence the behavior of others, the leader should understand the impact of power on the various leadership styles. In today's world, many sources of power within organizations have been legislated, negotiated, or administered away. Leaders now have less of some types of power to draw from, so it is even more important to effectively use what is available. Because power bases drive leadership styles, using them appropriately can enhance your effectiveness as a leader.[3]

In spite of the widespread usage of the term *power* in management literature, there are many definitions.[4] James Hillman reports that power's "rather innocent definition is simply the agency to act, to do, to be, coming from the Latin *potere,* to be able . . . power can be defined as sheer potency or potentiality, not the doing, but the capacity to do."[5] David C. McClelland and David H. Burnham have defined power as "influencing others."[6] John B. Miner defined power as "the ability to induce a person to do something he or she would not otherwise have done."[7] Miner goes on to write, "Influence is a broader concept, referring to anything a person does to alter the behavior, attitudes, values, feelings, and such of another person. . . . Power is thus one form of influence."[8] Stephen P. Robbins suggests the following:

> Power refers to a capacity that A has to influence the behavior of B, so that B does something that he or she would not otherwise do. This definition implies (1) a *potential* that need not be actualized to be effective, (2) a *dependence relationship,* and (3) that B has some *discretion* over his or her own behavior.[9]

While each of these definitions can be accurate, we will use Rogers's simple definition of power as "the potential for influence."[10] Thus, power is a resource that may or may not be used. The use of power resulting in a change in the probability that a person or group will adopt the desired behavioral change is defined as "influence." Accepting Rogers's definition, we make the following distinction between leadership and power. . . . Leadership is defined as the process of influencing the activities of an individual or a group in efforts toward accomplishing a goal in a given situation. Therefore, leadership is any attempt to influence, and power is a leader's *influence potential.* It is the resource that enables a leader to influence.

Position Power and Personal Power

One of the characteristics of leadership is that leaders exercise power. Amitai Etzioni discussed the difference between position power and personal power. His distinction resulted from his concept of power as the ability to induce or influence behavior. He claimed that power is derived from an organizational office, personal influence, or both. Individuals who are able to induce other individuals to do a certain job because of their position in the organization are considered to have position power; individuals who derive their power from their followers are considered to have personal power. Some individuals can have both position power and personal power.[11]

Where do managers get the position power that is available to them? Although Etzioni would argue that it comes from the organizational office of a manager, we feel it comes from above and, therefore, is not inherent in the office. Managers occupying positions in an organization may have more or less position power than their predecessors or someone else in a similar position in the same organization. *Position power* is the extent to which those people to whom managers report are willing to delegate authority and responsibility down to them. So position power tends to flow down in an organization; it is not a matter of the office's having power. This is not to say that leaders do not have any impact on how much position power they accrue. They certainly do. The confidence and trust they develop with the people above them will often determine the willingness of upper management to delegate down to them. And remember, whatever power is delegated downward can be taken back. We have all seen this occur when managers still have the same responsibilities, but their authority (to distribute rewards and sanctions) to get the job done has been taken away.

"Commitment is nice, but doses of compliance may be necessary."

—Michael Beer, *Harvard Business Review*

Personal power is the extent to which followers respect, feel good about, and are committed to their leader and to which they see their own goals as being satisfied by the goals of their leader. In other words, personal power is the extent to which people are willing to follow a leader. As a result, personal power in an organizational setting comes from below—from the followers—and so flows up in an organization. Thus, we must be careful when we say that some leaders are charismatic or have personal power that flows from them. Personal power is not inherent in the leader. If it were, managers with personal power could take over any department and have the same commitment and rapport they had in their last department. We know that they can't. Although managers certainly can influence the amount of personal power they have by the way they treat their people, it is a subjective and volatile kind of power. It can be taken away rapidly by followers. Make a few dramatic mistakes and see how many people are willing to follow. Personal power is a day-to-day phenomenon; it can be earned and it can be taken away.

"The first duty of a leader is to make himself be loved without courting love. To be loved without 'playing up' to anyone—even to himself."

—Andre Malraux

"Dignity does not come in possessing honors, but in deserving them."

—Aristotle

Etzioni suggested that the best situation for leaders is when they have both personal power and position power. But in some cases it is not possible to build a relationship on both. Then the question becomes whether it is more important to have personal power or position power. Happiness and human relations have been culturally reinforced over the past several decades. With this emphasis, most people would pick personal power as being the most important, but there is another side to this coin.

In his 16th-century treatise *The Prince,* Machiavelli presented an interesting viewpoint when he raised the question of whether it is better to have a relationship based on love (personal power) or fear (position power).[12] Machiavelli contended, as did Etzioni, that it is best to be both loved and feared. If, however, one cannot have both, he suggested that a relationship based on love alone tends to be volatile, short lived, and easily terminated when there is no fear of retaliation. On the other hand, a relationship based on fear tends to be longer lasting because the individual must be ready to incur the sanction (pay the price) before terminating the relationship. This is a difficult concept for many people to accept. One of the most difficult roles for leaders—whether they be a supervisor, teacher, or parent—is disciplining someone about whom they care. Yet to be effective at enhancing others' growth and development, leaders sometimes have to sacrifice short-term friendship for long-term respect. Machiavelli warned, however, that one should be careful that this fear (amount of position power) does not lead to hatred. Hatred often evokes overt behavior in terms of retaliation, undermining, and attempts to overthrow.

In summary, position power can be thought of as the authority, which is delegated down, to use rewards and sanctions. Personal power is the cohesiveness, commitment, and rapport between leaders and followers. It is also affected by the extent to which followers see their own goals as being the same, similar to, or at least dependent on the accomplishment of the leader's goals.

Although personal and position power are distinct, they are an interacting influence system. Often, followers are affected by their perceptions of both the leader's ability to provide rewards, punishments, and sanctions and the leader's ability to influence up the organization. The extent to which people above you in the organization are willing to delegate position power is often dependent on their perception of the followers' commitment to you. So it is not sufficient to have either position or personal power alone—a leader needs to work at gaining both.

Selling Within Your Own Organization

It is important to keep in mind that no matter where you are within your organization, you are trying to influence people.[13] If you are managing, you can use both position power and personal power to influence the people who report directly to you. When attempting to influence your supervisor, senior executives, and associates, however, you must depend almost exclusively on personal power. Therefore, you are selling. When you have little or no position power, you must learn to develop rapport through personal power because it is through this trust and confidence that an effective relationship can be built. Figure 1 illustrates this important idea. Keep in mind that power is a real-world issue. People who understand and know how to use power are more effective than those who do not or will not. Recognition of the fact that all managers are in the business of selling is an important aspect of this understanding.

Additional Bases of Power

Although position power and personal power are important and useful concepts in examining power, they are limited because they force you to divide "the pie" into just two pieces. R. L. Peabody named four categories of power on the basis of statements of questionnaire respondents in a police department, a welfare office, and an elementary school: power of legitimacy (laws, rules, policies); of position; of competence (professional and technical expertise); and of person.[14]

Figure 1
Selling Up/Managing Down

Supervisor / Associates

Staff Members / Employees

Source: Adapted from Paul Hersey, *Situational Selling* (Escondido, CA: Center for Leadership Studies, 1985), p. 15. Reprinted with permission.

A study by A. C. Filley and A. J. Grimes identified 11 reasons an individual would seek a decision from another on various work-related matters in a professional organization.[15] These reasons, from most frequently to least frequently mentioned, were:

- responsibility and function (the person is responsible for the particular matter)
- formal authority (the person is in a position to make decisions generally)
- control of resources (the person controls money, information, and so on)
- collegial (a group of peers has the right to be consulted)
- manipulation (the person can get the decision made in the manner desired)
- default or avoidance (the person is available and will deal with the problem)
- bureaucratic rules (the rules specify the person to consult)
- traditional rules (custom, tradition, or seniority specify the person to consult)
- equity (the person is a fair decision maker)
- friendship (the person is personally liked)
- expertise (the person has superior knowledge of the subject)

Many other power base classification systems have been developed, but the framework devised by J. R. P. French and B. Raven appears to be the most widely accepted.[16, 17] They proposed that there are five bases of power: coercive power, expert power, legitimate power, referent power, and reward power. Later, Raven, collaborating with W. Kruglanski, identified a sixth power base—information power.[18] Hersey and Walt Natemeyer modified some of the definitions of French, Raven, and Kruglanski and proposed a seventh base of power—connection power.[19] We will define each of these seven power bases shortly.

The Perception of Power

In the following discussion of power bases, we use the word *perceived* in such instances as "coercive power—the perceived ability to provide sanctions." We do this because the key issue in the concept of power is that it is not based on the reality of how much power the manager has but rather on the followers' perception of that power. Truth and reality evoke no behavior. All behavior is based on people's perception and interpretation of truth and reality. For example, when a couple has a fight, it does not matter whether the cause was real or imagined— it was just as much of a fight. In a similar fashion, it is the perception others hold about power that gives people the ability to influence.

We operate using psychological maps. No matter how hard we work or how detailed our psychological map, no matter how much information and specificity it contains, the map is not the actual territory. It is a mere representation. However, the closer we match our psychological map to the territory, the higher the probability that we will be able to operate effectively within that territory.

Get the Information Out

People must not only perceive you as having power, but also see you as able and willing to use it. It's not enough to have access to power; you have to let people know you're willing to use it. Information has value only when you get it out to the end user in a fashion that can be understood and accepted.

Consider a father examining his son's report card and suffering heart palpitations as he sees a solid column of Ds. Outraged that a product of his genes could so disgrace the family, he confronts his son: "Dave, this just won't do. I can't tolerate these grades, and if you don't show me an immediate turnaround, you're going to be grounded!" Six weeks later, Dave brings home another report card. This time the Ds are written in red ink with exclamation points. The father says, "David, get in here! I'm really upset, and now you have no choice at all. Hit those books hard or you're definitely going to be grounded!"

Next time it's the same except that the teacher has added some pointed remarks about Dave's inattentive behavior in class. Dave's father turns crimson, puts down the remote control and shouts, "David Ralph, this is it . . . last chance city . . . you're in real trouble with the old man now!" What has Dave learned? He has learned that his father, who has the ability to ground him, won't use the power. Because of his father's reluctance to follow through with his threatened punishments, Dave knows that all he has to do is take heat for six minutes and he's off the hook for six weeks!

Power is a matter of perception; use it or lose it!

Performance Readiness, Styles, and Power Bases

The relationship between performance readiness, leadership style, and the power base that drives that style will now be explained.

Coercive Power—The Perceived Ability to Provide Sanctions, Punishment, or Consequences for Not Performing

Followers at performance readiness level R1 need guidance and direction. Too much supportive behavior with people at this level who are not currently performing may be perceived as permissive or as rewarding the lack of performance. Without some coercive power to drive the telling style (S1), attempts to influence will most likely be ineffective. Followers who don't perform need to know that if they do not respond appropriately, there may be some costs, sanctions, or other consequences. These may take the form of a reprimand, cut in pay, transfer, demotion, or even termination.

Managers often erode their coercive power by not following through. They may, for instance, have the ability to impose sanctions but for one reason or another be unwilling to do so. This reluctance to use sanctions can result in a loss of power. Another way to erode coercive power is by not differentiating in the use of sanctions on the basis of performance. If people feel that they will be punished regardless of performance, coercive power has little impact on a leader's ability to influence them.

It is even possible to "talk" coercive power away. Let's say that a manager begins a performance appraisal interview with a low performer by saying, "Now, look, both of us know that you've been here over 20 years and I can't fire you." In those few words, the manager has stripped away any coercive power the follower might have perceived.

Connection Power—The Perceived Association of the Leader with Influential Persons or Organizations

Connection power is an important driver for telling (S1) and selling (S2) leadership styles. Usually, followers at R1 and R2 want to avoid the sanctions or gain the favor they associate with powerful connections. The important issue is not whether there is a real connection, but whether there is a perception of a real connection.

For example, a first-level supervisor may be regarded as having limited power. But if that supervisor is married to a relative of the company president, the perceived connection may provide added influence with others in the organization.

Reward Power—The Perceived Ability to Provide Things That People Would Like to Have

Reward power is enhanced if managers are seen as having the ability to give appropriate rewards. Followers who are unable to currently perform a certain task but are willing to make an effort (R2) are most likely to try on new behaviors if they feel increases in performance will be rewarded. Rewards may include raises, bonuses, promotions, or transfers to more desirable positions. They may also include intangibles such as a pat on the back or feedback on accomplishment. In the final analysis, managers get what they reward. Therefore, it matters not only that the reward be offered in a timely manner, but also that the reward be perceived as such by the receiver. More pointedly, what constitutes a reward is indeed in the eye of the beholder.

A significant amount of reward power has been legislated, negotiated, and administered away over the past few decades. This has resulted from companies endeavoring to avoid costly litigation when they are forced to downsize, restructure, and cut costs in response to the increasingly competitive global environment. Consequently, we often have to remind managers that reward power is tied to not only monetary rewards. This may require some creative thinking, but discovering what intangibles actually motivate followers can have an enormous impact on a leader's reward power. Managers, however, often erode what little reward power they have by making promises they don't keep. Consider, for example, the following:

> *Salesperson:* I did it! I made the 15 percent over quota with room to spare. When am I going to get that 10 percent bonus?

> *Sales Manager:* I'm sorry, but economic conditions are such that we'll have to postpone it for a while. But don't worry, if you keep up the good work, I promise I'll make it up to you.

Other managers erode their reward power by "hoping for A but rewarding B."[20] An example might be an organization that gives all salespeople a 10 percent cost-of-living adjustment and yet the difference between reward for average sales and outstanding sales is only 1 or 2 percent. In this case, "hanging around" for another year is significantly rewarded. This practice often results in high performers losing their motivation and commitment or looking outside the company for opportunities. A problem with power derived from rewards is that rewards will often run their course. The manager will be left with an employee who is no longer motivated through the use of rewards and an organization that can no longer provide rewards.

Legitimate Power—The Perception That it is Appropriate for the Leader to Make Decisions because of Title, Role, or Position in the Organization

Legitimate power can be a useful driver for both the selling and participating leadership styles but ineffective for followers who are both unable and unwilling or insecure (R1), who generally don't care whether someone's title is manager, regional manager, or vice president. Similarly, followers high in performance readiness (R4) are far less impressed with title or position than they are with expertise or information. However followers in the moderate ranges of performance readiness (R2 or R3) can often be influenced if they feel it is appropriate for a person in that position with that title to make that decision. For example, a salesperson might comment to a peer about the department's recent reorganization: "Pat should be making those kinds of decisions . . . that's what the sales manager gets paid to do."

Referent Power—The Perceived Attractiveness of Interacting with the Leader

In attempting to influence people who are able but insecure or unwilling (R3), high-relationship behavior is necessary. If people have a confidence problem, the manager needs to provide encouragement. If they have a motivation problem, the manager needs to discuss and problem solve. In either case, if the manager has not taken time to build rapport, attempts to participate may be perceived as adversarial rather than helpful. Confidence, trust, and rapport are important ingredients necessary for influencing people. If a follower feels that the manager will provide encouragement and help when it is needed, referent power can make an important difference in the success of the influence attempt. Referent power is based on the manager's personal traits, such as integrity and honesty. A manager high in referent power is generally liked and admired by others because of personality. It is this liking for, admiration for, and identification with the manager that influences others.

"Men are more often bribed by their loyalties and ambitions than by money."

—Robert H. Jackson, U.S. Supreme Court Justice

Information Power—The Perceived Access to, or Possession of, Useful Information

The styles that tend to effectively influence followers at above-average performance readiness levels (R3 and R4) are participating (S3) and delegating (S4). Information power is most helpful in driving these styles. The use of this power source has grown significantly since the inception of the Internet. In fact, it has continued to grow in importance as more data becomes available and accessible. Those who know how to access the information needed in a timely manner tend to be the ones that others seek out, and sharing that information provides an opportunity for those knowledge holders to influence the behaviors of others.

Information power is based on perceived access to data. This is different from expert power, which is the understanding of or ability to use data. For example, one study found that secretaries in a major corporate office had a significant amount of information power but little expert power in some technical areas. They were able to help gain or prevent access to information but, with the exception of a few technical areas, had little expertise themselves.

Expert Power—The Perception That the Leader Has Relevant Education, Experience, and Expertise

Followers who are competent and confident require little direction or supportive behavior. They are able and willing to perform on their own. The driver for influencing these followers is expert power. With followers who are able and confidently willing (R4), leaders are more effective if they possess the expertise, skill, and knowledge that followers respect and regard as important. An apt example is Al Smith, former governor of New York State. When he was a freshman legislator, he spent his nights studying the New York State budget instead of attending the many social events. As Tom Peters, well-known author and commentator on the management scene, described it, "His matchless command of the fine print [of the budget] launched an extraordinary career."[21]

Is There a Best Type of Power?

The French and Raven initial classification system motivated a number of scholars to try to answer the following question: Given the wide variety of power bases available to the leader, which type of power should be emphasized in order to maximize effectiveness? In any attempt to answer this question, it is important to remember the definition of effectiveness. . . . Organizational effectiveness, as well as leader effectiveness, is a function of both output variables and intervening variables.

K. R. Student studied 40 production groups in two plants of a company that manufactured home appliances.[22] Employees rated the extent to which they complied with their foremen because of each of the five French and Raven power bases. Legitimate power was found to be the strongest reason for compliance, followed by expert power, reward power, referent power, and last, coercive power.

Student also related the foremen's power base use (as perceived by the workers) to a number of measures of performance. He found that legitimate power, while most important among the reasons for compliance, was not related to the performance of the work groups. Reward and coercive power were positively related to some performance measures (suggestions submitted, supply cost performance) but negatively related to others (average earnings, maintenance cost performance). Expert and referent power were significantly and positively related to four and five measures of performance, respectively, and thus emerged as the two most effective bases of supervisory power. Student explained these results by suggesting that expert and referent power are qualitatively different from legitimate, reward, and coercive power. Expert and referent power are considered idiosyncratic in character and dependent on an individual's unique role behavior, whereas legitimate, reward, and coercive power are organizationally determined and designed to be equal for supervisors at the same hierarchical level. Implicit in Student's conclusions is the contention that followers are more responsive to and satisfied with a leader whose influence attempts are not based entirely on position-based power (that is, legitimate, reward, and coercive).

Similar results were obtained in a study by J. G. Bachman, C. G. Smith, and J. A. Slesinger.[23] Data were obtained from 36 branch offices of a national sales organization. Each office was managed by a single office supervisor. Employees were asked to rank each of the five power bases according to the extent to which it was a reason for compliance. These results were then correlated with satisfaction and performance measures. Legitimate and expert power again emerged as first and second in importance, followed by referent, reward, and coercive power, in that order.

In those offices in which referent and expert power predominated, performance and satisfaction were high. In those offices in which reward power was high, performance tended to be poor and there was marked dissatisfaction. Coercive and legitimate bases of power were associated with dissatisfaction, but they were unrelated to performance.

The findings of Student and Bachman and others were included in a comparative study of five organizations by Bachman, D. G. Bowers, and P. M. Marcus.[24] In addition to the appliance firm and the sales organization, other organizations examined were 12 liberal arts colleges, 40 agencies of a life insurance company, and 21 work groups of a large Midwestern utility company. A ranking procedure was used to ascertain the strength of the supervisors' power bases in the colleges and the utility company, while an independent rating procedure for each power base was used with the life insurance agencies.

Expert and legitimate power were again the most important reasons for complying with supervisors in all three organizations. Expert power was most important, and legitimate power, second, in the colleges and insurance agencies. The order was reversed in the utility company. Referent power was third in importance in the colleges, fourth in the insurance agencies, and fifth in the utility companies. Reward power was third in importance in the utility company and the agencies and fourth in the colleges. Finally, coercive power was least important in the colleges and the insurance agencies and fourth in the utility company.

Expert and referent power were again strongly and positively related to satisfaction in these three additional organizations, whereas reward and legitimate power were not strongly related to the satisfaction measures. Coercive power was consistently related to dissatisfaction. Performance data were obtained from the insurance agencies but not from the colleges or utility company. Expert and reward power were positively related to insurance agency performance measures, and coercive, legitimate, and referent power yielded insignificant correlations.

J. M. Ivancevich and J. H. Donnelly studied salespersons' perceptions of their managers' power bases in 31 branches of a large firm that produces food products.[25] The employees were asked to rank the power bases in order of importance for compliance. Expert power was most important, followed by legitimate, reward, referent, and coercive power. Referent and expert power were positively related to performance; reward, legitimate, and coercive power showed no relationship.

R. J. Burke and D. S. Wilcox conducted a study of leader power bases and follower satisfaction in six offices of a large public utility company.[26] A one-to-five ranking method was used. Expert power emerged as most important, followed by legitimate, coercive, referent, and reward power. Referent and expert power were associated with greatest satisfaction, legitimate and reward power were intermediate, and coercive power was associated with least satisfaction.

In summarizing a review of the most important research relating supervisory power bases to follower satisfaction and performance, Walter Natemeyer made the following general conclusion: Although expert and legitimate power bases appear to be the most important reason for compliance, and expert and referent power bases tend to be often strongly and consistently related to follower performance and satisfaction measures, the results are not clear enough to generalize about a best power base.[27] In fact, the results suggest that the appropriate power base is largely affected by situational variables. In other words, leaders may need various power bases, depending on the situation.

Power Bases and Performance Readiness Level

Hersey, Natemeyer, and Blanchard suggest that there is a direct relationship between the level of performance readiness of individuals and groups and the kind of power bases that have a high probability of gaining compliance from those people.[28] Situational Leadership views performance readiness as the ability and willingness of individuals or groups to take responsibility for directing their own behavior in a particular situation. Thus, it must be reemphasized that performance readiness is a task-specific concept and depends on what the leader is attempting to accomplish.

As people move from lower to higher levels of performance readiness, their competence and confidence to do things increase. The seven power bases appear to have significant impact on the behavior of people at various levels of performance readiness, as seen in Figure 2.

Figure 2
The Impact of Power Bases
at Various Levels of Performance Readiness

High Performance Readiness

Expert
Information
Referent
Legitimate
Reward
Connection
Coercive

Low Performance Readiness

Integrating Power Bases, Performance Readiness Level, and Leadership Style through Situational Leadership®

Situational Leadership® provides the context for understanding the potential impact of each power base. It is our contention that the performance readiness of the follower not only dictates which style of leadership will have the highest probability of success, but also determines the power base that the leader should use in order to induce compliance or influence behavior to maximize performance.

The Situational Use of Power

Even if the leader is using the appropriate leadership style for a given performance readiness level, that style may not be maximizing the leader's probability of success if it does not reflect the appropriate power base. Therefore, just as an effective leader should vary leadership style according to the performance readiness level of the follower, it is appropriate to vary the use of power in a similar manner. The power bases that may influence people's behavior at various levels of performance readiness are shown in Figure 3.

Figure 3
Power Bases Necessary to Influence People's Behavior
at Various Levels of Performance Readiness

Performance Readiness Level

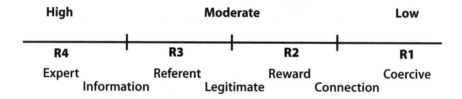

Figure 3 shows a relationship only between power bases and performance readiness level. However, there also appears to be a direct relationship between the kind of power bases a person has and the corresponding leadership style that will be effective for that person in influencing the behavior of others at various performance readiness levels.

Coercive Power.   A follower low in performance readiness generally needs strong directive behavior in order to become productive. To engage effectively in this telling style (S1), the leader may have to use coercive power. The behavior of people at low levels of performance readiness (R1) seems to be generally influenced by the awareness that costs will be incurred if they do not learn and follow the rules of the game. Thus, sanctions—the perceived power to fire, transfer, demote, and so on—may be an important way that a leader can induce compliance from people who are unable and unwilling. The leader's coercive power may motivate the followers to avoid the punishment or "cost" by doing what the leader tells them to do.

Connection Power.   As a follower begins to move from performance readiness level R1 to R2, directive behavior is still needed, but increases in supportive behavior are also important at this juncture. The telling (S1) and selling (S2) leadership styles appropriate for these levels of performance readiness may become more effective if the leader has connection power. The possession of this power base may induce compliance because a follower at these performance readiness levels tends to engage in behaviors geared toward avoiding punishments or gaining rewards that are perceived to be available through the powerful connection.

Reward Power. A follower at a low to moderate level of performance readiness often needs high amounts of supportive behavior and directive behavior (S2). This selling style is often enhanced by reward power. Since individuals at this performance readiness level are willing to try on new behaviors, the leader needs to be perceived as having access to rewards in order to gain compliance and to reinforce growth in the desired direction.

Legitimate Power. The leadership styles that tend to influence effectively those at both moderate levels of performance readiness (R2 and R3) are selling (S2) and participating (S3). Legitimate power seems to be helpful in the effective use of these styles. By the time a follower reaches these moderate levels of performance readiness, the power of the leader has become legitimized. That is, the leader is able to induce compliance or influence behavior by virtue of the leader's position in the organizational hierarchy.

Referent Power. A follower at a moderate to high level of performance readiness (R3) tends to need little direction but still requires a high level of communication and support from the leader. This participating style (S3) may be more effectively utilized if the leader has referent power. This source of power is based on good personal relations with the follower. With people who are able but insecure or unwilling, this power base tends to be an important means of instilling confidence and providing encouragement, recognition, and other supportive behavior. When that occurs, followers will generally respond in a positive way, permitting the leader to influence them because they like, admire, or identify with the leader.

Information Power. The leadership styles that tend to motivate followers effectively at above-average performance readiness levels (R3 and R4) are participating (S3) and delegating (S4). Information power seems to be particularly helpful in using these two styles in that people at these levels of performance readiness look to the leader for information to maintain or improve performance. The transition from moderate to high performance readiness may in fact be facilitated if the follower knows that the leader is available to clarify or explain issues and provide access to pertinent data, reports, and correspondence when needed. Through this information power, the leader is able to influence people who are both willing and able.

Expert Power. A follower who develops to a high level of performance readiness often requires little direction or support. This follower is able and willing (R4) to perform the tasks required and tends to respond most readily to a delegating leadership style (S4) and through the leader's judicious use of expert power. Thus, a leader may gain respect from and influence most readily a person who has both competence and confidence by possessing expertise, skill, and knowledge that this follower recognizes as important.

Power bases can be very subjective. We can draw conclusions about which power base tends to be most effective with each performance readiness level. However, there may be more than one power base driving the influence behavior. An easy way to think about sources of power in terms of making diagnostic judgments is to draw a triangle, as shown in Figure 4, around the three power bases necessary to influence below-average, average, and above-average levels of performance readiness.

Figure 4
Power Bases Necessary to Influence People
at Various Readiness Levels

A way to examine the high-probability power base for a specific performance readiness level is to draw triangles, as shown in Figure 5. Note that R1 and R4, the extreme performance readiness levels, include only two power bases instead of three.

Figure 5
Power Bases Necessary to Influence People's Behavior
at Specific Levels of Performance Readiness

Developing Sources of Power

Although these seven power bases are potentially available to any leader as a means of influencing the behavior of others, it is important to note that there is significant variance in the powers that leaders may actually possess. Some leaders have a great deal of power; others have very little. Part of the variance in actual power is due to the organization and the leader's position in the organization (position power), and part is due to individual differences among the leaders themselves (personal power), as shown in Figure 6.

Figure 6
Summary of Relationships among Power Bases,
Performance Readiness Level, and Leadership Style

The power bases that are most relevant at the below-average levels of performance readiness tend to be those that the organization or others can bestow on the leader. The power bases that influence people who are above average in performance readiness must, to a large degree, be earned from the people the leader is attempting to influence. Therefore, we suggest that position power and the phrase *power over* are most descriptive with coercive, connection, reward, and legitimate power bases, and we suggest that personal power and the phrase *power with* more accurately describe the effect on behavior from referent, information, and expert power.

Sources of Power

Just as some leaders start off with little power and gradually build and develop various power sources, other leaders gradually let their power bases erode and lose them. Why? Before we answer that question, managers need to understand the sources of position and personal power.

As we discussed earlier, position power can be thought of as the authority that is delegated down in an organization. Managers do, however, have some impact on how much position (coercive, connection, reward, and legitimate) power they get. The extent to which they develop rapport, confidence, and trust between themselves and senior management will determine how willing those above them will be to delegate power. In that sense, position power is something that a manager has to earn on a day-to-day basis.

The same can be said about personal power, except that the personal power (reward, information, and expert) that managers possess depends on the confidence and trust those managers generate from the people they are attempting to influence. For example, people might think that some leaders have charisma and other leaders don't. Leaders don't have charisma; followers give leaders charisma. We have all seen that phenomenon with elected officials. They are often carried into office because of their charisma, but when their actions do not gain general approval, they may lose their charisma overnight. Again, this is not to say that managers do not have some impact on how much personal power they get, but it's something that they have to earn on a day-to-day basis.

Position power and personal power bases together constitute an interaction-influence system. That is, power does not develop in a vacuum. Each power base tends to affect each of the other power bases. Thus, the extent to which people are willing to grant personal power to a manager depends a great deal on their perception of a leader's ability to provide rewards, punishment, or sanctions (position power). At the same time, the willingness of managers above a leader to delegate position power is often determined by the extent to which they perceive that leader as being liked and respected and having information and expertise (personal power) with their people. Keep in mind that we did not say how much personal power or position power affects whether leaders will be delegated authority or treated with respect. As we have noted before, it is the perception that others have of those power bases that is crucial. So the key word, perhaps, in the whole area of the behavioral sciences is *perception.*

Eroding Sources of Power

Since leaders have only a limited amount of power available to them, one would hope that they would hold on to whatever power bases they have. Yet some leaders who start off with significant power gradually lose their power bases and let them erode. The key to avoiding such erosion is to use your power bases. For example, a leader could have a significant amount of coercive power but gradually lose it by threatening followers with some kind of punishment and not follow through. In this context, people will start to think that the leader really does not have any coercive power. Similarly, leaders can lose their reward power if everyone gets the same reward whether they perform or not, or just because they have seniority in industry, or are older in the family. Some parents establish age requirements when kids can get to do things. "When you're 13, you'll be able to stay out past 10 o'clock. When you're 16, you'll be able to stay home alone." The problem with using age as a factor in determining when people can do things is that all they have to do is get older. When age is used as the determining factor, reward power as a parent or a leader is lost because what is happening is that people are getting rewards for being older, not for being more ready to take responsibility.

Connection power can be eroded when people begin to see that the sponsor or connection does not make any disciplinary interventions or provide any favors or sanctions. In other words, to be maintained, connection power needs occasional interventions from the sponsor. Similarly, managers can lose their legitimate power by not making decisions that people think they ought to make, given their position. Erosion of this power base can also occur if a manager continually makes decisions that are not fruitful. After a while, their staff members will no longer look to them to make decisions even if they have the title of senior research scientist or department manager.

This process also works with referent power. When you give praise or recognition to those who are performing and the same praise or recognition to those who are not performing, you begin to erode your referent power. If people do not have to earn praise and recognition, then you no longer have referent power.

Leaders also have to be careful about eroding their information and expert power, particularly if they give away expertise and information to people whose goals are not organizational goals. If you give away too much information and knowledge, eventually those people will not need you. The only way you can get around this problem is to continually develop new information and new expertise so they have to come back to the source.

If leaders let their power bases erode, they will also reduce the effectiveness of their leadership attempts. For example, an effective telling (S1) leadership style depends on having some coercive power. If leaders are not seen as being able to deliver punishments and sanctions, their use of that style is limited.

The same can be said about a selling (S2) style. Without some control over rewards, leaders are seen as not being able to reinforce or compensate for increased performance as people grow and develop their skills.

A participating (S3) style won't work if people don't like and respect a manager. Additionally, if a manager has let reward power erode by not being particularly responsive to people, then a participative, high-relationship style is going to be seen not as a reward, but as a punishment. Suppose a manager has ignored a staff member for a long time then, suddenly, when that person's family life begins to deteriorate, the manager tries to comfort and console the staffer. Since the manager has eroded available referent power, these supportive leadership attempts are not seen as rewards, but as sanctions and punishments. Time with the boss is not seen as a positive experience.

A manager who is supervising highly competent and motivated people needs to have some expert power to make any kind of significant intervention. If the manager has eroded information and expert power, the possibility of influencing these people in any significant way will be very limited. . . .

The Power Perception Profile

To provide leaders with feedback on their power bases so they can determine which power bases they already have and which they need to develop, Hersey and Natemeyer developed the Power Perception Profile.[29] There are two versions of this instrument: one measures self-perception of power, and the other determines perceptions of another's power.

Development of the Power Perception Profile

The Power Perception Profile contains 21 forced-choice pairs of reasons often given by people when asked why they do things that a leader suggests or wants them to do.

After completing the Power Perception Profile, respondents are able to obtain a score of the relative strength of each of the seven bases of power. This score represents the perception of influence for themselves or some other leader.

One of the shortcomings of most forced-choice instruments is that they provide comparisons only between items or categories, but they do not offer any perspective on the overall scope of the concepts. In other words, a leader might score high or low on a certain power base when compared with each of the other power bases, but no indication is given of how that power base score compares with the score another leader might receive. For example, even if a leader's score on coercive power is low in relation to the other six power bases, the leader may be relatively high in coercive power when compared with other leaders the respondent has known. To correct this deficiency, the Power Perception Profile goes one step further than most forced-choice questionnaires and asks respondents to compare the leader with other leaders they have known in reference to each of the seven power bases.

Uses of the Power Perception Profile

The Power Perception Profile can be used to gather data in actual organizational settings or any learning environment—for example, student or training groups. In learning groups, the instrument is particularly helpful in groups that have developed some history—that is, they have spent a considerable amount of time interacting with each other while analyzing or solving cases and/or participating in simulations or other training exercises. In this kind of situation, it is recommended that the group fill out one instrument together, using a particular member as the subject and arriving at a consensus on each of the items on the instrument. During each discussion, the person whose power bases are being examined should play a nonparticipant role. That person should not ask any questions or attempt to clarify, justify, or explain actions. An appropriate response might be, "Could you tell me more about that?" or "I'd like to hear more on that point." Then, at the end of the group's assessment, the person whose power bases were being examined is given an opportunity to respond to the group's discussion. This process is repeated until every participant has had a turn to get feedback from the group.

If the Power Perception Profile is being used to gather data in an organization, each organizational member from whom perceptions are desired should fill out a separate instrument. In this case, it is strongly suggested that the leaders not collect the data themselves. Instead, a third party who has the trust and confidence of all involved—such as a representative from human resources—should administer the questionnaire. It is also important to assure respondents that only generalized data will be shared with the leader, not the scores from any particular person. These suggestions are important because if leaders collect their own data, even if the instruments are anonymous, there is a tendency for some respondents to answer according to what they feel the leaders want or do not want to hear. Thus, to help establish a valid data base, leaders may want to have their data gathered by a third party.

Understanding power bases is important. If you understand which power bases tend to influence a group of people, you have some insight into who should be given a particular project assignment or responsibility. The person you assign to a particular task should have the power bases and be comfortable in using the appropriate leadership styles that are required in a particular setting. If someone really wants an assignment and doesn't have the appropriate power bases, it's a problem of self-development. You can work out a program to build that power base or appropriate style. What all this means is that we can increase the probability of success of a particular manager if we understand the territory—if we know what power bases and corresponding leadership styles are needed to influence the people involved effectively. That's the whole concept of team building. . . .

Notes

[1] R. M. Stogdill, *Handbook of Leadership* (New York: Free Press, 1974).

[2] Many of the concepts in this chapter were first published in Paul Hersey, Kenneth H. Blanchard, and Walter E. Natemeyer, "Situational Leadership, Perception, and the Impact of Power," *Group and Organizational Studies* 4, no. 4 (December 1979): 418–428.

[3] Adapted from Paul Hersey, *The Situational Leader* (Escondido, CA: Center for Leadership Studies, 1985), 27.

[4] This section on defining power and other concepts originated with Walter E. Natemeyer, "An Empirical Investigation of the Relationships between Leader Behavior, Leader Power Bases, and Subordinate Performance and Satisfaction" (PhD diss., University of Houston, August 1975).

[5] James Hillman, *Kinds of Power* (New York: Currency-Doubleday, 1995), 97.

[6] David C. McClelland and David H. Burnham, "Power Is the Great Motivator," *Harvard Business Review,* January–February 1995, 134.

[7] John B. Miner, *Organizational Behavior* (New York: Random House, 1988), 481.

[8] Ibid.

[9] Stephen P. Robbins, *Essentials of Organizational Behavior,* 4th ed. (Englewood Cliffs, NJ: Prentice Hall, 1994), 152.

[10] M. F. Rogers, "Instrumental and Infra-Resources: The Bases of Power," *American Journal of Sociology* 79, 6 (1973): 1418–1433.

[11] Amitai Etzioni, *A Comparative Analysis of Complex Organizations* (New York: Free Press, 1961).

[12] Niccolo Machiavelli, "Of Cruelty and Clemency, Whether It Is Better to Be Loved or Feared," *The Prince and the Discourses* (New York: Random House, 1950).

[13] This section is adapted from Paul Hersey, *Situational Selling* (Escondido, CA: Center for Leadership Studies, 1985), 14–15.

[14] R. L. Peabody, "Perceptions of Organizational Authority: A Comparative Analysis," *Administrative Quarterly* 6 (1962): 463–482.

[15] A. C. Filley and A. J. Grimes, "The Bases of Power in Decision Processes," *Reprint Series 104* (Industrial Relations Research Institute, University of Wisconsin, 1967).

[16] K. D. Beene, *A Conception of Authority* (New York: Teachers College, Columbia University, 1943).

[17] John R. P. French and B. Raven, "The Bases of Social Power," in D. Cartright, ed., *Studies in Social Power* (Ann Arbor: University of Michigan, Institute for Social Research, 1959).

[18] B. H. Raven and W. Kruglanski, "Conflict and Power," in P. G. Swingle, ed., *The Structure of Conflict* (New York: Academic Press, 1975), 177–219.

[19] Paul Hersey and Walt Natemeyer, "The Changing Role of Performance Management," *Training and Development Journal* (April 1980).

[20] Steven Kerr, "On the Folly of Rewarding A, While Hoping for B," *Academy of Management Journal* 18 (1975): 769–783. Reprinted with commentary in *The Academy of Management Executive* 9, no. 1 (February 1995): 7–14 and an informal survey, "More on the Folly," 15–16.

[21] Tom Peters, "Power: Get It and Use It with These 13 Secrets," *Star Tribune,* August 2, 1994, 2D.

[22] K. R. Student, "Supervisory Influence and Work-Group Performance," *Journal of Applied Psychology* 52, no. 3 (1968): 188–194.

[23] J. G. Bachman, C. G. Smith, and J. A. Slesinger, "Control, Performance, and Satisfaction: An Analysis of Structural and Individual Effects," *Journal of Personality and Social Psychology* 4, no. 2 (1966): 127–136.

[24] J. G. Bachman, D. G. Bowers, and P. M. Marcus, "Bases of Supervisory Power: A Comparative Study in Five Organizational Settings," in Arnold S. Tannenbaum, ed., *Control in Organizations* (New York: McGraw-Hill, 1968).

[25] J. M. Ivancevich and J. H. Donnelly, "Leader Influence and Performance," *Personnel Psychology* 23, no. 4 (1970): 539–549.

[26] R. J. Burke and D. S. Wilcox, "Bases of Supervisory Power and Subordinate Job Satisfactions," *Canadian Journal of Behavioral Science* (1971).

[27] Natemeyer, "An Empirical Investigation."

[28] Hersey, Blanchard, and Natemeyer, "Situational Leadership and Power."

[29] This instrument was developed by Paul Hersey and Walter E. Natemeyer. Published by the Center for Leadership Studies, Escondido, CA 92025.

Organizations, Work Processes, and People

S ince the inception of the field, management studies have addressed the relationships between organizations, work processes, and people. These issues have also interested scholars outside of management, including German philosopher and organizational theorist Max Weber. The first reading is a translation of Weber's classic analysis of bureaucracy. He describes the advantages of a clearly defined organizational structure with stable rules and set roles and responsibilities. "Bureaucracy" helped bring order to many types of organizations and was particularly relevant during times of stable growth and simple technologies.

Chris Argyris, in "The Individual and the Organization," contends that the formal structure of organizations is often incompatible with the needs of the human personality. He argues that various aspects of formal organizations (such as task specialization, unity of direction, chain of command, and span of control) tend to inhibit the development of psychologically healthy, mature adults. This failure to integrate the individual and the organization results in negative consequences for both the organization and its employees. The article reprinted here summarizes his landmark 1957 book, *Personality and Organization.*

In "Mechanistic and Organic Systems," Tom Burns and G. M. Stalker suggest that a more rigid "mechanistic" management system is appropriate for stable organizational environments, but that a more adaptable "organic" form is appropriate for dynamic conditions. Their ideas popularized the notion that the appropriate organizational structure depends on the unique situation facing the organization.

Rensis Likert, one of the pioneering researchers and theorists in the field of organizational development, is perhaps best known for his classification and discussion of management systems. This reading from Likert's well-known book, *The Human Organization,* provides the reader with the opportunity to diagnose organizations using the Systems 1 through 4 framework. Likert contends that high-performing organizations typically possess System 4 characteristics such as a high level of trust, open communication, and motivation through participation and employee involvement.

The fifth article in section VI is entitled "Management by Objectives" by George Odiorne. He defines management by objectives (MBO) as a process whereby leaders and followers jointly identify common goals, define each individual's major areas of responsibility in terms of the results expected, and then use these measures as guides for operating the unit and assessing the contribution of each person. Odiorne contends that MBO must start at the top of the organization. He provides specific guidelines for implementing the MBO system including: setting goals with subordinates, measuring results against those goals, reviewing organizational performance, and defining goals for the next year. He lists the following essential ingredients for successfully implementing MBO:

- Secure top management support.
- Clarify common goals before individual goals.
- Change the organization structure (if necessary) in accordance with your goals.

Odiorne concludes with a number of "do's" and "don'ts" in the MBO cycle.

The groundbreaking work of Paul Lawrence and Jay Lorsch is exemplified in the article "Differentiation and Integration." Organizational subunits, such as sales or production, are shown to be more effective when their operational features fit with the degree of uncertainty characterized by their environment. Subunits within the organization become different as they change to match their environment, and this degree of differentiation determines which methods of integration are required. If subunits are very different, then supplemental integrating (coordinating) processes such as cross-functional teams will be needed, and this has direct implications for where and how conflict will be resolved.

The next reading is entitled "What's Missing in MBO?" by Paul Hersey and Ken Blanchard. The authors suggest that what is often missing in MBO is the development of a psychological contract between the leader and follower regarding the role of the leader in helping the follower accomplish his or her goals. They suggest that the leader's failure to provide the appropriate amount of direction and support to the follower could lead to the follower's lack of success. Hersey and Blanchard discuss how Situational Leadership can be a useful tool in avoiding this problem by discussing the follower's readiness level and mutually deciding what leadership style is needed. The leader and follower make a contract for the appropriate direction and support the leader must provide in order for the employee to succeed. This approach clarifies the leader's important role in ensuring that followers achieve their goals.

In "Reengineering Work Processes," Michael Hammer and James Champy contend that many organizations in today's business environment have become overly complicated and inefficient. These organizations need to "reengineer" or they may go out of business. Traditional organizational structures and work processes are based on concepts of division of labor and hierarchical control that evolved with the Industrial Revolution and mass production. This approach works in a world of stable growth and simple technologies but does not fit the demands of today's dynamic business environment. The authors define reengineering as the fundamental rethinking and radical redesign of business processes to achieve dramatic improvement in performance. A business process is a collection of activities that takes one or more inputs and creates an output that has value to the customer. By streamlining work processes, tremendous cost savings and increased efficiencies can be achieved.

1

Bureaucracy

Max Weber

Characteristics of Bureaucracy

Modern officialdom functions in the following specific manner:

I. *There is the principle of fixed and official jurisdictional areas, which are generally ordered by rules, that is, by laws or administrative regulations.* [Italics added]

1. The regular activities required for the purposes of the bureaucratically governed structure are distributed in a fixed way as official duties.

2. The authority to give the commands required for the discharge of these duties is distributed in a stable way and is strictly delimited by rules concerning the coercive means, physical, sacerdotal, or otherwise, which may be placed at the disposal of officials.

3. Methodical provision is made for the regular and continuous fulfillment of these duties and for the execution of the corresponding rights; only persons who have the generally regulated qualifications to serve are employed.

In public and lawful government these three elements constitute "bureaucratic authority." In private economic domination, they constitute bureaucratic "management." Bureaucracy, thus understood, is fully developed in political and ecclesiastical communities only in the modern state, and, in the private economy, only in the most advanced institutions of capitalism. Permanent and public office authority, with fixed jurisdiction, is not the historical rule but rather the exception. This is so even in large political structures such as those of the ancient Orient, the Germanic and Mongolian empires of conquest, or of many feudal structures of state. In all these cases, the ruler executes the most important measures through personal trustees, table-companions, or court-servants. Their commissions and authority are not precisely delimited and are temporarily called into being for each case.

Reprinted from *Essays in Sociology,* pp. 196–204, "Bureaucracy" by Max Weber (1946, 1958). Edited by Gerth, H. H. and Wright, C. (trans.). Reprinted by permission of Oxford University Press.

II. *The principles of office hierarchy and of levels of graded authority mean a firmly ordered system of super- and subordination in which there is a supervision of the lower offices by the higher ones.* Such a system offers the governed the possibility of appealing the decision of a lower office to its higher authority, in a definitely regulated manner. With the full development of the bureaucratic type, the office hierarchy is monocratically organized. The principle of hierarchical office authority is found in all bureaucratic structures: in state and ecclesiastical structures as well as in large party organizations and private enterprises. It does not matter for the character of bureaucracy whether its authority is called "private" or "public."

When the principle of jurisdictional "competency" is fully carried through, hierarchical subordination—at least in public office—does not mean that the "higher" authority is simply authorized to take over the business of the "lower." Indeed, the opposite is the rule. Once established and having fulfilled its task, an office tends to continue in existence and be held by another incumbent.

III. *The management of the modern office is based upon written documents ("the files"), which are preserved in their original or draught form.* There is, therefore, a staff of subaltern officials and scribes of all sorts. The body of officials actively engaged in a "public" office, along with the respective apparatus of material implements and the files, make up a "bureau." In private enterprise, "the bureau" is often called "the office."

In principle, the modern organization of the civil service separates the bureau from the private domicile of the official, and, in general, bureaucracy segregates official activity as something distinct from the sphere of private life. Public monies and equipment are divorced from the private property of the official. This condition is everywhere the product of a long development. Nowadays, it is found in public as well as in private enterprises; in the latter, the principle extends even to the leading entrepreneur. In principle, the executive office is separated from the household, business from private correspondence, and business assets from private fortunes. The more consistently the modern type of business management has been carried through the more are these separations the case. The beginnings of this process are to be found as early as the Middle Ages.

It is the peculiarity of the modern entrepreneur that he conducts himself as the "first official" of his enterprise, in the very same way in which the ruler of a specifically modern bureaucratic state spoke of himself as "the first servant" of the state. The idea that the bureau activities of the state are intrinsically different in character from the management of private economic offices is a continental European notion and, by way of contrast, is totally foreign to the American way.

IV. *Office management, at least all specialized office management—and such management is distinctly modern—usually presupposes thorough and expert training.* This increasingly holds for the modern executive and employee of private enterprises, in the same manner as it holds for the state official.

V. *When the office is fully developed, official activity demands the full working capacity of the official, irrespective of the fact that his obligatory time in the bureau may be firmly delimited.* In the normal case, this is only the product of a long development, in the public as well as in the private office. Formerly, in all cases, the normal state of affairs was reversed: official business was discharged as a secondary activity.

VI. *The management of the office follows general rules, which are more or less stable, more or less exhaustive, and which can be learned.* Knowledge of these rules represents a special technical learning which the officials possess. It involves jurisprudence, or administrative or business management.

The reduction of modern office management to rules is deeply embedded in its very nature. The theory of modern public administration, for instance, assumes that the authority to order certain matters by decree—which has been legally granted to public authorities—does not entitle the bureau to regulate the matter by commands given for each case, but only to regulate the matter abstractly. This stands in extreme contrast to the regulation of all relationships through individual privileges and bestowals of favor, which is absolutely dominant in patrimonialism, at least in so far as such relationships are not fixed by sacred tradition.

The Position of the Official

All this results in the following for the internal and external position of the official:

I. *Office holding is a "vocation."* This is shown, first, in the requirement of a firmly prescribed course of training, which demands the entire capacity for work for a long period of time, and in the generally prescribed and special examinations which are prerequisites of employment. Furthermore, the position of the official is in the nature of a duty. This determines the internal structure of his relations, in the following manner: Legally and actually, office holding is not considered a source to be exploited for rents or emoluments, as was normally the case during the Middle Ages and frequently up to the threshold of recent times. Nor is office holding considered a usual exchange of services for equivalents, as is the case with free labor contracts. Entrance into an office, including one in the private economy, is considered an acceptance of a specific obligation of faithful management in return for a secure existence. It is decisive for the specific nature of modern loyalty to an office that, in the pure type, it does not establish a relationship to a *person*, like the vassal's or disciple's faith in feudal or in patrimonial relations of authority. Modern loyalty is devoted to impersonal and functional purposes. Behind the functional purposes, of course, "ideas of culture-values" usually stand. These are *ersatz* for the earthly or supra-mundane personal master: ideas such as "state," "church," "community," "party," or "enterprise" are thought of as being realized in a community; they provide an ideological halo for the master.

The political official—at least in the fully developed modern state—is not considered the personal servant of a ruler. Today, the bishop, the priest, and the preacher are in fact no longer, as in early Christian times, holders of purely personal charisma. The supra-mundane and sacred values which they offer are given to everybody who seems to be worthy of them and who asks for them. In former times, such leaders acted upon the personal command of their master; in principle, they were responsible only to him. Nowadays, in spite of the partial survival of the old theory, such religious leaders are officials in the service of a functional purpose, which in the present-day "church" has become routinized and, in turn, ideologically hallowed.

II. *The personal position of the official is patterned in the following way:*

1. Whether he is in a private office or a public bureau, the modern official always strives for and usually enjoys a distinct *social esteem* as compared with the governed. His social position is guaranteed by the prescriptive rules of rank order and, for the political official, by special definitions of the criminal code against "insults of officials" and "contempt" of state and church authorities.

The actual social position of the official is normally highest where, as in old civilized countries, the following conditions prevail: a strong demand for administration by trained experts; a strong and stable social differentiation, where the official predominantly derives from socially and economically privileged strata because of the social distribution of power; or where the costliness of the required training and status conventions are binding upon him. The possession of educational certificates—to be discussed elsewhere—are usually linked with qualification for office. Naturally, such certificates or patents enhance the "status element" in the social position of the official. For the rest this status factor in individual cases is explicitly and impassively acknowledged; for example, in the prescription that the acceptance or rejection of an aspirant to an official career depends upon the consent ("election") of the members of the official body. This is the case in the German army with the officer corps. Similar phenomena, which promote this guildlike closure of officialdom, are typically found in patrimonial and, particularly, in prebendal officialdoms of the past. The desire to resurrect such phenomena in changed forms is by no means infrequent among modern bureaucrats. For instance, they have played a role among the demands of the quite proletarian and expert officials (the *tretyj* element) during the Russian revolution.

Usually the social esteem of the officials as such is especially low where the demand for expert administration and the dominance of status conventions are weak. This is especially the case in the United States; it is often the case in new settlements by virtue of their wide fields for profitmaking and the great instability of their social stratification.

2. The pure type of bureaucratic official is *appointed* by a superior authority. An official elected by the governed is not a purely bureaucratic figure. Of course, the formal existence of an election does not by itself mean that no appointment hides behind the election—in the state, especially, appointment by party chiefs. Whether or not this is the case does not depend upon legal statutes but upon the way in which the party mechanism functions. Once firmly organized, the parties can turn a formally free election into the mere acclamation of a candidate designated by the party chief. As a rule, however, a formally free election is turned into a fight, conducted according to definite rules, for votes in favor of one of two designated candidates.

In all circumstances, the designation of officials by means of an election among the governed modifies the strictness of hierarchical subordination. In principle, an official who is so elected has an autonomous position opposite the superordinate official. The elected official does not derive his position "from above" but "from below," or at least not from a superior authority of the official hierarchy but from powerful party men ("bosses"), who also determine his further career. The career of the elected official is not, or at least not primarily, dependent upon his chief in the administration. The official who is not elected but appointed by a chief normally functions more exactly, from a technical point of view, because, all other circumstances being equal, it is more likely that purely functional points of consideration and qualities will determine his selection and career. As laymen, the governed can become acquainted with the extent to which a candidate is expertly qualified for office only in terms of experience, and hence only after his service. Moreover, in every sort of selection of officials by election, parties quite naturally give decisive weight not to expert considerations but to the services a follower renders to the party boss. This holds for all kinds of procurement of officials by elections, for the designation of formally free, elected officials by party bosses when they determine the slate of candidates, or the free appointment by a chief who has himself been elected. The contrast, however, is relative: substantially similar conditions hold where legitimate monarchs and their subordinates appoint officials, except that the influence of the followings are then less controllable.

Where the demand for administration by trained experts is considerable, and the party followings have to recognize an intellectually developed, educated, and freely moving "public opinion," the use of unqualified officials falls back upon the party in power at the next election. Naturally, this is more likely to happen when the officials are appointed by the chief. The demand for a trained administration now exists in the United States, but in the large cities, where immigrant votes are "corralled," there is, of course, no educated public opinion. Therefore, popular elections of the administrative chief and also of his subordinate officials usually endanger the expert qualification of the official as well as the precise functioning of the bureaucratic mechanism. It also weakens the dependence of the officials upon the hierarchy. This holds at least for the large administrative bodies that are difficult to supervise. The superior qualification and integrity of federal judges, appointed by the President, as over against elected judges in the United States is well known, although both types of officials have been selected primarily in terms of party considerations. The great changes in American metropolitan administrations demanded by reformers have proceeded essentially from elected mayors working with an apparatus of officials who were appointed by them. These reforms have thus come about in a "Caesarist" fashion. Viewed technically, as an organized form of authority, the efficiency of "Caesarism," which often grows out of democracy, rests in general upon the position of the "Caesar" as a free trustee of the masses (of the army or of the citizenry), who is unfettered by tradition. The "Caesar" is thus the unrestrained master of a body of highly qualified military officers and officials whom he selects freely and personally without regard to tradition or to any other considerations. This "rule of the personal genius," however, stands in contradiction to the formally "democratic" principle of a universally elected officialdom.

3. Normally, the position of the official is held for life, at least in public bureaucracies; and this is increasingly the case for all similar structures. As a factual rule, *tenure for life* is presupposed, even where the giving of notice or periodic reappointment occurs. In contrast to the worker in a private enterprise, the official normally holds tenure. Legal or actual life-tenure, however, is not recognized as the official's right to the possession of office, as was the case with many structures of authority in the past. Where legal guarantees against arbitrary dismissal or transfer are developed, they merely serve to guarantee a strictly objective discharge of specific office duties free from all personal considerations. In Germany, this is the case for all juridical and, increasingly, for all administrative officials.

Within the bureaucracy, therefore, the measure of "independence," legally guaranteed by tenure, is not always a source of increased status for the official whose position is thus secured. Indeed, often the reverse holds, especially in old cultures and communities that are highly differentiated. In such communities, the stricter the subordination under the arbitrary rule of the master, the more it guarantees the maintenance of the conventional seigneurial style of living for the official. Because of the very absence of these legal guarantees of tenure, the conventional esteem for the official may rise in the same way as, during the Middle Ages, the esteem of the nobility of office rose at the expense of esteem for the freemen, and as the king's judge surpassed that of the people's judge. In Germany, the military officer or the administrative official can be removed from office at any time, or at least far more readily than the "independent judge," who never pays with loss of his office for even the grossest offense against the "code of honor" or against social conventions of the salon. For this very reason, if other things are equal, in the eyes of the master stratum the judge is considered less qualified for social intercourse than are officers and administrative officials, whose greater dependence on the master is a greater guarantee of their conformity with status conventions. Of course, the average official strives for a civil-service law, which would materially secure his old age and provide increased guarantees against his arbitrary removal from office. This striving, however, has its limits. A very strong development of the "right to the office" naturally makes it more difficult to staff them with regard to technical efficiency, for such a development decreases the career-opportunities of ambitious candidates for office. This makes for the fact that officials, on the whole, do not feel their dependency upon those at the top. This lack of a feeling of dependency, however, rests primarily upon the inclination to depend upon one's equals rather than upon the socially inferior and governed strata. The present conservative movement among the Badenia clergy, occasioned by the anxiety of a presumably threatening separation of church and state, has been expressly determined by the desire not to be turned "from a master into a servant of the parish."

4. The official receives the regular *pecuniary* compensation of a normally fixed *salary* and the old age security provided by a pension. The salary is not measured like a wage in terms of work done, but according to "status," that is,

according to the kind of function (the "rank") and, in addition, possibly, according to the length of service. The relatively great security of the official's income, as well as the rewards of social esteem, make the office a sought-after position, especially in countries which no longer provide opportunities for colonial profits. In such countries, this situation permits relatively low salaries for officials.

5. The official is set for a *"career"* within the hierarchical order of the public service. He moves from the lower, less important, and lower paid to the higher positions. The average official naturally desires a mechanical fixing of the conditions of promotion: if not of the offices, at least of the salary levels. He wants these conditions fixed in terms of "seniority," or possibly according to grades achieved in a developed system of expert examinations. Here and there, such examinations actually form a character *indelebilis* of the official and have lifelong effects on his career. To this is joined the desire to qualify the right to office and the increasing tendency toward status group closure and economic security. All of this makes for a tendency to consider the offices as "prebends" of those who are qualified by educational certificates. The necessity of taking general personal and intellectual qualifications into consideration, irrespective of the often subaltern character of the educational certificate, has led to a condition in which the highest political offices, especially the positions of "ministers," are principally filled without reference to such certificates.

2

The Individual and the Organization

Chris Argyris

It is a fact that most industrial organizations have some sort of formal structure within which individuals must work to achieve the organization's objectives.[1] Each of these basic components of organization (the formal structure and the individuals) has been and continues to be the subject of much research, discussion, and writing. An extensive search of the literature leads us to conclude, however, that most of these inquiries are conducted by persons typically interested in one or the other of the basic components. Few focus on both the individual and the organization.

Since in real life the formal structure and the individuals are continuously interacting and transacting, it seems useful to consider a study of their simultaneous impact upon each other. It is the purpose of this paper to outline the beginnings of a systematic framework by which to analyze the nature of the relationship between formal organization and individuals and from which to derive specific hypotheses regarding their mutual impact.[2] Although a much more detailed definition of formal organization will be given later, it is important to emphasize that this analysis is limited to those organizations whose original formal structure is defined by such traditional principles of organization as "chain of command," "task specialization," "span of control," and so forth. Another limitation is that since the nature of individuals varies from culture to culture, the conclusions of this paper are also limited to those cultures wherein the proposed model of personality applies (primarily American and some Western European cultures).

The method used is a simple one designed to take advantage of the existing research on each component. The first objective is to ascertain the basic properties of each component. Exactly what is known and agreed upon by the experts about each of the components? Once this information has been collected, the second objective follows logically. When the basic properties of each of these components

From Chris Argyris, "The Individual and the Organization: Some Problems of Mutual Adjustment," *Administrative Science Quarterly*, Vol. 2, No. 1 (June 1957), pp. 1–24. Copyright © 1957 *Administrative Science Quarterly*. Reprinted by permission.

are known, what predictions can be made regarding their impact upon one another once they are brought together?

Some Properties of Human Personality

The research on the human personality is so great and voluminous that it is indeed difficult to find agreement regarding its basic properties.[3] It is even more difficult to summarize the agreements once they are inferred from the existing literature. Because of space limitations it is only possible to discuss in detail one of several agreements which seems to the writer to be the most relevant to the problem at hand. The others may be summarized briefly as follows. Personality is conceptualized as (1) being an organization of parts where the parts maintain the whole and the whole maintains the parts; (2) seeking internal balance (usually called adjustment) and external balance (usually called adaptation); (3) being propelled by psychological (as well as physical) energy; (4) located in the need systems; and (5) expressed through the abilities. (6) The personality organization may be called "the self" which (7) acts to color all the individual's experiences, thereby causing him to live in "private worlds," and which (8) is capable of defending (maintaining) itself against threats of all types.

The self, in this culture, tends to develop along specific trends which are operationally definable and empirically observable. The basic developmental trends may be described as follows. The human being, in our culture:

1. tends to develop from a state of being passive as an infant to a state of increasing activity as an adult. (This is what E. H. Erikson has called self-initiative and Urie Bronfenbrenner has called self-determination.) [4]

2. tends to develop from a state of dependence upon others as an infant to a state of relative independence as an adult. Relative independence is the ability to "stand on one's own two feet" and simultaneously to acknowledge healthy dependencies.[5] It is characterized by the individual's freeing himself from his childhood determiners of behavior (*e.g.,* the family) and developing his own set of behavioral determiners. The individual does not tend to react to others (*e.g.,* the boss) in terms of patterns learned during childhood.[6]

3. tends to develop from being capable of behaving in only a few ways as an infant to being capable of behaving in many different ways as an adult.[7]

4. tends to develop from having erratic, casual, shallow, quickly dropped interests as an infant to possessing a deepening of interests as an adult. The mature state is characterized by an endless series of challenges where the reward comes from doing something for its own sake. The tendency is to analyze and study phenomena in their full-blown wholeness, complexity, and depth.[8]

5. tends to develop from having a short-time perspective (*i.e.,* the present largely determines behavior) as an infant to having a much longer time perspective as an adult (*i.e.,* the individual's behavior is more affected by the past and the future).[9]

6. tends to develop from being in a subordinate position in the family and society as an infant to aspiring to occupy at least an equal and/or superordinate position relative to his peers.

7. tends to develop from having a lack of awareness of the self as an infant to having an awareness of and control over the self as an adult. The adult who experiences adequate and successful control over his own behavior develops a sense of integrity (Erikson) and feelings of self-worth (Carl R. Rogers).[10]

These characteristics are postulated as being descriptive of a basic multidimensional developmental process along which the growth of individuals in our culture may be measured. Presumably every individual, at any given moment in time, could have his degree of development plotted along these dimensions. The exact location on each dimension will probably vary with each individual and even with the same individual at different times. Self-actualization may now be defined more precisely as the individual's plotted scores (or profile) along the above dimensions.[11]

A few words of explanation may be given concerning these dimensions of personality development:

1. They are only one aspect of the total personality. All the properties of personality mentioned above must be used in trying to understand the behavior of a particular individual. For example, much depends upon the individual's self-concept, his degree of adaptation and adjustment, and the way he perceives his private world.

2. The dimensions are continua, where the growth to be measured is assumed to be continuously changing in degree. An individual is presumed to develop continuously in degree from infancy to adulthood.

3. The only characteristic assumed to hold for all individuals is that, barring unhealthy personality development, they will move from the infant toward the adult end of each continuum. This description is a model outlining the basic growth trends. As such, it does not make any predictions about any specific individual. It does, however, presume to supply the researcher with basic developmental continua along which the growth of any individual in our culture may be described and measured.

4. It is postulated that no individual will ever obtain maximum expression of all these developmental trends. Clearly all individuals cannot be maximally independent, active, and so forth all the time and still maintain an organized society. It is the function of culture (*e.g.,* norms, mores, and so forth) to inhibit maximum expression and to help an individual adjust and adapt by finding his optimum expression.

   A second factor that prevents maximum expression and fosters optimum expression are the limits set by the individual's own personality. For example, some people fear the same amount of independence and activity that others desire, and some people do not have the necessary abilities to perform certain tasks. No given individual is known to have developed all known abilities to their full maturity.

5. The dimensions described above are constructed in terms of latent or genotypical characteristics. If one states that an individual needs to be dependent, this need may be ascertained by clinical inference, because it is one that individuals are not usually aware of. Thus one may observe an employee acting as if he were independent, but it is possible that if one goes below the behavioral surface the individual may be quite dependent. The obvious example is the employee who always seems to behave in a manner contrary to that desired by management. Although this behavior may look as if he is independent, his contrariness may be due to his great need to be dependent upon management which he dislikes to admit to himself and to others.

One might say that an independent person is one whose behavior is not caused by the influence others have over him. Of course, no individual is completely independent. All of us have our healthy dependencies (*i.e.,* those which help us to be creative and to develop). One operational criterion to ascertain whether an individual's desire to be, let us say, independent and active is truly a mature manifestation is to ascertain the extent to which he permits others to express the same needs. Thus an autocratic leader may say that he needs to be active and independent; he may also say that he wants subordinates who are the same. There is ample research to suggest, however, that his leadership pattern only makes him and his subordinates more dependence-ridden.

Some Basic Properties of Formal Organization

The next step is to focus the analytic spotlight on the formal organization. What are its properties? What are its basic "givens"? What probable impact will they have upon the human personality? How will the human personality tend to react to this impact? What sorts of chain reactions are probable when these two basic components are brought together?

Formal Organizations as Rational Organizations

Probably the most basic property of formal organization is its logical foundation or, as it has been called by students of administration, its essential rationality. It is the planners' conception of how the intended consequences of the organization may best be achieved. The underlying assumption made by the creators of formal organization is that within respectable tolerances man will behave rationally, that is, as the formal plan requires him to behave. Organizations are formed with particular objectives in mind, and their structures mirror these objectives. Although man may not follow the prescribed paths, and consequently the objectives may never be achieved, Herbert A. Simon suggests that by and large man does follow these prescribed paths:

Organizations are formed with the intention and design of accomplishing goals; and the people who work in organizations believe, at least part of the time, that they are striving toward these same goals. We must not lose sight of the fact that however far organizations may depart from the traditional description . . . nevertheless most behavior in organizations is intendedly rational behavior. By "intended rationality" I mean the kind of adjustment of behavior to goals of which humans are capable—a very incomplete and imperfect adjustment, to be sure, but one which nevertheless does accomplish purposes and does carry out programs.[12]

In an illuminating book, L. Urwick eloquently describes this underlying characteristic.[13] He insists that the creation of a formal organization requires a logical "drawing-office" approach. Although he admits that "nine times out of ten it is impossible to start with a clean sheet," the organizer should sit down and in a "cold-blooded, detached spirit . . . draw an ideal structure." The section from which I quote begins with Urwick's description of how the formal structure should be planned. He then continues:

Manifestly that is a drawing-office job. It is a designing process. And it may be objected with a great deal of experience to support the contention that organization is never done that way . . . human organization. Nine times out of ten it is impossible to start with a clean sheet. The organizer has to make the best possible use of the human material that is already available. And in 89 out of those 90 percent of cases he has to adjust jobs around to fit the man; he can't change the man to fit the job. He can't sit down in a cold-blooded, detached spirit and draw an ideal structure, an optimum distribution of duties and responsibilities and relationships, and then expect the infinite variety of human nature to fit into it.

To which the reply is that he can and he should. If he has not got a clean sheet, that is no earthly reason why he should not make the slight effort of imagination required to assume that he has a clean sheet. It is not impossible to forget provisionally the personal facts—that old Brown is admirably methodical but wanting in initiative, that young Smith got into a mess with Robinson's wife and that the two men must be kept at opposite ends of the building, that Jones is one of those creatures who can think like a Wrangler about other people's duties but is given to periodic amnesia about certain aspects of his own.[14]

The task of the organizer, therefore, is to create a logically ordered world where, as Fayol suggests, there is a "proper order" and in which there is a "place for everything (everyone)."[15]

The possibility that the formal organization can be altered by personalities, as found by Conrad M. Arensberg and Douglas McGregor[16] and Ralph M. Stogdill and Katheleen Koehler,[17] is not denied by formal organizational experts. Urwick, for example, states in the passage below that the planner must take into account the human element. But it is interesting to note that he perceives these adjustments as "temporary deviations from the pattern in order to deal with idiosyncrasy of personality." If possible, these deviations should be minimized by careful preplanning.

He [the planner] should never for a moment pretend that these (human) difficulties don't exist. They do exist; they are realities. Nor, when he has drawn
up an ideal plan of organization, is it likely that he will be able to fit in all the
existing human material perfectly. There will be small adjustments of the job
to the man in all kinds of directions. But those adjustments are deliberate and
temporary deviations from the pattern in order to deal with idiosyncrasy.
There is a world of difference between such modification and drifting into an
unworkable organization because Green has a fancy for combining bits of
two incompatible functions, or White is "empire-building" . . . or Black has
always looked after the canteen, so when he is promoted to Sales Manager,
he might as well continue to sell buns internally, though the main product of
the business happens to be battleships.

What is suggested is that problems of organization should be handled *in
the right order*. Personal adjustments must be made, insofar as they are necessary. But fewer of them will be necessary and they will present fewer deviations from what is logical and simple, if the organizer first makes a plan, a
design—to which he would work if he had the ideal human material. He
should expect to be driven from it here and there. But he will be driven from
it far less and his machine will work much more smoothly if he *starts* with a
plan. If he starts with a motley collection of human oddities and tries to organize to fit them all in, thinking first of their various shapes and sizes and colors, he may have a patchwork quilt; he will not have an organization.[18]

The majority of experts on formal organization agree with Urwick. Most of
them emphasize that no organizational structure will be ideal. None will exemplify
the maximum expression of the principles of formal organization. A satisfactory
aspiration is for optimum expression, which means modifying the ideal structure to
take into account the individual (and any environmental) conditions. Moreover,
they urge that the people must be loyal to the formal structure if it is to work effectively. Thus Taylor emphasizes that scientific management would never succeed
without a "mental revolution."[19] Fayol has the same problem in mind when he
emphasizes the importance of *esprit de corps*.

It is also true, however, that these experts have provided little insight into *why*
they believe that people should undergo a "mental revolution," or why an *esprit de
corps* is necessary if the principles are to succeed. The only hints found in the literature are that resistance to scientific management occurs because human beings
"are what they are" or "because it's human nature." But *why* does "human nature"
resist formal organizational principles? Perhaps there is something inherent in the
principles which causes human resistance. Unfortunately too little research specifically assesses the impact of formal organizational principles upon human beings.

Another argument for planning offered by the formal organizational experts is
that the organization created by logical, rational design, in the long run, is more
human than one created haphazardly. They argue that it is illogical, cruel, wasteful,
and inefficient not to have a logical design. It is illogical because design must come
first. It does not make sense to pay a large salary to an individual without clearly
defining his position and its relationship to the whole. It is cruel because, in the long
run, the participants suffer when no clear organizational structure exists. It is wasteful

because, unless jobs are clearly predefined, it is impossible to plan logical training, promotion, resigning, and retiring policies. It is inefficient because the organization becomes dependent upon personalities. The personal touch leads to playing politics, which Mary Follett has described as a "deplorable form of coercion."[20]

Unfortunately, the validity of these arguments tends to be obscured in the eyes of the behavioral scientist because they imply that the only choice left, if the formal, rational, predesigned structure is not accepted, is to have no organizational structure at all, with the organizational structure left to the whims, pushes, and pulls of human beings. Some human-relations researchers, on the other hand, have unfortunately given the impression that formal structures are "bad" and that the needs of the individual participants should be paramount in creating and administering an organization. A recent analysis of the existing research, however, points up quite clearly that the importance of the organization is being recognized by those who in the past have focused largely upon the individual.[21]

In the past, and for the most part in the present, the traditional organizational experts based their "human architectural creation" upon certain basic principles or assumptions about the nature of organization. These principles have been described by such people as Urwick,[22] Mooney, Holden *et al.*, Fayol, Dennison, Brown, Gulick, White, Gaus, Stene, Hopf, and Taylor. Although these principles have been attacked by behavioral scientists, the assumption is made in this paper that to date no one has defined a more useful set of formal organization principles. Therefore the principles are accepted as givens. This frees us to inquire about their probable impact upon people, *if they are used as defined.*

Task (Work) Specialization

As James J. Gillespie suggests, the roots of these principles of organization may be traced back to certain principles of industrial economics, the most important of which is the basic economic assumption held by builders of the industrial revolution that "the concentration of effort on a limited field of endeavor increases quality and quantity of output."[23] It follows from the above that the necessity for specialization should increase as the quantity of similar things to be done increases.

If concentrating effort on a limited field of endeavor increases the quality and quantity of output, it follows that organizational and administrative efficiency is increased by the specialization of tasks assigned to the participants of the organization.[24] Inherent in this assumption are three others. The first is that the human personality will behave more efficiently as the task that it is to perform becomes specialized. Second is the assumption that there can be found a one best way to define the job so that it is performed at greater speed.[25] Third is the assumption that any individual differences in the human personality may be ignored by transferring more skill and thought to machines.[26]

A number of difficulties arise concerning these assumptions when the properties of the human personality are recalled. First, the human personality we have seen is always attempting to actualize its unique organization of parts resulting from a continuous, emotionally laden, ego-involving process of growth. It is difficult, if not impossible, to assume that this process can be choked off and the resultant unique differences of individuals ignored. This is tantamount to saying that self-actualization can be ignored. The second difficulty is that task specialization requires the individual to use only a few of his abilities. Moreover, as specialization increases, the less complex motor abilities are used more frequently. These, research suggests, tend to be of lesser psychological importance to the individual. Thus the principle violates two basic givens of the healthy adult human personality. It inhibits self-actualization and provides expression for few, shallow, superficial abilities that do not provide the "endless challenge" desired by the healthy personality.

Harold L. Wilensky and Charles N. Lebeaux correctly point out that task specialization causes what little skill is left in a job to become very important.[27] Now small differences in ability may make enormous differences in output. Thus two machine-shovel operators or two drill-press operators of different degrees of skill can produce dramatically different outputs. Ironically, the increasing importance of this type of skill for the healthy, mature worker means that he should feel he is performing self-satisfying work while using a small number of psychologically unchallenging abilities, when in actuality he may be predisposed to feel otherwise. Task specialization, therefore, requires a healthy adult to behave in a less mature manner, but it also requires that he feel good about it!

Not only is the individual affected, but the social structure as well is modified as a result of the situation described above. Wilensky and Lebeaux, in the same analysis, point out that placing a great emphasis on ability makes "Who you are" become less important that "What you can do." Thus the culture begins to reward relatively superficial, materialistic characteristics.

Chain of Command

The principle of task specialization creates an aggregate of parts, each performing a highly specialized task. An aggregate of parts, each busily performing its particular objective, does not form an organization, however. A pattern of parts must be formed so that the interrelationships among the parts create the organization. Following the logic of specialization, the planners create a new function (leadership) the primary responsibility of which is to control, direct, and coordinate the interrelationships of the parts and to make certain that each part performs its objective adequately. Thus the planner makes the assumption that administrative and organizational efficiency is increased by arranging the parts in a determinate hierarchy of authority in which the part on top can direct and control the part on the bottom.

If the parts being considered are individuals, then they must be motivated to accept direction, control, and coordination of their behavior. The leader, therefore, is assigned formal power to hire, discharge, reward, and penalize the individuals in order to mold their behavior in the pattern of the organization's objectives.

The impact of such a state of affairs is to make the individuals dependent upon, passive, and subordinate to the leader. As a result, the individuals have little control over their working environment. At the same time their time perspective is shortened because they do not control the information necessary to predict their futures. These requirements of formal organization act to inhibit four of the growth trends of the personality, because to be passive, subordinate, and to have little control and a short time perspective exemplify in adults the dimensions of immaturity, not adulthood.

The planners of formal organization suggest three basic ways to minimize this admittedly difficult position. First, ample rewards should be given to those who perform well and who do not permit their dependence, subordination, passivity, and so forth to influence them in a negative manner. The rewards should be material and psychological. Because of the specialized nature of the worker's job, however, few psychological rewards are possible. It becomes important, therefore, that adequate material rewards are made available to the productive employee. This practice can lead to new difficulties, since the solution is, by its nature, not to do anything about the on-the-job situation (which is what is causing the difficulties) but to pay the individual for the dissatisfactions he experiences. The result is that the employee is paid for his dissatisfaction while at work and his wages are given to him to gain satisfactions outside his work environment.

Thus the management helps to create a psychological set which leads the employees to feel that basic causes of dissatisfaction are built into industrial life, that the rewards they receive are wages for dissatisfaction, and that if satisfaction is to be gained, the employee must seek it outside the organization.

To make matters more difficult, there are three assumptions inherent in the above solution that also violate the basic givens of human personality. First, the solution assumes that a whole human being can split his personality so that he will feel satisfied in knowing that the wages for his dissatisfaction will buy him satisfaction outside the plant. Second, it assumes that the employee is primarily interested in maximizing his economic gains. Third, it assumes that the employee is best rewarded as an individual producer. The work group in which he belongs is not viewed as a relevant factor. If he produces well, he should be rewarded. If he does not, he should be penalized even though he may be restricting production because of informal group sanctions.

The second solution suggested by the planners of formal organization is to have technically competent, objective, rational, loyal leaders. The assumption is made that if the leaders are technically competent presumably they cannot have "the wool pulled over their eyes" and that therefore the employees will have a high respect for them. The leaders should be objective and rational and personify the rationality inherent in the formal structure. Being rational means that they must avoid becoming emotionally involved. As one executive states, "We try to keep our personality out of the job." The leader must also be impartial; he must not permit his feelings to operate when he is evaluating others. Finally, the leader must be loyal to the organization so that he can inculcate the loyalty in the employees that Taylor, Fayol, and others believe is so important.

Admirable as this solution may be, it also violates several of the basic properties of personality. If the employees are to respect an individual for what he does rather than for who he is, the sense of integrity based upon evaluation of the total self which is developed in people is lost. Moreover, to ask the leader to keep his personality out of his job is to ask him to stop actualizing himself. This is not possible as long as he is alive. Of course, the executive may want to feel that he is not involved, but it is a basic given that the human personality is an organism always actualizing itself. The same problem arises with impartiality. No one can be completely impartial. As has been shown, the self concept always operates when we are making judgments. In fact, as Rollo May has pointed out, the best way to be impartial is to be as partial as one's needs predispose one to be but to be aware of this partiality in order to correct for it at the moment of decision.[28] Finally, if a leader can be loyal to an organization under these conditions, there may be adequate grounds for questioning the health of his personality make-up.

The third solution suggested by many adherents to formal organizational principles is to motivate the subordinates to have more initiative and to be more creative by placing them in competition with one another for the positions of power that lie above them in the organizational ladder. This solution is traditionally called "the rabble hypothesis." Acting under the assumption that employees will be motivated to advance upward, the adherents of formal organizations further assume that competition for the increasingly (as one goes up the ladder) scarcer positions will increase the effectiveness of the participants. D. C. S. Williams, conducting some controlled experiments, shows that the latter assumption is not necessarily valid. People placed in competitive situations are not necessarily better learners than those placed in noncompetitive situations.[29] M. Deutsch, as a result of extensive controlled experimental research, supports Williams' results and goes much further to suggest that competitive situations tend to lead to an increase in tension and conflict and a decrease in human effectiveness.[30]

Unity of Direction

If the tasks of everyone in a unit are specialized, then it follows that the objective or purpose of the unit must be specialized. The principle of unity of direction states that organizational efficiency increases if each unit has a single activity (or homogeneous set of activities) that is planned and directed by the leader.[31]

This means that the goal toward which the employees are working, the path toward the goal, and the strength of the barriers they must overcome to achieve the goal are defined and controlled by the leader. Assuming that the work goals do not involve the egos of the employees (*i.e.,* they are related to peripheral, superficial needs), then ideal conditions for psychological failure have been created. The reader may recall that a basic given of a healthy personality is the aspiration for psychological success. Psychological success is achieved when each individual is able to define his own goals, in relation to his inner needs and the strength of the barriers to be overcome in order to reach these goals. Repetitive as it may sound, it is nevertheless true that the principle of unity of direction also violates a basic given of personality.

Span of Control

The principle of span of control[32] states that administrative efficiency is increased by limiting the span of control of a leader to no more than five or six subordinates whose work interlocks.[33]

It is interesting to note that Ernest Dale, in an extensive study of organizational principles and practices in one hundred large organizations, concludes that the actual limits of the executive span of control are more often violated than not,[34] while in a recent study James H. Healey arrives at the opposite conclusion.[35] James C. Worthy reports that it is formal policy in his organization to extend the span of control of the top management much further than is theoretically suggested.[36] Finally, W. W. Suojanen, in a review of the current literature on the concept of span of control, concludes that it is no longer valid, particularly as applied to the larger government agencies and business corporations.[37]

In a recent article, however, Urwick criticizes the critics of the span-of-control principle.[38] For example, he notes that in the case described by Worthy, the superior has a large span of control over subordinates whose jobs do not interlock. The buyers in Worthy's organization purchase a clearly defined range of articles; therefore they find no reason to interlock with others.

Simon criticizes the span-of-control principle on the grounds that it increases the "administrative distance" between individuals. An increase in administrative distance violates, in turn, another formal organizational principle that administrative efficiency is enhanced by keeping at a minimum the number of organizational levels through which a matter must pass before it is acted on.[39] Span of control, continues Simon, inevitably increases red tape, since each contact between agents must be carried upward until a common superior is found. Needless waste of time and energy result. Also, since the solution of the problem depends upon the superior, the subordinate is in a position of having less control over his own work situation. This places the subordinate in a work situation in which he is less mature.

Although the distance between individuals in different units increases (because they have to find a common superior), the administrative distance between superior and subordinate within a given unit decreases. As Whyte correctly points out, the principle of span of control, by keeping the number of subordinates at a minimum, places great emphasis on close supervision.[40] Close supervision leads the subordinates to become dependent upon, passive toward, and subordinate to, the leader. Close supervision also tends to place the control in the superior. Thus we must conclude that span of control, if used correctly, will tend to increase the subordinate's feelings of dependence, submissiveness, passivity, and so on. In short, it will tend to create a work situation which requires immature, rather than mature, participants.

An Incongruency between the Needs of a Mature Personality and of Formal Organization

Bringing together the evidence regarding the impact of formal organizational principles upon the individual, we must conclude that there are some basic incongruencies between the growth trends of a healthy personality in our culture and the requirements of formal organization. If the principles of formal organization are used as ideally defined, then the employees will tend to work in an environment where (1) they are provided minimal control over their work-a-day world, (2) they are expected to be passive, dependent, subordinate, (3) they are expected to have a short-time perspective, (4) they are induced to perfect and value the frequent use of a few superficial abilities, and (5) they are expected to produce under conditions leading to psychological failure.

All of these characteristics are incongruent to the ones healthy human beings are postulated to desire. They are much more congruent with the needs of infants in our culture. In effect, therefore, formal organizations are willing to pay high wages and provide adequate seniority if mature adults will, for eight hours a day, behave in a less mature manner. If this analysis is correct, this inevitable incongruency increases (1) as the employees are of increasing maturity, (2) as the formal structure (based upon the above principles) is made more clear-cut and logically tight for maximum formal organizational effectiveness, (3) as one goes down the line of command, and (4) as the jobs become more and more mechanized (*i.e.,* take on assembly-line characteristics).

As in the case of the personality developmental trends, this picture of formal organization is also a model. Clearly, no company actually uses the formal principles of organization exactly as stated by their creators. There is ample evidence to suggest that they are being modified constantly in actual situations. Those who expound these principles, however, probably would be willing to defend their position that this is the reason that human-relations problems exist; the principles are not followed as they should be.

In the model of the personality and the formal organization, we are assuming the extreme of each in order that the analysis and its results can be highlighted. Speaking in terms of extremes helps us to make the position sharper. In doing this, we make no assumption that all situations in real life are extreme (*i.e.,* that the individuals will always want to be more mature and that the formal organization will always tend to make people more dependent, passive, and so forth, all the time).[41] The model ought to be useful, however, to plot the degree to which each component tends toward extremes and then to predict the problems that will tend to arise.

Returning to the analysis, it is not difficult to see why some students of organization suggest that immature and even mentally retarded individuals probably would make excellent employees in certain jobs. There is very little documented experience to support such a hypothesis. One reason for this lack of information is probably the delicacy of the subject. Examples of what might be obtained if a systematic study were made may be found in a recent work by Mal Brennan.[42] He cites the Utica Knitting Mill, which made arrangements during 1917 with the Rome Institution for Mentally Defective Girls to employ twenty-four girls whose mental age ranged from six to ten years of age. The girls were such excellent workers that they were employed after the war emergency ended. In fact, the company added forty more in another of their plants. It is interesting to note that the managers praised the subnormal girls highly. According to Brennan, in several important reports they said that:

> when business conditions required a reduction of the working staff, the hostel girls were never "laid off" in disproportion to the normal girls; that they were more punctual, more regular in their habits, and did not indulge in as much "gossip and levity." They received the same rate of pay, and they had been employed successfully at almost every process carried out in the workshops.

In another experiment reported by Brennan, the Works Manager of the Radio Corporation, Ltd., reported that of five young [mentally challenged people] employed, "the three girls compared very favorably with the normal class of employee in that age group. The boy employed in the store performed his work with satisfaction. . . . Although there was some doubt about the fifth child, it was felt that getting the most out of him was just a matter of right placement." In each of the five cases, the [employees] were reported to be quiet, respectful, well behaved, and very obedient. The Works Manager was especially impressed by their truthfulness. A year later the same Works Manager was still able to advise that "in every case, the girls proved to be exceptionally well-behaved, particularly obedient, and strictly honest and trustworthy. They carried out work required of them to such a degree of efficiency that *we were surprised they were classed as subnormals for their age.*"[43]

Summary of Findings

If one were to put these basic findings in terms of propositions, one could state:

Proposition I. *There Is a Lack of Congruency between the Needs of Healthy Individuals and the Demands of the Formal Organization.*

If one uses the traditional formal principles of organization (*i.e.,* chain of command, task specialization, and so on) to create a social organization, and if one uses as an input agents who tend toward mature psychological development (*i.e.,* who are predisposed toward relative independence, activeness, use of important abilities, and so on), then one creates a disturbance, because the needs of healthy individuals listed above are not congruent with the requirements of formal organization, which tends to require the agents to work in situations where they are dependent, passive, use few and unimportant abilities, and so forth.

Corollary 1. The disturbance will vary in proportion to the degree of incongruency between the needs of the individuals and the requirements of the formal organization.[44]

An administrator, therefore, is always faced with a tendency toward continual disturbance inherent in the work situation of the individuals over whom he is in charge.

Drawing on the existing knowledge of the human personality, a second proposition can be stated.

Proposition II. *The Results of This Disturbance Are Frustration, Failure, Short-Time Perspective, and Conflict.*[45]

If the agents are predisposed to a healthy, mature self-actualization, the following results will occur:

1. They will tend to experience frustration because their self-actualization will be blocked.

2. They will tend to experience failure because they will not be permitted to define their own goals in relation to their central needs, the paths to these goals, and so on.

3. They will tend to experience short-time perspective, because they have no control over the clarity and stability of their future.

4. They will tend to experience conflict, because, as healthy agents, they will dislike the frustration, failure, and short-time perspective which is characteristic of their present jobs. If they leave, however, they may not find new jobs easily, and even if new jobs are found, they may not be much different.[46]

Based upon the analysis of the nature of formal organization, one may state a third proposition.

Proposition III. *The Nature of the Formal Principles of Organization Cause the Subordinate, at Any Given Level, to Experience Competition, Rivalry, Intersubordinate Hostility, and to Develop a Focus toward the Parts Rather than the Whole.*

1. Because of the degree of dependence, subordination, and so on of the subordinates upon the leader, and because the number of positions above any given level always tends to decrease, the subordinates aspiring to perform effectively and to advance will tend to find themselves in competition with, and receiving hostility from, each other.[47]

2. Because, according to the formal principles, the subordinate is directed toward and rewarded for performing his own task well, the subordinate tends to develop an orientation toward his own particular part rather than toward the whole.

3. This part-orientation increases the need for the leader to coordinate the activity among the parts in order to maintain the whole. This need for the leader, in turn, increases the subordinates' degree of dependence, subordination, and so forth. This is a circular process whose impact is to maintain and/or increase the degree of dependence, subordination, and so on, as well as to stimulate rivalry and competition for the leader's favor.

A Bird's-Eye, Cursory Picture of Some Other Related Findings

It is impossible in the short space available to present all of the results obtained from the analysis of the literature. For example, it can be shown that employees tend to adapt to the frustration, failure, short-time perspective, and conflict involved in their work situations by any one or a combination of the following acts:

1. Leaving the organization.

2. Climbing the organizational ladder.

3. Manifesting defense reactions such as daydreaming, aggression, ambivalence, regression, projection, and so forth.

4. Becoming apathetic and disinterested toward the organization, its make-up, and its goals. This leads to such phenomena as: (a) employees reducing the number and potency of the needs they expect to fulfill while at work; (b) employees goldbricking, setting rates, restricting quotas, making errors, cheating, slowing down, and so on.

5. Creating informal groups to sanction the defense reactions and the apathy, disinterest, and lack of self-involvement.

6. Formalizing the informal group.

7. Evolving group norms that perpetuate the behavior outlined in (3), (4), (5), and (6).

8. Evolving a psychological set in which human or nonmaterial factors become increasingly unimportant while material factors become increasingly important.

9. Acculturating youth to accept the norms outlined in (7) and (8).

Furthermore, it can also be shown that many managements tend to respond to the employees' behavior by:

1. Increasing the degree of their pressure-oriented leadership.

2. Increasing the degree of their use of management controls.

3. Increasing the number of "pseudo"-participation and communication programs.

These three reactions by management actually compound the dependence, subordination, and so on that the employees experience, which in turn cause the employees to increase their adaptive behavior, the very behavior management desired to curtail in the first place.

Is there a way out of this circular process? The basic problem is the reduction in the degree of dependency, subordination, submissiveness, and so on experienced by the employee in his work situation. It can be shown that job enlargement and employee-centered (or democratic or participative) leadership are elements which, if used correctly, can go a long way toward ameliorating the situation. These are limited, however, because their success depends upon having employees who are ego-involved and highly interested in the organization. This dilemma between individual needs and organization demands is a basic, continual problem posing an eternal challenge to the leader. How is it possible to create an organization in which the individuals may obtain optimum expression and, simultaneously, in which the organization itself may obtain optimum satisfaction of its demands? Here lies a fertile field for future research in organizational behavior.

Notes

[1] Temporarily, "formal structure" is defined as that which may be found on the organization charts and in the standard operating procedures of an organization.

[2] This analysis is part of a larger project whose objectives are to integrate by the use of a systematic framework much of the existing behavioral-science research related to organization. The total report

will be published by Harper & Brothers as a book, tentatively entitled *The Behavioral Sciences and Organization*. The project has been supported by a grant from the Foundation for Research on Human Behavior, Ann Arbor, Michigan, for whose generous support the writer is extremely grateful.

[3] The relevant literature in clinical, abnormal, child, and social psychology, and in personality theory, sociology, and anthropology was investigated. The basic agreements inferred regarding the properties of personality are assumed to be valid for most contemporary points of view. Allport's "trait theory," Cattell's factor analytic approach, and Kretschmer's somatotype framework are not included. For lay description see the author's *Personality Fundamentals for Administrators*, rev. ed. (New Haven, 1954).

[4] E. H. Erikson, *Childhood and Society* (New York, 1950); Urie Bronfenbrenner, "Toward an Integrated Theory of Personality," in Robert R. Blake and Glenn V. Ramsey, *Perception* (New York, 1951), pp. 206–257. See also R. Kotinsky, *Personality in the Making* (New York, 1952), pp. 8–25.

[5] This is similar to Erikson's sense of autonomy and Bronfenbrenner's state of creative interdependence.

[6] Robert W. White, *Lives in Progress* (New York, 1952), pp. 339 ff.

[7] Lewin and Kounin believe that as the individual develops needs and abilities the boundaries between them become more rigid. This explains why an adult is better able than a child to be frustrated in one activity and behave constructively in another. See Kurt Lewin, *A Dynamic Theory of Personality* (New York, 1935) and Jacob S. Kounin, "Intellectual Development and Rigidity," in R. Barker, J. Kounin, and H. R. Wright, eds., *Child Behavior and Development* (New York, 1943), pp. 179–198.

[8] Robert White, *op. cit.*, pp. 347 ff.

[9] Lewin reminds those who may believe that a long-time perspective is not characteristic of the majority of individuals of the billions of dollars that are invested in insurance policies. Kurt Lewin, *Resolving Social Conflicts* (New York, 1948), p. 105.

[10] Carl R. Rogers, *Client-Centered Therapy* (New York, 1951).

[11] Another related but discrete set of developmental dimensions may be constructed to measure the protective (defense) mechanisms individuals tend to create as they develop from infancy to adulthood. Exactly how these would be related to the above model is not clear.

[12] Herbert A. Simon, *Research Frontiers in Politics and Government* (Washington, DC, 1955), ch. ii, p. 30.

[13] L. Urwick, *The Elements of Administration* (New York, 1944).

[14] *Ibid.*, pp. 36–39.

[15] Cited in Harold Koontz and Cyril O'Donnell, *Principles of Management* (New York, 1955), p. 24.

[16] Conrad M. Arensberg and Douglas McGregor, Determination of Morale in an Industrial Company, *Applied Anthropology*, Vol. 1 (Jan.-March 1942), 12–34.

[17] Ralph M. Stogdill and Katheleen Koehler, *Measures of Leadership Structure and Organization Change* (Columbus, OH, 1952).

[18] *Ibid.*, pp. 36–39.

[19] For a provocative discussion of Taylor's philosophy, see Reinhard Bendix, *Work and Authority in Industry* (New York, 1956), pp. 274–319.

[20] Quoted in *ibid.*, pp. 36–39.

[21] Chris Argyris, *The Present State of Research in Human Relations* (New Haven, 1954), ch. i.

[22] Urwick, *op. cit.*

[23] James J. Gillespie, *Free Expression in Industry* (London, 1948), pp. 34–37.

[24] Herbert A. Simon, *Administrative Behavior* (New York, 1947), pp. 80–81.

[25] For an interesting discussion see Georges Friedman, *Industrial Society* (Glencoe, IL, 1955), pp. 54 ff.

[26] *Ibid.*, p. 20. Friedman reports that 79 percent of Ford employees had jobs for which they could be trained in one week.

[27] Harold L. Wilensky and Charles N. Lebeaux, *Industrialization and Social Welfare* (New York, 1955), p. 43.

[28] Rollo May, "Historical and Philosophical Presuppositions for Understanding Therapy," in O. H. Mowrer, *Psychotherapy Theory and Research* (New York, 1953), pp. 38–39.

[29] D. C. S. Williams, Effects of Competition between Groups in a Training Situation, *Occupational Psychology*, Vol. 30 (April 1956), 85–93.

[30] M. Deutsch, An Experimental Study of the Effects of Cooperation and Competition upon Group Process, *Human Relations*, Vol. 2 (1949), 199–231.

[31] The sacredness of these principles is questioned by a recent study. Gunnar Heckscher concludes that the principles of unity of command and unity of direction are formally violated in Sweden: "A fundamental principle of public administration in Sweden is the duty of all public agencies to cooperate directly without necessarily passing through a common superior. This principle is even embodied in the constitution itself, and in actual fact it is being employed daily. It is traditionally one of the most important characteristics of Swedish administration that especially central agencies, but also central and local agencies of different levels, cooperate freely and that this is being regarded as a perfectly normal procedure" (*Swedish Public Administration at Work* [Stockholm, 1955], p. 12).

[32] First defined by V. A. Graicunas in an article entitled "Relationship in Organization," in L. Gulick and L. Urwick, eds., *Papers on the Science of Administration*, 2d ed. (New York, 1947), pp. 183–187.

[33] L. Urwick, *Scientific Principles and Organization* (New York, 1938), p. 8.

[34] Ernest Dale, *Planning and Developing the Company Organization Structure* (New York, 1952), ch. xx.

[35] James H. Healey, Coordination and Control of Executive Functions, *Personnel*, Vol. 33 (Sept. 1956), 106–117.

[36] James C. Worthy, Organizational Structure and Employee Morale, *American Sociological Review*, Vol. 15 (April 1950), 169–179.

[37] W. W. Suojanen, The Span of Control—Fact or Fable?, *Advanced Management*, Vol. 20 (1955), 5–13.

[38] L. Urwick, The Manager's Span of Control, *Harvard Business* Review, Vol. 34 (May-June 1956), 39–47.

[39] Simon, *op. cit.*, pp. 26–28.

[40] William Whyte, "On the Evolution of Industrial Sociology" (mimeographed paper presented at the 1956 meeting of the American Sociological Society).

[41] In fact, much evidence is presented in the book from which this article is drawn to support contrary tendencies.

[42] Mal Brennan, *The Making of a Moron* (New York, 1953), pp. 13–18.

[43] Mr. Brennan's emphasis.

[44] This proposition does not hold under certain conditions.

[45] In the full analysis, specific conditions are derived under which the basic incongruency increases or decreases.

[46] These points are taken, in order, from: Roger G. Barker, T. Dembo, and K. Lewin, "Frustration and Regression: An Experiment with Young Children," *Studies in Child Welfare*, Vol. XVIII, No. 2 (Iowa City, IA, 1941); John Dollard *et al., Frustration and Aggression* (New Haven, 1939); Kurt Lewin *et al.,* "Level of Aspiration," in J. McV. Hunt, ed., *Personality and the Behavior Disorders* (New York, 1944), pp. 333–378; Ronald Lippitt and Leland Bradford, Employee Success in Work Groups, *Personnel Administration*, Vol. 8 (Dec. 1945), 6–10; Kurt Lewin, "Time Perspective and Morale," in Gertrud Weiss Lewin, ed., *Resolving Social Conflicts* (New York, 1948), pp. 103–124; and Theodore M. Newcomb, *Social Psychology* (New York, 1950), pp. 361–373.

[47] These problems may not arise for the subordinate who becomes apathetic, disinterested, and so on.

3

Mechanistic and Organic Systems

Tom Burns and G. M. Stalker

We are now at the point at which we may set down the outline of the two management systems which represent for us . . . the two polar extremities of the forms
which such systems can take when they are adapted to a specific rate of technical
and commercial change. The case we have tried to establish from the literature is
that the different forms assumed by a working organization do exist objectively and
are not merely interpretations offered by observers of different schools.

Both types represent a "rational" form of organization, in that they may both,
in our experience, be explicitly and deliberately created and maintained to exploit
the human resources of a concern in the most efficient manner feasible in the circumstances of the concern. Not surprisingly, however, each exhibits characteristics
which have been hitherto associated with different kinds of interpretation. For it is
our contention that empirical findings have usually been classified according to
sociological ideology rather than according to the functional specificity of the
working organization to its task and the conditions confronting it.

We have tried to argue that these are two formally contrasted forms of management system. These we shall call the mechanistic and organic forms.

A *mechanistic* management system is appropriate to stable conditions. It is
characterized by:

(a) the specialized differentiation of functional tasks into which the problems
and tasks facing the concern as a whole are broken down;

(b) the abstract nature of each individual task, which is pursued with techniques and purposes more or less distinct from those of the concern as a whole; *i.e.,*
the functionaries tend to pursue the technical improvement of means, rather than
the accomplishment of the ends of the concern;

(c) the reconciliation, for each level in the hierarchy, of these distinct performances by the immediate superiors, who are also, in turn, responsible for seeing
that each is relevant in his own special part of the main task;

Reprinted from *The Management of Innovation,* pp. 119–125, by Tom Burns and G. M. Stalker
(1961). Reprinted by permission of Oxford University Press.

(d) the precise definition of rights and obligations and technical methods attached to each functional role;

(e) the translation of rights and obligations and methods into the responsibilities of a functional position;

(f) hierarchic structure of control, authority and communication;

(g) a reinforcement of the hierarchic structure by the location of knowledge of actualities exclusively at the top of the hierarchy, where the final reconciliation of distinct tasks and assessment of relevance is made.[1]

(h) a tendency for interaction between members of the concern to be vertical, *i.e.,* between superior and subordinate;

(i) a tendency for operations and working behavior to be governed by the instructions and decisions issued by superiors;

(j) insistence on loyalty to the concern and obedience to superiors as a condition of membership;

(k) a greater importance and prestige attaching to internal (local) than to general (cosmopolitan) knowledge, experience, and skill.

The *organic* form is appropriate to changing conditions, which give rise constantly to fresh problems and unforeseen requirements for action which cannot be broken down or distributed automatically arising from the functional roles defined within a hierarchic structure. It is characterized by:

(a) the contributive nature of special knowledge and experience to the common task of the concern;

(b) the "realistic" nature of the individual task, which is seen as set by the total situation of the concern;

(c) the adjustment and continual redefinition of individual tasks through interaction with others;

(d) the shedding of "responsibility" as a limited field of rights, obligations and methods. (Problems may not be posted upwards, downwards, or sideways as being someone else's responsibility);

(e) the spread of commitment to the concern beyond any technical definition;

(f) a network structure of control, authority, and communication. The sanctions which apply to the individual's conduct in his working role derive more from presumed community of interest with the rest of the working organization in the survival and growth of the firm, and less from a contractual relationship between himself and a non-personal corporation, represented for him by an immediate superior;

(g) omniscience no longer imputed to the head of the concern; knowledge about the technical or commercial nature of the here and now task may be located anywhere in the network; this location becoming the *ad hoc* center of control authority and communication;

(h) a lateral rather than a vertical direction of communication through the organization, communication between people of different rank, also, resembling consultation rather than command;

(i) a content of communication which consists of information and advice rather than instructions and decisions;

(j) commitment to the concern's task and to the "technological ethos" of material progress and expansion is more highly valued than loyalty and obedience;

(k) importance and prestige attach to affiliations and expertise valid in the industrial and technical and commercial milieus external to the firm.

One important corollary to be attached to this account is that while organic systems are not hierarchic in the same sense as are mechanistic, they remain stratified. Positions are differentiated according to seniority—*i.e.,* greater expertise. The lead in joint decisions is frequently taken by seniors, but it is an essential presumption of the organic system that the lead, *i.e.,* "authority," is taken by whoever shows himself most informed and capable, *i.e.,* the "best authority." The location of authority is settled by consensus.

A second observation is that the area of commitment to the concern—the extent to which the individual yields himself as a resource to be used by the working organization—is far more extensive in organic than in mechanistic systems. Commitment, in fact, is expected to approach that of the professional scientist to his work, and frequently does. One further consequence of this is that it becomes far less feasible to distinguish "informal" from "formal" organization.

Thirdly, the emptying out of significance from the hierarchic command system, by which co-operation is ensured and which serves to monitor the working organization under a mechanistic system, is countered by the development of shared beliefs about the values and goals of the concern. The growth and accretion of institutionalized values, beliefs, and conduct, in the form of commitments, ideology, and manners, around an image of the concern in its industrial and commercial setting make good the loss of formal structure.

Finally, the two forms of systems represent a polarity, not a dichotomy; there are, as we have tried to show, intermediate stages between the extremities empirically known to us. Also, the relation of one form to the other is elastic, so that a concern oscillating between relative stability and relative change may also oscillate between the two forms. A concern may (and frequently does) operate with a management system which includes both types.

The organic form, by departing from the familiar clarity and fixity of the hierarchic structure, is often experienced by the individual manager as an uneasy, embarrassed, or chronically anxious quest for knowledge about what he should be doing, or what is expected of him, and similar apprehensiveness about what others are doing. Indeed, as we shall see later, this kind of response is necessary if the organic form of organization is to work effectively. Understandably, such anxiety finds expression in resentment when the apparent confusion besetting him is not explained. In these situations, all managers some of the time, and many managers all the time, yearn for more definition and structure.

On the other hand, some managers recognize a rationale of nondefinition, a reasoned basis for the practice of those successful firms in which designation of status, function, and line of responsibility and authority has been vague or even avoided.

The desire for more definition is often in effect a wish to have the limits of one's task more neatly defined—to know what and when one doesn't have to bother about as much as to know what one does have to. It follows that the more definition is given, the more omniscient the management must be, so that no functions are left whole or partly undischarged, no person is overburdened with undelegated responsibility, or left without the authority to do his job properly. To do this, to have all the separate functions attached to individual roles fitting together and comprehensively, to have communication between persons constantly maintained on a level adequate to the needs of each functional role, requires rules or traditions of behavior proved over a long time and an equally fixed, stable task. The omniscience which may then be credited to the head of the concern is expressed throughout its body through the lines of command, extending in a clear, explicitly titled hierarchy of officers and subordinates.

The whole mechanistic form is instinct with this twofold principle of definition and dependence which acts as the frame within which action is conceived and carried out. It works, unconsciously, almost in the smallest minutiae of daily activity. "How late is late?" The answer to this question is not to be found in the rule book, but in the superior. Late is when the boss thinks it is late. Is he the kind of man who thinks 8:00 is the time, and 8:01 is late? Does he think that 8:15 is all right occasionally if it is not a regular thing? Does he think that everyone should be allowed a five-minute grace after 8:00 but after that they are late?

Settling questions about how a person's job is to be done in this way is nevertheless simple, direct, and economical of effort. We shall later examine more fully the nature of the protection and freedom (in other respects than his job) which this affords the individual.

One other feature of mechanistic organization needs emphasis. It is a necessary condition of its operation that the individual "works on his own," functionally isolated; he "knows his job," he is "responsible for seeing it's done." He works at a job which is in a sense artificially abstracted from the realities of the situation the concern is dealing with, the accountant "dealing with the costs side," the works manager "pushing production," and so on. As this works out in practice, the rest of the organization becomes part of the problem situation the individual has to deal with in order to perform successfully; *i.e.,* difficulties and problems arising from work or information which has been handed over the "responsibility barrier" between two jobs or departments are regarded as "really" the responsibility of the person from whom they were received. As a design engineer put it,

> When you get designers handing over designs completely to production, it's "their responsibility" now. And you get tennis games played with the responsibility for anything that goes wrong. What happens is that you're constantly getting unsuspected faults arising from characteristics which you didn't think important in the design. If you get to hear of these through a sales person, or a production person, or somebody to whom the design was handed over to in the dim past, then, instead of being a design problem, it's an annoyance caused by that particular person, who can't do his own job—because you'd thought you were finished with that one, and you're on to something else now.

When the assumptions of the form of organization make for preoccupation with specialized tasks, the chances of career success, or of greater influence, depend rather on the relative importance which may be attached to each special function by the superior whose task it is to reconcile and control a number of them. And, indeed, to press the claims of one's job or department for a bigger share of the firm's resources is in many cases regarded as a mark of initiative, of effectiveness, and even of "loyalty to the firm's interests." The state of affairs thus engendered squares with the role of the superior, the man who can see the wood instead of just the trees, and gives it the reinforcement of the aloof detachment belonging to a court of appeal. The ordinary relationship prevailing between individual managers "in charge of" different functions is one of rivalry, a rivalry which may be rendered innocuous to the persons involved by personal friendship or the norms of sociability, but which turns discussion about the situations which constitute the real problems of the concern—how to make the products more cheaply, how to sell more, how to allocate resources, whether to curtail activity in one sector, whether to risk expansion in another, and so on—into an arena of conflicting interests.

The distinctive feature of the second, organic system is the pervasiveness of the working organization as an institution. In concrete terms, this makes itself felt in a preparedness to combine with others in serving the general aims of the concern. Proportionately to the rate and extent of change, the less can the omniscience appropriate to command organizations be ascribed to the head of the organization; for executives, and even operatives, in a changing firm it is always theirs to reason why. Furthermore, the less definition can be given to status, roles, and modes of communication, the more do the activities of each member of the organization become determined by the real tasks of the firm as he sees them than by instruction and routine. The individual's job ceases to be self-contained; the only way in which "his" job can be done is by his participating continually with others in the solution of problems which are real to the firm, and put in a language of requirements and activities meaningful to them all. Such methods of working put much heavier demands on the individual.

We have endeavored to stress the appropriateness of each system to its own specific set of conditions. Equally, we desire to avoid the suggestion that either system is superior under all circumstances to the other. In particular, nothing in our experience justifies the assumption that mechanistic systems should be superseded by organic in conditions of stability.[2] The beginning of administrative wisdom is the awareness that there is no one optimum type of management system.

Notes

[1] This functional attribute to the head of a concern often takes on a clearly expressive aspect. It is common enough for concerns to instruct all people with whom they deal to address correspondence to the firm (*i.e.,* to its formal head) and for all outgoing letters and orders to be signed by the head of the concern. Similarly, the printed letter heading used by Government departments carries instructions for the replies to be addressed to the Secretary, etc. These instructions are not always taken seriously, either by members of the organization or their correspondents, but in one company this practice was insisted upon and was taken to somewhat unusual lengths; *all* correspondence was delivered to the managing director, who would thereafter distribute excerpts to members of the staff, synthesizing their replies into the letter of reply which he eventually sent. Telephone communication was also controlled by limiting the numbers of extensions, and by monitoring incoming and outgoing calls.

[2] A recent instance of this assumption is contained in H. A. Shepard's paper addressed to the Symposium on the Direction of Research Establishments, 1956. "There is much evidence to suggest that the optimal use of human resources in industrial organizations requires a different set of conditions, assumptions, and skills from those traditionally present in industry. Over the past twenty-five years, some new orientations have emerged from organizational experiments, observations, and inventions. The new orientations depart radically from doctrines associated with 'Scientific Management' and traditional bureaucratic patterns.

The central emphases in this development are as follows:

1. Wide participation in decision-making, rather than centralized decision-making.
2. The face-to-face group, rather than the individual, as the basic unit of organization.
3. Mutual confidence, rather than authority, and the integrative force in organization.
4. The supervisor as the agent for maintaining intragroup and intergroup communication, rather than as the agent of higher authority.
5. Growth of members of the organization to greater responsibility, rather than external control of the member's performance or their tasks."

4

Management Systems 1–4

Rensis Likert

This article will be more interesting and more readily understood if a few minutes are taken now to complete the following form in accordance with these directions:

"Please think of the highest-producing department, division, or organization you have known well. Then place the letter H on the line under each organizational variable in the following table to show where this organization would fall. Treat each item as a continuous variable from the left extreme of System 1 to the right extreme of System 4."

Now that you have completed the form (table 1) to describe the highest-producing department or unit you know well, please think of the *least* productive department, division, or organization you know well. Preferably it should be about the same size as your most productive unit and engaged in the same general kind of work. Then put the letter L on the line under each organizational variable in table 1 to show where, in the light of your observations, you feel this least-productive organization falls on that item. As before, treat each item as a continuous variable from the left extreme of System 1 to the right extreme of System 4.

After you have completed table 1 to describe both the most and the least productive departments you know well, compare the relative position of your two answers on each item. You are very likely to discover that on all items, or virtually all, your L's are to the left of your H's, i.e., that your high-producing department has a management system more to the right in the table and your low-producing department is characterized by having a management system more to the left.

Many different groups of managers, totaling several hundred persons, have completed table 1 describing both the highest- and lowest-producing departments which they knew well. They have varied in their descriptions of the most productive departments; some are quite far to the right, the H's being largely under System 4.

Table 1

Table of Organizational and Performance Characteristics of Different Management Systems

Organizational Variable	System 1	System 2	System 3	System 4
1. Leadership processes used Extent to which superiors have confidence and trust in *subordinates*	Have no confidence and trust in subordinates	Have condescending confidence and trust, such as master has to servant	Substantial but not complete confidence and trust; still wishes to keep control of decisions	Complete confidence and trust in all matters
Extent to which superiors behave so that subordinates feel free to discuss important things about their jobs with their immediate superior	Subordinates do not feel at all free to discuss things about the job with their superior	Subordinates do not feel very free to discuss things about the job with their superior	Subordinates feel rather free to discuss things about the job with their superior	Subordinates feel completely free to discuss things about the job with their superior
Extent to which immediate superior in solving job problems generally tries to get subordinates' ideas and opinions and make constructive use of them	Seldom gets ideas and opinions of subordinates in solving job problems	Sometimes gets ideas and opinions of subordinates in solving job problems	Usually gets ideas and opinions and usually tries to make constructive use of them	Always gets ideas and opinions and always tries to make constructive use of them

(continued)

Table 1 (continued)

Organizational Variable	System 1	System 2	System 3	System 4
2. Character of motivational forces				
Manner in which motives are used	Fear, threats, punishment, and occasional rewards	Rewards and some actual or potential punishment	Rewards, occasional punishment, and some involvement	Economic rewards based on compensation system developed through participation; group participation and involvement in setting goals, improving methods, appraising progress toward goals, etc.
Amount of responsibility felt by each member of organization for achieving organization's goals	High levels of management feel responsibility; lower levels feel less; rank and file feel little and often welcome opportunity to behave in ways to defeat organization's goals	Managerial personnel usually feel responsibility; rank and file usually feel relatively little responsibility for achieving organization's goals	Substantial proportion of personnel, especially at high levels, feel responsibility and generally behave in ways to achieve the organization's goals	Personnel at all levels feel real responsibility for organization's goals and behave in ways to implement them
3. Character of communication process				
Amount of interaction and communication aimed at achieving organization's objectives	Very little	Little	Quite a bit	Much with both individuals and groups

(continued)

Table 1 (continued)

Organizational Variable	System 1	System 2	System 3	System 4
Direction of information flow	Downward	Mostly downward	Down and up	Down, up, and with peers
Extent to which downward communications are accepted by subordinates	Viewed with great suspicion	May or may not be viewed with suspicion	Often accepted but at times viewed with suspicion; may or may not be openly questioned	Generally accepted, but if not, openly and candidly questioned
Accuracy of upward communication via line	Tends to be inaccurate	Information that boss wants to hear flows; other information is restricted and filtered	Information that boss wants to hear flows; other information may be limited or cautiously given	Accurate
Psychological closeness of superiors to subordinates (i.e., how well does superior know and understand problems faced by subordinates?)	Has no knowledge or understanding of problems of subordinates	Has some knowledge and understanding of problems of subordinates	Knows and understands problems of subordinates quite well	Knows and understands problems of subordinates very well

(continued)

Table 1 (continued)

Organizational Variable	System 1	System 2	System 3	System 4
4. Character of interaction-influence process				
Amount and character of interaction	Little interaction and always with fear and distrust	Little interaction and usually with some condescension by superiors; fear and caution by subordinates	Moderate interaction, often with fair amount of confidence and trust	Extensive, friendly interaction with high degree of confidence and trust
Amount of cooperative teamwork present	None	Relatively little	A moderate amount	Very substantial amount throughout the organization
5. Character of decision-making process				
At what level in organization are decisions formally made?	Bulk of decisions at top of organization	Policy at top, many decisions within prescribed framework made at lower levels	Broad policy and general decisions at top, more specific decisions at lower levels	Decision making widely done throughout organization, although well integrated through linking process provided by overlapping groups
To what extent are decision makers aware of problems, particularly those at lower levels in the organization?	Often are unaware or only partially aware	Aware of some, unaware of others	Moderately aware of problems	Generally quite well aware of problems

(continued)

Table 1 (continued)

Organizational Variable	System 1	System 2	System 3	System 4
Extent to which technical and professional knowledge is used in decision making	Used only if possessed at higher levels	Much of what is available in higher and middle levels is used	Much of what is available in higher, middle, and lower levels is used	Most of what is available anywhere within the organization is used
To what extent are subordinates involved in decisions related to their work?	Not at all	Never involved in decisions; occasionally consulted	Usually are consulted but ordinarily not involved in the decision making	Are involved fully in all decisions related to their work
Are decisions made at the best level in the organization so far as the motivational consequences (i.e., does the decision-making process help to create the necessary motivations in those persons who have to carry out the decisions)?	Decision making contributes little or nothing to the motivation to implement the decision, usually yields adverse motivation	Decision making contributes relatively little motivation	Some contribution by decision making to motivation to implement	Substantial contribution by decision-making processes to motivation to implement

(continued)

Table 1 (continued)

Organizational Variable	System 1	System 2	System 3	System 4
6. Character of goal setting or ordering				
Manner in which usually done	Orders issued	Orders issued, opportunity to comment may or may not exist	Goals are set or orders issued after discussion with subordinate(s) of problems and planned action	Except in emergencies, goals are usually established by means of group participation
Are there forces to accept, resist, or reject goals?	Goals are overtly accepted but are covertly resisted strongly	Goals are overtly accepted but often covertly resisted to at least a moderate degree	Goals are overtly accepted but at times with some covert resistance	Goals are fully accepted both overtly and covertly
7. Character of control processes				
Extent to which the review and control functions are concentrated	Highly concentrated in top management	Relatively highly concentrated, with some delegated control to middle and lower levels	Moderate downward delegation of review and control processes; lower as well as higher levels feel responsible	Quite widespread responsibility for review and control, with lower units at times imposing more rigorous reviews and tighter controls than top management

(continued)

Table 1 (continued)

Organizational Variable	System 1	System 2	System 3	System 4
Extent to which there is an informal organization present and opposing or supporting goals of formal organization	Informal organization present and opposing goals of formal organization	Informal organization usually present and partially resisting goals	Informal organization may be present and may either support or partially resist goals of formal organization	Informal and formal organization are one and the same; hence all social forces support efforts to achieve organization's goals
Extent to which control data (e.g., accounting, productivity, cost, etc.) are used for self-guidance or group problem solving by managers and non-supervisory employees; or used by superiors in a punitive, policing manner	Used for policing and in punitive manner	Used for policing coupled with reward and punishment; sometimes punitively; used somewhat for guidance but in accord with orders	Largely used for policing with emphasis usually on reward but with some punishment; used for guidance in accord with orders; some use also for self-guidance	Used for self-guidance and for coordinated problem solving and guidance; not used punitively

For others, the most productive unit was largely under System 3. The striking fact, however, is that irrespective of where the H's describing the high-producing unit fall in the table, the L's for the low-producing department fall to the left. Quite consistently, the high-producing department is seen as toward the right end of the table.

For the vast majority of managers, this has been the pattern for every item in the table irrespective of the field of experience of the manager—production, sales, financial, office, etc.—and regardless of whether he occupies a staff or a line position. In about one case in twenty, a manager will place the low-producing unit to the right of the high on one or two items. But with very few exceptions, high-producing departments are seen as using management systems more to the right (toward System 4) and low-producing units as more to the left (toward System 1).

One would expect that such extraordinary consensus would lead managers to manage in ways consistent with it. When managers or non-supervisory employees are asked, however, to use table 1 to describe their own organization as they experience it, the answers obtained show that most organizations are being managed with systems appreciably more to the left than that which managers quite generally report is used by the highest-producing departments.

Parenthetically, some low-producing managers, although they display the same pattern of answers as other managers, believe that a manager should move toward System 4 *after* he has achieved high levels of productivity. They feel that the way to move from low to high productivity is to use a management system well toward the left (e.g., System 1 or 2) and move toward System 4 only after high productivity is achieved. Their view is essentially that of the supervisor of a low-producing unit who said: "This interest in people approach is all right, but it is a luxury. I've got to keep pressure on for production, and when I get production up, then I can afford to take time to show an interest in my employees and their problems." Research results show that managers who hold this view are not likely to achieve high productivity in their units.

The impressively consistent pattern of answers to table 1 obtained from most managers poses important and perplexing questions: Why do managers use a system of management which they recognize is less productive than an alternate system which they can describe correctly and presumably could use? All these managers keenly want to achieve outstanding success. What keeps them from using the management system which they recognize yields the highest productivity, lowest costs, and best performance? There are two related questions which should be considered.

A significant finding emerges when experienced managers are asked the following: "In your experience what happens in a company when the senior officer becomes concerned about earnings and takes steps to cut costs, increase productivity, and improve profits? Does top management usually continue to use the management system it has been employing, or does it shift its operation to a management system more toward System 1 or more toward System 4?" Most managers report that, when top management seeks to reduce costs, it shifts its system more toward System 1, i.e., toward a system which they know from their own observations and experience yields poorer productivity and higher costs, on the average and over the long run, than does the existing management system of the company.

What causes the top management of a firm, when it wishes to reduce costs, to take steps which shift its management system in the direction which will actually increase costs over the long run rather than reduce them? What are the inadequacies in the accounting methods and in the financial reports which lead managers and boards of directors to believe that with the shift toward System 1 their costs and earnings are improving, when the actual facts are to the contrary? Why are not the reported increases in earnings shown for what they really are: cash income derived from what is usually an even greater liquidation of corporate human assets?

These are extremely important questions which affect the success or even the survival of companies.

5

Management by Objectives

George S. Odiorne

The systems concept is primarily a way of thinking about the job of managing.

—R. Johnson, F. A. Kast, and J. E. Rosensweig

At the outset, let's make it plain that the system of management by objectives goes beyond being a set of rules, a series of procedures, or even a set method of managing. As the above quotation points out, it is a particular way of thinking about management. Let's begin, then, by placing our system in its conceptual framework:

1. The basic structure of the corporation is the organizational form often called a *hierarchy*. This is the familiar arrangement of boxes showing the boss in the top box, with two, three, or more subordinates in the boxes one level down. Management by objectives is a system for making that structure work, and to bring about more vitality and personal involvement of the people in the hierarchy.

2. Management by objectives provides for the maintenance and orderly growth of the organization by means of statements of what is expected for everyone involved, and measurement of what is actually achieved. It assigns risks to all responsible leaders and makes their progress—even their tenure—dependent upon their producing results. It stresses the ability and achievements of leaders rather than their personality.

3. As a system, management by objectives is especially applicable to professional and managerial employees. It can extend as far down as first-line supervisors, and also cover many staff and technical positions. Though the same basic system (measuring results against standards) is

Reprinted from *Management by Objectives: A System of Managerial Leadership,* pp. 54–56 and 68–79, by George Odiorne. Copyright © 1969 Prentice-Hall, Inc. Reproduced by permission of Pearson Education, Inc.

used in managing hourly rated or clerical workers, the methods of setting standards and measuring results are significantly different.

4. Management by objectives helps overcome many of the chronic problems of managing managers and professionals. For example:

   a. It provides a means of measuring the true contribution of managerial and professional personnel.

   b. By defining the common goals of people and organizations and measuring individual contributions to them, it enhances the possibility of obtaining coordinated effort and teamwork without eliminating personal risk taking.

   c. It provides solutions to the key problem of defining the major areas of responsibility for each person in the organization, including joint or shared responsibilities.

   d. Its processes are geared to achieving the results desired, both for the organization as a whole and for the individual contributors.

   e. It eliminates the need for people to change their personalities, as well as for appraising people on the basis of their personality traits.

   f. It provides a means of determining each manager's span of control.

   g. It offers an answer to the key question of salary administration— "How should we allocate pay increases from available funds, if we want to pay for results?"

   h. It aids in identifying potential for advancement and in finding promotable people.

A Brief Definition

In brief, the system of management by objectives can be described as a process whereby the superior and subordinate managers of an organization jointly identify its common goals, define each individual's major areas of responsibility in terms of the results expected of him, and use these measures as guides for operating the unit and assessing the contribution of each of its members.

The words we shall use in describing this system will be those every manager knows. We'll talk about authority, responsibility, delegation, and so on. We'll refer to such familiar procedures as the performance review, the salary review, cost accounting, and other everyday management terms. The reader will not be called upon to master a new glossary or to grapple with the jargon of social science. Why? Because management by objectives is essentially a system of incorporating into a more logical and effective pattern the things many people are already doing, albeit in a somewhat chaotic fashion, or in a way that obscures personal risk and responsibility.

The primary effects of operating by management by objectives are to be seen in such tangible results as improved profit, more growth, lower costs, and increased revenues. On a more intangible plane, it also makes bureaucracy less tenable by affecting such secondary variables as production, quality, housekeeping, sales volume, staff work, and research effectiveness. Its tertiary effects are visible in such areas as better morale, more promotable people, improved quality of service, and improved delegation of decision making. . . .

The Necessary Conditions

The primary condition that must be met in installing a system of management by objectives is the support, endorsement, or permission of the principal manager in the organizational unit where the system is to be used. The premise that success for every subordinate means "helping his boss to succeed" means also that the boss must be in accord with the goals of the subordinate and must not oppose the methods he uses to achieve them.

Hence, the place to begin an installation is with the top man in the organization where it is to be started. If the system is to be used at the corporate officer level, this will probably be the company president. At the divisional level, it must include the general manager, if the key functional heads are to use it as a way of managing. In manufacturing, sales, and engineering departments, it must include the plant manager, sales manager, or chief engineer of each of these functional units if it is to work effectively in them.

This doesn't preclude any manager whose boss is not opposed to his using the system from going ahead on his own and installing it in his own department or unit, so long as he has discretionary power over methods of managing.

The installation of management by objectives in the national sales organization of Honeywell's Micro-Switch division, for example, was successfully carried out because the division's national sales manager decided that the system had strong possibilities for his group, and his general manager enthusiastically backed him up. In numerous other companies, personnel, R & D, and accounting departments, legal staffs, and other units have successfully installed management by objectives where the top man in the unit was free to do so, and wanted it to be done. Usually the installation proceeds through the following phases:

1. Familiarization of the top man and his key executives (those reporting directly to him) with the system and how it operates.

2. Following the decision to install the system, the top man and his subordinates program measures of organization performance.

3. Goal-setting methods are then extended down through the organization to the first-line supervisory level through a successive series of meetings between the various organizational units and their superiors.

4. The necessary changes are made in such areas as the appraisal system, the salary and bonus procedures, and the delegation of responsibility. Ambiguous policies are clarified and procedures that may be blocking effective operation of the system are amended. Other changes, such as the installation of a system of "responsibility accounting" by the cost department, are also made.

The Stages of Installation for the Individual Manager

For every manager starting out to install this system in his own activity, the questions naturally arise: "How and where do I start? What steps are involved?" Following is a workable procedure for the individual manager at any level:

Actually two distinct but related activities are involved:

1. At the beginning of each budget year the manager and each of his subordinates agree on the subordinate's targets of performance for that year.

2. At the end of the year they take out these targets and jointly review the subordinate's performance against them.

Let's look a little more closely at each of these activities and see what the manager does to accomplish them.

Setting Goals with Subordinates

The following steps are undertaken at the beginning of each budget period for which goals are to be established:

Step One. Identify the common goals of the whole organizational unit for the coming period. This is based on your desired goals for the whole organization, which are stated in terms of the measures of organization performance you intend to apply at the end of the period. Some typical areas in which a statement of common goals may be needed are:

Profitability

Competitive position

Productivity

Technological leadership

Employee development

Public responsibility

Employee relations

Usually the economic goals are stated in terms of the controllable areas of responsibility for the head of the unit concerned.

Unit	Economic Goal
General management	Profit
Sales	Revenues, margins, or contribution
Service	Cost of unit of service delivered
Manufacturing	Cost of product made
Staff or research	Budget and program promised

Step Two. Clarify your working organization chart. Sketch the actual organization of the group under your supervision showing titles, duties, relationships, and impending changes.

As a manager you are responsible for achieving organizational results and personal responsibilities. You work out performance budgets only for those reporting directly to you. Those below that level should work out their budgets with their own immediate supervisor.

Your objectives are your own goals plus the major goals of those reporting directly to you. Don't pyramid into one set of goals all the many responsibilities of all the people below you in the organization. Carry the goal-setting process to your immediate subordinates. Take individual stock of the men with whom you'll be setting performance budgets. (Review each man's past work assignment, appraisals, salary progress. Note any special factors about him and his work; his major responsibilities, what's going to be expected of him, and so on.)

Step Three.   Set objectives for the next budget year with each man individually. Here's how you go about this:

    a. Ask the subordinate to make notes on what objectives *he* has in mind for next year and set a date when you'd like to discuss these with him. Normally, these goals will fall into four categories:

> Routine duties
> Problem-solving goals
> Creative goals
> Personal goals

    b. Before the meeting, list some objectives you'd like to see him include for the next year and have them ready. Note especially any innovations and improvements required of his function.

    c. In your personal conference, review the man's own objectives in detail, then offer your own suggestions or changes.

    d. Have two copies of the final draft of his objectives typed; give him one and keep one yourself.

    e. Working from the final agreement, ask him what *you* can do to help him accomplish his targets. Note his suggestions, keep them with your copy, and include them in your objectives, if pertinent.

Step Four.   During the year check each subordinate's goals as promised milestones are reached:

    a. Is he meeting his targets? Time, cost, quantity, quality, and service should be measured here.

    b. Should his targets be amended? Don't hesitate to eliminate inappropriate goals, or to add new targets if a special opportunity arises.

    c. Are you delivering on your part in helping him?

    d. Use the jointly agreed-upon goals as a tool for coaching, developing, and improving each man's performance on a continuous basis. Reinforce good results by feedback of *success* when you see it. Allow a man to make some mistakes (don't hound him for them) but use his failures as a platform for coaching.

Measuring Results against Goals

These steps are undertaken as the end of the budget year draws near:

Step One.   Near the end of the budget year, ask each subordinate to prepare a brief "statement of performance against budget" using his copy of his performance budget as a guide. Tell him not to rewrite the whole statement, but to submit a written estimate (giving relevant figures, where possible) of his accomplishments compared with his targets. In this statement he should also give reasons for any variances and list additional accomplishments not budgeted for.

Step Two.   Set a date to go over this report in detail. Search for causes of variances. Ask yourself:

a. Was it your fault?

b. Was it some failure on his part?

c. Was it beyond anyone's control?

Then get his agreement on just how good his performance was and where he fell down.

Step Three.   At this meeting, also, you can cover other things that may be on his mind. If he's so disposed, you might discuss such matters as relationships on the job, opportunity, job-related personal problems, and so on. But don't rush this. If he'd prefer, set another date for talking about these things.

Step Four.   Set the stage for establishing the subordinate's performance budget for the coming year.

Reviewing Organization Performance and Defining Goals for the Coming Year

Here, of course, the manager finds himself back at Step One of the goal-setting stage, but better equipped by reason of his experience, to set more realistic goals for the next budget period.

Unfortunately, simply setting forth a stark outline of this type may give rise to the misleading impression that the installation of the system calls for no more than slavish adherence to the prescribed pattern. Actually, any mere statement of procedure overlooks the factors of time and judgment, and of the willingness to move with the deliberate speed required to overcome the cultural patterns that oppose the introduction of change.

Technical assistance teams in underdeveloped nations, industrial engineers in inefficient factories, and community development experts in rural America, have all had to learn the hard way that people everywhere cling to expectations that offer them fulfillment of the values they hold dear. In the executive suites of the nation, as in the villages of India, the natives are under the sway of gods, graves, ghosts, sacred books, and high priests. No procedure can sweep these aside with a weapon forged from the feeble material of logic alone. The procedure must allow for local customs and cultural idiosyncrasies and go forward at a pace determined by the elimination of these barriers, rather than by the dictates of pure logic.

Still, technical and logical progress must be made.

Some Indispensable Preliminaries

In installing the system, managers would do well to look to the experience of others if they wish to avoid the costs of trial and error. When, in the hope of reaping quick gains, what others have learned is ignored, a certain amount of "backing up" and redoing will almost certainly become necessary, as many companies have found in trying to shortcut some of these essential steps:

Secure Top Management Backing

If the often-delicate negotiations that are necessary to obtain the endorsement of the top manager are omitted, the subsequent steps are likely to fail pretty badly. Unless the top man and the key men in each department know and accept what is being done, the staff man who would personally favor the use of the system might as well *defer his hopes until such endorsement is forthcoming*. It's no secret that there are many successful managers who enjoy personalized control, and don't mind at all if things appear chaotic as long as control is effectively centered in their hands. Such leaders resist systemization for a variety of personal reasons. Where they also possess abundant energy and long experience, and run the business with vigor and zest, the results will probably be good. The question, though, is whether they are succeeded by men who are their equals in ability, experience, and energy. It may also be questioned whether such people are, in fact, using their talents to best advantage.

When a company is, in effect, run by one man, this usually means that several conditions exist that can hardly be considered favorable to the organization or the top man himself. He's probably tied closely to the present, and is doing too little innovation. This isn't always true, however. Many charismatic leaders are great innovators, continually pushing the organization into new—and not always appropriate—fields. At the same time, the innovative powers of others may be stultified by this domination.

Most leaders who practice personalized control are prisoners of their subordinates and the job. The prisoner and the guard are both in jail. The puppetmaster and the puppets are both tied to the same string.

Usually the personalized style of leadership results in the leader's working at projects below his best abilities. As a rule, these are "vocational hobbies"—things the leader particularly enjoys doing because he excels at them. Perhaps he once held the job now being done by a subordinate, and over-supervises him. Perhaps he gains personal satisfaction from a particular line of work and dallies with it, though he is paying someone else to do it. The process of weaning managers away from such vocational hobbies is in part accelerated by a systematic approach to management.

Trying to obtain the endorsement, support, or permission of the leading figure in the organization to install management by objectives will be of little avail if he resists giving up personal control. If he is intractable in accepting systemization, is successful, has strong successors coming along, and innovates, it may as well be accepted that a new system is likely to add little to the company's immediate profit and growth and had better be deferred.

In any event, if management by objectives doesn't promise to achieve some beneficial effects that can be measured, it shouldn't be pressed into use at that time.

Clarify Common Goals Before Individual Goals

One of the more important reasons for involving the top leaders of the organization in the process is to engage them in setting common goals for the whole organization. This is more than a simple cumulation of the individual goals of subordinates. Such common goals may come from past history, from competitive records, from industry standards, or from higher levels of management, such as the board of directors.

Much of the literature of the social scientists who have studied and written about management by objectives has stressed "productivity" as a single measure of success. Experienced managers recognize this as but one of a dozen or so possible goals for an organization. These common goals might be in any one of the following areas:

Amount of profit

Rate of profit

Profit as a percent of sales

Profit as a return on investment

Profit as a return on equity

Growth in assets, sales, or profit

Market position or product-mix pattern

Share of market

Quantity and quality of service provided

Productivity of people, machines, or capital

Revenue levels

Contributions to profit

Employee relations, attitudes, turnover, etc.

Public relations

The necessity of setting organization measures of performance before setting individual management measures of performance lies in this simple fact:

Not all organization goals will be divisible into the personal goals of managers at lower levels.

Decisions taken at the highest level—as, for example, to buy rather than to manufacture (or vice versa); to accelerate growth through merger and acquisition; to increase productivity through automation or instrumentation—may affect the objectives of individuals in subordinate positions in a variety of ways. Individual managers at lower levels must know what these decisions are, and what limitations they place on their discretionary powers before they can be asked to propose their own goals. Otherwise, superiors may find themselves seeking opinions or suggestions that, in fact, cannot be used because they conflict with decisions previously made higher up. It is far better never to have asked subordinates to participate in decisions that affect them, than to ask them—and then ignore what they have to say.

For example, a grocery company found that its marketing methods of calling on grocers were drastically changed by the rapid rise of the food store and chain. The buyers had become more like purchasing agents of quantity lots than individual mom-and-pop grocers of the past. It became evident to top management that a complete revamping of the marketing plan was needed. Among the envisaged changes were early retirement for a substantial number of salesmen, the release of others, and the demotion of many sales managers. The pure use of participative management ("How do you think we should organize to fit the new marketing situation facing us?") produced a vast array of resistance to the drastic upheaval that was obviously called for. As a result, a great deal of bitterness ensued when the necessary change was enforced from the top. But what really irked the managers was that they had been asked their views and given them freely, had then been ignored, and had had the inevitable ill effects upon the sales group forced on them anyway.

The establishment of measures of organization performance before individual measures are set *defines the boundaries* within which subordinates can legitimately propose goals. Once these boundaries are known, individual goals and budgets should be solicited, and to the extent possible should be used to *adapt to organization goals.*

In brief, *the establishment of measures of organization performance should precede goal-setting meetings between managers and subordinates.* These measures of organization performance delineate the areas of decision of both parties in the joint goal-setting process.

While many of the measures of organizational performance will be summations of the individual goals of managers, those which are not should be clearly identified.

Change the Organization Structure in Accordance with Goals

The sketching out of the actual organization structure follows goals. The reason for this is similarly logical. If goals are being changed, there may be organization changes that will be required as well. In the case cited above it was the goal which shaped the organization and not the reverse. Changes in organization will lead to changes in individual areas of responsibility and authority and should be clarified before subordinate managers are asked to work out their performance goals and measures for the coming period.

The Management-by-Objectives Cycle

As Figure 1 shows, the system of management by objectives is a cycle. In this cycle, the newest feature is the *joint establishment* of subordinate goals. This is also the phase of the process that requires the most time from the most people.

Figure 1
The Cycle of Management by Objectives

This use of time on the manager's part is an important aspect of management by objectives, and depends heavily upon three points of emphasis:

1. *Management by objectives is a system of managing, not an addition to the manager's job....* [If] Manager M ... is to identify common goals, restructure his organization, jointly set goals with his major subordinates (A, B, and C), and use these goals as measures of results, both for the entire period and for periodic review, he will be too busy doing all this to do much else. In other words, he will be too busy managing to do much else.

2. *The manager who adopts management by objectives as a system of managing must plan to drop some of his more time-consuming vocational hobbies.* This is another way of saying that the manager must delegate, or relinquish personal control of certain activities that he has hitherto personally manipulated or overseen in too much detail. The difference here in his behavior is that he adds the teaching of the subordinate to his duties, and his rate of relinquishing personal control is identical with the rate at which he teaches the subordinate to perform as an independent operator. Thus the *learning curve* for the subordinate is the *delegation curve* for the superior. His former hobbies become responsibilities of the subordinate.

3. *The system of management by objectives entails a behavior change on the part of both superior and subordinate.* The subordinate moves in a more results-oriented fashion because he knows what his goals are. His superior provides the instruction, help, and behavior that will help him succeed. The superior must constantly ask, "What can I do, or do differently, or stop doing, to help you achieve the goals we've agreed on for your position?"

What Not To Do

There are certain key points in the foregoing procedure that can make or break the system. Here is a brief rundown of the major "don'ts":

1. Don't get involved in personality discussions. It's becoming increasingly recognized that the chart-rating type of performance review is based on unsound premises, and achieves no behavioral change of a predictable or productive nature. Confine your talk to the job, the results, and the reasons for variances.

2. Don't discuss salary and performance at the same meeting. . . . Suffice it to say here that the two subjects involve many different facets and should be discussed at different times.

3. Don't discuss potential and promotability at the same time as you are working on the man's responsibilities and results. Make that a separate discussion also. . . .

4. Don't hold a man accountable for things that are totally beyond his control.

5. Don't dwell on isolated incidents at the expense of overall results.

6. Don't make up your mind about the results a man has achieved until you've had your discussion with him.

7. Don't nag. By nagging we mean berating a subordinate for his failure to do things he didn't clearly know were expected of him.

6

Differentiation and Integration

Paul R. Lawrence and Jay W. Lorsch

It is no mystery that organizations must carry on transactions with their environment simply to survive, and, even more importantly, to grow. We identified the quality of these transactions as posing one of the fundamental developmental problems of any organization. Other analysts of organizational affairs have consistently mentioned transactions with the environment as a crucial if not the most crucial issue. It is an issue that has been dealt with extensively by economists and by specialists in business policy and strategy. They have dealt primarily with the content of these relationships—the actual kind and amount of goods, services, and funds that are part of these transactions. But the issue has not been extensively studied by specialists in the application of behavioral sciences, and attention has not been focused on such human aspects affecting the quality of these transactions as: What is the quality of the information exchanged across the organizational boundaries? What are the major determinants of the quality? What are its consequences? Such questions have been asked many times of the relations between individuals and groups within the organization, but the boundary-spanning relations have simply not been subjected to comparable scrutiny. It is not surprising therefore, that systematic efforts to diagnose and improve the quality of these organization-environment relations have also lagged behind the effort applied to improving internal relations. It is worth speculating about the reasons for this lack of attention.

Perhaps the focus has been placed on internal transactions because both parties to a faulty relation, being within the institution, tend to bring their troubles to a single source—their shared superior up the chain of command. This focuses attention on the costs of unsatisfactory work relations and triggers corrective action. There is less likelihood that this will happen in connection with boundary transactions. It is, moreover, not so easy to collect information about the status of the

From *Developing Organizations: Diagnosis and Action,* pp. 11–14 and 23–30, by Paul R. Lawrence and Jay W. Lorsch. Copyright © 1969. Reprinted with permission of Pearson Education, Inc.

boundary-spanning relation since the outside participants may feel no obligation to cooperate. The relative neglect may also be due to the traditional division of labor between academic disciplines. It may be automatically assumed that economists are the experts on boundary transactions while the psychologist and the sociologist are expected to confine their efforts to internal relations. Even within business schools, it is traditional for the functional specialties, such as marketing and finance, to have exclusive concern with the quality of salesman-customer and treasurer-banker relationships. Only recently have such specialists drawn on behavioral disciplines to aid them in the study of these matters.

The authors themselves became involved in the study and improvement of relations at this interface by approaching the topic through the back door. We had been concerned for some years with the quality of intergroup relations in organizations. This interest led us to the observation that major groups in industry displayed some distinctive characteristics that persisted in spite of efforts from top management toward consistency. We came to the conclusion that this persistence could be accounted for if these groups needed these characteristics to conduct favorable transactions with the segment of the firm's environment with which they were especially involved. So, in order to account for some important sources of intergroup conflict, we began to study each group's relations with its special segment of the environment. Our research findings tended strongly to confirm our theory. This, in turn, led us into a new interest not only in understanding these transactions from a behavioral standpoint, but also in helping organizations and their managers diagnose the quality of these relations and improve them.

The Certainty-Uncertainty Continuum

Our research findings with specific relevance to this interface can be quickly summarized. We started our inquiry with the simple notion that the characteristics of an organizational unit would in some way need to match up with those of its segment of the environment if healthy transactional relations were to prevail. We were particularly interested in information flows across these boundaries. It seemed to us that if the sector of the environment involved was in a fairly steady, unchanging state, the amount and complexity of the information needed would be much less than if the opposite were true—namely, if there existed a high degree of uncertainty and change in the relevant part of the environment. As the environment varies along this certainty-uncertainty continuum, we expected to find matching differences in the organizational unit concerned if the transactions were to be sound. We identified four measurable features of groups that we thought might vary with the certainty-uncertainty of their parts of the environment. These were:

1. the degree of reliance on formalized rules and formal communication channels within the unit;

2. the time horizon of managers and professionals in the groups;

3. their orientation toward goals, either diffuse or concentrated; and

4. their interpersonal style, either relationship- or task-oriented.

Using measures of these four characteristics, we made a study of high- and low-performance companies in three different industries, and arrived at the specific conclusion that there was a closer fit in the high-performing organizations than in the low performers between the attributes of each unit and the demands of its relevant part of the environment.

One way to visualize the meaning of these findings is to think again in terms of information flows. In order to relate effectively to its environment, any organization must have reasonably accurate and timely information about the environment and especially about environmental changes. This is clearly an easier job if the environment is relatively stable. The job can be specified in a predetermined set of operating rules. The necessary messages can be handled through the traditional superior-subordinate channels, which may be few and constricted but are probably less subject to error and relatively inexpensive. Fairly short time horizons are usually adequate to take account of the reactions of such an environment to the firm's actions. This makes it sensible to use a straightforward, task-oriented approach in managerial style.

On the other hand, life in an organizational unit must become more complex in order to deal adequately with an uncertain and rapidly changing sector of the environment. To have more points of contact with the environment, a flatter organization is employed. Formal rules cannot be formulated that will be suitable for any appreciable time period, so it seems better not to rely heavily on them. More of an all-to-all communications pattern is indicated, which can keep environmental clues moving throughout the unit for interpretation at all points instead of just through superior-subordinate channels. A longer time orientation is usually needed. The growth of this necessarily more complex and sophisticated (as well as more costly) communication network is fostered by an interpersonal style that emphasizes building strong relationships rather than just accomplishing the task, per se.

Stability vs. Change in the Environment

Securing and processing relevant information from the environment, while highly critical, is not the only requirement for high-quality transactions at the organization-environment interface. In addition to exchanging information, people at these interfaces must frequently negotiate the terms of exchange of tangible goods and less tangible services of many kinds. These bargaining and/or problem-solving kinds of relationships can also be analyzed in terms of the findings of research. Fouraker has used his findings from experimental research to develop the idea that organizational units with different internal features are more or less effective depending upon whether their environment is characterized by harsh competition for scarce resources or by more beneficent circumstances. In a relatively unchanging environment, it is likely that time has brought more competitors into the struggle and that therefore resources are scarce. In this circumstance, he argues that the organizations which can conduct more favorable transactions will operate with tighter internal controls, more rules, and simpler channels of communication. In short, they will have closed ranks and geared up for a competitive fight. Again, it is a matching process.

At the other extreme is an organization unit dealing with a rapidly changing environment. The resources are plentiful and diverse, but the organization must be capable of creative and flexible problem-solving to discover potential opportunities for conducting more favorable transactions. Here again that unit will thrive which relies not on rules but on a more complex and flatter communication network which serves to stimulate new ideas. Such a unit would be oriented to a longer time perspective. It would thus be matched with the features of its environment as it works at solving the problem of defining and continually redefining the terms of its environmental transactions.

These, then, are the highlights of current research on the matching of organizational units with their respective sectors of the environment. Good matching seems to foster sound transactions at this organization-environment interface. In our research we studied this interface only for the important functions of sales, research, and production; but table 1 indicates how many additional interfaces of this type are relevant to most business organizations. Similar lists could be drawn for other types of organizations.

One of the ways of evolving an overall strategy for any organization is to develop within the organization the capacity to carry on fully adequate transactions at each of these important interfaces, with some special advantages in regard to one or two of them where a favorable exchange is possible. These are areas of "distinctive competence," to use Selznick's term. An organization in which each of its boundary-spanning units is well matched with its corresponding environmental sector is in a desirable position to detect opportunities for new kinds of favorable transactions with the environment and to anticipate newly developing hazards in the environment. This matching process is a highly flexible way to maintain the kind of continuous search that is recommended by a pioneering study recently conducted by Aguilar on how business firms scan their relevant environments.

Table 1

Organizational Unit	Relevant Environmental Sector
Sales	Customers and competitors
Research	Science and technology
Production and engineering	Technology and equipment suppliers
Purchasing	Suppliers
Finance	Financial institutions
Personnel	Labor and professional markets
Public relations	The press and legislative bodies
Legal	Governmental regulatory agencies

As the relevant environment changes, however, organizations not only need suitable matched units, but on occasion also need to establish new units to address emerging environmental facts and to regroup old units. For instance, the emergence of the computer as a new environmental fact has led many firms to create a new unit such as management-information services; and the development of newly relevant mathematical techniques has led to the emergence of operations-research groups and long-range planning groups. Such new groups not only draw together people with different technical skills, but also they often need different orientations, structures, and styles to transact their business successfully.

In addition, as firms grow in terms of product variety and geographical coverage, a need frequently arises to switch the first big structural division of work in the company from the traditional functional basis, implicit in our discussion so far, to some other basis. Valid arguments can be mustered for various choices of first-level structural division, but the soundest arguments will be based on environmental facts. For instance, if different geographical areas require quite different ways of marketing, while the products of a firm are quite similar technically, a first-level split by *geography* is usually indicated, and vice versa. If, on the other hand, the products and the geographical conditions are relatively homogeneous, an initial division by *function* is probably the soundest basis.

This analysis of differences and similarities needs to be complemented by an analysis of the intensity of the interdependencies between various units to find the best possible trade-off. Once the primary basis for structurally dividing work is selected, secondary means can be provided not only at lower levels but also by staff groups. In some instances where two factors, such as functions and products, are both highly different and critical, some firms, as in the aerospace industry, are turning to a matrix organization. In such an organization two bases are used simultaneously as a first-level division of labor.

We have seen that whether we view the environmental transaction primarily as a problem of information exchange or as one of bargaining and problem solving, we are pointed toward a matching of organizational traits and orientations with environmental features. We are now in a position to explain how we use this method of analysis as a practical tool in helping specific organizations improve the quality of their environmental transactions. We will do this by examining several specific cases.

The first set of cases involves situations where mismatches could be directly addressed by making adjustments in the internal arrangements of the unit concerned. A second set of cases will also be examined where other types of adjustments were needed to improve the matching process:

1. by releasing counterpressures in the organization for consistency among all units;
2. by adjusting units to accommodate shifts in the environment;
3. by creating new units to meet newly important environmental conditions; and
4. by realigning units to cope with the increased scope of the business.

In reviewing these cases emphasis will be given to the variety of variables in the organizational systems that were selected as the initial means of implementing planned change.

Before turning to the cases, however, we need to get a feel for the way problems at this interface are likely to first present themselves to managers and in turn to behaviorally-oriented consultants. Problems at the environment-organization interface are likely to manifest themselves eventually through economic results. For example, at the sales-customer interface, it is in a loss of sales volume; in research and development, it is in a drop in the flow of new products, etc. However, these indicators of interface trouble are fairly slow to show up, and managers learn to be sensitive to earlier clues of difficulty. These often take the form of complaints from the outside—letters from customers, a private word dropped at lunch by a banker, an important move by a competitor that caught everyone flatfooted. The customer may be saying that your organization is unresponsive, that you cannot seem to tailor your products to his needs, that he is getting tired of fighting his way through your red tape. In other cases, the concern will develop because a competitor seems too frequently to be first with a new-product introduction, or a new marketing technique. Perhaps in the production area it is a failure to realize economies through process innovation or falling behind in the race with rising wages and salaries. Another clue might be that the best specialists are not staying in the company—there is a worrisome amount of turnover among the more promising professionals in the physical or managerial sciences. These are the clues that might well be traced back to human problems at the environment-organization interface.

The Differentiation-and-Integration Model

The notions of differentiation and integration and associated concepts dealing with the management of intergroup conflict have been presented as a comprehensive conceptual model elsewhere. We want only briefly to summarize them here. In doing so, we need to emphasize two points.

1. The model is based on empirical study of ten organizations in three different environments. Further, these findings have been corroborated by our consulting activities in several additional settings.

2. The model is fully consistent with the view of organizations as systems. That is, instead of providing a universal prescription of the one best way to organize, it provides a framework, based on the demands of the organization's environment, by which we can understand what organizational characteristics are required if an organization is to perform effectively in its particular environment.

Differentiation

To understand the environmental demands on an organization, we start first by looking at how much differentiation should exist among the various groups. As already suggested, this depends upon what internal characteristics each group must develop to carry out planned transactions with its assigned part of the environment. More specifically, it depends primarily upon the extent to which the certainty of information within the various parts of the environment is similar or different. If these parts of the environment (e.g., the market, scientific knowledge, technoeconomic manufacturing factors) are fairly homogeneous in their degree of certainty, the units will need to be fairly similar in formal organizational practices and members' orientations. If these parts of the environment have quite different degrees of certainty, the units will need to be more differentiated. Our evidence indicates that these needed differences are not minor variations in outlook but, at times, involve fundamental ways of thinking and behaving.

Integration

This model focuses attention not only upon the degree of differentiation necessary but also upon the integration required among organizational units. We need to be concerned with two aspects of the integration issue: which units are required to work together and how tight the requirement is for interdependence among them. But there is a strong inverse relationship between differentiation and integration. As we have suggested, when units (because of their particular tasks) are highly differentiated, it is more difficult to achieve integration among them than when the individuals in the units have similar ways of thinking and behaving. As a result, when groups in an organization need to be highly differentiated, but also require tight integration, it is necessary for the organization to develop more complicated integrating mechanisms. The *basic* organizational mechanism for achieving integration is, of course, the management hierarchy. In organizations with low differentiation, we have found that this is often sufficient to achieve the required intergroup collaboration. However, organizations faced with the requirement for both a high degree of differentiation and tight integration must develop *supplemental* integrating devices, such as individual coordinators, cross-unit teams, and even whole departments of individuals whose basic contribution is achieving integration among other groups. By using this model, then, we are able to understand not only the pattern of differentiation and integration required to deal effectively with a particular environment, but also the formal structural devices needed to achieve this pattern.

Conflict Management Variables

This model also points to another set of variables which are important—the behavior patterns used to manage intergroup conflict. As individuals with different points of view attempt to attain unity of effort, conflicts inevitably arise. How well the organization will succeed in achieving integration, therefore, depends to a great extent upon how the individuals resolve their conflicts. Our work indicates that the pattern of behavior which leads to effective conflict resolution varies in certain respects depending upon environmental demands, and in other respects is the same *regardless* of variations in environmental demands.

Those conflict management factors which vary with environmental demands include the pattern of influence or power within and among groups. The influence within groups means the organizational level *at which influence or power resides* to make decisions leading to the resolution of conflict. If conflict is to be managed effectively, this influence must be concentrated at the point in the various group hierarchies where the *knowledge* to reach such decisions also exists. Obviously, this will vary depending upon the certainty of information in various parts of a particular environment. The required pattern of influence among groups also varies with environmental demands. The groups which have more critical knowledge about environmental conditions are the ones which need to have high influence in resolving intergroup conflict if the organization is to be effective in resolving such conflict.

The factors which lead to effective conflict-resolution under all environmental conditions are the mode of conflict resolution and the basis from which influence is derived. In organizations existing in quite different environments, we have found that effective conflict management occurs when the individuals deal openly with conflict and work the problem until they reach a resolution which is best in terms of total organizational goals. In essence, effective organizations confront internal conflicts, rather then smoothing them over or exercising raw power or influence to force one party to accept a solution.

In organizations dealing effectively with conflict, we have also found that the individuals primarily involved in achieving integration, whether they be common superiors or persons in coordinating roles, need to have influence based largely upon their perceived *knowledge and competence.* They are followed not just because they have formal positional influence, but because they are seen as knowledgeable about the issues which have to be resolved.

To summarize, the differentiation and integration model provides a set of concepts which enable us to understand what characteristics an organization must have to be effective in a particular set of environmental circumstances. It directs our attention to environmental demands on the organization in terms of the degree of differentiation, the pattern and degree of integration, integrative mechanisms, and conflict-resolving behaviors. In sum, it provides a way of understanding much of what needs to happen at both the organization-and-environment and group-to-group interfaces.

7

What's Missing in MBO?

Paul Hersey and Kenneth H. Blanchard

Of all the management concepts and techniques that have been developed over the past decades, few have received such widespread attention as management by objectives (MBO). Managers in all kinds of organizational settings are attempting to run their organizations with MBO as a basic underlying management concept. Unfortunately, however, MBO success stories do not occur as often as anticipated by theorists who have written about MBO or practitioners who have applied it.

It is our contention that there has been a major missing link to more successful implementation of MBO: contracting for leadership style. In most MBO programs, an effort is made only to reach agreement on performance goals; there is little thought given to developing a psychological contract between the leader and the subordinates regarding the role of the leader in helping these subordinates accomplish their objectives.

Management by objectives, as it is practiced in most organizations, begins with agreement by superiors and subordinates of an enterprise on the common goals of the entire organization. At this time, any changes needed in the organization's structure—for example, changes in title, duties, or span of control—are made. Next, superior and subordinate independently propose time-oriented goals for the subordinate's job and the methods to be used to evaluate on-the-job performance. These are discussed and jointly agreed on by the superior and the subordinate. Checkpoints also are established: times when superior and subordinate together will compare the performance goals with what has actually been accomplished. If there is a discrepancy between the goals and the accomplishments, they discuss and determine the cause of the problem, then take steps to overcome it.

From *Managerial Review,* October 1974, pp. 25–32, by Paul Hersey and Kenneth H. Blanchard.

The Missing Link

The unique aspect of MBO is that superior and subordinate participate both in the establishment of performance goals and in the review or evaluation that takes place in relation to the agreed-upon goals. It has been found that participation in the formulation of objectives tends to make subordinates feel more personal responsibility for goal attainment and is thus more effective than having objectives imposed by an authority figure in the organization. The problem with MBO—and the reason why few effective implementations occur—is that the role of the leader in helping subordinates accomplish objectives is not clearly defined.

MBO could be a powerful tool for productivity improvement if superiors negotiated with their subordinates not only the goals toward which the subordinates would work but also the leadership style they would use to help their subordinates meet their objectives. Just as golfers, with the aid of their caddies, select a club depending on their lie on the course, so managers, with the help of their subordinates, should select the leadership style to be used according to the objectives and the needs of the subordinate in achieving the agreed-upon objectives. The Life Cycle Theory of Leadership—a situational leadership theory developed at Ohio University's Center for Leadership Studies—should help in this selection.

This theory grew out of earlier leadership models that were based on two kinds of behavior central to the concept of leadership style: *task behavior* and *relationship behavior.* Task behavior is the extent to which a leader explains what each subordinate is to do as well as when, where, and how tasks are to be accomplished. Relationship behavior is the extent to which a leader engages in behaviors such as emotional support, communication, facilitation, and interpersonal relations. The two dimensions of leader behavior, plotted on two separate axes, are shown in Figure 1.

Research in the last several decades has clearly indicated that there is no "best" style of leadership that can be universally applied. Thus, any of the four basic styles shown in Figure 1 may be effective or ineffective depending on the situation. The situational aspect of leadership is taken into consideration in the Life Cycle Theory of Leadership—which is based on the relationship among (1) task behavior—or the amount of direction a leader gives, (2) relationship behavior—or the amount of socio-emotional support a leader provides, and (3) the "maturity" of the leader's followers or group.

Maturity is defined in Life Cycle Theory as the capacity to set high but attainable goals, the willingness and the ability to take responsibility, and the education and/or experience of an individual or a group. These variables of maturity should be considered in relation to a specific task to be performed. A salesperson may be very responsible in closing sales but very irresponsible when it comes to completing the paperwork that has to be filed on every sale.

According to Life Cycle Theory, as the level of maturity of one's followers *increases* in terms of accomplishing a specific task, leaders should begin to *reduce* their task behavior and *increase* their relationship behavior until the individual or the group is sufficiently mature for the leaders to *reduce* their relation-

Figure 1
Basic Leader Behavior Styles

ship behavior as well. This cycle is illustrated in Figure 2 by the bell-shaped curve going through the four leadership quadrants.

Benchmarks of maturity are provided for determining appropriate leadership style by dividing the maturity continuum into three categories—below average, average, and above average. When working with people of below average maturity in terms of accomplishing a specific task, a high-task style (quadrant 1) has the best possibility of success. Moderate-task and moderate- to high-socioemotional styles (quadrants 2 and 3) appear to be most appropriate in dealing with people who are of average maturity in terms of accomplishing a specific task, while low-task and low-relationship styles (quadrant 4) have the best possibility of success in working with people of above average maturity.

Modifying Levels of Maturity

In attempting to help an individual or a group mature—that is, to take on more and more responsibility for a specific task—a leader should be careful not to delegate responsibility and/or increase socio-emotional support too rapidly. If the leader does either of these things, the individual or the group can take advantage and view him as a "soft touch." The leader should slowly develop the capability of subordinates on each task, using less task behavior and more relationship behavior as they mature and become more willing and able to assume responsibility.

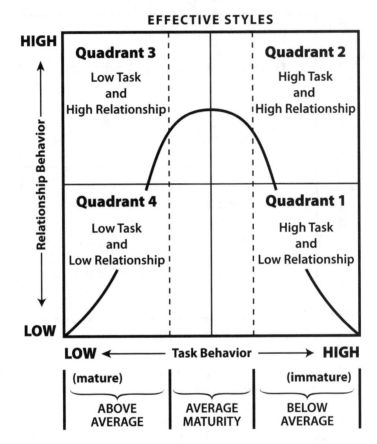

Figure 2
Life Cycle Theory of Leadership

Also, to obtain the desired behavior, a leader should reward as soon as possible behaviors exhibited by the individual in the desired direction and continue this process as the individual's behavior comes closer and closer to the leader's expectations of good performance. For example, suppose a sales manager wants to move a salesperson through the cycle so that he or she assumes significantly more responsibility. If the salesperson is normally very dependent on the manager to close a sale, the sales manager's best bet initially is to reduce some of the structure or close supervision by giving the salesperson the opportunity to assume some responsibility for, say, setting up the closing meeting. If this is done well, he should reinforce the behavior with increases in socio-emotional support or relationship behavior.

This process should continue until the salesperson is assuming significant responsibility and performing as a mature individual in closing sales. This does not mean that the salesperson's work will have less structure, but rather that the structure will now be internally imposed by the individual instead of being externally imposed by the sales manager. The cycle would be depicted in Figure 2 as a backward-bending curve moving into quadrant 4 (low-task behavior and low-relationship behavior). The salesperson is able not only to structure many of the activities in which he is engaged, but also to provide his own satisfaction for interpersonal and emotional needs. At this stage of maturity, individuals are positively reinforced for their accomplishments by the leader's *not* looking over their shoulder on a specific task and leaving them more and more on their own.

Of course, when people begin to behave less maturely for whatever reason—say, a crisis at home or a change in work technology—the leader should adjust behavior backward through the curve to meet the present maturity of his or her group. Suppose, for example, that a salesperson who is presently working well alone faces a family crisis that begins to affect performance on the job. In this situation, it may be necessary for the manager to increase structure and socio-emotional support until the individual regains composure.

Negotiating for Leadership Style

In the case of MBO, once a superior and a subordinate have agreed upon certain goals for the subordinate, the next logical step (but not often used) is for both parties involved—the superior and subordinate—to negotiate the appropriate leadership style that the superior will use in helping the subordinate accomplish each objective. The subordinate should participate in this selection not only because it will increase his feeling of personal responsibility for goal attainment but also because he can bring input to the decision making that will help in the selection of the appropriate leadership style.

Failure to select the right leadership style can lead to problems. For example, if the superior uses a low-task, low-relationship leadership style and leaves the subordinate completely alone in an area where the subordinate lacks sufficient technical skill and knowhow, the result may be failure—and the superior may not know about it until the next interim check period. Conversely, if a leader continually hovers over and directs the activities of subordinates working in areas where they are competent and capable of working alone, that leader may alienate them.

In areas where a subordinate is experienced and has been successful in accomplishing similar objectives over a period of time, superior and subordinate should negotiate a contract calling for the boss to leave the subordinate on his or her own. Rather than direct and closely supervise the subordinate, the boss should make sure that the resources necessary for accomplishing the goal are available and should coordinate the results of the project with other projects under his or her supervision. In those instances where the subordinate is working on a project with which he or she has very little experience and the boss does have some expertise, the subordinate and the superior should negotiate significant structure, direction, and supervision from the boss until the subordinate is familiar with the task. For a subordinate to accomplish every agreed-upon goal, a boss may have to use a variety of leadership styles depending on the subordinate's maturity in relation to the specific tasks involved.

Two things should be remembered in negotiating leadership style. First, the contract should always be open for renegotiation by either party. A subordinate may find that working without supervision on a particular task is not realistic or a superior may find that the style being used with an individual on a particular task is not producing results—and the two should be able to renegotiate for more supervision.

Second, it is important to remember that boss-subordinate negotiation over leadership style implies a shared responsibility if goals are not met. This means that a boss, if he or she has contracted for close supervision, cannot withhold help from a subordinate (even though work may pile up on another project) without sharing some of the responsibility for lack of accomplishment of that goal.

An Example of Contracting

Integrating the negotiation of leadership styles with management by objectives is a new concept but one that is already meeting with some initial success in industrial and educational settings. Take the case of an elementary school we studied in eastern Massachusetts. In many school systems, the principal of a school is required by school policy to visit each of his or her classrooms a certain number of times each year. This visitation policy is dysfunctional for principals who recognize that their teachers vary in their experience and competence and therefore have varying needs for supervision. If a principal decides to schedule visitations according to his or her perception of the competence of the teachers, problems can occur with teachers at either end of the extreme. Left alone, a highly experienced teacher may be confused by the lack of contact with the principal and may even interpret it as a lack of interest. By the same token, an inexperienced teacher may interpret frequent visits of the principal as a sign of lack of trust and confidence.

These potential problems were eliminated in this particular elementary school when the principal shared Life Cycle Theory of Leadership with the staff, then proceeded to negotiate what his leadership style should be with each of the teachers. It was found that when a low task-low relationship "hands off" leadership style was negotiated between the principal and a teacher because both agreed that the teacher was capable of working on his or her own, infrequent visits from the principal were perceived by the teacher in a positive rather than a negative manner.

The same thing held true at the other end of the continuum. It was found that when negotiation for leadership style took place with an inexperienced teacher who realized that the system was designed to help teachers learn to work on their own, the teacher was less reluctant to share anxieties about certain aspects of his or her teaching. If the negotiation resulted in close supervision initially, the teacher was able to view this interaction as positive, not punitive, because it was a temporary situation and demonstrated the principal's interest in helping the teacher to operate without much supervision.

Establishing objectives and reaching consensus over performance criteria for subordinates in a traditional management-by-objectives program are often the first steps toward providing the structure for individual and organizational accomplishment. Recent experiences indicate that if this initial negotiation procedure is combined with a similar process for negotiating the appropriate leadership style a superior should use to facilitate goal accomplishment, the whole MBO process may become more effective. Contracting for leadership styles can also help establish the interpersonal relations necessary for accomplishment of meaningful long-term objectives.

8

Reengineering Work Processes

Michael Hammer and James Champy

A set of principles laid down more than two centuries ago has shaped the structure, management, and performance of American businesses throughout the nineteenth and twentieth centuries. In this book, we say that the time has come to retire those principles and to adopt a new set. The alternative is for corporate America to close its doors and go out of business.

The choice is that simple and that stark.

American entrepreneurs, executives, and managers created and operated companies that for more than one hundred years met the expanding demand for mass market products and services. American managers and the companies they ran set the performance standard for the rest of the business world. Sadly, that is no longer the case.

This chapter describes a conceptually new business model and an associated set of techniques that American executives and managers will have to use to reinvent their companies for competition in a new world.

To reinvent their companies, American managers must throw out their old notions about how businesses should be organized and run. They must abandon the organizational and operational principles and procedures they are now using and create entirely new ones.

The new organizations won't look much like today's corporations, and the ways in which they buy, make, sell, and deliver products and services will be very different. They will be companies designed specifically to operate in today's world and tomorrow's, not institutions carried over from an earlier, glorious, but no longer relevant age.

For two hundred years people have founded and built companies around Adam Smith's brilliant discovery that industrial work should be broken down into its simplest and most basic *tasks*. In the postindustrial business age we are now entering, corporations will be founded and built around the idea of reunifying those tasks into coherent business *processes*.

In this chapter we demonstrate how existing corporations can reinvent themselves. We call the techniques they can use to accomplish this *business reengineering*, and it is to the next revolution of business what the specialization of labor was to the last. America's largest corporations—even the most successful and promising among them—must embrace and apply the principles of business reengineering, or they will be eclipsed by the greater success of those companies that do.

Reengineering isn't another idea imported from Japan. It isn't another quick fix that American managers can apply to their organizations. It isn't a new trick that promises to boost the quality of a company's product or service or shave a percentage off costs. Business reengineering isn't a program to hike worker morale or to motivate the sales force. It won't push an old computer system to work faster. Business reengineering isn't about *fixing* anything.

Business reengineering means starting all over, starting from scratch.

Reengineering—The Path to Change

When someone asks us for a quick definition of business reengineering, we say that it means "starting over." It *doesn't* mean tinkering with what already exists or making incremental changes that leave basic structures intact. It isn't about making patchwork fixes—jury-rigging existing systems so that they work better. It does mean abandoning long-established procedures and looking afresh at the work required to create a company's product or service and deliver value to the customer. It means asking this question: "If I were re-creating this company today, given what I know and given current technology, what would it look like?" Reengineering a company means tossing aside old systems and starting over. It involves going back to the beginning and inventing a better way of doing work.

This informal definition is fine for conversation, because it gives people an idea of what we mean by business reengineering. But anyone who wants to apply reengineering to a company needs something more.

How does a company reengineer its business processes? Where does it begin? Who gets involved? Where do the ideas for radical change come from?

We have watched companies use trial and error to answer these questions about radical change. We have served as advisers to companies that have made such changes and have observed others. Out of their experiences and our own emerged the concept of business reengineering, which we have developed into a process for reinventing a company. To perform this process, we and the companies with which we have worked have developed a body of techniques. These are not formulas, but tools that companies can use to reinvent the way their work gets done.

Our experiences and those of our clients with these techniques are encouraging. Used properly—that is, with intelligence and imagination—they work and can lead to breathtaking improvements in performance. The balance of this chapter is about business reengineering and how people can make it succeed in their companies.

Reengineering Formally Defined

Let's begin, then, with a better definition. "Reengineering," properly, is "the fundamental rethinking and radical redesign of business processes to achieve dramatic improvements in critical, contemporary measures of performance, such as cost, quality, service, and speed." This definition contains four key words.

Key Word: Fundamental

The first key word is "fundamental." In doing reengineering, businesspeople must ask the most basic questions about their companies and how they operate: *Why* do we do what we do? And why do we do it the way we do? Asking these fundamental questions forces people to look at the tacit rules and assumptions that underlie the way they conduct their businesses. Often, these rules turn out to be obsolete, erroneous, or inappropriate.

Reengineering begins with no assumptions and no givens; in fact, companies that undertake reengineering must guard against the assumptions that most processes already have embedded in them. To ask "How can we perform customer credit checks more efficiently?" assumes that customer credit must be checked. In many instances, the cost of checking may, in fact, exceed the bad-debt losses that checking avoids. Reengineering first determines *what* a company must do, then *how* to do it. Reengineering takes nothing for granted. It ignores what *is* and concentrates on what *should be*.

Key Word: Radical

The second key word in our definition is radical, which is derived from the Latin word "radix," meaning root. Radical redesign means getting to the root of things: not making superficial changes or fiddling with what is already in place, but throwing away the old. In reengineering, radical redesign means disregarding all existing structures and procedures and inventing completely new ways of accomplishing work. Reengineering is about business *reinvention*—not business improvement, business enhancement, or business modification.

Key Word: Dramatic

The third key word is *dramatic*. Reengineering isn't about making marginal or incremental improvements but about achieving quantum leaps in performance. If a company falls 10 percent short of where it should be, if its costs come in 10 percent too high, if its quality is 10 percent too low, if its customer service performance needs a 10-percent boost, that company does *not* need reengineering. More conventional methods, from exhorting the troops to establishing incremental quality programs, can dig a company out of a 10-percent hole. Reengineering should be brought in only when a need exists for heavy blasting. Marginal improvement requires fine-tuning; dramatic improvement demands blowing up the old and replacing it with something new.

From our experience, we have identified three kinds of companies that undertake reengineering. First are companies that find themselves in deep trouble. They have no choice. If a company's costs are an order of magnitude higher than the competition's or than its business model will allow, if its customer service is so abysmal that customers openly rail against it, if its product failure rate is twice, three times, or five times as great as the competition's, if, in other words, it needs order-of-magnitude improvement, that company clearly needs business reengineering. Ford Motor Company in the early 1980s is a case in point.

Second are companies that are not yet in trouble but whose management has the foresight to see trouble coming. Aetna Life & Casualty in the last half of the 1980s is an example. For the time being, financial results may appear satisfactory, but looming in the distance are storm clouds—new competitors, changing customer requirements or characteristics, an altered regulatory or economic environment—that threaten to sweep away the foundations of the company's success. These companies have the vision to begin reengineering in advance of running into adversity.

The third type of company undertaking reengineering are those that are in peak condition. They have no discernible difficulties, either now or on the horizon, but their managements are ambitious and aggressive. Examples include Hallmark and Wal-Mart. Companies in this third category see reengineering as an opportunity to further their lead over their competitors. By enhancing their performance, they seek to raise the competitive bar even higher and make life even tougher for everyone else. Clearly, reengineering from a position of strength is hard to do. Why rewrite the rules when you're already winning the game? It has been said that the hallmark of the truly successful company is a willingness to abandon what has long been successful. A truly great company is never satisfied with its current performance. A truly great company willingly abandons practices that have long worked well in the hope and expectation of coming up with something better.

We sometimes explain the distinctions among these three kinds of companies this way: Companies in the first category are desperate; they have hit the wall and are lying injured on the ground. Companies in the second category are cruising along at high speed, but see something rushing toward them in their headlamps. Could it be a wall? Companies in the third category are out for a drive on a clear afternoon, with no obstacles in sight. What a splendid time, they decide, to stop and build a wall for the other guys.

Key Word: Processes

The fourth key word in our definition is *processes*. Although this word is the most important in our definition, it is also the one that gives most corporate managers the greatest difficulty. Most businesspeople are not "process-oriented"; they are focused on tasks, on jobs, on people, on structures, but not on processes.

We define a business process as a collection of activities that takes one or more kinds of input and creates an output that is of value to the customer. A process talked about is order fulfillment, which takes an order as its input and results in the delivery of the ordered goods. In other words, the delivery of the ordered goods to the customer's hands is the value that the process creates.

Under the influence of Adam Smith's notion of breaking work into its simplest tasks and assigning each of these to a specialist, modern companies and their managers focus on the individual tasks in this process—receiving the order form, picking the goods from the warehouse, and so forth—and tend to lose sight of the larger objective, which is to get the goods into the hands of the customer who ordered them. The individual tasks within this process are important, but none of them matters one whit to the customer if the overall process doesn't work—that is, if the process doesn't deliver the goods.

We will use three examples of reengineering to illustrate how it works and what it can accomplish for companies. In reading these examples, it is helpful to keep in mind the four key words that characterize reengineering—fundamental, radical, dramatic, and process—but especially process. Task-based thinking—the fragmentation of work into its simplest components and their assignment to specialist workers—has influenced the organizational design of companies for the last two hundred years. The shift to process-based thinking is already underway, and that shift is illustrated in the radical changes that mainstream companies such as IBM Credit, Ford Motor, and Kodak have made.

Example: IBM Credit. Our first case concerns IBM Credit Corporation, a wholly owned subsidiary of IBM, which, if it were independent, would rank among the *Fortune 100* service companies. IBM Credit is in the business of financing the computers, software, and services that the IBM Corporation sells. It is a business of which IBM is fond, since financing customers' purchases is an extremely profitable business.

In its early years, IBM Credit's operation was positively Dickensian. When an IBM field salesperson called in with a request for financing, he or she reached one of fourteen people sitting around a conference room table in Old Greenwich, Connecticut. The person taking the call logged the request for a deal on a piece of paper. That was step one.

In step two, someone carted that piece of paper upstairs to the credit department, where a specialist entered the information into a computer system and checked the potential borrower's creditworthiness. The specialist wrote the results of the credit check on the piece of paper and dispatched it to the next link in the chain, which was the business practices department.

The business practices department, step three, was in charge of modifying the standard loan covenant in response to customer request. Business practices had its own computer system. When done, a person in that department would attach the special terms to the request form.

Next, the request went to a pricer, step four, who keyed the data into a personal computer spreadsheet to determine the appropriate interest rate to charge the customer. The pricer wrote the rate on a piece of paper, which, with the other papers, was delivered to a clerical group, step five.

There, an administrator turned all this information into a quote letter that could be delivered to the field sales representative by Federal Express.

The entire process consumed six days on average, although it sometimes took as long as two weeks. From the sales reps' point of view, this turnaround was too long, since it gave the customer six days to find another source of financing, to be seduced by another computer vendor, or simply to call the whole deal off. So the rep would call—and call and call—to ask, "Where is my deal, and when are you going to get it out?" Naturally, no one had a clue, since the request was lost somewhere in the chain.

In their efforts to improve this process, IBM Credit tried several fixes. They decided, for instance, to install a control desk, so they could answer the rep's questions about the status of the deal. That is, instead of each department forwarding the credit request to the next step in the chain, it would return it to the control disk where the calls were originally taken. There, an administrator logged the completion of each step before sending the paper out again. This fix did indeed solve one problem: The control desk knew the location of each request in the labyrinth and could give the rep the information he or she wanted. Unfortunately, this information was purchased at the cost of adding more time to the turnaround.

Eventually, two senior managers at IBM Credit had a brainstorm. They took a financing request and walked it themselves through all five steps, asking personnel in each office to put aside whatever they were doing and to process this request as they normally would, only without the delay of having it sit in a pile on someone's desk. They learned from their experiments that performing the actual work took in total only *ninety minutes*—one and one half hours. The remainder—now more than seven days on the average—was consumed by handing the form off from one department to the next. Management had begun to look at the heart of the issue, which was the overall credit issuance process. Indeed, if by the wave of some magic wand the company were able to double the personal productivity of each individual in the organization, total turnaround time would have been reduced by only forty-five minutes. The problem did not lie in the tasks and the people performing them, but in the structure of the process itself. In other words, it was the process that had to change, not the individual steps.

In the end, IBM Credit replaced its specialists—the credit checkers, pricers, and so on—with generalists. Now, instead of sending an application from office to office, one person called a deal structurer processes the entire application from beginning to end: No handoffs.

How could one generalist replace four specialists? The old process design was, in fact, founded on a deeply held (but deeply hidden) assumption: that every bid request was unique and difficult to process, thereby requiring the intervention of four highly trained specialists. In fact, this assumption was false; most requests were simple and straightforward. The old process had been overdesigned to handle the most difficult applications that management could imagine. When IBM Credit's senior managers closely examined the work the specialists did, they found that most of it was little more than clerical: finding a credit rating in a database, plugging numbers into a standard model, pulling boilerplate clauses from a file. These tasks fall well within the capability of a single individual when he or she is supported by an easy-to-use computer system that provides access to all the data and tools the specialists would use.

IBM Credit also developed a new, sophisticated computer system to support the deal structurers. In most situations, the system provides the deal structurer with the guidance needed to proceed. In really tough situations, he or she can get help from a small pool of real specialists—experts in credit checking, pricing, and so forth. Even here handoffs have disappeared because the deal structurer and the specialists he or she calls in work together as a team.

The performance improvement achieved by the redesign is extraordinary. IBM Credit slashed its seven-*day* turnaround to four *hours.* It did so *without* an increase in head count—in fact, it has achieved a small head-count reduction. At the same time, the number of deals that it handles has increased a hundredfold. Not 100 percent, but *one hundred times.*

What IBM Credit accomplished—a 90-percent reduction in cycle time and a hundredfold improvement in productivity—easily meets our definition of reengineering. The company achieved a *dramatic* performance breakthrough by making a *radical* change to the *process* as a whole. IBM Credit did not ask, "How do we improve the calculation of a financing quote? How do we enhance credit checking?" It asked instead, "How do we improve the credit issuance process?" Furthermore, in making its radical change, IBM Credit shattered the assumption that it needed specialists to perform specialized steps.

Example: Ford Motor.   Our second example of reengineering involves changes to a different category of process. We defined a process as a series of activities that delivers value to a customer and cited order fulfillment and credit issuance as examples. However, the customer of a process is not necessarily a customer of the company. The customer may be inside the company, as it is, for instance, for the materials acquisition or purchasing process, which supplies materials to a company's manufacturing operations. Reengineering can apply to these processes, too, as Ford Motor Company learned.

In the early 1980s, Ford, like many other American corporations, was searching for ways to cut overhead and administrative costs. One of the places Ford believed it could reduce costs was in its accounts payable department, the organization that paid the bills submitted by Ford's suppliers. At that time, Ford's North American accounts payable department employed more than five hundred people. By using computers to automate some functions, Ford executives believed that they could attain a 20 percent head-count reduction in the department, bringing the number of clerks down to four hundred. By our definition, this incremental improvement, achieved by automating the existing manual process, would not qualify as business reengineering. Nonetheless, Ford managers thought 20 percent sounded pretty good—until they visited Mazda.

Ford had recently acquired a 25 percent equity interest in the Japanese company. The Ford executives noted that the admittedly smaller company took care of its accounts payable chores with only *five* people. The contrast—Ford's five hundred people to Mazda's five—was too great to attribute just to the smaller company's size, *esprit de corps,* company songs, or morning calisthenics. Automating to achieve a 20 percent personnel reduction clearly would not put Ford on a cost-par with Mazda, so the Ford executives were forced to rethink the entire process in which the accounts payable department took part.

This decision marked a critical shift in perspective for Ford, because companies can reengineer only business processes, not the administrative organizations that have evolved to accomplish them. "Accounts payable" cannot be reengineered, because it is not a process. It is a department, an organizational artifact of a particular process design. The accounts payable department consists of a group of clerks sitting in a room and passing paper amongst themselves. *They* cannot be reengineered, but what they *do* can be—and the way they are eventually reorganized to accomplish the new work process will follow from the requirements of the reengineered process itself.

We cannot emphasize this crucial distinction enough. Reengineering must focus on redesigning a fundamental business process, not on departments or other organizational units. Define a reengineering effort in terms of an organizational unit, and the effort is doomed. Once a real work process is reengineered, the shape of the organizational structure required to perform the work will become apparent. It probably will not look much like the old organization; some departments or other organizational units may even disappear, as they did at Ford.

The process that Ford eventually reengineered was not "accounts payable," but "procurement." That process took as input a purchase order from, say, a plant that needed parts, and provided that plant (the process customer) with bought-and-paid-for goods. The procurement process included the accounts payable function, but it also encompassed purchasing and receiving.

Ford's old parts acquisition process was remarkably conventional. It began with the purchasing department sending a purchase order to a vendor, with a copy going to accounts payable. When the vendor shipped the goods and they arrived at Ford, a clerk at the receiving dock would complete a form describing the goods and send it to accounts payable. The vendor, meanwhile, sent accounts payable an invoice.

Accounts payable now had three documents relating to those goods—the purchase order, the receiving document, and the invoice. If all three matched, a clerk issued payment. Most of the time, that is what happened, but occasionally Vilfredo Pareto intervened.

Pareto, an early twentieth-century Italian economist, formulated what most of us call the 80–20 rule, technically known as the law of maldistribution. This rule states that 80 percent of the effort expended in a process is caused by only 20 percent of the input. In the case of Ford's accounts payable department, clerks there spent the great majority of their time straightening out the infrequent situations in which the documents—purchase order, receiving document, and invoice—did not match. Sometimes, the resolution required weeks of time and enormous amounts of work in order to trace and clarify the discrepancies.

Ford's new accounts payable process looks radically different. Accounts payable clerks no longer match purchase order with invoice with receiving document, primarily because the new process eliminates the invoice entirely. The results have proved dramatic. Instead of five hundred people, Ford now has just 125 people involved in vendor payment.

The new process looks like this: When a buyer in the purchasing department issues a purchase order to a vendor, that buyer simultaneously enters the order into an on-line database. Vendors, as before, send goods to the receiving dock. When they arrive, someone in receiving checks a computer terminal to see whether the received shipment corresponds to an outstanding purchase order in the database. Only two possibilities exist: It does or it doesn't. If it does, the clerk at the dock accepts the goods and pushes a button on the terminal keyboard that tells the database that the goods have arrived. Receipt of the goods is now recorded in the database, and the computer will automatically issue and send a check to the vendor at the appropriate time. If, on the other hand, the goods do not correspond to an outstanding purchase order in the database, the clerk on the dock will refuse the shipment and send it back to the vendor.

The basic concept of the change at Ford is simple. Payment authorization, which used to be performed by accounts payable, is now accomplished at the receiving dock. The old process fostered Byzantine complexities: searches, suspense files, ticklers—enough to keep five hundred clerks more or less busy. The new process does not. In fact, the new process comes close to eliminating the need for an accounts payable department altogether. In some parts of Ford, such as the Engine Division, the head count in accounts payable is now just 5 percent of its former size. Only a handful of people remains to handle exceptional situations.

The reengineered process at Ford breaks hard and fast rules that formerly applied there. Every business has these rules, deeply ingrained in the operation of the organization, whether they are explicitly spelled out or not.

For instance, Rule One at Ford's accounts payable department was: We pay when we receive the invoice. While this rule was rarely articulated, it was the frame around which the old process was formed. When Ford's managers reinvented this process, they were effectively asking whether they still wanted to live by this rule. The answer was no. The way to break this rule was to eliminate invoices. Instead of "We pay when we receive the *invoice*," the new rule at Ford is, "We pay when we receive the *goods*." Altering just that one word established the basis for a major business change. Other one-word changes in old rules at Ford are having similar effects today.

In one of its truck plants, for instance, instead of "We pay when we receive the goods," Ford has implemented an even newer rule: "We pay when we *use* the goods." The company has said in effect to one of its brake suppliers, "We like your brakes, and we will continue to install them on our trucks, but until we do, they are *your* brakes, not ours. The brakes only become ours when we use them, and that's when we'll pay for them. Every time a truck comes off the line with a set of your brakes on it, we'll mail you a check." This change has simplified even further Ford's purchasing and receiving procedures. (It also has paid off in other ways, from reducing inventory levels to improving cash flow.)

The new process for brake acquisition shatters another rule at Ford, the one that requires the company always to maintain multiple sources of supply. At least with regard to truck brakes, the new rule is, "We shall have a *single* source of supply and work *very* closely with that vendor."

One might wonder why the brake supplier agreed to this change, since it is now, for practical purposes, financing Ford's brake inventory. What benefit does the supplier derive from the new arrangement?

First, it now gets all of Ford's truck brake business instead of just some of it. Second, because the supplier is now privy to Ford's computerized manufacturing schedule, it does not have to depend on the unreliable forecasts of Ford's brake demands that it previously got from its own sales force. The brake supplier can better schedule its own production and reduce the size of its own inventory.

The reengineering of procurement at Ford illustrates another characteristic of a true reengineering effort: Ford's changes would have been impossible without modern *information technology*—which is likewise true for the reengineering effort at IBM Credit. The new processes at both companies are not just the old processes with new wrinkles. They are entirely new processes that could not exist without today's information technology.

In the reengineered procurement process, for example, Ford's receiving clerk could not authorize vendor payment when goods arrived without the on-line database of purchase orders. In fact, absent the database, the receiving clerk would be just as much in the dark as ever about what goods Ford had actually ordered. The clerk's only option when goods arrived would have been, as previously, to assume that they had been ordered, accept them, and leave it to accounts payable to reconcile the receiving document, the purchase order, and the invoice. In theory, purchasing could have sent a photocopy of every purchase order to every receiving dock in the company, and receiving clerks could have checked arriving goods against these, but for obvious reasons such a paper-based system would prove impractical. Technology has enabled Ford to create a radically new mode of operation. Similarly, at IBM Credit technology permits generalists to have easy access to information previously available only to specialists.

We say that in reengineering, information technology acts as an *essential enabler.* Without information technology, the process could not be reengineered.

Example: Kodak.   Another example of reengineering is the product development process that Kodak created in response to a competitive challenge. In 1987, Kodak's arch-rival, Fuji, announced a new 35mm, single-use camera, the sort that the customer buys loaded with film, uses once, and then returns to the manufacturer, who processes the film and breaks down the camera into parts for reuse. Kodak had no competitive offering, nor even one in the works, and its traditional product design process would have taken seventy weeks to produce a rival to Fuji's camera. Such a time delay would have handed Fuji an enormous head start and advantage in a new market. To slash its time-to-market, Kodak reengineered its product development process.

Most product development processes are either sequential, which makes them slow, or parallel, which also makes them slow, but for a different reason. In a sequential development process, individuals or groups working on one part of a product wait until the previous step is completed before beginning their own. Camera body designers, for example, may do their work first, followed by shutter designers, then the film advance mechanism designers, and so on. It is no mystery why this process is slow.

In a parallel design process, all the parts are designed simultaneously and integrated at the end. But this method engenders its own problem: Usually, the subsystems will not fit together because, even though all the groups were working from the same basic camera design, changes—often improvements—occurred along the way but were not communicated to the other groups. Then, when the camera is supposed to be ready to go to production, it's back to square one in design.

Kodak's old product development process was partly sequential and partly parallel but entirely slow. Designing the camera was conducted in parallel, with that method's attendant problems, and the design of the manufacturing tooling was tacked on, sequentially, at the end. At Kodak, the manufacturing engineers did not even begin their work until twenty-eight weeks after the product designers had started.

Kodak reengineered its product development process through the innovative use of a technology called CAD/CAM—Computer Aided Design/Computer Aided Manufacturing. This technology allows engineers to design at computer workstations instead of at drafting tables. Just working at a screen instead of on paper would have made the designers individually more productive, but such use of the technology would have had only marginal effect on the process as a whole.

The technology that has enabled Kodak to reengineer its process is an integrated product design database. Each day this database collects each engineer's work and combines all the individual efforts into a coherent whole. Each morning, design groups and individuals inspect the database to see whether someone else's work yesterday has created a problem for them or for the overall design. If so, they resolve the problem *immediately*, instead of after weeks or months of wasted work. Moreover, this technology permits manufacturing engineers to begin their tooling design just ten weeks into the development process, as soon as the product designers have given the first prototype some shape.

Kodak's new process, called concurrent engineering, has been used widely in the aerospace and automotive industries and is now starting to attract adherents in consumer goods companies. Kodak exploited concurrent engineering to cut nearly in half—to thirty-eight weeks—the time required to move the 35mm, single-use camera from concept to production. Furthermore, because the reengineered process allows tooling designers to get involved before product design is finished, their expertise can be tapped to create a design that is more easily and inexpensively manufactured. Kodak has reduced its tooling and manufacturing costs for the single-use camera by 25 percent.

In these three examples, we have seen illustrations of true *business reengineering,* even though some of them occurred before we had coined the term. These examples illustrate the four requisite characteristics of a reengineering effort and fulfill the definition that reengineering is the *fundamental* rethinking and *radical* redesign of business *processes* to achieve *dramatic* improvements in critical, contemporary measures of performance, such as cost, quality, service, and speed.

Several themes, listed below, emerge in these three cases.

- Process orientation
  The improvements that IBM Credit, Ford, and Kodak effected did not come about by attending to narrowly defined tasks and working within predefined organizational boundaries. Each was achieved by looking at an entire process—credit issuance, procurement, and product development—that cut across organizational boundaries.

- Ambition
  Minor improvements would not have been sufficient in any of these situations. All three companies aimed for breakthroughs. In reengineering its accounts payable process, Ford, for example, skipped the 20 percent fix and went for the 80 percent solution.

- Rule-breaking
  Each of these companies broke with old traditions as they reengineered their processes. Assumptions of specialization, sequentiality, and timing were deliberately abandoned.

- Creative use of information technology
  The agent that enabled these companies to break their old rules and create new process models was modern information technology. Information technology acts as an enabler that allows organizations to do work in radically different ways.

What Reengineering Isn't

People with hearsay knowledge of reengineering and those just being introduced to the concept often jump to the conclusion that it is much the same as other business improvement programs with which they are already familiar. "Oh, I get it. Reengineering," they may say, "is another name for downsizing." Or they equate it with restructuring or some other business fix of the month. Not at all. Reengineering has little or nothing in common with any of these other programs and differs in significant ways even from those with which it does share some common premises.

First, despite the prominent role played by information technology in business reengineering, it should by now be clear that reengineering is not the same as automation. Automating existing processes with information technology is analogous to paving cow paths. Automation simply provides more efficient ways of doing the wrong kinds of things.

Nor should people confuse business reengineering with so-called software reengineering, which means rebuilding obsolete information systems with more modern technology. Software reengineering often produces nothing more than sophisticated computerized systems that automate obsolete processes.

Reengineering is not restructuring or downsizing. These are just fancy terms for reducing capacity to meet current, lower demand. When the market wants fewer GM cars, GM reduces its size to better match demand. But downsizing and restructuring only mean doing less with less. Reengineering, by contrast, means doing *more* with less.

Reengineering also is not the same as reorganizing, delayering, or flattening an organization, although reengineering may, in fact, produce a flatter organization. As we have argued above, the problems facing companies do not result from their *organizational* structures but their *process* structures. Overlaying a new organization on top of an old process is pouring soured wine into new bottles.

Companies that earnestly set out to "bust" bureaucracies are holding the wrong end of the stick. Bureaucracy is not the problem. On the contrary, bureaucracy has been the solution for the last two hundred years. If you dislike bureaucracy in your company, try getting by without it. Chaos will result. Bureaucracy is the glue that holds traditional corporations together. The underlying problem, to which bureaucracy has been and remains a solution, is that of fragmented processes. The way to eliminate bureaucracy and flatten the organization is by reengineering the processes so that they are no longer fragmented. Then the company can manage nicely without its bureaucracy.

Nor is reengineering the same as quality improvement, total quality management (TQM), or any other manifestation of the contemporary quality movement. To be sure, quality programs and reengineering share a number of common themes. They both recognize the importance of processes, and they both start with the needs of the process customer and work backwards from there. However, the two programs also differ fundamentally. Quality programs work within the framework of a company's existing processes and seek to enhance them by means of what the Japanese call *kaizen*, or continuous incremental improvement. The aim is to do what we already do, only to do it better. Quality improvement seeks steady incremental improvement to process performance. Reengineering, as we have seen, seeks breakthroughs, not by enhancing existing processes, but by discarding them and replacing them with entirely new ones. Reengineering involves, as well, a different approach to change management from that needed by quality programs.

Finally, we can do no better than to return to our original two-word definition for reengineering: starting over. Reengineering is about beginning again with a clean sheet of paper. It is about rejecting the conventional wisdom and received assumptions of the past. Reengineering is about inventing new approaches to process structure that bear little or no resemblance to those of previous eras.

Fundamentally, reengineering is about reversing the industrial revolution. Reengineering rejects the assumptions inherent in Adam Smith's industrial paradigm—the division of labor, economies of scale, hierarchical control, and all the other appurtenances of an early-stage developing economy. Reengineering is the search for new models of organizing work. Tradition counts for nothing. Reengineering is a new beginning.

Increasing Leadership and Organizational Effectiveness

I n today's complex and dynamic environment, organizations must learn to continually adapt to new conditions if they are to remain viable and avoid organizational "paradigm paralysis." Consequently, the processes of leadership development and organizational development have received increasing attention. The classic selections presented in this section provide guidelines for leaders and organizations as they seek to maintain effectiveness in a turbulent world.

The first selection is entitled "Skills of an Effective Administrator" by Robert Katz. He identifies and discusses three basic skills that every successful manager must have:

- technical skill,
- human skill, and
- conceptual skill.

Katz then discusses how the relative importance of these three skills varies depending on one's level within the organization. At the supervisory level, technical skill is most critical since these leaders manage the hands-on work. Human skill is viewed as critical at all levels. Conceptual skill is seen as most important at the top of the organization since these are the managers who make decisions that affect the organization as a whole. Katz then discusses some implications of his three-skill approach for executive development, executive placement, and executive selection. Finally, he concludes by providing suggestions for developing each of these three basic skills.

The second reading is entitled "Leadership Effectiveness Can Be Learned" and is from Peter Drucker's best-selling book, *The Effective Executive.* Drucker

543

contends that executives are paid to be effective and that managerial effectiveness can be learned. He suggests several important steps toward increasing one's effectiveness:

- Record how you spend your time (which will lead to focusing on high priority actions).
- Clarify the contribution you should make to your organization.
- Build on your strengths.
- Do "first things first."
- Make decisions in an effective manner.

Drucker concludes by stating that executives must devote time and energy to their self-development. Doing so will lead to an increase in both personal and organizational effectiveness.

In "Organization Development," Wendell French defines organization development as a long-range effort to improve an organization's problem-solving capabilities. The article addresses the typical objectives, assumptions, attitudes, and strategies of OD programs. French contends that in order to maximize effectiveness, management must learn to adapt to changes in their environment. To accomplish this, an open and flexible organizational climate must be created to stimulate the growth and development of an organization's most important resource—its people.

"In Search of Excellence," by Tom Peters and Bob Waterman, reviews the findings of their classic McKinsey study of consistently high-performing large companies. The authors discuss eight distinguishing characteristics of excellent companies and contend that the absence of these desirable attributes greatly limits the effectiveness of many organizations.

In the next selection, Peter M. Senge describes the components of "The Learning Organization"—one that continually enhances its capacity to cope with change and uncertainty. These organizations utilize systems thinking, personal mastery, mental models, building a shared vision, and team learning. Central to learning organizations is a shift in thinking that recognizes the role of the organization in creating problems previously viewed as external, and discovery of how the organization can change its own reality.

In "Competing for the Future," Gary Hamel and C. K. Prahalad contend that many organizations have attempted to increase organizational effectiveness and profitability by reducing costs through reengineering work processes and downsizing. While this approach can lead to short-term improvements, long-term success requires developing a sound strategy for growing a business, shaping the future of the industry, and maximizing the potential of human resources. Hamel and Prahalad provide a checklist for assessing how prepared an organization is to thrive in the future. They also review some examples of how focusing time and energy on the future can lead to significant benefits for the organization.

The next reading is "Emotional Intelligence" by Daniel Goleman. He suggests that while IQ and technical skill are important, the most critical requirement for effective leadership is "emotional intelligence." The five components of emotional intelligence are discussed (self-awareness, self-regulation, motivation, empathy, and social skill). Goleman concludes that with persistence, practice, and feedback from others, emotional intelligence can be learned.

In "The Level 5 Leader," Jim Collins shares the findings of five years of research on companies that sustained superlative performance. Collins suggests that "good-to-great" transformations don't happen without "Level 5 leaders" at the helm. He reviews the characteristics of five levels of capabilities:

- Level 1—highly capable individual who makes productive contributions through talent, knowledge, skills, and good work habits.
- Level 2—contributing team member who contributes to the achievement of group objectives and works effectively with others.
- Level 3—competent manager who organizes people and resources toward the effective and efficient pursuit of predetermined objectives.
- Level 4—effective leader who catalyzes commitment to and vigorous pursuit of a clear and compelling vision, and stimulates the group to high performance standards.
- Level 5—executive who builds enduring greatness through a combination of personal humility and professional will.

Collins elaborates on the elements of personal humility and professional will. Personal humility is characterized by:

- Demonstrating modesty, shunning public adulation, and never boasting.
- Acting with quiet, calm determination and relying on inspired standards to motivate.
- Channeling ambition into the company rather than into oneself.
- Accepting responsibility for poor performance rather than blaming others.

Professional will is characterized by:

- Creating superb results.
- Demonstrating an unwavering resolve to do what must be done to produce the best long-term results.
- Setting the standard of building an enduring great company.
- Giving credit to others for the success of the company.

Collins concludes by suggesting that many people don't have the Level 5 "seed" within them and will never subjugate their own needs to the greater ambition of something larger and more lasting than themselves. Other people have the potential to evolve. Under the right circumstances (self-reflection, mentoring, a significant life experience), the seed can develop into Level 5 leadership.

In "Feedforward," Marshall Goldsmith, a well-known executive coach, suggests that there is a fundamental problem with all types of feedback (down, up, sideways): it focuses on the past and is therefore limited and static as opposed to expansive and dynamic. An alternative approach is to provide "feedforward" by giving someone else suggestions for the future and helping them in their efforts to improve.

Goldsmith provides numerous reasons why "feedforward" is preferable to feedback:

- We can change the future. We can't change the past.
- It can be more productive to help people be "right," than prove they were "wrong."
- Feedforward is especially suited to successful people.
- Feedforward can come from anyone who knows about the task. It does not require personal experience with the individual.
- People do not take feedforward as personally as feedback.
- Feedback can reinforce personal stereotyping and negative self-fulfilling prophecies.
- Most of us hate getting negative feedback, and we don't like to give it.
- Feedforward can cover almost all of the same "material" as feedback.
- Feedforward tends to be much faster and more efficient than feedback.
- Feedforward can be a useful tool to apply with managers, peers, and team members.
- People tend to listen more attentively to feedforward than feedback.

Feedforward can drastically improve the quality of communication within the organization and positively impact both individual and organizational performance.

1

Skills of an Effective Administrator

Robert L. Katz

Although the selection and training of good administrators is widely recognized as one of American industry's most pressing problems, there is surprisingly little agreement among executives or educators on what makes a good administrator. The executive development programs of some of the nation's leading corporations and colleges reflect a tremendous variation in objectives.

At the root of this difference is industry's search for the traits or attributes which will objectively identify the "ideal executive" who is equipped to cope effectively with any problem in any organization. As one observer of American industry recently noted:

> The assumption that there is an executive type is widely accepted, either openly or implicitly. Yet any executive presumably knows that a company needs all kinds of managers for different levels of jobs. The qualities most needed by a shop superintendent are likely to be quite opposed to those needed by a coordinating vice president of manufacturing. The literature of executive development is loaded with efforts to define the qualities needed by executives, and by themselves these sound quite rational. Few, for instance, would dispute the fact that a top manager needs good judgment, the ability to make decisions, the ability to win respect of others, and all the other well-worn phrases any management man could mention. But one has only to look at the successful managers in any company to see how enormously their particular qualities vary from any ideal list of executive virtues.[1]

Yet this quest for the executive stereotype has become so intense that many companies, in concentrating on certain specific traits or qualities, stand in danger of losing sight of their real concern: *what a man can accomplish.*

It is the purpose of this article to suggest what may be a more useful approach to the selection and development of administrators. This approach is based not on what good executives are (their innate traits and characteristics), but rather on what they do (the kinds of skills which they exhibit in carrying out their jobs effectively). As used here, a skill implies an ability which can be developed, not necessarily inborn, and which is manifested in performance, not merely in potential. So the principal criterion of skillfulness must be effective action under varying conditions.

This approach suggests that effective administration rests on *three basic developable skills* which obviate the need for identifying specific traits and which may provide a useful way of looking at and understanding the administrative process. This approach is the outgrowth of firsthand observation of executives at work coupled with study of current field research in administration.

In the sections which follow, an attempt will be made to define and demonstrate what these three skills are; to suggest that the relative importance of the three skills varies with the level of administrative responsibility; to present some of the implications of this variation for selection, training, and promotion of executives; and to propose ways of developing these skills.

Three-Skill Approach

It is assumed here that an administrator is one who (a) directs the activities of other persons and (b) undertakes the responsibility for achieving certain objectives through these efforts. Within this definition, successful administration appears to rest on three basic skills, which we will call *technical, human,* and *conceptual.* It would be unrealistic to assert that these skills are not interrelated, yet there may be real merit in examining each one separately, and in developing them independently.

Technical Skill

As used here, technical skill implies an understanding of, and proficiency in, a specific kind of activity, particularly one involving methods, processes, procedures, or techniques. It is relatively easy for us to visualize the technical skill of the surgeon, the musician, the accountant, or the engineer when each is performing his own special function. Technical skill involves specialized knowledge, analytical ability within that specialty, and facility in the use of the tools and techniques of the specific discipline.

Of the three skills described in this article, technical skill is perhaps the most familiar because it is the most concrete, and because, in our age of specialization, it is the skill required of the greatest number of people. Most of our vocational and on-the-job training programs are largely concerned with developing this specialized technical skill.

Human Skill

As used here, human skill is the executive's ability to work effectively as a group member and to build cooperative effort within the team he leads. As *techni-*

cal skill is primarily concerned with working with "things" (processes or physical objects), so *human* skill is primarily concerned with working with people. This skill is demonstrated in the way the individual perceives (and recognizes the perceptions of) his superiors, equals, and subordinates, and in the way he behaves subsequently.

The person with highly developed human skill is aware of his own attitudes, assumptions, and beliefs about other individuals and groups; he is able to see the usefulness and limitations of these feelings. By accepting the existence of viewpoints, perceptions, and beliefs which are different from his own, he is skillful in understanding what others really mean by their words and behavior. He is equally skillful in communicating to others, in their own contexts, what he means by *his* behavior.

Such a person works to create an atmosphere of approval and security in which subordinates feel free to express themselves without fear of censure or ridicule, by encouraging them to participate in the planning and carrying out of those things which directly affect them. He is sufficiently sensitive to the needs and motivations of others in his organization so that he can judge the possible reactions to, and outcomes of, various courses of action he may undertake. Having this sensitivity, he is able and willing to *act* in a way which takes these perceptions by others into account.

Real skill in working with others must become a natural, continuous activity, since it involves sensitivity not only at times of decision making but also in the day-by-day behavior of the individual. Human skill cannot be a "sometime thing." Techniques cannot be randomly applied, nor can personality traits be put on or removed like an overcoat. Because everything which an executive says and does (or leaves unsaid or undone) has an effect on his associates, his true self will, in time, show through. Thus, to be effective, this skill must be naturally developed and unconsciously, as well as consistently, demonstrated in the individual's every action. It must become an integral part of his whole being.

Because human skill is so vital a part of everything the administrator does, examples of inadequate human skill are easier to describe than are highly skillful performances. Perhaps consideration of an actual situation would serve to clarify what is involved:

> When a new conveyor unit was installed in a shoe factory where workers had previously been free to determine their own work rate, the production manager asked the industrial engineer who had designed the conveyor to serve as foreman, even though a qualified foreman was available. The engineer, who reported directly to the production manager, objected, but under pressure he agreed to take the job "until a suitable foreman could be found," even though this was a job of lower status than his present one. Then the following conversation took place:
>
> **PRODUCTION MANAGER:** "I've had a lot of experience with conveyors. I want you to keep this conveyor going at all times except for rest periods, and I want it going at top speed. Get these people thinking in terms of 2 pairs of shoes a minute, 70 dozen pairs a day, 350 dozen pairs a week. They are all experienced operators on their individual jobs, and it's just a matter of getting them to do their jobs in a little different way. I want you to make that base rate of 250 dozen pair a week work!" [Base rate was established at

slightly under 75% of the maximum capacity. This base rate was 50% higher than under the old system.]

ENGINEER: "If I'm going to be foreman of the conveyor unit, I want to do things my way. I've worked on conveyors, and I don't agree with you on first getting people used to a conveyor going at top speed. These people have never seen a conveyor. You'll scare them. I'd like to run the conveyor at one-third speed for a couple of weeks and then gradually increase the speed.

"I think we should discuss setting the base rate [production quota before incentive bonus] on a daily basis instead of a weekly basis. [Workers had previously been paid on a daily straight piecework basis.]

"I'd also suggest setting a daily base rate at 45 or even 40 dozen pair. You have to set a base rate low enough for them to make. Once they know they can make the base rate, they will go after the bonus."

PRODUCTION MANAGER: "You do it your way on the speed; but remember it's the results that count. On the base rate, I'm not discussing it with you; I'm telling you to make the 250 dozen pair a week work. I don't want a daily base rate."[2]

Here is a situation in which the production manager was so preoccupied with getting the physical output that he did not pay attention to the people through whom that output had to be achieved. Notice, first, that he made the engineer who designed the unit serve as foreman, apparently hoping to force the engineer to justify his design by producing the maximum output. However, the production manager was oblivious to (a) the way the engineer perceived this appointment, as a demotion, and (b) the need for the engineer to be able to control the variables if he was to be held responsible for output. Instead the production manager imposed a production standard and refused any changes in the work situation.

Moreover, although this was a radically new situation for the operators, the production manager expected them to produce immediately at well above their previous output—even though the operators had an unfamiliar production system to cope with, the operators had never worked together as a team before, the operators and their new foreman had never worked together before, and the foreman was not in agreement with the production goals or standards. By ignoring all these human factors, the production manager not only placed the engineer in an extremely difficult operating situation but also, by refusing to allow the engineer to "run his own show," discouraged the very assumption of responsibility he had hoped for in making the appointment.

Under these circumstances, it is easy to understand how the relationship between these two men rapidly deteriorated, and how production, after two months' operation, was at only 125 dozen pairs per week (just 75% of what it had been under the old system).

Conceptual Skill

As used here, conceptual skill involves the ability to see the enterprise as a whole; it includes recognizing how the various functions of the organization depend on one another, and how changes in any one part affect all the others; and it extends to visualizing the relationship of the individual business to the industry, the community, and the political, social, and economic forces of the nation as a whole. Recognizing these relationships and perceiving the significant elements in any situation, the administrator should then be able to act in a way which advances the over-all welfare of the total organization.

Hence, the success of any decision depends on the conceptual skill of the people who make the decision and those who put it into action. When, for example, an important change in marketing policy is made, it is critical that the effects on production, control, finance, research, and the people involved be considered. And it remains critical right down to the last executive who must implement the new policy. If each executive recognizes the over-all relationships and significance of the change, he is almost certain to be more effective in administering it. Consequently the chances for succeeding are greatly increased.

Not only does the effective coordination of the various parts of the business depend on the conceptual skill of the administrators involved, but so also does the whole future direction and tone of the organization. The attitudes of a top executive color the whole character of the organization's response and determine the "corporate personality" which distinguishes one company's ways of doing business from another's. These attitudes are a reflection of the administrator's conceptual skill (referred to by some as his "creative ability")—the way he perceives and responds to the direction in which the business should grow, company objectives and policies, and stockholders' and employees' interests.

Conceptual skill, as defined above, is what Chester I. Barnard, former president of the New Jersey Bell Telephone Company, implies when he says: ". . . the essential aspect of the [executive] process is the sensing of the organization as a whole and the total situation relevant to it."[3] Examples of inadequate conceptual skill are all around us. Here is one instance:

> In a large manufacturing company which had a long tradition of job-shop type operations, primary responsibility for production control had been left to the foremen and other lower-level supervisors. "Village" type operations with small working groups and informal organizations were the rule. A heavy influx of orders following World War II tripled the normal production requirements and severely taxed the whole manufacturing organization. At this point, a new production manager was brought in from outside the company, and he established a wide range of controls and formalized the entire operating structure.
>
> As long as the boom demand lasted, the employees made every effort to conform with the new procedures and environment. But when demand subsided to prewar levels, serious labor relations problems developed, friction was high among department heads, and the company found itself saddled with a heavy indirect labor cost. Management sought to reinstate its old procedures; it fired the production manager and attempted to give greater authority to the foremen once again. However, during the four years of formalized control, the foremen had grown away from their old practices, many had left the company, and adequate replacements had not been developed. Without strong foreman leadership, the traditional job-shop operations proved costly and inefficient.

In this instance, when the new production controls and formalized organizations were introduced, management did not foresee the consequences of this action in the event of a future contraction of business. Later, when conditions changed and it was necessary to pare down operations, management was again unable to recognize the implications of its action and reverted to the old procedures, which, under existing circumstances, were no longer appropriate. This compounded *conceptual* inadequacy left the company at a serious competitive disadvantage.

Because a company's over-all success is dependent on its executives' conceptual skill in establishing and carrying out policy decisions, this skill is the unifying, coordinating ingredient of the administrative process, and of undeniable over-all importance.

Relative Importance

We may notice that, in a very real sense, conceptual skill embodies consideration of both the technical and human aspects of the organization. Yet the concept of *skill,* as an ability to translate knowledge into action, should enable one to distinguish between the three skills of performing the technical activities (technical skill), understanding and motivating individuals and groups (human skill), and coordinating and integrating all the activities and interests of the organization toward a common objective (conceptual skill).

This separation of effective administration into three basic skills is useful primarily for purposes of analysis. In practice, these skills are so closely interrelated that it is difficult to determine where one ends and another begins. However, just because the skills are interrelated does not imply that we cannot get some value from looking at them separately, or by varying their emphasis. In playing golf the action of the hands, wrists, hips, shoulders, arms, and head are all interrelated; yet in improving one's swing it is often valuable to work on one of these elements separately. Also, under different playing conditions the relative importance of these elements varies. Similarly, although all three are of importance at every level of administration, the technical, human, and conceptual skills of the administrator vary in relative importance at different levels of responsibility.

At Lower Levels

Technical skill is responsible for many of the great advances of modern industry. It is indispensable to efficient operation. Yet it has greatest importance at the lower levels of administration. As the administrator moves further and further from the actual physical operation, this need for technical skill becomes less important, provided he has skilled subordinates and can help them solve their own problems. At the top, technical skill may be almost nonexistent, and the executive may still be able to perform effectively if his human and conceptual skills are highly developed. For example:

> In one large capital-goods producing company, the controller was called on to replace the manufacturing vice president who had been stricken suddenly with a severe illness. The controller had no previous production experience,

but he had been with the company for more than 20 years and knew many of the key production personnel intimately. By setting up an advisory staff, and by delegating an unusual amount of authority to his department heads, he was able to devote himself to coordination of the various functions. By so doing, he produced a highly efficient team. The results were lower costs, greater productivity, and higher morale than the production division had ever before experienced. Management had gambled that this man's ability to work with people was more important than his lack of a technical production background, and the gamble paid off.

Other examples are evident all around us. We are all familiar with those "professional managers" who are becoming the prototypes of our modern executive world. These men shift with great ease, and with no apparent loss in effectiveness, from one industry to another. Their human and conceptual skills seem to make up for their unfamiliarity with the new job's technical aspects.

At Every Level

Human skill, the ability to work with others, is essential to effective administration at every level. One recent research study has shown that human skill is of paramount importance at the foreman level, pointing out that the chief function of the foreman as an administrator is to attain collaboration of people in the work group.[4] Another study reinforces this finding and extends it to the middle-management group, adding that the administrator should be primarily concerned with facilitating communication in the organization.[5] And still another study, concerned primarily with top management, underscores the need for self-awareness and sensitivity to human relationships by executives at that level.[6] These findings would tend to indicate that human skill is of great importance at every administrative level, but notice the difference in emphasis.

Human skill seems to be most important at lower levels, where the number of direct contacts between administrators and subordinates is greatest. As we go higher and higher in the administrative echelons, the number and frequency of these personal contacts decrease, and the need for human skill becomes proportionately, although probably not absolutely, less. At the same time, conceptual skill becomes increasingly more important with the need for policy decisions and broad-scale action. The human skill of dealing with individuals then becomes subordinate to the conceptual skill of integrating group interests and activities into a coordinated whole.

In fact, a recent research study by Professor Chris Argyris of Yale University has given us the example of an extremely effective plant manager who, although possessing little human skill as defined here, was nonetheless very successful:

> This manager, the head of a largely autonomous division, made his supervisors, through the effects of his strong personality and the "pressure" he applied, highly dependent on him for most of their "rewards, penalties, authority, perpetuation, communication, and identification."
>
> As a result, the supervisors spent much of their time competing with one another for the manager's favor. They told him only the things they thought he wanted to hear, and spent much time trying to find out his desires. They

depended on him to set their objectives and to show them how to reach them. Because the manager was inconsistent and unpredictable in his behavior, the supervisors were insecure and continually engaged in interdepartmental squabbles which they tried to keep hidden from the manager.

Clearly, human skill, as defined here, was lacking. Yet, by the evaluation of his superiors and by his results in increasing efficiency and raising profits and morale, this manager was exceedingly effective. Professor Argyris suggests that employees in modern industrial organizations tend to have a "built-in" sense of dependence on superiors which capable and alert men can turn to advantage.[7]

In the context of the three-skill approach, it seems that this manager was able to capitalize on this dependence because he recognized the interrelationships of all the activities under his control, identified himself with the organization, and sublimated the individual interests of his subordinates to *his* (the organization's) interest, set his goals realistically, and showed his subordinates how to reach these goals. This would seem to be an excellent example of a situation in which strong conceptual skill more than compensated for a lack of human skill.

At the Top Level

Conceptual skill, as indicated in the preceding sections, becomes increasingly critical in more responsible executive positions where its effects are maximized and most easily observed. In fact, recent research findings lead to the conclusion that at the top level of administration this conceptual skill becomes the most important ability of all. As Herman W. Steinkraus, president of Bridgeport Brass Company, said:

> One of the most important lessons which I learned on this job [the presidency] is the importance of coordinating the various departments into an effective team, and, secondly, to recognize the shifting emphasis from time to time of the relative importance of various departments to the business.[8]

It would appear, then, that at lower levels of administrative responsibility, the principal need is for technical and human skills. At higher levels, technical skill becomes relatively less important while the need for conceptual skill increases rapidly. At the top level of an organization, conceptual skill becomes the most important skill of all for successful administration. A chief executive may lack technical or human skills and still be effective if he has subordinates who have strong abilities in these directions. But if his conceptual skill is weak, the success of the whole organization may be jeopardized.

Implications for Action

This three-skill approach implies that significant benefits may result from redefining the objectives of executive development programs, from reconsidering the placement of executives in organizations, and from revising procedures for testing and selecting prospective executives.

Executive Development

Many executive development programs may be failing to achieve satisfactory results because of their inability to foster the growth of these administrative skills. Programs which concentrate on the mere imparting of information or the cultivation of a specific trait would seem to be largely unproductive in enhancing the administrative skills of candidates.

A strictly informative program was described to me recently by an officer and director of a large corporation who had been responsible for the executive development activities of his company, as follows:

> What we try to do is to get our promising young men together with some of our senior executives in regular meetings each month. Then we give the young fellows a chance to ask questions to let them find out about the company's history and how and why we've done things in the past.

It was not surprising that neither the senior executives nor the young men felt this program was improving their administrative abilities.

The futility of pursuing specific traits becomes apparent when we consider the responses of an administrator in a number of different situations. In coping with these varied conditions, he may appear to demonstrate one trait in one instance—e.g., dominance when dealing with subordinates—and the directly opposite trait under another set of circumstances—e.g., submissiveness when dealing with superiors. Yet in each instance he may be acting appropriately to achieve the best results. Which, then, can we identify as a desirable characteristic? Here is a further example of this dilemma:

> A Pacific Coast sales manager had a reputation for decisiveness and positive action. Yet when he was required to name an assistant to understudy his job from among several well-qualified subordinates, he deliberately avoided making a decision. His associates were quick to observe what appeared to be obvious indecisiveness.
>
> But after several months had passed, it became clear that the sales manager had very unobtrusively been giving the various salesmen opportunities to demonstrate their attitudes and feelings. As a result, he was able to identify strong sentiments for one man whose subsequent promotion was enthusiastically accepted by the entire group.

In this instance, the sales manager's skillful performance was improperly interpreted as "indecisiveness." Their concern with irrelevant traits led his associates to overlook the adequacy of his performance. Would it not have been more appropriate to conclude that his human skill in working with others enabled him to adapt effectively to the requirements of a new situation?

Cases such as these would indicate that it is more useful to judge an administrator on the results of his performance than on his apparent traits. Skills are easier to identify than are traits and are less likely to be misinterpreted. Furthermore, skills offer a more directly applicable frame of reference for executive development, since any improvement in an administrator's skills must necessarily result in more effective performance.

Still another danger in many existing executive development programs lies in the unqualified enthusiasm with which some companies and colleges have embraced courses in "human relations." There would seem to be two inherent pitfalls here: (1) Human relations courses might only be imparting information or specific techniques, rather than developing the individual's human skill. (2) Even if individual development does take place, some companies, by placing all of their emphasis on human skill, may be completely overlooking the training requirements for top positions. They may run the risk of producing men with highly developed human skill who lack the conceptual ability to be effective top-level administrators.

It would appear important, then, that the training of a candidate for an administrative position be directed at the development of those skills which are most needed at the level of responsibility for which he is being considered.

Executive Placement

This three-skill concept suggests immediate possibilities for the creating of management teams of individuals with complementary skills. For example, one medium-size midwestern distributing organization has as president a man of unusual conceptual ability but extremely limited human skill. However, he has two vice presidents with exceptional human skill. These three men make up an executive committee which has been outstandingly successful, the skills of each member making up for deficiencies of the others. Perhaps the plan of two-man complementary conference leadership proposed by Robert F. Bales, in which the one leader maintains "task leadership" while the other provides "social leadership," might also be an example in point.[9]

Executive Selection

In trying to predetermine a prospective candidate's abilities on a job, much use is being made these days of various kinds of testing devices. Executives are being tested for everything from "decisiveness" to "conformity." These tests, as a recent article in *Fortune* points out, have achieved some highly questionable results when applied to performance on the job.[10] Would it not be much more productive to be concerned with skills of doing rather than with a number of traits which do not guarantee performance?

This three-skill approach makes trait testing unnecessary and substitutes for it procedures which examine a man's ability to cope with the actual problems and situations he will find on his job. These procedures, which indicate what a man can *do* in specific situations, are the same for selection and for measuring development. They will be described in the section on developing executive skills which follows.

This approach suggests that executives should *not* be chosen on the basis of their apparent possession of a number of behavior characteristics or traits, but on the basis of their possession of the requisite skills for the specific level of responsibility involved.

Developing the Skills

For years many people have contended that leadership ability is inherent in certain chosen individuals. We talk of "born leaders," "born executives," "born salesmen." It is undoubtedly true that certain people, naturally or innately, possess greater aptitude or ability in certain skills. But research in psychology and physiology would also indicate, first, that those having strong aptitudes and abilities can improve their skill through practice and training, and, secondly, that even those lacking the natural ability can improve their performance and effectiveness.

The *skill* conception of administration suggests that we may hope to improve our administrative effectiveness and to develop better administrators for the future. This skill conception implies *learning by doing*. Different people learn in different ways, but skills are developed through practice and through relating learning to one's own personal experience and background. If well done, training in these basic administrative skills should develop executive abilities more surely and more rapidly than through unorganized experience. What, then, are some of the ways in which this training can be conducted?

Technical Skill

Development of technical skill has received great attention for many years by industry and educational institutions alike, and much progress has been made. Sound grounding in the principles, structures, and processes of the individual specialty, coupled with actual practice and experience during which the individual is watched and helped by a superior, appear to be most effective. In view of the vast amount of work which has been done in training people in the technical skills, it would seem unnecessary in this article to suggest more.

Human Skill

Human skill, however, has been much less understood, and only recently has systematic progress been made in developing it. Many different approaches to the development of human skill are being pursued by various universities and professional men today. These are rooted in such disciplines as psychology, sociology, and anthropology.

Some of these approaches find their application in "applied psychology," "human engineering," and a host of other manifestations requiring technical specialists to help the businessman with his human problems. As a practical matter, however, the executive must develop his own human skill, rather than lean on the advice of others. To be effective, he must develop his own personal point of view toward human activity, so that he will (a) recognize the feelings and sentiments which he brings to a situation; (b) have an attitude about his own experiences which will enable him to re-evaluate and learn from them; (c) develop ability in understanding what others by their actions and words (explicit or implicit) are trying to communicate to him; and (d) develop ability in successfully communicating his ideas and attitudes to others.[11]

This human skill can be developed by some individuals without formalized training. Others can be individually aided by their immediate superiors as an integral part of the "coaching" process to be described later. This aid depends for effectiveness, obviously, on the extent to which the superior possesses the human skill.

For larger groups, the use of case problems coupled with impromptu role playing can be very effective. This training can be established on a formal or informal basis, but it requires a skilled instructor and organized sequence of activities.[12] It affords as good an approximation to reality as can be provided on a continuing classroom basis and offers an opportunity for critical reflection not often found in actual practice. An important part of the procedure is the self-examination of the trainee's own concepts and values, which may enable him to develop more useful attitudes about himself and about others. With the change in attitude, hopefully, there may also come some active skill in dealing with human problems.

Human skill has also been tested in the classroom, within reasonable limits, by a series of analyses of detailed accounts of actual situations involving administrative action, together with a number of role-playing opportunities in which the individual is required to carry out the details of the action he has proposed. In this way an individual's understanding of the total situation and his own personal ability to do something about it can be evaluated.

On the job, there should be frequent opportunities for a superior to observe an individual's ability to work effectively with others. These may appear to be highly subjective evaluations and to depend for validity on the human skill of the rater. But does not every promotion, in the last analysis, depend on someone's subjective judgment? And should this subjectivity be berated, or should we make a greater effort to develop people within our organizations with the human skill to make such judgments effectively?

Conceptual Skill

Conceptual skill, like human skill, has not been very widely understood. A number of methods have been tried to aid in developing this ability, with varying success. Some of the best results have always been achieved through the "coaching" of subordinates by superiors.[13] This is no new idea. It implies that one of the key responsibilities of the executive is to help his subordinates to develop their administrative potentials. One way a superior can help "coach" his subordinate is by assigning a particular responsibility, and then responding with searching questions or opinions, rather than giving answers, whenever the subordinate seeks help. When Benjamin F. Fairless, now chairman of the board of the United States Steel Corporation, was president of the corporation, he described his coaching activities as follows:

> When one of my vice presidents or the head of one of our operating companies comes to me for instructions, I generally counter by asking him questions. First thing I know, he has told me how to solve the problem himself.[14]

Obviously, this is an ideal and wholly natural procedure for administrative training, and applies to the development of technical and human skill, as well as to that of conceptual skill. However, its success must necessarily rest on the abilities and willingness of the superior to help the subordinate.

Another excellent way to develop conceptual skill is through trading jobs, that is, by moving promising young men through different functions of the business but at the same level of responsibility. This gives the man the chance literally to "be in the other fellow's shoes."

Other possibilities include: special assignments, particularly the kind which involve inter-departmental problems; and management boards, such as the McCormick Multiple Management plan, in which junior executives serve as advisers to top management on policy matters.

For larger groups, the kind of case-problems course described above, only using cases involving broad management policy and interdepartmental coordination, may be useful. Courses of this kind, often called "General Management" or "Business Policy," are becoming increasingly prevalent.

In the classroom, conceptual skill has also been evaluated with reasonable effectiveness by presenting a series of detailed descriptions of specific complex situations. In these the individual being tested is asked to set forth a course of action which responds to the underlying forces operating in each situation and which considers the implications of this action on the various functions and parts of the organization and its total environment.

On the job, the alert supervisor should find frequent opportunities to observe the extent to which the individual is able to relate himself and his job to the other functions and operations of the company.

Like human skill, conceptual skill, too, must become a natural part of the executive's makeup. Different methods may be indicated for developing different people, by virtue of their backgrounds, attitudes, and experience. But in every case that method should be chosen which will enable the executive to develop his own personal skill in visualizing the enterprise as a whole and in coordinating and integrating its various parts.

Conclusion

The purpose of this article has been to show that effective administration depends on three basic personal skills, which have been called *technical, human,* and *conceptual.* The administrator needs: (a) sufficient technical skill to accomplish the mechanics of the particular job for which he is responsible; (b) sufficient human skill in working with others to be an effective group member and to be able to build cooperative effort within the team he leads; (c) sufficient conceptual skill to recognize the interrelationships of the various factors involved in his situation, which will lead him to take that action which achieves the maximum good for the total organization.

The relative importance of these three skills seems to vary with the level of administrative responsibility. At lower levels, the major need is for technical and human skills. At higher levels, the administrator's effectiveness depends largely on human and conceptual skills. At the top, conceptual skill becomes the most important of all for successful administration.

This three-skill approach emphasizes that good administrators are not necessarily born; they may be developed. It transcends the need to identify specific traits in an effort to provide a more useful way of looking at the administrative process. By helping to identify the skills most needed at various levels of responsibility, it may prove useful in the selection, training, and promotion of executives.

Notes

[1] Perrin Stryker, "The Growing Pains of Executive Development," *Advanced Management,* August 1954, p. 15.

[2] From a mimeographed case in the files of the Harvard Business School; copyrighted by the President and Fellows of Harvard College.

[3] *Functions of the Executive* (Cambridge, Harvard University Press, 1948), p. 235.

[4] A. Zaleznik, *Foreman Training in a Growing Enterprise* (Boston, Division of Research, Harvard Business School, 1951).

[5] Harriet O. Ronken and Paul R. Lawrence, *Administering Changes* (Boston, Division of Research, Harvard Business School, 1952).

[6] Edmund P. Learned, David H. Ulrich, and Donald R. Booz, *Executive Action* (Boston, Division of Research, Harvard Business School, 1950).

[7] *Executive Leadership* (New York, Harper & Brothers, 1953); see also "Leadership Pattern in the Plant," HBR, January–February 1953, p. 63.

[8] "What Should a President Do?" *Dun's Review,* August 1951, p. 21.

[9] "In Conference," HBR, March–April 1954, p. 44.

[10] William H. Whyte, Jr., "The Fallacies of 'Personality' Testing," *Fortune,* September 1954, p. 117.

[11] For a further discussion of this point, see F. J. Roethlisberger, "Training Supervisors in Human Relations," HBR, September 1951, p. 47.

[12] See, for example, A. Winn, "Training in Administration and Human Relations," *Personnel,* September 1953, p. 139; see also, Kenneth R. Andrews, "Executive Training by the Case Method," HBR, September 1951, p. 58.

[13] For a more complete development of the concept of "coaching," see Myles L. Mace, *The Growth and Development of Executives* (Boston, Division of Research, Harvard Business School, 1950).

[14] "What Should a President Do?" *Dun's Review,* July 1951, p. 14.

2

Leadership Effectiveness Can Be Learned

Peter F. Drucker

This book rests on two premises:

- The executive's job is to be effective; and
- Effectiveness can be learned.

The executive is paid for being effective. He owes effectiveness to the organization for which he works. What then does the executive have to learn and have to do to deserve being an executive? In trying to answer this question, this book has, on the whole, taken organizational performance and executive performance to be goals in and by themselves.

Effectiveness can be learned is the second premise. The book has therefore tried to present the various dimensions of executive performance in such sequence as to stimulate readers to learn for themselves how to become effective executives. This is not a textbook, of course—if only because effectiveness, while capable of being learned, surely cannot be taught. Effectiveness is, after all, not a "subject," but a self-discipline. But throughout this book, and implicit in its structure and in the way it treats its subject matter, is always the question: "What makes for effectiveness in an organization and in any of the major areas of an executive's day and work?" Only rarely is the question asked: "Why should there be effectiveness?" The goal of effectiveness is taken for granted.

In looking back on the arguments and flow of these chapters and on their findings, another and quite different aspect of executive effectiveness emerges, however. Effectiveness reveals itself as crucial to a man's self-development; to organization development; and to the fulfillment and viability of modern society.

1. The first step toward effectiveness is a procedure: *recording where the time goes*. This is mechanical if not mechanistic. The executive need not

even do this himself; it is better done by a secretary or assistant. Yet if this is all the executive ever does, he will reap a substantial improvement. The results should be fast, if not immediate. If done with any continuity, recording one's time will also prod and nudge a man toward the next steps for greater effectiveness.

The analysis of the executive's time, the elimination of the unnecessary time-wasters, already requires some action. It requires some elementary decisions. It requires some changes in a man's behavior, his relationships, and his concerns. It raises searching questions regarding the relative importance of different uses of time, of different activities and of their goals. It should affect the level and the quality of a good deal of work done. Yet this can perhaps still be done by going down a checklist every few months, that is, by following a form. It still concerns itself only with efficiency in the utilization of a scarce resource—namely, time.

2. The next step, however, in which the executive is asked to *focus his vision on contribution* advances from the procedural to the conceptual, from mechanics to analysis, and from efficiencies to concern with results. In this step the executive disciplines himself to think through the reason why he is on the payroll and the contribution he ought to make. There is nothing very complicated about this. The questions the executive asks himself about his contribution are still straightforward and more or less schematic. But the answers to these questions should lead to high demands on himself, to thinking about his own goals and those of the organization, and to concern with values. They should lead to demands on himself for high standards. Above all, these questions ask the executive to assume responsibility, rather than to act the subordinate, satisfied if he only "pleases the boss." In focusing himself and his vision on contribution the executive, in other words, has to think through purpose and ends rather than means alone.

3. *Making strengths productive* is fundamentally an attitude expressed in behavior. It is fundamentally respect for the person—one's own as well as others. It is a value system in action. But it is again "learning through doing" and self-development through practice. In making strengths productive, the executive integrates individual purpose and organization needs, individual capacity and organization results, individual achievement and organization opportunity.

4. . . . "First Things First," serves as antiphon to . . . "Know Thy Time." These two . . . might be called the twin pillars between which executive effectiveness is suspended and on which it rests. But the procedure here no longer deals with a resource, time, but with the end product, the performance of organization and executive. What is being recorded and analyzed is no longer what happens to us but what we should try to make happen in the environment around us. And what is being developed here is not information, but character: foresight, self-reliance,

courage. What is being developed here, in other words, is leadership—not the leadership of brilliance and genius, to be sure, but the much more modest yet more enduring leadership of dedication, determination, and serious purpose.

5. The *effective decision* . . . is concerned with rational action. There is no longer a broad and clearly marked path which the executive only has to walk down to gain effectiveness. But there are still clear surveyor's benchmarks to give orientation and guidance how to get from one to the next. How the executive, for instance, is to move from identifying a pattern of events as constituting a generic problem to the setting of the boundary conditions which the decision has to satisfy, is not spelled out. This has to be done according to the specific situation encountered. But what needs to be done and in what sequence should be clear enough. In following these benchmarks, the executive, it is expected, will develop and train himself in responsible judgment. Effective decision-making requires both procedure and analysis, but its essence is an ethics of action.

There is much more to the self-development of an executive than his training in effectiveness. He has to acquire knowledges and skills. He has to learn a good many new work habits as he proceeds along his career, and he will occasionally have to unlearn some old work habits. But knowledges, skills, and habits, no matter how accomplished, will avail the executive little unless he first develops himself in effectiveness.

There is nothing exalted about being an effective executive. It is simply doing one's job like thousands of others. There is little danger that anyone will compare this essay on training oneself to be an effective executive with, say, Kierkegaard's great self-development tract, *Training in Christianity*. There are surely higher goals for a man's life than to become an effective executive. But only because the goal is so modest can we hope at all to achieve it; that is, to have the large number of effective executives modern society and its organizations need. If we required saints, poets, or even first-rate scholars to staff our knowledge positions, the large-scale organization would simply be absurd and impossible. The needs of large-scale organization have to be satisfied by common people achieving uncommon performance. This is what the effective executive has to make himself able to do. Though this goal is a modest one, one that everyone should be able to reach if he works at it, the self-development of an effective executive is true development of the person. It goes from mechanics to attitudes, values and character, from procedure to commitment.

Self-development of the effective executive is central to the development of the organization, whether it be a business, a government agency, a research laboratory, a hospital, or a military service. It is the way toward performance of the organization. As executives work toward becoming effective, they raise the performance level of the whole organization. They raise the sights of people—their own as well as others.

As a result, the organization not only becomes capable of doing better. It becomes capable of doing different things and of aspiring to different goals. Developing executive effectiveness challenges directions, goals, and purposes of the organization. It raises the eyes of its people from preoccupation with problems to a vision of opportunity, from concern with weakness to exploitation of strengths. This, in turn, wherever it happens, makes an organization attractive to people of high ability and aspiration, and motivates people to higher performance and higher dedication. Organizations are not more effective because they have better people. They have better people because they motivate to self-development through their standards, through their habits, through their climate. And these, in turn, result from systematic, focused, purposeful self-training of the individuals in becoming effective executives. . . .

3

Organization Development

Wendell French

Organization development refers to a long-range effort to improve an organization's problem solving capabilities and its ability to cope with changes in its external environment with the help of external or internal behavioral-scientist consultants, or change agents, as they are sometimes called. Such efforts are relatively new but are becoming increasingly visible within the United States, England, Japan, Holland, Norway, Sweden, and perhaps in other countries. A few of the growing number of organizations which have embarked on organization development (OD) efforts to some degree are Union Carbide, Esso, TRW Systems, Humble Oil, Weyerhaeuser, and Imperial Chemical Industries Limited. Other kinds of institutions, including public school systems, churches, and hospitals, have also become involved.

Organization development activities appear to have originated about 1957 as an attempt to apply some of the values and insights of laboratory training to total organizations. The late Douglas McGregor, working with Union Carbide, is considered to have been one of the first behavioral scientists to talk systematically about and to implement an organization development program.[1] Other names associated with such early efforts are Herbert Shepard and Robert Blake who, in collaboration with the Employee Relations Department of the Esso Company, launched a program of laboratory training (sensitivity training) in the company's various refineries. This program emerged in 1957 after a headquarters human relations research division began to view itself as an internal consulting group offering services to field managers rather than as a research group developing reports for top management.[2]

Objectives of Typical OD Programs

Although the specific interpersonal and task objectives of organization development programs will vary according to each diagnosis of organizational problems,

Reprinted from the *California Management Review*, Vol. 12, No. 2. Copyright © 1969 by The Regents of the University of California. Reprinted by permission of The Regents.

a number of objectives typically emerge. These objectives reflect problems which are very common in organizations:

1. To increase the level of trust and support among organizational members.

2. To increase the incidence of confrontation of organizational problems, both within groups and among groups, in contrast to "sweeping problems under the rug."

3. To create an environment in which authority of assigned role is augmented by authority based on knowledge and skill.

4. To increase the openness of communications laterally, vertically, and diagonally.

5. To increase the level of personal enthusiasm and satisfaction in the organization.

6. To find synergistic solutions[3] to problems with greater frequency. (Synergistic solutions are creative solutions in which 2 plus 2 equals more than 4, and through which all parties gain more through cooperation than through conflict.)

7. To increase the level of self and group responsibility in planning and implementation.[4]

Difficulties in Categorizing

Before describing some of the basic assumptions and strategies of organization development, it would be well to point out that one of the difficulties in writing about such a "movement" is that a wide variety of activities can be and are subsumed under this label. These activities have varied all the way from inappropriate application of some "canned" management development program to highly responsive and skillful joint efforts between behavioral scientists and client systems.

Thus, while labels are useful, they may gloss over a wide range of phenomena. The "human relations movement," for example, has been widely written about as though it were all bad or all good. To illustrate, some of the critics of the movement have accused it of being "soft" and a "handmaiden of the Establishment," of ignoring the technical and power systems of organizations, and of being too naively participative. Such criticisms were no doubt warranted in some circumstances, but in other situations may not have been at all appropriate. Paradoxically, some of the major insights of the human relations movement, e.g., that the organization can be viewed as a social system and that subordinates have substantial control over productivity have been assimilated by its critics.

In short, the problem is to distinguish between appropriate and inappropriate programs, between effectiveness and ineffectiveness, and between relevancy and irrelevancy. The discussion which follows will attempt to describe the "ideal" circumstances for organization development programs, as well as to point out some pitfalls and common mistakes in organization change efforts.

Relevancy to Different Technologies and Organization Subunits

Research by Joan Woodward[5] suggests that organization development efforts might be more relevant to certain kinds of technologies and organizational levels, and perhaps to certain workforce characteristics, than to others. For example, OD efforts may be more appropriate for an organization devoted to prototype manufacturing than for an automobile assembly plant. However, experiments in an organization like Texas Instruments suggest that some manufacturing efforts which appear to be inherently mechanistic may lend themselves to a more participative, open management style than is often assumed possible.[6]

However, assuming the constraints of a fairly narrow job structure at the rank-and-file level, organization development efforts may inherently be more productive and relevant at the managerial levels of the organization. Certainly OD efforts are most effective when they start at the top. Research and development units—particularly those involving a high degree of interdependency and joint creativity among group members—also appear to be appropriate for organization development activities, if group members are currently experiencing problems in communicating or interpersonal relationships.

Basic Assumptions

Some of the basic assumptions about people which underlie organization development programs are similar to "Theory Y" assumptions[7] and will be repeated only briefly here. However, some of the assumptions about groups and total systems will be treated more extensively. The following assumptions appear to underlie organization development efforts.[8]

About People

Most individuals have drives toward personal growth and development, and these are most likely to be actualized in an environment which is both supportive and challenging. Most people desire to make, and are capable of making, a much higher level of contribution to the attainment of organization goals than most organizational environments will permit.

About People in Groups

Most people wish to be accepted and to interact cooperatively with at least one small reference group, and usually with more than one group, e.g., the work group, the family group.

One of the most psychologically relevant reference groups for most people is the work group, including peers and the superior.

Most people are capable of greatly increasing their effectiveness in helping their reference groups solve problems and in working effectively together.

For a group to optimize its effectiveness, the formal leader cannot perform all of the leadership functions in all circumstances at all times, and all group members must assist each other with effective leadership and member behavior.

About People in Organizational Systems

Organizations tend to be characterized by overlapping, interdependent work groups, and the "linking pin" function of supervisors and others needs to be understood and facilitated.[9]

What happens in the broader organization affects the small work group and vice versa.

What happens to one subsystem (social, technological, or administrative) will affect and be influenced by other parts of the system.

The culture in most organizations tends to suppress the expression of feelings which people have about each other and about where they and their organizations are heading.

Suppressed feelings adversely affect problem solving, personal growth, and job satisfaction.

The level of interpersonal trust, support, and cooperation is much lower in most organizations than is either necessary or desirable.

"Win-lose" strategies between people and groups, while realistic and appropriate in some situations, are not optimal in the long run to the solution of most organizational problems.

Synergistic solutions can be achieved with a much higher frequency than is actually the case in most organizations.

Viewing feelings as data important to the organization tends to open up many avenues for improved goal setting, leadership, communications, problem solving, intergroup collaboration, and morale.

Improved performance stemming from organization development efforts needs to be sustained by appropriate changes in the appraisal, compensation, training, staffing, and task-specialization subsystem—in short, in the total personnel system.

Value and Belief Systems of Behavioral Scientist-Change Agents

While scientific inquiry, ideally, is value-free, the applications of science are not value-free. Applied behavioral scientist-organization development consultants tend to subscribe to a comparable set of values, although we should avoid the trap of assuming that they constitute a completely homogenous group. They do not.

One value, to which many behavioral scientist-change agents tend to give high priority, is that the needs and aspirations of human beings are the reasons for organized effort in society. They tend, therefore, to be developmental in their outlook and concerned with the long-range opportunities for the personal growth of people in organizations.

A second value is that work and life can become richer and more meaningful, and organized effort more effective and enjoyable, if feelings and sentiments are permitted to be a more legitimate part of the culture. A third value is a commitment to an action role, along with a commitment to research, in an effort to improve the effectiveness of organizations.[10] A fourth value—or perhaps a belief—is that improved competency in interpersonal and intergroup relationship will result in more effective organizations.[11] A fifth value is that behavioral science research and an examination of behavioral science assumptions and values are relevant and important in considering organizational effectiveness. While many change agents are perhaps overly action-oriented in terms of the utilization of their time, nevertheless, as a group they are paying more and more attention to research and to the examination of ideas.[12]

The value placed on research and inquiry raises the question as to whether the assumptions stated earlier are values, theory, or "facts." In my judgment, a substantial body of knowledge, including research on leadership, suggests that there is considerable evidence for these assumptions. However, to conclude that these assumptions are facts, laws, or principles would be to contradict the value placed by behavioral scientists on continuous research and inquiry. Thus, I feel that they should be considered theoretical statements that are based on provisional data.

This also raises the paradox that the belief that people are important tends to result in their being important. The belief that people can grow and develop in terms of personal and organizational competency tends to produce this result. Thus, values and beliefs tend to be self-fulfilling, and the question becomes "What do you choose to want to believe?" While this position can become Pollyannaish in the sense of not seeing the real world, nevertheless, behavioral scientist-change agents, at least this one, tend to place a value on optimism. It is a kind of optimism that says people can do a better job of goal setting and facing up to and solving problems, not an optimism that says the number of problems is diminishing.

It should be added that it is important that the values and beliefs of each behavioral science-change agent be made visible both to himself and to the client. In the first place, neither can learn to adequately trust the other without such exposure—a hidden agenda handicaps both trust building and mutual learning. Second, and perhaps more pragmatically, organizational change efforts tend to fail if a prescription is applied unilaterally and without proper diagnosis.

Strategy in OD: An Action Research Model

A frequent strategy in organization development programs is based on what behavioral scientists refer to as an "action research model." This model involves extensive collaboration between the consultant (whether an external or an internal change agent) and the client group, data gathering, data discussion, and planning. While descriptions of this model vary in detail and terminology from author to author, the dynamics are essentially the same.[13]

Figure 1 summarizes some of the essential phases of the action research model, using an emerging organization development program as an example. The key aspects of the model are diagnosis, data gathering, feedback to the client group, data discussion and work by the client group, action planning, and action. The sequence tends to be cyclical, with the focus on new or advanced problems as the client group learns to work more effectively together. Action research should also be considered a process, since, as William Foote Whyte says, it involves "a continuous gathering and analysis of human relations research data and the feeding of the findings into the organization in such a manner as to change behavior."[14] (Feedback we will define as nonjudgmental observations of behavior.)

Figure 1
An Action Research Model for Organization Development

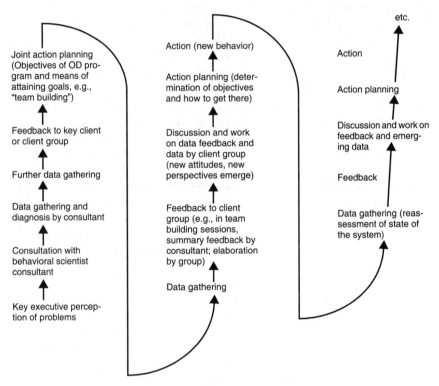

Ideally, initial objectives and strategies of organization development efforts stem from a careful diagnosis of such matters as interpersonal and intergroup problems, decision-making processes, and communication flow which are currently being experienced by the client organization. As a preliminary step, the behavioral scientist and the key client (the president of a company, the vice president in charge of a division, the works manager or superintendent of a plant, a superintendent of schools, etc.), will make a joint initial assessment of the critical problems which need working on. Subordinates may also be interviewed in order to provide supplemental data. The diagnosis may very well indicate that the central problem is technological or that the key client is not at all willing or ready to examine the organization's problem-solving ability or his own managerial behavior.[15] Either could be a reason for postponing or moving slowly in the direction of organization development activities, although the technological problem may easily be related to deficiencies in interpersonal relationships or decision making. The diagnosis might also indicate the desirability of one or more additional specialists (in engineering, finance, or electronic data processing, for example) to simultaneously work with the organization.

This initial diagnosis, which focuses on the expressed needs of the client, is extremely critical. As discussed earlier, in the absence of a skilled diagnosis, the behavioral scientist-change agent would be imposing a set of assumptions and a set of objectives which may be hopelessly out of joint with either the current problems of the people in the organization or their willingness to learn new modes of behavior. In this regard, it is extremely important that the consultant hear and understand what the client is trying to tell him. This requires a high order of skill.[16]

Interviews are frequently used for data gathering in OD work for both initial diagnosis and subsequent planning sessions, since personal contact is important for building a cooperative relationship between the consultant and the client group. The interview is also important since the behavioral scientist-consultant is interested in spontaneity and in feelings that are expressed as well as cognitive matters. However, questionnaires are sometimes successfully used in the context of what is sometimes referred to as survey feedback, to supplement interview data.[17]

Data gathering typically goes through several phases. The first phase is related to diagnosing the state of the system and to making plans for organizational change. This phase may utilize a series of interviews between the consultant and the key client, or between a few key executives and the consultant. Subsequent phases focus on problems specific to the top executive team and to subordinate teams (see figure 2).

Typical questions in data gathering or "problem sensing" would include: What problems do you see in your group, including problems between people, that are interfering with getting the job done the way you would like to see it done?; and what problems do you see in the broader organization? Such open-ended questions provide wide latitude on the part of the respondents and encourage a reporting of problems as the individual sees them. Such interviewing is usually conducted privately, with a commitment on the part of the consultant that the information will be

Figure 2
Organization Development Phases in a Hypothetical Organization

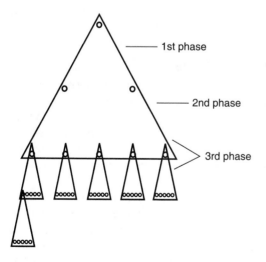

—— 1st phase

—— 2nd phase

—— 3rd phase

1st phase. Data gathering, feedback and diagnosis—consultant and top executive only.

2nd phase. Data gathering, feedback, and revised diagnosis—consultant and two or more key staff or line people.

3rd phase. Data gathering and feedback to total top executive team in "team-building" laboratory, with or without key subordinates from level below.

4th and additional phases. Data gathering and team-building sessions with 2nd or 3rd level teams.
Subsequent phases. Data gathering, feedback, and interface problem-solving sessions across groups.
Simultaneous phases. Several managers may attend "stranger" T-Groups, courses in the management development program may supplement this learning.

used in such a way as to avoid unduly embarrassing anyone. The intent is to find out what common problems or themes emerge, with the data to be used constructively for both diagnostic and feedback purposes.

Two- or three-day offsite team-building or group problem-solving sessions typically become a major focal point in organization development programs. During these meetings the behavioral scientist frequently provides feedback to the group in terms of the themes which emerged in the problem-sensing interviews.[18] He may also encourage the group to determine which items or themes should have priority in terms of maximum utilization of time. These themes usually provide substantial and meaningful data for the group to begin work on. One-to-one interpersonal matters, both positive and negative, tend to emerge spontaneously as the participants gain confidence from the level of support sensed in the group.

Different consultants will vary in their mode of behavior in such sessions, but will typically serve as "process" observers and as interpreters of the dynamics of the group interaction to the degree that the group expresses a readiness for such intervention. They also typically encourage people to take risks, a step at a time, and to experiment with new behavior in the context of the level of support in the group. Thus, the trainer-consultant(s) serves as a stimulant to new behavior but also as a protector. The climate which I try to build, for example, is: "Let's not tear down any more than we can build back together."[19] Further, the trainer-consultant typically works with the group to assist team members in improving their skills in diagnosing and facilitating group progress.[20]

It should be noted, however, that different groups will have different needs along a task-process continuum. For example, some groups have a need for intensive work on clarifying objectives; others may have the greatest need in the area of personal relationships. Further, the consultant or the chief consultant in a team of consultants involved in an organization development program will play a much broader role than serving as a T-group or team-building trainer. He will also play an important role in periodic data gathering and diagnosis and in joint long-range planning of the change efforts.[21]

Laboratory Training and OD

Since organization development programs have largely emerged from T-group experience, theory, and research, and since laboratory training in one form or another tends to be an integral part of most such programs, it is important to focus on laboratory training per se. As stated earlier, OD programs grew out of a perceived need to relate laboratory training to the problems of ongoing organizations and a recognition that optimum results could only occur if major parts of the total social system of an organization were involved.

Laboratory training essentially emerged around 1946, largely through a growing recognition by Leland Bradford, Ronald Lippitt, Kenneth Benne, and others, that human relations training which focused on the feelings and concerns of the participants was frequently a much more powerful and viable form of education than the lecture method. Some of the theoretical constructs and insights from which these laboratory training pioneers drew stemmed from earlier research by Lippitt, Kurt Lewin, and Ralph White. The term "T-Group" emerged by 1949 as a shortened label for "Basic Skill Training Group"; these terms were used to identify the programs which began to emerge in the newly formed National Training Laboratory in Group Development (now NTL Institute for Applied Behavioral Science).[22] "Sensitivity Training" is also a term frequently applied to such training.

Ordinarily, laboratory training sessions have certain objectives in common. The following list, by two internationally known behavioral scientists,[23] is probably highly consistent with the objectives of most programs:

Self-Objectives

Increased awareness of own feelings and reactions, and own impact on others.

Increased awareness of feelings and reactions of others, and their impact on self.

Increased awareness of dynamics of group action.

Changed attitudes toward self, others and groups, i.e., more respect for, tolerance for, and faith in self, others, and groups.

Increased interpersonal competence, i.e., skill in handling interpersonal and group relationships toward more productive and satisfying relationships.

Role Objectives

Increased awareness of own organizational role, organizational dynamics, dynamics of larger social systems, and dynamics of the change process in self, small groups, and organizations.

Changed attitudes toward own role, role of others, and organizational relationships, i.e., more respect for and willingness to deal with others with whom one is interdependent, greater willingness to achieve collaborative relationships with others based on mutual trust.

Increased interpersonal competence in handling organizational role relationships with superiors, peers, and subordinates.

Organizational Objectives

Increased awareness of, changed attitudes toward, and increased interpersonal competence about specific organizational problems existing in groups or units which are interdependent.

Organizational improvement through the training of relationships or groups rather than isolated individuals.

Over the years, experimentation with different laboratory designs has led to diverse criteria for the selection of laboratory participants. Probably a majority of NTL-IABS human relations laboratories are "stranger groups," i.e., involving participants who come from different organizations and who are not likely to have met earlier. However, as indicated by the organizational objectives above, the incidence of special labs designed to increase the effectiveness of persons already working together appears to be growing. Thus terms like "cousin labs," i.e., labs involving people from the same organization but not the same subunit, and "family labs" or "team-building" sessions, i.e., involving a manager and all of his subordinates, are becoming familiar. Participants in labs designed for organizational members not of the same unit may be selected from the same rank level ("horizontal slice") or selected so as to constitute a heterogeneous grouping by rank ("diagonal slice"). Further, NTL-IABS is now encouraging at least two members from the same organization to attend NTL Management Work Conferences and Key Executive Conferences in order to maximize the impact of the learning in the back-time situation.[24]

In general, experienced trainers recommend that persons with severe emotional illness should not participate in laboratory training, with the exception of programs designed specifically for group therapy. Designers of programs make the assumptions, as Argyris states them,[25] that T-Group participants should have:

1. A relatively strong ego that is not overwhelmed by internal conflicts.

2. Defenses which are sufficiently low to allow the individual to hear what others say to him.

3. The ability to communicate thought and feelings with minimal distortion.

As a result of such screening, the incidence of breakdown during laboratory training is substantially less than that reported for organizations in general.[26] However, since the borderline between "normalcy" and illness is very indistinct, most professionally trained staff members are equipped to diagnose severe problems and to make referrals to psychiatrists and clinical psychologists when appropriate. Further, most are equipped to give adequate support and protection to participants whose ability to assimilate and learn from feedback is low. In addition, group members in T-Group situations tend to be sensitive to the emotional needs of the members and to be supportive when they sense a person experiencing pain. Such support is explicitly fostered in laboratory training.

The duration of laboratory training programs varies widely. "Micro-Labs," designed to give people a brief experience with sensitivity training, may last only one hour. Some labs are designed for a long weekend. Typically, however, basic human relations labs are of two weeks duration, with participants expected to meet mornings, afternoons, and evenings, with some time off for recreation. While NTL Management Work Conferences for middle managers and Key Executive Conferences run for one week, team-building labs, from my experience, typically are about three days in length. However, the latter are usually only a part of a broader organization development program involving problem sensing and diagnosis, and the planning of action steps and subsequent sessions. In addition, attendance at stranger labs for key managers is frequently a part of the total organization development effort.

Sensitivity training sessions typically start with the trainer making a few comments about his role—that he is there to be of help, that the group will have control of the agenda, that he will deliberately avoid a leadership role, but that he might become involved as both a leader and a member from time to time, etc. The following is an example of what the trainer might say:

This group will meet for many hours and will serve as a kind of laboratory where each individual can increase his understanding of the forces which influence individual behavior and the performance of groups and organizations. The data for learning will be our own behavior, feelings, and reactions. We begin with no definite structure or organization, no agreed-upon procedures, and no specific agenda. It will be up to us to fill the vacuum created by the lack of these familiar elements and to study our group as we evolve. My role will be to help the group to learn from its own experience, but not to act as a traditional chairman nor to suggest how we should organize, what our procedure should be, or exactly what our agenda will include. With these few comments, I think we are ready to begin in whatever way you feel will be most helpful.[27]

The trainer then lapses into silence. Group discomfort then precipitates a dialogue which, with skilled trainer assistance, is typically an intense but generally highly rewarding experience for group members. What goes on in the group becomes the data for the learning experience.

Interventions by the trainer will vary greatly, depending upon the purpose of the lab and the state of learning on the part of the participants. A common intervention, however, is to encourage people to focus on and own up to their own feelings about what is going on in the group, rather than to make judgments about others. In this way, the participants begin to have more insight into their own feelings and to understand how their behavior affects the feelings of others.

While T-Group work tends to be the focal point in human relations laboratories, laboratory training typically includes theory sessions and frequently includes exercises such as role playing or management games.[28] Further, family labs of subunits of organizations will ordinarily devote more time to planning action steps for back on the job than will stranger labs.

Robert J. House has carefully reviewed the research literature on the impact of T-Group training and has concluded that the research shows mixed results. In particular, research on changes as reflected in personality inventories is seen as inconclusive. However, studies which examine the behavior of participants upon returning to the job are generally more positive.[29] House cites six studies, all of which utilized control groups, and concludes:

All six studies revealed what appear to be important positive effects of T-Group training. Two of the studies report negative effects as well . . . all of the evidence is based on observations of the behavior of the participants in the actual job situations. No reliance is placed on participant response; rather, evidence is collected from those having frequent contact with the participant in his normal work activities.[30]

John P. Campbell and Marvin D. Dunnette,[31] on the other hand, while conceding that the research shows that T-Group training produces changes in behavior, point out that the usefulness of such training in terms of job performance has yet to be demonstrated. They urge research toward "forging the link between training-induced behavior changes and changes in job performance effectiveness."[32] As a summary comment, they state:

... the assumption that T-Group training has positive utility for organizations must necessarily rest on shaky ground. It has been neither confirmed nor disconfirmed. The authors wish to emphasize ... that utility for the organization is not necessarily the same as utility for the individual.[33]

At least two major reasons may account for the inconclusiveness of research on the impact of T-Group training on job performance. One reason is simply that little research has been done. The other reason may center around a factor of cultural isolation. To oversimplify, a major part of what one learns in laboratory training, in my opinion, is how to work more effectively with others in group situations, particularly with others who have developed comparable skills. Unfortunately, most participants return from T-Group experiences to environments including colleagues and superiors who have not had the same affective (emotional, feeling) experiences, who are not familiar with the terminology and underlying theory, and who may have anxieties (usually unwarranted) about what might happen to them in a T-Group situation.

This cultural distance which laboratory training can produce is one of the reasons why many behavioral scientists are currently encouraging more than one person from the same organization to undergo T-Group training and, ideally, all of the members of a team and their superior to participate in some kind of laboratory training together. The latter assumes that a diagnosis of the organization indicates that the group is ready for such training and assumes such training is reasonably compatible with the broader culture of the total system.

Conditions and Techniques for Successful OD Programs

Theory, research, and experience to date suggest to me that successful OD programs tend to evolve in the following way and that they have some of these characteristics (these statements should be considered highly tentative, however):

- There is strong pressure for improvement from both outside the organization and from within.[34]

- An outside behavioral scientist-consultant is brought in for consultation with the top executives and to diagnose organizational problems.

- A preliminary diagnosis suggests that organization development efforts, designed in response to the expressed needs of the key executives, are warranted.

- A collaborative decision is made between the key client group and the consultant to try to change the culture of the organization, at least at the top initially. The specific goals may be to improve communications, to secure more effective participation from subordinates in problem solving, and to move in the direction of more openness, more feedback, and more support. In short, a decision is made to change the culture to help the company meet its organizational goals and to provide better avenues for initiative, creativity, and self-actualization on the part of organization members.

- Two or more top executives, including the chief executive, go to laboratory training sessions. (Frequently, attendance at labs is one of the facts which precipitates interest in bringing in the outside consultant.)

- Attendance in T-Group program is voluntary. While it is difficult to draw a line between persuasion and coercion, OD consultants and top management should be aware of the dysfunctional consequences of coercion (see the comments on authentic behavior below). While a major emphasis is on team-building laboratories, stranger labs are utilized both to supplement the training going on in the organization and to train managers new to the organization or those who are newly promoted.

- Team-building sessions are held with the top executive group (or at the highest point where the program is started). Ideally, the program is started at the top of the organization, but it can start at levels below the president as long as there is significant support from the chief executive, and preferably from other members of the top power structure as well.

- In a firm large enough to have a personnel executive, the personnel-industrial relations vice president becomes heavily involved at the outset.

- One of two organizational forms emerges to coordinate organization development efforts, either (a) a coordinator reporting to the personnel executive (the personnel executive himself may fill this role), or (b) a coordinator reporting to the chief executive. The management development director is frequently in an ideal position to coordinate OD activities with other management development activities.

- Ultimately, it is essential that the personnel-industrial relations group, including people in salary administration, be an integral part of the organization development program. Since OD groups have such potential for acting as catalysts in rapid organizational change, the temptation is great to see themselves as "good guys" and the other personnel people as "bad guys" or simply ineffective. Any conflicts between a separate organization development group and the personnel and industrial relations groups should be faced and resolved. Such tensions can be the "Achilles heel" for either program. In particular, however, the change agents in the organization development program need the support of the other people who are heavily involved in human resources administration and vice versa; what is done in the OD program needs to be compatible with what is done in selection, promotion, salary administration, appraisal, and vice versa. In terms of systems theory, it would seem imperative that one aspect of the human resources function such as any organization development program must be highly interdependent with the other human resources activities including selection, salary administration, etc. (TRW Systems is an example of an organization which involves top executives plus making the total personnel and industrial relations group an integral part of the OD program.[35])

- Team-building labs, at the request of the various respective executives, with laboratory designs based on careful data gathering and problem diagnosis, are conducted at successively lower levels of the organization with the help of outside consultants, plus the help of internal consultants whose expertise is gradually developed.

- Ideally, as the program matures, both members of the personnel staff and a few line executives are trained to do some organization development work in conjunction with the external and internal professionally trained behavioral scientists. In a sense, then, the external change agent tries to work himself out of a job by developing internal resources.

- The outside consultant(s) and the internal coordinator work very carefully together and periodically check on fears, threats, and anxieties which may be developing as the effort progresses. Issues need to be confronted as they emerge. Not only is the outside change agent needed for his skills, but the organization will need someone to act as a "governor"—to keep the program focused on real problems and to urge authenticity in contrast to gamesmanship. The danger always exists that the organization will begin to punish or reward involvement in T-Group kinds of activities per se, rather than focus on performance.

- The OD consultants constantly work on their own effectiveness in interpersonal relationships and their diagnostic skills so they are not in a position of "do as I say, but not as I do." Further, both consultant and client work together to optimize the consultant's knowledge of the organization's unique and evolving culture structure, and web of interpersonal relationships.

- There needs to be continuous audit of the results, both in terms of checking on the evolution of attitudes about what is going on and in terms of the extent to which problems which were identified at the outset by the key clients are being solved through the program.

- As implied above, the reward system and other personnel systems need to be readjusted to accommodate emerging changes in performance in the organization. Substantially improved performance on the part of individuals and groups is not likely to be sustained if financial and promotional rewards are not forthcoming. In short, management needs to have a "systems" point of view and to think through the interrelationships of the OD effort with the reward and staffing systems and the other aspects of the total human resources subsystem.

In the last analysis, the president and the "line" executives of the organization will evaluate the success of the OD effort in terms of the extent to which it assists the organization in meeting its human and economic objectives. For example, marked improvements on various indices from one plant, one division, one department, etc., will be important indicators of program success. While human resources administration indices are not yet perfected, some of the measuring devices being developed by Likert, Mann, and others show some promise.[36]

Summary Comments

Organization development efforts have emerged through attempts to apply laboratory training values and assumptions to total systems. Such efforts are organic in the sense that they emerge from and are guided by the problems being experienced by the people in the organization. The key to their viability (in contrast to becoming a passing fad) lies in an authentic focus on problems and concerns of the members of the organization and in their confrontation of issues and problems.

Organization development is based on assumptions and values similar to "Theory Y" assumptions and values but includes additional assumptions about total systems and the nature of the client-consultant relationship. Intervention strategies of the behavioral scientist-change agent tend to be based on an action-research model and tend to be focused more on helping the people in an organization learn to solve problems rather than on prescriptions of how things should be done differently.

Laboratory training (or "sensitivity training") or modifications of T-group seminars typically are a part of the organizational change efforts, but the extent and format of such training will depend upon the evolving needs of the organization. Team-building seminars involving a superior and subordinates are being utilized more and more as a way of changing social systems rapidly and avoiding the cultural-distance problems which frequently emerge when individuals return from stranger labs. However, stranger labs can play a key role in change efforts when they are used as part of a broader organization development effort.

Research has indicated that sensitivity training generally produces positive results in terms of changed behavior on the job, but has not demonstrated the link between behavior changes and improved performance. Maximum benefits are probably derived from laboratory training when the organizational culture supports and reinforces the use of new skills in ongoing team situations.

Successful organization development efforts require skillful behavioral scientist interventions, a systems view, and top management support and involvement. In addition, changes stemming from organization development must be linked to changes in the total personnel subsystem. The viability of organization development efforts lies in the degree to which they accurately reflect the aspirations and concerns of the participating members.

In conclusion, successful organization development tends to be a total system effort; a process of planned change—not a program with a temporary quality; and aimed at developing the organization's internal resources for effective change in the future.

Notes

[1] Richard Beckhard, W. Warner Burke, and Fred I. Steele, "The Program for Specialists in Organization Training and Development," mimeographed, NTL Institute for Applied Behavioral Science, Dec. 1967, p. ii; and John Paul Jones, "What's Wrong With Work?" in *What's Wrong With Work?* (New York: National Association of Manufacturers, 1967), p. 8. For a history of NTL Institute for Applied Behavioral Science, with which Douglas McGregor was long associated in addition to his professorial appointment at M.I.T. and which has been a major factor in the history of organization development, see Leland P. Bradford, "Biography of an Institution," *Journal of Applied Behavioral*

Science, III:2 (1967), 127–143. While we will use the word "program" from time to time, ideally organization development is a "process," not just another new program of temporary quality.

[2] Harry D. Kolb, Introduction to *An Action Research Program for Organization Improvement* (Ann Arbor: Foundation for Research in Human Behavior, 1960), p. i.

[3] Cattell defines synergy as "The sum total of the energy which a group can command." Daniel Katz and Robert L. Kahn, *The Social Psychology of Organizations* (New York: John Wiley and Sons, 1966), p. 33.

[4] For a similar statement of objectives, see "What is OD?" *NTL Institute: News and Reports from NTL Institute for Applied Behavioral Science*, II (June 1968), 1–2. Whether OD programs increase the overall level of authority in contrast to redistributing authority is a debatable point. My hypothesis is that both a redistribution and an overall increase occur.

[5] Joan Woodward, *Industrial Organization: Theory and Practice* (London: Oxford University Press, 1965).

[6] See M. Scott Myers, "Every Employee a Manager," *California Management* Review, X (Spring 1968), 9–20.

[7] See Douglas McGregor, *The Human Side of Enterprise* (New York: McGraw-Hill Book Company, 1960), pp. 47–48.

[8] In addition to influence from the writings of McGregor, Likert, Argyris, and others, this discussion has been influenced by "Some Assumptions About Change in Organizations," in notebook "Program for Specialists in Organization Training and Development," NTL Institute for Applied Behavioral Science, 1967; and by staff members who participated in that program.

[9] For a discussion of the "linking pin" concept, see Rensis Likert, *New Patterns of Management* (New York: McGraw-Hill Book Company, 1961).

[10] Warren G. Bennis sees three major approaches to planned organizational change, with the behavioral scientists associated with each all having "a deep concern with applying social science knowledge to create more viable social systems; a commitment to action, as well as to research . . . and a belief that improved interpersonal and group relationships will ultimately lead to better organizational performance." Bennis, "A New Role for the Behavioral Sciences: Effecting Organizational Change," *Administrative Science Quarterly*, VIII (Sept. 1963), 157–158; and Herbert A. Shepard, "An Action Research Model," in *An Action Research Program for Organization Improvement*, pp. 31–35.

[11] Bennis, "A New Role for the Behavioral Sciences," 158.

[12] For a discussion of some of the problems and dilemmas in behavioral science research, see Chris Argyris, "Creating Effective Relationships in Organizations," in Richard N. Adams and Jack J. Preiss, eds., *Human Organization Research* (Homewood, IL: The Dorsey Press, 1960), pp. 109–123; and Barbara A. Benedict, *et al.*, "The Clinical Experimental Approach to Assessing Organizational Change Efforts," *Journal of Applied Behavioral Science,* (Nov. 1967), 347–380.

[13] For further discussion of action research, see Edgar H. Schein and Warren G. Bennis, *Personal and Organizational Change through Group Methods* (New York: John Wiley and Sons, 1966), pp. 272–274.

[14] William Foote Whyte and Edith Lentz Hamilton, Action Research for Management (Homewood, IL: Richard D. Irwin, 1964), p. 2.

[15] Jeremiah J. O'Connell appropriately challenges the notion that there is "one best way" of organizational change and stresses that the consultant should choose his role and intervention strategies on the basis of "the conditions existing when he enters the client system" (*Managing Organizational Innovation* [Homewood, IL: Richard D. Irwin, 1968], pp. 10–11).

[16] For further discussion of organization diagnosis, see Richard Beckhard, "An Organization Improvement Program in a Decentralized Organization," *Journal of Applied Behavioral Science*, II (Jan–March 1966), 3–4, "OD as a Process," in W*hat's Wrong with Work?*, pp. 12–13.

[17] For example, see Floyd C. Mann, "Studying and Creating Change," in Timothy W. Costello and Sheldon S. Zalkind, eds., *Psychology in Administration—A Research Orientation* (Englewood Cliffs: Prentice-Hall, 1963), pp. 321–324. See also Delbert C. Miller, "Using Behavioral Science to Solve Organization Problems," *Personnel Administration*, XXXI (Jan.-Feb. 1968), 21–29.

[18] For a description of feedback procedures used by the Survey Research Center, Univ. of Michigan, see Mann and Likert, "The Need for Research on the Communication of Research Results," in *Human Organization Research*, pp. 57–66.

[19] This phrase probably came from a management workshop sponsored by NTL Institute for Applied Behavioral Science.

[20] For a description of what goes on in team-building sessions, see Beckhard, "An Organizational Improvement Program," 9–13; and Newton Margulies and Anthony P. Raia, "People in Organizations–A Case for Team Training," *Training and Development Journal*, XXII (August 1968), 2–11. For a description of problem-solving sessions involving the total management group (about 70) of a company, see Beckhard, "The Confrontation Meeting," *Harvard Business Review*, XLV (March–April 1967), 149–155.

[21] For a description of actual organization development programs, see Paul C. Buchanan, "Innovative Organizations—A Study in Organization Development," in *Applying Behavioral Science Research in Industry* (New York: Industrial Relations Counselors, 1964), pp. 87–107; Sheldon A. Davis, "An Organic Problem-Solving Method of Organizational Change," *Journal of Applied Behavioral Science*, III:1 (1967), 3–21; Cyril Sofer, *The Organization from Within* (Chicago: Quadrangle Books, 1961); Alfred J. Marrow, David G. Bowers, and Stanley E. Seashore, *Management by Participation* (New York: Harper and Row, 1967); Robert R. Blake, Jane S. Mouton, Louis B. Barnes, and Larry E. Greiner, "Breakthrough in Organization Development," *Harvard Business Review*, XLII (Nov.-Dec. 1964), 133–155; Alton C. Bartlett, "Changing Behavior as a Means to Increased Efficiency," *Journal of Applied Behavioral Science*, III:3 (1967), 381–403; Larry E. Greiner, "Antecedents of Planned Organization Change," *ibid.*, III:1 (1967), 51–85; and Robert R. Blake and Jane Mouton, *Corporate Excellence Through Grid Organization Development* (Houston, TX: Gulf Publishing Company, 1968).

[22] From Bradford, "Biography of an Institution." See also Kenneth D. Benne, "History of the T Group in the Laboratory Setting," in Bradford, Jack R. Gibb, and Benne, eds., *T/Group Theory and Laboratory Method* (New York: John Wiley and Sons, 1964), pp. 80–135.

[23] Schein and Bennis, p. 37.

[24] For further discussion of group composition in laboratory training, see Schein and Bennis, pp. 63–69. NTL-LABS now include the Center for Organization Studies, the Center for the Development of Educational Leadership, the Center for Community Affairs, and the Center for International Training to serve a wide range of client populations and groups.

[25] Chris Argyris, "T-Groups for Organizational Effectiveness" *Harvard Business Review*, XLII (March–April 1964), 60–74.

[26] Based on discussions with NTL staff members. One estimate is that the incidence of "serious stress and mental disturbance" during laboratory training is less than one percent of participants and in almost all cases occurs in persons with a history of prior disturbance (Charles Seashore, "What Is Sensitivity Training," *NTL Institute News and Reports*, II [April 1968], 2).

[27] *Ibid.*, 1.

[28] For a description of what goes on in T-groups, see Schein and Bennis, pp. 10–27; Bradford, Gibb, and Benne, pp. 55–67; Dorothy S. Whitaker, "A Case Study of a T-Group," in Galvin Whitaker, ed., *T-Group Training: Group Dynamics in Management Education*, A.T.M. Occasional, Papers, (Oxford: Basil Blackwell, 1965), pp. 14–22; Irving R. Weschler and Jerome Relsel, *Inside a Sensitivity Training Group* (Berkeley: University of California, Institute of Industrial Relations, 1959); and William F. Glueck, "Reflections on a T-Group Experience," *Personnel Journal*, XLVII (July 1968), 501–504. For use of cases or exercises based on research results ("instrumented training") see Robert R. Blake and Jane S. Mouton, "The Instrumented Training Laboratory," in Irving R. Weschler and Edgar H. Schein, eds., *Five Issues in Training* (Washington: National Training Laboratories, 1962), pp. 61–76; and W. Warner Burke and Harvey A. Hornstein, "Conceptual vs. Experimental Management Training," *Training and Development Journal*, XXI (Dec. 1967), 12–17.

[29] Robert J. House, "T-Group Education and Leadership Effectiveness: A Review of the Empiric Literature and a Critical Evaluation," *Personnel Psychology*, XX (Spring 1967), 1–32. See also Dorothy Stock, "A Survey of Research on T-Groups," in Bradford, Gibb, and Benne, pp. 395–441.

[30] House, *ibid.*, pp. 18–19.

[31] John P. Campbell and Marvin D. Dunnette, "Effectiveness of T-Group Experiences in Managerial Training and Development," *Psychological Bulletin*, LXX (August 1968), 73–104.

[32] *Ibid.*, 100.

[33] *Ibid.,* 101. See also the essays by Dunnette and Campbell and Chris Argyris in *Industrial Relations*, VIII (Oct. 1968), 1–45.

[34] On this point, see Larry E. Greiner, "Patterns of Organization Change," *Harvard Business Review*, XLV (May–June 1967), 119–130.

[35] See Sheldon A. Davis, "An Organic Problem-Solving Method."

[36] See Rensis Likert, *The Human Organization: Its Management and Value* (New York: McGraw-Hill Book Company, 1967).

4

In Search of Excellence

Thomas J. Peters and Robert H. Waterman

We put together a team and undertook a full-blown project on the subject of excellence as we had defined it—continuously innovative big companies. This was mainly funded by McKinsey, with some support from interested clients. At that point we chose seventy-five highly regarded companies, and in the winter of 1979–80 conducted intense, structured interviews in about half these organizations. The remainder we initially studied through secondary channels, principally press coverage and annual reports for the last twenty-five years; we have since conducted intensive interviews with more than twenty of those companies. (We also studied some underachieving companies for purposes of comparison, but we didn't concentrate much on this, as we felt we had plenty of insight into underachievement through our combined twenty-four years in the management consulting business.)

Our findings were a pleasant surprise. The project showed, more clearly than could have been hoped for, that the excellent companies were, above all, brilliant on the basics. Tools didn't substitute for thinking. Intellect didn't overpower wisdom. Analysis didn't impede action. Rather, these companies worked hard to keep things simple in a complex world. They persisted. They insisted on top quality. They fawned on their customers. They listened to their employees and treated them like adults. They allowed their innovative product and service "champions" long tethers. They allowed some chaos in return for quick action and regular experimentation.

The eight attributes that emerged to characterize most nearly the distinction of the excellent, innovative companies go as follows:

1. *A bias for action*, for getting on with it. Even though these companies may be analytical in their approach to decision making, they are not paralyzed by that fact (as so many others seem to be). In many of these companies the standard operating procedure is "Do it, fix it, try it." Says a Digital Equipment Corporation senior executive, for example, "When

we've got a big problem here, we grab ten senior guys and stick them in a room for a week. They come up with an answer *and* implement it." Moreover, the companies are experimenters supreme. Instead of allowing 250 engineers and marketers to work on a new product in isolation for fifteen months, they form bands of 5 to 25 and test ideas out on a customer, often with inexpensive prototypes, within a matter of weeks. What is striking is the host of practical devices the excellent companies employ, to maintain corporate fleetness of foot and counter the stultification that almost inevitably comes with size.

2. *Close to the customer.* These companies learn from the people they serve. They provide unparalleled quality, service, and reliability—things that work and last. They succeed in differentiating—*à la* Frito-Lay (potato chips), Maytag (washers), or Tupperware—the most commodity-like products. IBM's marketing vice president, Francis O. (Buck) Rodgers, says, "It's a shame that, in so many companies, whenever you get good service, it's an exception." Not so at the excellent companies. Everyone gets into the act. Many of the innovative companies got their best product ideas from customers. That comes from listening, intently and regularly.

3. *Autonomy and entrepreneurship.* The innovative companies foster many leaders and many innovators throughout the organization. They are a hive of what we've come to call champions; 3M has been described as "so intent on innovation that its essential atmosphere seems not like that of a large corporation but rather a loose network of laboratories and cubbyholes populated by feverish inventors and dauntless entrepreneurs who let their imaginations fly in all directions." They don't try to hold everyone on so short a rein that he can't be creative. They encourage practical risk taking, and support good tries. They follow Fletcher Byrom's ninth commandment: "Make sure you generate a reasonable number of mistakes."

4. *Productivity through people.* The excellent companies treat the rank and file as the root source of quality and productivity gain. They do not foster we/they labor attitudes or regard capital investment as the fundamental source of efficiency improvement. As Thomas J. Watson, Jr., said of his company, "IBM's philosophy is largely contained in three simple beliefs. I want to begin with what I think is the most important: *our respect for the individual.* This is a simple concept, but in IBM it occupies a major portion of management time." Texas Instruments' chairman Mark Shepherd talks about it in terms of every worker being "seen as a source of ideas, not just acting as a pair of hands"; each of his more than *9,000* People Involvement Program, or PIP, teams (TI's quality circles) does contribute to the company's sparkling productivity record.

5. *Hands-on, value driven.* Thomas Watson, Jr., said that "the basic philosophy of an organization has far more to do with its achievements than

do technological or economic resources, organizational structure, innovation and timing." Watson and HP's William Hewlett are legendary for walking the plant floors. McDonald's Ray Kroc regularly visits stores and assesses them on the factors the company holds dear, Q.S.C. & V. (Quality, Service, Cleanliness, and Value).

6. *Stick to the knitting.* Robert W. Johnson, former Johnson & Johnson chairman, put it this way: "Never acquire a business you don't know how to run." Or as Edward O. Harness, past chief executive at Procter & Gamble, said, "This company has never left its base. We seek to be anything but a conglomerate." While there were a few exceptions, the odds for excellent performance seem strongly to favor those companies that stay reasonably close to businesses they know.

7. *Simple form, lean staff.* As big as most of the companies we have looked at are, none when we looked at it was formally run with a matrix organization structure, and some which had tried that form had abandoned it. The underlying structural forms and systems in the excellent companies are elegantly simple. Top-level staffs are lean; it is not uncommon to find a corporate staff of fewer than 100 people running multi-billion-dollar enterprises.

8. *Simultaneous loose-tight properties.* The excellent companies are both centralized and decentralized. For the most part, as we have said, they have pushed autonomy down to the shop floor or product development team. On the other hand, they are fanatic centralists around the few core values they hold dear. 3M is marked by barely organized chaos surrounding its product champions. Yet one analyst argues, "The brainwashed members of an extremist political sect are no more conformist in their central beliefs." At Digital the chaos is so rampant that one executive noted, "Damn few people know who they work for." Yet Digital's fetish for reliability is more rigidly adhered to than any outsider could imagine.

Most of these eight attributes are not startling. Some, if not most, are "motherhoods." But as Rene McPherson says, "Almost everybody agrees, 'people are our most important asset.' Yet almost none really lives it." The excellent companies live their commitment to people, as they also do their preference for action—any action—over countless standing committees and endless 500-page studies, their fetish about quality and service standards that others, using optimization techniques, would consider pipe dreams; and their insistence on regular initiative (practical autonomy) from tens of thousands, not just 200 designated $75,000-a-year thinkers.

Above all, the *intensity itself,* stemming from strongly held beliefs, marks these companies. During our first round of interviews, we could "feel it." The language used in talking about people was different. The expectation of regular contributions was different. The love of the product and customer was palpable. And we felt different ourselves, walking around an HP or 3M facility watching groups at work and play, from the way we had in most of the more bureaucratic institutions we have had experience with. It was watching busy bands of engineers, salesmen, and manufacturers casually hammering out problems in a conference room in St. Paul in February; even a customer was there. It was seeing an HP division manager's office ($100 million unit), tiny, wall-less, on the factory floor, shared with a secretary. It was seeing Dana's new chairman, Gerald Mitchell, bearhugging a colleague in the hall after lunch in the Toledo headquarters. It was very far removed from silent board rooms marked by dim lights, somber presentations, rows of staffers lined up along the walls with calculators glowing, and the endless click of the slide projector as analysis after analysis lit up the screen.

We should note that not all eight attributes were present or conspicuous to the same degree in all of the excellent companies we studied. But in every case at least a preponderance of the eight was clearly visible, quite distinctive. We believe, moreover, that the eight are conspicuously absent in most large companies today. Or if they are not absent, they are so well disguised you'd hardly notice them, let alone pick them out as distinguishing traits. Far too many managers have lost sight of the basics, in our opinion: quick action, service to customers, practical innovation, and the fact that you can't get any of these without virtually everyone's commitment.

5

The Learning Organization

Peter M. Senge

Today, I believe, five new "component technologies" are gradually converging to innovate learning organizations. Though developed separately, each will, I believe, prove critical to the others' success, just as occurs with any ensemble. Each provides a vital dimension in building organizations that can truly "learn," that can continually enhance their capacity to realize their highest aspirations:

Systems Thinking. A cloud masses, the sky darkens, leaves twist upward, and we know that it will rain. We also know that after the storm, the runoff will feed into groundwater miles away, and the sky will grow clear by tomorrow. All these events are distant in time and space, and yet they are all connected within the same pattern. Each has an influence on the rest, an influence that is usually hidden from view. You can only understand the system of a rainstorm by contemplating the whole, not any individual part of the pattern.

Business and other human endeavors are also systems. They, too, are bound by invisible fabrics of interrelated actions, which often take years to fully play out their effects on each other. Since we are part of that lacework ourselves, it's doubly hard to see the whole pattern of change. Instead, we tend to focus on snapshots of isolated parts of the system and wonder why our deepest problems never seem to get solved. Systems thinking is a conceptual framework, a body of knowledge and tools that has been developed over the past fifty years, to make the full patterns clearer, and to help us see how to change them effectively.

Though the tools are new, the underlying worldview is extremely intuitive; experiments with young children show that they learn systems thinking very quickly.

Personal Mastery. Mastery might suggest gaining dominance over people or things. But mastery can also mean a special level of proficiency. A master craftsman doesn't dominate pottery or weaving. People with a high level of personal mastery are able to consistently realize the results that matter most deeply to them—in effect, they approach their life as an artist would approach a work of art. They do that by becoming committed to their own lifelong learning.

Personal mastery is the discipline of continually clarifying and deepening our personal vision, of focusing our energies, of developing patience, and of seeing reality objectively. As such, it is an essential cornerstone of the learning organization—the learning organization's spiritual foundation. An organization's commitment to and capacity for learning can be no greater than that of its members. The roots of this discipline lie in both Eastern and Western spiritual traditions, and in secular traditions as well.

But surprisingly few organizations encourage the growth of their people in this manner. This results in vast untapped resources: "'People enter business as bright, well-educated, high-energy people, full of energy and desire to make a difference,'" says Hanover's O'Brien. "By the time they are 30, a few are on the 'fast track' and the rest 'put in their time' to do what matters to them on the weekend. They lose the commitment, the sense of mission, and the excitement with which they started their careers. We get damn little of their energy and almost none of their spirit."

And surprisingly few adults work to rigorously develop their own personal mastery. When you ask most adults what they want from their lives, they often talk first about what they'd like to get rid of: "I'd like my mother-in-law to move out," they say, or "I'd like my back problems to clear up." The discipline of personal mastery, by contrast, starts with clarifying the things that really matter to us, of living our lives in the service of our highest aspirations.

Here, I am most interested in the connections between personal learning and organizational learning, in the reciprocal commitments between individual and organization, and in the special spirit of an enterprise made up of learners.

Mental Models. "Mental models" are deeply ingrained assumptions, generalizations, or even pictures or images that influence how we understand the world and how we take action. Very often, we are not consciously aware of our mental models or the effects they have on our behavior. For example, we may notice that a coworker dresses elegantly, and say to ourselves, "She's a country club person." About someone who dresses shabbily, we may feel, "He doesn't care about what others think." Mental models of what can or cannot be done in different management settings are no less deeply entrenched. Many insights into new markets or outmoded organizational practices fail to get put into practice because they conflict with powerful, tacit mental models.

Royal Dutch/Shell, one of the first large organizations to understand the advantages of accelerating organizational learning, came to this realization when they discovered how pervasive was the influence of hidden mental models, especially those that become widely shared. Shell's extraordinary success in managing through the dramatic changes and unpredictability of the world oil business in the 1970s and 1980s came in large measure from learning how to surface and challenge managers' mental models. (In the early 1970s Shell was the weakest of the big seven oil companies; by the late 1980s it was the strongest.) Arie de Geus, Shell's recently retired Coordinator of Group Planning, says that continuous adaptation and growth in a changing business environment depends on "institutional learning, which is the process whereby management teams change their shared mental models of the company, their markets, and their competitors. For this reason, we think of planning as learning and of corporate planning as institutional learning."

The discipline of working with mental models starts with turning the mirror inward; learning to unearth our internal pictures of the world, to bring them to the surface and hold them rigorously to scrutiny. It also includes the ability to carry on "learningful" conversations that balance inquiry and advocacy, where people expose their own thinking effectively and make that thinking open to the influence of others.

Building Shared Vision.   If any one idea about leadership has inspired organizations for thousands of years, it's the capacity to hold a shared picture of the future we seek to create. One is hard pressed to think of any organization that has sustained some measure of greatness in the absence of goals, values, and missions that become deeply shared throughout the organization. IBM had "service"; Polaroid had instant photography; Ford had public transportation for the masses and Apple had computing power for the masses. Though radically different in content and kind, all these organizations managed to bind people together around a common identity and sense of destiny.

When there is a genuine vision (as opposed to the all-too-familiar "vision statement"), people excel and learn, not because they are told to, but because they want to. But many leaders have personal visions that never get translated into shared visions that galvanize an organization. All too often, a company's shared vision has revolved around the charisma of a leader, or around a crisis that galvanizes everyone temporarily. But, given a choice, most people opt for pursuing a lofty goal, not only in times of crisis but at all times. What has been lacking is a discipline for translating individual vision into shared vision—not a "cookbook" but a set of principles and guiding practices.

The practice of shared vision involves the skills of unearthing shared "pictures of the future" that foster genuine commitment and enrollment rather than compliance. In mastering this discipline, leaders learn the counterproductiveness of trying to dictate a vision, no matter how heartfelt.

Team Learning.   How can a team of committed managers with individual IQs above 120 have a collective IQ of 63? The discipline of team learning confronts this paradox. We know that teams can learn; in sports, in the performing arts, in science, and even, occasionally, in business, there are striking examples where the intelligence of the team exceeds the intelligence of the individuals in the team, and where teams develop extraordinary capacities for coordinated action. When teams are truly learning, not only are they producing extraordinary results but the individual members are growing more rapidly than could have occurred otherwise.

The discipline of team learning starts with "dialogue," the capacity of members of a team to suspend assumptions and enter into a genuine "thinking together." To the Greeks *dia-logos* meant a free-flowing of meaning through a group, allowing the group to discover insights not attainable individually. Interestingly, the practice of dialogue has been preserved in many "primitive" cultures, such as that of the American Indian, but it has been almost completely lost to modern society. Today, the principles and practices of dialogue are being rediscovered and put into a contemporary context. (Dialogue differs from the more common "discussion," which has its roots with "percussion" and "concussion," literally a heaving of ideas back and forth in a winner-takes-all competition.)

The discipline of dialogue also involves learning how to recognize the patterns of interaction in teams that undermine learning. The patterns of defensiveness are often deeply engrained in how a team operates. If unrecognized, they undermine learning. If recognized and surfaced creatively, they can actually accelerate learning.

Team learning is vital because teams, not individuals, are the fundamental learning unit in modern organizations. This where "the rubber meets the road"; unless teams can learn, the organization cannot learn.

If a learning organization were an engineering innovation, such as the airplane or the personal computer, the components would be called "technologies." For an innovation in human behavior, the components need to be seen as *disciplines*. By "discipline," I do not mean an "enforced order" or "means of punishment," but a body of theory and technique that must be studied and mastered to be put into practice. A discipline is a developmental path for acquiring certain skills or competencies. As with any discipline, from playing the piano to electrical engineering, some people have an innate "gift," but anyone can develop proficiency through practice.

To practice a discipline is to be a lifelong learner. You "never arrive"; you spend your life mastering disciplines. You can never say, "We are a learning organization," any more than you can say, "I am an enlightened person." The more you learn, the more acutely aware you become of your ignorance. Thus, a corporation cannot be "excellent" in the sense of having arrived at a permanent excellence; it is always in the state of practicing the disciplines of learning, of becoming better or worse.

That organizations can benefit from disciplines is not a totally new idea. After all, management disciplines such as accounting have been around for a long time. But the five learning disciplines differ from more familiar management disciplines in that they are "personal" disciplines. Each has to do with how we think, what we truly want, and how we interact and learn with one another. In this sense, they are more like artistic disciplines than traditional management disciplines. Moreover, while accounting is good for "keeping score," we have never approached the subtler tasks of building organizations, of enhancing their capabilities for innovation and creativity, of crafting strategy and designing policy and structure through assimilating new disciplines. Perhaps this is why, all too often, great organizations are fleeting, enjoying their moment in the sun, then passing quietly back to the ranks of the mediocre.

Practicing a discipline is different from emulating "a model." All too often, new management innovations are described in terms of the "best practices" of so-called leading firms. While interesting, I believe such descriptions can often do more harm than good, leading to piecemeal copying and playing catch-up. I do not believe great organizations have ever been built by trying to emulate another, any more than individual greatness is achieved by trying to copy another "great person."

When the five component technologies converged to create the DC-3 the commercial airline industry began. But the DC-3 was not the end of the process. Rather, it was the precursor of a new industry. Similarly, as the five component learning disciplines converge they will not create *the* learning organization but rather a new wave of experimentation and advancement.

The Fifth Discipline

It is vital that the five disciplines develop as an ensemble. This is challenging because it is much harder to integrate new tools than simply apply them separately. But the payoffs are immense.

This is why systems thinking is the fifth discipline. It is the discipline that integrates the disciplines, fusing them into a coherent body of theory and practice. It keeps them from being separate gimmicks or the latest organization change fads. Without a systemic orientation, there is no motivation to look at how the disciplines interrelate. By enhancing each of the other disciplines, it continually reminds us that the whole can exceed the sum of its parts.

For example, vision without systems thinking ends up painting lovely pictures of the future with no deep understanding of the forces that must be mastered to move from here to there. This is one of the reasons why many firms that have jumped on the "vision bandwagon" in recent years have found that lofty vision alone fails to turn around a firm's fortunes. Without systems thinking, the seed of vision falls on harsh soil. If nonsystemic thinking predominates, the first condition for nurturing vision is not met: a genuine belief that we can make our vision real in the future. We may say, "We can achieve our vision" (most American managers are conditioned to this belief), but our tacit view of current reality as a set of conditions created by somebody else betrays us.

But systems thinking also needs the disciplines of building shared vision, mental models, team learning, and personal mastery to realize its potential. Building shared vision fosters a commitment to the long term. Mental models focus on the openness needed to unearth shortcomings in our present ways of seeing the world. Team learning develops the skills of groups of people to look for the larger picture that lies beyond individual perspectives. And personal mastery fosters the personal motivation to continually learn how our actions affect our world. Without personal mastery, people are so steeped in the reactive mindset ("someone/something else is creating my problems") that they are deeply threatened by the systems perspective.

Lastly, systems thinking makes understandable the subtlest aspect of the learning organization—the new way individuals perceive themselves and their world. At the heart of a learning organization is a shift of mind—from seeing ourselves as separate from the world to connected to the world, from seeing problems as caused by someone or something "out there" to seeing how our own actions create the problems, we experience. A learning organization is a place where people are continually discovering how they create their reality. And how they can change it. As Archimedes has said, "Give me a lever long enough . . . and single-handed I can move the world."

6

Competing for the Future

Gary Hamel and C. K. Prahalad

Look around your company. Look at the high-profile initiatives that have recently been launched, the issues preoccupying senior management, the criteria and benchmarks by which progress is measured, your track record of new-business creation. Look into the faces of your colleagues, and consider their ambitions and fears. Look toward the future, and ponder your company's ability to shape that future in the years and decades to come.

Now ask yourself: Do senior managers in my company have a clear and shared understanding of how the industry may be different ten years from now? Is my company's point of view about the future unique among competitors?

These are not rhetorical questions. Get a pencil and score your company.

How does senior management's point of view about the future compare with that of your competitors?

Conventional and reactive . . . . .Distinctive and farsighted

Which business issue absorbs more senior-management attention?

Reengineering core processes . . . . .Regenerating core strategies

How do competitors view your company?

Mostly as a rule follower . . . . Mostly as a rule maker

What is your company's strength?

Operational efficiency . . . . Innovation and growth

What is the focus of your company's advantage-building efforts?

Mostly catching up. . . . . Mostly getting out in front

What has set your transformation agenda?

Our competitors . . . . .Our foresight

Do you spend the bulk of your time as a maintenance engineer preserving the status quo or as an architect designing the future?

Mostly as an engineer . . . . Mostly as an architect

If your scores fall somewhere in the middle or off to the left, your company may be devoting too much energy to preserving the past and not enough to creating the future.

When we talk to senior managers about competing for the future, we ask them three questions. First, what percentage of your time is spent on external rather than internal issues—on understanding, for example, the implications of a particular new technology instead of debating corporate overhead allocations? Second, of this time spent looking outward, how much do you spend considering how the world may change in five or ten years rather than worrying about winning the next big contract or responding to a competitor's pricing move? Third, of the time devoted to looking outward *and* forward, how much do you spend working with colleagues to build a deeply shared, well-tested perspective on the future as opposed to a personal and idiosyncratic view?

The answers to these questions typically conform to what we call the "40/30/20 Rule." In our experience, about 40% of a senior executive's time is devoted to looking outward and, of this time, about 30% is spent peering three, four, five, or more years into the future. Of that time spent looking forward, no more than 20% is devoted to building a collective view of the future (the other 80% is spent considering the future of the manager's particular business). Thus, on average, senior managers devote less than 3% (40% x 30% x 20%) of their time to building a *corporate* perspective on the future. In some companies, the figure is less than 1%. Our experience suggests that to develop a distinctive point of view about the future, senior managers must be willing to devote considerably more of their time. And after the initial burst of energy that they must expend to develop a distinct view of the future, managers must be willing to adjust that perspective as the future unfolds.

Such commitment as well as substantial and sustained intellectual energy is required to answer such questions as: What new core competencies will we need to build? What new product concepts should we pioneer? What alliances will we need to form? What nascent development programs should we protect? What long-term regulatory initiatives should we pursue?

We believe such questions have received far too little attention in many companies, not because senior managers are lazy—most are working harder than ever—but because they won't admit, to themselves or to their employees, that they are less than fully in control of their companies' future. Difficult questions go unanswered because they challenge the assumption that top management really is in control, really does have more accurate foresight than anyone else in the corporation, and already has a clear and compelling view of the company's future. Senior managers are often unwilling to confront these illusions. So the urgent drives out the important; the future is left largely unexplored; and the capacity to act, rather than to think and imagine, becomes the sole measure of leadership.

Beyond Restructuring

The painful upheavals in so many companies in recent years reflect the failure of one-time industry leaders to keep up with the accelerating pace of industry change. For decades, the changes undertaken at Sears, General Motors, IBM, Westinghouse, Volkswagen, and other incumbents were, if not exactly glacial in speed, more or less linear extrapolations of the past. Those companies were run by managers, not leaders, by maintenance engineers, not architects.

If the future is not occupying senior managers, what is? Restructuring and reengineering. While both are legitimate and important tasks, they have more to do with shoring up today's businesses than with building tomorrow's industries. Any company that is a bystander on the road to the future will watch its structure, values, and skills become progressively less attuned to industry realities. Such a discrepancy between the pace of industrial change and the pace of company change gives rise to the need for organizational transformation.

A company's organizational transformation agenda typically includes downsizing, overhead reduction, employee empowerment, process redesign, and portfolio rationalization. When a competitiveness problem (stagnant growth, declining margins, and falling market share, for example) can no longer be ignored, most executives pick up a knife and begin the painful work of restructuring. The goal is to carve away layers of corporate fat and amputate underperforming businesses. Executives who don't have the stomach for emergency-room surgery, like John Akers at IBM or Robert Stempel at GM, soon find themselves out of a job.

Masquerading behind terms like refocusing, delayering, decluttering, and right-sizing (Why is the "right" size always smaller?), restructuring always results in fewer employees. In 1993, large U.S. companies announced nearly 600,000 layoffs—25% more than were announced in 1992 and nearly 10% more than in 1991, the year in which the U.S. recession hit its lowest point. While European companies have long tried to put off their own day of reckoning, bloated payrolls and out-of-control employment costs have made downsizing as inevitable in the old world as it is in the new. Despite excuses about global competition and the impact of productivity-enhancing technology, most layoffs at large U.S. companies have been the fault of senior managers who fell asleep at the wheel and missed the turn-off for the future.

With no growth or slow growth, companies soon find it impossible to support their burgeoning employment rosters and traditional R&D budgets and investment programs. The problems of low growth are often compounded by inattentiveness to ballooning overheads (IBM's problem), diversification into unrelated businesses (Xerox's foray into financial services), and the paralysis imposed by an unfailingly conservative staff. It is not surprising that shareholders are giving moribund companies unequivocal marching orders: "Make this company lean and mean;" "Make the assets sweat;" "Get back to basics." In most companies, return on capital employed, shareholder value, and revenue per employee have become the primary arbiters of top management performance.

Although perhaps inescapable and in many cases commendable, restructuring has destroyed lives, homes, and communities in the name of efficiency and productivity. While it is impossible to argue with such objectives, pursuing them single-mindedly does the cause of competitiveness as much harm as good. Let us explain.

Imagine a CEO who is fully aware that if he or she doesn't make effective use of corporate resources, someone else will be given the chance. So the chief executive launches a tough program to improve return on investment. Now, ROI (or return on net assets or return on capital employed) has two components: a numerator—net income—and a denominator—investment, net assets, or capital employed. (In a service industry, a more appropriate denominator may be head count.) Managers know that raising net income is likely to be harder than cutting assets and head count. To increase the numerator, top management must have a sense of where new opportunities lie, must be able to anticipate changing customer needs, must have invested in building new competencies, and so on. So under intense pressure for a quick ROI improvement, executives reach for the lever that will bring the fastest, surest result: the denominator.

The United States and Britain have produced an entire generation of managers obsessed with denominators. They can downsize, declutter, delayer, and divest better than any other managers. Even before the current wave of downsizing, U.S. and British companies had, on average, the highest asset-productivity ratios of any companies in the world. Denominator management is an accountant's shortcut to asset productivity.

Don't misunderstand. A company must get to the future not only first but also for less. But there is more than one route to productivity improvement. Just as any company that cuts the denominator and maintains revenues will reap productivity gains, so too will any company that succeeds in increasing its revenue stream atop a slower-growing or constant capital and employment base. Although the first approach may be necessary, we believe the second is usually more desirable.

In a world in which competitors are capable of achieving 5%, 10%, or 15% real growth in revenues, aggressive denominator reduction under a flat revenue stream is simply a way to sell market share and the future of the company. Marketing strategists term this a *harvest strategy* and consider it a no-brainer. Between 1969 and 1991, for example, Britain's manufacturing output (the numerator) went up by only 10% in real terms. Yet over this same period, the number of people employed in British manufacturing (the denominator) was nearly halved. The result was that during the early and mid-1980s, the Thatcher years, British manufacturing productivity increased faster than that of any other major industrialized country except Japan. Though Britain's financial press and Conservative ministers trumpeted this as a "success," it was, of course, bittersweet. While new legislation limited the power of trade unions, and the liberalization of statutory impediments to workforce reduction enabled management to excise inefficient and outmoded work practices, British companies demonstrated scant ability to create new markets at home and abroad. In effect, British companies surrendered global market share. One almost expected to pick up the *Financial Times* and find that Britain had finally matched Japan's manufacturing productivity—and that the last remaining person at work in British manufacturing was the most productive son of a gun on the planet.

The social costs of such denominator-driven job losses are high. Although an individual company may be able to avoid some of those costs, society cannot. In Britain, the service sector could not absorb all the displaced manufacturing workers and underwent its own vicious downsizing in the recession that began in 1989. Downsizing also causes employee morale to plummet. What employees hear is that "people are our most important asset." What they see is that people are the most expendable asset.

Moreover, restructuring seldom results in fundamental business improvements. At best, it buys time. One study of 16 large U.S. companies with at least three years of restructuring experience found that while restructuring usually did raise a company's share price, such improvement was almost always temporary. Three years into restructuring, the share prices of the companies surveyed were, on average, lagging even further behind index growth rates than they had been when the restructuring effort began.

Beyond Reengineering

Downsizing attempts to correct the mistakes of the past, not to create the markets of the future. But getting smaller is not enough. Recognizing that restructuring is a dead end, smart companies move on to reengineering. The difference between restructuring and reengineering is that the latter offers at least the hope, if not always the reality, of getting better as well as getting leaner. Yet in many companies, reengineering is more about catching up than getting out in front.

For example, Detroit automakers are catching up with Japanese rivals on quality and cost. Supplier networks have been reconstituted, product-development processes redesigned, and manufacturing processes reengineered. However, the cheerful headlines heralding Detroit's comeback miss the deeper story—among the losses have been hundreds of thousands of jobs, 20-some percentage points of market share in the United States, and any hope of U.S. automakers beating Japanese rivals in the booming Asian markets anytime soon.

Catching up is not enough. In a survey taken at the end of the 1980s, nearly 80% of U.S. managers polled believed that quality would be a fundamental source of competitive advantage in the year 2000, but barely half of Japanese managers agreed. Their primary goal was to create new products and businesses.[1] Does this mean that Japanese managers will turn their backs on quality? Of course not. It merely indicates that by the year 2000, quality will be the price of market entry, not a competitive differentiator. Japanese managers realize that tomorrow's competitive advantages will be different from today's. It remains to be seen whether Detroit will set the pace in the next round of competition and produce vehicles as exciting as they are fuel efficient and reliable or will once again rest on its laurels.

We come across far too many top managers whose advantage-building agenda is still dominated by quality, time-to-market, and customer responsiveness.

While such advantages are prerequisites for survival, they are hardly a testimony to management foresight. Though managers often try to make a virtue out of imitation, dressing it up in the fashionable colors of "adaptiveness," what they are adapting to all too often are the preemptive strategies of more imaginative competitors.

Consider Xerox. During the 1970s and 1980s, Xerox surrendered a substantial amount of market share to Japanese competitors, such as Canon and Sharp. Recognizing that the company was on the slippery slope to oblivion, Xerox benchmarked its competitors and fundamentally reengineered its processes. By the early 1990s, the company had become a textbook example of how to reduce costs, improve quality, and satisfy customers. But amid all the talk of the new "American Samurai," two issues were overlooked. First, although Xerox halted the erosion of its market share, it has not fully recaptured share lost to its Japanese competitors: Canon remains one of the largest copier manufacturers in the world. Second, despite pioneering research in laser printing, networking, icon-based computing, and the laptop computer, Xerox has not created any substantial new businesses outside its copier core. Although Xerox may have invented the office as we know it today and as it's likely to be, the company has actually profited very little from its creation.

In fact, Xerox has probably left more money on the table, in the form of underexploited innovation, than any other company in history. Why? Because to create new businesses, Xerox would have had to regenerate its core strategy: the way it defined its market, its distribution channels, its customers, its competitors, the criteria for promoting managers, the metrics used to measure success, and so on. A company surrenders today's businesses when it gets smaller faster than it gets better. A company surrenders tomorrow's businesses when it gets better without changing.

We meet many managers who describe their companies as "market leaders." (With enough creativity in delimiting market boundaries, almost any company can claim to be a market leader.) But market leadership today certainly doesn't equal market leadership tomorrow. Think about two sets of questions:

Today	In the Future
Which customers do you serve today?	Which customers will you serve in the future?
Through what channels do you reach customers today?	Through what channels will you reach customers in the future?
Who are your competitors today?	Who will your competitors be in the future?
What is the basis for your competitive advantage today?	What will be the basis for your competitive advantage in the future?
Where do your margins come from today?	Where will your margins come from in the future?
What skills or capabilities make you unique today?	What skills or capabilities will make you unique in the future?

If senior executives don't have reasonably detailed answers to the "future" questions, and if the answers they have are not significantly different from the "today" answers, there is little chance that their companies will remain market leaders. The market a company dominates today is likely to change substantially over the next ten years. There's no such thing as "sustaining" leadership; it must be regenerated again and again.

Creating the Future

Organizational transformation must be driven by a point of view about the future of the industry: How do we want this industry to be shaped in five or ten years? What must we do to ensure that the industry evolves in a way that is maximally advantageous for us? What skills and capabilities must we begin building now if we are to occupy the industry high ground in the future? How should we organize for opportunities that may not fit neatly within the boundaries of current business units and divisions? Since most companies don't start with a shared view of the future, seniors managers' first task is to develop a process for pulling together the collective wisdom within an organization. Concern for the future, a sense of where opportunities lie, and an understanding of organizational change are not the province of any group; people from all levels of a company can help define the future.

One company that developed a process for establishing a point of view about the future is Electronic Data Systems (EDS), based in Plano, Texas. In 1992, EDS's position seemed unassailable. With $8.2 billion in sales, EDS had recorded its thirtieth consecutive year of record earnings and looked forward to the ever-growing demand for computer-services outsourcing. EDS expected to become at least a $25 billion company by the year 2000.

But some top executives, including Chairman Lester Alberthal, foresaw problems. Margins were under intense pressure from new competitors, such as Andersen Consulting. Customers were demanding hefty discounts in their long-term service contracts. Fewer new customers could be found among leading-edge IT users in the United States. And future business needs would involve desktop computers, not the mainframes EDS specialized in, while the most exciting new information-network services would focus on the home, not the office.

The company's top officers, known as the Leadership Council, concluded that EDS was no more immune from "great company disease" than any other successful enterprise. Council members committed themselves to rebuilding industry leadership for the 1990s and beyond.

As it happened, others in the company were already thinking along similar lines. Back in 1990, a small band of EDS managers, none of them yet corporate officers, had created a Corporate Change Team. Despite their lack of an official charter, team members believed EDS needed to rethink its direction and its deepest assumptions. They soon realized this would require far more resources, both temporal and intellectual, than could be mustered by one small team.

After talking with the Leadership Council about its goals, the Corporate Change Team developed a unique approach to company renewal. From across the company and around the world, 150 EDS managers—key resource holders as well as less-senior managers who were known to be challenging, bright, and unconventional—gathered in Dallas, 30 at a time, to begin creating the future. Each of the five "waves" considered in detail the economic threats to EDS and the opportunities afforded by the digital revolution. Each wave was given an assignment. The first wave studied the discontinuities that EDS could use to change the shape of the industry. The second and third waves tried to develop a view of the company's competencies that was substantially independent from current definitions of EDS's served markets. They then benchmarked those competencies against EDS's strongest competitors. Drawing on the work of the previous waves, wave four explored opportunities on the horizon. And wave five considered how to devote more company resources to building competencies and developing opportunities.

Each wave's output was thoroughly debated by the other waves and with the Leadership Council. Finally, a team composed of members from all the waves produced a draft corporate strategy, which, again, was debated throughout the company.

EDS's new strategy is captured in three words: globalize, informationalize, and individualize. The strategy is based on the company's ability to use information technology to span geographical, cultural, and organizational boundaries; to help customers convert data into information, information into knowledge, and knowledge into action; and to mass-customize and enable individuals to mass-customize information services and products.

The process of developing this strategy for the future was full of frustrations, surprises, unexpected insights, and missed deadlines. More than 2,000 people participated in the creation of EDS's new strategy, and nearly 30,000 person-hours were devoted to the exercise. (More than one-third of the time investment was made outside the company's normal business hours.)

EDS emerged from the process with a view of its industry and its role that was substantially broader, more creative, and more prescient than it had been 12 months earlier. This view was held not only by a few technical gurus or corporate visionaries but by every senior EDS manager. Indeed, those who participated in the process thought it contributed as much to leadership development as it did to strategy development.

The Quest for Foresight

To create the future as EDS has done requires industry foresight. Why do we talk of foresight rather than vision? Vision connotes a dream or an apparition, and there is more to industry foresight than a blinding flash of insight. Industry foresight is based on deep insights into trends in technology, demographics, regulations, and lifestyles, which can be harnessed to rewrite industry rules and create new competitive space. While understanding the potential implications of such trends requires creativity and imagination, any "vision" that is not based on a solid foundation is likely to be fantastical.

For this reason, industry foresight is a synthesis of many people's visions. Often, journalists or sycophantic employees have described foresight as the "vision" of one person. Much of the credit for NEC's visionary concept of "computers and communication" may have gone to Akira Kobayashi, but the idea of exploiting the convergence between the two industries synthesized the thinking of many in the company. Senior executives are not the only ones with industry foresight. In fact, their primary role is to capture and exploit the foresight that exists throughout the organization.

Given that change is inevitable, the real issue for managers is whether that change will happen belatedly, in a crisis atmosphere, or with foresight, in a calm and considered manner; whether the transformation agenda will be set by a company's more prescient competitors or by its own point of view; whether transformation will be spasmodic and brutal or continuous and peaceful. Palace coups make great press copy, but the real objective is a transformation that is revolutionary in result and evolutionary in execution.

Developing a point of view about the future should be an ongoing project sustained by continuous debate within a company, not a massive one-time effort. Unfortunately, most companies consider the need to regenerate their strategies and reinvent their industries only when restructuring and reengineering fail to halt the process of corporate decline. To get ahead of the industry change curve, to have the chance of conducting a bloodless revolution, top managers must recognize that the real focus for their companies is the opportunity to compete for the future.

Note

[1] Donald Hambrick, *Reinventing the CEO: 21st Century Repair* (New York: Korn Ferry International and the Columbia University Graduate School of Business, 1989).

7

Emotional Intelligence

Daniel Goleman

Every businessperson knows a story about a highly intelligent, highly skilled executive who was promoted into a leadership position only to fail at the job. And they also know a story about someone with solid—but not extraordinary—intellectual abilities and technical skills who was promoted into a similar position and then soared.

Such anecdotes support the widespread belief that identifying individuals with the "right stuff" to be leaders is more art than science. After all, the personal styles of superb leaders vary: Some leaders are subdued and analytical; others shout their manifestos from the mountaintops. And just as important, different situations call for different types of leadership. Most mergers need a sensitive negotiator at the helm, whereas many turnarounds require a more forceful authority.

I have found, however, that the most effective leaders are alike in one crucial way: They all have a high degree of what has come to be known as *emotional intelligence*. It's not that IQ and technical skills are irrelevant. They do matter, but mainly as "threshold capabilities"; that is, they are the entry-level requirements for executive positions. But my research, along with other recent studies, clearly shows that emotional intelligence is the sine qua non of leadership. Without it, a person can have the best training in the world, an incisive, analytical mind, and an endless supply of smart ideas, but he still won't make a great leader.

In the course of the past year, my colleagues and I have focused on how emotional intelligence operates at work. We have examined the relationship between emotional intelligence and effective performance, especially in leaders. And we have observed how emotional intelligence shows itself on the job. How can you tell if someone has high emotional intelligence, for example, and how can you recognize it in yourself? In the following pages, we'll explore these questions, taking each of the components of emotional intelligence—self-awareness, self-regulation, motivation, empathy, and social skill—in turn.

Evaluating Emotional Intelligence

Most large companies today have employed trained psychologists to develop what are known as "competency models" to aid them in identifying, training, and promoting likely stars in the leadership firmament. The psychologists have also developed such models for lower-level positions. And in recent years, I have analyzed competency models from 188 companies, most of which were large and global and included the likes of Lucent Technologies, British Airways, and Credit Suisse.

In carrying out this work, my objective was to determine which personal capabilities drove outstanding performance within these organizations, and to what degree they did so. I grouped capabilities into three categories: purely technical skills like accounting and business planning; cognitive abilities like analytical reasoning; and competencies demonstrating emotional intelligence, such as the ability to work with others and effectiveness in leading change.

To create some of the competency models, psychologists asked senior managers at the companies to identify the capabilities that typified the organization's most outstanding leaders. To create other models, the psychologists used objective criteria, such as a division's profitability, to differentiate the star performers at senior levels within their organizations from the average ones. Those individuals were then extensively interviewed and tested, and their capabilities were compared. This process resulted in the creation of lists of ingredients for highly effective leaders. The lists ranged in length from seven to 15 items and included such ingredients as initiative and strategic vision.

When I analyzed all this data, I found dramatic results. To be sure, intellect was a driver of outstanding performance. Cognitive skills such as big-picture thinking and long-term vision were particularly important. But when I calculated the ratio of technical skills, IQ, and emotional intelligence as ingredients of excellent performance, emotional intelligence proved to be twice as important as the others for jobs at all levels.

Moreover, my analysis showed that emotional intelligence played an increasingly important role at the highest levels of the company, where differences in technical skills are of negligible importance. In other words, the higher the rank of a person considered to be a star performer, the more emotional intelligence capabilities showed up as the reason for his or her effectiveness. When I compared star performers with average ones in senior leadership positions, nearly 90% of the difference in their profiles was attributable to emotional intelligence factors rather than cognitive abilities.

Other researchers have confirmed that emotional intelligence not only distinguishes outstanding leaders but can also be linked to strong performance. The findings of the late David McClelland, the renowned researcher in human and organizational behavior, are a good example. In a 1996 study of a global food and beverage company, McClelland found that when senior managers had a critical mass of emotional intelligence capabilities, their divisions outperformed yearly earnings goals by 20%. Meanwhile, division leaders without that critical mass underperformed by almost the same amount. McClelland's findings, interestingly, held as true in the company's U.S. divisions as in its divisions in Asia and Europe.

In short, the numbers are beginning to tell us a persuasive story about the link between a company's success and the emotional intelligence of its leaders. And just as important, research is also demonstrating that people can, if they take the right approach, develop their emotional intelligence. (See the sidebar "Can Emotional Intelligence Be Learned?")

Self-Awareness

Self-awareness is the first component of emotional intelligence—which makes sense when one considers that the Delphic oracle gave the advice to "know thyself" thousands of years ago. Self-awareness means having a deep understanding of one's emotions, strengths, weaknesses, needs, and drives. People with strong self-awareness are neither overly critical nor unrealistically hopeful. Rather, they are honest—with themselves and with others.

People who have a high degree of self-awareness recognize how their feelings affect them, other people, and their job performance. Thus, a self-aware person who knows that tight deadlines bring out the worst in him plans his time carefully and gets his work done well in advance. Another person with high self-awareness will be able to work with a demanding client. She will understand the client's impact on her moods and the deeper reasons for her frustration. "Their trivial demands take us away from the real work that needs to be done," she might explain. And she will go one step further and turn her anger into something constructive.

Self-awareness extends to a person's understanding of his or her values and goals. Someone who is highly self-aware knows where he is headed and why; so, for example, he will be able to be firm in turning down a job offer that is tempting financially but does not fit with his principles or long-term goals. A person who lacks self-awareness is apt to make decisions that bring on inner turmoil by treading on buried values. "The money looked good so I signed on," someone might say two years into a job, "but the work means so little to me that I'm constantly bored." The decisions of self-aware people mesh with their values; consequently, they often find work to be energizing.

How can one recognize self-awareness? First and foremost, it shows itself as candor and an ability to assess oneself realistically. People with high self-awareness are able to speak accurately and openly—although not necessarily effusively or confessionally—about their emotions and the impact they have on their work. For instance, one manager I know of was skeptical about a new personal-shopper service that her company, a major department-store chain, was about to introduce. Without prompting from her team or her boss, she offered them an explanation: "It's hard for me to get behind the rollout of this service," she admitted, "because I really wanted to run the project, but I wasn't selected.

Bear with me while I deal with that." The manager did indeed examine her feelings; a week later, she was supporting the project fully.

Such self-knowledge often shows itself in the hiring process. Ask a candidate to describe a time he got carried away by his feelings and did something he later regretted. Self-aware candidates will be frank in admitting to failure—and will often tell their tales with a smile. One of the hallmarks of self-awareness is a self-deprecating sense of humor.

Self-awareness can also be identified during performance reviews. Self-aware people know—and are comfortable talking about—their limitations and strengths, and they often demonstrate a thirst for constructive criticism. By contrast, people with low self-awareness interpret the message that they need to improve as a threat or a sign of failure.

Self-aware people can also be recognized by their self-confidence. They have a firm grasp of their capabilities and are less likely to set themselves up to fail by, for example, overstretching on assignments. They know, too, when to ask for help. And the risks they take on the job are calculated. They won't ask for a challenge that they know they can't handle alone. They'll play to their strengths.

Consider the actions of a midlevel employee who was invited to sit in on a strategy meeting with her company's top executives. Although she was the most junior person in the room, she did not sit there quietly, listening in awestruck or fearful silence. She knew she had a head for clear logic and the skill to present ideas persuasively, and she offered cogent suggestions about the company's strategy. At the same time, her self-awareness stopped her from wandering into territory where she knew she was weak.

Despite the value of having self-aware people in the workplace, my research indicates that senior executives don't often give self-awareness the credit it deserves when they look for potential leaders. Many executives mistake candor about feelings for "wimpiness" and fail to give due respect to employees who openly acknowledge their shortcomings. Such people are too readily dismissed as "not tough enough" to lead others.

In fact, the opposite is true. In the first place, people generally admire and respect candor. Furthermore, leaders are constantly required to make judgment calls that require a candid assessment of capabilities—their own and those of others. Do we have the management expertise to acquire a competitor? Can we launch a new product within six months? People who assess themselves honestly—that is, self-aware people—are well suited to do the same for the organizations they run.

Self-Regulation

Biological impulses drive our emotions. We cannot do away with them—but we can do much to manage them. Self-regulation, which is like an ongoing inner conversation, is the component of emotional intelligence that frees us from being prisoners of our feelings. People engaged in such a conversation feel bad moods and emotional impulses just as everyone else does, but they find ways to control them and even to channel them in useful ways.

Imagine an executive who has just watched a team of his employees present a botched analysis to the company's board of directors. In the gloom that follows, the executive might find himself tempted to pound on the table in anger or kick over a chair. He could leap up and scream at the group. Or he might maintain a grim silence, glaring at everyone before stalking off.

But if he had a gift for self-regulation, he would choose a different approach. He would pick his words carefully, acknowledging the team's poor performance without rushing to any hasty judgment. He would then step back to consider the reasons for the failure. Are they personal—a lack of effort? Are there any mitigating factors? What was his role in the debacle? After considering these questions, he would call the team together, lay out the incident's consequences, and offer his feelings about it. He would then present his analysis of the problem and a well-considered solution.

Why does self-regulation matter so much for leaders? First of all, people who are in control of their feelings and impulses—that is, people who are reasonable—are able to create an environment of trust and fairness. In such an environment, politics and infighting are sharply reduced and productivity is high. Talented people flock to the organization and aren't tempted to leave. And self-regulation has a trickle-down effect. No one wants to be known as a hothead when the boss is known for her calm approach. Fewer bad moods at the top mean fewer throughout the organization.

Second, self-regulation is important for competitive reasons. Everyone knows that business today is rife with ambiguity and change. Companies merge and break apart regularly. Technology transforms work at a dizzying pace. People who have mastered their emotions are able to roll with the changes. When a new program is announced, they don't panic; instead, they are able to suspend judgment, seek out information, and listen to the executives as they explain the new program. As the initiative moves forward, these people are able to move with it.

Sometimes they even lead the way. Consider the case of a manager at a large manufacturing company. Like her colleagues, she had used a certain software program for five years. The program drove how she collected and reported data and how she thought about the company's strategy. One day, senior executives announced that a new program was to be installed that would radically change how information was gathered and assessed within the organization. While many people in the company complained bitterly about how disruptive the change would be, the manager mulled over the reasons for the new program and was convinced of its potential to improve performance. She eagerly attended training sessions—some of her colleagues refused to do so—and was eventually promoted to run several divisions, in part because she used the new technology so effectively.

I want to push the importance of self-regulation to leadership even further and make the case that it enhances integrity, which is not only a personal virtue but also an organizational strength. Many of the bad things that happen in companies are a function of impulsive behavior. People rarely plan to exaggerate profits, pad expense accounts, dip into the till, or abuse power for selfish ends. Instead, an opportunity presents itself, and people with low impulse control just say yes.

By contrast, consider the behavior of the senior executive at a large food company. The executive was scrupulously honest in his negotiations with local distributors. He would routinely lay out his cost structure in detail, thereby giving the distributors a realistic understanding of the company's pricing. This approach meant the executive couldn't always drive a hard bargain. Now, on occasion, he felt the urge to increase profits by withholding information about the company's costs. But he challenged that impulse—he saw that it made more sense in the long run to counteract it. His emotional self-regulation paid off in strong, lasting relationships with distributors that benefited the company more than any short-term financial gains would have.

The signs of emotional self-regulation, therefore, are easy to see: a propensity for reflection and thoughtfulness; comfort with ambiguity and change; and integrity—an ability to say no to impulsive urges.

Like self-awareness, self-regulation often does not get its due. People who can master their emotions are sometimes seen as cold fish—their considered responses are taken as a lack of passion. People with fiery temperaments are frequently thought of as "classic" leaders—their outbursts are considered hallmarks of charisma and power. But when such people make it to the top, their impulsiveness often works against them. In my research, extreme displays of negative emotion have never emerged as a driver of good leadership.

Can Emotional Intelligence Be Learned?

For ages, people have debated if leaders are born or made. So too goes the debate about emotional intelligence. Are people born with certain levels of empathy, for example, or do they acquire empathy as a result of life's experiences? The answer is both. Scientific inquiry strongly suggests that there is a genetic component to emotional intelligence. Psychological and developmental research indicates that nurture plays a role as well. How much of each perhaps will never be known, but research and practice clearly demonstrate that emotional intelligence can be learned.

One thing is certain: Emotional intelligence increases with age. There is an old-fashioned word for the phenomenon: maturity. Yet even with maturity, some people still need training to enhance their emotional intelligence. Unfortunately, far too many training programs that intend to build leadership skills—including emotional intelligence—are a waste of time and money. The problem is simple: They focus on the wrong part of the brain.

Emotional intelligence is born largely in the neurotransmitters of the brain's limbic system, which governs feelings, impulses, and drives. Research indicates that the limbic system learns best through motivation, extended practice, and feedback. Compare this with the kind of learning that goes on in the neocortex, which governs analytical and technical ability. The neocortex grasps concepts and logic. It is the part of the brain that figures out how to use a computer or make a sales call by reading a book. Not surprisingly—but mistakenly—it is also the part of the brain targeted by most training programs aimed at enhancing emotional intelligence. When such programs take, in effect, a neocortical approach, my research with the Consortium for Research on Emotional Intelligence in Organizations has shown they can even have a *negative* impact on people's job performance.

To enhance emotional intelligence, organizations must refocus their training to include the limbic system. They must help people break old behavioral habits and establish new ones. That not only takes much more time than conventional training programs, it also requires an individualized approach.

Imagine an executive who is thought to be low on empathy by her colleagues. Part of that deficit shows itself as an inability to listen; she interrupts people and doesn't pay close attention to what they're saying. To fix the problem, the executive needs to be motivated to change, and then she needs practice and feedback from others in the company. A colleague or coach could be tapped to let the executive know when she has been observed failing to listen. She would then have to replay the incident and give a better response; that is, demonstrate her ability to absorb what others are saying. And the executive could be directed to observe certain executives who listen well and to mimic their behavior.

With persistence and practice, such a process can lead to lasting results. I know one Wall Street executive who sought to improve his empathy—specifically his ability to read people's reactions and see their perspectives. Before beginning his quest, the executive's subordinates were terrified of working with him. People even went so far as to hide bad news from him. Naturally, he was shocked when finally confronted with these facts. He went home and told his family—but they only confirmed what he had heard at work. When their opinions on any given subject did not mesh with his, they, too, were frightened of him.

Enlisting the help of a coach, the executive went to work to heighten his empathy through practice and feedback. His first step was to take a vacation to a foreign country where he did not speak the language. While there, he monitored his reactions to the unfamiliar and his openness to people who were different from him. When he returned home, humbled by his week abroad, the executive asked his coach to shadow him for parts of the day, several times a week, to critique how he treated people with new or different perspectives. At the same time, he consciously used on-the-job interactions as opportunities to practice "hearing" ideas that differed from his. Finally, the executive had himself videotaped in meetings and asked those who worked for and with him to critique his ability to acknowledge and understand the feelings of others. It took several months, but the executive's emotional intelligence did ultimately rise, and the improvement was reflected in his overall performance on the job.

It's important to emphasize that building one's emotional intelligence cannot—will not—happen without sincere desire and concerted effort. A brief seminar won't help; nor can one buy a how-to manual. It is much harder to learn to empathize—to internalize empathy as a natural response to people—than it is to become adept at regression analysis. But it can be done. "Nothing great was ever achieved without enthusiasm," wrote Ralph Waldo Emerson. If your goal is to become a real leader, these words can serve as a guidepost in your efforts to develop high emotional intelligence.

Motivation

If there is one trait that virtually all effective leaders have, it is motivation. They are driven to achieve beyond expectations—their own and everyone else's. The key word here is *achieve*. Plenty of people are motivated by external factors, such as a big salary or the status that comes from having an impressive title or being part of a prestigious company. By contrast, those with leadership potential are motivated by a deeply embedded desire to achieve for the sake of achievement.

If you are looking for leaders, how can you identify people who are motivated by the drive to achieve rather than by external rewards? The first sign is a passion for the work itself—such people seek out creative challenges, love to learn, and take great pride in a job well done. They also display an unflagging energy to do things better. People with such energy often seem restless with the status quo. They are persistent with their questions about why things are done one way rather than another; they are eager to explore new approaches to their work.

A cosmetics company manager, for example, was frustrated that he had to wait two weeks to get sales results from people in the field. He finally tracked down an automated phone system that would beep each of his salespeople at 5 PM every day. An automated message then prompted them to punch in their numbers—how many calls and sales they had made that day. The system shortened the feedback time on sales results from weeks to hours.

That story illustrates two other common traits of people who are driven to achieve. They are forever raising the performance bar, and they like to keep score. Take the performance bar first. During performance reviews, people with high levels of motivation might ask to be "stretched" by their superiors. Of course, an employee who combines self-awareness with internal motivation will recognize her limits—but she won't settle for objectives that seem too easy to fulfill.

And it follows naturally that people who are driven to do better also want a way of tracking progress—their own, their team's, and their company's. Whereas people with low achievement motivation are often fuzzy about results, those with high achievement motivation often keep score by tracking such hard measures as profitability or market share. I know of a money manager who starts and ends his day on the Internet, gauging the performance of his stock fund against four industry-set benchmarks.

Interestingly, people with high motivation remain optimistic even when the score is against them. In such cases, self-regulation combines with achievement motivation to overcome the frustration and depression that come after a setback or failure. Take the case of another portfolio manager at a large investment company. After several successful years, her fund tumbled for three consecutive quarters, leading three large institutional clients to shift their business elsewhere.

Some executives would have blamed the nosedive on circumstances outside their control; others might have seen the setback as evidence of personal failure. This portfolio manager, however, saw an opportunity to prove she could lead a turnaround. Two years later, when she was promoted to a very senior level in the company, she described the experience as "the best thing that ever happened to me; I learned so much from it."

The Five Components of Emotional Intelligence at Work

	Definition	Hallmarks
Self-Awareness	• the ability to recognize and understand your moods, emotions, and drives, as well as their effect on others	• self-confidence • realistic self-assessment • self-deprecating sense of humor
Self-Regulation	• the ability to control or redirect disruptive impulses and moods • the propensity to suspend judgment—to think before acting	• trustworthiness and integrity • comfort with ambiguity • openness to change
Motivation	• a passion to work for reasons that go beyond money or status • a propensity to pursue goals with energy and persistence	• strong drive to achieve • optimism, even in the face of failure • organizational commitment
Empathy	• the ability to understand the emotional makeup of other people • skill in treating people according to their emotional reactions	• expertise in building and retaining talent • cross-cultural sensitivity • service to clients and customers
Social Skill	• proficiency in managing relationships and building networks • an ability to find common ground and build rapport	• effectiveness in leading change • persuasiveness • expertise in building and leading teams

Executives trying to recognize high levels of achievement motivation in their people can look for one last piece of evidence: commitment to the organization. When people love their jobs for the work itself, they often feel committed to the organizations that make that work possible. Committed employees are likely to stay with an organization even when they are pursued by headhunters waving money.

It's not difficult to understand how and why a motivation to achieve translates into strong leadership. If you set the performance bar high for yourself, you will do the same for the organization when you are in a position to do so. Likewise, a drive to surpass goals and an interest in keeping score can be contagious. Leaders with these traits can often build a team of managers around them with the same traits. And of course, optimism and organizational commitment are fundamental to leadership—just try to imagine running a company without them.

Empathy

Of all the dimensions of emotional intelligence, empathy is the most easily recognized. We have all felt the empathy of a sensitive teacher or friend; we have all been struck by its absence in an unfeeling coach or boss. But when it comes to business, we rarely hear people praised, let alone rewarded, for their empathy. The very word seems unbusinesslike, out of place amid the tough realities of the marketplace.

But empathy doesn't mean a kind of "I'm OK, you're OK" mushiness. For a leader, that is, it doesn't mean adopting other people's emotions as one's own and trying to please everybody. That would be a nightmare—it would make action impossible. Rather, empathy means thoughtfully considering employees' feelings—along with other factors—in the process of making intelligent decisions.

For an example of empathy in action, consider what happened when two giant brokerage companies merged, creating redundant jobs in all their divisions. One division manager called his people together and gave a gloomy speech that emphasized the number of people who would soon be fired. The manager of another division gave his people a different kind of speech. He was up-front about his own worry and confusion, and he promised to keep people informed and to treat everyone fairly.

The difference between these two managers was empathy. The first manager was too worried about his own fate to consider the feelings of his anxiety-stricken colleagues. The second knew intuitively what his people were feeling, and he acknowledged their fears with his words. Is it any surprise that the first manager saw his division sink as many demoralized people, especially the most talented, departed? By contrast, the second manager continued to be a strong leader, his best people stayed, and his division remained as productive as ever.

Empathy is particularly important today as a component of leadership for at least three reasons: the increasing use of teams; the rapid pace of globalization; and the growing need to retain talent.

Consider the challenge of leading a team. As anyone who has ever been a part of one can attest, teams are cauldrons of bubbling emotions. They are often charged with reaching a consensus—which is hard enough with two people and much more difficult as the numbers increase. Even in groups with as few as four or five members, alliances form and clashing agendas get set. A team's leader must be able to sense and understand the viewpoints of everyone around the table.

That's exactly what a marketing manager at a large information technology company was able to do when she was appointed to lead a troubled team. The group was in turmoil, overloaded by work and missing deadlines. Tensions were high among the members. Tinkering with procedures was not enough to bring the group together and make it an effective part of the company.

So the manager took several steps. In a series of one-on-one sessions, she took the time to listen to everyone in the group—what was frustrating them, how they rated their colleagues, whether they felt they had been ignored. And then she directed the team in a way that brought it together: She encouraged people to speak more openly about their frustrations, and she helped people raise constructive complaints during meetings. In short, her empathy allowed her to understand her team's emotional makeup. The result was not just heightened collaboration among members but also added business, as the team was called on for help by a wider range of internal clients.

Globalization is another reason for the rising importance of empathy for business leaders. Cross-cultural dialogue can easily lead to miscues and misunderstandings. Empathy is an antidote. People who have it are attuned to subtleties in body language; they can hear the message beneath the words being spoken. Beyond that, they have a deep understanding of both the existence and the importance of cultural and ethnic differences.

Consider the case of an American consultant whose team had just pitched a project to a potential Japanese client. In its dealings with Americans, the team was accustomed to being bombarded with questions after such a proposal, but this time it was greeted with a long silence. Other members of the team, taking the silence as disapproval, were ready to pack and leave. The lead consultant gestured them to stop. Although he was not particularly familiar with Japanese culture, he read the client's face and posture and sensed not rejection but interest—even deep consideration. He was right: When the client finally spoke, it was to give the consulting firm the job.

Finally, empathy plays a key role in the retention of talent, particularly in today's information economy. Leaders have always needed empathy to develop and keep good people, but today the stakes are higher. When good people leave, they take the company's knowledge with them.

That's where coaching and mentoring come in. It has repeatedly been shown that coaching and mentoring pay off not just in better performance but also in increased job satisfaction and decreased turnover. But what makes coaching and mentoring work best is the nature of the relationship. Outstanding coaches and mentors get inside the heads of the people they are helping. They sense how to give effective feedback. They know when to push for better performance and when to hold back. In the way they motivate their protégés, they demonstrate empathy in action.

In what is probably sounding like a refrain, let me repeat that empathy doesn't get much respect in business. People wonder how leaders can make hard decisions if they are "feeling" for all the people who will be affected. But leaders with empathy do more than sympathize with people around them: They use their knowledge to improve their companies in subtle but important ways.

Social Skill

The first three components of emotional intelligence are self-management skills. The last two, empathy and social skill, concern a person's ability to manage relationships with others. As a component of emotional intelligence, social skill is not as simple as it sounds. It's not just a matter of friendliness, although people with high levels of social skill are rarely mean-spirited. Social skill, rather, is friendliness with a purpose: moving people in the direction you desire, whether that's agreement on a new marketing strategy or enthusiasm about a new product.

Socially skilled people tend to have a wide circle of acquaintances, and they have a knack for finding common ground with people of all kinds—a knack for building rapport. That doesn't mean they socialize continually; it means they work according to the assumption that nothing important gets done alone. Such people have a network in place when the time for action comes.

Social skill is the culmination of the other dimensions of emotional intelligence. People tend to be very effective at managing relationships when they can understand and control their own emotions and can empathize with the feelings of others. Even motivation contributes to social skill. Remember that people who are driven to achieve tend to be optimistic, even in the face of setbacks or failure. When people are upbeat, their "glow" is cast upon conversations and other social encounters. They are popular, and for good reason.

Because it is the outcome of the other dimensions of emotional intelligence, social skill is recognizable on the job in many ways that will by now sound familiar. Socially skilled people, for instance, are adept at managing teams—that's their empathy at work. Likewise, they are expert persuaders—a manifestation of self-awareness, self-regulation, and empathy combined. Given those skills, good persuaders know when to make an emotional plea, for instance, and when an appeal to reason will work better. And motivation, when publicly visible, makes such people excellent collaborators; their passion for the work spreads to others, and they are driven to find solutions.

But sometimes social skill shows itself in ways the other emotional intelligence components do not. For instance, socially skilled people may at times appear not to be working while at work. They seem to be idly schmoozing—chatting in the hallways with colleagues or joking around with people who are not even connected to their "real" jobs. Socially skilled people, however, don't think it makes sense to arbitrarily limit the scope of their relationships. They build bonds widely because they know that in these fluid times, they may need help someday from people they are just getting to know today.

For example, consider the case of an executive in the strategy department of a global computer manufacturer. By 1993, he was convinced that the company's future lay with the Internet. Over the course of the next year, he found kindred spirits and used his social skill to stitch together a virtual community that cut across levels, divisions, and nations. He then used this de facto team to put up a corporate Web site, among the first by a major company. And, on his own initiative, with no budget or formal status, he signed up the company to participate in an annual Internet industry convention. Calling on his allies and persuading various divisions to donate funds, he recruited more than 50 people from a dozen different units to represent the company at the convention.

Management took notice: Within a year of the conference, the executive's team formed the basis for the company's first Internet division, and he was formally put in charge of it. To get there, the executive had ignored conventional boundaries, forging and maintaining connections with people in every corner of the organization.

Is social skill considered a key leadership capability in most companies? The answer is yes, especially when compared with the other components of emotional intelligence. People seem to know intuitively that leaders need to manage relationships effectively; no leader is an island. After all, the leader's task is to get work done through other people, and social skill makes that possible. A leader who cannot express her empathy may as well not have it at all. And a leader's motivation will be useless if he cannot communicate his passion to the organization. Social skill allows leaders to put their emotional intelligence to work.

It would be foolish to assert that good-old-fashioned IQ and technical ability are not important ingredients in strong leadership. But the recipe would not be complete without emotional intelligence. It was once thought that the components of emotional intelligence were "nice to have" in business leaders. But now we know that, for the sake of performance, these are ingredients that leaders "need to have."

It is fortunate, then, that emotional intelligence can be learned. The process is not easy. It takes time and, most of all, commitment. But the benefits that come from having a well-developed emotional intelligence, both for the individual and for the organization, make it worth the effort.

8

The Level 5 Leader

Jim Collins

In 1971, a seemingly ordinary man named Darwin E. Smith was named chief executive of Kimberly-Clark, a stodgy old paper company whose stock had fallen 36% behind the general market during the previous 20 years. Smith, the company's mild-mannered in-house lawyer, wasn't so sure the board had made the right choice—a feeling that was reinforced when a Kimberly-Clark director pulled him aside and reminded him that he lacked some of the qualifications for the position. But CEO he was, and CEO he remained for 20 years.

What a 20 years it was. In that period, Smith created a stunning transformation at Kimberly-Clark, turning it into the leading consumer paper products company in the world. Under his stewardship, the company beat its rivals Scott Paper and Procter & Gamble. And in doing so, Kimberly-Clark generated cumulative stock returns that were 4.1 times greater than those of the general market, outperforming venerable companies such as Hewlett-Packard, 3M, Coca-Cola, and General Electric.

Smith's turnaround of Kimberly-Clark is one the best examples in the twentieth century of a leader taking a company from merely good to truly great. And yet few people—even ardent students of business history—have heard of Darwin Smith. He probably would have liked it that way. Smith is a classic example of a Level 5 leader—an individual who blends extreme personal humility with intense professional will. According to our five-year research study, executives who possess this paradoxical combination of traits are catalysts for the statistically rare event of transforming a good company into a great one. (The research is described in the sidebar "One Question, Five Years, 11 Companies.")

"Level 5" refers to the highest level in a hierarchy of executive capabilities that we identified during our research. Leaders at the other four levels in the hierarchy can produce high degrees of success but not enough to elevate companies from mediocrity to sustained excellence. (For more details about this concept, see the exhibit "The Level 5 Hierarchy.") And while Level 5 leadership is not the only requirement for transforming a good company into a great one—other factors include getting the right people on the bus (and the wrong people off the bus) and creating a culture of discipline—our research shows it to be essential. Good-to-great transformations don't happen without Level 5 leaders at the helm. They just don't.

Not What You Would Expect

Our discovery of Level 5 leadership is counterintuitive. Indeed, it is countercultural. People generally assume that transforming companies from good to great requires larger-than-life leaders—big personalities like Lee Iacocca, Al Dunlap, Jack Welch, and Stanley Gault, who make headlines and become celebrities.

Compared with those CEOs, Darwin Smith seems to have come from Mars. Shy, unpretentious, even awkward, Smith shunned attention. When a journalist

---

The Level 5 Hierarchy

The Level 5 leader sits on top of a hierarchy of capabilities and is, according to our research, a necessary requirement for transforming an organization from good to great. But what lies beneath? Four other layers, each one appropriate in its own right but none with the power of Level 5. Individuals do not need to proceed sequentially through each level of the hierarchy to reach the top, but to be a full-fledged Level 5 requires the capabilities of all the lower levels, plus the special characteristics of Level 5.

Level 5
Executive
Builds enduring greatness through a paradoxical
combination of personal humility plus professional will.

Level 4
Effective Leader
Catalyzes commitment to and vigorous pursuit of a clear and
compelling vision; stimulates the group to high performance standards.

Level 3
Competent Manager
Organizes people and resources toward the effective
and efficient pursuit of predetermined objectives.

Level 2
Contributing Team Member
Contributes to the achievement of group objectives;
works effectively with others in a group setting.

Level 1
Highly Capable Individual
Makes productive contributions through talent,
knowledge, skills, and good work habits.

One Question, Five Years, 11 Companies

The Level 5 discovery derives from a research project that began in 1996, when my research teams and I set out to answer one question: Can a good company become a great company and, if so, how? Most great companies grew up with superb parents—people like George Merck, David Packard, and Walt Disney—who instilled greatness early on. But what about the vast majority of companies that wake up partway through life and realize that they're good but not great?

To answer that question, we looked for companies that had shifted from good performance to great performance—and sustained it. We identified comparison companies that had failed to make that sustained shift. We then studied the contrast between the two groups to discover common variables that distinguished those who made and sustained a shift from those who could have but didn't.

More precisely, we searched for a specific pattern: cumulative stock returns at or below the general stock market for 15 years, punctuated by a transition point, then cumulative returns at least three times the market over the next 15 years. (See the accompanying exhibit.) We used data from the University of Chicago Center for Research in Security Prices and adjusted for stock splits and all dividends reinvested. The shift had to be distinct from the industry; if the whole industry showed the same shift, we'd drop the company. We began with 1,435 companies that appeared on the *Fortune 500* from 1965 to 1995; we found 11 good-to-great examples. That's not a sample; that's the total number that jumped all our hurdles and passed into the study.

Those that made the cut averaged cumulative stock returns 6.9 times the general stock market for the 15 years after the point of transition. To put that in perspective, General Electric under Jack Welch outperformed the general stock market by 2.8:1 during his tenure from 1986 to 2000. One dollar invested in a mutual fund of the good-to-great companies in 1965 grew to $470 by 2000 compared with $56 in the general stock market. These are remarkable numbers, made all the more so by the fact that they came from previously unremarkable companies.

For each good-to-great example, we selected the best direct comparison, based on similarity of business, size, age, customers, and performance leading up to the transition. We also constructed a set of six "unsustained" comparisons (companies that showed a short-lived shift but then fell off) to address the question of sustainability. To be conservative, we consistently picked comparison companies that, if anything, were in better shape than the good-to-great companies were in the years just before the transition.

With 22 research associates working in groups of four to six at a time from 1996 to 2000, our study involved a wide range of both qualitative and quantitative analyses. On the qualitative front, we collected nearly 6,000 articles, conducted 87 interviews with key executives, analyzed companies' internal strategy documents, and culled through analysts' reports. On the quantitative front, we ran financial metrics, examined executive compensation, compared patterns of management turnover, quantified company layoffs and restructurings, and calculated the effect of acquisitions and divestitures, and calculated the effect of acquisitions and divesti-

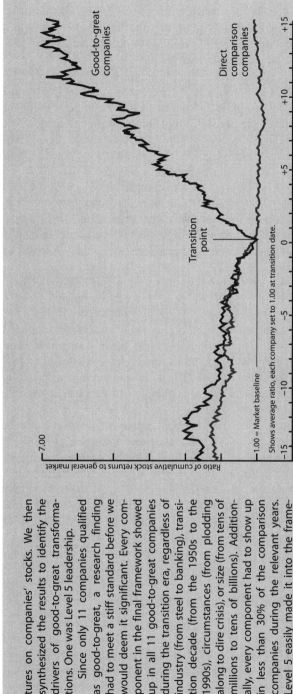

tures on companies' stocks. We then synthesized the results to identify the drivers of good-to-great transformations. One was Level 5 leadership.

Since only 11 companies qualified as good-to-great, a research finding had to meet a stiff standard before we would deem it significant. Every component in the final framework showed up in all 11 good-to-great companies during the transition era, regardless of industry (from steel to banking), transition decade (from the 1950s to the 1990s), circumstances (from plodding along to dire crisis), or size (from tens of millions to tens of billions). Additionally, every component had to show up in less than 30% of the comparison companies during the relevant years. Level 5 easily made it into the framework as one of the strongest, most consistent contrasts between the good-to-great and the comparison companies.

asked him to describe his management style, Smith just stared back at the scribe from the other side of his thick black-rimmed glasses. He was dressed unfashionably, like a farm boy wearing his first J.C. Penney suit. Finally, after a long and uncomfortable silence, he said, "Eccentric." Needless to say, the *Wall Street Journal* did not publish a splashy feature on Darwin Smith.

But if you were to consider Smith soft or meek, you would be terribly mistaken. His lack of pretense was coupled with a fierce, even stoic, resolve toward life. Smith grew up on an Indiana farm and put himself through night school at Indiana University by working the day shift at International Harvester. One day, he lost a finger on the job. The story goes that he went to class that evening and returned to work the very next day. Eventually, this poor but determined Indiana farm boy earned admission to Harvard Law School.

He showed the same iron will when he was at the helm of Kimberly-Clark. Indeed, two months after Smith became CEO, doctors diagnosed him with nose and throat cancer and told him he had less than a year to live. He duly informed the board of his illness but said he had no plans to die anytime soon. Smith held to his demanding work schedule while commuting weekly from Wisconsin to Houston for radiation therapy. He lived 25 more years, 20 of them as CEO.

Smith's ferocious resolve was crucial to the rebuilding of Kimberly-Clark, especially when he made the most dramatic decision in the company's history: selling the mills.

To explain: Shortly after he took over, Smith and his team had concluded that the company's traditional core business—coated paper—was doomed to mediocrity. Its economics were bad and the competition weak. But, they reasoned, if Kimberly-Clark were thrust into the fire of the consumer paper products business, better economics and world-class competition like Procter & Gamble would force it to achieve greatness or perish.

And so, like the general who burned the boats upon landing on enemy soil, leaving his troops to succeed or die, Smith announced that Kimberly-Clark would sell its mills—even the namesake mill in Kimberly, Wisconsin. All proceeds would be thrown into the consumer business, with investments in brands like Huggies diapers and Kleenex tissues. The business media called the move stupid, and Wall Street analysts downgraded the stock. But Smith never wavered. Twenty-five years later, Kimberly-Clark owned Scott Paper and beat Procter & Gamble in six of eight product categories. In retirement, Smith reflected on his exceptional performance, saying simply, "I never stopped trying to become qualified for the job."

Not What We Expected, Either

We'll look in depth at Level 5 leadership, but first let's set an important *context* for our findings. We were not looking for Level 5 or anything like it. Our original question was, Can a good company become a great one and, if so, how? In fact, I gave the research teams explicit instructions to downplay the role of top executives in their analyses of this question so we wouldn't slip into the simplistic "credit the leader" or "blame the leader" thinking that is so common today.

But Level 5 found us. Over the course of the study, research teams kept saying, "We can't ignore the top executives even if we want to. There *is* something consistently unusual about them." I would push back, arguing, "The comparison companies also had leaders. So what's different here?" Back and forth the debate raged. Finally, as should always be the case, the data won. The executives at companies that went from good to great and sustained that performance for 15 years or more were all cut from the same cloth—one remarkably different from that which produced the executives at the comparison companies in our study. It didn't matter whether the company was in crisis or steady state, consumer or industrial, offering services or products. It didn't matter when the transition took place or how big the company. The successful organizations all had a Level 5 leader at the time of transition.

Furthermore, the absence of Level 5 leadership showed up consistently across the comparison companies. The point: Level 5 is an empirical finding, not an ideological one. And that's important to note, given how much the Level 5 finding contradicts not only conventional wisdom but much of management theory to date. (For more about our findings on good-to-great transformations, see the sidebar "Not by Level 5 Alone.")

Humility + Will = Level 5

Level 5 leaders are a study in duality: modest and willful, shy and fearless. To grasp this concept, consider Abraham Lincoln, who never let his ego get in the way of his ambition to create an enduring great nation. Author Henry Adams called him "a quiet, peaceful, shy figure." But those who thought Lincoln's understated manner signaled weakness in the man found themselves terribly mistaken—to the scale of 250,000 Confederate and 360,000 Union lives, including Lincoln's own.

Not by Level 5 Alone

Level 5 leadership is an essential factor for taking a company from good to great, but it's not the only one. Our research uncovered multiple factors that deliver companies to greatness. And it is the combined package—Level 5 plus these other drivers—that takes companies beyond unremarkable. There is a symbiotic relationship between Level 5 and the rest of our findings: Level 5 enables implementation of the other findings, and practicing the other findings may help you get to Level 5. We've already talked about who Level 5 leaders are; the rest of our findings describe what they do. Here is a brief look at some of the other key findings.

First Who

We expected that good-to-great leaders would start with the vision and strategy. Instead, they attended to people first, strategy second. They got the right people on the bus, moved the wrong people off, ushered the right people to the right seats—and then they figured out where to drive it.

(continued)

Stockdale Paradox

This finding is named after Admiral James Stockdale, winner of the Medal of Honor, who survived seven years in a Vietcong POW camp by hanging on to two contradictory beliefs: His life couldn't be worse at the moment, and his life would someday be better than ever. Like Stockdale, people at the good-to-great companies in our research confronted the most brutal facts of their current reality, yet simultaneously maintained absolute faith that they would prevail in the end. And they held both disciplines—faith and facts—at the same time, all the time.

Buildup-Breakthrough Flywheel

Good-to-great transformations do not happen overnight or in one big leap. Rather, the process resembles relentlessly pushing a giant, heavy flywheel in one direction. At first, pushing it gets the flywheel to turn once. With consistent effort, it goes two turns, then five, then ten, building increasing momentum until—bang!—the wheel hits the breakthrough point, and the momentum really kicks in. Our comparison companies never sustained the kind of breakthrough momentum that the good-to-great companies did; instead, they lurched back and forth with radical change programs, reactionary moves, and restructurings.

The Hedgehog Concept

In a famous essay, philosopher and scholar Isaiah Berlin described two approaches to thought and life using a simple parable: The fox knows a little about many things, but the hedgehog knows only one big thing very well. The fox is complex; the hedgehog simple. And the hedgehog wins. Our research shows that breakthroughs require a simple, hedgehog-like understanding of three intersecting circles: what a company can be the best in the world at, how its economics work best, and what best ignites the passions of its people. Breakthroughs happen when you get the hedgehog concept and become systematic and consistent with it, eliminating virtually anything that does not fit in the three circles.

Technology Accelerators

The good-to-great companies had a paradoxical relationship with technology. On the one hand, they assiduously avoided jumping on new technology bandwagons. On the other, they were pioneers in the application of carefully selected technologies, making bold, farsighted investments in those that directly linked to their hedgehog concept. Like turbochargers, these technology accelerators create an explosion in flywheel momentum.

A Culture of Discipline

When you look across the good-to-great transformations, they consistently display three forms of discipline: disciplined people, disciplined thought, and disciplined action. When you have disciplined people, you don't need hierarchy. When you have disciplined thought, you don't need bureaucracy. When you have disciplined action, you don't need excessive controls. When you combine a culture of discipline with an ethic of entrepreneurship, you get the magical alchemy of great performance.

It might be a stretch to compare the 11 Level 5 CEOs in our research to Lincoln, but they did display the same kind of duality. Take Colman M. Mockler, CEO of Gillette from 1975 to 1991. Mockler, who faced down three takeover attempts, was a reserved, gracious man with a gentle, almost patrician manner. Despite epic battles with raiders—he took on Ronald Perelman twice and the former Coniston Partners once—he never lost his shy, courteous style. At the height of crisis, he maintained a calm business-as-usual demeanor, dispensing first with ongoing business before turning to the takeover.

And yet, those who mistook Mockler's outward modesty as a sign of inner weakness were beaten in the end. In one proxy battle, Mockler and other senior executives called thousands of investors, one by one, to win their votes. Mockler simply would not give in. He chose to fight for the future greatness of Gillette even though he could have pocketed millions by flipping his stock.

Consider the consequences had Mockler capitulated. If a share flipper had accepted the full 44% price premium offered by Perelman and then invested those shares in the general market for ten years, he still would have come out 64% behind a shareholder who stayed with Mockler and Gillette. If Mockler had given up the fight, it's likely that none of us would be shaving with Sensor, Lady Sensor, or the Mach III—and hundreds of millions of people would have a more painful battle with daily stubble.

Sadly, Mockler never had the chance to enjoy the full fruits of his efforts. In January 1991, Gillette received an advance copy of *Forbes*. The cover featured an artist's rendition of the publicity-shy Mockler standing on a mountaintop, holding a giant razor above his head in a triumphant pose. Walking back to his office just minutes after seeing this public acknowledgment of his 16 years of struggle, Mockler crumpled to the floor and died of a massive heart attack.

Even if Mockler had known he would die in office, he could not have changed his approach. His placid persona hid an inner intensity, a dedication to making anything he touched the best—not just because of what he would get but because he couldn't imagine doing it any other way. Mockler could not give up the company to those who would destroy it, any more than Lincoln would risk losing the chance to build an enduring great nation.

A Compelling Modesty

The Mockler story illustrates the modesty typical of Level 5 leaders. (For a summary of Level 5 traits, see the exhibit "The Yin and Yang of Level 5.") Indeed, throughout our interviews with such executives, we were struck by the way they talked about themselves—or rather, didn't talk about themselves. They'd go on and on about the company and the contributions of other executives, but they would instinctively deflect discussion about their own role. When pressed to talk about themselves, they'd say things like, "I hope I'm not sounding like a big shot," or "I don't think I can take much credit for what happened. *We* were blessed with marvelous people." One Level 5 leader even asserted, "There are a lot of people in this company who could do my job better than I do."

By contrast, consider the courtship of personal celebrity by the comparison CEOs. Scott Paper, the comparison company to Kimberly-Clark, hired Al Dunlap as CEO—a man who would tell anyone who would listen (and many who would have preferred not to) about his accomplishments. After 19 months atop Scott Paper, Dunlap said in *Business Week,* "The Scott story will go down in the annals of American business history as one of the most successful, quickest turnarounds ever. It makes other turnarounds pale by comparison." He personally accrued $100 million for 603 days of work at Scott Paper—about $165,000 per day—largely by slashing the workforce, halving the R&D budget, and putting the company on growth steroids in preparation for sale. After selling off the company and pocketing his quick millions, Dunlap wrote an autobiography in which he boastfully dubbed himself "Rambo in pinstripes." It's hard to imagine Darwin Smith thinking, "Hey, that Rambo character reminds me of me," let alone stating it publicly.

Granted, the Scott Paper story is one of the more dramatic in our study, but it's not an isolated case. In more than two-thirds of the comparison companies, we noted the presence of a gargantuan ego that contributed to the demise or continued mediocrity of the company. We found this pattern particularly strong in the unsustained comparison companies—the companies that would show a shift in performance under a talented yet egocentric Level 4 leader, only to decline in later years.

Lee Iacocca, for example, saved Chrysler from the brink of catastrophe, performing one of the most celebrated (and deservedly so) turnarounds in U.S. business history. The automaker's stock rose 2.9 times higher than the general market about halfway through his tenure. But then Iacocca diverted his attention

The Yin and Yang of Level 5

Personal Humility	**Professional Will**
Demonstrates a compelling modesty, shunning public adulation; never boastful.	Creates superb results, a clear catalyst in the transition from good to great.
Acts with quiet, calm determination; relies principally on inspired standards, not inspiring charisma, to motivate.	Demonstrates an unwavering resolve to do whatever must be done to produce the best long-term results, no matter how difficult.
Channels ambition into the company, not the self; sets up successors for even more greatness in the next generation.	Sets the standard of building an enduring great company; will settle for nothing less.
Looks in the mirror, not out the window, to apportion responsibility for poor results, never blaming other people, external factors, or bad luck.	Looks out the window, not in the mirror, to apportion credit for the success of the company—to other people, external factors, and good luck.

to transforming himself. He appeared regularly on talk shows like the *Today Show* and *Larry King Live,* starred in more than 80 commercials, entertained the idea of running for president of the United States, and promoted his autobiography, which sold 7 million copies worldwide. Iacocca's personal stock soared, but Chrysler's stock fell 31% below the market in the second half of his tenure.

And once Iacocca had accumulated all the fame and perks, he found it difficult to leave center stage. He postponed his retirement so many times that Chrysler's insiders began to joke that Iacocca stood for "I Am Chairman of Chrysler Corporation Always." When he finally retired, he demanded that the board continue to provide a private jet and stock options. Later, he joined forces with noted takeover artist Kirk Kerkorian to launch a hostile bid for Chrysler. (It failed.) Iacocca did make one final brilliant decision: He picked a modest yet determined man—perhaps even a Level 5—as his successor. Bob Eaton rescued Chrysler from its second near-death crisis in a decade and set the foundation for a more enduring corporate transition.

An Unwavering Resolve

Besides extreme humility, Level 5 leaders also display tremendous professional will. When George Cain became CEO of Abbott Laboratories, it was a drowsy, family-controlled business sitting at the bottom quartile of the pharmaceutical industry, living off its cash cow, erythromycin. Cain was a typical Level 5 leader in his lack of pretense; he didn't have the kind of inspiring personality that would galvanize the company. But he had something much more powerful: inspired standards. He could not stand mediocrity in any form and was utterly intolerant of anyone who would accept the idea that good is good enough. For the next 14 years, he relentlessly imposed his will for greatness on Abbott Labs.

Among Cain's first tasks was to destroy one of the root causes of Abbott's middling performance: nepotism. By systematically rebuilding both the board and the executive team with the best people he could find, Cain made his statement. Family ties no longer mattered. If you couldn't become the best executive in the industry within your span of responsibility, you would lose your paycheck.

Such near-ruthless rebuilding might be expected from an outsider brought in to turn the company around, but Cain was an 18-year insider—and a part of the family, the son of a previous president. Holiday gatherings were probably tense for a few years in the Cain clan—"Sorry I had to fire you. Want another slice of turkey?"—but in the end, family members were pleased with the performance of their stock. Cain had set in motion a profitable growth machine. From its transition in 1974 to 2000, Abbott created shareholder returns that beat the market 4.5:1, outperforming industry superstars Merck and Pfizer by a factor of two.

Another good example of iron-willed Level 5 leadership comes from Charles R. "Cork" Walgreen III, who transformed dowdy Walgreen's into a company that outperformed the stock market 16:1 from its transition in 1975 to 2000. After years of dialogue and debate within his executive team about what to do with Walgreen's food-service operations, this CEO sensed the team had finally reached a watershed: The company's brightest future lay in convenient drug-stores, not in food service. Dan Jorndt, who succeeded Walgreen in 1988, describes what happened next:

> Cork said at one of our planning committee meetings, "Okay, now I am going to draw the line in the sand. We are going to be out of the restaurant business completely in five years." At the time we had more than 500 restau-rants. You could have heard a pin drop. He said, "I want to let everybody know the clock is ticking." Six months later we were at our next planning committee meeting and someone mentioned just in passing that we had only five years to be out of the restaurant business. Cork was not a real vociferous fellow. He sort of tapped on the table and said, "Listen, you now have four and a half years. I said you had five years six months ago. Now you've got four and a half years." Well, that next day things really clicked into gear for winding down our restaurant business. Cork never wavered. He never doubted. He never second-guessed.

Like Darwin Smith selling the mills at Kimberly-Clark, Cork Walgreen required stoic resolve to make his decisions. Food service was not the largest part of the business, although it did add substantial profits to the bottom line. The real problem was more emotional than financial. Walgreen's had, after all, invented the malted milk shake, and food service had been a long-standing family tradition dating back to Cork's grandfather. Not only that, some food-service outlets were even named after the CEO—for example, a restaurant chain named Corky's. But no matter; if Walgreen had to fly in the face of family tradition in order to refocus on the one arena in which Walgreen's could be the best in the world—convenient drugstores—and terminate everything else that would not produce great results, then Cork would do it. Quietly, doggedly, simply.

One final, yet compelling, note on our findings about Level 5: Because Level 5 leaders have ambition not for themselves but for their companies, they routinely select superb successors. Level 5 leaders want to see their companies become even more successful in the next generation and are comfortable with the idea that most people won't even know that the roots of that success trace back to them. As one Level 5 CEO said, "I want to look from my porch, see the company as one of the great companies in the world someday, and be able to say, 'I used to work there.'" By contrast, Level 4 leaders often fail to set up the company for enduring success. After all, what better testament to your own personal greatness than that the place falls apart after you leave?

In more than three-quarters of the comparison companies, we found execu-tives who set up their successors for failure, chose weak successors, or both. Consider the case of Rubbermaid, which grew from obscurity to become one of *Fortune's* most admired companies—and then, just as quickly, disintegrated into such sorry shape that it had to be acquired by Newell.

The architect of this remarkable story was a charismatic and brilliant leader named Stanley C. Gault, whose name became synonymous in the late 1980s with Rubbermaid's success. Across the 312 articles collected by our research team about the company, Gault comes through as a hard-driving, egocentric executive.

In one article, he responds to the accusation of being a tyrant with the statement, "Yes, but I'm a sincere tyrant." In another, drawn directly from his own comments on leading change, the word "I" appears 44 times, while the word "we" appears 16 times. Of course, Gault had every reason to be proud of his executive success: Rubbermaid generated 40 consecutive quarters of earnings growth under his leadership—an impressive performance, to be sure, and one that deserves respect.

But Gault did not leave behind a company that would be great without him. His chosen successor lasted a year on the job and the next in line faced a management team so shallow that he had to temporarily shoulder four jobs while scrambling to identify a new number-two executive. Gault's successors struggled not only with a management void but also with strategic voids that would eventually bring the company to its knees.

Of course, you might say—as one *Fortune* article did—that the fact that Rubbermaid fell apart after Gault left proves his greatness as a leader. Gault was a tremendous Level 4 leader, perhaps one of the best in the last 50 years. But he was not at Level 5, and that is one crucial reason why Rubbermaid went from good to great for a brief, shining moment and then just as quickly went from great to irrelevant.

The Window and the Mirror

As part of our research, we interviewed Alan L. Wurtzel, the Level 5 leader responsible for turning Circuit City from a ramshackle company on the edge of bankruptcy into one of America's most successful electronics retailers. In the 15 years after its transition date in 1982, Circuit City outperformed the market 18.5:1.

We asked Wurtzel to list the top five factors in his company's transformation, ranked by importance. His number one factor? Luck. "We were in a great industry, with the wind at our backs," he said. But wait a minute, we retorted, Silo—your comparison company—was in the same industry, with the same wind and bigger sails. The conversation went back and forth, with Wurtzel refusing to take much credit for the transition, preferring to attribute it largely to just being in the right place at the right time. Later, when we asked him to discuss the factors that would sustain a good-to-great transformation, he said, "The first thing that comes to mind is luck. I was lucky to find the right successor."

Luck. What an odd factor to talk about. Yet the Level 5 leaders we identified invoked it frequently. We asked an executive at steel company Nucor why it had such a remarkable track record for making good decisions. His response? "I guess we were just lucky." Joseph F. Cullman III, the Level 5 CEO of Philip Morris, flat out refused to take credit for his company's success, citing his good fortune to have great colleagues, successors, and predecessors. Even the book he wrote about his career—which he penned at the urging of his colleagues and which he never intended to distribute widely outside the company—had the unusual title *I'm a Lucky Guy.*

At first, we were puzzled by the Level 5 leaders' emphasis on good luck. After all, there is no evidence that the companies that had progressed from good to great were blessed with more good luck (or more bad luck, for that matter) than the comparison companies. But then we began to notice an interesting pattern in the executives at the comparison companies: They often blamed their situations on bad luck, bemoaning the difficulties of the environment they faced.

Compare Bethlehem Steel and Nucor, for example. Both steel companies operated with products that are hard to differentiate, and both faced a competitive challenge from cheap imported steel. Both companies paid significantly higher wages than most of their foreign competitors. And yet executives at the two companies held completely different views of the same environment.

Bethlehem Steel's CEO summed up the company's problems in 1983 by blaming the imports: "Our first, second, and third problems are imports." Meanwhile, Ken Iverson and his crew at Nucor saw the imports as a blessing: "Aren't we lucky; steel is heavy, and they have to ship it all the way across the ocean, giving us a huge advantage." Indeed, Iverson saw the first, second, and third problems facing the U.S. steel industry not in imports but in management. He even went so far as to speak out publicly against government protection against imports, telling a gathering of stunned steel executives in 1977 that the real problems facing the industry lay in the fact that management had failed to keep pace with technology.

The emphasis on luck turns out to be part of a broader pattern that we have come to call "the window and the mirror." Level 5 leaders, inherently humble, look out the window to apportion credit—even undue credit—to factors outside themselves. If they can't find a specific person or event to give credit to, they credit good luck. At the same time, they look in the mirror to assign responsibility, never citing bad luck or external factors when things go poorly. Conversely, the comparison executives frequently looked out the window for factors to blame but preened in the mirror to credit themselves when things went well.

The funny thing about the window-and-mirror concept is that it does not reflect reality. According to our research, the Level 5 leaders were responsible for their companies' transformations. But they would never admit that. We can't climb inside their heads and assess whether they deeply believed what they saw through the window and in the mirror. But it doesn't really matter, because they acted as if they believed it, and they acted with such consistency that it produced exceptional results.

Born or Bred?

Not long ago, I shared the Level 5 finding with a gathering of senior executives. A woman who had recently become chief executive of her company raised her hand. "I believe what you've told us about Level 5 leadership," she said, "but I'm disturbed because I know I'm not there yet, and maybe I never will be. Part of the reason I got this job is because of my strong ego. Are you telling me that I can't make my company great if I'm not Level 5?"

"Let me return to the data," I responded. "Of 1,435 companies that appeared on the *Fortune* 500 since 1965, only 11 made it into our study. In those 11, all of them had Level 5 leaders in key positions, including the CEO role, at the pivotal time of transition. Now, to reiterate, we're not saying that Level 5 is the only element required for the move from good to great, but it appears to be essential."

She sat there, quiet for a moment, and you could guess what many people in the room were thinking. Finally, she raised her hand again. "Can you learn to become Level 5?" I still do not know the answer to that question. Our research, frankly, did not delve into how Level 5 leaders come to be, nor did we attempt to explain or codify the nature of their emotional lives. We speculated on the unique psychology of Level 5 leaders. Were they "guilty" of displacement—shifting their own raw ambition onto something other than themselves? Were they sublimating their egos for dark and complex reasons rooted in childhood trauma? Who knows? And perhaps more important, do the psychological roots of Level 5 leadership matter any more than do the roots of charisma or intelligence? The question remains: Can Level 5 be developed?

My preliminary hypothesis is that there are two categories of people: those who don't have the Level 5 seed within them and those who do. The first category consists of people who could never in a million years bring themselves to subjugate their own needs to the greater ambition of something larger and more lasting than themselves. For those people, work will always be first and foremost about what they get—the fame, fortune, power, adulation, and so on. Work will never be about what they build, create, and contribute. The great irony is that the animus and personal ambition that often drives people to become a Level 4 leader stands at odds with the humility required to rise to Level 5.

When you combine that irony with the fact that boards of directors frequently operate under the false belief that a larger-than-life, egocentric leader is required to make a company great, you can quickly see why Level 5 leaders rarely appear at the top of our institutions. We keep putting people in positions of power who lack the seed to become a Level 5 leader, and that is one major reason why there are so few companies that make a sustained and verifiable shift from good to great.

The second category consists of people who could evolve to Level 5; the capability resides within them, perhaps buried or ignored or simply nascent. Under the right circumstances—with self-reflection, a mentor, loving parents, a significant life experience, or other factors—the seed can begin to develop. Some of the Level 5 leaders in our study had significant life experiences that might have sparked development of the seed. Darwin Smith fully blossomed as a Level 5 after his near-death experience with cancer. Joe Cullman was profoundly affected by his World War II experiences, particularly the last-minute change of orders that took him off a doomed ship on which he surely would have died; he considered the next 60-odd years a great gift. A strong religious belief or conversion might also nurture the seed. Colman Mockler, for example, converted to evangelical Christianity while getting his MBA at Harvard, and later, according to the book *Cutting Edge* by Gordon McKibben, he became a prime mover in a group of Boston business executives that met frequently over breakfast to discuss the carryover of religious values to corporate life.

We would love to be able to give you a list of steps for getting to Level 5—other than contracting cancer, going through a religious conversion, or getting different parents—but we have no solid research data that would support a credible list. Our research exposed Level 5 as a key component inside the black box of what it takes to shift a company from good to great. Yet inside that black box is another—the inner development of a person to Level 5 leadership. We could speculate on what that inner box might hold, but it would mostly be just that: speculation.

In short, Level 5 is a very satisfying idea, a truthful idea, a powerful idea, and, to make the move from good to great, very likely an essential idea. But to provide "ten steps to Level 5 leadership" would trivialize the concept.

My best advice, based on the research, is to practice the other good-to-great disciplines that we discovered. Since we found a tight symbiotic relationship between each of the other findings and Level 5, we suspect that conscientiously trying to lead using the other disciplines can help you move in the right direction. There is no guarantee that doing so will turn executives into full-fledged Level 5 leaders, but it gives them a tangible place to begin, especially if they have the seed within.

We cannot say for sure what percentage of people have the seed within, nor how many of those can nurture it enough to become Level 5. Even those of us on the research team who identified Level 5 do not know whether we will succeed in evolving to its heights. And yet all of us who worked on the finding have been inspired by the idea of trying to move toward Level 5. Darwin Smith, Colman Mockler, Alan Wurtzel, and all the other Level 5 leaders we learned about have become role models for us. Whether or not we make it to Level 5, it is worth trying. For like all basic truths about what is best in human beings, when we catch a glimpse of that truth, we know that our own lives and all that we touch will be the better for making the effort to get there.

9

Feedforward

Marshall Goldsmith

Providing feedback has long been considered to be an essential skill for leaders. As they strive to achieve the goals of the organization, employees need to know how they are doing. They need to know if their performance is in line with what their leaders expect. They need to learn what they have done well and what they need to change. Traditionally, this information has been communicated in the form of "downward feedback" from leaders to their employees. Just as employees need feedback from leaders, leaders can benefit from feedback from their employees. Employees can provide useful input on the effectiveness of procedures and processes as well as input to managers on their leadership effectiveness. This "upward feedback" has become increasingly common with the advent of 360° multi-rater assessments.

But there is a fundamental problem with all types of feedback: it focuses on *the past*, on what has already occurred, not on the infinite variety of opportunities that can happen in the future. As such, feedback can be limited and static, as opposed to expansive and dynamic.

Over the past several years, I have observed more than ten thousand leaders as they participated in a fascinating experiential exercise. In the exercise, participants are each asked to play two roles. In one role, they are asked to provide *feedforward**—that is, to give someone else suggestions for the future and *help as much as they can*. In the second role, they are asked to accept *feedforward*—that is, to listen to the suggestions for the future and *learn as much as they can*. The exercise typically lasts for 10–15 minutes, and the average participant has 6–7 dialogue sessions. In the exercise participants are asked to:

---

*The term "feedforward" was coined in a discussion that I had with Jon Katzenbach, author of *The Wisdom of Teams, Real Change Leaders,* and *Peak Performance.*

- Pick one behavior that they would like to change. *Change in this behavior should make a significant, positive difference in their lives.*
- Describe this behavior to randomly selected fellow participants.
- This is done in one-on-one dialogues. It can be done quite simply, such as, "I want to be a better listener."
- Ask for *feedforward* for two suggestions for the future that might help them achieve a positive change in their selected behavior. *If participants have worked together in the past, they are not allowed to give ANY feedback about the past. They are only allowed to give ideas for the future.*
- Listen attentively to the suggestions and take notes. *Participants are not allowed to comment on the suggestions in any way. They are not allowed to critique the suggestions or even to make positive judgmental statements, such as, "That's a good idea."*
- Thank the other participants for their suggestions.
- Provide *feedforward*—two suggestions aimed at helping the other person change.
- Say, "You are welcome," when thanked for the suggestions. *The entire process of both giving and receiving feedforward usually takes about two minutes.*

Find another participant and keep repeating the process until the exercise is stopped.

When the exercise is finished, I ask participants to provide one word that best describes their reaction to this experience. I ask them to complete the sentence, "This exercise was . . . ." The words provided are almost always extremely positive, such as "great," "energizing," "useful" or "helpful." The most common word mentioned is "fun!"

What is the *last* word that most of us think about when we receive feedback, coaching, and developmental ideas? Fun!

Participants are then asked why this exercise is seen as fun and helpful as opposed to painful, embarrassing, or uncomfortable. Their answers provide a great explanation of why feedforward can often be more useful than feedback as a developmental tool.

Eleven Reasons to Try Feedforward

1. *We can change the future. We can't change the past.* Feedforward helps people envision and focus on a positive future, not a failed past. Athletes are often trained using feedforward. Racecar drivers are taught to "look at the road ahead, not at the wall." Basketball players are taught to envision the ball going in the hoop and to imagine the perfect shot. By giving people ideas on how they can be even more successful, we can increase their chances of achieving this success in the future.

2. *It can be more productive to help people be "right," than prove they were "wrong."* Negative feedback often becomes an exercise in "let me prove

you were wrong." This tends to produce defensiveness on the part of the receiver and discomfort on the part of the sender. Even constructively delivered feedback is often seen as negative as it necessarily involves a discussion of mistakes, short-falls, and problems. Feedforward, on the other hand, is almost always seen as positive because it focuses on solutions—not problems.

3. *Feedforward is especially suited to successful people.* Successful people like getting ideas that are aimed at helping them achieve their goals. They tend to resist negative judgment. We all tend to accept feedback that is consistent with the way we see ourselves. We also tend to reject or deny feedback that is incon-sistent with the way we see ourselves. Successful people tend to have a very pos-itive self-image. I have observed many successful executives respond to (and even enjoy) feedforward. I am not sure that these same people would have had such a positive reaction to feedback.

4. *Feedforward can come from anyone who knows about the task. It does not require personal experience with the individual.* One very common positive reaction to the previously described exercise is that participants are amazed by how much they can learn from people that they don't know! For example, if you want to be a better listener, almost any fellow leader can give you ideas on how you can improve. They don't have to know you. Feedback requires knowing about the person. Feedforward just requires having good ideas for achieving the task.

5. *People do not take feedforward as personally as feedback.* In theory, constructive feedback is supposed to "focus on the performance, not the person." In practice, almost all feedback is taken personally (no matter how it is deliv-ered). Successful people's sense of identity is highly connected with their work. The more successful people are, the more this tends to be true. It is hard to give a dedicated professional feedback that is not taken personally. Feedforward cannot involve a personal critique, since it is discussing something that has not yet hap-pened! Positive suggestions tend to be seen as objective advice—personal cri-tiques are often viewed as personal attacks.

6. *Feedback can reinforce personal stereotyping and negative self-fulfilling prophecies.* Feedforward can reinforce the possibility of change. Feedback can reinforce the feeling of failure. How many of us have been "helped" by a spouse, significant other or friend, who seems to have a near-photographic memory of our previous "sins" that they share with us in order to point out the history of our shortcomings. Negative feedback can be used to reinforce the message, "this is just the way you are." Feedforward is based on the assumption that the receiver of suggestions can make positive changes in the future.

7. *Face it! Most of us hate getting negative feedback, and we don't like to give it.* I have reviewed summary 360° feedback reports for over 50 companies. The items, "provides developmental feedback in a timely manner" and "encour-ages and accepts constructive criticism" almost always score near the bottom on co-worker satisfaction with leaders. Traditional training does not seem to make a great deal of difference. If leaders got better at providing feedback every time the performance appraisal forms were "improved," most should be perfect by now!

Leaders are not very good at giving or receiving negative feedback. It is unlikely that this will change in the near future.

8. *Feedforward can cover almost all of the same "material" as feedback.* Imagine that you have just made a terrible presentation in front of the executive committee. Your manager is in the room. Rather than make you "relive" this humiliating experience, your manager might help you prepare for future presentations by giving you suggestions for the future. These suggestions can be very specific and still be delivered in a positive way. In this way your manager can "cover the same points" without feeling embarrassed and without making you feel even more humiliated.

9. *Feedforward tends to be much faster and more efficient than feedback.* An excellent technique for giving ideas to successful people is to say, "Here are four ideas for the future. Please accept these in the positive spirit that they are given. If you can only use two of the ideas, you are still two ahead. Just ignore what doesn't make sense for you." With this approach almost no time gets wasted on judging the quality of the ideas or "proving that the ideas are wrong." This "debate" time is usually negative; it can take up a lot of time, and it is often not very productive. By eliminating judgment of the ideas, the process becomes much more positive for the sender, as well as the receiver. Successful people tend to have a high need for self-determination and will tend to accept ideas that they "buy" while rejecting ideas that feel "forced" upon them.

10. *Feedforward can be a useful tool to apply with managers, peers, and team members.* Rightly or wrongly, feedback is associated with judgment. This can lead to very negative—or even career-limiting—unintended consequences when applied to managers or peers. Feedforward does not imply superiority or judgment. It is more focused on being a helpful "fellow traveler" than an "expert." As such it can be easier to hear from a person who is not in a position of power or authority. An excellent team-building exercise is to have each team member ask, "How can I better help our team in the future?" and listen to feedforward from fellow team members (in one-on-one dialogues).

11. *People tend to listen more attentively to feedforward than feedback.* One participant in the feedforward exercise noted, "I think that I listened more effectively in this exercise than I ever do at work!" When asked why, he responded, "Normally, when others are speaking, I am so busy *composing* a reply that will make sure that I sound smart—that I am not fully *listening* to what the other person is saying. In feedforward the only reply that I am allowed to make is 'thank you.' Since I don't have to worry about composing a clever reply, I can focus all of my energy on listening to the other person!"

In summary, the intent of this article is not to imply that leaders should never give feedback or that performance appraisals should be abandoned. The intent is to show how feedforward can often be preferable to feedback in day-to-day interactions. Aside from its effectiveness and efficiency, feedforward can make life a lot more enjoyable. When managers are asked, "How did you feel the last time you received feedback?" their most common responses are very negative. When managers are asked how they felt after receiving feedforward, they reply that feedforward was not only useful, it was also fun!

Quality communication—between and among people at all levels and every department and division—is the glue that holds organizations together. By using feedforward, and by encouraging others to use it, leaders can dramatically improve the quality of communication in their organizations, ensuring that the right message is conveyed, and that those who receive it are receptive to its content. The result is a much more dynamic, much more open organization—one whose employees focus on the promise of the future rather than dwelling on the mistakes of the past.